MODERN REAL ESTATE
PRACTICE IN
ILLINOIS

THIRD EDITION

FILLMORE W. GALATY

WELLINGTON J. ALLAWAY

ROBERT C. KYLE

JOYCE BEA STERLING, Consulting Editor

DEARBORN™
A **Kaplan Professional** Company

Vice President: Carol L. Luitjens
Executive Editor: Diana Faulhaber
Senior Development Editor: Robert A. Porché
Associate Real Estate Writer: Nikki Loosemore
Managing Editor: Ronald J. Liszkowski
Art and Design Manager: Lucy Jenkins
Cover Design: DePinto Studios

Published by Real Estate Education Company®/Chicago,
a division of Dearborn Financial Publishing, Inc.®,
a Kaplan Professional Company
155 North Wacker Drive
Chicago, IL 60606-1719
(312) 836-4400
http://www.dearborn.com

Printed in the United States of America.

99   00   01   10   9   8   7   6   5   4   3   2   1

Library of Congress Cataloging-in-Publication Data

Galaty, Fillmore W.
    Modern real estate practice in Illinois / Fillmore W. Galaty,
Wellington J. Allaway, Robert C. Kyle ; Joyce Bea Sterling,
consulting editor. — 3rd ed.
        p.   cm.
    Includes index.
    ISBN 0-7931-3307-6
    1. Real Estate business—Law and legislation—Illinois.   2. Real
estate agents—Licenses—Illinois.   3. Vendors and purchasers—
Illinois.   4. Conveyancing—Illinois.   I. Allaway, Wellington J.
II. Kyle, Robert C.   III. Sterling, Joyce Bea.   IV. Title.
KFI1482.R4G35   1999   99-28196
346.77304'3—dc21   CIP

Contents

Handwritten notes:

FOR THE BUYERS
3 POINTS = 3% OF LOAN AMOUNT
FOR LENDER OR INVESTER
3 POINT INCREASE YIELDS BY 3/8%
ANY EXAMINATION THAT ASK WHAT IS THE
EFFECTS OF POINTS ANSWER :- IT INCREAM
LENDER YEILDS & EFFFET IS
P DISCOUNTED LOAN

Preface

Whether you are preparing for the Illinois licensing examination, fulfilling a college or university requirement, looking for specific guidance about buying a home or investment property or simply expanding your understanding of this fascinating field, you can rely on *Modern Real Estate Practice in Illinois,* 3rd Edition, for accurate and comprehensive information in a format that is easy to use.

TEXT FEATURES

- *Illinois-specific laws and practice issues* are clearly highlighted for easy study and classroom emphasis.
- The *For Example* feature adds real-life examples and case studies to illustrate key concepts.
- *Math Concepts* help students learn basic real estate math skills and their real-life applications.
- *Margin notes* direct readers' attention to important vocabulary terms, concepts and study tips for more efficient and effective studying.
- A *Key Terms* list appears at the beginning of each chapter, alerting readers to the important vocabulary words that will be discussed. When each key word appears for the first time within the text, it is set in boldface. A *Glossary* appears at the end of the book as a useful summary of these terms.
- Each chapter contains a *Summary,* which reinforces the material that has just been covered.

NEW TO THE THIRD EDITION

- Exam preparation expert *Joyce Bea Sterling* has joined in preparing this edition of the book to ensure compliance with the question format and content outline of the new Illinois Applied Measurement Professionals testing service. Also look for the new *AMP examination outline,* reprinted in the back of the book, which references each topic to the appropriate chapter in *Modern Real Estate Practice in Illinois.*
- *Chapter Review* and *Sample Exam* questions have been thoroughly revised and replaced where necessary to comply with the new *AMP* exam standards. The questions have been carefully designed to demonstrate

the types of questions students will be likely to encounter on the new Illinois state licensing exams. There are even more demanding fact-pattern problems that encourage students to understand and apply information rather than just memorize—an important test-taking and exam-preparation skill. The **Answer Key** includes specific page references to the text.

- We've divided the **agency** and **brokerage** chapter into two distinct chapters so students can focus on each of these important topics separately.
- The chapter on **Broker Employment Contracts** has been revised to cover more of the essential listing and buyer representation agreement topics.
- The homestead and capital gains tax laws have been thoroughly updated to reflect the **1997 Taxpayer Relief Act** and its 1998 amendment.
- The Math Review Appendix is **totally NEW** and offers comprehensive coverage of typical math concepts for students wishing further study and review.
- For easier readability, all of the **situational examples** and questions have been rewritten with names—rather than letters—as the characters.

One thing, however, has stayed the same. The two fundamental goals of *Modern Real Estate Practice in Illinois* are to help students understand the dynamics of the real estate industry in Illinois and pass their state licensing exams. In this edition, we've met that challenge, providing the critical information students need to pass the real estate examination, buy or sell property or establish a real estate career.

A FINAL NOTE

We like to hear from our readers. Like the hundreds of instructors who have helped us develop each edition, like the real estate professionals who have been willing to share their expertise, you are a partner in the *Modern Real Estate Practice* series. The only way we can be sure we've succeeded—and know what we need to improve—is if you tell us.

Your comments help us evaluate the current edition and continue to improve future ones. Please take a few moments to let us know what you thought of this edition of *Modern Real Estate Practice in Illinois*. Did it help you? Has your understanding of the real estate industry increased? How did you do in your course or on your license exam? What additional or different information would improve the book? Please indicate that you used the 3rd Edition of *Modern Real Estate Practice in Illinois* and send your comments to Real Estate Education Company, Attention: Editorial Group, 155 North Wacker Drive, Chicago, Illinois 60606-1719.

Thank you for your help and for joining the ranks of successful users of *Modern Real Estate Practice in Illinois*.

Acknowledgments

CONSULTING EDITOR

The authors would like to express special appreciation to Joyce Bea Sterling for her invaluable review and analysis of the question bank, ensuring its compliance with the standards and content outline established by Applied Measurement Professionals, Inc. (AMP). She is the author of Real Estate Education Company's successful *Your Guide to Passing the AMP Real Estate Exam*, the first guide specifically designed for the AMP exam.

A real estate exam preparation expert, Ms. Sterling has been an instructor since 1986 and has helped thousands of students pass their exams. Currently, she teaches prelicensing classes in Kentucky (previously an AMP exam state), exam review courses in Ohio and is a mortgage consultant for Referral Mortgage, Ltd. She's authored test-taking packages and a real estate vocabulary workbook and tape set. She's also co-authored exam review audio tapes for the states of North Carolina, New York and Pennsylvania, and is the coauthor and on-camera cohost of the *Mastering Real Estate Math* video, all published by Real Estate Education Company.

REVIEWERS

Like a real estate transaction, this book is the product of teamwork and cooperation among professionals. The authors express their gratitude and appreciation to the instructors and other real estate professionals whose invaluable suggestions and advice help *Modern Real Estate Practice in Illinois*, 3rd Edition, remain the state's leading real estate principles text. Whether they responded to instructor surveys, provided reviews and suggestions for improving the previous edition or reviewed the manuscript for this edition, the participation of these professionals—and their willingness to share their expertise—is greatly appreciated.

The authors gratefully acknowledge the assistance of the following professionals who have contributed their knowledge to the third edition:

Maureen Cain, Attorney and Chicago Association of REALTORS® Instructor
William F. Carmody, Esq., College of DuPage
Lee E. Dillenbeck, Elgin Community College

Michael Fair, Director, Illinois Academy of Real Estate
Sue Miranda, Miranda Real Estate, Inc.
Mary Wezeman, Coldwell Banker School of Real Estate

Each new edition of *Modern Real Estate Practice in Illinois* builds on earlier
editions. The authors would like to thank these individuals for their assistance
with prior editions of this book:

Elyse Berns   Clarke Marquis
Sandra CeCe   Rose McDonald
Maureen LeVanti   Wayne Paprocki
Vincent C. Lopez   Dawn Svennigsen
Laurie MacDougal   Alan Toban

                              Fillmore W. Galaty
                              Wellington J. Allaway
                              Robert C. Kyle

Part One

PRINCIPLES

CHAPTER 1

Introduction to the Real Estate Business

KEY TERMS   broker   property manager   supply and demand
                market   salesperson

A VERY BIG BUSINESS

Real estate transactions are taking place all around you, all the time. When a commercial leasing company rents space in a mall or the owner of a building rents an apartment to a retired couple, it's a real estate transaction. If an appraiser gives an expert opinion of the value of farmland or a bank lends money to a professional corporation to purchase an office building, it's a real estate transaction. Most common of all, when American families sell their old homes and buy new ones, they take part in the real estate industry. Consumers of real estate services include buyers and sellers of homes, tenants and landlords, investors and developers. Nearly everyone, at some time, is involved in a real estate transaction.

All this adds up to really big business—complex transactions that involve billions of dollars every year in the United States alone. The services of millions of highly trained individuals are required: attorneys, bankers, trust company representatives, abstract and title insurance company agents, architects, surveyors, accountants, tax experts and many others, in addition to buyers and sellers. All these people depend on the skills and knowledge of licensed real estate professionals.

REAL ESTATE: A BUSINESS OF MANY SPECIALIZATIONS

Despite the size and complexity of the real estate business, many people think of it as being made up of only brokers and salespersons. Actually, the real estate industry is much bigger than that. Appraisal, property management, financing, subdivision and development, counseling and education are all separate businesses within the real estate field. To succeed in a complex industry, every real estate professional must have a basic knowledge of these specialties and the terms associated with them.

Brokerage—*Brokerage* is the business of bringing people together in a real estate transaction. A **broker** acts as a point of contact between two or more people in negotiating the sale, purchase or rental of property. A broker may be the agent of the buyer or the seller (or both), or the broker may not be anyone's agent. The property may be residential, commercial or industrial. A **salesperson** is a licensee employed by or associated with the broker. The salesperson conducts brokerage activities on behalf of the broker. The broker, however, is ultimately responsible for the salesperson's acts.

Appraisal—*Appraisal* is the process of estimating a property's market value based on established methods and the appraiser's professional judgment. Although their training will give brokers some understanding of the valuation process, lenders generally require a professional appraisal, and property sold by court order requires an appraiser's expertise. Appraisers must have detailed knowledge of the methods of valuation. In many states, appraisers must be licensed or certified to carry out local transactions. Appraisers must be licensed or certified for any federally related transactions.

Property management—A **property manager** is a person hired to maintain and manage property on behalf of its owner. By hiring a property manager, the owner is relieved of such day-to-day management tasks as finding new tenants, collecting rents, altering or constructing new space for tenants, ordering repairs and generally maintaining the property. The scope of the manager's work depends on the terms of the individual employment contract, known as a management agreement. Whatever tasks are specified, the basic responsibility of the property manager is to protect the owner's investment and maximize the owner's return on his or her investment.

Financing—*Financing* is the business of providing the funds that make real estate transactions possible. Most transactions are financed by means of mortgage loans or trust deed loans secured by the property. Individuals involved in financing real estate may work in commercial banks, savings associations and mortgage banking and mortgage brokerage companies. A growing number of real estate brokerage firms affiliate with mortgage brokers to provide consumers with "one-stop-shopping" real estate services.

Subdivision and development—*Subdivision* is the splitting of a single property into smaller parcels. Development involves the construction of improvements on the land. These improvements may be either on-site or off-site. Off-site improvements, such as water lines and storm sewers, are made on public lands to serve the new development. On-site improvements, such as new homes or swimming pools, are made on individual parcels. While subdivision and development normally are related, they are independent processes that can occur separately.

Counseling—*Counseling* involves providing clients with competent independent advice based on sound professional judgment. A real estate counselor helps clients choose among the various alternatives involved in purchasing, using or investing in property. A counselor's role is to furnish clients with the information needed to make informed decisions. Professional real estate counselors must have a high degree of industry expertise.

Education—*Real estate education* is available to both practitioners and consumers. Colleges and universities, private schools and trade organizations all conduct real estate courses and seminars, from the principles of a prelicensing program to the technical aspects of tax and exchange law. State licensing laws establish the minimum educational requirements for obtaining—and keeping—a real estate license. Continuing education helps ensure that licensees keep their skills and knowledge current.

Other areas—Many other real estate career options are available. Practitioners will find that real estate specialists are needed in a variety of business settings. *Lawyers* who specialize in real estate are always in demand. Large corporations with extensive land holdings often have their own *real estate and property tax departments.* Local governments must staff both *zoning boards and assessment offices.*

PROFESSIONAL ORGANIZATIONS

Many trade organizations serve the real estate business. The largest is the National Association of REALTORS® (NAR). NAR is composed of state, regional and local associations. NAR also sponsors various affiliated organizations that offer professional designations to brokers, salespersons and others who complete required courses in areas of special interest. Members subscribe to a Code of Ethics and are entitled to be known as REALTORS® or REALTOR®-ASSOCIATES®. The National Association of REALTORS® also has state affiliates, such as the Illinois Association of REALTORS®, and local organizations, such as the Chicago Board of REALTORS®. These REALTOR® associations have ongoing political and educational activities as valuable member services.

Among the other professional associations is the National Association of Real Estate Brokers (NAREB), whose members also subscribe to a code of ethics. Members of NAREB are known as Realtists. Other professional associations include the Appraisal Institute, the American Society of Appraisers (ASA), the National Association of Independent Fee Appraisers (NAIFA) and the Real Estate Educators Association (REEA). The growth in buyer brokerage led to the formation of organizations such as the Real Estate Buyer's Agent Council (REBAC), now associated with NAR, and the National Association of Exclusive Buyer's Agents (NAEBA). Other organizations include the Building Owners and Managers Association (BOMA), the Institute of Real Estate Management (IREM), the Commercial Investment Real Estate Institute (CIREI), the Association of Real Estate License Law Officials (ARELLO) and the American Society of Real Estate Counselors (ASREC).

TYPES OF REAL PROPERTY

Five Categories of Real Property

1. Residential
2. Commercial
3. Industrial
4. Agricultural
5. Special purpose

Just as there are areas of specialization within the real estate industry, there are different types of property in which to specialize. Real estate can be classified as

- *residential*—all property used for single-family or multifamily housing, whether in urban, suburban or rural areas;
- *commercial*—business property, including office space, shopping centers, stores, theaters, hotels and parking facilities;
- *industrial*—warehouses, factories, land in industrial districts and power plants;
- *agricultural*—farms, timberland, ranches and orchards; or
- *special purpose*—churches, schools, cemeteries and government-held lands.

The market for each of these types of property can be subdivided into the sales market, which involves the transfer of title and ownership rights, and the rental market, in which space is used temporarily by lease.

In Practice   Although it is possible for a single real estate firm or an individual real estate professional to perform all the services and handle all the classes of property discussed in this chapter (unless restricted by Illinois law), this rarely is done. While such general services may be available in small towns, most firms and professionals specialize to some degree, especially in urban areas. Some licensees perform only one service for one type of property, such as residential sales or commercial leasing.

THE REAL ESTATE MARKET

A **market** is a place where goods can be bought and sold. A market may be a specific place, such as the village square. It may also be a vast, complex, worldwide economic system for moving goods and services around the globe. In either case, the function of a market is to provide a setting in which supply and demand can establish market value, making it advantageous for buyers and sellers to trade.

Supply and Demand

The operation of **supply and demand** in the market is how prices for goods and services are set. Essentially, when supply increases and demand remains stable, prices go down; when demand increases and supply remains stable, prices go up. Greater supply means producers need to attract more buyers, so they lower prices. Greater demand means producers can raise their prices because buyers compete for the produt.

> When supply increases and demand remains stable, prices go down. When demand increases and supply remains stable, prices go up.

FOR EXAMPLE Here's how one downstate broker describes market forces: "In my 17 years in real estate, I've seen supply and demand in action many times. When a car maker relocated its factory to my region a few years back, hundreds of people wanted to buy the few higher-bracket houses for sale at the time. Those sellers were able to ask ridiculously high prices for their properties, and two houses actually sold for more than the asking prices! On the other hand, when the naval base closed and 2,000 civilian jobs were transferred to other parts of the country, it seemed like every other house in town was for sale. We were practically giving houses away to the few people who were buying."

> *Uniqueness* and *immobility* are the two characteristics of land that have the most impact on market value.

Supply and demand in the real estate market. Two characteristics of real estate govern the way the market reacts to the pressures of supply and demand: uniqueness and immobility. *Uniqueness* means that, no matter how identical they may appear, no two parcels of real estate are ever exactly alike; each occupies its own unique geographic location. *Immobility* refers to the fact that property cannot be relocated to satisfy demand where supply is low. Nor can buyers always relocate to areas with greater supply. For these reasons, real estate markets are local markets: each geographic area has different types of real estate and different conditions that drive prices. In these well-defined small areas, real estate offices can keep track of both what type of property is in demand and what parcels are available.

In Practice   Technological advances and market changes have widened the real estate professional's local market. No longer limited to a single small area, brokers and salespersons must track trends and conditions in a variety of different and sometimes distant local markets. Computers—including information networks and laptop PCs, cellular phones, fax machines and a growing arsenal of other technologies—help real estate practitioners stay on top of their wide-ranging markets.

Because of real estate's uniqueness and immobility, the market generally adjusts slowly to the forces of supply and demand. Though a home offered for sale can be withdrawn in response to low demand and high supply, it is much more likely that oversupply will result in lower prices. When supply is low, on the other hand, a high demand may not be met immediately because development and construction are lengthy processes. As a result, development tends to occur in uneven spurts of activity.

Even when supply and demand can be forecast with some accuracy, natural disasters such as hurricanes and earthquakes can disrupt market trends. Similarly, sudden changes in financial markets or local events such as plant relocations or environmental factors can dramatically disrupt a seemingly stable market.

Factors Affecting Supply

Factors that tend to affect the supply side of the real estate market's supply and demand balance include the labor force, construction and material costs, and government controls and financial policies.

Labor force and construction costs. A shortage of skilled labor or building materials or an increase in the cost of materials can decrease the amount of new construction. High transfer costs (such as taxes) and construction permit fees also can discourage development. Increased construction costs may be passed along to buyers and tenants in the form of higher prices and increased rents, which can further slow the market.

Government controls and financial policies. The government's monetary policy can have a substantial impact on the real estate market. The Federal Reserve Board establishes a discount rate of interest for the money it lends to commercial banks. That rate has a direct impact on the interest rates the banks in turn charge to borrowers. These interest rates play a significant part in people's ability to buy homes. Such government agencies as the Federal Housing Administration (FHA), the Government National Mortgage Association (GNMA) and the Federal Home Loan Mortgage Corporation (FHLMC) can affect the amount of money available to lenders for mortgage loans. These government agencies will be discussed in greater detail in Chapter 16.

> Factors that affect the supply of real estate are
>
> - labor force,
> - construction costs,
> - government controls, and
> - government financial policies.

Virtually any government action has some effect on the real estate market. For instance, federal environmental regulations may increase or decrease the supply and value of land in a local market.

Real estate taxation is one of the primary sources of revenue for local governments. Policies on taxation of real estate can have either positive or negative effects. High taxes may deter investors. On the other hand, tax incentives can attract new businesses and industries. And, of course, along with these enterprises come increased employment and expanded residential real estate markets.

Local governments also can influence supply. Land-use controls, building codes and zoning ordinances help shape the character of a community and control the use of land. Careful planning helps stabilize and even increase real estate values. The dedication of land to such amenities as forest preserves, schools and parks also helps shape the market.

Factors Affecting Demand

Factors that tend to affect the demand side of the real estate market include population, demographics and employment and wage levels.

Population. Shelter is a basic human need, so the demand for housing grows with the population. Although the total population of the country continues to rise, the demand for real estate increases faster in some areas than in others. In some locations, however, growth has ceased altogether or the population has declined. This may be due to economic changes (such as plant closings), social concerns (such as the quality of schools or a desire for more open space) or population changes (such as population shifts from colder to warmer climates). The result can be a drop in demand for real estate in one area, matched by an increase in demand elsewhere.

Demographics. Demographics is the study and description of a population. The population of a community is a major factor in determining the quantity and type of housing in that community. Family size, the ratio of adults to children, the ages of children, the number of retirees, family income, lifestyle and the growing number of single-parent and empty-nester households are all demographic factors that contribute to the amount and type of housing needed.

Employment and wage levels. Decisions about whether to buy or rent and how much to spend on housing are closely related to income. When job opportunities are scarce or wage levels low, demand for real estate usually drops. The market might, in fact, be affected drastically by a single major employer moving in or shutting down. Licensees must be aware of the business plans of local employers.

As we've seen, the real estate market depends on a variety of economic forces, such as interest rates and employment levels. To be successful, licensees must follow economic trends and anticipate where they will lead. How people use their income depends on consumer confidence. Consumer confidence is based not only on perceived job security but also on the availability of credit and the impact of inflation. General trends in the economy, such as the availability of mortgage money and the rate of inflation, will influence an individual's decision about how to spend his or her income.

> Factors that affect the demand for real estate are
>
> • population,
> • demographics, and
> • employment and wage levels.

SUMMARY

Although brokerage is the most widely recognized real estate activity, the industry provides many other services. These include appraisal, property management, property development, counseling, property financing and education. Most real estate firms specialize in only one or two of these areas; however, the highly complex and competitive nature of our society requires that a real estate person be an expert in a number of fields.

Real property can be classified by its general use as residential, commercial, industrial, agricultural or special purpose. Although many brokers deal with more than one type of real property, they usually specialize to some degree.

A market is a place where goods and services can be bought and sold and where price levels can be established based on supply and demand. Because of its unique characteristics, real estate is relatively slow to adjust to the forces of supply and demand.

The supply of and demand for real estate are affected by many factors, including changes in population and demographics, wage and employment levels, construction costs, availability of labor and governmental monetary policy and controls.

QUESTIONS

1. Commercial real estate includes all of the following EXCEPT:
   A. office buildings for sale.
   B. a house for rent.
   C. retail space for lease.
   D. fast-food restaurants for lease.

2. In general, when the supply of a certain commodity increases:
   A. prices tend to rise.
   B. prices tend to drop.
   C. demand tends to rise.
   D. demand is unchanged.

3. All of the following factors tend to affect supply EXCEPT:
   A. the labor force.
   B. construction costs.
   C. government controls.
   D. demographics.

4. Factors that influence the demand for real estate include:
   A. the number of real estate brokers in the area.
   B. the number of full-time real estate salespersons in the area.
   C. wage levels and employment opportunities for the area.
   D. the price of new homes being built in the area.

5. Property management, appraisal, financing and development are all examples of:
   A. factors affecting demand.
   B. specializations within the real estate industry.
   C. non–real estate professions.
   D. government regulation of the real estate industry.

6. A REALTOR® is:
   A. a specially licensed real estate professional who acts as a point of contact between two or more people in negotiating the sale, purchase or rental of property.
   B. any real estate broker or salesperson who assists buyers, sellers, landlords or tenants in any real estate transaction.
   C. a member of the National Association of Real Estate Brokers who specializes in residential properties.
   D. a real estate licensee who is a member of the National Association of REALTORS®.

7. A major manufacturer of automobiles announces that it will relocate one of its factories, along with 2,000 employees, to Smallville. What effect will this announcement likely have on Smallville's housing market?
   A. Houses likely will become less expensive as a result of the announcement.
   B. Houses likely will become more expensive as a result of the announcement.
   C. The announcement involves an issue of demographics, not a supply and demand issue; housing prices will stay the same.
   D. The announcement involves an industrial property; residential housing will not be affected.

8. Mario holds a real estate license and has several years of experience in the industry. However, Mario has "retired" from actively marketing properties. Now Mario helps clients choose among the various alternatives involved in purchasing, using or investing in property. What is Mario's profession?
   A. Real estate counselor
   B. Real estate appraiser
   C. Real estate educator
   D. REALTOR®

CHAPTER 2

Real Property and the Law

accession
air rights
bundle of legal rights
chattels
emblement

fixture
improvement
land
personal property
real estate

real property
severance
subsurface rights
surface rights
trade fixture

LAND, REAL ESTATE AND REAL PROPERTY

The words *land, real estate* and *real property* often are used interchangeably. To most people, they mean the same thing. Strictly speaking, however, the terms refer to different aspects of the same idea. To fully understand the nature of real estate and the laws that affect it, licensees must be aware of these subtle yet important differences in meaning.

Land
Land is defined as *the earth's surface extending downward to the center of the earth and upward to infinity.* The term includes permanent natural objects such as trees and water. (See Figure 2.1.)

Land, then, means not only the surface of the earth but also the underlying soil. It refers to things that are *naturally* attached to the land, such as boulders and plants. It includes the minerals and substances that lie far below the earth's surface. Land even includes the air above the earth, all the way up into space. These are known respectively as the *subsurface* and the *airspace*.

Real Estate
Real estate is defined as *land at, above and below the earth's surface, plus all things permanently attached to it, whether natural or artificial.* (See Figure 2.1.)

The term *real estate* is similar to the term *land,* but it means much more. *Real estate* includes not only the natural components of the land but also all man-made improvements. An **improvement** is any artificial thing attached to land, such as a building or a fence. The term *improvement,* as used in the real estate industry, refers to any addition to the land. The word is neutral. It doesn't matter whether the artificial attachment makes the property better looking or more useful; the land still is said to be improved. Land also may be improved

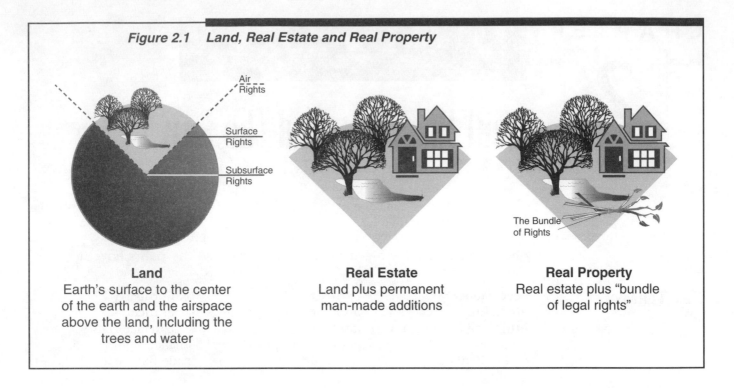

Figure 2.1   Land, Real Estate and Real Property

Air
Rights

Surface
Rights

Subsurface
Rights

Land
Earth's surface to the center
of the earth and the airspace
above the land, including the
trees and water

Real Estate
Land plus permanent
man-made additions

The Bundle
of Rights

Real Property
Real estate plus "bundle
of legal rights"

by streets, utilities, sewers and other additions that make it suitable for building.

Real Property   **Real property** is defined as *the interests, benefits and rights that are automatically included in the ownership of land and real estate.* (See Figure 2.1.)

The term *real property* is the broadest of all. It includes both land and real estate. Real property includes the surface, subsurface and airspace, any improvements and the *bundle of legal rights*—the legal rights of ownership that attach to ownership of a parcel of real estate (discussed later in this chapter). Real property includes the surface rights, subsurface rights and air rights, all of which can be owned by different individuals.

Real property often is coupled with the word *appurtenance.* An appurtenance is anything associated with the property, although not necessarily a part of it. Typical appurtenances include parking spaces in multiunit buildings, easements, water rights and other improvements. An appurtenance is connected to the property, and ownership of the appurtenance normally passes with the property itself.

[handwritten: IT IS ANYTHING RUNS WITH LAND PASSES WITH THE DEED]

In Practice   When people talk about buying or selling homes, office buildings and land, they usually call these things *real estate.* For all practical purposes, the term is synonymous with *real property* as defined here. Thus, in everyday usage, *real estate* includes the legal rights of ownership specified in the definition of real property. Sometimes people use the term *realty* instead.

Subsurface and air rights. The right to use the surface of the earth is referred to as a **surface right.** However, real property ownership also can include **subsurface rights,** which are the rights to the natural resources lying below the earth's surface. Although it may be difficult to imagine, the two rights are distinct: an owner may transfer his or her surface rights without transferring the subsurface rights.

FOR EXAMPLE Annie sells the rights to any oil and gas found beneath her farm to an oil company. Later, she sells the remaining interests (the surface, air and limited subsurface rights) to Bradley, reserving the rights to any coal that may be found in the land. Bradley sells the remaining land to Charles, but Bradley retains the farmhouse, stable and pasture. After these sales, four parties have ownership interests in the same real estate: (1) the oil company owns all the oil and gas; (2) Annie owns all the coal; (3) Bradley owns the farmhouse, stable and pasture; and (4) Charles owns the rights to the remaining real estate.

The rights to use the air above the land, provided the rights have not been preempted by law, may be sold or leased independently. Air rights can be an important part of real estate, particularly in large cities, where air rights over railroads must be purchased to construct office buildings such as the Met Life Building in New York City and the Prudential Building in Chicago. To construct such a building, the developer must purchase not only the air rights but also numerous small portions of the land's surface for the building's foundation supports.

Before air travel was common, a property's air rights were considered to be unlimited, extending upward into the farthest reaches of outer space. Today, however, the courts permit reasonable interference with these rights, such as that necessary for aircraft (and presumably spacecraft), as long as the owner's right to use and occupy the land is not unduly lessened. Governments and airport authorities often purchase adjacent air rights to provide approach patterns for air traffic.

With the continuing development of solar power, air rights—and, more specifically, light or solar rights—are being closely examined by the courts. A new tall building that blocks sunlight from a smaller, existing building may be held to be interfering with the smaller building's right to sunlight, particularly if the smaller building is solar powered.

REAL PROPERTY AND PERSONAL PROPERTY

Personal property, sometimes called *personalty,* is all property that does not fit the definition of *real property.*

An important distinction between the two is that personal property is movable. Items of personal property, also referred to as **chattels,** include such tangibles as chairs, tables, clothing, money, bonds and bank accounts. Trade fixtures, discussed below, are included in this category.

Mobile Homes The distinction between real and personal property is not always obvious. A mobile home, for example, generally is considered personal property even though its mobility may be limited to a single trip to a mobile-home park. A mobile home may, however, be considered real property if it becomes permanently affixed to the land. The distinction generally is one of state law. Real estate licensees should be familiar with local laws before attempting to sell mobile homes. Some states permit only mobile-home dealers to sell them; others require no special licensing.

In Illinois . . .

Because they can be moved, mobile homes are generally considered personal property in Illinois unless they have been permanently affixed to their foundation. ■

Plants

Trees and crops generally fall into one of two classes. Trees, perennial shrubbery and grasses that do not require annual cultivation are considered real estate. Annual plantings or crops of wheat, corn, vegetables and fruit, known as **emblements,** generally are considered personal property. As long as an annual crop is growing, it will be transferred as part of the real property unless other provisions are made in the sales contract. That is, a farmer won't have to dig up growing corn plants and haul them away unless the sales contract says so: the young corn remains on the land. The farmer may come back and harvest the corn when it's ready. The former owner or tenant is entitled to harvest the crops that result from his or her labor.

In Illinois . . .

When Illinois farmland is sold, it is customary for possession to be transferred to the buyer on March 1, which is normally after the last year's crops have been harvested and before the new crops are planted. Usually, no special provisions are required regarding the annual crops. However, when possession is transferred to the buyer on March 1, it also is customary for the buyer to assume full payment of the current year's tax bill without proration to date of sale because he or she will get the full benefit of the new crop for that tax year.

If the sale is closed at another time during the year and before the crops are harvested, the sales contract should indicate whether the growing crops are included in the sales price. Sometimes, when the crop is included in the sale, the buyer reimburses the seller for out-of-pocket costs of the crop already incurred, such as seed, planting, fertilizing and spraying. ■

An item of real property can become personal property by **severance.** For example, a growing tree is real estate until the owner cuts it down, literally severing it from the property. Similarly, an apple becomes personal property once it is picked from a tree, and a wheat crop becomes personal property once it is harvested.

> The term used in the law for plants that do not require annual cultivation (such as trees and shrubbery) is *fructus naturales* (fruits of nature); emblements are known in the law as *fructus industriales* (fruits of industry).

It also is possible to change personal property into real property. If, for example, a landowner buys cement, stones and sand, mixes them into concrete and constructs a sidewalk across his or her land, the landowner has converted personal property (cement, stones and sand) into real property (a sidewalk). This process is called *annexation.*

Licensees need to know whether property is real or personal for many reasons. An important distinction arises, for instance, when the property is transferred from one owner to another. Real property is conveyed by deed, while personal property is conveyed by a bill of sale.

Classifications of Fixtures

In considering the differences between real and personal property, it is necessary to distinguish between a *fixture* and personal property.

Fixtures. A **fixture** is an item of *personal property that has been so attached to land or a building that, by law, it becomes part of the real estate.* Examples of fixtures are heating systems, elevator equipment in highrise buildings, radiators, kitchen cabinets, light fixtures and plumbing fixtures. Almost any item that has been added as a permanent part of a building is considered a fixture.

During the course of time, the same materials may be both real and personal property, depending on their use and location.

Legal tests of a fixture. Courts use four basic tests to determine whether an item is a fixture (real property) or personal property:

Legal Tests of a Fixture
1. Intent
2. Method of annexation
3. Adaptation to real estate
4. Agreement

1. *Intent*—Did the person who installed the item intend for it to remain permanently on the property or for it to be removable in the future?
2. *Method of annexation*—How permanent is the method of attachment? Can the item be removed without causing damage to the surrounding property?
3. *Adaptation to real estate*—Is the item being used as real property or personal property?
4. *Agreement*—Have the parties agreed in writing on whether the item is real or personal property?

Although these tests may seem simple, court decisions have been inconsistent. Property that appears to be permanently affixed sometimes has been ruled to be personal property, while property that seems removable has been ruled a fixture. It is important that an owner clarify what is to be sold with the real estate at the very beginning of the sales process.

In Practice

At the time a property is listed, the seller and listing agent should discuss which items will be included in the sale. The written sales contract between the buyer and the seller should list specifically all articles that are being included in the sale, particularly if any doubt exists as to whether they are personal property or fixtures (for instance, built-in bookcases, chandeliers, ceiling fans or exotic shrubbery). This will avoid misunderstanding between the parties that could result in the collapse of the transaction and expensive lawsuits.

Trade fixtures. A special category of fixtures includes property used in the course of business. An article owned by a tenant and attached to a rented space or building or used in conducting a business is a **trade fixture,** or a *chattel fixture.* Some examples of trade fixtures are bowling alleys, store shelves, bars and restaurant equipment. Agricultural fixtures, such as chicken coops and toolsheds, also are included in this category. Trade fixtures must be removed on or before the last day the property is rented. The tenant is responsible for any damage caused by the removal of a trade fixture. Trade fixtures that are not removed become the real property of the landlord. Acquiring the property in this way is known as **accession.**

FOR EXAMPLE Paul's Pizza leases space in a small shopping center. Paul bolted a large iron oven to the floor of the unit. When Paul's Pizza goes out of business or relocates, Paul will be able to take his pizza oven with him if he can repair the bolt holes in the floor.

Trade fixtures differ from other fixtures in these ways:

- Fixtures belong to the owner of the real estate, but trade fixtures are usually owned and installed by a tenant for the tenant's use.
- Fixtures are considered a permanent part of a building, but trade fixtures are removable. Trade fixtures may be attached to a building so they appear to be fixtures.
- Legally, fixtures are real property, so they are included in any sale or mortgage. Trade fixtures, however, are considered personal property and are not included in the sale or mortgage of real estate, except by special agreement.

OWNERSHIP OF REAL PROPERTY

Traditionally, real property is described as a bundle of legal rights. In other words, a purchaser of real estate actually buys the rights of ownership held by the seller. These rights include the

- right of possession;
- right to control the property within the framework of the law;
- right of enjoyment (that is, to use the property in any legal manner);
- right of exclusion (to keep others from entering or using the property); and
- right of disposition (to sell, will, transfer or otherwise dispose of or encumber the property).

The concept of a *bundle of rights* comes from old English law. In the Middle Ages, a seller transferred property by giving the purchaser a handful of earth or a bundle of bound sticks from a tree on the property, symbolizing the whole property. The purchaser, who accepted the bundle in a formal ceremony, then owned the tree from which the sticks came and the land to which the tree was attached. Because the rights of ownership (like the sticks) can be separated and individually transferred, the sticks became symbolic of those rights. (See Figure 2.2.)

CHARACTERISTICS OF REAL ESTATE

Real estate possesses seven basic characteristics that define its nature and affect its use. These characteristics fall into two broad categories—*economic* characteristics and *physical* characteristics.

Economic Characteristics

The economic characteristics of land affect its investment value. They are scarcity, improvements, permanence of investment and area preference.

> **Economic Characteristics of Real Estate**
>
> 1. Scarcity
> 2. Improvements
> 3. Permanence of investment
> 4. Area prefererance

Scarcity. We usually do not consider land a rare commodity, but think about it: only about a quarter of the earth's surface is dry land; the rest is water. The total supply of land, then, is not limitless. While a considerable amount of land remains unused or uninhabited, the supply in a given location or of a particular quality is generally considered to be finite.

Improvements. Building an improvement on one parcel of land can affect the land's value and use as well as that of neighboring tracts and whole communities. For example, constructing a new shopping center or selecting

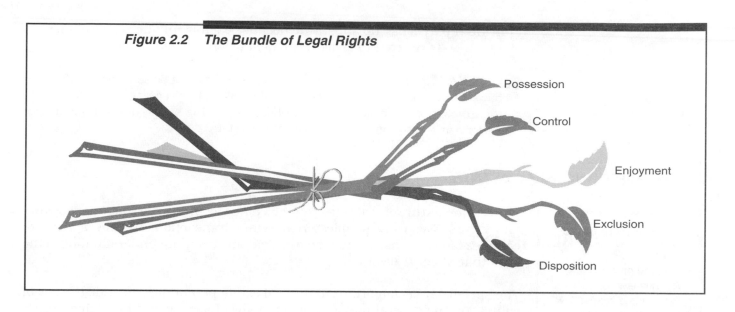

Figure 2.2   The Bundle of Legal Rights

- Possession
- Control
- Enjoyment
- Exclusion
- Disposition

a site for a nuclear power plant or toxic waste dump can dramatically change the value of land in a large area.

Permanence of investment. The capital and labor used to build an improvement represent a large fixed investment. Although even a well-built structure can be razed to make way for a newer building, improvements such as drainage, electricity, water and sewerage remain. The return on such investments tends to be long term and relatively stable.

Area preference. This economic characteristic, sometimes called *situs,* does not refer to a geographic location but rather to people's preferences for given areas. It is the unique quality of these preferences that results in different values for similar units. Area preference is the most important economic characteristic of land.

Physical Characteristics

Land has certain physical characteristics: immobility, indestructibility and uniqueness.

Physical Characteristics of Real Estate

1. Immobility
2. Indestructibility
3. Uniqueness

Immobility. It is true that some of the substances of land are removable and that topography can be changed, but *the geographic location of any given parcel of land can never be changed.* It is fixed.

Indestructibility. Land also is *indestructible.* It may be changed, but it cannot be destroyed. This permanence of land, coupled with the long-term nature of improvements, tends to stabilize investments in real estate.

The fact that land is indestructible does not, however, change the fact that the improvements on land depreciate and can become obsolete, which may dramatically reduce the land's value. This gradual depreciation should not be confused with the knowledge that the economic desirability of a given location can change.

Uniqueness. No two parcels of land are ever exactly the same. Although they may be substantially similar, all parcels differ geographically because each parcel has its own location. The characteristics of each measurable unit of property, no matter how small, differ from those of every other unit. An individual parcel has no substitute because each is unique. The uniqueness of land also is referred to as its *heterogeneity* or *nonhomogeneity*.

FOR EXAMPLE Because of the uniqueness of property, a person who contracted to buy a new condominium apartment, Unit 305, cannot be given Unit 307 at the closing, even though the two units appear to be identical. The buyer could sue for specific performance based on the uniqueness of real estate.

LAWS AFFECTING REAL ESTATE

Real Estate Laws

- Contract law
- General property law
- Agency law
- Real estate license law
- Federal regulations
- Federal, state and local tax laws
- Zoning and land use laws
- Federal, state and local environmental regulations

7 Sources of Law

1. United States Constitution
2. Laws passed by Congress
3. Rules of the regulatory agencies
4. State constitutions
5. State statutes
6. Local ordinances
7. Common law

The unique nature of real estate has given rise to an equally unique set of laws and rights. Even the simplest real estate transaction involves a body of complex laws. Licensees must have a clear and accurate understanding of the laws that affect real estate.

The specific areas important to the real estate practitioner include the law of contracts, the general property law, the law of agency and his or her state's real estate license law. All of these will be discussed in this text. Federal regulations (such as environmental laws), as well as federal, state and local tax laws, also play an important role in real estate transactions. State and local land-use and zoning laws have a significant effect on the practice of real estate, too.

Laws come from seven different sources. They are the United States Constitution, laws passed by Congress, rules of the regulatory agencies, state constitutions, state statutes, local ordinances and common law (common usage and court decisions).

Obviously, a real estate practitioner can't be an expert in all areas of real estate law. However, licensees should know and understand some basic principles. Perhaps most important is the ability to recognize problems that should be referred to a competent attorney. Only attorneys are trained and licensed to prepare documents defining or transferring rights in property and to give advice on matters of law. Under no circumstances may a broker or salesperson act as an attorney unless he or she is also a licensed attorney representing a client in that capacity.

Because brokers and salespersons are involved with other people's real estate and money, the need for regulation of their activities has long been recognized. The purpose of real estate license laws is to protect the public from fraud, dishonesty and incompetence in real estate transactions. All 50 states, the District of Columbia and all Canadian provinces have passed laws that require that real estate brokers and salespersons be licensed. Although state license laws are similar in many respects, they differ in some details, such as the amount and type of prelicense education required.

In Illinois . . .

The practice of real estate in Illinois is governed by the Real Estate License Act of 1983, as amended from time to time by the legislature, and by the rules established by the Office of Banks and Real Estate. The license law may be found at 255 Illinois Compiled Statutes 455/1. Other laws affecting real estate in Illinois are found throughout the Illinois Compiled Statutes, although many property issues are addressed in 765 ILCS generally. ■

SUMMARY

Although most people think of land as the surface of the earth, land includes the earth's surface, the mineral deposits under the earth and the air above it. The term *real estate* further expands this definition to include all natural and man-made improvements attached to the land. The term *real property* describes real estate plus the bundle of legal rights associated with its ownership.

The various rights to the same parcel of real estate may be owned and controlled by different parties, for instance, one owning the surface rights, one owning the air rights and one owning the subsurface rights.

All property that does not fit the definition of real estate is classified as personal property, or chattels. When articles of personal property are affixed to land, they may become fixtures and as such are considered part of the real estate. However, personal property attached to real estate by a tenant for business purposes is classified as a trade, or chattel, fixture and remains personal property.

The special nature of land as an investment is apparent in both its economic and physical characteristics. The economic characteristics are scarcity, improvements, permanence of investment and area preference. The physical characteristics of land are that it is immobile, indestructible and unique.

Even the simplest real estate transactions reflect a complex body of laws. A buyer of real estate actually purchases from the seller the legal rights to use the land in certain ways.

Every U.S. state and Canadian province has some type of licensing requirement for real estate brokers and salespersons. Students must become familiar with the real estate laws and licensing requirements not only of their own states but of those into which their practice may extend as well.

QUESTIONS

1. The major difference between real estate and personal property is:
   A. real estate includes land and all things permanently attached, while personal property includes property that is movable.
   B. real estate includes land and the rights and interests inherent in the ownership of land, while personal property only includes personal items such as furniture, cars, clothes, etc.
   C. real estate includes trees and air rights, while personal property includes streets and utilities.
   D. real estate includes annual crops, while personal property includes mineral rights.

2. Helen owns a building in a commercial area of town. Trudy rents space in the building and operates a bookstore. In Trudy's bookstore, there are large tables fastened to the walls, where customers are encouraged to sit and read. Shelves create aisles from the front of the store to the back. The shelves are bolted to both the ceiling and the floor. Which of the following best characterizes the contents of Trudy's bookstore?
   A. The shelves and tables are trade fixtures and will be sold when Helen sells the building.
   B. The shelves and tables are trade fixtures and must be removed before Trudy's lease expires.
   C. Because Trudy is a tenant, the shelves and tables are fixtures and may not be removed except with Helen's permission.
   D. Because the shelves and tables are attached to the building, they are treated the same as other fixtures.

3. The term *nonhomogeneity* refers to:
   A. scarcity.
   B. immobility.
   C. uniqueness.
   D. indestructibility

4. All of the following could be examples of trade fixtures EXCEPT:
   A. store shelves and restaurant equipment.
   B. sewers and utilities.
   C. furniture and machinery.
   D. a marker board and a slide projector.

5. The bundle of legal rights includes all of the following EXCEPT:
   A. the right to exclude someone from the property.
   B. the right to enjoy the property within the framework of the law.
   C. the right to sell or otherwise convey the property.
   D. the right to use the property for any purpose, legal or otherwise.

6. Omar inherited Rolling Hills from his uncle. The first thing Omar did with the vacant property was to remove all the topsoil, which he sold to a landscaping company. Omar then removed a thick layer of limestone and sold it to a construction company. Finally, Omar dug 40 feet into the bedrock and sold it for gravel. When Omar died, he left Rolling Hills to his daughter, Patty. Which of the following statements is true?
   A. Patty inherits nothing, because Rolling Hills no longer exists.
   B. Patty inherits a large hole in the ground, but it is still Rolling Hills, down to the center of the earth.
   C. Patty owns the gravel, limestone and topsoil, no matter where it is.
   D. Omar's estate must restore Rolling Hills to its original condition.

7. A buyer and seller of a home are debating whether a certain item is real or personal property. The buyer says it is real property and should convey along with the house; the seller says it is personal property and may be conveyed separately through a bill of sale. In determining whether an item is real or personal property, a court would consider all the following EXCEPT:
   A. the cost of the item when it was purchased.
   B. the method of its attachment to other real property.
   C. the intention of the person who installed the item that it become a permanent part of the property.
   D. the manner in which the item is actually used with other real property.

8. Which of the following would BEST describe the economic characteristics of real estate?
   A. Location, uniqueness and indestructibility
   B. Scarcity, immobility, and improvements
   C. Heterogeneity, location and improvements
   D. Scarcity, improvements and area preference

9. An owner decides to sell her house and take the garage door opener with her when she moves. Is the owner allowed to remove the garage door opener?
   A. Yes, the owner can remove the garage door opener, and the act would be known as *accession.*
   B. Yes, the owner can remove the garage door opener, and the act would be known as *severance.*
   C. Yes, the owner can remove the garage door opener, and the act would be known as *conversion.*
   D. Yes, the owner can remove the garage door opener, and the act would be known as *separation.*

10. When the buyer moved into a newly purchased home, the buyer discovered that the seller had taken the electric lighting fixtures that were installed over the vanity in the bathroom. The seller had not indicated that the fixtures would be removed. Which of the following is true?
    A. Lighting fixtures normally are considered to be real estate.
    B. The lighting fixtures belong to the seller because he installed them.
    C. These lighting fixtures are considered trade fixtures.
    D. Original lighting fixtures are real property, but replacement fixtures would be personal property.

11. Jamal is building a new enclosed front porch on his home. A truckload of lumber has been left on Jamal's driveway for use in building the porch. At this point, the lumber is considered what kind of property?
    A. A fixture, because it will be permanently affixed to existing real property
    B. Personal property
    C. A chattel that is real property
    D. A trade, or chattel, fixture

12. Intent of the parties, method of annexation, adaptation to real estate and agreement between the parties are the legal tests for determining whether an item is:
    A. a trade fixture or personal property.
    B. real property or real estate.
    C. a fixture or personal property.
    D. an improvement.

13. Parking spaces in multiunit buildings, water rights and other improvements are classified as:
    A. trade fixtures.
    B. emblements.
    C. subsurface rights.
    D. appurtenances.

14. Yolanda purchases Greenacre, a parcel of natural forest. She immediately cuts down all the trees and constructs a large shed out of old sheets of rusted tin. Yolanda uses the shed to store turpentine, varnish and industrial waste products. Which of the following statements is true?
    A. Yolanda's action constitutes improvement of the property.
    B. Yolanda's shed is personal property.
    C. If Yolanda is in the business of storing toxic substances, her shed is a trade fixture.
    D. Altering the property in order to construct a shed is not included in the bundle of legal rights.

CHAPTER

3

Concepts of Home Ownership

KEY TERMS

capital gain
coinsurance clause
equity

homeowner's
insurance policy

liability coverage
replacement cost

HOME OWNERSHIP

People buy their own homes for psychological as well as financial reasons. To many, home ownership is a sign of financial stability. It is an investment that can appreciate in value and provide federal income tax deductions. Home ownership also offers benefits that may be less tangible but are no less valuable: pride, security and a sense of belonging to the community.

Types of Housing

As our society evolves, the needs of its homebuyers become more specialized. The following paragraphs describe the types of housing currently available to meet these needs. Some housing types are not only innovative uses of real estate but also incorporate a variety of ownership concepts. Notice as you read how the different forms of housing respond to the demands of a diverse marketplace.

Apartment complexes are groups of apartment buildings with any number of units in each building. The buildings may be lowrise or highrise, and the amenities may include parking, security, clubhouses, swimming pools, tennis courts and even golf courses.

The *condominium* is a popular form of residential ownership, particularly for people who want the security of owning property without the care and maintenance a house demands. Condominium owners share ownership of common facilities, such as halls, elevators, swimming pools, clubhouses, tennis courts and surrounding grounds. Management and maintenance of building exteriors and common facilities are provided by the governing association and outside contractors, with expenses paid out of monthly assessments charged to owners.

A *cooperative* is similar to a condominium in that it also can have units that share common facilities. The owners, however, do not actually own the units. Instead, they buy shares of stock in the corporation that holds title to the building. Owners receive proprietary leases that entitle them to occupy particular units. Like condominium unit owners, cooperative unit owners pay their share of the building's expenses.

Planned unit developments (PUDs), sometimes called *master-planned communities,* merge such diverse land uses as housing, recreation and commercial units in one self-contained development. PUDs are planned under special zoning ordinances. These ordinances permit maximum use of open space by reducing lot sizes and street areas. Owners do not have direct ownership interest in the common areas. A community association is formed to maintain these areas, with fees collected from the owners.

Retirement communities, many of them in temperate climates, often are structured as PUDs. They may provide shopping, recreational opportunities and health-care facilities in addition to residential units.

Highrise developments, sometimes called *mixed-use developments* (MUDs), combine office space, stores, theaters and apartment units in a single vertical community. MUDs usually are self-contained and offer laundry facilities, restaurants, food stores, valet shops, beauty parlors, barbershops, swimming pools and other attractive and convenient features.

Converted-use properties are factories, warehouses, office buildings, hotels, schools, churches and other structures that have been converted to residential use. Developers often find renovation of such properties more aesthetically and economically appealing than demolishing a perfectly sound structure to build something new. An abandoned warehouse may be transformed into luxury loft condominium units, a closed hotel may reopen as an apartment building, and an old factory may be recycled into a profitable shopping mall.

Mobile homes were once considered useful only as temporary residences or for travel. Now, however, such homes are more often permanent principal residences or stationary vacation homes. Relatively low cost, coupled with the increased living space available in the newer models, has made such homes an attractive option for many people. Increased sales have resulted in growing numbers of "housing parks" in some communities. These parks offer complete residential environments with permanent community facilities as well as semipermanent foundations and hookups for gas, water and electricity.

Modular homes also are gaining popularity as the price of newly constructed homes rises. Each room is preassembled at a factory, driven to the building site on a truck, then lowered onto its foundation by a crane. Later, workers finish the structure and connect plumbing and wiring. Entire developments can be built at a fraction of the time and cost of conventional construction.

Through *time-shares,* multiple purchasers share ownership of a single property, usually a vacation home. Each owner is entitled to use the property for a certain period of time each year, usually a specific week. In addition to the purchase price, each owner pays an annual maintenance fee.

HOUSING AFFORDABILITY

Housing affordability has become a major issue. Real estate prices have risen, making it difficult for many potential buyers to save the down payment and closing costs needed for a conventional loan. Because more homeowners mean more business opportunities, real estate and related industry groups have a vital interest in ensuring affordable housing for all segments of the population. Congress, state legislatures and local governments have been working to increase the availability of affordable housing.

Certainly not everyone wants to own a home. Home ownership involves substantial commitment and responsibility, and the flexibility of renting suits some individuals' needs. People whose work requires frequent moves or whose financial position is uncertain particularly benefit from renting. Renting also provides more leisure time by freeing tenants from management and maintenance.

Those who choose home ownership must evaluate many factors before they make a final decision to purchase a particular property. And the purchasing decision must be weighed carefully in light of each individual's financial circumstances.

Mortgage Terms

Liberalized mortgage terms and payment plans offer many people the option of purchasing a home. Low-down-payment mortgage loans are available under programs sponsored by the Federal Housing Administration (FHA) and the Department of Veterans Affairs (VA).

An increasing number of creative mortgage loan programs are being offered by various government agencies and private lenders. Adjustable-rate loans, whose lower initial interest rate makes it possible for many buyers to qualify for a mortgage loan, are now common. Specific programs may offer lower closing costs or deferred interest or principal payments for purchasers in targeted neighborhoods or for first-time buyers. Many innovative loans are tailored to suit the younger buyer, who may need a low interest rate to qualify but whose income is expected to increase in coming years.

Ownership Expenses and Ability To Pay

Home ownership involves many expenses, including utilities (such as electricity, natural gas and water), trash removal, sewer charges and maintenance and repairs. Owners also must pay real estate taxes and buy property insurance, and they must repay the mortgage loan with interest.

MEMORY TIP

The basic costs of owning a home—mortgage *Principal, Interest, Taxes* and *Insurance*—can be remembered by the acronym **PITI.**

To determine whether a prospective buyer can afford a certain purchase, lenders traditionally have used a "rule of thumb" formula: The monthly cost of buying and maintaining a home (mortgage payments—both principal and interest—plus taxes and insurance impounds) should not exceed 28 percent of gross (pretax) monthly income. The payments on all debts should not exceed 36 percent of monthly income. Expenses such as insurance premiums, utilities and routine medical care are not included in the 36 percent figure but are considered to be covered by the remaining 64 percent of the buyer's monthly income. These formulas may vary, however, depending on the type of loan program and the borrower's earnings, credit history, number of dependents and other factors.

FOR EXAMPLE A prospective homebuyer wants to know how much house he or she can afford to buy. The buyer has a gross monthly income of $3,000. The buyer's allowable housing expense may be calculated as follows:

$3,000 gross monthly income × 28% = $840 total housing expense allowed
$3,000 gross monthly income × 36% = $1,080 total housing and other debt expense allowed

These formulas allow for other debts of 8 percent of gross monthly income—the difference between the 36 percent and 28 percent figures. If actual debts exceed the amount allowed and the borrower is unable to reduce them, the monthly payment would have to be lowered proportionately because the debts and housing payment combined cannot exceed 36 percent of gross monthly income. So, in the example above, if the homebuyer has $300 in monthly debts, he or she can afford only $780 for PITI ($1,080 – $300), not $840. However, lower debts would not result in a higher allowable housing payment; rather, it would be considered a compensating factor for approval of the loan.

Investment Considerations

Purchasing a home offers several financial advantages to a buyer. First, if the property's value increases, a sale could bring in more money than the owner paid—a long-term gain. Second, as the total mortgage debt is reduced through monthly payments, the owner's actual ownership interest in the property increases. This increasing ownership interest is called **equity** and represents the paid-off share of the property, held free of any mortgage. A tenant accumulates nothing except a good credit rating by paying the rent on time; a homeowner's mortgage payments build equity and so increase his or her net worth. Equity builds even further when the property's value rises. The third financial advantage of homeownership is the tax deductions available to homeowners but not to renters.

Current market value –
Property debt = Equity

Tax Benefits

To encourage home ownership, the federal government allows homeowners certain income tax advantages. Homeowners may deduct from their income some or all of the mortgage interest paid as well as real estate taxes and certain other expenses. They may even defer or eliminate tax on the profit received from selling the home. Tax considerations may be an important part of any decision to purchase a home.

Beginning in 1997, several federal tax reforms were enacted that significantly changed the importance of tax considerations for most homesellers. For instance, while the amount of a homeowner's **capital gain** on the sale of a residence was once an important tax factor, the federal government now excludes $500,000 from capital gains tax for profits on the sale of a principal residence by taxpayers who file jointly. Taxpayers who file singly are entitled to a $250,000 exclusion. The exemption may be used repeatedly, as long as the homeowners have occupied the property as their residence for at least two years.

For most homeowners, the net result of the law is that they will never pay capital gains tax on the sale of their homes. Of course, sellers of higher-bracket homes or those who have accumulated profits over time that exceed $500,000 will continue to face federal capital gains taxation. Individual state tax laws may or may not change to reflect the federal reforms.

In addition, a new law passed in 1998 reduces the required holding period for a noncorporate taxpayer from 18 months to 12 months for long-term capital gain. The mid-term type of capital gain effective prior to 1997 has been eliminated.

Another reform will benefit the real estate market by making it easier for people to obtain down payments. First-time home buyers may make penalty-free withdrawals from their tax-deferred individual retirement funds (IRAs) for a down payment on their home. The limit on such withdrawals is $10,000. Other reforms eliminate the one-time over-55 exclusion (that permitted homeowners over 55 to exclude the gain from the sale of their home one time during their lives) and eliminate the automatic rollover of gains from old to newer properties. In short, the present trend is to reform and simplify federal taxes that affect homeownership—good news for real estate professionals.

Tax deductions. Homeowners may deduct from their gross income

- real estate taxes on all property owned;
- mortgage interest payments on most first and second homes (interest);
- loan origination fees in the year of purchase (interest paid up front) (rules differ for refinance and equity loans);
- loan discount points in the year of purchase (interest paid up front) (rules differ for refinance and equity loans); and
- loan prepayment penalties (interest charged for paying off a loan).

When a homeowner fixes up his or her property in preparation for its sale, the homeowner may deduct certain expenses from his or her gain in determining the adjusted sales price for capital gains purposes.

The cost of materials, such as paint, carpeting and wallpaper, and other repairs may be deducted if the expense meets specific IRS requirements.

HOMEOWNER'S INSURANCE

A home is frequently the biggest investment many people ever make. Most homeowners see the wisdom in protecting such an important investment by insuring it. Lenders usually require that a homeowner obtain insurance when the debt is secured by the property. While owners can purchase individual policies that insure against destruction of property by fire or windstorm, injury to others and theft of personal property, most buy packaged **homeowner's insurance policies** to cover all these risks.

Coverage and Claims   The most common homeowner's policy is called a *basic form.* It provides property coverage against

- fire and lightning,
- glass breakage,
- windstorm and hail,
- explosion,
- riot and civil commotion,
- damage by aircraft,
- damage from vehicles,
- damage from smoke,
- vandalism and malicious mischief,
- theft and
- loss of property removed from the premises when it is endangered by fire or other perils.

A broad-form policy also is available. It covers

- falling objects;
- damage due to the weight of ice, snow or sleet;
- collapse of all or part of the building;
- bursting, cracking, burning or bulging of a steam or hot water heating system or of appliances used to heat water;

- accidental discharge, leakage or overflow of water or steam from within a plumbing, a heating or an air-conditioning system;
- freezing of plumbing, heating and air-conditioning systems and domestic appliances; and
- injury to electrical appliances, devices, fixtures and wiring from short circuits or other accidentally generated currents.

Further insurance is available from policies that cover almost all possible perils. Special apartment and condominium policies generally provide fire and windstorm, theft and public **liability coverage** for injuries or losses sustained within the unit. However, they do not usually cover losses or damages to the structure. The basic structure is insured by either the landlord or the condominium owners' association.

A third party, such as an insurance company, may make a payment to settle a claim covered by a policy. When this happens, the third party generally acquires the right to any remedy or damages available to the insured. This right is called *subrogation*.

Most homeowner's insurance policies contain a **coinsurance clause.** This provision usually requires that the owner maintain insurance equal to at least 80 percent of the **replacement cost** of the dwelling (not including the price of the land). An owner who has this type of policy may make a claim for the full cost of the repair or replacement of the damaged property without deduction for depreciation.

If the homeowner carries less than 80 percent of the full replacement cost, however, the claim will be handled in one of two ways. Either the loss will be settled for the actual cash value (replacement cost less depreciation) or it will be prorated by dividing the percentage of replacement cost actually covered by the policy by the minimum coverage requirement (usually 80 percent).

FEDERAL FLOOD INSURANCE PROGRAM

The National Flood Insurance Act of 1968 was enacted by Congress to help owners of property in flood-prone areas by subsidizing flood insurance and by taking land-use and land-control measures to improve future management for floodplain areas. The Federal Emergency Management Agency (FEMA) administers the flood program. The Army Corps of Engineers has prepared maps that identify specific flood-prone areas throughout the country. Owners in flood-prone areas must obtain flood insurance to finance property with federal or federally related mortgage loans. If they do not obtain the insurance (either they don't want it or they don't qualify because their communities have not properly entered the program), they are not eligible for this financial assistance.

In designated areas, flood insurance is required on all types of buildings—residential, commercial, industrial and agricultural—for either the value of the property or the amount of the mortgage loan, subject to the maximum limits available. Policies are written annually and can be purchased from any licensed property insurance broker, the National Flood Insurance Program or the designated servicing companies in each state. However, if a borrower can produce a survey showing that the lowest part of the building is located above the 100-year flood mark, the borrower may be exempted from the flood insurance requirement, even if the property is in a flood-prone area.

SUMMARY

Current trends in home ownership include single-family homes, apartment complexes, condominiums, cooperatives, planned unit developments, retirement communities, highrise developments, converted-use properties, modular homes, mobile homes and time-shares.

Prospective buyers should be aware of both the advantages and disadvantages of home ownership. While a homeowner gains financial security and pride of ownership, the costs of ownership—the initial price and the continuing expenses—must be considered.

One of the income tax benefits available to homeowners is the ability to deduct mortgage interest payments (with certain limitations) and property taxes from their federal income tax returns. The federal government now excludes $500,000 from capital gains tax for profits on the sale of a principal residence by taxpayers who file jointly. Taxpayers who file singly are entitled to a $250,000 exclusion. The exemption may be used repeatedly, as long as the homeowners have occupied the property as their residence for at least two years.

To protect their investment in real estate, most homeowners purchase insurance. A standard homeowner's insurance policy covers fire, theft and liability and can be extended to cover many types of less common risks. Another type of insurance, which covers personal property only, is available to people who live in apartments and condominiums.

Many homeowner's policies contain a coinsurance clause that requires that the policyholder maintain insurance in an amount equal to 80 percent of the replacement cost of the home. If this percentage is not met, the policyholder may not be reimbursed for the full repair costs if a loss occurs.

In addition to homeowner's insurance, the federal government requires flood insurance for people living in flood-prone areas who wish to obtain federally regulated or federally insured mortgage loans.

QUESTIONS

1. The real cost of owning a home includes certain costs or expenses that many people tend to overlook. All of the following are costs or expenses of owning a home EXCEPT:
   A. interest paid on borrowed capital.
   B. homeowner's insurance.
   C. maintenance and repairs.
   D. taxes on personal property.

2. Mr. and Mrs. Homeowner paid $56,000 for their property 20 years ago. Today the market value is $119,000 and they owe $5,000 on their mortgage. In regards to this situation, which of the following is true?
   A. The $63,000 difference between the original investment and the market value is their tax basis.
   B. The $114,000 difference between the market value and the mortgage is their equity.
   C. The $63,000 difference between the original investment and the market value will be used to compute the capital gains.
   D. The $114,000 difference between the market value and the mortgage is their replacement cost.

3. A building that is remodeled into residential units and is no longer used for the purpose for which it was originally built is an example of a(n):
   A. converted-use property.
   B. urban homesteading.
   C. planned unit development.
   D. modular home.

4. A highrise development that includes office space, stores, theaters and apartment units is an example of which of the following?
   A. Planned unit development
   B. Mixed-use development
   C. Converted-use property
   D. Special cluster zoning

5. Theresa, a single person, bought her home 18 months ago, and has found a new job in another city. Ursula and Vincent are a married couple who file jointly but have owned their nine-bedroom home for only three years. Now, Ursula and Vincent want to move to a small condominium unit. Walter, a single person, has owned his home for 17 years, and will use the proceeds from his sale to purchase a larger house. Based on these facts, which of these people is entitled to the $500,000 exclusion?
   A. Theresa only
   B. Ursula and Vincent only
   C. Ursula, Vincent and Walter only
   D. Walter and Theresa only

6. If a jointly filing homeowner realizes a profit from the sale of his or her home that exceeds $500,000, what is the result?
   A. The homeowner will not pay capital gains tax if he or she is over 55.
   B. Up to $125,000 of the excess profit will be taxed as a capital gain.
   C. The excess gain will be taxed at the homeowner's income tax rate.
   D. The excess gain will be taxed at the current applicable capital gains rate.

7. A typical homeowner's insurance policy covers all of the following EXCEPT:
   A. the cost of medical expenses for a person injured in the policyholder's home.
   B. theft.
   C. vandalism.
   D. flood damage.

8. One result of the new tax law enacted in 1997 is that most homeowners:
   A. will pay capital gains tax at an 8 percent lower rate on their home sales.
   B. may use a one-time $500,000 exclusion if they file their taxes jointly.
   C. will never pay capital gains tax on the sale of their homes.
   D. will be permitted to use the $125,000 over-55 exclusion more than once.

9. In 1998 Lorenzo purchased his home and paid two discount points at the closing. Which of the following is NOT deductible from his gross income?
   A. Mortgage interest payments on a principal residence
   B. Real estate taxes (except for interest on overdue taxes)
   C. The gain realized from the sale or exchange of a principal residence
   D. Loan discount points

10. A lot is valued at $25,000 and the house is valued at $75,000. If the house is totally destroyed by fire, under a standard insurance policy, which of the following would MOST LIKELY occur?
    A. The insurance company would pay $100,000 to the owner.
    B. The insurance company would pay $75,000 to the owner.
    C. The insurance company would pay $60,000 to the owner.
    D. The insurance company would pay $80,000 to the owner.

11. Janis has a basis of $30,000 in her primary residence. She sells the house for $45,000. The broker's commission was 6.5 percent, and other selling expenses amounted to $400. What is Janis's gain on this transaction?
    A. $11,450
    B. $11,500
    C. $11,675
    D. $14,025

12. Marco incurs the following expenses: (1) $9,500 in interest on a mortgage loan on his residence; (2) $800 in real estate taxes plus a $450 late payment penalty; and (3) a $1,000 loan origination fee paid in the course of purchasing his home. How much may be deducted from Marco's gross income?
    A. $9,800
    B. $10,500
    C. $11,300
    D. $11,750

Real Estate Agency

KEY TERMS

agency
agency coupled with
   an interest
agent
buyer agency
buyer agency
   agreement
client
common-law law of
   agency
customer

designated agent
dual agency
express agreement
fiduciary relationship
fraud
general agent
implied agreement
latent defect
law of agency
listing agreement
ministerial acts

negligent
   misrepresentation
principal
puffing
ready, willing and
   able buyer
single agency
special agent
subagent
universal agent

INTRODUCTION TO REAL ESTATE AGENCY

The relationship between a real estate licensee and the parties involved in a real estate transaction is not a simple one. In addition to the parties' assumptions and expectations, the licensee is subject to a wide range of legal and ethical requirements designed to protect the seller, the buyer and the transaction itself. **Agency** is the word used to describe that special relationship between a real estate licensee and the person he or she represents. Agency is governed by two kinds of law: *common law* (the rules of a society established by tradition and court decisions) and *statutory law* (the laws, rules and regulations enacted by legislatures and other governing bodies). Article 4 of the License Act establishes agency rules and regulations in Illinois.

The History of Agency

The basic framework of the law that governs the legal responsibilities of the broker to the people he or she represents is known as the **common-law law of agency.** The fundamentals of agency law have remained largely unchanged for hundreds of years. However, the application of the law has changed dramatically, particularly in residential transactions and especially in recent years. As states enact legislation that defines and governs the broker-client relationship, brokers are reevaluating their services. They must determine whether they will represent the seller, the buyer or both in a transaction. They also must decide how they will cooperate with other brokers, depending on which party each broker represents. In short, the brokerage business is undergoing many changes as brokers focus on ways to enhance their services to buyers and sellers.

Even as the laws change, however, the underlying assumptions that govern the agency relationship remain intact. The principal-agent relationship evolved from the master-servant relationship under English common law. In that relationship, the servant owed absolute loyalty to the master. This loyalty superseded the servant's personal interests as well as any loyalty the servant might owe to others. In a modern-day agency relationship, the agent owes the principal similar loyalty. As masters used the services of servants to accomplish what they could not or did not want to do for themselves, principals use the services of agents. The agent is regarded as an expert on whom the principal can rely for specialized professional advice.

COMMON LAW OF AGENCY

The **law of agency** defines the rights and duties of the principal and the agent. It applies to a variety of business transactions. In real estate transactions, contract law and real estate licensing laws—in addition to the law of agency—interpret the relationship between licensees and their clients. The law of agency is a common-law concept; it may be (and increasingly is) superseded by state statute.

Definitions

Real estate brokers and salespersons commonly are called **agents.** Legally, however, the term refers to strictly defined legal relationships. In the case of real estate, it is a relationship with buyers and sellers or with landlords and tenants. In the common law of agency, the following terms have specific definitions. A general understanding of these terms is essential before considering their applications in Illinois.

> An agent is a person authorized to act on behalf of another.

- **Agent**—the individual who is authorized and consents to represent the interests of another person. In the real estate business, a firm's broker is the agent, and he or she shares this responsibility with the licensees who work for the firm.
- **Subagent**—the agent of an agent. If the original agency agreement permits it, an agent may delegate some of his or her authority or responsibility to a third party. The subagent also is an agent of the principal. *In Illinois, subagents are not allowed in multiple-listing service arrangements.*
- **Principal**—the individual who hires the agent and delegates to him or her the responsibility of representing the principal's interests. In the real estate business, the principal is the buyer or seller, landlord or tenant.
- **Agency**—the fiduciary relationship between the principal and the agent.
- **Fiduciary**—the relationship in which the agent is held in a position of special trust and confidence by the principal; also, the individual who is placed in the position of trust.
- **Client**—the principal.
- **Customer**—the third party for whom some level of service is provided and who is entitled to fairness and honesty.
- **Nonagent**—(also referred to as a *facilitator, transactional broker, transactional coordinator* or *contract broker*) an intermediary between a buyer and seller (or landlord and tenant) who assists both parties with the transaction without representing either party's interests. Nonagents are often subject to specific statutory responsibilities.

January 1995

In Illinois . . .

Agency relationships in Illinois are governed by statute. The Illinois Brokerage Relationships in Real Estate Transactions Law (255 ILCS 455/38.1 et seq.) applies "to the exclusion of the common law concepts of principal and agent and to the fiduciary duties, which have . . . been applied to real estate brokers, salespersons, and real estate brokerage services." In this chapter, however, we will discuss both the traditional common-law relationships and the Illinois statute.

The general terms of the law of agency under the Illinois statute (255 ILCS 455/38.1–38.65) are defined as follows:

- **Agency**—a relationship in which a real estate broker or licensee, whether directly or through an affiliated licensee, represents a consumer by the consumer's consent, whether express or implied, in a real property transaction. *Exclusive in writing*
- **Brokerage agreement**—a written or oral agreement for brokerage services to be provided to a consumer in return for compensation or the right to receive compensation from another.
- **Client**—a person who is being represented by a licensee.
- **Consumer**—a person or entity who seeks or receives real estate brokerage services. *goods or services*
- **Customer**—a consumer who is not being represented by a licensee, but for whom the licensee is performing ministerial acts.
- **Ministerial acts**—those acts that a licensee may perform for a consumer that are informative in nature and do not rise to the level of active representation. For instance, responding to inquiries about a property's price or location; responding to questions at an open house; or completing business or factual information for a consumer on an offer or contract to purchase a client's property. ■

> An agent works *for* the *client* and *with* the *customer*.

There is a distinction between the level of services an agent provides to a **client** and the level of services the agent provides to a **customer.** The client is the **principal** to whom the agent gives advice and counsel. The agent is entrusted with certain confidential information and has fiduciary responsibilities (discussed in greater detail later) to the principal. In contrast, the customer is entitled to factual information and fair and honest dealings as a consumer but does not receive advice and counsel or confidential information about the principal. The agent works for the principal and with the customer. Essentially, the agent is an advocate for the principal, not for the customer.

The relationship between the principal and agent must be consensual; that is, the principal delegates authority, and the agent consents to act as the agent of the principal. Alternatively, the broker may designate a salesperson to act as agent. The parties must agree to form the relationship. An agent may be authorized by the principal to use the assistance of others.

Just as the agent owes certain duties to the principal, the principal has responsibilities toward the agent. The principal's primary duties are to comply with the agency agreement and cooperate with the agent; that is, the principal must not hinder the agent and must deal with the agent in good faith. The principal also must compensate the agent according to the terms of the agency agreement.

Fiduciary Responsibilities

The agency agreement usually authorizes the broker to act for the principal. The law of agency requires that the broker make a reasonable effort to carry out the assumed agency duties successfully. The agent's **fiduciary relationship** of trust and confidence with the principal means that the broker owes the principal certain specific duties. These duties are not simply moral or ethical; they are the law—the common law of agency or the statutory law governing real estate transactions. *Under the common law of agency, an agent owes the principal the five duties of care, obedience, accounting, loyalty (including confidentiality) and disclosure.*

Reasonable skill and care. The agent must exercise a reasonable degree of care while transacting the business entrusted to him or her by the principal. The principal expects the agent's skill and expertise in real estate matters to be superior to that of the average person. The most fundamental way in which the agent exercises care is to use that skill and knowledge in the principal's behalf. The agent should know all facts pertinent to the principal's affairs, such as the physical characteristics of the property being transferred and the type of financing being used.

If the agent represents the seller, care and skill include helping the seller arrive at an appropriate and realistic listing price, discovering and disclosing facts that affect the seller and properly presenting the contracts that the seller signs. It also means making reasonable efforts to market the property, such as advertising and holding open houses, and helping the seller evaluate the terms and conditions of offers to purchase.

An agent who represents the buyer is expected to help the buyer locate suitable property and evaluate property values, neighborhood and property conditions, financing alternatives and offers and counteroffers with the buyer's interest in mind.

An agent who does not make a reasonable effort to properly represent the interests of the principal could be found by a court to have been negligent. The agent is liable to the principal for any loss resulting from the agent's negligence or carelessness. The standard of care will vary from market to market and depends on the expected behavior for a particular type of transaction in a particular area.

In Practice

Because real estate licensees have, under the law, enormous exposure to liability, some brokers purchase what are known as errors and omissions (E&O) insurance policies for their firms. Similar to malpractice insurance in the medical and legal fields, E&O policies cover liability for errors and negligence in the usual listing and selling activities of a real estate office. Individual salespersons also might be insured. Licensing laws in several states now require E&O insurance for brokers and, in some cases, for individual salespersons as well. However, no insurance policy will protect a licensee from litigation arising from criminal acts. Insurance companies normally exclude coverage for violation of civil rights and antitrust laws as well.

Obedience. The fiduciary relationship obligates the agent to act in good faith at all times, obeying the principal's instructions in accordance with the contract.

However, that obedience is not absolute. The agent may not obey instructions that are unlawful or unethical. Because illegal acts do not serve the principal's

---

MEMORY TIP

The five common-law fiduciary duties may be remembered by the acronym **COALD:** *Care, Obedience, Accounting, Loyalty* and *Disclosure.*

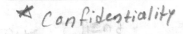 ✱ *Confidentiality*

best interests, obeying such instructions violates the broker's duty of loyalty. On the other hand, an agent who exceeds the authority assigned in the contract will be liable for any losses that the principal suffers as a result.

FOR EXAMPLE   A seller tells the listing agent, "I don't want you to show this house to any, you know, minorities." Because refusing to show a property to someone on the basis of race is illegal, the agent may not follow the seller's instructions.

Accounting. Most states' license laws require that agents periodically report the status of all funds or property received from or on behalf of the principal. Similarly, most state license laws require that brokers give accurate copies of all documents to all affected parties and keep copies on file for a specified period of time.

In Illinois . . .

Illinois brokers are required to deliver true copies of all documents to the people who signed them *within 24 hours.* In Illinois, all funds entrusted to a broker must be deposited in a special escrow account by the next business day following the signing of a sale contract or lease. Commingling such monies with the broker's personal or general business funds is illegal. Records of escrow account transactions must be kept on file for three years.   ■

Loyalty. The duty of loyalty requires that the agent place the principal's interests above those of all others, including the agent's own self-interest. The agent must be particularly sensitive to any possible conflicts of interest. Confidentiality about the principal's personal affairs is a key element of loyalty. An agent may not, for example, disclose the principal's financial condition. When the principal is the seller, the agent may not reveal such things as the principal's willingness to accept less than the listing price or his or her anxiousness to sell unless the principal has authorized the disclosure. If the principal is the buyer, the agent may not disclose, for instance, that the buyer will pay more than the offered price if necessary or that the buyer is under a tight moving schedule or any other fact that might harm the principal's bargaining position.

In Illinois . . .

While an agent may not disclose personal information about his or her principal, known material facts about the property's condition must be disclosed.

Because the agent may not act out of self-interest, the negotiation of a sales contract must be conducted without regard to how much the agent will earn in commission. All states forbid agents to buy property listed with them for their own accounts or for accounts in which they have a personal interest without first disclosing that interest and receiving the principal's consent. Neither brokers nor salespersons may sell property in which they have a personal interest without informing the purchaser of that interest.   ■

Disclosure. It is the agent's duty to keep the principal informed of all facts or information that could affect a transaction. Duty of disclosure includes relevant information or material facts that the agent knows or should have known.

The agent is obligated to discover facts that a reasonable person would feel are important in choosing a course of action, regardless of whether those facts are favorable or unfavorable to the principal's position. The agent may be held liable for damages for failing to disclose such information.

An agent for the buyer must disclose deficiencies of a property as well as sales contract provisions and financing that do not suit the buyer's needs. The agent would suggest the lowest price the buyer should pay based on comparable values, regardless of the listing price. The agent also would disclose information about how long a property has been listed or why the owner is selling that would affect the buyer's ability to negotiate the lowest purchase price possible. If the agent represents the seller, of course, disclosure of any of this information would violate the agent's fiduciary duty to the seller.

In Illinois . . .

These duties, based on (but replacing) agency common law, are set forth in Article IX of the Illinois Real Estate License Act. According to this statute, the agent must

1. perform the terms of the brokerage agreement.
2. promote the best interests of the client by
   - seeking a transaction at the price and terms stated in the brokerage agreement or at a price and terms otherwise acceptable to the client;
   - timely presenting all offers to and from the client, unless the client has waived this duty;
   - disclosing to the client material facts concerning the transaction of which the licensee has actual knowledge, unless that information is confidential information;
   - timely accounting for all money and property received in which the client has, may have or should have an interest;
   - obeying specific directions of the client that are not otherwise contrary to applicable statutes, ordinances or rules; and
   - acting in a manner consistent with promoting the client's best interests as opposed to a licensee's or any other person's self-interest.
3. exercise reasonable skill and care in the performance of brokerage services.
4. keep confidential all confidential information received from the client. Confidentiality is not limited to the term of the agreement; client confidentiality is forever.
5. comply with all the requirements of the law, including fair housing and civil rights.

Although based on common law, these duties are statutory. ■

Creation of Agency

An agency relationship may be based on a formal agreement between the parties (an *express agency*) or it may result from the parties' behavior (an *implied agency*).

Express agency. The principal and agent may enter into a contract, or an **express agreement,** in which the parties formally express their intention to establish an agency and state its terms and conditions. The agreement may be either oral or written. An agency relationship between a seller and a broker generally is created by a written employment contract, commonly referred to as a **listing agreement,** which authorizes the broker to find a buyer or tenant for the owner's property. An express agency relationship between a buyer and a broker is created by a **buyer agency agreement.** Similar to a listing agreement, it stipulates the activities and responsibilities the buyer expects from the broker in finding the appropriate property for purchase or rent.

In Illinois . . .

Illinois law does not require written listing agreements; however, it is a good idea to have them in writing. A listing agreement cannot be enforced in court unless it is in writing. ■ *all Exiuesive must be written*

Implied agency. An agency also may be created by **implied agreement.** This occurs when the actions of the parties indicate that they have mutually consented to an agency. A person acts on behalf of another as agent; the other person, as principal, delegates the authority to act. The parties may not have consciously planned to create an agency relationship. Nonetheless, one can result unintentionally, inadvertently or accidentally by their actions.

F **OR EXAMPLE** Nancy tells Phillip, a real estate broker, that she is thinking about selling her home. Phillip immediately contacts several prospective buyers. One of them makes an attractive offer without even seeing the property. Phillip goes to Nancy's house and presents the offer, which Nancy accepts. Although no formal agency agreement was entered into either orally or in writing, Phillip's actions implied to prospective buyers that Phillip was acting as Nancy's agent.

In Illinois . . .

Even though licensees may be required to disclose whom they represent to the parties, it often is difficult for customers to understand the complexities of the law of agency. To resolve some of this confusion, Article 15 of the Illinois Real Estate License Act (referred to as the *Illinois Brokerage Relationships in Real Estate Transactions Law*) was enacted. Under this law, the licensee is presumed to be the agent of the consumer with whom the licensee is working unless

- there is a written agreement between the broker and the consumer providing for a different relationship or
- the licensee is performing only ministerial acts on behalf of the consumer.

Ministerial acts are defined as acts that are informative in nature—that is, acts that do not rise to the level of active representation. Examples of ministerial acts include

- responding to phone inquiries by consumers as to the availability and pricing of brokerage services;
- responding to phone inquiries from a consumer concerning the price or location of property;
- attending an open house and responding to questions about the property from a consumer;
- setting an appointment to view property;
- responding to questions of consumers walking into a licensee's office concerning brokerage services offered or a particular property;
- accompanying an appraiser, inspector, contractor or similar third party on a visit to a property;
- completing business or factual information for a consumer on an offer or contract to purchase on behalf of a client;
- showing a client through a property being sold by an owner on his or her own behalf; or
- referring to another broker or service provider.

On the other hand, if a licensee prequalifies a consumer to determine what price of housing the consumer can afford, searches for suitable properties for the consumer to view, shows the properties to the consumer, helps negotiate a sales price for the consumer and walks the consumer through the closing process, the licensee would be going beyond the definition of ministerial acts and would be considered the agent of that consumer. ■

Compensation. The source of compensation does not determine agency. An agent does not necessarily represent the person who pays his or her commission. In fact, agency can exist even if no fee is involved (called a *gratuitous agency*). Buyers and sellers can agree however they choose to compensate the broker, regardless of which is the agent's principal. For instance, a seller could agree to pay a commission to the buyer's agent. The written agency agreement should state how the agent is being compensated and explain all the alternatives available.

Termination of Agency

An agency may be terminated for any of the following reasons:

- Death or incapacity of either the client or the broker (notice of death is not necessary)
- Destruction or condemnation of the property
- Expiration of the terms of the agency
- Mutual agreement by all parties to the contract
- Breach by one of the parties, such as abandonment by the agent or revocation by the principal (in which case the breaching party might be liable for damages)
- By operation of law, as in bankruptcy of the principal (bankruptcy terminates the agency contract, and title to the property transfers to a court-appointed receiver)
- Completion, performance or fulfillment of the purpose for which the agency was created

In Illinois . . .

A definite termination date must be included in an agency agreement under Illinois law. Automatic extension clauses are illegal in Illinois. ■

An **agency coupled with an interest** is an agency relationship in which the agent is given an interest in the subject of the agency, such as the property being sold. An agency coupled with an interest cannot be revoked by the principal or be terminated on the principal's death.

FOR EXAMPLE A broker agrees to provide the financing for a condominium building being constructed by a developer in exchange for the exclusive right to sell the units once the building is completed. The developer may not revoke the listing agreement once the broker has provided the financing because this is an agency coupled with an interest.

TYPES OF AGENCY RELATIONSHIPS

What an agent may do as the principal's representative depends solely on what the principal authorizes the agent to do.

Limitations on an Agent's Authority

A **universal agent** is a person empowered to do anything the principal could do personally. The universal agent's authority to act on behalf of the principal is virtually unlimited. In Illinois, a written power of attorney agreement is necessary to create a universal agency.

working for owner property agency

A **general agent** may represent the principal in a broad range of matters related to a particular business or activity. The general agent may, for example, bind the principal to any contract within the scope of the agent's authority. This type of agency can be created by a general power of attorney, which makes the agent an attorney-in-fact. A real estate broker typically does not have this scope of authority as an agent in a real estate transaction. A property manager often is a general agent.

working for seller, buyer

> A general agent represents the principal *generally;* a special agent represents the principal only for *special occasions,* such as the sale of a house.

A **special agent** is authorized to represent the principal in one specific act or business transaction only, under detailed instructions. A real estate broker usually is a special agent. If hired by a seller, the broker is limited to finding a **ready, willing and able buyer** for the property. A special agent for a buyer would have the limited responsibility of finding a property that fits the buyer's criteria. As a special agent, the broker may not bind the principal to any contract. A special power of attorney is another means of authorizing an agent to carry out only a specified act or acts.

> Special agency—working for a
> - seller in a listing agreement
> - buyer in a buyer's agreement
> - tenant in a rental finder's agreement
>
> General agency—working for an
> - owner in a property management agreement

FOR EXAMPLE You are very busy with an important project, so you give your colleague $5 and ask him to buy your lunch. Your colleague is your general agent: you have limited his scope of activity to a particular business (buying your lunch) and established the amount that may be spent (up to $5). Still, he has broad discretion in selecting what you will eat and where he will buy it. However, if you had told your colleague, "Please buy me a Number 3 salad at Lettuce Eat Lettuce," you would have further limited his authority to a very specific task. Your colleague, therefore, would have been your special agent.

Finally, a **designated agent** is a person authorized by the broker to act as the agent of a specific principal. A designated agent is the only agent in the company who has a fiduciary responsibility toward the principal. When one salesperson in the company is a designated agent, the others are free to act as agents for the other party in a transaction. Thus, two salespersons from the same real estate company may end up representing opposite sides in a property sale.

In Illinois . . .

Designated agency is permitted in Illinois. A broker may designate individual salespersons or associated brokers within his or her brokerage business as being the exclusive agents of a client. The broker will not be considered a dual agent as long as the designated agents represent only one party in a single transaction. ■

Single Agency

In **single agency,** the agent represents only one party in any single transaction. The agent owes fiduciary duties exclusively to one principal, who may be either the buyer or the seller (or the landlord or tenant) in a transaction. Any third party is a customer. (See Figure 4.1.)

While a single agency broker may represent both sellers and buyers, he or she cannot represent both in the same transaction. This avoids conflicts and results in client-based service and loyalty to only one client. On the other hand, it precludes the sale of in-house listings to represented buyers. The

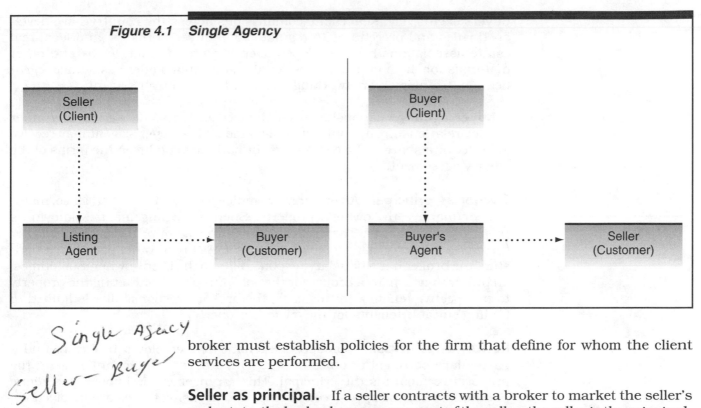

Figure 4.1   Single Agency

Single Agency
Seller — Buyer

broker must establish policies for the firm that define for whom the client services are performed.

Seller as principal.   If a seller contracts with a broker to market the seller's real estate, the broker becomes an agent of the seller; the seller is the principal, the broker's client. In single agency, a buyer who contacts the broker to review properties listed with the broker's firm is the broker's customer. Though obligated to deal fairly with all parties to a transaction and to comply with all aspects of the license law, the broker is strictly accountable only to the principal—in this case, the seller. The customer (in this case, the buyer) usually will be the client of another agent.

The listing contract usually authorizes the broker to use licensees employed by the broker as well as the services of other, cooperating brokers in marketing the seller's real estate.

The relationship of a salesperson or an associate broker to an employing broker also is an agency. These licensees are thus agents of the broker in addition to being subagents of the principal.

Buyer as principal.   When a buyer contracts with a broker to locate property and represent his or her interests in a transaction, the buyer is the principal—the broker's client. The broker, as agent, is strictly accountable to the buyer. The seller is the customer and may be the client of another agent or a *FSBO* (pronounced "fizz-boe," it means *for sale by owner*).

In the past, it was simple: brokers always represented sellers, and buyers were expected to look out for themselves. With the widespread use of multiple-listing services, a buyer often had the mistaken impression that the subagent was the buyer's agent, although the reality was that the agent represented the seller's interests.

Today, however, many residential brokers and salespersons are discovering opportunities of buyer representation. Some brokers and salespersons have become specialists in the emerging field of buyer brokerage, representing buyers exclusively. Real estate commissions across the country have developed rules and procedures to regulate such buyer's brokers, and local real estate associations have developed agency representation forms and other materials for them to use. Professional organizations offer assistance, certification, training and networking opportunities for buyer's agents.

A **buyer agency** relationship is established in the same way as any other agency relationship: by contract or agreement. The buyer's agent may receive a flat fee or a share of the commission or both, depending on the terms of the agency agreement.

Owner as principal. An owner may employ a broker to market, lease, maintain or manage the owner's property. Such an arrangement is known as *property management.* The broker is made the agent of the property owner through a property management agreement. As in any other agency relationship, the broker has a fiduciary responsibility to the client-owner. Sometimes, an owner may employ a broker for the sole purpose of marketing the property to prospective tenants. In this case, the broker's responsibility is limited to finding suitable tenants for the owner's property.

Renter as principal. A prospective tenant may employ a broker to find a particular apartment or office to rent. The broker is the tenant's agent; the prospective tenant is the principal. This arrangement is known as a *rental finding service,* and special contractual and licensing issues are involved.

Dual Agency

In **dual agency,** the agent represents two principals in the same transaction. Dual agency requires equal loyalty to two separate principals at the same time. The challenge is to fulfill the fiduciary obligations to one principal without compromising the interests of the other, especially when the parties' interests may not only be separate but even opposite. While practical methods of ensuring fairness and equal representation exist, it should be noted that a dual agent can never fully represent either party's interests. (See Figure 4.2.)

Because of the obvious risks inherent in dual agency—ranging from conflicts of interest to outright abuse of trust—the practice is illegal in some states. In Illinois, dual agency is permitted; however, all parties must give their informed written consent.

FOR EXAMPLE   *Martin,* a real estate broker, is the agent for the owner of Roomy Manor, a large mansion. *Josef,* a prospective buyer, comes into *Martin's* office and asks *Martin* to represent him in his search for a modest home. After several weeks of activity, including two offers unsuccessfully negotiated by *Martin, Josef* spots the For Sale sign in front of Roomy Manor. She tells *Martin* she wants to make an offer and asks for *Martin's* advice on a likely price range. *Martin* is now in the difficult position of being a dual agent: *Martin* represents the seller (who naturally is interested in receiving the highest possible price) and the buyer (who is interested in making a successful low offer).

Disclosed dual agency.   Real estate licensing laws may permit dual agency only if the buyer and seller are informed and consent to the broker's representation of both in the same transaction. Although the possibility of conflict of interest still exists, disclosure is intended to minimize the risk for the broker by ensuring that both principals are aware of the effect of dual agency on their respective interests. The disclosure alerts the principals that they may have to assume greater responsibility for protecting their interests than they would if they had independent representation. The broker must reconcile how, as

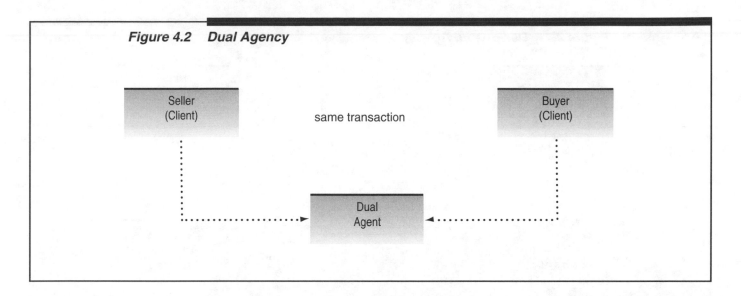

Figure 4.2   Dual Agency

agent, he or she will discharge the fiduciary duties on behalf of both principals, particularly providing loyalty and protecting confidential information. See Figure 4.3 for the required Illinois Consensual Dual Agency form.

Considerable debate focuses on whether brokers can properly represent both the buyer and seller in the same transaction, even though the dual agency is disclosed. As discussed previously, several states have passed laws that permit a broker to designate certain licensees within the firm who act as the legal representatives of a principal—a practice known as *designated agency.* The broker is not considered a dual agent as long as the designated agent for each principal in the transaction is not the same salesperson. In effect, these laws create a split-interest agency, which is quite a departure from the traditional common law. It is likely that there will be additional legislative developments as the states wrestle with this issue.

Figure 4.3   Consensual Dual Agency

The undersigned *(insert name(s)),* ("licensee"), may undertake a dual representation (represent both the seller or landlord and the buyer or tenant) for the sale or lease of the property located at *(insert address).* The under-signed acknowledge they were informed of the possibility of this type of representation. Before signing this document please read the following:

Representing more than one party to a transaction presents a conflict of interest since both clients may rely upon licensee's advice and the client's respective interests may be adverse to each other. Licensee will undertake this representation only with the written consent of ALL clients in the transaction.

Any agreement between the clients as to a final contract price and other terms is a result of negotiations between the clients acting in their own best interests and on their own behalf. You acknowledge that licensee has explained the implications of dual representation, including the risks involved, and understand that you have been advised to seek independent advice from your advisors or attorneys before signing any documents in this transaction.

_____   _____
Buyer   Seller

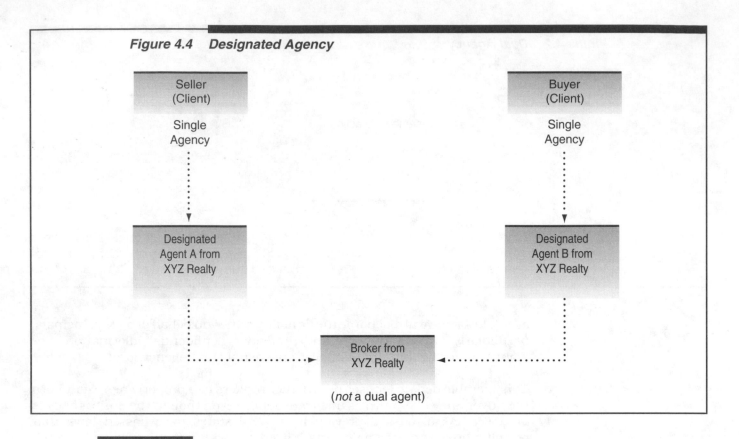

Figure 4.4   Designated Agency

(*not* a dual agent)

In Illinois . . .

Designated agency. In an attempt to avoid dual agency, particularly when the buyer-principal wants to purchase a property listed by the same broker-agent (known as an *in-house sale*), Illinois allows a broker to designate certain licensees within the firm as the legal representatives of a principal. The broker is not considered a dual agent unless he or she is working with a buyer and seller who are his or her personal clients, in which case the broker is a designated agent. (See Figure 4.4.)

A designated agent must take care to protect confidential information disclosed by the client. However, a designated agent may disclose to his or her sponsoring broker confidential information for the purpose of seeking advice or assistance in regards to the transaction for the benefit of the client. ■

Undisclosed dual agency. A broker may not intend to create a dual agency. However, a salesperson's words and actions may create a dual agency unintentionally or inadvertently. Sometimes the cause is carelessness. Other times the salesperson does not fully understand his or her fiduciary responsibilities. Some salespeople lose sight of legal obligations when they focus intensely on bringing buyers and sellers together. For example, a salesperson representing the seller might tell a buyer that the seller will accept less than the listing price. Or the salesperson might promise to persuade the seller to accept an offer that is in the buyer's interest. Giving the buyer any specific advice on how much to offer can lead the buyer to believe that the salesperson is an advocate for the buyer. These actions create an implied agency with the buyer and violate the duties of loyalty and confidentiality to the principal-seller. Because neither party has been informed of that situation and been given the opportunity to seek separate representation, the interests of both are jeopardized. This undisclosed dual agency is a violation of licensing laws. It can result in rescission of the sales contract, forfeiture of commission or filing of a suit for damages.

In Illinois . . .

One of the purposes of Article IV of the Illinois Real Estate License Act is to reduce the incidence of undisclosed dual agency by creating a statutory presumption that the licensee is representing the party he or she is actually working with. ■

Disclosure of Agency

A licensee is required to reveal who his or her client is. Understanding the scope of the service a party can expect from the agent allows a customer to make an informed decision about whether to seek his or her own representation.

Mandatory agency disclosure laws now exist in every state. These laws stipulate when, how and to whom disclosures must be made. They may, for instance, dictate that a particular type of written form be used. The laws might state what information an agent must provide to gain informed consent where disclosed dual agency is permitted. The laws even might go so far as to require that all agency alternatives be explained, including the brokerage firm's policies regarding its services. Frequently, printed brochures outlining agency alternatives are available to a firm's clients and customers.

In Illinois . . .

Licensees are presumed to be representing the consumer with whom they are working as the consumer's designated agent, unless there is a written agreement between them specifying another relationship or if the licensee is performing only ministerial acts on the consumer's behalf. If the other party is represented by another agent, no disclosures are necessary. A licensee who is acting as the designated agent of a party must disclose *in writing* to any customer that the agency relationship exists. (See Figure 4.5.) Understanding the scope of the service a party can expect from the broker allows customers to make an informed decision about whether to seek their own representation.

According to Article IV of the Illinois Real Estate License Act, a consumer must receive the following disclosures no later than the time when a brokerage agreement is entered into:

- That a designated agency relationship will exist unless there is a written agreement providing otherwise
- Any other agency relationships available through the broker
- The names of any designated agents
- The amount and manner of the broker's compensation
- Whether or not the broker will share the compensation with brokers who represent other parties in a transaction

A licensee must disclose to an unrepresented *customer* in writing that the licensee is not acting as the customer's agent. The disclosure must be made at a time intended to prevent disclosure of confidential information by the customer to the licensee, but the disclosure must be made no later than the preparation of an offer to purchase or lease real property. A licensee may perform ministerial acts for a customer without violating any brokerage agreement with a client. Merely performing ministerial acts does not create a brokerage agreement.

Figure 4.5   Illinois Designated Agency Disclosure Form

ILLINOIS ASSOCIATION OF REALTORS®
NOTICE OF DESIGNATED AGENCY

Thank you for giving _____ ("Sales Associate")

the opportunity to_____
(Insert description of work, ie. listing presentation)

in regard to_____ .
(Property address)

    Sales Associate's broker has previously entered into a contract with a client to provide certain real estate brokerage services through a Sales Associate who acts as that client's designated agent. As a result, Sales Associate will not be acting as your agent but as the agent of the_____(buyer or seller).

THIS DISCLOSURE IS BEING PROVIDED AS REQUIRED BY STATE LAW.

_____   Date_____
Sales Associate

Date Acknowledged _____

_____   _____
Customer   Customer

Form 346 12/94   Copyright© by Illinois Association of REALTORS®

If the broker is representing two principals in the same transaction, the impact on both parties must be explained and the written consent of both parties must be obtained.

As discussed earlier, Illinois law allows a broker to designate certain licensees within the firm as the legal representatives of a principal. The broker is not considered a dual agent as long as the designated agent for each principal in the transaction is not the same salesperson. ∎

CUSTOMER-LEVEL SERVICES

Even though an agent's primary responsibility is to the principal, the agent also has duties to third parties. Any time a licensee works with a third party, or customer, the licensee is responsible for adhering to state and federal consumer protection laws as well as the ethical requirements imposed by professional associations and state regulators.

In Illinois . . .

An agent owes a *customer* the duties of *reasonable care* and *skill; honest* and *fair dealing;* and *disclosure of known facts.*

✱ all material Inf.
about the prop

An agent's primary responsibility is to the principal, and Illinois courts have long held that the contractual principal-agent relationship as defined in the listing contract gives the seller a cause of action (basis for a lawsuit) against the licensee who breaches his or her fiduciary duties to the client. The courts have not demanded fiduciary duty to third parties. However, Illinois license law sets forth the duties that licensees owe to third-party customers (buyers or sellers). Licensees are to treat all customers honestly. They cannot negligently or knowingly give customers false information. Finally, licensees must disclose all material adverse facts about the physical condition of the property to the customer that are actually known by the licensee and that could not be discovered by a reasonably diligent inspection of the property by the customer.

In Illinois, a licensee may be held liable at common law to a seller or buyer if the licensee misrepresents material facts about a property and if the seller or buyer suffers monetary loss through reliance on these statements. The licensee's loyalty to the principal is no defense, even though the principal may have ordered the agent to misrepresent. Licensees have a duty to prospective sellers and buyers to disclose all material information within their knowledge. If the licensee knowingly makes untrue statements, Illinois courts will have no difficulty in finding the licensee liable to the buyer or seller.

Furthermore, liability may be imposed when the licensee is aware of facts that tend to indicate he or she is making a false statement; if the seller tells his or her agent/licensee that "the roof was replaced last year," and the agent has good reason to believe that statement to be untrue, the licensee should attempt to ascertain the truth and/or not pass the information on to the buyer. However, a licensee will not be liable to a customer for providing false information if that false information was provided by the client and the licensee did not have knowledge that the information was false.

Brokers who attempt to avoid liability to buyers through the use of a waiver or an exculpatory clause in the sales contract will probably be unsuccessful. In the Illinois Appellate Court case of *Zimmerman v. Northfield Real Estate, Inc.,* 1st Dist. (1986), the broker included the following language in the sales contract:

> "Purchaser acknowledges . . . that neither the seller, broker or any of their agents have made any representations with respect to any material fact relating to the real estate unless such representations are in writing and further that the purchaser has made such investigations as purchaser deems necessary or appropriate to satisfy that there has been no deception, fraud, false pretenses, misrepresentations, concealments, suppressions or omission of any material fact by the seller, the broker, or any of their agents relating to the real estate, its improvements and included personal property."

The court refused to enforce the clause because it clearly violated public policy, particularly that expressed within the Illinois license act and the general rules. ■

Opinion versus Fact

Brokers, salespersons and other staff members always must be careful about the statements they make. They must be sure that the customer understands whether the statement is an opinion or a fact. Statements of opinion are permissible only as long as they are offered as opinions and without any intention to deceive.

Statements of fact, however, must be accurate. Exaggeration of a property's benefits is called **puffing.** While puffing is legal, licensees must ensure that none of their statements can be interpreted as fraudulent. **Fraud** is the intentional misrepresentation of a material fact in such a way as to harm or take advantage of another person. That includes not only making false statements about a property but also intentionally concealing or failing to disclose important facts.

The misrepresentation or omission does not have to be intentional to result in broker liability. A **negligent misrepresentation** occurs when the broker should have known that a statement about a material fact was false. The fact that the broker actually may be ignorant about the issue is no excuse. If the buyer relies on the broker's statement, the broker is liable for any damages that result. Similarly, if a broker accidentally fails to perform some act—for instance, he or she forgets to deliver a counteroffer—the broker may be liable for damages that result from such a negligent omission.

FOR EXAMPLE 1. While showing a potential buyer a very average-looking house, Broker *Quinn* described even its plainest features as "charming" and "beautiful." Because the statements were obviously *Quinn's* personal opinions, designed to encourage a positive feeling about the property (or puff it up), their truth or falsity is not an issue.

2. Broker *Georgia* was asked by a potential buyer if a particular neighborhood was safe. Although *Georgia* knew that the area was experiencing a skyrocketing rate of violent crime, *Georgia* assured the buyer that no problem existed. *Georgia* also neglected to inform the buyer that the lot next to the house the buyer was considering had been sold to a waste disposal company for use as a toxic dump. Both are examples of fraudulent misrepresentation.

If a contract to purchase real estate is obtained as a result of fraudulent misstatements, the contract may be disaffirmed or renounced by the purchaser. In such a case, the broker not only loses a commission but can be liable for damages if either party suffers loss because of the misrepresentation. If the licensee's misstatements were based on the owner's own inaccurate statements and the licensee had no independent duty to investigate their accuracy, the broker may be entitled to a commission, even if the buyer rescinds the sales contract.

In Illinois . . .

An Illinois licensee may be held liable to the buyer under the Illinois Consumer Fraud and Deceptive Practices Act. Licensees found in violation of this act may be required to pay the plaintiff's attorney's fees and court costs in addition to damages. The act prohibits the use, within a trade or profession, of any deception, fraud, false promise, misrepresentation or concealment, suppression or omission of any material fact with the intent that others rely on it. A real estate brokerage business clearly fits within the meaning of the act, and the courts of Illinois have ruled accordingly. ■

Latent Defects

The seller has a duty to discover and disclose any known latent defects that threaten structural soundness or personal safety. A **latent defect** is a hidden

Patent defect = discoverable

structural defect that would not be discovered by ordinary inspection. Buyers have been able to either rescind the sales contract or receive damages when a seller fails to reveal known latent defects. For instance, sellers were found liable where a house was built over a ditch covered with decaying timber; a buried drain tile caused water to accumulate; and a driveway was built partly on adjoining property. The courts also have decided in favor of the buyer when the seller neglected to reveal violations of zoning or building codes.

In addition to the seller's duty to disclose latent defects, in some states the agent has an independent duty to conduct a reasonably competent and diligent inspection of the property. It is the licensee's duty to discover any material facts that may affect the property's value or desirability, whether or not they are known to or disclosed by the seller. Any such material facts discovered by the licensee must be disclosed to prospective buyers. If the licensee should have known about a substantial defect that is detected later by the buyer, the agent may be liable to the buyer for any damages resulting from that defect.

FOR EXAMPLE Broker *Kelley* knew that a house had been built on a landfill. A few days after the house was listed, one of *Kelley's* salespersons noticed that the living room floor was uneven and sagging in places. Both *Kelley* and the salesperson have a duty to conduct further investigations into the structural soundness of the property. They cannot simply ignore the problem or place throw rugs over particularly bad spots and hope buyers won't look underneath.

In Illinois . . .

The Illinois Appellate Court, in *Munjal v. Baird & Warner, Inc. et al.,* 2nd Dist. (1985), held that a broker or salesperson has no duty to discover "latent material defects" in a property if a seller has not disclosed these defects to him or her prior to sale. This decision underscored the need to find ways by which a broker could obtain relevant information about a listed property from the seller to avoid future litigation from unhappy buyers. In Illinois, the *Residential Real Property Disclosure Act* took effect in October 1994, and requires that all sellers fill out property disclosure forms for buyers that reveal any material defects in the real estate for sale. The completed form should be given to the buyer before an offer is made; if it is offered later with any negative disclosures, the buyer has three days to cancel the contract. Furthermore, if the seller learns of a new problem *after* a contract is signed, disclosure must be made in writing to the buyer, but the buyer does *not* have the power to cancel or change the contract. ■

Stigmatized Properties

In recent years, questions have been raised about stigmatized properties— properties that society has branded undesirable because of events that occurred there. Typically, the stigma is a criminal event, such as homicide, illegal drug manufacturing or gang-related activity, or a tragedy, such as suicide. However, properties even have been stigmatized by rumors that they are haunted. Because of the potential liability to a licensee for inadequately researching and disclosing material facts concerning a property's condition, licensees should seek competent counsel when dealing with a stigmatized property. Some states have laws regarding the disclosure of information about such properties, designed to protect sellers and local property values against a baseless psychological reaction. In other states, the licensee's responsibility may be difficult to define because the issue is not a physical defect but merely a perception that a property is undesirable.

In Illinois . . .

Section 31 of the Illinois Real Estate License Act states that in dealing with specific situations related to disclosure, "no cause of action shall arise against a licensee for the failure to disclose that an occupant of that property was inflicted with HIV or that the property was the site of an act or occurrence which had no effect on the physical condition of the property or its environment or the structures located thereon." However, because of the potential liability to a broker for inadequately researching the facts concerning a property's condition and the responsibility to disclose material facts, brokers should seek competent counsel when dealing with a stigmatized property. ■

SUMMARY

The law of agency governs the principal-agent relationship. Agency relationships may be expressed either by the words of the parties or by written agreement, or they may be implied by the parties' actions. In single agency relationships, the broker or agent represents one party, either the buyer or the seller, in the transaction. If the agent elicits the assistance of other brokers who cooperate in the transaction, the other brokers may become subagents of the principal. Many states have adopted statutes that replace the common law of agency and that establish the responsibilities and duties of the parties.

Representing two opposing parties in the same transaction constitutes dual agency. Licensees must be careful not to create dual agency when none was intended. This unintentional or inadvertent dual agency can result in the sales contract being rescinded and the commission being forfeited or in a lawsuit. Disclosed dual agency requires that both principals be informed of and consent to the broker's multiple representation. In any case, the prospective parties in the transaction should be informed about the agency alternatives and how client-level versus customer-level services differ. Many states have mandatory agency disclosure laws. The source of compensation for the client services does not determine which party is represented.

Licensees have certain duties and obligations to their customers as well. Consumers are entitled to fair and honest dealings and to the information necessary for them to make informed decisions. This includes accurate information about the property. Some states have mandatory property disclosure laws.

Real estate license laws and regulations govern the professional conduct of brokers and salespersons. The license laws are enacted to protect the public by ensuring a standard of competence and professionalism in the real estate industry.

In Illinois . . .

There has been a new statutory law of agency in effect in Illinois since January 1995. Real estate transactions have been removed from the impact of common law agency rules by the substitution of statutory agency rules. Illinois agency law presumes that a salesperson who is working with a seller represents the seller; a salesperson working with a buyer is presumed to represent the buyer. Agency disclosure is required for any other arrangement.

Illinois statute establishes rules of behavior governing permitted dual agency.

Merely designating one salesperson to represent sellers and another to represent buyers does not constitute dual agency. Dual agency occurs only if the same broker or salesperson is the representative of both parties in a transaction.   ■

QUESTIONS

MONONE

1. Which of the following best describes a fiduciary?
   A. A person who gives someone else the legal power to act on his or her behalf
   B. A person who is in a customer-agent relationship
   C. A person who is placed in a position of trust and confidence
   D. Two agents who work for the same brokerage firm

2. Sam just listed his property with SXS Realty. The agency relationship between Sam and the broker would be what type of agency?
   A. Special
   B. General
   C. Implied
   D. Universal

3. Which of the following statements is true of a real estate broker acting as the agent of the seller?
   A. The broker is obligated to render faithful service to the seller.
   B. The broker can disclose personal information to a buyer if it increases the likelihood of a sale.
   C. The broker can agree to a change in price without the seller's approval.
   D. The broker can accept a commission from the buyer without the seller's approval.

4. Louise is a real estate broker. Kristen lists a home with Louise for $89,500. Later that same day, Jerry comes into Louise's office and asks for general information about homes for sale in the $30,000 to $40,000 price range. Based on these facts, which of the following statements is true?
   A. Both Kristen and Jerry are Louise's customers.
   B. Kristen is Louise's client; Jerry is a customer.
   C. Louise owes fiduciary duties to both Kristen and Jerry.
   D. If Jerry asks Louise to be Jerry's buyer representative, Louise must decline because of the preexisting agreement with Kristen.

5. A licensee who has contracted with a condominium owner to find renters for his highrise apartments is probably a:
   A. transactional broker.
   B. buyer's agent.
   C. general agent.
   D. special agent.

6. Which of the following events will terminate an agency in a broker-seller relationship?
   A. The broker discovers that the market value of the property is such that he or she will not make an adequate commission.
   B. The owner declares personal bankruptcy.
   C. The owner abandons the property.
   D. The broker appoints other brokers to help sell the property.

In Illinois . . .

7. In Illinois, a real estate broker hired by an owner to sell a parcel of real estate must comply with:
   A. the federal common law of agency, although a state agency statute may exist that abrogates common law.
   B. undisclosed dual agency requirements.
   C. the concept of caveat emptor as codified in Illinois law.
   D. the Illinois statute governing agency relationships.

8. Broker Andre is hired by a first-time buyer to help the buyer purchase a home. The buyer confides to Andre that being approved for a mortgage loan may be complicated by the fact that the buyer filed for bankruptcy two years ago. When the buyer offers to buy Mr. and Mrs. Thompson's home, what is Andre's responsibility?
   A. Andre should discuss with the buyer Andre's duty to disclose the buyer's financial situation to the local multiple-listing service.
   B. Andre has a duty of fair dealing toward Mr. and Mrs. Thompson and must discuss the buyer's finances with them honestly, although in the best possible terms.
   C. Andre should have the buyer qualified by a lender, and then politely refuse to answer any questions that would violate the duty of confidentiality.
   D. Andre has no responsibility toward Mr. and Mrs. Thompson because Andre is the buyer's agent.

9. Broker David lists Kim's residence. For various reasons, Kim must sell the house quickly. To expedite the sale, David tells a prospective purchaser that Kim will accept at least $5,000 less than the asking price for the property. Based on these facts, which of the following statements is true?
   A. David has not violated his agency responsibilities to Kim.
   B. David should have disclosed this information, regardless of its accuracy.
   C. The disclosure was improper, regardless of David's motive.
   D. The relationship between David and Kim is referred to as a *general agency relationship*.

10. A buyer who is a client of the broker wants to purchase a house that the broker has listed for sale. Which of the following statements is true?
    A. Illinois law no longer regulates this situation.
    B. The broker should refer the buyer to another broker to negotiate the sale.
    C. The seller and buyer must be informed of the situation and agree to the broker's representing both of them.
    D. The buyer should not have been shown a house listed by the broker.

11. Bob is a real estate broker. Saul is a FSBO who has a home advertised for $98,000. Vera comes into Bob's office and asks Bob to represent her while she searches for a home in the $90,000 to $100,000 price range. Bob calls Saul and asks if he can show Saul's home to Vera. Based on these facts, which of the following statements is true?
    A. Both Saul and Vera are Bob's customers.
    B. Saul is Bob's customer; Vera is a client.
    C. Vera is Bob's customer; Saul is Bob's client.
    D. Bob is now a dual agent.

12. A real estate licensee was representing a buyer. At their first meeting, the buyer explained that he planned to operate a dog-grooming business out of any house he bought. The licensee did not check the local zoning ordinances to determine in which parts of town such a business could be conducted. Which common-law agency duty did the licensee violate?
    A. Care
    B. Obedience
    C. Loyalty
    D. Accountability

13. Broker Elliot tells a prospective buyer, "This property has the most beautiful river view." In fact, the view includes the back of a shopping center. In a separate transaction, broker Phyllis fails to mention to some enthusiastic potential buyers that a six-lane highway is planned for construction within ten feet of a house the buyers think is perfect. Based on these facts, which of the following statements is true?
    A. Broker Elliot has committed fraud.
    B. Broker Phyllis has committed puffing.
    C. Both broker Elliot and broker Phyllis are guilty of intentional misrepresentation.
    D. Broker Elliot merely is puffing; broker Phyllis has misrepresented the property.

14. Under Illinois agency law, which of the following is true?
    A. The law codifies the common-law concept of caveat emptor by eliminating any assumption of a buyer's right to representation or disclosure.
    B. Brokers may designate which agent represents which party.
    C. Sellers are not legally obligated to make any disclosures regarding the known physical condition of the property.
    D. Dual agency is outlawed.

15. A broker listed and sold Martin's home. Martin told the broker that the home was structurally sound. This information was passed on to a prospective buyer by the broker's salesperson. If the broker has no way of knowing that this information is false, who will likely be held liable if a latent defect is later discovered?
    A. Only the salesperson
    B. The seller
    C. The seller and the salesperson
    D. The buyer will lose because a buyer must carefully inspect or bear the loss

CHAPTER 5

Real Estate Brokerage

KEY TERMS

allocation of
   customers or
   markets
antitrust laws
brokerage
commission

employee
group boycotting
independent
   contractor
price-fixing

procuring cause
real estate assistant
salesperson
tie-in agreement
transactional broker

PURPOSE OF LICENSE LAWS

All 50 states, the District of Columbia and all Canadian provinces license and regulate the activities of real estate brokers and salespersons. While the laws share a common purpose, the details vary from state to state. Uniform policies and standards for administering and enforcing state license laws are promoted by an organization of state license law officials known as ARELLO—the Association of Real Estate License Law Officials.

Real estate license laws have been enacted to protect the public by ensuring a standard of competence and professionalism in the real estate industry. The laws achieve this goal by

- establishing basic requirements for obtaining a real estate license and, in many cases, requiring continuing education to keep a license;
- defining which activities require licensing;
- describing the acceptable standards of conduct and practice for licensees; and
- enforcing those standards through a disciplinary system.

The purpose of these laws is not merely to regulate the real estate industry. Their main objective is to make sure that the rights of purchasers, sellers, tenants and owners are protected from unscrupulous or sloppy practices.

The laws are not intended to prevent licensees from conducting their businesses successfully or to interfere in legitimate transactions. Laws cannot create an ethical or a moral marketplace. However, by establishing minimum levels of competency and limits of permitted behavior, laws can make the marketplace safer and more honest.

Each state has a licensing authority—a commission, a department, a division, a board or an agency—for real estate brokers and salespersons. This authority has the power to issue licenses, make real estate information available to licensees and the public and enforce the statutory real estate law.

In Illinois . . .

Illinois has had a Real Estate License Act since January 1, 1921. The law, administered through the Director of Real Estate under the Illinois Office of Banks and Real Estate, governs the licensing and activities of brokers and salespeople "for the protection of the public and to evaluate the competency of real estate professionals." Illinois license law consists of the act itself and rules promulgated by the Office of Banks and Real Estate to interpret and implement the act. Throughout this book, reference will be made to the act and to the general rules. ■

REAL ESTATE BROKERAGE

A **brokerage** business may take many forms. It may be a sole proprietorship (a single-owner company), a corporation or a partnership with another broker. The office may be independent or part of a regional or national franchise. The business may consist of a single office or multiple branches. The broker's office may be located in a downtown highrise, a suburban shopping center or the broker's home. A typical real estate brokerage may specialize in one kind of transaction or service or may offer an array of services.

No matter what form it takes, however, a real estate brokerage has the same demands, expenses and rewards as any other small business. The real estate industry, after all, is made up of thousands of small businesses operating in defined local markets. A real estate broker faces the same challenges as an entrepreneur in any other industry. In addition to mastering the complexities of real estate transactions, the broker must be able to handle the day-to-day details of running a business. He or she must set effective policies for every aspect of the brokerage operation: maintaining space and equipment, hiring employees and salespersons, determining compensation, directing staff and sales activities and implementing procedures to follow in carrying out agency duties. The real estate license laws and regulations establish the business activities and methods of doing business that are permitted.

In Practice

At each step in a real estate transaction, the broker should advise the parties to secure legal counsel to protect their interests. Although real estate brokers and salespersons may bring buyers and sellers together and may fill in preprinted blank purchase agreement forms, only an attorney may offer legal advice or prepare legal documents. Licensees who are not attorneys are prohibited from practicing law.

Real Estate Assistants and Technologies

A **real estate assistant** (also known as a personal assistant or professional assistant) is a combination office manager, marketer, organizer and facilitator with a fundamental understanding of the real estate industry. An assistant may or may not have a real estate license. The extent to which the assistant can help the broker or salesperson with transactions is often determined by state license laws. Depending on state law, an assistant may perform duties ranging from clerical and secretarial functions to office management, telemarketing, market strategy development and direct contact with clients and customers. A licensed assistant can set up and host open houses and assist in all aspects of a real estate transaction.

In Illinois . . . Section 1450.95 of the administrative rules specifies the permitted activities in which an unlicensed real estate assistant may engage. (See Figure 5.1.) ■

In addition to assistants, a wide range of technologies is available to help a real estate licensee do his or her job more efficiently and effectively. Computers are a necessary ingredient in any modern real estate brokerage. Multiple-listing services (MLSs) and mortgage information are accessible to consumers and licensees on the Internet. Numerous software packages have been designed specifically for real estate professionals, and generic word-processing and spreadsheet software is available. Some of these programs help real estate brokers and salespersons with such office management tasks as billing, accounting and timekeeping. Other software assists with marketing and advertising properties and services. In some states, continuing education requirements can be met through the use of specially designed continuing education software. Real estate web sites, home pages and computer networks help licensees keep in touch; and some cable and satellite television channels are dedicated solely to real estate programming for both consumers and professionals.

Real estate brokers and salespersons can carry laptop computers with portable modems that link them with their offices, an MLS or a mortgage company from virtually anywhere. Portable fax machines, pagers and cellular phones make licensees available to their offices and clients 24 hours a day. Voicemail systems can track caller response to advertisements and give callers information about specific properties when the broker or salesperson is unavailable. And yard signs are available that broadcast details about a property on an AM radio band, so drivers passing by can tune in for tempting information.

All this technology is a great boon to practitioners, but real estate brokers and salespersons must make careful decisions about which technologies best suit their needs. Furthermore, they must keep up with the rapidly changing world of high-tech real estate tools to remain competitive.

In Practice   Home listings are becoming available to the general public on the Internet, through such web sites as Realtor.com (http://www.realtor.com) and Microsoft Network's Homeadvisor (http://homeadvisor.msn.com/ie/). By accessing these services, potential buyers can preview photographs of properties and narrow their searches by price range, number of bedrooms, amenities, neighborhood or school district.

Broker-Salesperson Relationship   Although brokerage firms vary widely in size, few brokers today perform their duties without the assistance of salespersons. Consequently, much of the business's success hinges on the broker-salesperson relationship.

A real estate **salesperson** is any person licensed to perform real estate activities on behalf of a licensed real estate broker. The broker is fully responsible for the actions performed in the course of the real estate business by all persons licensed under the broker. In turn, all of a salesperson's

Figure 5.1

An Unlicensed Real Estate Assistant May . . .	An Unlicensed Real Estate Assistant May NOT. . .
• answer the telephone, take messages, and forward calls	• host open houses, kiosks, home show booths or other promotional displays
• submit listings and changes to a multiple-listing service	• show property
• follow up on a transaction after a contract has been signed	• interpret information on listings, titles, financing documentation, contracts, closing papers or other information related to a real estate transaction
• assemble documents for a closing	
• obtain public information documents from official sources	
• have keys made for a listing	• explain or interpret a contract, listing, lease agreement or other real estate document with anyone outside the employing licensee's firm
• draft advertising and promotional materials ✔	
• purchase and place advertising in media	
• record and deposit earnest money, security deposits and rents	• negotiate or agree to any commission, commission split or management or referral fee on behalf of a licensee
• monitor licenses and personnel files	
• complete contract forms with factual information ✔	
• compute commission checks	• perform any activity for which a real estate license is required by law
• perform bookkeeping activities	• place telemarketing calls or other solicitations on the licensee's behalf
• place yard signs on property	
• order items of routine repair ✔	
• act as a courier	
• prepare and distribute flyers and promotional materials ✔	
• place routine telephone calls on late rent payments	
• schedule appointments for the licensee	
• respond to questions by quoting from published information	
• gather feedback on showings	
• perform general administrative, clerical and personal activities on the licensee's behalf	

✔ = Licensee supervision and approval specifically required

SOURCE: 1450.95, Rules for the Administration of the Real Estate License Act of 1983

activities must be performed in the name of the supervising broker. The salesperson can carry out only those responsibilities assigned by the broker with whom he or she is licensed and can receive compensation only from that broker. As an agent of the broker, the salesperson has no authority to make contracts with or receive compensation from any other party. The broker is liable for the acts of the salesperson within the scope of the employment agreement.

ILL LAW REQUIRES A WRITEN CONTRACT

Independent contractor versus employee. The employment agreement between a broker and a salesperson should define the nature, obligations and responsibilities of the relationship. Essentially, the salesperson may be an employee or an independent contractor. State license laws generally treat the salesperson as the employee of the broker, regardless of whether the salesperson is considered to be an employee or an independent contractor for income tax purposes. Whether a salesperson is treated as an employee or an independent contractor affects the structure of the salesperson's responsibilities and the broker's liability to pay and withhold taxes from the salesperson's earnings.

A broker can exercise certain controls over salespersons who are **employees.** The broker may require that an employee follow rules governing such matters as working hours, office routine, attendance at sales meetings, assignment of sales quotas and adherence to dress codes. As an employer, a broker is required by the federal government to withhold Social Security tax and income tax from wages paid to employees. The broker also is required to pay unemployment compensation tax on wages paid to one or more employees, as defined by state and federal laws. In addition, employees might receive benefits such as health insurance, profit-sharing plans and workers' compensation.

A broker's relationship with a salesperson who is an **independent contractor** is very different. As the name implies, an independent contractor operates more independently than an employee, and a broker may not exercise the same degree of control over the salesperson's activities. While the broker may control what the independent contractor does, the broker cannot dictate how to do it. The broker cannot require that the independent contractor keep specific office hours or attend sales meetings. Independent contractors are responsible for paying their own income and Social Security taxes and receive nothing from brokers that could be construed as an employee benefit, such as health insurance or paid vacation time. As a rule, independent contractors use their own materials and equipment. (See Figure 5.2.)

 test?

The Internal Revenue Service often investigates the independent contractor/employee situation in real estate offices. Under the qualified real estate agent category in the Internal Revenue Code, meeting three requirements can establish an independent contractor status:

1. The individual must have a current real estate license.
2. He or she must have a written contract with the broker that specifies that the salesperson will not be treated as an employee for federal tax purposes.
3. At least 90 percent of the individual's income as a licensee must be based on sales production and not on the number of hours worked.

In Practice   A broker must have a standardized employment agreement drafted and reviewed by an attorney to ensure its compliance with federal law. The broker also should be aware that written agreements carry little weight with an IRS auditor if the actions of the parties contradict the provisions of the contract. Specific legal and tax questions regarding independent contractors should be referred to a competent attorney or accountant.

Figure 5.2 *Employee or Independent Contractor? IRS General Considerations*

Factors Indicating Control *Note: These factors are only possible indicators of a worker's status. Each case must be determined on its own facts, based on all the information.*	Employee	Independent Contractor
Is the worker required to comply with **employer instructions** about when, where and how work is to be performed?	Yes	No
Is the worker required to undergo **training?**	Yes	No
Does the worker hire, supervise and pay **others** to perform work for which he or she is responsible?	No	Yes
Must the worker's job be performed during **certain set hours?**	Yes	No
Must the worker devote **full time** to the job?	Yes	No
Must the work be performed **on the employer's property?**	Yes	No
Must tasks be performed in a **certain order** set by the employer?	Yes	No
Is the individual required to submit **regular written or oral reports** to the employer?	Yes	No
Is **payment** by the **hour, week** or **month?**	Yes	No
Is **payment** in a **lump sum?**	No	Yes
Are the worker's **business and travel expenses** paid by the employer?	Yes	No
Does the employer furnish the **tools and materials** required for the job?	Yes	No
Does the worker rent his or her own **office or working space?**	No	Yes
Will the worker realize a **profit or loss** as a result of his or her services?	No	Yes
Does the worker make his or her services **available to the general public?**	No	Yes
Does the employer have the **right to fire** the worker?	Yes	No
Does the worker have the **right to quit** the job at any time, whether or not a particular task is complete?	Yes	No

Broker's Compensation

The broker's compensation is specified in the contract with the principal. License laws may stipulate that a written agreement must establish the compensation to be paid. Compensation can be in the form of a commission or brokerage fee (computed as a percentage of the total sales price), a flat fee or an hourly rate. The amount of a broker's **commission** is negotiable in every case. Attempting, however subtly, to impose uniform commission rates is a clear violation of state and federal antitrust laws (discussed later in this chapter). A broker may, however, set the minimum rate acceptable for that broker's firm. The important point is for broker and client to agree on a rate before the agency relationship is established.

In Illinois . . .

Only a licensed broker may collect a commission in Illinois. To collect a commission on a real estate transaction, a licensed broker must be hired by having a listing agreement in which his or her principal agrees to pay a specified commission. The percentage or dollar amount of commission must be expressed clearly in the listing agreement.

> To be a *procuring cause,* the broker must have started a chain of events that resulted in a sale.

A commission is usually considered to be earned when the work for which the broker was hired has been accomplished. In Illinois, this means that the listing broker generally is entitled to a commission after procuring a full-price offer with no contingencies from a buyer who is ready, willing and able to buy on the seller's terms as set forth in the listing. To be considered the **procuring cause** of sale, the broker must have taken action to start or to cause a chain of events that resulted in the sale. Courts may prevent the broker from receiving a commission if the broker knew the buyer was unable to perform. When terms other than those offered by the original listing are agreed to as indicated by a contract of sale signed by both buyer and seller, the broker is entitled to a commission. ■

> A *ready, willing and able buyer* is one prepared to buy on the seller's terms and ready to complete the transactions.

Most sales commissions are payable when the sale is consummated by delivery of the seller's deed. This provision generally is included in the listing agreement or in the real estate sales contract. When the sales or listing agreement specifies no time for the payment of the broker's commission, the commission generally is earned when a completed sales contract has been executed by a ready, willing and able buyer; when it has been accepted and executed by the seller; and when copies of the contract are in the possession of all parties.

In Illinois . . .

The closing of the sale is the usual proof in a court of law that the broker has produced a buyer and earned a commission. ■

Even if the transaction is not consummated, the broker may still be entitled to a commission if the seller

- has a change of mind and refuses to sell,
- has a spouse who refuses to sign the deed,
- has a title with uncorrected defects,
- commits fraud with respect to the transaction,
- is unable to deliver possession within a reasonable time,
- insists on terms not in the listing (for example, the right to restrict the use of the property) or
- has a mutual agreement with the buyer to cancel the transaction.

In other words, a broker generally is due a commission if a sale is not consummated because of the ~~principal's~~ *seller* default.

Salesperson's Compensation

The amount of compensation a salesperson receives is set by mutual agreement between the broker and the salesperson. A broker may agree to pay a fixed salary or a share of the commissions from transactions originated by a salesperson. In some cases, a salesperson may draw from an account against earned shares of commissions. Some brokers require that salespersons pay all or part of the expenses of advertising listed properties.

In many states, including Illinois, it is illegal for a broker to pay a commission to anyone other than the salesperson licensed with the broker or to another broker. Fees, commissions or other compensation cannot be paid to unlicensed persons for services requiring a real estate license. Other compensation includes gifts of certain items of personal property, such as a new television, or other premiums, such as vacations. This is not to be confused with referral fees paid between brokers for "leads," which are legal as long as the individuals are licensed. ■

Some firms have adopted a 100 percent commission plan. Salespersons in these offices pay a monthly service charge to their brokers to cover the costs of office space, telephones and supervision in return for keeping 100 percent of the commissions from the sales they negotiate. The 100 percent commission salesperson pays all of his or her own expenses.

Other companies have graduated commission splits based on a salesperson's achieving specified production goals. For instance, a broker might agree to split commissions 50/50 up to a $25,000 salesperson's share; 60/40 for shares from $25,000 to $30,000; and so on. Commission splits as generous as 80/20 or 90/10 are possible, however, particularly for high producers.

However the salesperson's compensation is structured, only the employing broker can pay it. In cooperating transactions, the commission first must be received by the employing broker and then paid to the salesperson, unless otherwise permitted by license laws and agreed to by the employing broker.

In Illinois . . .

In Illinois the commission first must be paid to the employing broker for payment to the salesperson. The license laws of some states permit otherwise, but even then the employing broker must agree to a different arrangement. An exception to this rule would occur if a salesperson had earned a commission but his or her employment had been terminated prior to the payment of the commission. In this situation, the former employing broker may pay the commission directly to the former associate, even if that former associate has a new sponsoring broker. ■

MATH CONCEPTS

Sharing Commissions

A commission might be shared by many people: the listing broker, the listing salesperson, the selling broker and the selling salesperson. Drawing a diagram can help you determine which person is entitled to receive what amount of the total commission.

For example, salesperson Elizabeth, while working for broker Harold, took a listing on a $73,000 house at a 6 percent commission rate. Salesperson Tim, while working for broker Mary, found the buyer for the property. If the property sold for the listed price, the listing broker and the selling broker shared the commission equally and the selling broker kept 45 percent of what he received, how much did salesperson Tim receive? (If the broker retained 45 percent of the total commission he received, his salesperson would receive the balance: 100% − 45% = 55%.) Broker Harold will pay Salesperson Elizabeth 50%.

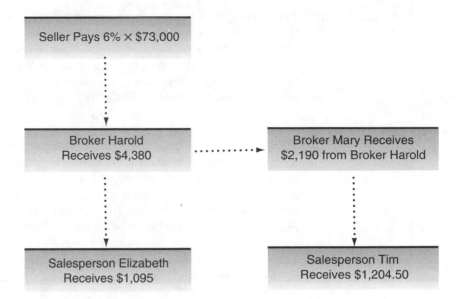

Transactional Brokerage

A **transactional broker** (also referred to as a *nonagent, facilitator, coordinator or contract broker*) is not an agent of either party. A transactional broker's job is simply to help both the buyer and the seller with the necessary paperwork and formalities involved in transferring ownership of real property. The buyer and the seller negotiate the sale without representation.

The transactional broker is expected to treat all parties honestly and competently, to locate qualified buyers or suitable properties, to help the parties arrive at mutually acceptable terms and to assist in the closing of the transaction. Transactional brokers are equally responsible to both parties and must disclose known defects in a property. However, they may not negotiate on behalf of either the buyer or the seller, and they must not disclose confidential information to either party.

Legal Rights and Obligations

As each contract is prepared for signature during a real estate transaction, the broker should advise the parties of the desirability of securing legal counsel to protect their interests. As mentioned earlier, only a lawyer can offer legal advice. Licensees who are not lawyers are prohibited from practicing law.

In Illinois . . .

In *Chicago Bar Association et al. v. Quinlan and Tyson, Inc.,* 34 Ill.2d116 (1966), the Illinois Supreme Court held that real estate licensees could complete preprinted forms that were in general usage in the area of the broker's practice, but that only attorneys could prepare additional clauses and conveyancing documents. ■

ANTITRUST LAWS

Antitrust violations include

• price-fixing;
• group boycotting;
• allocation of customers;
• allocation of markets; and
• tie-in agreements

The real estate industry is subject to federal and state **antitrust laws.** These laws prohibit monopolies as well as any contracts, combinations and conspiracies that unreasonably restrain trade—that is, acts that interfere with the free flow of goods and services in a competitive marketplace. The most common antitrust violations are price-fixing, group boycotting, allocation of customers or markets and tie-in agreements.

RESTRAIN OF TRADE

Price-Fixing

Price-fixing is the practice of setting prices for products or services rather than letting competition in the open market establish those prices. In real estate, price-fixing occurs when competing brokers agree to set sales commissions, fees or management rates. Price-fixing is illegal. Brokers must independently determine commission rates or fees for their own firms only. These decisions must be based on a broker's business judgment and revenue requirements without input from other brokers.

MLSs, Boards of REALTORS® and other professional organizations may not set fees or commission splits. Nor can they deny membership to brokers based on the fees the brokers charge. Either practice could lead the public to believe that the industry not only sanctions the unethical practice of withholding cooperation from certain brokers but also encourages the illegal practice of restricting open-market competition.

The broker's challenge is to avoid even the impression of price fixing. Hinting to prospective clients that there is a "going rate" of commission or a "normal" fee implies that rates are, in fact, standardized. The broker must make it clear to clients that the rate stated is only what his or her firm charges.

Group Boycotting

Group boycotting occurs when two or more businesses *Sales person* conspire against another business or agree to withhold their patronage to reduce competition. Group boycotting is illegal under the antitrust laws.

Allocation of Customers or Markets

Allocation of customers or markets involves an agreement between brokers to divide their markets and refrain from competing for each other's business. Allocations may be made on a geographic basis, with brokers agreeing to specific territories within which they will operate exclusively. The division also may occur by markets, such as by price range or category of housing. These agreements result in reduced competition.

FOR EXAMPLE Lilly and Nick, the only real estate brokers in Potterville, agree that there are too many apartment-finder services in town. They decide to refer all prospective tenants to the service operated by Lilly's niece rather than handing out a list of all providers, as they have done in the past. As a result, Lilly's niece runs the only apartment-finder service in Potterville by the end of the year.

Tie-In Agreements

Finally, **tie-in agreements** (also known as *tying agreements*) are agreements to sell one product only if the buyer purchases another product as well. The sale of the first (desired) product is "tied" to the purchase of a second (less desirable) product.

Penalties

The penalties for violating antitrust laws are severe. For instance, under the Federal Sherman Antitrust Act, people who fix prices or allocate markets may be subject to a maximum $100,000 fine and three years in prison. For corporations, the penalty may be as high as $1 million. In a civil suit, a person who has suffered a loss because of the antitrust activities of a guilty party may recover triple the value of the actual damages plus attorney's fees and costs.

FOR EXAMPLE Dion, a real estate broker, owns a vacant lot in a popular area of town. Brent, a builder, wants to buy the lot and build three new homes on it. Dion refuses to sell the lot to the builder unless Brent agrees to list the improved lot with Dion so that Dion can sell the homes. This sort of list-back arrangement violates antitrust laws.

SUMMARY

Real estate license laws and regulations govern the professional conduct of brokers and salespersons. The license laws are enacted to protect the public by ensuring a standard of competence and professionalism in the real estate industry.

Real estate brokerage is the act of bringing people together, for a fee or commission, who wish to buy, sell, exchange or lease real estate.

Real estate assistants and technologies are changing the way that brokerage offices are managed and operated.

The broker's compensation in a real estate sale may take the form of a commission, a flat fee or an hourly rate. The broker is considered to have earned a commission when he or she procures a ready, willing and able buyer for a seller.

A broker may hire salespersons to assist in this work. The salesperson works on the broker's behalf as either an employee or an independent contractor.

Federal and state antitrust laws prohibit brokers from conspiring to fix prices, engage in boycotts, allocate customers or markets or establish tie-in agreements.

Restraon trade

QUESTIONS

1. Which of the following statements best explains the meaning of this sentence: "To recover a commission for brokerage services, a broker must be employed as the agent of the seller"?
   A. The broker must work in a real estate office.
   B. The seller must have made an express or implied agreement to pay a commission to the broker for selling the property.
   C. The broker must have asked the seller the price of the property and then found a ready, willing and able buyer.
   D. The broker must have a salesperson employed in the office.

2. An Illinois real estate salesperson who is engaged as an independent contractor:
   A. is considered an employee by the IRS for tax purposes.
   B. must have a written contract with the broker.
   C. must be covered by workers' compensation.
   D. may work as an independent contractor for two or more brokers.

3. In Illinois, the usual "proof" that the listing broker has earned his or her commission is the:
   A. submission to the seller of a signed offer from a ready, willing and able buyer.
   B. closing of the sale.
   C. signing of an exclusive listing contract.
   D. deposit of the buyer's earnest money into escrow.

4. Broker Sierra listed Brock's home for $100,000. Before the listing contract expired, Sierra brought Brock a full-price offer on his terms, containing no contingencies. Brock then decided not to sell. Which of the following statements is true?
   A. Sierra has no reason to collect a commission in this case.
   B. Brock probably is liable for the commission.
   C. Sierra must immediately file suit against Brock.
   D. Brock's only liability is to the buyer.

5. Gerald is an unlicensed real estate assistant. Under Illinois law, Gerald may do all the following EXCEPT:
   A. submit listings and changes to listings to a local or regional multiple-listing service.
   B. prepare and distribute flyers and promotional materials to market the services of an employing licensed real estate broker.
   C. place yard signs on property.
   D. host an open house.

6. According to the Illinois license law, a real estate salesperson may not:
   A. represent both buyer and seller.
   B. buy or sell real estate for himself or herself.
   C. accept a commission from another broker unless previously earned.
   D. show property in another state.

7. Broker Janet has taken a $300,000 home listing. Her friend Carol refers a buyer to Janet, who in turn purchases the home. Janet is very grateful and would like to share her commission with Carol as a way of saying thank you. When is the soonest that Janet may pay Carol?
   A. Janet may not share her commission with Carol.
   B. At closing.
   C. Thirty days after the offer to purchase is signed.
   D. As soon as the earnest money deposit is received.

8. Broker Mark and Broker David agreed to boycott the services of the MNM Title Company so that the new TSK Title Company could gain market share. What is the act that Mark and David are violating?
   A. Washington Antiboycotting Act
   B. Illinois Lincoln Antitrust Act
   C. Federal Sherman Antitrust Act
   D. Land of Lincoln Fair Trade Act

Broker Employment Contracts

KEY TERMS

buyer agency
   agreement
competitive market
   analysis
exclusive-agency
   listing

exclusive right-to-sell
   listing
market value
multiple-listing
   service

net listing
open listing
option listing

Special Agus

If you work For

Seller (Listus)

Buyer   Buyer bro

Listing and buyer representation agreements are *employment contracts* rather than real estate contracts. They are contracts for the personal professional services of the broker, not for the transfer of real estate. In most states, either by their statutes of frauds or by specific rules from their real estate licensing authorities, the listing must be in writing to be enforceable in court. However, oral listings are sometimes permitted.

In Illinois . . .

PROPARTY manager

General Agus

Illinois law does not require written agreements with buyers or sellers. However, any exclusive agreement must be in writing to be enforceable. ■
IN WRITING

Employment contracts with buyers and sellers create special agency relationships between the principal (the person who is being represented by the broker) and the broker (the agent). As agent, the broker is authorized to represent the principal to third parties.

Under both the law of agency and most state license laws, only a broker can act as agent to list, sell, rent or purchase another person's real estate and provide other services to a principal. A salesperson who performs these acts does so only in the name and under the supervision of the broker. Throughout this chapter, unless otherwise stated, the terms *broker, agent* and *firm* are intended to include both the broker and a salesperson working under the broker. However, the only parties to a broker employment contract are the principal and the broker.

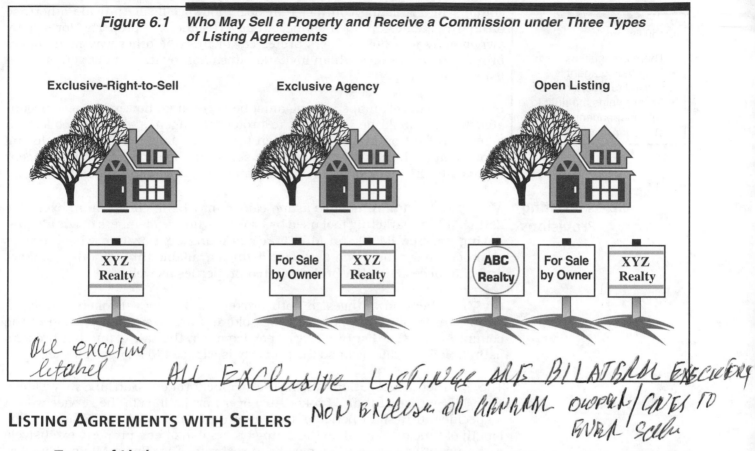

Figure 6.1   *Who May Sell a Property and Receive a Commission under Three Types of Listing Agreements*

Exclusive-Right-to-Sell

Exclusive Agency

Open Listing

[handwritten: One exception Litated]

[handwritten: ALL EXCLUSIVE LISTINGS ARE BILATERAL EXCEPTING NON EXCLUSIV OR GENERAL OWNER/GIVES TO EVERY Selen]

LISTING AGREEMENTS WITH SELLERS

Types of Listing Agreements

Several types of listing agreements exist. The type of contract determines the specific rights and obligations of the parties. (See Figure 6.1.)

Exclusive right to sell.   In an **exclusive-right-to-sell listing,** one broker is appointed as the seller's sole agent. The broker is given the exclusive right, or *authorization,* to market the seller's property. If the property is sold while the listing is in effect, the seller must pay the broker a commission *regardless of who sells the property.* In other words, if the seller finds a buyer without the broker's assistance, the seller still must pay the broker a commission. Sellers benefit from this form of agreement because the broker feels freer to spend time and money actively marketing the property, making a timely and profitable sale more likely. From the broker's perspective, an exclusive-right-to-sell listing offers the greatest opportunity to receive a commission. The majority of residential listing agreements in Illinois are exclusive-right-to-sell listing agreements.

> **Exclusive right to sell:**
>
> One authorized agent—broker receives a commission regardless of who sells the property.

Exclusive-agency listing.   In an **exclusive-agency listing,** one broker is authorized to act as the exclusive agent of the principal. However, the seller retains the right to sell the property without obligation to the broker. The seller is obligated to pay a commission to the broker only if the broker has been the procuring cause of a sale.

> **Exclusive-agency listing:**
>
> - There is one authorized agent.
> - Broker receives a commission only if he or she is the procuring cause.
> - Seller retains the right to sell without obligation.

[handwritten: ↗ NON EXCLUSIV OR GENERAL]

Open listing.   In an **open listing** (also known in some areas as a *nonexclusive listing* or a *general listing*), the seller retains the right to employ any number of brokers as agents. The brokers can act simultaneously, and the seller is obligated to pay a commission to only that broker who successfully produces a ready, willing and able buyer. If the seller personally sells the property without the aid of any of the brokers, the seller is not obligated to pay a

---

Open listing:

• There are multiple agents.
• Only selling agent is entitled to a commission.
• Seller retains the right to sell independently without obligation.

---

commission. A listing contract that does not specifically provide otherwise ordinarily creates an open listing. An advertisement of property "for sale by owner" may indicate "brokers protected" or in some other way invite offers brought by brokers. Such an invitation does not, by itself, however, create a listing agreement.

Even the terms of an open listing must be negotiated, however. These negotiated terms should be in writing to protect the agent's ability to collect an agreed-on fee from the seller. Written terms may be in the form of a listing agreement (if the agent represents the seller) or a fee agreement (if the agent represents the buyer or the seller does not wish to be represented).

Special Listing Provisions

Multiple listing. *A multiple-listing clause* may be included in an exclusive listing. It is a marketing tool used by brokers who are members of a **multiple-listing service** (MLS). An MLS is a marketing organization whose broker members make their own exclusive listings available through other brokers and gain access to other brokers' listed properties as well.

An MLS offers advantages to both brokers and sellers. Brokers develop a sizable inventory of properties to be sold and are assured a portion of the commission if they list property or participate in the sale of another broker's listing. Sellers gain because the property is exposed to a larger market.

The contractual obligations among the member brokers of an MLS vary widely. Most MLSs require that a broker turn over new listings to the service within a specific, fairly short period of time after the broker obtains the listing. The length of time during which the listing broker can offer a property exclusively without notifying the other member brokers varies. Some MLSs, however, permit a broker up to five days before he or she must submit the listing to the service.

Under the provisions of most MLSs, a participating broker makes a unilateral offer of cooperation and compensation to other member brokers. The broker must have the written consent of the seller to include the property in an MLS. If a broker chooses to be an agent for the buyer of a property in the MLS, that broker must notify the listing broker before any communication with the seller takes place. All brokers must determine the appropriate way to proceed to protect their clients.

In Illinois . . .

Under Illinois law, a broker is not considered to be a subagent of another broker's client solely by being affiliated with an MLS. An offer of subagency may not be made through an MLS in Illinois. ■

In Practice

Technology has enhanced the benefits of MLS membership. In addition to providing instant access to information about the status of listed properties, MLSs often offer a broad range of other useful information about mortgage loans, real estate taxes and assessments, and municipalities and school districts. They are equally helpful to the licensee who needs to make a competitive market analysis to determine the value of a particular property before suggesting an appropriate range of listing prices. Computer-assisted searches also help buyers select properties that best meet their needs.

> In a *net listing,* the broker is entitled to any amount exceeding the seller's stated net; in an *option listing,* the broker has the right to purchase the property.

Net listing. A **net listing** provision specifies that the seller will receive a net amount of money from any sale, with the excess going to the listing broker as commission. The broker is free to offer the property at any price greater than that net amount. Because a net listing can create a conflict of interest between the broker's fiduciary responsibility to the seller and the broker's profit motive, however, net listings are illegal in many states and are discouraged in others.

In Illinois . . .

While net listings are not specifically prohibited in Illinois, they are considered undesirable and potentially unethical: the risk of fraud involved makes them incompatible with the service-based nature of the brokerage business. ■

Option listing. An option listing provision gives the broker the right to purchase the listed property. Use of an option listing may open the broker to charges of fraud unless the broker is scrupulous in fulfilling all obligations to the property owner. In some states, a broker who chooses to exercise such an option must first inform the property owner of the broker's profit in the transaction and secure in writing the owner's agreement to it. An option listing differs from an option contract.

In Illinois . . .

Sometimes, brokers and sellers enter into *guaranteed sale agreements*, in which the broker agrees to buy the listed property if it fails to sell before the end of the listing period. Typically, these guarantees are made to the seller as an inducement to list the property with the broker. In Illinois, any such agreement must be in writing and is subject to other legal requirements. ■

EXPIRATION OF LISTING PERIOD

All listings should specify a definite period of time during which the broker is to be employed.

Courts have discouraged the use of automatic extension clauses in exclusive listings, such as a clause providing for a base period of 90 days that "continues thereafter until terminated by either party hereto by 30 days' notice in writing." Extension clauses are illegal in some states, and many listing contract forms specifically provide that there can be no automatic extensions of the agreement. Some courts have held that an extension clause actually creates an open listing rather than an exclusive-agency agreement.

In Illinois . . .

The failure to specify a definite termination date in a listing agreement is grounds for suspension or revocation of a real estate license. Illinois law forbids automatic extension clauses. ■

Some listing contracts contain a *broker protection clause.* This clause provides that the property owner will pay the listing broker a commission if, within a specified number of days after the listing expires, the owner transfers the property to someone the broker originally introduced to the owner. This clause protects a broker who was the procuring cause from losing a commission because the transaction was completed after the listing expired. The time for such a clause usually parallels the terms of the listing agreement: a six-month listing may carry a broker protection clause of six months after the listing's expiration, for example. To protect the owner and prevent any liability of the owner for two separate commissions, most of these clauses stipulate that they cannot be enforced if the property is relisted under a new contract either with the original listing broker or with another broker.

THE LISTING PROCESS

Before signing a contract, the broker and seller must discuss a variety of issues. The seller's most critical concerns typically are the selling price of the property and the net amount the seller can expect to receive from the sale. The broker has several professional tools to provide information about a property's value and to calculate the proceeds from a sale.

Pricing the Property

A *competitive market analysis* is an analysis of market activity among comparable properties; it is *not* the same as a formal appraisal.

While it is the responsibility of the broker or salesperson to advise and assist, it is the seller who must determine the listing price for the property. Because the average seller does not have the resources needed to make an informed decision about a reasonable listing price, real estate agents must be prepared to offer their knowledge, information and expertise.

A salesperson can help the seller determine a listing price for the property by using a **competitive market analysis** (CMA). This is a comparison of the prices of properties recently sold, properties currently on the market and properties that did not sell. The comparisons must be made with properties similar in location, size, age, style and amenities to the seller's property. Although a CMA is not a formal appraisal, the salesperson uses many of the same methods and techniques an appraiser uses in arriving at a reasonable value range. If no adequate comparisons can be made, or if the property is unique in some way, the seller may prefer that a professional appraiser conduct a detailed, formal estimate of the property's value.

Market Value

The most probable price property would bring in an arm's-length transaction under normal conditions on the open market.

Whether a CMA or a formal appraisal is used, the figure sought is the property's market value. **Market value** is the most probable price property would bring in an arm's-length transaction under normal conditions on the open market. A CMA estimates market value as likely to fall within a range of values (for instance, $135,000 to $140,000). A CMA, however, should not be confused with a formal appraisal, which will indicate a specific value rather than a range.

In Practice

When helping a seller determine an appropriate listing price, the broker must give an estimate of value that is as reasonable, conservative and accurate as possible. Overpriced listings cost the broker time and money in wasted marketing and advertising and give sellers false hopes of riches to come. Ultimately, failing to move overpriced listings will cost the broker future business opportunities as well.

While it is the property owner's privilege to set whatever listing price he or she chooses, a broker should consider rejecting any listing in which the price is substantially exaggerated or severely out of line with the indications of the CMA or appraisal. These tools provide the best indications of what a buyer will likely pay for the property. An unrealistic listing price will make it difficult for the broker to properly market the seller's property within the agreed-on listing period. Furthermore, a seller who is unreasonable about the property's value may prove uncooperative on other issues later on.

Seller's Return   The broker easily can calculate roughly how much the seller will net from a given sales price or what sales price will produce a desired net amount. (The Math Concepts accompanying this section illustrate how the formulas are applied.)

Calculating Sales Prices, Commissions and Nets to Sellers

When a property sells, the sales price equals 100 percent of the money being transferred. Therefore, if a broker is to receive a 6 percent commission, 94 percent will remain for the seller's other expenses and equity. To calculate a commission using a sales price of $80,000 and a commission rate of 6 percent, multiply the sales price by the commission rate:

$$\$80{,}000 \times 6\% = \$80{,}000 \times .06 = \$4{,}800 \text{ commission}$$

To calculate a sales price using a commission of $4,550 and a commission rate of 7 percent, divide the commission by the commission rate:

$$\$4{,}550 \div 7\% = \$4{,}550 \div .07 = \$65{,}000 \text{ sales price}$$

To calculate a commission rate using a commission of $3,200 and a sales price of $64,000, divide the commission by the sales price:

$$\$3{,}200 \div \$64{,}000 = .05, \text{ or } 5\% \text{ commission rate}$$

To calculate the net to the seller using a sales price of $85,000 and a commission rate of 8 percent, multiply the sales price by 100 percent minus the commission rate:

$$\$85{,}000 \times (100\% - 8\%) = \$85{,}000 \times (1 - .08) = \$85{,}000 \times .92 = \$78{,}200$$

The same result could be achieved by calculating the commission ($85,000 × .08 = $6,800) and deducting it from the sales price ($85,000 − $6,800 = $78,200); however, this involves unnecessary extra calculations.

You may use this circle formula to help you with these calculations. If you know two of the figures, you can determine the third.

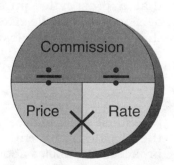

In summary: sales price × commission rate = commission
commission ÷ commission rate = sales price
commission ÷ sales price = commission rate
sales price × (100% − commission rate) = net to seller

Information Needed for Listing Agreements

Once the real estate licensee and the owner agree on a listing price, the licensee must obtain specific, detailed information about the property. Obtaining as many facts as possible ensures that most contingencies can be anticipated. This is particularly important when the listing will be shared with other brokers through an MLS and the other licensees must rely on the information taken by the lister.

The information needed for a listing agreement generally includes

- the names and relationship, if any, of the owners;
- the street address and legal description of the property;
- the size, type, age and construction of improvements;
- the number of rooms and their sizes;
- the dimensions of the lot;
- existing loans, including such information as the name and address of each lender, the type of loan, the loan number, the loan balance, the interest rate, the monthly payment and what it includes (principal, interest, real estate tax impounds, hazard insurance impounds, mortgage insurance premiums), whether the loan may be assumed by the buyer and under what circumstances and whether the loan may be prepaid without penalty;
- the possibility of seller financing;
- the amount of any outstanding special assessments and whether they will be paid by the seller or assumed by the buyer;
- the zoning classification of the property;
- the current (or most recent year's) property taxes;
- neighborhood amenities (for instance, schools, parks and recreational areas, churches and public transportation);
- any real property to be removed from the premises by the seller and any personal property to be included in the sale for the buyer (both the listing contract and the subsequent purchase contract should be explicit on these points);
- any additional information that would make the property more appealing and marketable; and
- any required disclosures concerning agency representation and property conditions.

Disclosures

Disclosure of agency relationships and property conditions has become the focus of consumer safeguards in recent years. Property condition disclosures normally cover a wide range of structural, mechanical and other conditions that a prospective purchaser should know about to make an informed decision. It is the licensee's responsibility to see that the seller complies with these mandatory disclosures. Agents should caution sellers to make truthful disclosures to avoid litigation arising from fraudulent or careless misrepresentations.

In Illinois . . .

Like most other states, Illinois requires that agents disclose whose interests they legally represent. It is important that the seller be informed of the brokerage's policies about cooperating with other brokers. Seller disclosure of property conditions is also required by Illinois law. (See Figure 6.2.) ■

THE LISTING CONTRACT FORM

A wide variety of listing contract forms are available. Some brokers have attorneys draft contracts, some use forms prepared by their MLSs and some use forms produced by their state real estate licensing authorities. Some brokers use a separate information sheet (also known as a *profile* or *data sheet*) for recording property features. That sheet is wed to a second form containing the contractual obligations between the seller and the broker: listing price, duration of the agreement, signatures of the parties and so forth. Other brokers use a single form. A sample listing agreement appears in Figure 6.3.

In Illinois . . .

Illinois law requires that the following disclosures be included in listing contracts:

Disclosure of material facts. A licensee must not withhold material facts concerning a property of which he or she has knowledge from any purchaser, prospective purchaser, seller, lessee, lessor or other party to the transaction. *Material facts* are any facts on which a reasonable person would base a contractual decision. However, the rules respect the fiduciary relationship between broker and principal. Licensees are not required to violate any duty imposed by the laws of agency.

Disclosure of interest. A licensee must disclose in writing to the parties to the transaction his or her status as a licensee and any direct or indirect interest he or she has or may have in the subject property. For example, if the buyer or seller is a licensed salesperson or broker, it must be clearly stated in the contract.

Disclosure of special compensation. A licensee is prohibited from accepting "any finder fees, commissions, discounts, kickbacks or other compensation from any financial institution, title insurance company or any other person other than another licensee, without full disclosure in writing of such receipt to all parties to the transaction." (In any event all sales agents may receive additional compensation only through their respective brokers.)

Earnest money and purchaser default. When any written listing includes a provision that the seller will not receive the earnest money deposit if the purchaser defaults, this fact must appear emphasized in letters larger than those otherwise used in the listing agreement.

Disclosure of property condition. Seller disclosure of property conditions is required by law in Illinois. These disclosures normally cover a wide range of structural, mechanical and other conditions that a prospective purchaser should know about to make an informed decision. It is the licensee's responsibility to see that the seller complies with these disclosures. Agents should caution sellers to make truthful disclosures to avoid litigation arising from fraudulent or careless misrepresentations. A property disclosure form appears in Figure 6.2. The form must be given to the buyer before an offer is made, or the buyer will have three days in which to rescind the offer, based on any negtive disclosures.

Figure 6.2   Illinois Property Condition Disclosure Form

MAP MULTIPLE LISTING SERVICE
SELLER PROPERTY DISCLOSURE

This form is provided as a convenience feature to the Seller. The real estate agency/agent assume no responsibility for the information conveyed by the seller.

THE PURPOSE OF THIS REPORT IS TO PROVIDE PROSPECTIVE BUYERS WITH INFORMATION ABOUT MATERIAL DEFECTS IN THE RESIDENTIAL REAL PROPERTY. THIS REPORT DOES NOT LIMIT THE PARTIES RIGHT TO CONTRACT FOR THE SALE OF RESIDENTIAL REAL PROPERTY IN "AS IS" CONDITION. UNDER COMMON LAW SELLERS WHO DISCLOSE MATERIAL DEFECTS MAY BE UNDER A CONTINUING OBLIGATION TO ADVISE THE PROSPECTIVE BUYERS ABOUT THE CONDITION OF THE RESIDENTIAL REAL PROPERTY EVEN AFTER THE REPORT IS DELIVERED TO THE PROSPECTIVE BUYER. COMPLETION OF THIS REPORT BY SELLER CREATES LEGAL OBLIGATIONS ON SELLER; THEREFORE, SELLER MAY WISH TO CONSULT AN ATTORNEY PRIOR TO COMPLETION OF THIS REPORT.

Property Address:_____
City, State & Zip Code:_____
Seller's Name:_____

This report is a disclosure of certain conditions of the residential real property listed above in compliance with the Residential Real Property Disclosure Act. This information is provided as of _____ , 19__, and does not reflect any changes made or occurring after that date or information that becomes known to the seller after that date. The disclosures herein shall not be deemed warranties of any kind by the seller or any person representing any party in this transaction.

In this form, "am aware" means to have actual notice or actual knowledge without any specific investigation or inquiry. In this form a "material defect" means a condition that would have a substantial adverse effect on the value of the residential real property or that would significantly impair the health or safety of future occupants of the residential real property unless the seller reasonably believes that the condition has been corrected.

The seller discloses the following information with the knowledge that even though the statements herein are not deemed to be warranties, prospective buyers may choose to rely on this information in deciding whether or not and on what terms to purchase the residential real property.

The seller represents that to the best of his or her actual knowledge, the following statements have been accurately noted as "yes", (correct), "no" (incorrect) or "not applicable" to the property being sold. If the seller indicates that the response to any statement, except number 1, is yes or not applicable, the seller shall provide an explanation, in the additional information area of this form.

	YES	NO	N/A	
1.	___	___	___	Seller has occupied the property within the last 12 months. (No explanation is needed.)
2.	___	___	___	I am aware of flooding or recurring leakage problems in the crawlspace or basement.
3.	___	___	___	I am aware that the property is located in a flood plain or that I currently have flood hazard insurance on the property.
4.	___	___	___	I am aware of material defects in the basement or foundation (including cracks and bulges).
5.	___	___	___	I am aware of leaks or material defects in the roof, ceilings or chimney.
6.	___	___	___	I am aware of material defects in the walls or floors.
7.	___	___	___	I am aware of material defects in the electrical system.
8.	___	___	___	I am aware of material defects in the plumbing system (includes such things as water heater, sump pump, water treatment system, sprinkler system, and swimming pool).
9.	___	___	___	I am aware of material defects in the well or well equipment.
10.	___	___	___	I am aware of unsafe conditions in the drinking water.
11.	___	___	___	I am aware of material defects in the heating, air conditioning, or ventilating systems.
12.	___	___	___	I am aware of material defects in the fireplace or woodburning stove.
13.	___	___	___	I am aware of material defects in the septic, sanitary sewer, or other disposal system.
14.	___	___	___	I am aware of unsafe concentrations of radon on the premises.
15.	___	___	___	I am aware of unsafe concentrations of or unsafe conditions relating to asbestos on the premises.
16.	___	___	___	I am aware of unsafe concentrations of or unsafe conditions relating to lead paint, lead water pipes, lead plumbing pipes or lead in the soil on the premises.
17.	___	___	___	I am aware of mine subsidence, underground pits, settlement, sliding, upheaval, or other earth stability defects on the premises.
18.	___	___	___	I am aware of current infestations of termites or other wood boring insects.
19.	___	___	___	I am aware of a structural defect caused by previous infestations of termites or other wood boring insects.
20.	___	___	___	I am aware of underground fuel storage tanks on the property.
21.	___	___	___	I am aware of boundary or lot line disputes.
22.	___	___	___	I have received notice of violation of local, state or federal laws or regulations relating to this property, which violation has not been corrected.

Note: These disclosures are not intended to cover the common elements of a condominium, but only the actual residential real property including limited common elements allocated to the exclusive use thereof that form an integral part of the condominium unit.

Note: These disclosures are intended to reflect the current condition of the premises and do not include previous problems, if any, that the seller reasonably believes have been corrected.

If any of the above are marked "not applicable" or "yes", please explain here or use additional pages, if necessary.

_____
_____
_____

Check here if additional pages used:_____

Seller certifies that seller has prepared this statement and certifies that the information provided is based on the actual notice or actual knowledge of the seller without any specific investigation or inquiry on the part of the seller. The seller hereby authorizes any person representing any principal in this transaction to provide a copy of this report, and to disclose any information in the report, to any person in connection with any actual or anticipated sale of the property.

Seller:_____ Date:_____ _____
Seller:_____ Date:_____ _____

PROSPECTIVE BUYER IS AWARE THAT THE PARTIES MAY CHOOSE TO NEGOTIATE AN AGREEMENT FOR THE SALE OF THE PROPERTY SUBJECT TO ANY OR ALL MATERIAL DEFECTS DISCLOSED IN THIS REPORT ("AS IS"). THIS DISCLOSURE IS NOT A SUBSTITUTE FOR ANY INSPECTIONS OR WARRANTIES THAT THE PROSPECTIVE BUYER OR SELLER MAY WISH TO OBTAIN OR NEGOTIATE. THE FACT THAT THE SELLER IS NOT AWARE OF A PARTICULAR CONDITION OR PROBLEM IS NO GUARANTEE THAT IT DOES NOT EXIST. PROSPECTIVE BUYER IS AWARE THAT HE MAY REQUEST AN INSPECTION OF THE PREMISES PERFORMED BY A QUALIFIED PROFESSIONAL.

Prospective Buyer:_____ Date:_____ Time:_____

Prospective Buyer:_____ Date:_____ Time:_____

DF REV. 9/98   COPYRIGHT MAP/MLS

Figure 6.2 Illinois Property Condition Disclosure Form (Continued)

RESIDENTIAL REAL PROPERTY DISCLOSURE ACT
SENATE BILL 828 (PUBLIC ACT 88-111) EFFECTIVE OCTOBER 1, 1994

AN ACT relating to disclosure by the seller of residential real property.

Section 1. Short title. This Act may be cited as the Residential Real Property Disclosure Act.

Section 5. As used in this Act, unless the context otherwise requires the following terms have the meaning given in this section:

"Residential real property" means real property improved with not less than one nor more than four residential dwelling units; units in residential cooperatives; or, condominium units including the limited common elements allocated to the exclusive use thereof that form an integral part of the condominium unit.

"Seller" means every person or entity who is an owner, beneficiary of a trust, contract purchaser or lessee of a ground lease, who has an interest (legal or equitable) in residential real property. However, "seller" shall not include any person who has both (i) never occupied the residential real property and (ii) never had the management responsibility for the residential real property nor delegated such responsibility for the residential real property to another person or entity.

"Prospective buyer" means any person or entity negotiating or offering to become an owner or lessee of residential real property by means of a transfer for value to which this Act applies.

Section 10. Except as provided in Section 15, this Act applies to any transfer by sale, exchange, installment land sale-contract, assignment of beneficial interest, lease with an option to purchase, ground lease or assignment of ground lease of residential real property.

Section 15. The provisions of this Act do not apply to the following:

(1) Transfers pursuant to court order, including, but not limited to, transfers ordered by a probate court in administration of an estate, transfers between spouses resulting from a judgment of dissolution of marriage or legal separation, transfers pursuant to an order of possession, transfers by a trustee in bankruptcy, transfers by eminent domain and transfers resulting from a decree for specific performance.

(2) Transfers from a mortgagor to a mortgagee by deed in lieu of foreclosure or consent judgement, transfer by judicial deed issued pursuant to a foreclosure sale to the successful bidder or the assignee of a certificate of sale, transfer by a collateral assignment of a beneficial interest of a land trust, or a transfer by a mortgagee or a successor in interest to the mortgagee's secured position or a beneficiary under a deed in trust who has acquired the real property by deed in lieu of foreclosure, consent judgement or judicial deed issued pursuant to a foreclosure sale.

(3) Transfers by a fiduciary in the course of the administration of a decedent's estate, guardianship, conservatorship, or trust.

(4) Transfers from one co-owner to one or more other co-owners.

(5) Transfers pursuant to testate or intestate succession.

(6) Transfers made to a spouse, or to a person or persons in the lineal line of consanguinity of one or more of the sellers.

(7) Transfers from an entity that has taken title to residential real property from a seller for the purpose of assisting in the relocation of the seller, so long as the entity makes available to all prospective buyers a copy of the disclosure form furnished to the entity by the seller.

(8) Transfers to or from any governmental entity.

(9) Transfers of newly constructed residential real property that has not been occupied.

Section 20. A seller of residential real property shall complete all applicable items in the disclosure document described in Section 35 of this Act. The seller shall deliver to the prospective buyer the written disclosure statement required by this Act before the signing of a written agreement by the seller and prospective buyer that would, subject to the satisfaction of any negotiated contingencies, require the prospective buyer to accept a transfer of the residential real property.

Section 25. Liability of seller. (a) The seller is not liable for any error, inaccuracy, or omission of any information delivered pursuant to this Act if (i) the seller had no knowledge of the error, inaccuracy, or omission, (ii) the error, inaccuracy, or omission was based on a reasonable belief that a material defect or other matter not disclosed had been corrected, or (iii) the error, inaccuracy, or omission was based on information provided by a public agency or by a licensed engineer, land surveyor, structural pest control operator, or by a contractor about matters within the scope of the contractor's occupation and the seller had no knowledge of the error, inaccuracy or omission.

(b) The seller shall disclose material defects of which the seller has actual knowledge.

(c) The seller is not obligated by this Act to make any specific investigation or inquiry in an effort to complete the disclosure statement.

Section 30. Disclosure supplement. If prior to closing, any seller has actual knowledge of an error, inaccuracy, or omission in any prior disclosure document after delivery of that disclosure document to a prospective buyer, that seller shall supplement the prior disclosure document with a written supplemental disclosure.

Section 35. Disclosure report form. The disclosures required of a seller by this Act, shall be made in the following form: [form on reverse side]

Section 40. Material defect. If a material defect is disclosed in the Residential Real Property Disclosure Report, after acceptance by the prospective buyer of an offer or counter-offer made by a seller or after the execution of an offer made by a prospective buyer that is accepted by the seller for the conveyance of the residential real property, then the Prospective Buyer may, within three business days after receipt of that Report by the prospective buyer, terminate the contract or other agreement without any liability or recourse except for the return to prospective buyer of all earnest money deposits or down payments paid by prospective buyer in the transaction. If a material defect is disclosed in a supplement to this disclosure document, the prospective buyer shall not have a right to terminate unless the material defect results from an error, inaccuracy, or omission of which the seller had actual knowledge at the time the prior disclosure document was completed and signed by the seller. The right to terminate the contract, however, shall no longer exist after the conveyance of the residential real property. For purposes of this Act the termination shall be deemed to be made when written notice of termination is personally delivered to at least one of the sellers identified in the contract or other agreement or when deposited, certified or registered mail, with the United States Postal Service, addressed to one of the sellers at the address indicated in the contract or agreement, or, if there is not an address contained therein, then at the address indicated for the residential real property on the Report.

Section 45. This Act is not intended to limit or modify any obligation to disclose created by any other statute or that may exist in common law in order to avoid fraud, misrepresentation, or deceit in the transaction.

Section 50. Delivery of the Residential Real Property Disclosure Report provided by this Act shall be by:

1) personal or facsimile delivery to the prospective buyer;

2) depositing the report with the United States Postal Service, postage prepaid, first class mail, addressed to the prospective buyer at the address provided by the prospective buyer or indicated on the contract or other agreement, or

3) depositing the report with an alternative delivery service such as Federal Express, UPS, or Airborne, delivery charges prepaid, addressed to the Prospective buyer at the address provided by the prospective buyer or indicated on the contract or other agreement.

For purposes of this Act, delivery to one prospective buyer is deemed delivery to all prospective buyers. Delivery to authorized individual acting on behalf of a prospective buyer constitutes delivery to all prospective buyers. Delivery of the Report is effective upon receipt by the prospective buyer. Receipt may be acknowledged on the Report, in an agreement for the conveyance of the residential real property, or shown in any other verifiable manner.

Section 55. Violations and damages. If the seller fails or refuses to provide the disclosure document prior to the conveyance of the residential real property, the buyer shall have the right to terminate the contract. A person who knowingly violates or fails to perform any duty prescribed by any provision of this Act or who discloses any information on the Residential Real Property Disclosure Report that he knows to be false shall be liable in the amount of actual damages and court costs, and the court may award reasonable attorney fees incurred by the prevailing party.

Section 60. No action for violation of this Act may be commenced later than one year from the earlier of the date of possession, date of occupancy or date of recording of an instrument of conveyance of the residential real property.

Section 65. A copy of this Act, excluding Section 35, must be printed on or as a part of the Residential Real Property Disclosure Report form.

Section 99. This Act takes effect on October 1, 1994.

PUBLIC ACT (88-111), REPRINTED IN ITS ENTIRETY

As amended, effective date 1-1-98

Once a listing agreement has been finalized and signed by the broker and seller, Illinois law prohibits the licensee from making any addition to, deletion from or alteration of the written listing without the written consent of the principal. The licensee must give a true copy of this signed listing agreement to the principal within 24 hours of execution. ■

Listing Agreement Issues

Regardless of which standard form of listing agreement is used, the same considerations arise in most real estate transactions. This means that all listing contracts tend to require similar information. However, licensees should review the specific forms used in their areas and refer to their states' laws for any specific requirements. Some of the considerations covered in a typical contract are discussed in the following paragraphs.

In Illinois . . .

There is no required state form for any real estate contract in Illinois. However, all written exclusive listing agreements must include

- the list price of the property,
- the agreed basis of or amount of commission and the time of payment,
- the time duration of the agreement,
- the names of the broker and seller and
- the address or legal description of the property.

Licensees may not obtain written listings that contain blank spaces to be filled in later. In addition, the form must include a statement of nondiscrimination. A listing agreement form that complies with Illinois law is reprinted in Figure 6.3. ■

Type of listing agreement. The contract may be an exclusive-right-to-sell listing (the most common type), an exclusive-agency listing or an open listing. The type of listing agreement determines the extent of a broker's authority to act on the principal's behalf. Most MLSs do not permit open listings to be posted in the system.

Broker's authority and responsibilities. The contract should specify whether the broker may place a sign on the property and advertise and market the property. Another major consideration is whether the broker is permitted to authorize buyer's brokers through an MLS. Will the contract allow the broker to show the property at reasonable times and on reasonable notice to the seller? May the broker accept earnest money deposits on behalf of the seller, and what are the broker's responsibilities in holding the funds? Without the written consent of the seller, the broker cannot undertake any of these or other important activities.

No FOR SALES or Rent without WRITTEN consent of owner

Names of all parties to the contract. Anyone who has an ownership interest in the property must be identified and should sign the listing to validate it.

In Illinois . . .

If the listed property is being lived in by a married couple, both spouses must sign the listing *even if only one owns the property.* If the property is in the possession of a tenant, that should be disclosed and instructions given on how the property is to be shown to a prospective buyer. ■

Figure 6.3   Sample Listing Agreement

COOPERATIVE SELLING CONTRACT

EQUAL HOUSING
OPPORTUNITY

1 To _____ Broker   Date _____
2 In consideration of the following agreements and of your efforts to procure a purchaser for the property and improvements thereon described below
3 ("Property"), the undersigned ("Seller") grants to you ("Broker") as broker, the exclusive right to sell the property.

4 In accordance with the 1994 amendment to the Illinois Real Estate License Act of 1983 under Article IV, a licensee working with a client is considered
5 to be the Designated Agent of that client unless there is a written agreement as to a different relationship. Unless otherwise agreed to in a separate
6 rider, the licensed Responsible Broker of the above mentioned company hereby designates certain agent(s), as listed later herein, as the Designated
7 Agent(s) of the Client(s), to the exclusion of all other licensees, employees, owners or other similar persons associated with the Company. The Company
8 itself and the Responsible Broker are not Agents of the Client(s), but rather have a vendor/customer (service) relationship with the Client(s).

9 The Broker designates _____
10 as the Designated Agent of the Client(s). Broker may, from time to time, add Designated Agents, as may be required in day to day operations, by
11 notifying all interested parties in writing. All licensees designated as Agents of the Client(s) shall remain Agents of the Client(s) throughout the term
12 of this Contract unless released, in writing, by the Client(s) or because such licensee is no longer affiliated with the Broker. Should any Designated
13 Agent be released for any reason, such Designated Agent shall not be released from (his/her) duties of confidentiality.

14 (_____ / _____) The Client(s) acknowledge(s) that they have been advised as to any alternative agency relationship available through the Broker.
       Client(s) Initials Required.

15 Street Address (or legal description): _____
16 _____ PERMANENT REAL ESTATE INDEX NUMBER _____
17 Possession _____ Lot Approximately _____ X _____
18 (the parties reserve the right to attach the legal description at a later date) together with improvements thereon including ventilating and central air
19 conditioning equipment if on premises; heating, lighting and plumbing fixtures; cabinets, planted vegetation.
20 Price $ _____ or such lesser amount as Seller may agree to accept.
21 PERSONAL PROPERTY: The following is the personal property which is now located on the premises and for which a Bill of Sale is to be given at the
22 closing STRIKE INAPPLICABLE ITEM(S): screens, storm windows and doors as exist, drapery rods, attached TV antenna, water softener, garage door
23 receiver (opener) and transmitter(s).
24 _____
25 I give you, the Broker, the exclusive right to sell this property for a period of time beginning this date and that exclusive right shall continue in effect
26 until expiration of ONE YEAR. However, I, the owner, may cancel this Cooperative Selling Contract any time after_____, upon
27 a THIRTY (30) DAY ADVANCE WRITTEN NOTICE. You, the Broker, may cancel this Contract any time upon THIRTY DAYS ADVANCE WRITTEN
28 NOTICE.
29 BROKER SHALL: List the property with cooperating brokers and compensate said cooperating brokers including subagents, buyer agents, and other
30 brokers, of which any may represent other parties to the transaction, in accordance with MAP Multiple Listing Service rules and regulations.
31 Make a continued and earnest effort to sell the property as Broker deems it advisable to obtain prospective purchasers, including placing informa-
    tion on any Internet system of broker's choice.
32 Take such other action as Broker deems necessary and proper to carry out Broker's obligations under the Contract, including advertising and the placing
33 of "For Sale" signs on the property.
34 Within 48 hours of this date, or as per the MAP Multiple Listing Service Standard Operating Procedures, file information concerning this property with
35 MAP MULTIPLE LISTING SERVICE for distribution to the members of the Service. Members may use this information to make market studies,
36 give service to the public, and advise clients or customers.
37 SELLER SHALL: Cooperate fully with Broker; refer all inquiries to Broker; conduct all negotiations through Broker; furnish a commitment for title
38 insurance in the amount of the sale price; execute or cause to be executed a recordable warranty deed (or other appropriate deed if title is in trust or
39 in an estate) to the purchaser of the property; and pay a real estate brokerage commission to Broker of _____ % of the sale price; if (1)
40 Broker provides a purchaser ready, willing and able to purchase in accordance with this Contract; or (2) if the property is sold, exchanged, gifted, or
41 optioned by Broker or by or through any other person including the Seller during the period of this Contract; or (3) if it is sold directly or indirectly within
42 six (6) months after termination of this Contract to a purchaser to whom it was offered during the term thereof. However, the Seller shall not be
43 obligated to pay such fee if a valid listing agreement is entered into during the term of said six (6) month period with another licensed real estate broker,
44 and a sale, lease, exchange, gift or option to purchase the property is made during the term of said protection. This six (6) month protection period
45 will survive any subsequent listing by another broker which terminates for any reason.
46 The commission shall be paid at or before closing. In the event the Seller enters into articles of agreement for deed (contract sale), the commission
47 shall be payable at the date of possession of the premises. If there is no closing, then Seller agrees to pay such commission as may be due to Broker
48 under this Contract upon written demand to Seller by Broker.
49 In the event the premises is a condominium, the Seller shall comply with all requirements set forth in the Illinois Condominium Property Act.
50 Seller agrees at the closing of this property, or as otherwise agreed, the Broker may pay out of the escrow fund, if any, the commission
51 as set forth above and any additional expenses as agreed to by the Seller.
52 Seller shall indemnify and save and hold the real estate firm and its agents harmless from all claims, disputes, litigations, judgments and costs arising
53 from any misrepresentations made by Seller, incorrect information supplied by Seller or problems with the property, which would tend to decrease the
54 value of the property, or any other latent defects in the property, which are known to the Seller and Seller fails to disclose.
55 OTHER: No amendment or alteration of the terms of this Contract relating to the amount of the commission or the time of payment of the
56 commission is valid or binding unless in writing and signed by all parties hereto. All specific directions of the client are incorporated herein or in riders
57 attached hereto. Additional direction shall be considered an amendment to this Contract.
58 The Seller understands and agrees that Broker/Agent may from time to time work with other sellers in disposing of property similar to that of the
59 Seller's. The Seller expressly waives any claims including but not limited to breach of duty or breach of contract, based solely upon Broker's/Agent's
60 representation of other sellers who may be seeking to sell property similar to the Seller's.
61 Broker's sole duty is to effect a sale of the property and Broker is not charged with the custody of the property, its management, maintenance, upkeep
62 or repair, nor is Broker charged with any responsibility for the status or condition of the property or any appliances contained therein.
63 This Contract shall take precedence over any other listing agreement (whether exclusive or not) which is prior in time and which has expired in
64 accordance with its terms and conditions.
65 It is understood that it is illegal for either the Seller or Broker/Agent to refuse to display to, or sell to, any person because of their race, color, religion,
66 national origin, sex, physical disability, or marital status.
67 IF PURCHASER DEFAULTS, EARNEST MONEY SHALL BE APPLIED TO PAYMENT OF BROKER'S COMMISSION WHICH SHALL NOT EXCEED THE AMOUNT
68 OF THE EARNEST MONEY, AND ANY EXPENSE INCURRED, AND BALANCE PAID TO SELLER. IF SELLER DEFAULTS, EARNEST MONEY, AT THE OPTION
69 OF PURCHASER, SHALL BE REFUNDED TO PURCHASER, BUT SUCH REFUNDING SHALL NOT RELEASE SELLER FROM THE OBLIGATIONS OF THIS
70 CONTRACT, NOR FROM THE OBLIGATION TO PAY THE COMMISSION AS SET FORTH IN THIS CONTRACT.
71 IF A DISPUTE ARISES BETWEEN THE SELLER AND THE PURCHASER AS TO WHETHER A DEFAULT HAS OCCURRED, BROKER SHALL HOLD THE
72 EARNEST MONEY AND PAY IT OUT, LESS COMMISSION, IF ANY, AS AGREED IN WRITING BY SELLER AND PURCHASER. IN THE EVENT THAT
73 AGREEMENT CANNOT BE REACHED BY SELLER AND PURCHASER WITHIN THIRTY (30) DAYS AFTER WRITTEN NOTICE TO BROKER THAT SUCH
74 DISPUTE HAS ARISEN, IT IS AGREED THAT THE BROKER MAY DEPOSIT THE FUNDS WITH THE CLERK OF THE CIRCUIT COURT AND THAT SELLER
75 AGREES TO INDEMNIFY AND HOLD THE BROKER HARMLESS FROM ANY AND ALL CLAIMS AND DEMANDS, INCLUDING THE PAYMENT OF
76 REASONABLE ATTORNEY'S FEES, COSTS AND ANY EXPENSES ARISING OUT OF SUCH CLAIMS AND DEMANDS.
77 This Contract is subject to Rider(s)_____ attached hereto and made a part of this Contract.
78 It is mutually understood and agreed that, by law, Broker is only permitted to prepare a contract of sale. Seller agrees to furnish or have his attorney
79 furnish all legal documents necessary to close the transaction.
80 Broker shall have the right to release the selling price, terms, type of financing, and number of days to sell my property to the MAP MULTIPLE LISTING
81 SERVICE for use by its members, lending institutions, appraisers, and related industries at the time a valid contract is entered into though the settlement
82 day may be at a future date.
83 There are no unpaid special assessments and none confirmed relative to the property except those amounting to approximately $ _____
84 for _____ THE COMMISSION PAYABLE FOR THE SALE, LEASE OR MANAGEMENT OF
85 PROPERTY IS NOT SET BY MAP MULTIPLE LISTING SERVICE IN ANY MANNER AND IS NEGOTIABLE BETWEEN THE BROKER AND THE SELLER.
86 Seller warrants his/her authority to execute this Contract as herein provided.

_____   Owner: _____
Broker or Broker's Authorized Representative

                                                   Owner: _____

_____   Current Address: _____
Acceptance by Designated Agent
                                                   _____

FORM: C101 REV 4/98

Brokerage firm. The brokerage company name, the employing broker and, if appropriate, the salesperson taking the listing must all be identified.

Listing price. This is the proposed gross sales price. The seller's proceeds will be reduced by unpaid real estate taxes, special assessments, mortgage and trust deed debts and any other outstanding obligations.

Real property and personal property. Any personal property that will be left with the real estate when it is sold must be explicitly identified. Similarly, any items of real property that the seller expects to remove at the time of the sale must be specified as well. Some of these items may later become points of negotiation when a ready, willing and able buyer is found for the property. Typical items to consider include major appliances, swimming pool and spa equipment, fireplace accessories, storage sheds, window treatments, stacked firewood and stored heating oil.

Leased equipment. Will any leased equipment—security systems, cable television boxes, water softeners, special antennas—be left with the property? If so, the seller is responsible for notifying the equipment's lessor of the change of property ownership.

Description of the premises. In addition to the street address, the legal description, lot size and tax parcel number may be required for future insertion into a purchase offer.

In Illinois . . .

The street address of the property is sufficient for listing agreements to be valid and enforceable under Illinois law. ■

Proposed dates for the closing and the buyer's possession. These dates should be based on an anticipated sale date. The listing agreement should allow adequate time for the paperwork involved (including the buyer's qualification for any financing) and the physical moves to be arranged by the seller and the buyer.

Closing issues. Details of the closing—such as a closing attorney, title company or escrow company—should be considered even at this early stage. Will the designated party complete the settlement statements and disburse the funds? Will he or she file the proper forms, such as documents to be recorded, documents to be sent to the Internal Revenue Service and documents to be submitted for registering foreign owners?

Evidence of ownership. The most commonly used proofs of title are a warranty deed and either a title insurance policy or an abstract and legal opinion.

Encumbrances. Which liens will be paid in full at the closing by the seller and which liens will be assumed by the buyer?

Homeowner warranty program. In some situations, it may be advisable to offer a homeowner warranty with the property. If so, the listing contract should answer these questions: What items does the warranty cover? Is the seller willing to pay for it? If not, will it be available to the buyer at the buyer's expense? What are the deductibles?

Commission. The circumstances under which a commission will be paid must be stated specifically: Is payment earned only on the sale of the property, or on any transfer of interest created by the broker? Will it be a percentage or a flat fee? When will it be paid? Will it be paid directly by the seller or by the party handling the closing?

In Illinois . . .

By law, written listing agreements in Illinois must state that no change in the amount of the commission or time of payment will be valid or binding unless the change is made in writing and signed by the parties. ■

Termination of the contract. A contract should provide some way for the parties to end it. Under what circumstances will the contract terminate? Can the seller arbitrarily refuse to sell or cooperate with the listing broker?

Broker protection clause. As previously discussed, brokers may be well advised to protect their interests against possible fraud or a reluctant buyer's change of heart. Under what circumstances will the broker be entitled to a commission after the agreement terminates? How long will the clause remain in effect?

Warranties by the owner. The owner is responsible for certain assurances and disclosures that are vital to the agent's ability to market the property successfully. Is the property suitable for its intended purpose? Does it comply with the appropriate zoning and building codes? Will it be transferred to the buyer in essentially the same condition as it was originally presented, considering repairs or alterations to be made as provided for in a purchase contract? Are there any known defects?

Indemnification (hold harmless) wording. The seller and the broker may agree to hold each other harmless (that is, not to sue one another) for any incorrect information supplied by one to the other. Indemnification may be offered regardless of whether the inaccuracies are intentional or unintentional.

In Illinois . . .

A client shall not be vicariously liable for the acts or omissions of a salesperson or broker in providing brokerage services for or on behalf of the client. ■

Nondiscrimination (equal opportunity) wording. The seller must understand that the property will be shown and offered without regard to the race, color, creed or religious preference, national origin, family status, sex, sexual orientation, age, disability or source of income of the prospective buyer. Federal, state and local fair housing laws protect a variety of different groups and individuals.

In Illinois . . .

All Illinois written listing agreements must clearly state that it is illegal for either the owner or the broker to refuse to sell or show property to any person because of race, color, religion, national origin, sex, handicap or familial status. ■

Antitrust wording. The contract should indicate that all commissions have been negotiated between the seller and the broker. It is illegal for commissions to be set by any regulatory agency, trade association or other industry organization.

The signatures of the parties. All parties identified in the contract must sign it, including all individuals who have a legal interest in the property.

The date the contract is signed. This date may differ from the date the contract actually becomes effective, particularly if a salesperson takes the listing and then must have his or her broker sign the contract to accept employment under its terms.

In Practice	Anyone who takes a listing should use only the appropriate documents provided by the broker. Most brokers are conscientious enough to use only documents that have been carefully drafted or reviewed by an attorney so that their construction and legal language comply with the appropriate federal, state and local laws. Such contracts also should give consideration to local customs, such as closing dates and the proration of income and expenses, with which most real estate attorneys are familiar.

BUYER AGENCY AGREEMENTS

Like a listing agreement, a **buyer agency agreement** is an employment contract. In this case, however, the broker is employed as the buyer's agent. The buyer, rather than the seller, is the principal. The purpose of the agreement is to find a suitable property. An agency agreement gives the buyer a degree of representation possible only in a fiduciary relationship. A buyer's broker must protect the buyer's interests at all points in the transaction.

Types of Buyer Agency Agreements

Three basic types of buyer agency agreements exist:

1. **Exclusive buyer agency agreement**—This is a completely exclusive agency agreement. The buyer is legally bound to compensate the agent whenever the buyer purchases a property of the type described in the contract. The broker is entitled to payment regardless of whether he or she locates the property. Even if the buyer finds the property independently, the agent is entitled to payment. A sample exclusive buyer agency agreement appears in Figure 6.4.
2. **Exclusive-agency buyer agency agreement**—Like an exclusive buyer agency agreement, this is an exclusive contract between the buyer and the agent. However, this agreement limits the broker's right to payment. The broker is entitled to payment only if he or she locates the property the buyer ultimately purchases. The buyer is free to find a suitable property without obligation to pay the agent.
3. **Open buyer agency agreement**—This agreement is a nonexclusive agency contract between a broker and a buyer. It permits the buyer to enter into similar agreements with an unlimited number of brokers. The buyer is obligated to compensate only the broker who locates the property the buyer ultimately purchases.

Figure 6.4 *Illinois Exclusive Buyer Representation Form*

ILLINOIS ASSOCIATION OF REALTORS®

EXCLUSIVE BUYER REPRESENTATION/EXCLUSIVE RIGHT TO PURCHASE CONTRACT
(DESIGNATED AGENT)

In consideration of _____'s ("Broker") agreement to designate a sales associate affiliated with Broker to act as an agent of the Buyer for the purpose of identifying and negotiating to acquire real estate for _____ ("Buyer"), the Buyer hereby grants to Broker the relationship as marked in Section 1 of the Contract.

SECTION 1: TYPE OF REPRESENTATION
(Instruction: check the box next to desired choice):

☐ **Exclusive Representation**. Buyer understands that this exclusive right to represent Buyer (Exclusive Representation) means that if the Buyer makes an acquisition of property, whether through the efforts of Broker and his agents or through the efforts of another real estate office or agent, Buyer will be obligated to compensate Broker pursuant to Section 7 and 8 of this Contract. This Exclusive Agency shall be effective for the following area: _____
_____. The term "acquisition" shall include the purchase, lease, exchange or option of real estate.

☐ **Exclusive Right to Acquire**. Buyer understands that this "exclusive right to purchase" means that if Buyer acquires any property, whether through the efforts of the Buyer, another real estate agency besides Broker's, or other third party, Buyer will be obligated to compensate Broker pursuant to Section 7 of this Contract. This exclusive right to acquire shall be effective for the following area:_____. "Acquisition" shall include the purchase, lease, exchange or option of real estate.

Broker designates and Buyer accepts_____
("Buyer's Designated Agent") as the legal agent(s) of Buyer for the purpose of representing Buyer in the acquisition of real estate by Buyer. Buyer understands and agrees that neither Broker nor any other sales associates affiliated with Broker (except as provided for herein) will be acting as legal agent of the Buyer. Broker shall have the discretion to appoint a substitute designated agent for Buyer as Broker determines necessary. Buyer shall be advised within a reasonable time of any such substitution.

SECTION 2: TERM
This Contract shall be effective until 11:59 p.m. on _____, 19__, when it shall then terminate. This Contract is irrevocable and can be terminated prior to the termination date only by written agreement of the parties. If within ____ days after the termination of this Contract (i.e. the protection period), Buyer purchases any property to which Buyer was introduced by Buyer's Designated Agent, then Buyer agrees to pay Broker the compensation provided for in Section 7. However, no compensation will be due to Broker if, during this protection period, Buyer enters into a separate buyer representation agreement with another broker.

SECTION 3: BUYER'S DESIGNATED AGENT'S DUTIES
(a) To use Buyer's Designated Agent's best efforts to identify properties listed in the multiple listing service that meet the Buyer's specifications relating to location, price, features and amenities, as identified on the attached Buyer's Information Checklist.

(b) To arrange for inspections of properties identified by the Buyer as potentially appropriate for acquisition.

(c) To advise Buyer as to the pricing of comparable properties.

(d) To assist Buyer in the negotiation of a contract acceptable to the Buyer for the acquisition of property.

(e) To provide reasonable safeguards for confidential information that the Buyer discloses to Buyer's Designated Agent.

SECTION 4: BROKER'S DUTIES
(a) To provide Buyer's Designated Agent with assistance and advice as necessary in Buyer's Designated Agent's work on Buyer's behalf.

(b) To make the managing Broker, or his designated representative, available to consult with Buyer's Designated Agent as to Buyer's negotiations for the acquisition of real estate, who will maintain the confidence of Buyer's confidential information.

(c) To make other sales associates affiliated with Broker aware of Buyer's general specifications for real property.

(d) As needed, to designate one or more sales associates as Designated Agents of Buyer.

SECTION 5: BUYER'S DUTIES
(a) To complete the Buyer's checklist which will provide Buyer's specifications for the real estate Buyer is seeking.

(b) To work exclusively with Buyer's Designated Agent to identify and acquire real estate during the time that this Contract is in force.

(c) To supply relevant financial information that may be necessary to permit Buyer's Designated Agent to fulfill Agent's obligations under this Contract.

(d) To be available upon reasonable notice and at reasonable hours to inspect properties that seem to meet Buyer's specifications.

(e) To pay Broker according to the terms specified in Section 7 of this Contract.

Figure 6.4   Illinois Exclusive Buyer Representation Form (Continued)

SECTION 6: REPRESENTING OTHER BUYER
Buyer understands that Buyer's Designated Agent has no duty to represent only Buyer, and that Buyer's Designated Agent may represent other prospective buyers who may be interested in acquiring the same property or properties that Buyer is interested in acquiring.

SECTION 7: COMPENSATION
Broker and Buyer expect that Broker's commission will be paid by the seller or the seller's Broker, for Broker's acting as a cooperating agent. However, if Broker is not compensated by seller or seller's agent, then Buyer agrees to pay Broker a commission of _____% of the purchase price if, during the term of this Contract or the protection period, the Buyer enters into a contract to acquire real estate and such contract results in a closed transaction. Any modification of this section, including the commission to be paid to Broker, shall be done only by a separate written amendment to this Contract.

SECTION 8: PREVIOUS REPRESENTATION
Buyer understands that Broker and/or Designated Agent may have previously represented the seller from whom you wish to purchase property. During that representation, Broker and/or Designated Agent may have learned material information about the seller that is considered confidential. Under the law, neither Broker nor Designated Agent may disclose any such confidential information to you even though the Broker and Designated Agent now represent you as a buyer.

SECTION 9: FAILURE TO CLOSE
If a seller or lessor in an agreement made on behalf of Buyer fails to close such agreement, with no fault on the part of Buyer, the Buyer shall have no obligation to pay the commission provided for in Section 7. If such transaction fails to close because of any fault on the part of Buyer, such commission will not be waived, but will be due and payable immediately. In no case shall Broker or Buyer's Designated Agent be obligated to advance funds for the benefit of Buyer in order to complete a closing.

SECTION 10: DISCLAIMER
The Buyer acknowledges that Broker and Buyer's Designated Agent are being retained solely as real estate professionals, and not as attorneys, tax advisors, surveyors, structural engineers, home inspectors, environmental consultants, architects, contractors, or other professional service providers. The Buyer understands that such other professional service providers are available to render advice or services to the Buyer, if desired, at Buyer's expense.

SECTION 11: COSTS OF THIRD PARTY SERVICES OR PRODUCTS
Buyer agrees to reimburse Broker the cost of any products or services such as surveys, soil tests, title reports and engineering studies, furnished by outside sources immediately when payment is due.

SECTION 12: INDEMNIFICATION OF BROKER
Buyer agrees to indemnify Broker and Buyer's Designated Agent and to hold Broker and Buyer's Designated Agent harmless on account of any and all loss, damage, cost or expense, including attorneys' fees incurred by Broker or Buyer's Designated Agent, arising out of this Contract, or the collection of fees or commission due Broker pursuant to the terms and conditions of this Contract, provided the loss damage, cost, expense or attorneys' fees do not result because of Broker's or Buyer's Designated Agent's own negligence or willful and wanton misconduct.

SECTION 13: ASSIGNMENT BY BUYERS
No assignment of Buyer's interest under this Contract and no assignment of rights in real property obtained for Buyer pursuant to this Contract shall operate to defeat any of Broker's rights under this exclusive representation contract.

SECTION 14: NONDISCRIMINATION
THE PARTIES AGREE NOT TO DISCRIMINATE AGAINST ANY PROSPECTIVE SELLER OR LESSOR BECAUSE OF THE RACE, COLOR, SEX, AGE, RELIGION, DISABILITY, NATIONAL ORIGIN, ANCESTRY, MARITAL OR FAMILIAL STATUS OF SUCH PERSON. THE PARTIES AGREE TO COMPLY WITH ALL APPLICABLE FEDERAL, STATE, AND LOCAL FAIR HOUSING LAWS.

SECTION 15: MODIFICATION OF THIS CONTRACT
No modification of any of the terms of this Contract shall be valid and binding upon the parties or entitled to enforcement unless such modification has first been reduced to writing and signed by the parties.

SECTION 16: ENTIRE AGREEMENT
This Contract constitutes the entire agreement between the parties relating to the subject thereof, and any prior agreements pertaining hereto, whether oral or written have been merged and integrated into this Contract.

This Contract may be executed in multiple copies and my signature as Buyer hereon acknowledges that I have received a signed copy.

_____   Accepted by:

_____   _____
Buyer

_____   _____
Buyer   Broker

Buyer's Address: Date:_____

_____
                                          _____
_____   Buyer's Designated Agent

Date:_____   Date:_____

Form 338 10/94   Copyright© by Illinois Association of REALTORS®

**Buyer
Representation
Issues**

A number of issues must be discussed by a broker and a buyer before they sign a buyer agency agreement. For instance, the licensee should make the same disclosures to the buyer that the licensee would make in a listing agreement. The licensee should explain the forms of agency available and the parties' rights and responsibilities under each type. The specific services provided to a buyer-client should be clearly explained. Compensation issues need to be addressed, as well. Buyer's agents may be compensated in the form of a flat fee for services, an hourly rate or a percentage of the purchase price. The agent may require a retainer fee at the time the agreement is signed to cover initial expenses. The retainer is applied as a credit toward any fees due at the closing.

As in any agency agreement, the source of compensation is not the factor that determines the relationship. A buyer's agent may be compensated by either the buyer or the seller. Issues of compensation are always negotiable.

Because the agency contract employs the agent to represent the buyer and locate a suitable property, the licensee must obtain detailed financial information from the buyer. In addition, the buyer's agent needs information about the buyer's specific requirements for a suitable property.

In Practice

Buyer agency, like any other kind of real estate agency, increasingly is subject to detailed provisions of state law. If a state has adopted an agency statute, it is highly likely that the rights, duties and obligations of buyer's agents are specifically established.

TERMINATION OF BROKER EMPLOYMENT CONTRACTS

A broker employment agreement is a personal service contract between a broker and a property owner or buyer. Its success depends on the broker's personal, professional efforts. Because the broker's services are unique, he or she cannot turn over the contract to another broker without the principal's written consent. The client cannot force the broker to perform, but the broker's failure to work diligently toward fulfilling the contract's terms constitutes abandonment of the contract. In the event the contract is abandoned or revoked by the broker, the principal is entitled to sue the broker for damages.

Of course, the principal also might fail to fulfill the terms of the agreement. For instance, a property owner who refuses to cooperate with the broker's reasonable requests, such as allowing the broker to show the property to prospective buyers, or who refuses to proceed with a complete sales contract could be liable for damages to the broker. If either party cancels the contract, he or she may be liable for damages to the other.

An employment contract may be canceled for the following reasons:

- When the agreement's purpose is fulfilled.
- When the agreement's term expires without a successful transfer.

- If the property is destroyed or its use is changed by some force outside the client's control, such as a zoning change or condemnation by eminent domain.
- If title to the property is transferred by operation of law, as in the case of the client's bankruptcy.
- If the broker and client mutually agree to end the agreement or if one party ends it unilaterally (in which case he or she may be liable to the other party for damages).
- If either the broker or the client dies or becomes incapacitated.
- If either the broker or client breaches the contract, the agreement is terminated and the breaching or canceling party may be liable to the other for damages.

SUMMARY

To acquire an inventory of property to sell, brokers must obtain listings. Types of listings include exclusive-right-to-sell, exclusive-agency and open listings.

With an exclusive-right-to-sell listing, the seller employs only one broker and must pay that broker a commission regardless of whether it is the broker or the seller who finds a buyer, provided the buyer is found within the listing period.

Under an exclusive-agency listing, the broker is given the exclusive right to represent the seller, but the seller can avoid paying the broker a commission by selling the property to someone not procured by the broker.

With an open listing, the broker must find a ready, willing and able buyer on the seller's terms before the property is sold by the seller or another broker to obtain a commission.

A multiple-listing provision may appear in an exclusive-right-to-sell or an exclusive-agency listing. It gives the broker the additional authority and obligation to distribute the listing to other members of the broker's multiple-listing organization.

A net listing, which is outlawed in some states and considered unethical in most areas, is based on the net price the seller will receive if the property is sold. The broker is free to offer the property for sale at the highest available price and will receive as commission any amount exceeding the seller's stipulated net.

An option listing, which also must be handled with caution, gives the broker the option to purchase the listed property.

When listing a property for sale, the seller is concerned about the selling price and the net amount he or she will receive from the sale. A competitive market analysis compares the prices of recently sold properties that are similar to the seller's property. The CMA or a formal appraisal report can be used to help the seller determine a reasonable listing price. The amount the seller will net from the sale is calculated by subtracting the broker's commission, along with any existing liens and any other expenses that the seller incurs, from the selling price.

A wide variety of listing contract forms may be used, depending on the customs and laws in an area. Typically, they are preprinted forms that include such information as the type of listing agreement, the broker's authority and responsibility under the listing, the listing price, the duration of the listing, information about the property, terms for the payment of commission (including antitrust concerns and encumbrances) and the buyer's possession, and nondiscrimination laws. Detailed information about the property may be included in the listing contract or on a separate property data sheet. Disclosure of the broker's law of agency relationship and discussion of the broker's agency policies have become the focus of laws in many states. The seller also may be expected to comply with mandatory disclosure of property conditions.

A buyer agency agreement ensures that a buyer's interests will be represented. Different forms of buyer agency agreements exist. A buyer's broker is obligated to find a suitable property for the client, who is owed the traditional fiduciary duties. Buyer agency may be regulated by state agency laws.

A listing agreement may be terminated for the same reasons as any other agency relationship.

In Illinois . . .

In Illinois a written exclusive listing agreement must include the list price, the basis for and time of payment of the commission, the term of the listing, the names of the listing broker and seller and the address or legal description of the property. Detailed information about the property may be included in the listing contract or on a separate property data sheet. Disclosure of the broker's agency relationship, any interest the broker has in the subject property, material facts pertaining to the property and any special compensation or guaranteed sales agreement is required by Illinois law. ■

QUESTIONS

1. A listing taken by a real estate salesperson is an agreement between the seller and the:
   A. broker.
   B. local multiple-listing service.
   C. salesperson.
   D. salesperson and broker together.

2. Which of the following is a similarity between an exclusive-agency listing and an exclusive-right-to-sell listing?
   A. Under both, the seller retains the right to sell the real estate without the broker's help and without paying the broker a commission.
   B. Under both, the seller authorizes only one particular salesperson to show the property.
   C. Both types of listings give the responsibility of representing the seller to one broker only.
   D. Both types of listings are open listings.

3. The listing agreement between Broker Betty and Seller Theo states that it expires prior to May 2. All of the following events would terminate the listing EXCEPT:
   A. the agreement is not renewed prior to May 2.
   B. Betty dies on April 29.
   C. on April 15, Theo tells Betty that he is dissatisfied with Betty's marketing efforts.
   D. Theo's house is destroyed by fire on April 25.

4. The seller has listed his property under an exclusive-agency listing with the broker. If the seller sells the property himself during the term of the listing to someone introduced to the property by the seller, he will owe the broker:
   A. no commission.
   B. the full commission.
   C. a partial commission.
   D. only reimbursement for the broker's costs.

5. A broker sold a residence for $85,000 and received $5,950 as her commission in accordance with the terms of the listing. What was the broker's commission rate?
   A. 6 percent
   B. 7 percent
   C. 7.25 percent
   D. 7.5 percent

6. Under a listing agreement, the broker is entitled to sell the property for any price, as long as the seller receives $85,000. The broker may keep any amount over $85,000 as a commission. This type of listing is called a(n):
   A. exclusive-right-to-sell listing.
   B. exclusive-agency listing.
   C. open listing.
   D. net listing.

7. Which of the following is a similarity between an open listing and an exclusive-agency listing?
   A. Under both the seller avoids paying the broker a commission if the seller sells the property to someone the broker did not procure.
   B. Both grant a commission to any broker who procures a buyer for the seller's property.
   C. Under both the broker earns a commission regardless of who sells the property as long as it is sold within the listing period.
   D. Both grant an exclusive right to sell to whatever broker procures a buyer for the seller's property.

8. The listed price for a property should be determined by the:
   A. agent based on information from the local MLS.
   B. agent and the appraiser.
   C. agent and the buyer.
   D. seller based on the agent's CMAs.

9. Which of the following statements is true of a listing contract?
   A. It is an employment contract for the personal and professional services of the broker.
   B. It obligates the seller to convey the property if the broker procures a ready, willing and able buyer.
   C. It obligates the broker to work diligently for both the seller and the buyer.
   D. It automatically binds the owner, broker and MLS to the agreed provisions.

10. A real estate broker sold a property and received a 6.5 percent commission. The broker gave the listing salesperson 30 percent of the commission, or $3,575. What was the selling price of the property?
   A. $55,000   C. $152,580
   B. $95,775   D. $183,333

11. A seller hired Broker Nathan under the terms of an open listing. While that listing was still in effect, the seller, without informing Broker Nathan, hired Broker Frank under an exclusive-right-to-sell listing for the same property. If Broker Nathan produces a buyer for the property whose offer the seller accepts, then the seller must pay a:
   A. full commission only to Broker Nathan.
   B. full commission only to Broker Frank.
   C. full commission to both Broker Nathan and Broker Frank.
   D. half commission to both Broker Nathan and Broker Frank.

12. Seller Grace listed her residence with Broker Diane. Broker Diane brought an offer at full price and terms of the listing from buyers who were ready, willing and able to pay cash for the property. However, Seller Grace changed her mind and rejected the buyers' offer. In this situation, Seller Grace:
   A. must sell her property.
   B. owes a commission to Broker Diane.
   C. is liable to the buyers for specific performance.
   D. is liable to the buyers for compensatory damages.

13. All of the following are false regarding buyer agency EXCEPT:
   A. the buyer may enter into agreements with multiple brokers and is obligated to pay only the broker who locates the property that the buyer ultimately purchases.
   B. while the buyer may enter into agreements with multiple brokers, he or she is under no obligation to pay the broker; the seller bears all brokerage expenses.
   C. because multiple brokers may be involved, an open buyer agency agreement involves reduced fiduciary duties.
   D. the buyer may not look for or make offers on properties on his or her own.

14. Broker Jane and Buyer Bonnie enter into an exclusive-agency buyer agency agreement. This means:
   A. Bonnie is obligated to compensate Jane regardless of who locates the property ultimately purchased.
   B. Jane is entitled to payment only if she, or any broker acting under her authority, locates the property Bonnie ultimately purchases.
   C. Bonnie may enter into similar agreements with any number of other brokers.
   D. If Bonnie finds the property without any help from Jane, Bonnie must pay Jane a reduced compensation.

15. A competitive market analysis:
   A. is the same as an appraisal.
   B. can help the seller price the property.
   C. by law must be completed for each listing taken.
   D. should not be retained in the property's listing file.

16. A property was listed with a broker who belonged to a multiple-listing service and was sold by another member broker for $53,500. The total commission was 6 percent of the sales price. The selling broker received 60 percent of the commission, and the listing broker kept the balance. What was the listing broker's commission?
   A. $1,284   C. $1,926
   B. $1,464   D. $2,142

17. Shane signs a listing agreement with Broker Keith to sell Shane's home. The agreement states that Keith will receive a 7 percent commission. The home sells for $120,000. What is the net amount that Shane will receive from the sale?
    A. $36,000   C. $111,600
    B. $102,877   D. $120,000

18. A real estate broker and a seller enter into a listing agreement that contains the following language: "Seller will receive $100,000 from the sale of the subject property. Any amount greater than $100,000 will constitute Broker's sole and complete compensation." Which of the following statements is true regarding this agreement?
    A. This agreement is an example of an option listing.
    B. If the seller's home sells for exactly $100,000, the broker still will be entitled to receive the standard commission in the area.
    C. The broker may offer the property for any price over $100,000, but the agreement may be unethical.
    D. This type of listing is known as an *open listing*, because the selling price is left open.

19. All of the following would permit a listing agreement to be terminated EXCEPT:
    A. destruction of the listed property.
    B. seller dissatisfaction with the wording of a newspaper advertisement.
    C. seller refusal to permit showings of the property during any time other than early mornings.
    D. a breach by the broker.

20. Broker George enters into an agreement with a client. The agreement states, "In return for the compensation agreed upon, Broker will assist Client in locating and purchasing a suitable property. Broker will receive the agreed compensation regardless of whether Broker, Client or some other party locates the property ultimately purchased by Client." What kind of agreement is this?
    A. Exclusive-agency listing
    B. Exclusive-agency buyer agency agreement
    C. Exclusive buyer agency agreement
    D. Open buyer agency agreement

In Illinois . . .

21. Illinois salespeople may:
    A. submit a listing to the local MLS.
    B. refuse to show a property to racial minorities if their sellers so instruct them.
    C. advertise in their own name as long as they hold independent contractor status.
    D. never take open listings.

22. In Illinois, written listing agreements must include all of the following EXCEPT:
    A. the commission amount.
    B. a statement regarding the fact that discrimination is illegal.
    C. the address of the property.
    D. the license number of the broker.

CHAPTER 7

Interests in Real Estate

KEY TERMS

accretion
appurtenant
    easement
avulsion
condemnation
deed restrictions
doctrine of prior
    appropriation
easement
easement by
    condemnation
easement by
    necessity

easement by
    prescription
easement in gross
eminent domain
encroachment
encumbrance
erosion
escheat
estate in land
fee simple
fee simple absolute
fee simple defeasible
fee simple
    determinable

freehold estate
future interest
homestead
leasehold estate
license
lien
life estate
littoral rights
party wall
police power
remainder interest
reversionary interest
riparian rights
taxation

LIMITATIONS ON THE RIGHTS OF OWNERSHIP

An extensive bundle of rights goes along with owning real estate. However, many different interests in real estate can be acquired, and not all of them convey the entire bundle of legal rights to the owner. Licensees must take great care to ensure that prospective buyers understand exactly what interests a seller wishes to transfer.

Furthermore, ownership of real estate is not absolute. That is, a landowner's power to control his or her property is subject to other interests. Even the most complete ownership the law allows is limited by public and private restrictions. These are intended to ensure that one owner's use or enjoyment of his or her property does not interfere with others' use or enjoyment of their property or with the general welfare of the community. Licensees should have a working knowledge of the restrictions that might limit current or future owners. A zoning ordinance that will not allow a doctor's office to coexist with a residence, a condo association bylaw prohibiting resale without board approval or an easement allowing the neighbors to use the private beach may not only burden today's purchaser but also deter a future buyer.

This chapter puts the various interests in real estate in perspective—what rights they confer and how use of the ownership may be limited.

GOVERNMENT POWERS

Individual ownership rights are subject to certain powers, or rights, held by federal, state and local governments. These limitations on the ownership of real estate are imposed for the general welfare of the community and, therefore, supersede the rights or interests of the individual. Government powers include the following.

In Illinois . . .

The state and local government powers discussed in this section are all held by the state of Illinois and various county and municipal governing bodies. ■

Police Power

Every state has the power to enact legislation to preserve order, protect the public health and safety and promote the general welfare of its citizens. That authority is known as a state's **police power.** The state's authority is passed on to municipalities and counties through legislation called *enabling acts.*

> **MEMORY TIP**
>
> *The four government powers can be remembered as **PETE**: Police, Eminent domain, Taxation and Escheat.*

Of course, what is identified as being "in the public interest" varies widely from state to state and region to region. Generally, however, a state's police power is used to enact environmental protection laws, zoning ordinances and building codes. Regulations that govern the use, occupancy, size, location and construction of real estate also fall within the police powers of a state. Police powers may be used to achieve a community's needs or goals. A city that deems growth to be desirable, for instance, may exercise its police powers to enact laws encouraging the purchase and improvement of land. On the other hand, an area that wishes to retain its current character may enact laws that discourage development and population growth.

Like the rights of ownership, the states' power to regulate land use is not absolute. The laws must be uniform and nondiscriminatory; that is, they may not operate to the advantage or disadvantage of any one particular owner or owners.

Eminent Domain

Eminent domain is the right of the government to acquire privately owned real estate for public use or purpose. *Condemnation* is the process by which the government exercises this right, by either judicial or administrative proceedings. The proposed use must be for the public good, just compensation must be paid to the owner and the rights of the property owner must be protected by due process of law. Public use or purpose has been defined very broadly by the courts to include not only public facilities but also property that is no longer fit for use and must be closed or destroyed. In Hawaii, the housing authority took privately held land and gave it to a developer to build housing. Some common facilities that are created after properties are acquired by eminent domain include educational institutions, streets and public recreational facilities.

> *Eminent domain is the government's right to seize property; condemnation is the way the right is exercised.*

In Illinois . . .

Local units of government and quasi-governmental bodies are given the power of eminent domain by Article I, Section 15, of the Illinois Constitution and by the Illinois Code of Civil Procedure.

In certain situations, Illinois law permits a summary proceeding in which a plaintiff/condemnor may obtain immediate fee simple title to real property, including the rights of possession and use. Such a proceeding in Illinois is termed a *quick-take,* and the plaintiff must deposit a sum with the county treasurer that is preliminarily considered by the court to be *just compensation;* this can be litigated later. A quick-take might be appropriate, for instance, in the following circumstances:

- the state of Illinois or the Illinois Toll Highway Authority takes property to construct, maintain and operate highways;
- a sanitary district takes property to remove obstructions in a river, such as the Des Plaines River or Illinois River; or
- the St. Louis Metropolitan Area Airport Authority takes property to provide additional land for airport purposes. ■

Generally, the states delegate their power of eminent domain to quasi-public bodies and publicly held companies responsible for various facets of public service. For instance, a public housing authority might take privately owned land to build low-income housing; the state's land-clearance commission or redevelopment authority could use the power of eminent domain to make way for urban renewal. If there were no other feasible way to do so, a railway, utility company or state highway department might acquire farmland to extend a railroad track, bring electricity to a remote new development 'or build a highway. Again, all are allowable as long as the purpose contributes to the public good.

Ideally, the public agency and the owner of the property in question agree on compensation through direct negotiation, and the government purchases the property for a price considered fair by the owner. In some cases, the owner simply may dedicate the property to the government as a site for a school, park, library or other beneficial use. Sometimes, however, the owner's consent cannot be obtained. In those cases, the government agency can initiate **condemnation** proceedings to acquire the property.

Taxation

Taxation is a charge on real estate to raise funds to meet the public needs of a government.

Escheat

Although **escheat** is not actually a limitation on ownership, it is an avenue by which the state may acquire privately owned real or personal property. State laws provide for ownership to transfer, or escheat, to the state when an owner dies leaving no heirs (as defined by the law) and no will that directs how the real estate is to be distributed. In some states, real property escheats to the county where the land is located; in others, it becomes the property of the state. Escheat is intended to prevent property from being ownerless or abandoned.

In Illinois . . .

Real property will escheat to the county in which it is located rather than to the state. ■

ESTATES IN LAND

Historically, **estates in land** have been classified as *freehold estates* and *leasehold estates.* The two types of estates are distinguished primarily by their duration.

Freehold estates last for an indeterminable length of time, such as for a lifetime or forever. They include *fee simple* (also called an *indefeasible fee*), *defeasible fee* and *life estates.* The first two of these estates continue for an indefinite period and may be passed along to the owner's heirs. A life estate is based on the lifetime of a person and ends when that individual dies. Freehold estates are illustrated in Figure 7.1.

In Illinois . . . The traditional freehold estates are recognized under Illinois law. ■

Leasehold estates last for a fixed period of time. They include estates for years and estates from period to period. Estates at will and estates at sufferance also are leaseholds, though by their operation they are not generally viewed as being for fixed terms.

Fee Simple Estate

An estate in **fee simple** (or **fee simple absolute**) is the highest interest in real estate recognized by law. Fee simple ownership is absolute ownership: the holder is entitled to all rights to the property. It is limited only by public and private restrictions, such as zoning laws and restrictive covenants. Because this estate is of unlimited duration, it is said to run forever. Upon the death of its owner, it passes to the owner's heirs or as provided by will. A fee simple estate is also referred to as an *estate of inheritance* or simply as *fee ownership.*

Fee simple defeasible. A **fee simple defeasible** (or *defeasible fee*) estate is a qualified estate—that is, it is subject to the occurrence or nonoccurrence of some specified event. Two types of defeasible estates exist: those *subject to a condition subsequent* and those *qualified by a special limitation.*

A fee simple estate may be qualified by a *condition subsequent.* This means that the new owner must not perform some action or activity. The former owner retains a *right of reentry* so that *if the condition is broken, the former owner can retake possession of the property through legal action.* Conditions in a deed are different from restrictions or covenants because of the grantor's right to reclaim ownership, a right that does not exist under private restrictions.

FOR EXAMPLE   A grant of land "on the condition that" there be no consumption of alcohol on the premises is a fee simple subject to a condition subsequent. If alcohol is consumed on the property, the former owner has the right to reacquire full ownership. It will be necessary for the grantor (or the grantor's heirs or successors) to go to court to assert that right, however.

A fee simple estate also may be qualified by a *special limitation.* The estate ends automatically on the current owner's failure to comply with the limitation. The former owner retains a *possibility of reverter.* If the limitation is violated, the former owner (or his or her heirs or successors) reacquires full ownership, *with no need to reenter the land or go to court.* A fee simple with a special limitation is also called a **fee simple determinable** because it may

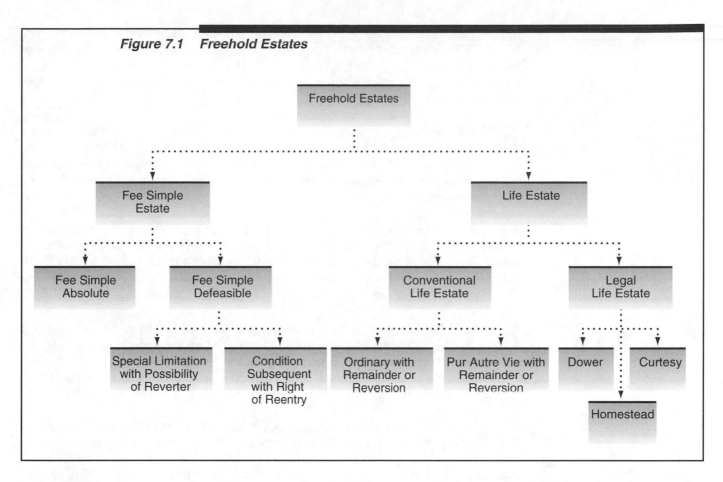

Figure 7.1 **Freehold Estates**

end automatically. The language used to distinguish a special limitation—the words *so long as* or *while* or *during*—is the key to creating this estate.

The right of entry and possibility of reverter may never take effect. If they do, it will be only at some time in the future. Therefore, both of these rights are considered **future interests.**

FOR EXAMPLE A grant of land from an owner to her church "so long as the land is used only for religious purposes" is a fee simple with a special limitation. If the church ever decides to use the land for a nonreligious purpose, title will revert to the previous owner (or her heirs or successors).

> Fee simple defeasible: "on the condition that"
>
> Fee siimple determinable:
> "so long as"
> "while"
> "during"

In Illinois . . . Because the right of reentry and possibility of reverter can happen only in the future, they are considered *future interests.* While the condition passes from owner to owner forever, Illinois allows the original grantor's right of reverter to continue for only 40 years. After that time, the condition still may be enforced but no longer by the threat of losing the property. ■

Life Estate A **life estate** is a freehold estate limited in duration to the life of the owner or the life of some other designated person or persons. Unlike other freehold estates, a life estate is not inheritable. It passes to future owners according to the provisions of the life estate.

Conventional life estate. A *conventional life estate* is created intentionally by the owner. It may be established either by deed at the time the ownership is transferred during the owner's life or by a provision of the owner's will after his or her death. The estate is conveyed to an individual who is called the *life tenant*. The life tenant has full enjoyment of the ownership for the duration of his or her life. When the life tenant dies, the estate ends and its ownership passes, usually as a fee simple, to another designated individual or returns to the previous owner.

FOR EXAMPLE Anna, who has a fee simple estate in Blackacre, conveys a life estate to Phil for Phil's lifetime. Phil is the life tenant. Upon Phil's death, the life estate terminates, and Anna once again owns Blackacre. If Phil's life estate had been created by Anna's will, however, subsequent ownership of Blackacre would be determined by the provisions of the will.

A life estate also may be based on the lifetime of a person other than the life tenant. This is known as a *life estate pur autre vie* ("for the life of another"). Although a life estate is not considered an estate of inheritance, a life estate pur autre vie provides for inheritance by the life tenant's heirs only until the death of the person against whose life the estate is measured.

FOR EXAMPLE Anna conveys a life estate in Blackacre to Phil as the life tenant for the duration of the life of David, Anna's elderly relative. Phil is still the life tenant, but the measuring life is David's. Upon David's death, the life estate ends. If Phil should die while David is still alive, Phil's heirs may inherit the life estate. However, when David dies, the heirs' estate ends.

A life tenant is entitled to the rights of ownership. That is, the life tenant can enjoy both possession and the ordinary use and profits arising from ownership, just as if the individual were a fee owner. The ownership may be sold, mortgaged or leased, but it always is subject to the limitation of the life estate.

A life tenant's ownership rights, however, are not absolute. The life tenant may not injure the property, such as by destroying a building or allowing it to deteriorate. In legal terms, this injury is known as *waste*. Those who eventually will own the property could seek an injunction against the life tenant or sue for damages.

Because the ownership will terminate on the death of the person against whose life the estate is measured, a purchaser, lessee or lender can be affected. The life tenant can sell, lease or mortgage only his or her interest—that is, ownership for a lifetime. Because the interest is obviously less desirable than a fee simple estate, the life tenant's rights are limited.

Remainder and reversion. The fee simple owner who creates a conventional life estate must plan for its future ownership. When the life estate ends, it is replaced by a fee simple estate. The future owner of the fee simple estate may be designated in one of two ways:

1. **Remainder interest:** The creator of the life estate may name a *remainderman* as the person to whom the property will pass when the life estate ends. ("Remainderman" is the legal term; neither the term *remainderperson* nor *remainderwoman* is used.) (See Figure 7.2.)
2. **Reversionary interest:** The creator of the life estate may choose *not* to name a remainderman. In that case, the creator will recapture ownership when the life estate ends. The ownership is said to revert to the original owner. (See Figure 7.3.)

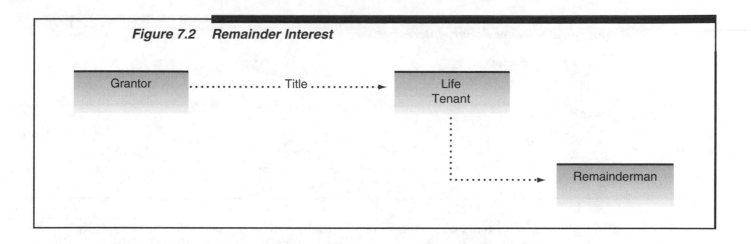

Figure 7.2   Remainder Interest

FOR EXAMPLE Anna conveys Blackacre to Phil for Phil's lifetime and designates Rhiann to be the remainderman. While Phil is still alive, Rhiann owns a remainder interest, which is a *nonpossessory estate;* that is, Rhiann does not possess the property, but has an interest in it nonetheless. This is a future interest in the fee simple estate. When Phil dies, Rhiann automatically becomes the fee simple owner. On the other hand, Anna may convey a life estate in Blackacre to Phil during Phil's life. On Phil's death, ownership of Blackacre reverts to Anna. Anna has retained a reversionary interest (also a nonpossessory estate). Anna has a future interest in the ownership and may reclaim the fee simple estate when Phil dies. If Anna dies before Phil, Anna's heirs (or other individuals specified in Anna's will) will assume ownership of Blackacre when Phil dies.

Legal life estate. A *legal life estate* is not created voluntarily by an owner. Rather, it is a form of life estate established by state law. It becomes effective automatically when certain events occur. *Dower, curtesy* and *homestead* are the legal life estates currently used in some states. Community property states have never used dower and curtesy.

In Illinois . . . Most separate property states, including Illinois, have abolished the common-law concepts of dower and curtesy in favor of the Uniform Probate Code, which gives the surviving spouse a right to an elective share upon the death of the other spouse. All rights to elect to take dower (and curtesy) were abolished by statute in Illinois on January 1, 1972. ■

Dower and curtesy provide the nonowning spouse with a means of support after the death of the owning spouse. *Dower* is the life estate that a wife has in the real estate of her deceased husband. *Curtesy* is an identical interest that a husband has in the real estate of his deceased wife. (In some states, dower and curtesy are referred to collectively as *either* dower or curtesy.)

Dower and curtesy provide that the nonowning spouse has a right to a one-half or one-third interest in the real estate for the rest of her or his life, even if the owning spouse wills the estate to others. Because a nonowning spouse might clam an interest in the future, both spouses may have to sign the proper documents when real estate is conveyed. The signature of the nonowning spouse would be needed to release any potential common-law interests in the property being transferred.

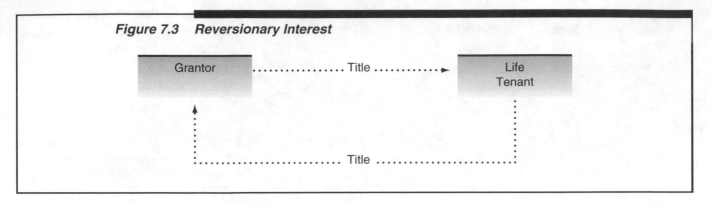

Figure 7.3   Reversionary Interest

A **homestead** is a legal life estate in real estate occupied as the family home. In effect, the home (or at least some part of it) is protected from creditors during the occupant's lifetime. In states that have homestead exemption laws, a portion of the area or value of the property occupied as the family home is exempt from certain judgments for debts such as charge accounts and personal loans. The homestead is not protected from real estate taxes levied against the property or a mortgage for the purchase or cost of improvements. That is, if the debt is secured by the property, the property cannot be exempt from a judgment on that debt.

In Illinois . . .

Every homeowner in Illinois is entitled to a homestead estate up to a value of $7,500 in the land and buildings he or she occupies as a principal residence. The estate extends to all types of residential property, both real and personal, including condominiums, cooperatives, beneficial interests in land trusts and leaseholds. Single persons, as well as householders with spouses and families, qualify.

There has been some confusion over the amount of the Illinois homestead exemption. One of the reasons for this confusion was disagreement over where the exemption was to be placed: in the property or in the individual. However, a 1987 court decision clearly placed the $7,500 exemption in the individual rather than the property. Therefore, in the case of *First National Bank of Moline v. Mohr, et al.*, 3rd Dist. (1987), the Illinois Appellate Court ruled that the homestead estates of a husband and wife could be combined to a total of $15,000. *Regardless, the answer to the question "How much of a homestead estate is an individual entitled to in his or her Illinois residence?" is* **$7,500.**

No notice has to be recorded or filed to establish a homestead in Illinois. Therefore, prospective purchasers, lienholders and other concerned parties are charged with inspecting a property to see if it serves as the residence of the potential debtor and if homestead estate rights can be claimed.   ■

How does the exemption actually work? Though the entire homestead is protected from being sold in a few states, usually the homestead merely reserves a certain amount of money for the family in the event of a court sale. Upon such a sale, any debts secured by the home, such as a mortgage, unpaid taxes or mechanics' liens (which are exceptions to homestead protection), will be paid from the proceeds first. Then the family will receive the amount reserved by the homestead exemption. Whatever remains will be applied to the family's unsecured debts.

In Illinois . . . A family can have only one homestead at any one time. The Illinois homestead exemption is not applicable between co-owners but is applicable to any cotenant's creditors. The exemption continues after the death of an individual for the benefit of the surviving spouse as long as she or he continues to occupy the homestead residence and extends for the benefit of all children living there until the youngest reaches 18 years of age.

A release, waiver or conveyance of homestead is not valid unless it is expressed in writing and signed by the individual and his or her spouse, if he or she has one. The signatures of both spouses should be required on residential sales contracts, listing agreements, notes, mortgages, deeds and other conveyances to release possible homestead rights, even if the property in question is owned solely by either the husband or the wife. ■

FOR EXAMPLE Greenacre is Tony's Illinois homestead. In Illinois, the homestead exemption is $7,500. At a court-ordered sale, the property is purchased for $60,000. First, Tony's remaining $15,000 mortgage balance is paid; then Tony receives $7,500. The remaining $37,500 is applied to Tony's unsecured debts. Of course, no sale would be ordered if the court could determine that nothing would remain from the proceeds for the creditors. If Greenacre could not be expected to bring more than $22,500, the priority of the mortgage lien and homestead exemption would make a sale pointless.

ENCUMBRANCES

An **encumbrance** is a claim, charge or liability that attaches to real estate. Simply put, it is a right or an interest held by someone other than the fee owner of the property that affects title to real estate. An encumbrance may lessen the value or obstruct the use of the property, but it does not necessarily prevent a transfer of title.

Encumbrances may be divided into two general classifications:

1. Encumbrances that affect title (*liens*–usually monetary charges) and
2. Encumbrances that affect the use or physical condition of the property (restrictions, easements and encroachments).

Liens A **lien** is a charge against property that provides security for a debt or an obligation of the property owner. If the obligation is not repaid, the lienholder is entitled to have the debt satisfied from the proceeds of a court-ordered or forced sale of the debtor's property. Real estate taxes, mortgages and trust deeds, judgments and mechanics' liens all represent possible liens against an owner's real estate.

Restrictions **Deed restrictions,** also referred to as *covenants, conditions and restrictions,* or *CC&Rs,* are private agreements that affect the use of land. They may be imposed by an owner of real estate and included in the seller's deed to the buyer. Typically, however, restrictive covenants are imposed by a developer or subdivider to maintain specific standards in a subdivision. Such restrictive covenants are listed in the original development plans for the subdivision filed in the public record.

Easements An **easement** is the right to use the land of another for a particular purpose. An easement may exist in any portion of the real estate, including the airspace above or a right-of-way across the land.

An **appurtenant easement** is annexed to the ownership of one parcel and allows the owner the use of a neighbor's land. For an appurtenant easement to exist, *two adjacent parcels of land must be owned by two different parties.* The parcel over which the easement runs is known as the *servient tenement;* the neighboring parcel that benefits is known as the *dominant tenement.* (See Figures 7.4 and 7.5.)

An appurtenant easement is part of the dominant tenement. If the dominant tenement is conveyed to another party, the easement transfers with the title. This type of easement is said to *run with the land.* It is an encumbrance on property and will transfer with the deed of the dominant tenement forever unless the holder of the dominant tenement somehow releases that right.

FOR EXAMPLE Kent and Lyle own adjoining parcels of land near a lake. Kent's property borders the lake, and Lyle's does not. Kent grants Lyle an easement, established by a deed properly delivered and accepted. The easement gives Lyle the right to cross Kent's property to reach the lake. This is an easement appurtenant. When Kent sells the lakefront property to Marion, the easement is automatically included, even if Kent's deed fails to mention it. Lyle's easement has become a limitation on the ownership rights of Kent's land.

Creating an easement. An easement is commonly created by a written agreement between the parties that establishes the easement right. It also may be created by the grantor in a deed of conveyance, where the grantor either reserves an easement over the sold land or grants the new owner an easement over the grantor's remaining land. An easement may be created by longtime usage, as in an easement by prescription, by necessity or by implication (that is, the situation or the parties' actions imply that they intend to create an easement).

The creation of an easement always involves two separate parties, one of whom is the owner of the land over which the easement runs. It is impossible for the owner of a parcel of property to have an easement over his or her own land.

Party wall easement. A **party wall** can be an exterior wall of a building that straddles the boundary line between two lots, or it can be a commonly shared partition wall between two connected properties. Each lot owner owns the half of the wall on his or her lot, and each has an appurtenant easement in the other half of the wall. A written party wall agreement must be used to create the easement rights. Expenses to build and maintain the wall usually are shared. A *party driveway* shared by and partly on the land of adjoining owners must also be created by written agreement, specifying responsibility for expenses.

Easement by necessity. An appurtenant easement that arises when an owner sells part of his or her land that has no access to a street or public way except over the seller's remaining land is an **easement by necessity.** An *easement by necessity is created by court order.* Such an easement arises because all owners have the right to enter and exit their land—they cannot be landlocked. Remember: this form of easement is called an easement by *necessity;* it is not merely for convenience and is not imposed simply to validate a shortcut.

Easement by prescription. When the claimant has made use of another's land for a certain period of time as defined by state law, an **easement by**

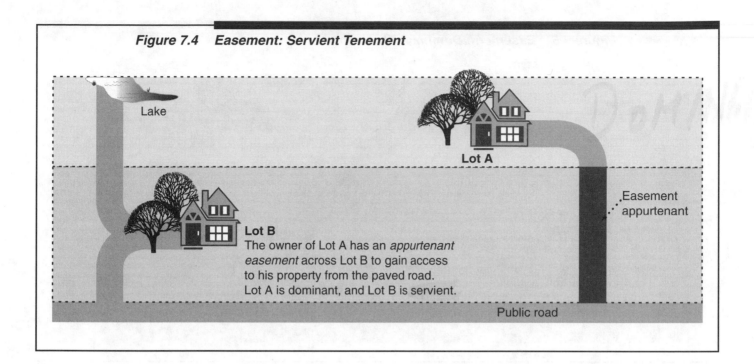

Figure 7.4 Easement: Servient Tenement

Lake

Lot A

Easement appurtenant

Lot B
The owner of Lot A has an *appurtenant easement* across Lot B to gain access to his property from the paved road. Lot A is dominant, and Lot B is servient.

Public road

prescription, or a *prescriptive easement,* may be acquired. The prescriptive period may be from 10 to 21 years. The claimant's use must have been continuous, exclusive and without the owner's approval. The use must be visible, open and notorious; that is, the owner must have been able to learn of it.

In Illinois . . . To establish an easement by prescription in Illinois, the use must be adverse, exclusive, under claim of right and continuous and uninterrupted for a period of *20 years.* Illinois law permits owners of pedestrian walkways in shopping centers and large commercial or industrial buildings to prevent the establishment of prescriptive easements by the public. The owner must display signs stating that access to the property is by permission (and thus not adverse). ■

The concept of *tacking* provides that successive periods of continuous occupation by different parties may be combined (tacked) to reach the required total number of years necessary to establish a claim for a prescriptive easement. To tack on one person's possession to that of another, the parties must have been successors in interest, such as an ancestor and his or her heir, a landlord and tenant, or a seller and buyer.

FOR EXAMPLE Jana's property is located in a state with a prescriptive period of 20 years. For the past 22 years, Frank has driven his car across Jana's front yard several times a day to reach his garage from a more comfortable angle. Frank has an easement by prescription. For 25 years, Linda has driven across Jana's front yard two or three times a year to reach her property when she's in a hurry. She does not have an easement by prescription because her use was not continuous. For 15 years, Elliot parked his car on Jana's property, next to Jana's garage. Six years ago, Elliot sold his house to Ned, who continued to park his car next to Jana's garage. Last year, Ned acquired an easement by prescription through tacking.

Easement in gross. An **easement in gross** is an individual interest in or right to use someone else's land. For instance, a railroad's right-of-way is an

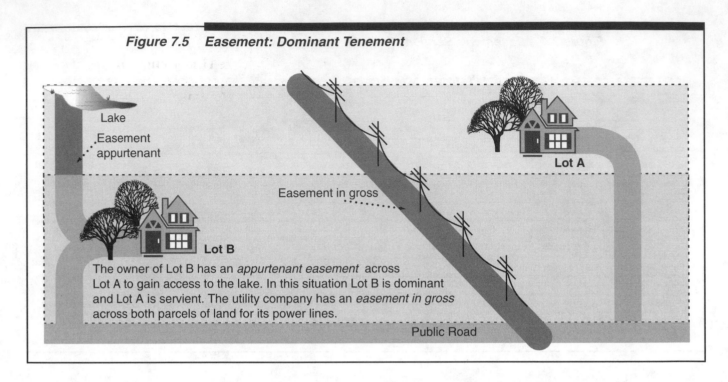

Figure 7.5   Easement: Dominant Tenement

Lake

Easement appurtenant

Lot A

Easement in gross

Lot B

The owner of Lot B has an *appurtenant easement* across Lot A to gain access to the lake. In this situation Lot B is dominant and Lot A is servient. The utility company has an *easement in gross* across both parcels of land for its power lines.

Public Road

easement in gross. So is the right-of-way for a pipeline or high-tension power line (utility easements). Commercial easements in gross may be assigned, conveyed and inherited. However, personal easements in gross usually are not assignable. Generally, a personal easement in gross terminates on the death of the easement owner. An easement in gross is often confused with the similar *personal right of license*, discussed later in this chapter.

Easement by condemnation. An **easement by condemnation** is acquired for a public purpose, through the right of *eminent domain*. The owner of the servient tenement must be compensated for any loss in property value.

Terminating an easement. An easement may be ended

- when the purpose for which the easement was created no longer exists;
- when the owner of either the dominant or the servient tenement becomes the owner of both—the properties are merged under one legal description (also known as *termination by merger*);
- by release of the right of easement to the owner of the servient tenement;
- by abandonment of the easement (the intention of the parties is the determining factor);
- by nonuse of a prescriptive easement;
- by adverse possession by the owner of the servient tenement;
- by destruction of the servient tenement (for instance, the demolition of a party wall);
- by lawsuit (an *action to quiet title*) against someone claiming an easement; or
- by excessive use, as when a residential use is converted to a commercial purpose.

Note that an easement may not automatically terminate for these reasons. Certain legal steps may be required.

Licenses

A **license** is a personal privilege to enter the land of another for a specific purpose. A license differs from an easement in that it can be terminated or canceled by the *licensor* (the person who granted the license). If a right to use another's property is given orally or informally, it generally is considered to be a license rather than a personal easement in gross. A license ends on the death of either party or the sale of the land by the licensor.

FOR EXAMPLE Paul asks Harold for permission to park a boat in Harold's driveway. Harold says, "Sure, go ahead!" Paul has a license, but Harold may tell Paul to move the boat at any time. Similarly, a ticket to a theater or sporting event is a license: the holder is permitted to enter the facility and is entitled to a seat. But if the ticketholder becomes rowdy or abusive, he or she may be asked to leave.

Encroachments

Physical Encumbrances

- Restrictions
- Easements
- Licenses
- Encroachments

An **encroachment** occurs when all or part of a structure (such as a building, fence or driveway) illegally extends beyond the land of its owner or beyond the legal building lines. An encroachment usually is disclosed by either a physical inspection of the property or a spot survey. A *spot survey* shows the location of all improvements located on a property and whether they extend over the lot or building lines. As a rule, a spot survey is more accurate and reliable than a simple physical inspection. If a building encroaches on adjoining land, the neighbor may be able to either recover damages or secure removal of the portion of the building that encroaches. Encroachments that exceed a state's prescriptive period, however, may give rise to easements by prescription.

In Practice

Because an undisclosed encroachment could make a title unmarketable, an encroachment should be noted in a listing agreement and the sales contract. An encroachment is not disclosed by the usual title evidence provided in a real estate sale unless a survey is submitted while the title examination is being made.

WATER RIGHTS

Whether for agricultural, recreational or other purposes, waterfront real estate has always been desirable. Each state has strict laws that govern the ownership and use of water as well as the adjacent land. The laws vary among the states, but all are closely linked to climatic and topographical conditions. Where water is plentiful, for instance, many states rely on the simple parameters set by the common-law doctrines of riparian and littoral rights. Where water is more scarce, a state may control all but limited domestic use of water according to the doctrine of prior appropriation.

Riparian Rights

MEMORY TIP

Riparian refers to rivers, streams and similar waterways; *Littoral* refers to lakes, oceans and similar bodies of water.

Riparian rights are common-law rights granted to owners of land along the course of a river, stream or similar body of water. Although riparian rights are governed by laws that vary from state to state, they generally include the unrestricted right to use the water. As a rule, the only limitation on the owner's use is that it cannot interrupt or alter the flow of the water or contaminate it in any way. In addition, an owner of land that borders a nonnavigable waterway (that is, a body of water unsuitable for commercial boat traffic) owns the land under the water to the exact center of the waterway. Land adjoining commercially navigable rivers, on the other hand, usually is owned to the water's edge, with the state holding title to the submerged land. (See

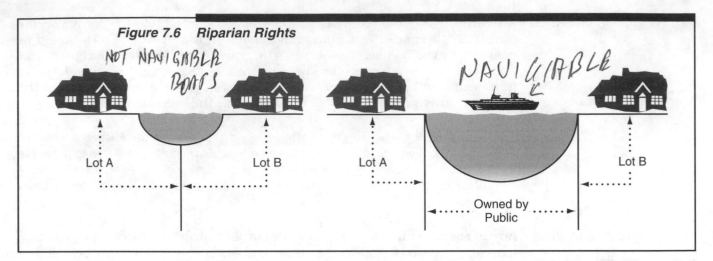

Figure 7.6   Riparian Rights

NOT NAVIGABLA BOATS

Lot A   Lot B

NAVIGABLE

Lot A   Lot B

Owned by Public

Figure 7.6.) Navigable waters are considered public highways in which the public has an easement or right to travel.

Littoral Rights

Closely related to riparian rights are the **littoral rights** of owners whose land borders commercially navigable lakes, seas and oceans. Owners with littoral rights enjoy unrestricted use of available waters, but own the land adjacent to the water only up to the mean (average) high-water mark. (See Figure 7.7.) All land below this point is owned by the government.

EROSION AVULSION) LOSS

Riparian and littoral rights are appurtenant (attached) to the land. The right to use the water belongs to whoever owns the bordering land and cannot be retained by a former owner after the land is sold.

Accretion, Erosion and Avulsion

The amount of land an individual owns may be affected by the natural action of water. An owner is entitled to all land created through **accretion**—increases in the land resulting from the deposit of soil by the water's action. (Such deposits are called *alluvion* or *alluvium*.) If water recedes, new land is acquired by *reliction.*

accretion RELICTION

On the other hand, an owner may lose land through **erosion.** Erosion is the gradual and imperceptible wearing away of the land by natural forces, such as wind, rain and flowing water. Fortunately, erosion usually takes hundreds or even thousands of years to have any noticeable effect on a person's property. Flash floods or heavy winds, however, can increase the speed of erosion.

If erosion is a slow natural process, **avulsion** is its opposite. Avulsion is the sudden removal of soil by an act of nature. It is an event that causes the loss of land much less subtly than does erosion. An earthquake or a mudslide, for instance, can cause an individual's land holding to become much smaller very quickly.

Doctrine of Prior Appropriation

In states where water is scarce (particularly in the western United States), ownership and use of water are often determined by the **doctrine of prior appropriation.** Under this doctrine, the right to use any water, with the exception of limited domestic use, is controlled by the state rather than by the landowner whose property lies adjacent to the water.

To secure water rights in prior appropriation states, a landowner must demonstrate to a state agency that she or he plans a *beneficial use* for the

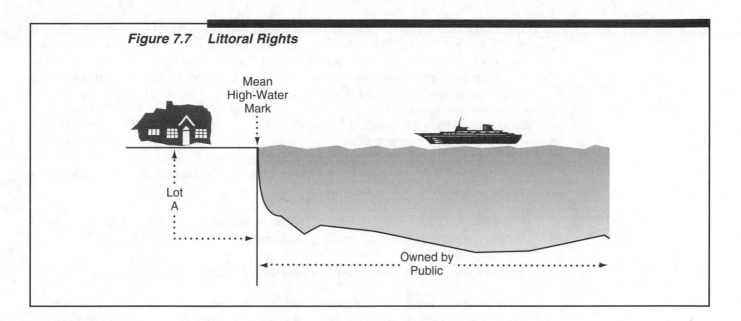

Figure 7.7   Littoral Rights

water, such as crop irrigation. If the state's requirements are met, the landowner receives a permit to use a specified amount of water for the limited purpose of the beneficial use. Although statutes governing prior appropriation vary from state to state, the priority of water rights is usually determined by the oldest recorded permit date.

Once granted, water rights attach to the land of the permitholder. The permitholder may sell a water right to another party.

Issuance of a water permit does not grant access to the water source. All access rights-of-way over the land of another (easements) must be obtained from the property owner.

SUMMARY

An individual's ownership rights are subject to the powers held by government. These powers include police power, by which states can enact legislation such as environmental protection laws and zoning ordinances. The government also may acquire privately owned land for public use through the power of eminent domain. Real estate taxes are imposed to raise government funds. When a property becomes ownerless, ownership of the property may transfer, or escheat, to the state.

An estate is the degree, quantity, nature and extent of interest a person holds in land. Freehold estates are estates of indeterminate length. Less-than-freehold estates are called leasehold estates, and they involve tenants.

A freehold estate may be a fee simple estate or a life estate. A fee simple estate can be absolute or defeasible on the happening of some event. A conventional life estate is created by the owner of a fee estate; a legal life estate is created by law. Legal life estates include curtesy, dower and homestead.

Encumbrances against real estate can be liens, deed restrictions, easements, licenses or encroachments.

An easement is the right acquired by one person to use another's real estate. Easements are classified as interests in real estate but are not estates in land.

There are two types of easements. Appurtenant easements involve two separately owned tracts. The tract benefited is known as the *dominant tenement;* the tract subject to the easement is called the *servient tenement.* An easement in gross is a personal right, such as that granted to utility companies to maintain poles, wires and pipelines.

Easements may be created by agreement, express grant or reservation in a deed, necessity, prescription or condemnation. An easement can be terminated when the purpose of the easement no longer exists, by merger of both interests, with an express intention to extinguish the easement by release or by abandonment of the easement.

A license is permission to enter another's property for a specific purpose. A license usually is created orally; it is temporary and can be revoked.

An encroachment is an unauthorized use of another's real estate.

Ownership of land encompasses not only the land itself but also the right to use the water on or adjacent to it. Many states subscribe to the common-law doctrine of riparian rights, which gives the owner of land adjacent to a nonnavigable stream ownership of the stream to its midpoint. Littoral rights are held by owners of land bordering large lakes and oceans and include rights to the water and ownership of the land up to the mean high-water mark. In states where water is scarce, water use is often decided by the doctrine of prior appropriation. Under prior appropriation, water belongs to the state, and it is allocated to users who have obtained permits.

In Illinois . . .

Local units of government and quasi-governmental bodies are granted the power of eminent domain by the Illinois Constitution. A quick-take is a summary proceeding to obtain title.

Real property escheats to the county in which it is located.

Dower and curtesy have been abolished since 1972.

The individual homestead entitlement is $7,500.

The period for an easement by prescription is 20 years. ■

QUESTIONS

1. A city decides to build a new library. Which of the following terms would best describe the action taken by the city to acquire the land for the new library?
   A. Zoning would allow the city to take the land by granting a variance for the library.
   B. County laws would allow the city to take the land by escheat and as long as the property owners were paid just compensation.
   C. The city has the right to take the land by eminent domain as long as just compensation is paid the property owners.
   D. The sheriff would sell the property at a public sale and pay the owners just compensation, and then the city could build the library.

2. A purchaser of real estate learned that his ownership rights could continue forever and that no other person claims to be the owner or has any ownership control over the property. This person owns a:
   A. fee simple interest.
   B. life estate.
   C. determinable fee estate.
   D. fee simple on condition.

3. Julia owned the fee simple title to a vacant lot adjacent to a hospital and was persuaded to make a gift of the lot. She wanted to have some control over its use, so her attorney prepared her deed to convey ownership of the lot to the hospital "so long as it is used for hospital purposes." After completion of the gift, the hospital will own a:
   A. fee simple absolute estate.
   B. license.
   C. fee simple determinable.
   D. leasehold estate.

4. After Dennis had purchased his house and moved in, he discovered that his neighbor regularly used Dennis's driveway to reach a garage located on the neighbor's property. Dennis's attorney explained that ownership of the neighbor's real estate includes an easement over the driveway. Dennis's property is properly called:
   A. the dominant tenement.
   B. a freehold.
   C. a leasehold.
   D. the servient tenement.

5. Bonnie is the owner of Blueacre. During her lifetime, Bonnie conveys a life estate in Blueacre to Carla. Under the terms of the grant, Carla's life estate will terminate when Bonnie's uncle dies. However, Carla dies shortly after moving to Blueacre, while Bonnie's uncle is still alive. Carla's will states, "I leave everything to Donald." Which of the following best describes the interests that the parties now hold?
   A. Carla possessed a life estate pur autre vie, measured by the life of Bonnie's uncle. Donald has the same interest as Carla had. Donald's interest in Blueacre will end when Bonnie's uncle dies. Bonnie has a reversionary interest in Blueacre.
   B. Carla possessed a life estate pur autre vie, measured by the life of Bonnie's uncle. Donald is the remainderman and holds a nonpossessory estate until Bonnie's uncle dies. When Bonnie's uncle dies, Blueacre will escheat to the state.
   C. Carla possessed a determinable life estate in Blueacre. Bonnie's uncle is the measuring life. When Carla died, her interest passed directly to Donald. When Bonnie's uncle dies, Bonnie may regain ownership of Blueacre only by suing Donald.
   D. Bonnie has a remainder interest in the conventional life estate granted to Carla. Because the grant was to Carla alone, the estate may not pass to Donald. When Carla died before Bonnie's uncle, the estate automatically ended and Bonnie now owns Blueacre in fee simple.

6. Wendell owns a home in a state that recognizes a limited homestead exemption. Which of the following statements is true if Wendell is sued by his creditors?
   A. The creditors can have the court sell Wendell's home and apply the full proceeds of sale to the debts.
   B. The creditors have no right to have Wendell's home sold.
   C. The creditors can force Wendell to sell the home to pay them.
   D. The creditors can request a court sale and apply the sale proceeds, in excess of the statutory exemption and secured debts, to Wendell's unsecured debts.

7. If the owner of real estate does not take action against a trespasser before the statutory period has passed, the trespasser may acquire:
   A. an easement by necessity.
   B. a license.
   C. title by eminent domain.
   D. an easement by prescription.

8. Mark wants to use water from a river that runs through his property to irrigate a potato field. In order to do so, Mark is required by his state's law to submit an application to the Department of Water Resources describing in detail the beneficial use he plans for the water. If the department approves Mark's application, he will receive a permit to divert a limited amount of river water into his field. Based on these facts, it can be assumed that Mark's state relies on which of the following rules of law?
   A. Common-law riparian rights
   B. Common-law littoral rights
   C. Doctrine of prior appropriation
   D. Doctrine of highest and best use

9. All of the following are powers of the government EXCEPT:
   A. easement in gross.
   B. police power.
   C. eminent domain.
   D. taxation.

10. Property deeded to a town so long as it is used "for recreational purposes" conveys a:
    A. fee simple absolute.
    B. fee simple on condition precedent.
    C. leasehold interest.
    D. fee simple determinable.

11. Tonya has the legal right to pass over the land owned by her neighbor. This is a(n):
    A. estate in land.   C. police power.
    B. easement.   D. encroachment.

12. All of the following are legal life estates EXCEPT:
    A. leasehold.
    B. husband's curtesy.
    C. homestead.
    D. wife's dower.

13. A father conveys ownership of his residence to his daughter but reserves for himself a life estate in the residence. The interest the daughter owns during her father's lifetime is:
    A. pur autre vie.
    B. a remainder.
    C. a reversion.
    D. a leasehold.

14. Kendra has just fenced her property. The fence extends one foot onto the property of a neighbor, Mary. The fence is an example of a(n):
    A. license.
    B. encroachment.
    C. easement by necessity.
    D. easement by prescription.

15. Encumbrances on real estate:
    A. include easements and encroachments.
    B. make it impossible to sell the encumbered property.
    C. must all be removed before the title can be transferred.
    D. are of no monetary value to those who own them.

16. Ken has permission from Aaron to hike on Aaron's property during the autumn months when the leaves are most colorful. Ken has a(n):
    A. easement by necessity.
    B. easement by prescription.
    C. determinable freehold interest.
    D. license.

In Illinois . . .

17. In Illinois, the homestead exemption:
    A. must be recorded with the county recorder.
    B. is limited to $7,500 per person.
    C. can never be released.
    D. is limited to $7,500 per residence.

18. A conveyance of residential real estate by a married person also should be executed by the conveyor's spouse:
    A. to ensure the release of any potential homestead rights.
    B. only if the property is owned by both parties.
    C. to release dower rights.
    D. to comply with Illinois's community property laws.

19. In Illinois, a prescriptive easement may be:
    A. established by 19 years of continuous, uninterrupted use under claim of right and without the owner's approval or permission.
    B. prevented by posting a "No Trespassing" sign in a prominent place on or near the boundary of the property.
    C. established by 20 years of continuous, uninterrupted, exclusive use under claim of right and without the owner's permission.
    D. defeated by showing that the adverse possession was not exercised by a single individual for the requisite period, but by successive parties in interest.

20. In Illinois, which of the following is true regarding the escheat of a decedent's real property?
    A. The decedent's heirs must receive just compensation for the property's fair market value, measured at the time of the decedent's death.
    B. The state laws of eminent domain apply.
    C. Ownership of the property goes to the county in which it is located.
    D. Ownership of the property goes to the state.

21. Evan died, leaving a lakefront cottage to his wife for her use as long as she lives, with the provision that title shall pass equally to their children upon her death. The estate that Evan's widow holds is a(n):
    A. fee simple estate.
    B. estate at will.
    C. determinable fee estate.
    D. life estate.

22. All of the following estates are recognized in Illinois, EXCEPT:
    A. curtesy.
    B. homestead.
    C. leasehold.
    D. fee simple determinable.

23. David made a gift of a house to Rhonda for Rhonda's lifetime, with a provision that the real estate will pass to Simone after Rhonda dies. Which of the following statements accurately describes these facts?
    A. Rhonda holds a life estate; Simone holds a reversionary interest; David has retained a reversionary interest.
    B. Rhonda holds a life estate; Simone holds a remainder interest.
    C. Rhonda holds an estate for years; Simone holds a life estate pur autre vie, measured by the life of Rhonda.
    D. Rhonda holds a life estate pur autre vie; Simone holds no interest in the house until after Rhonda dies; David has retained fee simple ownership under these facts.

24. In 1980, Gary conveyed Longacre to Ben in fee simple, on condition that Longacre is never used as a theme park. Under Illinois law, when may Ben open a theme park on Longacre without fear of automatically losing ownership of the property?
    A. In the year 2000, twenty years after the date of the original conveyance, Ben will own Longacre free of any condition or limitation.
    B. In the year 2020, forty years after the date of the original conveyance, Gary's limitation may still be enforced, but Gary's right of reverter will expire.
    C. In the year 2030, fifty years after the date of the original conveyance, Gary's limitation will no longer be enforceable, and Gary's right of reverter will expire.
    D. There is no expiration period on conveyances of real property in Illinois.

Forms of Real Estate Ownership

KEY TERMS

common elements
community property
condominium
cooperative
co-ownership
corporation
general partnership
joint tenancy
joint venture

limited liability
  company
limited partnership
partition
partnership
proprietary lease
right of survivorship
separate property
severalty

syndicate
tenancy by the
  entirety
tenancy in common
time-share estate
time-share use
time-sharing
trust

FORMS OF OWNERSHIP

As we've seen, many different interests in land exist—fee simple, life estates and easements, for instance. Licensees also need to understand how these interests in real property may be held. Although questions about forms of ownership always should be referred to an attorney, brokers and salespersons must understand the fundamental types of ownership so they will know who must sign various documents. They also must know what form of ownership a purchaser wants and what options are possible when more than one individual will take title.

Although the forms of ownership available are controlled by state laws, a fee simple estate may be held in three basic ways:

1. In *severalty*, where title is held by one individual
2. In *co-ownership*, where title is held by two or more individuals
3. In *trust*, where a third individual holds title for the benefit of another

ONE INDIVIDUAL
OUR CORP
OR ON PERSON

OWNERSHIP OR TENANCY IN SEVERALTY

OR GOVT

When title to real estate is owned by *one individual*, that individual is said to have ownership or tenancy in **severalty.** The term comes from the fact that this sole owner is "severed" or "cut off" from other owners. The severalty owner has sole rights to the ownership and sole discretion over the transfer of the ownership. When either a husband or wife owns property in severalty, state law may affect how ownership is held.

In Illinois . . .

Sole ownership of property is quite common in Illinois, and title held in severalty presents no unique legal problems. However, when either a husband or wife owns property in severalty, lenders, grantees and title insurers in Illinois usually do require that the spouse sign in order to release any potential homestead rights. A nonowning spouse who is a minor also will have to sign. In some other states, only the owner's signature is needed. ■

CO-OWNERSHIP

When title to one parcel of real estate is held by two or more individuals, those parties are called *co-owners* or *concurrent owners*. Most states commonly recognize various forms of **co-ownership.** Individuals may co-own property as tenants in common, joint tenants or tenants by the entirety, or they may co-own as community property.

In Illinois . . .

Illinois recognizes ownership in severalty and three of the four traditional forms of ownership discussed in this chapter (except community property), as well as ownership in trust, in partnership and by commercial entities such as corporations and limited liability companies. ■

Tenancy in Common

A parcel of real estate may be owned by two or more people as tenants in common. In a **tenancy in common,** each tenant holds an undivided fractional interest in the property. A tenant in common may hold, say, a one-half or one-third interest in a property. *The physical property, however, is not divided into a specific half or third.* The co-owners have *unity of possession;* that is, they are entitled to possession of the whole property. It is the ownership interest, not the property, that is divided.

> **Forms of Co-Ownership**
>
> 1. Tenancy in common
> 2. Joint tenancy
> 3. Tenancy by the entirety
> 4. Community property

The deed creating a tenancy in common may or may not state the fractional interest held by each co-owner. If no fractions are stated, the tenants are presumed to hold equal shares. For example, if five people hold title, each would own an undivided one-fifth interest.

In Illinois . . .

In Illinois, a single deed may show the proportional interests of each tenant in common, or a separate deed issued to each tenant may show his or her individual proportional interest. When a single deed is used, lack of a description of each tenant's share means all tenants hold equal, undivided shares. ■

Tenants in common also hold their ownership interests in *severalty*. That is, because the co-owners own separate interests, each can sell, convey, mortgage or transfer his or her interest without the consent of the other co-owners. However, no individual tenant may transfer the ownership of the entire property. When one co-owner dies, the tenant's undivided interest passes according to his or her will. (See Figure 8.1.)

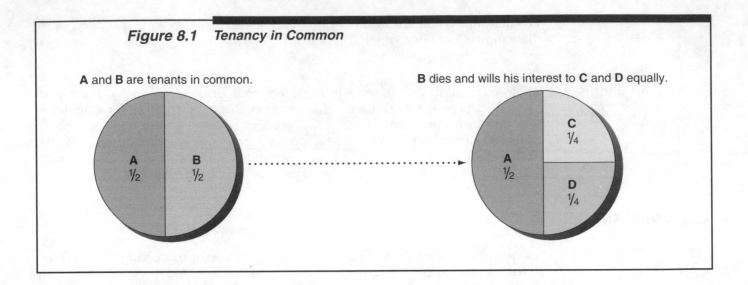

Figure 8.1   Tenancy in Common

A and B are tenants in common.

B dies and wills his interest to C and D equally.

In Illinois, the law presumes that two or more owners hold title as tenants in common if the deed giving them title does not mention the kind of ownership being acquired. No particular language is required to create a tenancy in common. Real estate conveyed to "*Arnold and Betty Campbell,* husband and wife" creates a tenancy in common. Special wording is necessary in a deed to give the owners joint tenancy or tenancy by the entirety. ■

Joint Tenancy

Most states recognize some form of **joint tenancy** in property owned by two or more people. The feature that distinguishes a joint tenancy from a tenancy in common is unity of ownership. Title is held as though all owners collectively constitute one unit. The death of one of the joint tenants does not destroy the ownership unit; it only reduces by one the number of people who make up the unit. This occurs because of the **right of survivorship.** The joint tenancy continues until only one owner remains. This owner then holds title in severalty. The right of survivorship applies only to the co-owners of the joint tenancy; it cannot pass to their heirs.

As each successive joint tenant dies, the surviving joint tenants acquire the deceased tenant's interest. The last survivor takes title in severalty and has all the rights of sole ownership, including the right to pass the property to his or her heirs. (See Figure 8.2.)

Creating joint tenancies. A joint tenancy can be created only by the intentional act of conveying a deed or giving the property by will. It cannot be implied or created by operation of law. The deed must specifically state the parties' intention to create a joint tenancy, and the parties must be explicitly identified as joint tenants. Some states, however, have abolished the right of survivorship as the distinguishing characteristic of joint tenancy. In these states, the deed must explicitly indicate the intention to create the right of survivorship for that right to exist.

Typical wording in a deed creating a joint tenancy would be: *"To A and B as joint tenants and not as tenants in common."*

Four "unities" are required to create a joint tenancy:

1. Unity of *possession*—all joint tenants holding an undivided right to possession
2. Unity of *interest*—all joint tenants holding equal ownership interests

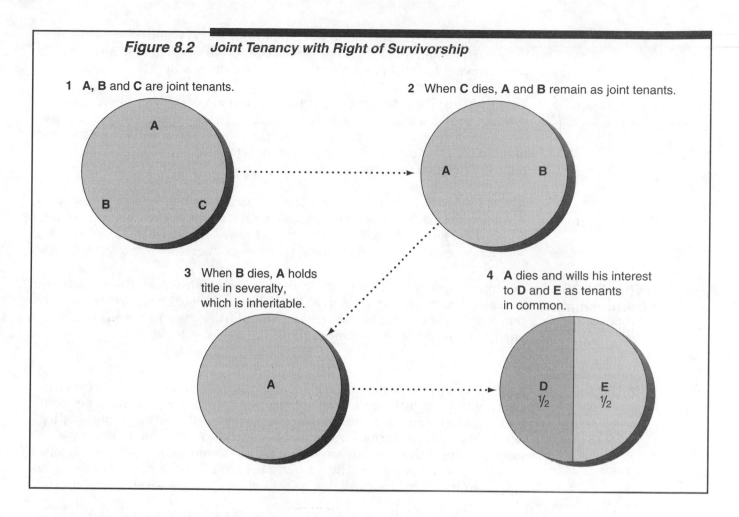

Figure 8.2   Joint Tenancy with Right of Survivorship

1   A, B and **C** are joint tenants.

2   When C dies, **A** and **B** remain as joint tenants.

3   When B dies, **A** holds title in severalty, which is inheritable.

4   A dies and wills his interest to **D** and **E** as tenants in common.

---

3. Unity of *time*—all joint tenants acquiring their interests at the same time
4. Unity of *title*—all joint tenants acquiring their interests by the same document

The four unities are present when the following requirements are met:

- Title is acquired by one deed.
- The deed is executed and delivered at one time.
- The deed conveys equal interests to all of the parties.
- The parties hold undivided possession of the property as joint tenants.

Because the unities must be satisfied, many states require the use of an intermediary when a sole owner wishes to create a joint tenancy between himself or herself and others. The owner conveys the property to a nominee, or straw man. Then the nominee conveys it back, naming all the parties as joint tenants in the deed. As a result, all the joint tenants acquire title at the same time by one deed.

In Illinois . . .

Illinois has eliminated this "legal fiction," and allows a sole owner to execute a deed to himself or herself and others "as joint tenants and not as tenants in common" in order to create a valid joint tenancy. In the 1983 Illinois Supreme Court case *Minonk State Bank v. Gassman,* the court held that a joint tenant may unilaterally sever the tenancy by conveying to himself or herself as a tenant in common even without the consent of co-owners. Of course, the tenancy also may be severed by mutual agreement of all cotenants, by conveying to third parties or through a partition suit. ■

Terminating joint tenancies. A joint tenancy is destroyed when any one of the four unities of joint tenancy is terminated. A joint tenant is free to convey his or her interest in the jointly held property, but doing so destroys the unity of interest. The new owner cannot become a joint tenant. Rights of other joint tenants, however, are unaffected.

FOR EXAMPLE *A, B* and *C* hold title to Blackacre as joint tenants. *A* conveys her interest to *D*. *D* now owns a fractional interest in Blackacre as a tenant in common with *B* and *C*, who continue to own their undivided interest as joint tenants. (See Figure 8.3.) *D* is presumed to have a one-third interest, which may be reconveyed or left to *D*'s heirs.

Termination of Co-Ownership by Partition Suit

Cotenants who wish to terminate their co-ownership may file an action in court to partition the property. **Partition** is a legal way to dissolve the relationship when the parties do not voluntarily agree to its termination. A partition suit is also sometimes referred to as a *suit to partition*.

In Illinois . . .

An Illinois partition suit may be filed by one or more of the owners in the circuit court of the county in which the subject parcel is located. The court appoints one or three commissioners who must, if possible, divide the property by legal description among the owners in title. If such division cannot be made without harming the rights of the co-owners, the commissioners must report a valuation of the property. The property is then offered for public sale for not less than two-thirds of the value as set by the commissioners.

All defendants to the suit (the co-owners who object to the partition) are required to pay their proportionate share of court costs and the lawyer fees of the plaintiff (the co-owner who is seeking partition). However, this requirement may be waived if the defendants have a sound and substantial defense. Upon completion of the sale, confirmation of the sale by the court and delivery of a proper conveyance to the purchaser at the sale, the proceeds of the sale are delivered to the former cotenants according to the court order. Generally, the proceeds of the sale are divided among the former owners according to their fractional interests. ■

Ownership by Married Couples

Tenancy by the entirety. Some states allow husbands and wives to use a special form of co-ownership called **tenancy by the entirety.** In this form of ownership, each spouse has an equal, undivided interest in the property. (The term *entirety* refers to the fact that the owners are considered one indivisible unit: under early common law, a married couple was viewed as one "legal person.") A husband and wife who are tenants by the entirety have rights of survivorship. During their lives, they can convey title only by a deed signed by both parties. One party may not convey a one-half interest, and generally they have no right to partition or divide. The main reason married couples own property by the entirety is that a lawsuit against one of the spouses will not put a lien on the house. A married couple owning property by the entirety would be eligible for homestead protection in the event of a judgment against either the husband or the wife. In addition, on the death of one spouse, the survivor automatically becomes the sole owner. Married couples often take title to property as tenants by the entirety so the surviving spouse can enjoy the benefits of ownership without the delay of probate proceedings.

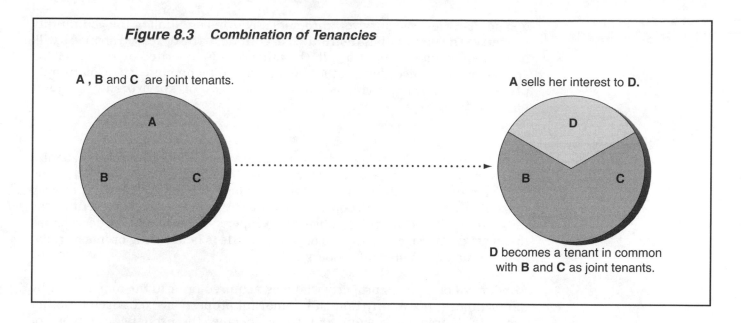

Figure 8.3   Combination of Tenancies

A, **B** and **C** are joint tenants.

A sells her interest to **D**.

D becomes a tenant in common
with **B** and **C** as joint tenants.

In Illinois . . .

Tenancy by the entirety has been recognized in Illinois since 1990. To create a tenancy by the entirety, the deed must

- identify the parties as husband and wife and
- indicate that the property is to be owned "not as joint tenants or tenants in common, but as tenants by the entirety." ■

A tenancy by the entirety may be terminated in several ways:

- By a court-ordered sale of the property to satisfy a judgment against the husband and wife as joint debtors (the tenancy is dissolved so that the property can be sold to pay the judgment)
- By the death of either spouse (the surviving spouse becomes sole owner in severalty)
- By agreement between both parties (through the execution of a new deed)
- By divorce (which leaves the parties as tenants in common)

> **MEMORY TIP**
>
> The methods of terminating a tenancy by the entirety may be remembered by the acronym *J's DAD: Judgment Sale, Death, Agreement* or *Divorce.*

Community property rights.   *Community property* laws are based on the idea that a husband and wife, rather than merging into one entity, are equal partners in the marriage. Any property acquired during a marriage is considered to be obtained by mutual effort. The states' community property laws vary widely. Essentially, however, they all recognize two kinds of property: separate property and community property.

Separate property is real or personal property that was owned solely by either spouse before the marriage. It also includes property acquired by gift or inheritance during the marriage, as well as any property purchased with separate funds during the marriage. Any income earned from a person's separate property remains part of his or her separate property. Separate property can be mortgaged or conveyed by the owning spouse without the signature of the nonowning spouse.

Community property consists of all other property, both real and personal, acquired by either spouse during the marriage. Any conveyance or encumbrance of community property requires the signatures of both spouses. When one spouse dies, the survivor automatically owns one-half of the community property. The other half is distributed according to the deceased spouse's will. If the spouse dies without a will, the other half is inherited by the surviving spouse or by the decedent's other heirs, depending on state law. Community property does not provide an automatic right of survivorship as joint tenancy does.

In Illinois . . .

Illinois is not a community property state. However, Illinois law does recognize that a husband and wife acquire joint rights in all property acquired after the date of marriage for the duration of the marriage. Illinois labels such property *marital property.* Marital property customarily is divided in the event of the dissolution of the marriage (divorce). Property acquired by either spouse during the marriage, regardless of whether title is held jointly or in severalty, is presumed to be marital property.

Nonmarital property is property that was acquired prior to the marriage or by gift or inheritance at any time. If nonmarital property is exchanged for other property, increases in value or returns income, the exchange, increase or income also would be considered nonmarital property. If nonmarital property is commingled with marital property, however, a presumption of *transmutation* is created: the resulting "mixed" property is presumed to be marital property. The spouses may execute an express contract agreeing to exclude certain property from being classified as marital property. ■

The *Illinois Marriage and Dissolution of Marriage Act* gives the courts flexibility in determining the precise division of marital property.

TRUSTS

A **trust** is a device by which one person transfers ownership of property to someone else to hold or manage for the benefit of a third party. Perhaps a grandfather wishes to ensure the college education of his granddaughter, so he transfers his oil field to the grandchild's mother. He instructs the mother to use its income to pay for the grandchild's college tuition. In this case, the grandfather is the *trustor*—the person who creates the trust. The granddaughter is the *beneficiary*—the person who benefits from the trust. The mother is the *trustee*—the party who holds legal title to the property and is entrusted with carrying out the trustor's instructions regarding the purpose of the trust. The trustee is a *fiduciary*, who acts in confidence or trust and has a special legal relationship with the beneficiary. The trustee's power and authority are limited by the terms of the trust agreement, will or deed in trust.

In Practice

The legal and tax implications of setting up a trust are complex and vary widely from state to state. Attorneys and tax experts should always be consulted on the subject of trusts.

Most states allow real estate to be held in trust. Depending on the type of trust and its purpose, the trustor, trustee and beneficiary can all be either people or legal entities, such as corporations. Trust companies are corporations set up for this specific purpose.

In Illinois . . .

Illinois permits real estate to be held in trust as part of a living or testamentary trust or as the sole asset in a land trust. ■

Real estate can be owned under living or testamentary trusts and land trusts. It also can be held by investors in a *real estate investment trust (REIT)*.

Living and Testamentary Trusts

A property owner may provide for his or her own financial care or for that of the owner's family by establishing a trust. This trust may be created by agreement during the property owner's lifetime (a living trust) or established by will after the owner's death (a testamentary trust).

The person who creates the trust conveys real or personal property to a trustee (usually a corporate trustee), with the understanding that the trustee will assume certain duties. These duties may include the care and investment of the trust assets to produce an income. After paying the trust's operating expenses and trustee's fees, the income is paid to or used for the benefit of the beneficiary. The trust may continue for the beneficiary's lifetime, or the assets may be distributed when the beneficiary reaches a certain age or when other conditions are met.

Land Trusts

A few states permit the creation of land trusts, in which real estate is the only asset. As in all trusts, the title to the property is conveyed to a trustee, and the beneficial interest belongs to the beneficiary. In the case of land trusts, however, the beneficiary usually is also the trustor. While the beneficial interest is personal property, the beneficiary retains management and control of the real property and has the right of possession and the right to any income or proceeds from its sale.

[handwritten note: Deed of Trust / Same as Mortgage / Both one / known Trust Deed]

One of the distinguishing characteristics of a land trust is that the public records usually do not name the beneficiary. A land trust may be used for secrecy when assembling separate parcels. There are other benefits as well. A beneficial interest in a land trust is personal property and can be transferred by assignment, making the formalities of a deed unnecessary. The beneficial interest in property can be pledged as security for a loan without having a mortgage recorded. Because the beneficiary's interest is personal, it passes at the beneficiary's death under the laws of the state in which the beneficiary lived. If the deceased owned property in several states, additional probate costs and inheritance taxes can be avoided.

In Illinois . . .

Land trusts are used extensively in Illinois. However, Illinois law requires that the trustee disclose the beneficiary's name to certain parties under specific circumstances:

- To the concerned housing authority within ten days after receiving a complaint of a violation of a building ordinance or law.
- When applying to any state of Illinois agency for a license or permit affecting the entrusted real estate.
- If selling the entrusted property by land contract.
- If the trustee is named as a defendant in a private lawsuit or criminal complaint regarding the subject real estate, the beneficiary's identity can be "discovered" by the plaintiff.
- A fire inspector or another officer has a statutory right to knowledge of beneficiaries during an arson investigation. ■

A land trust ordinarily continues for a definite term, such as 20 years. If the beneficiary does not extend the trust term when it expires, the trustee usually is obligated to sell the real estate and return the net proceeds to the beneficiary.

In Practice   Licensees should exercise caution in using the term *trust deed.* It can mean both a *deed in trust* (which relates to the creation of a living, testamentary or land trust) and a *deed of trust* (a financing document similar to a mortgage). Because these documents are not interchangeable, using an inaccurate term can cause serious misunderstandings.

OWNERSHIP OF REAL ESTATE BY BUSINESS ORGANIZATIONS

A business organization is a legal entity that exists independently of its members. Ownership by a business organization makes it possible for many people to hold an interest in the same parcel of real estate. Investors may be organized to finance a real estate project in various ways. Some provide for the real estate to be owned by the entity; others provide for direct ownership by the investors.

Partnerships   A **partnership** is an association of two or more persons who carry on a business for profit as co-owners. In a **general partnership,** all the partners participate in the operation and management of the business and share full liability for business losses and obligations. A **limited partnership,** on the other hand, consists of one or more general partners as well as limited partners. The business is run by the general partner or partners. The limited partners are not legally permitted to participate, and each can be held liable for business losses only to the extent of his or her investment. The limited partnership is a popular method of organizing investors because it permits investors with small amounts of capital to participate in large real estate projects with a minimum of personal risk.

Most states (including Illinois) have adopted the *Uniform Partnership Act (UPA),* which permits real estate to be held in the partnership name. The *Uniform Limited Partnership Act (ULPA)* has also been widely adopted. It establishes the legality of the limited partnership entity and provides that realty may be held in the limited partnership's name. Profits and losses are passed through the partnership to each partner, whose individual tax situation determines the tax consequences.

General partnerships are dissolved and must be reorganized if one partner dies, withdraws or goes bankrupt. In a limited partnership, however, the partnership agreement may provide for the continuation of the organization following the death or withdrawal of one of the partners.

Corporations   A **corporation** is a legal entity (an artificial person) created under the authority of the laws of the state from which it receives its charter. A corporation is managed and operated by its *board of directors.* The *charter* sets forth the powers of the corporation, including its right to buy and sell real estate (based on a resolution by the board of directors). Because the corporation is a legal entity, it can own real estate in severalty. Some corporations are permitted by their charters to purchase real estate for any purpose; others are limited to purchasing only the land necessary to fulfill the entities' corporate purposes.

In Illinois . . . The creation and regulation of corporations in Illinois are governed by the Illinois Business Corporation Act of 1983. ■

As a legal entity, a corporation continues to exist until it is formally dissolved. The death of one of the officers or directors does not affect title to property owned by the corporation.

Individuals participate, or invest, in a corporation by purchasing stock. Because stock is personal property, shareholders do not have direct ownership interest in real estate owned by a corporation. Each shareholder's liability for the corporation's losses is usually limited to the amount of his or her investment.

One of the main disadvantages of corporate ownership of income property is that the profits are subject to double taxation. As a legal entity, a corporation must file an income tax return and pay tax on its profits. The portion of the remaining profits distributed to shareholders as dividends is taxed again as part of the shareholders' individual incomes.

An alternative form of business ownership that provides the benefit of a corporation as a legal entity but avoids double taxation is known as an *S corporation* (in reference to Subchapter S of the Internal Revenue Code). Only the shares of the profits that are passed to the shareholders are taxed. The profits of the S corporation are not taxed. However, S corporations are subject to strict requirements regulating their structure, membership and operation. If the IRS determines that an S corporation has failed to comply with these detailed rules, the entity will be redefined as some other form of business organization, and its favorable tax treatment will be lost.

Syndicates and Joint Ventures Generally speaking, a **syndicate** is two or more people or firms joined together to make and operate a real estate investment. A syndicate is not in itself a legal entity; however, it may be organized into a number of ownership forms, including co-ownership (tenancy in common, joint tenancy), partnership, trust or corporation. A **joint venture** is a form of partnership in which two or more people or firms carry out a single business project. The joint venture is characterized by a time limitation resulting from the fact that the joint venturers do not intend to establish a permanent relationship.

Limited Liability Companies The **limited liability company** (LLC) is a relatively recent form of business organization. An LLC combines the most attractive features of limited partnerships and corporations. The members of an LLC enjoy the limited liability offered by a corporate form of ownership and the tax advantages of a partnership. In addition, the LLC offers flexible management structures without the complicated requirements of S corporations or the restrictions of limited partnerships. The structure and methods of establishing a new LLC, or of converting an existing entity to the LLC form, vary from state to state.

In Illinois . . . With passage of the *Illinois Limited Liability Company Act* in 1994, Illinois joined the majority of states that recognize limited liability companies as legitimate business organizations. ■

CONDOMINIUMS, COOPERATIVES AND TIME-SHARES

Home ownership does not refer only to ownership of a brick bungalow on a grassy lawn surrounded by a white picket fence. A growing urban population, diverse lifestyles, changing family structures and heightened mobility have created a demand for new forms of home and other property ownership. Condominiums, cooperatives and time-share arrangements are three types of real estate whose ownership addresses our society's changing needs and attitudes.

Condominium Ownership

The **condominium** form of ownership has become increasingly popular throughout the United States. Condominium laws, often called *horizontal property acts,* have been enacted in every state. Under these laws, the owner of each unit holds a fee simple title to the unit. The individual unit owners also own a specified share of the undivided interest in the remainder of the building and land, known as the **common elements.** Common elements typically include such items as land, courtyards, lobbies, the exterior structure, hallways, elevators, stairways and the roof, as well as recreational facilities such as swimming pools, tennis courts and golf courses. (See Figure 8.4.) The individual unit owners own these common elements as tenants in common. State law usually provides, however, that unit owners do not have the same right to partition that other tenants in common have.

Condominium ownership is not restricted to highrise buildings; lowrises, town houses and detached structures can all be held in the condominium form of ownership.

Creation of a condominium.   Many states have adopted the *Uniform Condominium Act (UCA).* Under its provisions, a condominium is created and established when the owner of an existing building (or the developer of unimproved property) executes and records a detailed report and description of the property called a *declaration of condominium.*

In Illinois . . .

Illinois has not adopted the Uniform Condominium Act. In Illinois, creation of condominiums is governed by the *Condominium Property Act.* Under this law, an owner/developer may elect to submit a parcel of real estate to condominium ownership by recording a declaration to which is attached a three-dimensional plat of survey of the parcel showing the location and size of all units in the building. *A building built on leased land may not be submitted for condominium ownership in Illinois.* Every unit purchaser acquires the fee simple title to that unit, together with the percentage of ownership of the common elements that is set forth in the declaration and that belongs to that unit. This percentage is computed on the basis of the initial list prices of each unit.

The survey required with each declaration of condominium ownership must indicate the dimensions of each unit. This survey will show the outlines of the lot, the size and shape of each apartment and the elevation or height above base datum for the upper surface of the floor level and the lower surface of ceiling level. The difference between these two levels represents the airspace owned in fee simple by the unit owner.

Many Illinois municipalities have adopted *conversion ordinances* to protect tenants in rental buildings whose owners decide to convert to condominiums.

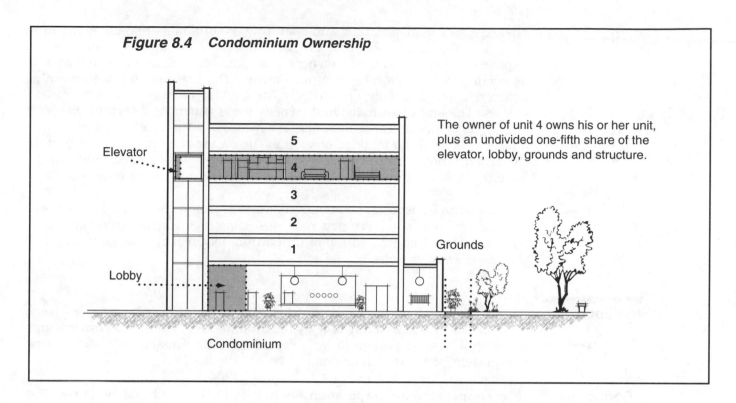

Figure 8.4 Condominium Ownership

The owner of unit 4 owns his or her unit, plus an undivided one-fifth share of the elevator, lobby, grounds and structure.

The ordinances also protect prospective purchasers. These laws typically allow tenants an opportunity to extend their leases and often guarantee first purchase rights. Additional protections often include disclosure of all material information, building and construction soundness, adequacy of parking and a variety of other concerns. These ordinances generally have been upheld by the courts as a valid exercise of police power. ∎

Ownership. Once the property is established as a condominium, each unit becomes a separate parcel of real estate that is owned in fee simple and may be held by one or more persons in any type of ownership or tenancy recognized by state law. A condominium unit may be mortgaged like any other parcel of real estate. The unit usually can be sold or transferred to whomever the owner chooses, unless the condominium association provides for a right of first refusal. In this case, the owner is required to offer the unit at the same price to the other owners in the condominium or the association before accepting an outside purchase offer.

Real estate taxes are assessed and collected on each unit as an individual property. Default in the payment of taxes or a mortgage loan by one unit owner may result in a foreclosure sale of that owner's unit. An owner's default, however, does not affect the other unit owners.

Operation and administration. The condominium property is administered by an *association of unit owners.* The association may be governed by a board of directors or another official entity, and it may manage the property on its own or hire a property manager.

The association must enforce any rules it adopts regarding the operation and use of the property. The association is responsible for the maintenance, repair, cleaning and sanitation of the common elements and structural portions of the property. It also must maintain fire, extended-coverage and liability insurance.

The expenses of maintaining and operating the building are paid by the unit owners in the form of fees and assessments. Both fees and assessments are imposed and collected by the owners' association. Recurring fees (referred to as *condo fees*) are paid by each unit owner. The fees may be due monthly, quarterly, semiannually or annually, depending on the provisions of the bylaws. The size of an individual owner's fee is generally determined by the size of his or her unit. For instance, the owner of a three-bedroom unit pays a larger share of the total expense than the owner of a one-bedroom unit. If the fees are not paid, the association may seek a court-ordered judgment to have the delinquent owner's unit sold to cover the outstanding amount.

Assessments are special payments required of unit owners to address some specific expense, such as a new roof. Assessments are structured like condo fees: owners of larger units pay proportionately higher assessments than owners of smaller units.

In Illinois . . .

Under the Condominium Property Act, the property may be removed from condominium status at any time by the unanimous consent of all owners and all lienholders, as evidenced by a recorded written instrument. All owners would then be tenants in common. ■

Cooperative Ownership

In a **cooperative,** a corporation holds title to the land and building. The corporation then offers shares of stock to prospective tenants. The price the corporation sets for each apartment becomes the price of the stock. The purchaser becomes a shareholder in the corporation by virtue of stock ownership and receives a **proprietary lease** to the apartment for the life of the corporation. *Because stock is personal property, the cooperative tenant-owners do not own real estate.* Instead, they own an interest in a corporation that has only one asset: the building.

Operation and management. The operation and management of a cooperative are determined by the corporation's bylaws. Through their control of the corporation, the shareholders of a cooperative control the property and its operation. They elect officers and directors who are responsible for operating the corporation and its real estate assets. Individual shareholders are obligated to abide by the corporation's bylaws.

An important issue in most cooperatives is the method by which shares in the corporation may be transferred to new owners. For instance, the bylaws may require that the board of directors approve any prospective shareholders. In some cooperatives, a tenant-owner must sell the stock back to the corporation at the original purchase price so that the corporation realizes any profits when the shares are resold.

FOR EXAMPLE In a highly publicized incident, former President Richard Nixon's attempt to move into an exclusive Manhattan cooperative apartment building was blocked by the cooperative's board. In refusing to allow the controversial ex-president to purchase shares, the board cited the unwanted publicity and media attention other tenants would suffer.

The corporation incurs costs in the operation and maintenance of the entire parcel, including both the common property and the individual apartments. These costs include real estate taxes and any mortgage payments the corporation may have. The corporation also budgets funds for such expenses as insurance, utilities, repairs and maintenance, janitorial and other services, replacement of equipment and reserves for capital expenditures. Funds for the budget are assessed to individual shareholders, generally in the form of monthly fees similar to those charged by a homeowners' association in a condominium.

Unlike in a condominium association, which has the authority to impose a lien on the title owned by someone who defaults on maintenance payments, the burden of any defaulted payment in a cooperative falls on the remaining shareholders. Each shareholder is affected by the financial ability of the others. For this reason, approval of prospective tenants by the board of directors frequently involves financial evaluation. If the corporation is unable to make mortgage and tax payments because of shareholder defaults, the property might be sold by court order in a foreclosure suit. This would destroy the interests of all shareholders, including those who have paid their assessments.

Advantages. Cooperative ownership, despite its risks, has become more desirable in recent years for several reasons. Lending institutions view the shares of stock as acceptable collateral for financing. The availability of financing expands the transferability of shares beyond wealthy cash buyers. As a tenant-owner, rather than a tenant who pays rent to a landlord, the shareholder has some control over the property. Tenants in cooperatives also enjoy certain income tax advantages from the payment of property taxes. Finally, owners enjoy freedom from maintenance.

In Practice   The laws in some states may prohibit real estate licensees from listing or selling cooperative interests because the owners own only personal property. Individuals who participate in these transactions may need a securities license appropriate for the type of cooperative interest involved.

In Illinois . . .

Illinois real estate brokers and salespersons are permitted to list and sell cooperative units and interests. ■

Time-Share Ownership   **Time-sharing** permits multiple purchasers to buy interests in real estate, usually a resort property. Each purchaser receives the right to use the facilities for a certain period of time. A time-share estate includes a real property interest in condominium ownership; a time-share use is a contract right under which the developer owns the real estate.

Fee simple INTEREST

In Illinois . . .

The promotion or sale of all time-share units is regulated by the *Illinois Real Estate Time-Share Act.* The act, regulated by the Office of Banks and Real Estate (OBRE), applies to both in-state and out-of-state time-share sales. ■

A **time-share estate** is a fee simple interest. The owner's occupancy and use of the property are limited to the contractual period purchased—for instance, the 17th complete week, Sunday through Saturday, of each calendar year. The owner is assessed for maintenance and common area expenses based on the ratio of the ownership period to the total number of ownership periods in

Not ownership lease holdbonds for year

the property. Time-share estates theoretically never end because they are real property interests. However, the physical life of the improvements is limited and must be looked at carefully when considering such a purchase.

The principal difference between a time-share estate and a time-share use lies in the interest transferred to an owner by the developer of the project. A **time-share use** consists of the right to occupy and use the facilities for a certain number of years. At the end of that time, the owner's rights in the property terminate. In effect, the developer has sold only a right of occupancy and use to the owner, not a fee simple interest.

In Illinois . . .

The Illinois Real Estate Time-Share Act distinguishes time-share estates and uses as follows:

- *Time-share estate:* Any arrangement in which the purchaser receives fee ownership in real property and the right to use the accommodations for a specified period of less than one year on a recurring basis of more than three years.
- *Time-share use:* Any arrangement, whether by lease, license, use agreement or any other means, in which the purchaser receives the right to use an accommodation in a time-share project for a specified period of less than one year on a recurring basis of more than three years but under which the purchaser does not receive a fee simple interest in any real property. ■

Some time-sharing programs specify certain months or weeks of the year during which the owner can use the property. Others provide a rotation system under which the owner can occupy the unit during different times of the year in different years. Some include a swapping privilege for transferring the ownership period to another property to provide some variety for the owner. Time-shared properties typically are used 50 weeks each year, with the remaining two weeks reserved for maintenance of the improvements.

In Illinois . . .

The Illinois Real Estate Time-Share Act requires that all developers and their agents must register with the Office of Banks and Real Estate. Each purchaser must be given a detailed *public offering statement* before signing the contract, disclosing extensive information about the property, time periods, percentage of common expenses for each unit, use and occupancy restrictions and total number of units. The statement also must include information about the developer and property management. Purchasers have three business days after signing in which to rescind the contract.

The act places developers and their agents under strict requirements regarding potential misrepresentation, such as predicting specific or immediate market value increases or disclosure of details of prizes offered. Violations can result in the suspension or revocation of a certificate or permit issued under the act. ■

Membership camping is similar to time-share use. The owner purchases the right to use the developer's facilities, which usually consist of an open area with minimal improvements (such as camper and trailer hookups and restrooms). Normally, the owner is not limited to a specific time for using the property; use is limited only by weather and access.

In Practice   The laws governing the development and sale of time-share units are complex. In addition, the sale of time-share properties may be subject to federal securities laws. In many states, time-share properties are now subject to subdivision requirements.

SUMMARY   Sole ownership, or ownership in severalty, means that title is held by one natural person or legal entity. Under co-ownership, title can be held concurrently by more than one person or legal entity in several ways.

Under tenancy in common, each party holds a separate title but shares possession with other tenants. Individual owners may sell their interests. Upon the death of a tenant in common, his or her interest passes to the tenant's heirs or according to a will. No special requirements for creating this interest exist. When two or more parties hold title to real estate, they do so as tenants in common unless they express another intention. Joint tenancy indicates two or more owners with the right of survivorship. The intention of the parties to establish a joint tenancy with right of survivorship must be stated clearly. The four unities of possession, interest, time and title must be present.

Tenancy by the entirety, in those states where it is recognized, actually is a joint tenancy between husband and wife. It gives the couple the right of survivorship in all lands they acquired during marriage. During their lives, both must sign the deed for any title to pass to a purchaser. Community property rights exist only in certain states and pertain only to land owned by husband and wife. Usually, the property acquired by combined efforts during the marriage is community property, and each spouse owns one-half. Properties acquired by a spouse before the marriage and through inheritance or gifts during the marriage are considered separate property.

Real estate ownership may be held in trust. To create a trust, the trustor conveys title to the property to a trustee.

Various types of business organizations may own real estate. A corporation is a legal entity and can hold title to real estate in severalty. While a partnership is technically not a legal entity, the Uniform Partnership Act and the Uniform Limited Partnership Act, adopted by most states, recognize a partnership as an entity that can own property in the partnership's name. A limited liability company (LLC) combines the limited liability offered by a corporate form and the tax advantages of a partnership without the complicated requirements of S corporations or the restrictions of limited partnerships. A syndicate is an association of two or more people or firms that invest in real estate. Many syndicates are joint ventures assembled for only a single project. A syndicate may be organized as a co-ownership trust, corporation or partnership.

Cooperative ownership indicates title in one entity (a corporation or trust) that must pay taxes, mortgage interest and principal and all operating expenses. Reimbursement comes from shareholders through monthly assessments. Shareholders have proprietary, long-term leases entitling them to occupy their apartments. Under condominium ownership, each owner-occupant holds fee simple title to a unit plus a share of the common elements. Each unit owner receives an individual tax bill and may mortgage the unit. Expenses for operating the building are collected by an owners' association through monthly assessments. Time-sharing enables multiple purchasers to own estates or use interests in real estate, with the right to use the property for a part of each year.

QUESTIONS

1. Which of the following is false regarding the forms of real estate ownership?
   A. Community property consists of all property, both real and personal, acquired by either spouse during marriage.
   B. Severalty ownership means sole ownership of property and would be an inheritable estate on the death of the owner.
   C. When two or more people own property as tenants in common, they each have an undivided interest in the entire property and it is an inheritable estate.
   D. Joint tenancy is characterized by the right of survivorship and the unities of time, interest, possession and person.

2. What is the difference between tenancy in common and joint tenancy?

   A. Tenancy in common is characterized by right of survivorship; joint tenancy is characterized by unity of possession.
   B. Tenancy in common ownership must contain specific wording; joint tenancy is presumed by the law when two or more people own property unless the deed states otherwise.
   C. Under tenancy in common ownership each owner has the right to sell, mortgage or lease his or her interest without the consent of the other owners; this is not true in joint tenancy.
   D. Tenancy is common is an inheritable estate; joint tenancy is characterized by the right of survivorship.

3. Martin, Bianca and Francine are joint tenants with rights of survivorship in a tract of land. Francine conveys her interest to Victor. Which of the following statements is true?
   A. Martin and Bianca are still joint tenants.
   B. Martin, Bianca and Victor are joint tenants.
   C. Martin, Bianca and Victor are tenants in common.
   D. Victor now has severalty ownership.

4. Hanna owns one of 20 townhouses in the Luxor Lakes development. Hanna owns the townhouse in fee simple and a 5 percent ownership share of the parking facilities, recreation center and grounds. What does Hanna own?
   A. Cooperative   C. Time-share
   B. Condominium   D. Land trust

5. John conveys a vineyard in trust to Raul, with the instruction that any income derived from the vineyard is to be used for Tina's medical care. Which of the following statements most accurately describes the relationship of these parties?
   A. John is the trustee, Raul is the trustor and Tina is the beneficiary.
   B. John is the trustor, Raul is the trustee and Tina is the beneficiary.
   C. John is the beneficiary, Raul is the trustor and Tina is the trustee.
   D. John is the trustor, Raul is the beneficiary and Tina is the trustee.

6. Dan and Sara are married. Under the laws of their state, any real property that either owns at the time of their marriage remains separate property. Further, any real property acquired by either party during the marriage (except by gift or inheritance) belongs to both of them equally. This form of ownership is called:
   A. a partnership.
   B. joint tenancy.
   C. tenancy by the entirety.
   D. community property.

7. Emma, Jack and Quincy were co-owners of a parcel of real estate. Jack died, and his interest passed according to his will to become part of his estate. Jack was a:
   A. joint tenant.
   B. tenant in common.
   C. tenant by the entirety.
   D. severalty owner.

8. A legal arrangement under which the title to real property is held to protect the interests of a beneficiary is a:
   A. trust.
   B. corporation.
   C. limited partnership.
   D. general partnership.

9. All of the following statements are true regarding a cooperative EXCEPT:
   A. title to the land and building are held by a corporation.
   B. unit owners hold personal property interests.
   C. costs of maintaining and operating the cooperative are incurred by the corporation from funds assessed to unit owners, generally in the form of monthly fees.
   D. because their proprietary leases are personal property, unit owners are exempt from the fees or assessments condominium owners are often required to pay to fund building maintenance and operation.

10. Ollie purchases an interest in a house in Beachfront. Ollie is entitled to the right of possession only between July 10 and August 4 of each year. Which of the following is most likely the type of ownership Ollie purchased?
   A. Cooperative   C. Time-share
   B. Condominium D. Trust

11. Because a corporation is a legal entity (an artificial person), real estate owned by it is owned in:
   A. trust.
   B. partnership.
   C. severalty.
   D. survivorship tenancy.

12. All of the following are forms of co-ownership EXCEPT:
   A. tenancy by the entirety.
   B. community property.
   C. tenancy in common.
   D. severalty.

13. Terri and Ron are married and co-own Blueacre, with a right of survivorship. Theirs is most likely:
   A. severalty ownership.
   B. community property.
   C. a tenancy in common.
   D. an estate by the entirety.

14. All of the following involve a fee simple interest EXCEPT a(n):
   A. ownership in severalty.
   B. tenancy for years.
   C. tenancy by the entirety.
   D. tenancy in common.

15. Goldacre is owned by Frank, George and Hank as tenants in common. When George dies, to whom will his interest pass?
   A. Frank and Hank equally
   B. George's heirs
   C. The state, by the law of escheat
   D. Frank and Hank in joint tenancy

16. Which of the following best proves the ownership in a cooperative?
   A. Tax bill for the individual unit
   B. Existence of a reverter clause
   C. Shareholder's stock certificate
   D. Right of first refusal

17. Shellie lives in the elegant Howell Tower. Her possessory interest is evidenced by a proprietary lease. What does Shellie own?
   A. Condominium unit
   B. Cooperative unit
   C. Time-share
   D. Leasehold

18. Which of the following statements applies to both joint tenancy and tenancy by the entirety?
   A. There is no right to file a partition suit.
   B. The survivor becomes a severalty owner.
   C. A deed signed by one owner will convey a fractional interest.
   D. A deed will not convey any interest unless signed by both spouses.

19. Theo owns a fee simple interest in a lakefront cottage, along with 5 percent of the parking lot, laundry room and boat house. Theo owns a:
   A. membership camping interest.
   B. time-share estate.
   C. cooperative unit.
   D. condominium unit.

20. If property is held by two or more owners as tenants with survivorship rights, the interest of a deceased cotenant will be passed to the:
    A. surviving owner or owners.
    B. heirs of the deceased.
    C. state under the law of escheat.
    D. trust under which the property was owned.

In Illinois . . .

21. Which of the following statements is true according to the Illinois Real Estate Time Share Act?
    A. Developers, but not their agents, are required to register with the Office of Banks and Real Estate.
    B. Purchasers must be given a disclosure statement about the property immediately after signing the purchase contract.
    C. Purchasers have 24 hours in which to request a disclosure statement from a developer.
    D. The statute guarantees purchasers a three-day right to rescind a time-share purchase contract.

22. The names of the beneficiaries of a land trust must be revealed by the trustee to:
    A. any member of the public who is interested in the beneficiary's identity.
    B. any Illinois agency when applying for a license or permit affecting the entrusted real estate.
    C. any unsecured creditor of the beneficiary.
    D. a licensed real estate broker, if the broker is assisting in the sale or rental of the entrusted property.

23. Every co-owner of real estate in Illinois has the right to file a suit for partition when the property is held in which of the following ways?
    A. Joint tenancy or tenancy in common
    B. Land trust
    C. Condominium or cooperative
    D. Time-share use or estate

24. Title to land in Illinois may be held and conveyed in which of the following ways?
    A. In the name of a partnership
    B. As joint tenants only if the property is owned by a husband and wife as their principal residence
    C. As tenants in common with rights of survivorship
    D. All of the above

25. If the deed of conveyance to Illinois land transfers title to two or more co-owners without defining the character of the co-ownership, which of the following statements is true?
    A. The property is construed as being held in joint tenancy.
    B. The co-owners are tenants in common.
    C. While proper in some states, such a deed would be an invalid conveyance under Illinois law.
    D. By statute, such co-owners would have the right of survivorship.

26. Ben and Cheri held title to an apartment building as joint tenants with rights of survivorship. Ben and Cheri had an argument, and Ben didn't like the possibility that Cheri would acquire total ownership of the building if Ben died. Therefore, Ben executed a deed to himself as a tenant in common and later willed his interest to Jenna. If these facts occurred in Illinois, which of the following statements accurately describes Ben's action?
    A. Ben's action is illegal under Illinois law.
    B. While not necessarily illegal, Ben's action has no effect on the joint tenancy.
    C. Ben's goal of severing the joint tenancy can be accomplished only by a partition suit.
    D. Ben's action legally severs the joint tenancy.

27. Which of the following is necessary to convert an apartment building to condominium ownership in Illinois?
    A. The owner records a condominium declaration with a three-dimensional plat.
    B. The owner must record a certificate stating that the current tenants have been duly surveyed and that a majority of all tenants are in favor of the conversion.
    C. The existing tenants elect a board of directors having the power to act as legal administrator for the property, and the board petitions the state under the Condominium Property Act for certification as a condominium.
    D. The owner must execute and record a declaration of condominium under the Uniform Condominium Act as adopted in Illinois.

Legal Descriptions

air lot	legal description	range
base line	lot-and-block (recorded	rectangular survey
bench mark	plat) system	system
correction line	metes and bounds	section
datum	monument	township
fractional section	plat map	township line
government check	point of beginning	township square
government lot	principal meridian	township tier

DESCRIBING LAND

People often refer to real estate by its street address, such as "1234 Main Street." While that usually is enough for the average person to find a particular building, it is not precise enough to be used on documents affecting the ownership of land. Sales contracts, deeds, mortgages and trust deeds, for instance, require a much more specific (or *legally sufficient*) description of property to be binding.

Courts have stated that a description is legally sufficient if it allows a competent surveyor to locate the parcel. In this context, however, *locate* means the surveyor must be able to define the exact boundaries of the property. The street address "1234 Main Street" would not tell a surveyor how large the property is or where it begins and ends. Several alternative systems of identification have been developed that express a **legal description** of real estate.

METHODS OF DESCRIBING REAL ESTATE

Three basic methods can be used to describe real estate:

1. Metes and bounds
2. Rectangular (or government) survey
3. Lot and block (recorded plat)

Although each method can be used independently, the methods may be combined in some situations. Some states use only one method; others use all three.

Metes-and-Bounds Method

The **metes-and-bounds** description is the oldest type of legal description. It relies on a property's physical features to determine the boundaries and measurements of the parcel. A metes-and-bounds description starts at a designated place on the parcel, called the **point of beginning** (POB). From there, the surveyor proceeds around the property's boundaries. The boundaries are recorded by referring to linear measurements, natural and artificial landmarks (called *monuments*) and directions. A metes-and-bounds description always ends back at the POB so that the tract being described is completely enclosed.

Monuments are fixed objects used to identify the POB, the ends of boundary segments or the location of intersecting boundaries. A monument may be a natural object, such as a stone, large tree, lake or stream. It may also be a manmade object, such as a street, highway, fence, canal or markers (iron pins or concrete posts) placed by surveyors. Measurements often include the words "more or less" because the location of the monuments is more important than the distance stated in the wording. The actual distance between monuments takes precedence over any linear measurements in the description.

An example of a metes-and-bounds description of a parcel of land (pictured in Figure 9.1) follows:

> A tract of land located in Red Skull, Boone County, Virginia, described as follows: Beginning at the intersection of the east line of Jones Road and the south line of Skull Drive; then east along the south line of Skull Drive 200 feet; then south 15° east 216.5 feet, more or less, to the center thread of Red Skull Creek; then northwesterly along the center line of said creek to its intersection with the east line of Jones Road; then north 105 feet, more or less, along the east line of Jones Road to the point of beginning.

When used to describe property within a town or city, a metes-and-bounds description may begin as follows:

> Beginning at a point on the southerly side of Kent Street, 100 feet easterly from the corner formed by the intersection of the southerly side of Kent Street and the easterly side of Broadway; then. . . .

In this description, the POB is given by reference to the corner intersection. *Again, the description must close by returning to the POB.*

In Practice

Metes-and-bounds descriptions can be complex and should be handled with extreme care. When they include detailed compass directions or concave and convex lines, they can be difficult to understand. Natural deterioration or destruction of the monuments in a description can make boundaries difficult to identify. For instance, "Raney's oak" may have died long ago, and "Hunter's Rock" may no longer exist. Computer programs are available that convert the data of the compass directions and dimensions to a drawing that verifies tat the description represents a closed figure. Professional surveyors should be consulted for definitive interpretations of any legal description.

Figure 9.1 Metes-and-Bounds Tract

In Illinois...

Metes-and-bounds descritions are used in Illinois when describing irregular tracts, portions of a recorded lot or fractions of a section. Such descriptions always incorporate the rectangular survey method and refer to the section, township, range and principal meridian of the land, described in the following section. ■

Rectangular (Government) Survey System

The **rectangular survey system,** sometimes called the *government survey system,* was established by Congress in 1785 to standardize the description of land acquired by the newly formed federal government. The system is based on two sets of intersecting lines: principal meridians and base lines. The **principal meridians** run north and south, and the **base lines** run east and west. Both are located by reference to degrees of longitude and latitude. Each principal meridian has a name or number and is crossed by a base line. Each principal meridian and its corresponding base line are used to survey a definite area of land, indicated on the map by boundary lines.

Each principal meridian describes only specific areas of land by boundaries. No parcel of land is described by reference to more than one principal meridian. The meridian used may not necessarily be the nearest one.

In Illinois . . .

Locations in Illinois are described by their relation to one of the three meridians shown on the map in Figure 9.2. Note that only two of these three meridians actually run through Illinois.

The *Second Principal Meridian* is located in Indiana and controls that portion of Illinois lying south and east of Kankakee. The *Third Principal Meridian* begins at Cairo, at the junction of the Ohio and Mississippi rivers, and extends northward toward Wisconsin and near Rockford to the Illinois-Wisconsin border. The *Fourth Principal Meridian* begins near Beardstown and extends northward to the Canadian border. Surveys of land located in the western portion of Illinois use a base line for the Fourth Principal Meridian at Beardstown. Surveys of land in Wisconsin and eastern Minnesota are made from the Fourth Principal Meridian using a base line that is the Illinois-Wisconsin border.

Not all property is described by reference to the nearest principal meridian. Looking at the Illinois map in Figure 9.2, you will see that a property on the western border of the Third Principal Meridian and just west of Rockford will nevertheless be described by reference to the Fourth Principal Meridian. There are no options with regard to the meridians and base lines used to describe a particular property; once made, a description will not change. ■

Figure 9.2   Rectangular Survey System Map

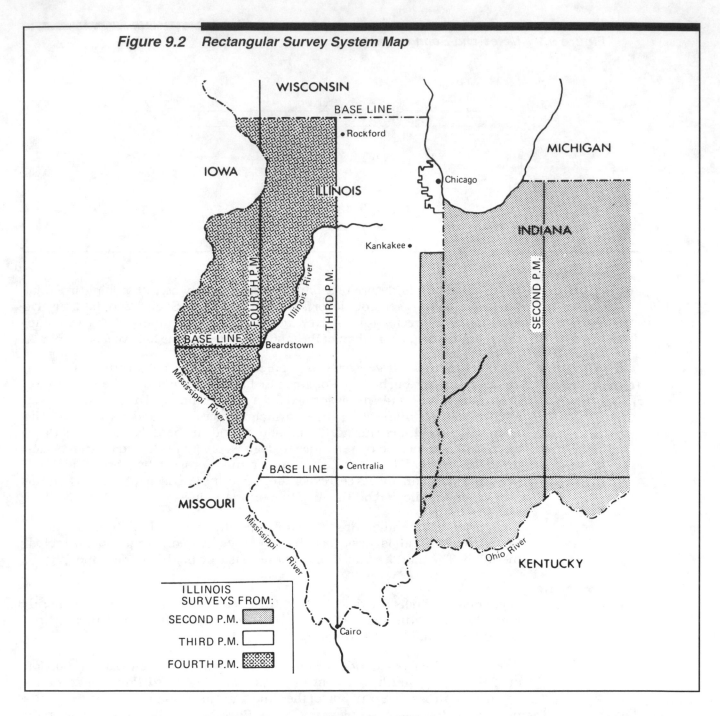

Further divisions are used in the same way as monuments in the metes-and-bounds method. They are

- townships,
- ranges,
- sections and
- quarter-section lines.

Township Tiers. Lines running east and west, parallel to the base line and six miles apart, are referred to as **township lines.** (See Figure 9.3.) They form strips of land called **township tiers.** These township tiers are designated by consecutive numbers north or south of the base line. For instance, the strip of land between 6 and 12 miles north of a base line is Township 2 North.

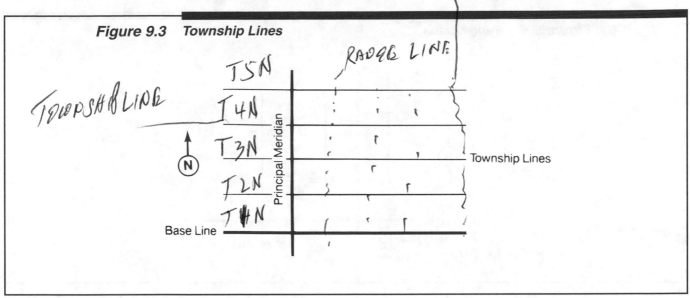

Figure 9.3 **Township Lines**

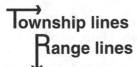

The directions of township lines and range lines may be easily remembered by thinking of the words this way:

Township lines
Range lines

Ranges. The land on either side of a principal meridian is divided into six-mile-wide strips by lines that run north and south, parallel to the meridian. These north-south strips of land are called **ranges.** (See Figure 9.4.) They are designated by consecutive numbers east or west of the principal meridian. For example, Range 3 East would be a strip of land between 12 and 18 miles east of its principal meridian.

Township squares. When the horizontal township lines and the vertical range lines intersect, they form squares. These **township squares** are the basic units of the rectangular survey system. (See Figure 9.5.) **Townships** are 6 miles square and contain 36 square miles (23,040 acres).

Note that although a township *square* is part of a township *tier,* the two terms do not refer to the same thing. In this discussion, the word *township* used by itself refers only to the *township square.*

Each township is given a legal description. The township's description includes the following:

- Designation of the township strip in which the township is located
- Designation of the range strip
- Name or number of the principal meridian for that area

FOR EXAMPLE In Figure 9.5, the township marked with an *X* is described as Township 3 North, Range 4 East of the Principal Meridian. This township is the third strip, or tier, north of the base line, and it designates the township number and direction. The township is also located in the fourth range strip (those running north and south) east of the principal meridian. Finally, reference is made to the principal meridian because the land being described is within the boundary of land surveyed from that meridian. This description is abbreviated as T3N, R4E 4th Principal Meridian.

Sections. Each township contains 36 **sections.** Each section is one square mile, or 640 acres. Sections are numbered 1 through 36, as shown in Figure 9.6. Section 1 is always in the northeast, or upper right-hand, corner. The numbering proceeds right to left to the upper left-hand corner. From there, the numbers drop down to the next tier and continue from left to right, then

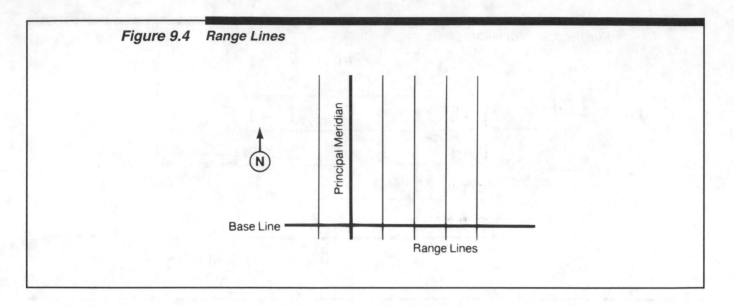

Figure 9.4 Range Lines

back from right to left. By law, each section number 16 is set aside for school purposes. The sale or rental proceeds from this land were originally available for township school use. The schoolhouse usually was located in this section so it would be centrally located for all of the students in the township. As a result, Section 16 is always referred to as a *school section.*

Sections (see Figure 9.7) are divided into halves (320 acres) and quarters (160 acres). In turn, each of those parts is further divided into halves and quarters. The southeast quarter of a section, which is a 160-acre tract, is abbreviated SE¼. The SE¼ of the SE¼ of the SE¼ of Section 1 would be a ten-acre square in the lower right-hand corner of Section 1.

The rectangular survey system sometimes uses a shorthand method in its descriptions. For instance, a comma may be used in place of the word *of:* SE¼, SE¼, SE¼, Section 1. It is possible to combine portions of a section, such as NE¼ of SW¼ and N½ of NW¼ of SE¼ of Section 1, which could also be written NE¼, SW¼; N½, NW¼, SE¼ of Section 1. A semicolon means *and.* Because of the word *and* in this description, the area is 60 acres.

Correction lines. Range lines are only parallel in theory. Owing to the curvature of the earth, range lines gradually approach each other. If they are extended northward, they eventually meet at the North Pole. The fact that the earth is not flat, combined with the crude instruments used in early days, means that few townships are exactly six-mile squares or contain exactly 36 square miles. The system compensates for this "round earth problem" with correction lines. (See Figure 9.8.) Every fourth township line, both north and south of the base line, is designated a **correction line.** On each correction line, the range lines are measured to the full distance of six miles apart. Guide meridians run north and south at 24-mile intervals from the principal meridian. A **government check** is the area bounded by two guide meridians and two correction lines—an area approximately 24 miles square.

Because most townships do not contain exactly 36 square miles, surveyors follow well-established rules of adjustment. These rules provide that any irregularity in a township must be adjusted in those sections adjacent to its north and west boundaries (Sections 1, 2, 3, 4, 5, 6, 7, 18, 19, 30 and 31). These are called *fractional sections* (discussed in the following paragraph). All

Townships are numbered the same way a field is plowed. (The word for such a system is *boustrophedonic*—literally, "turning like oxen pulling a plow.") Remember: *right to left, left to right, right to left.*

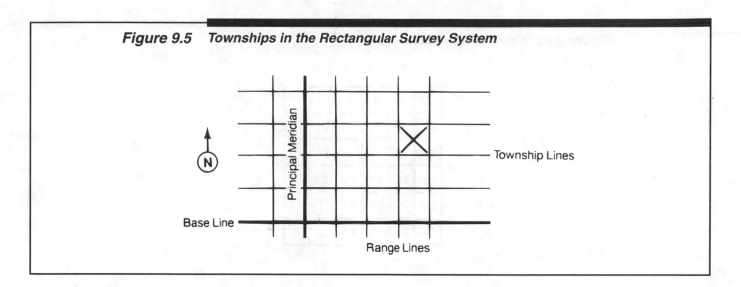

Figure 9.5 **Townships in the Rectangular Survey System**

other sections are exactly one square mile and are known as *standard sections.* These provisions for making corrections explain some of the variations in township and section acreage under the rectangular survey system of legal description.

Fractional sections and government lots. Undersized or oversized sections are classified as **fractional sections.** Fractional sections may occur for a number of reasons. In some areas, for instance, the rectangular survey may have been made by separate crews, and gaps less than a section wide remained when the surveys met. Other errors may have resulted from the physical difficulties encountered in the actual survey. For example, part of a section may be submerged in water.

Areas smaller than full quarter-sections were numbered and designated as **government lots** by surveyors. These lots can be created by the curvature of the earth, by land bordering or surrounding large bodies of water or by artificial state borders. An *overage* or a *shortage* was corrected whenever possible by placing the government lots in the north or west portions of the fractional sections. For example, a government lot might be described as *Government Lot 2 in the northwest quarter of fractional Section 18, Township 2 North, Range 4 East of the Salt Lake Meridian.*

Reading a rectangular survey description. To determine the location and size of a property described in the rectangular (or government) survey style, start at the end and work backward to the beginning, reading from right to left. For example, consider the following description:

> The S½ of the NW¼ of the SE¼ of Section 11, Township 8 North, Range 6 West of the Fourth Principal Meridian.

To locate this tract of land from the citation alone, first search for the Fourth Principal Meridian on a map of the United States. Then, on a regional map, find the township in which the property is located by counting six range strips west of the Fourth Principal Meridian and eight townships north of its corresponding base line. After locating Section 11, divide the section into quarters. Then divide the SE¼ into quarters, and then the NW¼ of that into halves. The S½ of that NW¼ contains the property in question.

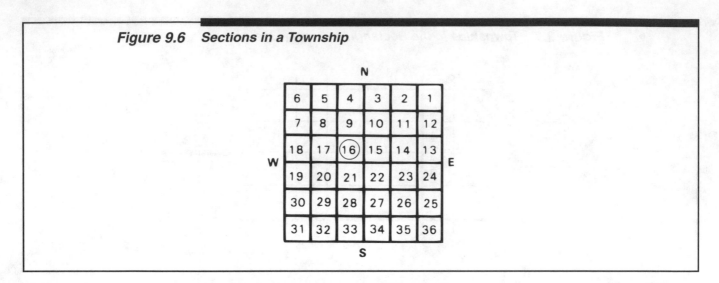

Figure 9.6   Sections in a Township

In computing the size of this tract of land, first determine that the SE¼ of the section contains 160 acres (640 acres divided by 4). The NW¼ of that quarter-section contains 40 acres (160 acres divided by 4), and the S½ of that quarter-section—the property in question—contains 20 acres (40 acres divided by 2).

In general, if a rectangular survey description does not use the conjunction *and* or a semicolon (indicating various parcels are combined), the *longer* the description, the *smaller* the tract of land it describes.

Legal descriptions should always include the name of the county and state in which the land is located because meridians often relate to more than one state and occasionally relate to two base lines. For example, the description "the southwest quarter of Section 10, Township 4 North, Range 1 West of the Fourth Principal Meridian" could refer to land in either Illinois or Wisconsin.

Metes-and-bounds descriptions within the rectangular survey system. Land in states that use the rectangular survey system also may require a metes-and-bounds description. This usually occurs in one of three situations: when describing an irregular tract; when a tract is too small to be described by quarter-sections; or when a tract does not follow the lot or block lines of a recorded subdivision or section, quarter-section lines or other fractional section lines. The following is an example of a combined metes-and-bounds and rectangular survey system description (see Figure 9.9):

> That part of the northwest quarter of Section 12, Township 10 North, Range 7 West of the Third Principal Meridian, bounded by a line described as follows: Commencing at the southeast corner of the northwest quarter of said Section 12 then north 500 feet; then west parallel with the south line of said section 1,000 feet; then south parallel with the east line of said section 500 feet to the south line of said northwest quarter; then east along said south line to the point of beginning.

In Illinois . . .

Metes-and-bounds descriptions may be included in the rectangular survey system used in Illinois when describing irregular or small tracts. ■

Lot-and-Block System

The third method of legal description is the **lot-and-block** (or **recorded plat**) **system.** This system uses *lot-and-block numbers* referred to in a **plat map** filed in the public records of the county where the land is located.

Township is 6xx sixtien
or 6 mile sq
or 36 sq mile

36 sec Pii

640 Acu

Figure 9.7 A Section

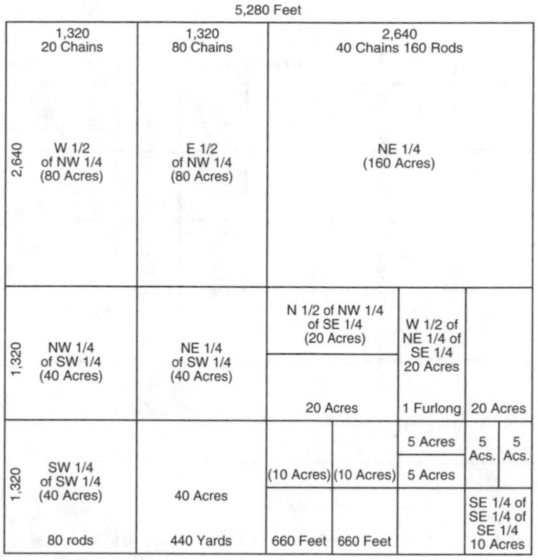

A lot-and-block survey is performed in two steps. First, a large parcel of land is described either by metes and bounds or by rectangular survey. Once this large parcel is surveyed, it is broken into smaller parcels. As a result, a lot-and-block legal description always refers to a prior metes-and-bounds or rectangular survey description. For each parcel described under the lot-and-block system, the *lot* refers to the numerical designation of any particular parcel. The *block* refers to the name of the subdivision under which the map is recorded. The block reference is drawn from the early 1900s, when a city block was the most common type of subdivided property.

The lot-and-block system starts with the preparation of a *subdivision plat* by a licensed surveyor or an engineer. (See Figure 9.10.) On this plat, the land is divided into numbered or lettered lots and blocks, and streets or access roads for public use are indicated. Lot sizes and street details must be described completely and must comply with all local ordinances and requirements. When properly signed and approved, the subdivision plat is recorded in the county in which the land is located. The plat becomes part of the legal description. In describing a lot from a recorded subdivision plat, three identifiers are used:

1. Lot-and-block number
2. Name or number of the subdivision plat
3. Name of the county and state

The following is an example of a lot-and-block description:

> Lot 71, Happy Valley Estates 2, located in a portion of the southeast quarter of Section 23, Township 7 North, Range 4 East of the Seward Principal Meridian in _____ County, State of _____.

Anyone who wants to locate this parcel would start with the map of the Seward Principal Meridian to identify the township and range reference. Then he or she would consult the township map of Township 7 North, Range 4 East, and

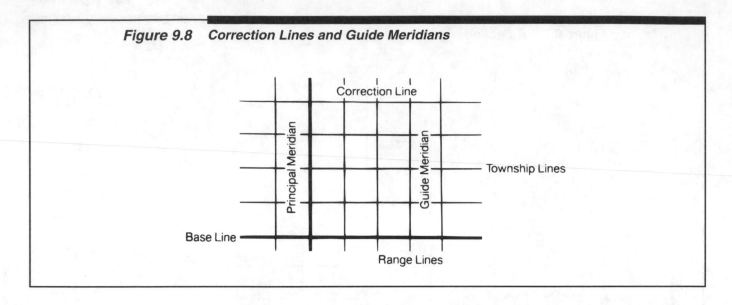

Figure 9.8 **Correction Lines and Guide Meridians**

the section map of Section 23. From there, he or she would look at the quarter-section map of the southeast quarter. The quarter-section map would refer to the plat map for the subdivision known as the second unit (second parcel subdivided) under the name of Happy Valley Estates.

Some subdivided lands are further divided by a later resubdivision. In the following example, one developer (Western View) purchased a large parcel from a second developer (Homewood). Western View then resubdivided the property into different-sized parcels:

> Lot 4, Western View Resubdivision of the Homewood Subdivision, located in a portion of the west half of Section 19, Township 10 North, Range 13 East of the Black Hills Principal Meridian, _____ County, State of _____.

In Illinois . . .

The lot-and-block system is now used to some degree in all states, including Illinois. Subdivision descriptions are the predominant method of describing developed land in this state. The plat of Prairie Acres Estates that appears in Figure 9.11 illustrates a subdivision map.

Under the *Illinois Plat Act,* when an owner divides a parcel of land into two or more parts, any of which is less than five acres, the parts must be surveyed and a plat of subdivision recorded. However, there are certain exceptions to this requirement: for instance, the division of lots or blocks of less than one acre in any recorded subdivision that does not involve the creation of any new streets or easements of access. When a conveyance is made, the county recorder may require an affidavit that an exception exists.

The provisions of the Illinois Plat Act are complicated and subject to interpretation by each county recorder. A licensee who is preparing to record a document conveying land under a metes-and-bounds description should consult a lawyer and the county recorder about the requirements inolved. ■

PREPARING A SURVEY

Legal descriptions should not be altered or combined without adequate information from a surveyor or title attorney. A licensed surveyor is trained

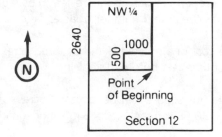

Figure 9.9   Metes and Bounds with Rectangular Survey

"Section 12, T10N, R7W, Third Principal Meridian"

"A tract of land beginning at SE1/4 of the NW1/4,
west 1000' then north 500' then east 1000' then
south 500' back to the point of beginning"

and authorized to locate and determine the legal description of any parcel of land. The surveyor does this by preparing two documents: a survey and a survey sketch. The *survey* states the property's legal description. The *survey sketch* shows the location and dimensions of the parcel. When a survey also shows the location, size and shape of buildings on the lot, it is referred to as a *spot survey.*

In Practice   Because legal descriptions, once recorded, affect title to real estate, they should be prepared only by a professional surveyor. Real estate licensees who attempt to draft legal descriptions create potential risks for themselves and their clients and customers.

Legal descriptions should be copied with extreme care. An incorrectly worded legal description in a sales contract may result in a conveyance of more or less land than the parties intended. Title problems can arise for the buyer who seeks to convey the property at a future date. Even if the contract can be corrected before the sale is closed, the licensee risks losing a commission and may be held liable for damages suffered by an injured party because of an improperly worded legal description.

MEASURING ELEVATIONS

Just as surface rights must be identified, surveyed and described, so must rights to the property above the earth's surface. As discussed earlier, land includes the space above the ground. In the same way land may be measured and divided into parcels, the air itself may be divided. An owner may subdivide the air above his or her land into air lots. **Air lots** are composed of the airspace within specific boundaries located over a parcel of land.

Land Acquisition Costs

To calculate the cost of purchasing land, use the same unit in which the cost is given. Costs quoted per square foot must be multiplied by the proper number of square feet; costs quoted per acre must be multiplied by the proper number of acres; and so on.

To calculate the cost of a parcel of land of three acres at $1.10 per square foot, convert the acreage to square feet before multiplying:

43,560 square feet per acre × 3 acres = 130,680 square feet
130,680 square feet × $1.10 per square foot = $143,748

To calculate the cost of a parcel of land of 17,500 square feet at $60,000 per acre, convert the cost per acre into the cost per square foot before multiplying by the number of square feet in the parcel:

$60,000 per acre ÷ 43,560 square feet per acre = $1.38 (rounded) per square foot
17,500 square feet × $1.38 per square foot = $24,150

Datum

A **datum** is a point, line or surface from which elevations are measured or indicated. For the purpose of the *U.S. Geological Survey (USGS)*, *datum* is defined as the mean sea level at New York Harbor. A surveyor would use a datum in determining the height of a structure or establishing the grade of a street.

The condominium laws passed in all states require that a registered land surveyor prepare a plat map that shows the elevations of floor and ceiling surfaces and the vertical boundaries of each unit with reference to an official datum (discussed below). A unit's floor, for instance, might be 60 feet above the datum, and its ceiling, 69 feet. Typically, a separate plat is prepared for each floor in the condominium building.

Subsurface rights can be legally described in the same manner as air rights. However, they are measured *below* the datum rather than above it. Subsurface rights are used not only for coal mining, petroleum drilling and utility line location but also for multistory condominiums—both residential and commercial—that have several floors below ground level.

In Illinois . . .

The general datum plane used by Illinois surveyors is the USGS datum. ■

Bench marks. As discussed earlier in this chapter, monuments traditionally are used to mark surface measurements between points. A monument could be a marker set in concrete, a piece of steel-reinforcing bar ("rebar"), a metal pipe driven into the soil or simply a wooden stake stuck in the dirt. Because such items are subject to the whims of nature and vandals, their accuracy is sometimes suspect. As a result, surveyors rely most heavily on bench marks to mark their work accurately and permanently.

Bench marks are permanent reference points that have been established throughout the United States. They are usually embossed brass markers set into solid concrete or asphalt bases. While used to some degree for surface measurements, their principal reference use is for marking datums.

Figure 9.10 Subdivision Plat Map

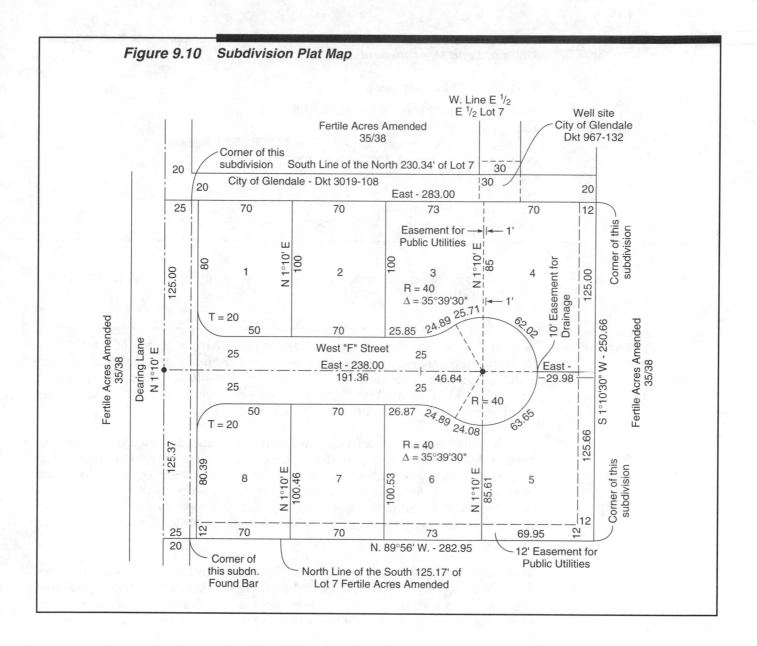

All large cities have established a local official datum used in place of the USGS datum. For instance, the official datum for Chicago is known as the *Chicago City Datum*. It is a horizontal plane that corresponds to the low-water level of Lake Michigan in 1847 (the year in which the datum was established) and is considered to be at zero elevation. Although a surveyor's measurement of elevation based on the USGS datum will differ from one computed according to a local datum, it can be translated to an elevation based on the USGS.

Cities with local datums also have designated official local benchmarks, which are assigned permanent identifying numbers. Local benchmarks simplify surveyors' work because the basic benchmarks may be miles away.

LAND UNITS AND MEASUREMENTS

It is important to understand land units and measurements because they are

Table 9.1 *Units of Land Measurement*

Unit	Measurement
mile	5,280 feet; 1,760 yards; 320 rods
rod	16.5 feet; 5.50 yards
sq. mile	640 acres (5,280 x 5,280 = 27,878,400 + 43,560)
acre	43,560 sq. feet; 160 sq. rods
cu. yard	27 cu. feet
sq. yard	9 sq. feet
sq. foot	144 sq. inches
chain	66 feet; 4 rods; 160 links

integral parts of legal descriptions. Some commonly used measurements are listed in Table 9.1.

SUMMARY

A legal description is a precise method of identifying a parcel of land. Three methods of legal description can be used: metes-and-bounds system, rectangular (or government) survey system and lot-and-block (plat map) system. A property's description should always be noted by the same method as the one used in previous documents.

A metes-and-bounds description uses direction and distance measurement to establish precise boundaries for a parcel. Monuments are fixed objects that establish these boundaries. Their actual location takes precedence over the written linear measurement in a document. When property is being described by metes and bounds, the description must always enclose a tract of land; that is, the boundary line must end at the point at which it started, the point of beginning.

The rectangular (or government) survey system is used in 30 states. It involves surveys based on 35 principal meridians. Under this system, each principal meridian and its corresponding base line are specifically located. Any parcel of land is surveyed from only one principal meridian and its base line.

East and west lines parallel with the base line form six-mile-wide strips called township tiers or strips. North and south lines parallel with the principal meridian form range strips. The resulting squares are 36 square miles in area and are called townships. Townships are designated by their township and range numbers and their principal meridians—for example, Township 3 North, Range 4 East of the Meridian. Townships are divided into 36 sections of one square mile each.

When a tract is irregular or its boundaries do not coincide with a section, regular fractions of a section, or a boundary of a lot or block in a subdivision, a surveyor can prepare a combination rectangular survey and metes-and-bounds description.

Land in every state can be subdivided into lots and blocks by means of a plat map. An approved plat of survey showing the division into blocks; giving the size, location and designation of lots; and specifying the location and size of streets to be dedicated for public use is filed for record in the recorder's office of the county in which the land is located. A subdivision plat gives the legal

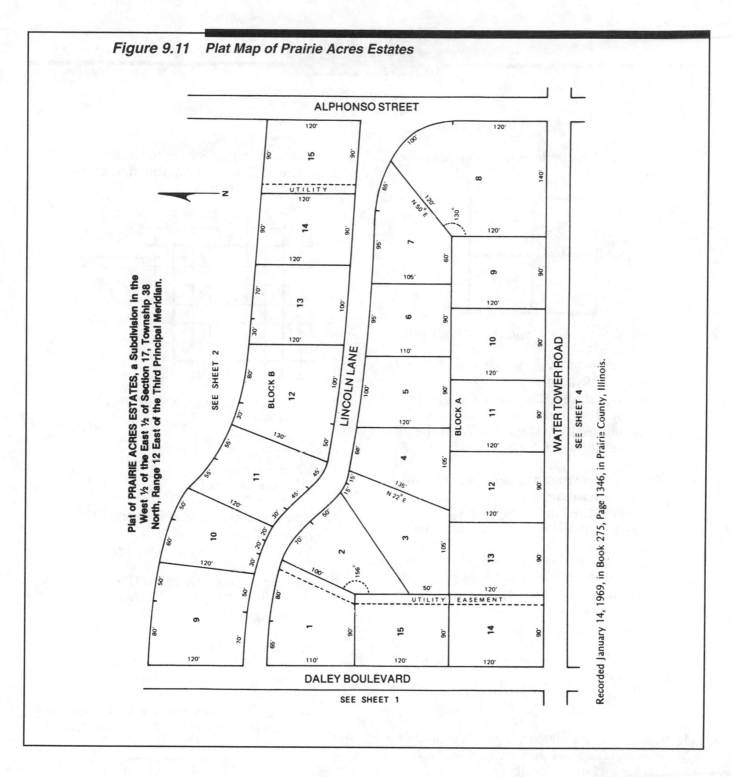

Figure 9.11   Plat Map of Prairie Acres Estates

description of a building site in a town or city by lot, block and subdivision in a section, township and range of a principal meridian in a county and state.

Air lots, condominium descriptions and other measurements of vertical elevations may be computed from the U.S. Geological Survey datum, which is the mean sea level in New York Harbor. Most large cities have established local survey datums for surveying within the areas. The elevations from these datums are further supplemented by reference points, called *bench marks,* placed at fixed intervals from the datums.

QUESTIONS

1. What is the proper description of this shaded area of a section?

   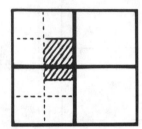

   A. SW¼ of the NE¼ and the N½ of the SE¼ of the SW¼
   B. N½ of the NE¼ of the SW¼ and the SE¼ of the NW¼
   C. SW¼ of the SE¼ of the NW¼ and the N½ of the NE¼ of the SW¼
   D. S½ of the SW¼ of the NE¼ and the NE¼ of the NW¼ of the SE¼

2. When surveying land, a surveyor refers to the principal meridian that is:
   A. nearest the land being surveyed.
   B. in the same state as the land being surveyed.
   C. not more than 40 townships or 15 ranges distant from the land being surveyed.
   D. within the rectangular survey system area in which the land being surveyed is located.

3. The N½ of the SW¼ of a section contains how many acres?
   A. 20   C. 60
   B. 40   D. 80

4. In describing real estate, the system that uses feet, degrees and natural and artificial markers as monuments is:
   A. rectangular survey.
   B. metes and bounds.
   C. government survey.
   D. lot and block.

Questions 5 through 8 refer to the following illustration of a whole township and parts of the adjacent townships.

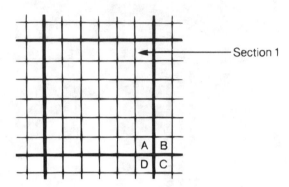

5. The section marked A is which of the following?
   A. School section
   B. Section 31
   C. Section 36
   D. Government lot

6. Which of the following is Section 6?
   A. A   C. C
   B. B   D. D

7. The section directly below C is:
   A. Section 7.   C. Section 25.
   B. Section 12.   D. Section 30.

8. Which of the following is Section D?
   A. Section 1   C. Section 31
   B. Section 6   D. Section 36

9. Which of these shaded areas of a section depicts the NE¼ of the SE¼ of the SW¼?

   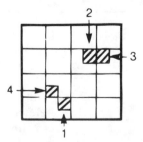

   A. Area 1   C. Area 3
   B. Area 2   D. Area 4

10. Janice purchases a one-acre parcel from Sheila for $2.15 per square foot. What is the selling price of the parcel?
    A. $344
    C. $1,376
    B. $774
    D. $93,654

11. The proper description of the shaded township area in this illustration is:

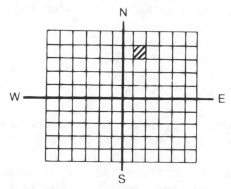

    A. T7N R7W.
    C. T4N R2E.
    B. T4W R7N.
    D. T4N R7E.

12. If a farm described as "the NW¼ of the SE¼ of Section 10, Township 2 North, Range 3 West of the 6th P.M." sold for $1,500 an acre, what would the sales price be?
    A. $30,000
    C. $45,000
    B. $15,000
    D. $60,000

13. The legal description "the northwest ¼ of the southwest ¼ of Section 6, Township 4 North, Range 7 West" is defective because there is no reference to:
    A. lot numbers.
    B. boundary lines.
    C. a principal meridian.
    D. a record of survey.

14. To keep the principal meridian and range lines as near to six miles apart as possible, a correction known as a government check is made. How large is a government check?
    A. One square mile
    B. Twenty square miles
    C. Six miles square
    D. Twenty-four miles square

15. Fractional sections in the rectangular survey system along the northern or western borders of a check that are less than a quarter-section in area are known as:
    A. fractional parcels.
    B. government lots.
    C. portional sections.
    D. fractional townships.

16. Tara purchased 4.5 acres of land for $78,400. An adjoining owner wants to purchase a strip of Tara's land measuring 150 feet by 100 feet. What should this strip cost the adjoining owner if Tara sells it for the same price per square foot originally paid for the property?
    A. $3,000
    C. $7,800
    B. $6,000
    D. $9,400

17. A property contained ten acres. How many 50-foot-by-100-foot lots could be subdivided from the property if 26,000 square feet were dedicated for roads?
    A. 80
    C. 82
    B. 81
    D. 83

18. A parcel of land is 400 feet by 640 feet. The parcel is cut in half diagonally by a stream. How many acres are there in each half of the parcel?
    A. 2.75
    C. 5.51
    B. 2.94
    D. 5.88

19. What is the shortest distance between Section 4 and Section 32 in the same township?
    A. 3 miles
    C. 5 miles
    B. 4 miles
    D. 6 miles

20. The section due west of Section 18, Township 5 North, Range 8 West, is:
    A. Section 19, T5N, R8W.
    B. Section 17, T5N, R8W.
    C. Section 13, T5N, R9W.
    D. Section 12, T5N, R7W.

21. In any township, which section is traditionally designated as the school section?
    A. 1
    C. 25
    B. 16
    D. 36

In Illinois . . .

22. Legal descriptions of land in Illinois usually are based on the:
    A. rectangular survey system.
    B. Third, Fourth and Fifth Principal Meridians.
    C. three base lines running through the central part of the state.
    D. nearest principal meridian.

23. Rebecca has a 10-acre tract of land. If she wants to divide the tract into four 2½-acre lots and sell the lots for residences, Rebecca must:
    A. establish a datum for the area.
    B. have a spot survey made of the proposed lots.
    C. record a copy of the plat before offering lots for sale.
    D. sell each of the lots before applying for a plot license.

24. Land in the northwest corner of Illinois is described with reference to which Principal Meridian?
    A. Second   C. Fourth
    B. Third   D. Fifth

Answer questions 26, 27 and 28 using the information given on the plat of Prairie Acres Estates in Figure 9.11.

25. How many lots have easements?
    A. 3   C. 6
    B. 4   D. 7

26. Which of the following lots has the most frontage on Lincoln Lane?
    A. Lot 10, block B
    B. Lot 11, block B
    C. Lot 7, block A
    D. Lot 8, block A

27. "Beginning at the intersection of the east line of Daley Boulevard and the south line of Lincoln Lane and running south along the east line of Daley Boulevard a distance of 230 feet; then easterly parallel to the north line of Water Tower Road a distance of 195 feet; then northeasterly on a course of N22°E a distance of 135 feet; and then northwesterly along the south line of Lincoln Lane to the point of beginning." Which lots are described here?
    A. Lots 13, 14 and 15, block A
    B. Lots 9, 10 and 11, block B
    C. Lots 1, 2, 3 and 15, block A
    D. Lots 7, 8 and 9, block A

CHAPTER

10

Real Estate Taxes and Other Liens

KEY TERMS

ad valorem tax	involuntary lien	special assessment
attachment	judgment	specific lien
equalization factor	judgment lien	statutory lien
equitable lien	lien	subordination
estate taxes	lis pendens	agreement
general lien	mechanic's lien	tax lien
general real estate tax	mill	tax sale
inheritance taxes	mortgage lien	voluntary lien

LIENS

A **lien** is a charge or claim against property, made to enforce the payment of money. Whenever someone borrows money, the lender generally requires some form of security. *Security* (also referred to as *collateral*) is something of value that the borrower promises to give the lender if the borrower fails to repay the debt. When the lender's security is in the form of real estate, the security is called a *lien.*

Liens are not limited to security for borrowed money (such as *mortgage liens*). Liens can be enforced against property by a government agency to recover taxes owed by the owner (*tax liens*). A lien can be used to compel the payment of an assessment or other special charge as well. A *mechanic's lien* represents an effort to recover payment for work performed. In all these ways, a person or an entity can use another's property to ensure payment for work performed, services rendered or debts incurred.

> All liens are encumbrances, but not all encumbrances are liens.

A lien represents only an interest in property; it does not constitute actual ownership of the property. It is an *encumbrance* on the owner's title. An encumbrance is any charge or claim that attaches to real property and lessens its value or impairs its use. An encumbrance does not necessarily prevent the transfer or conveyance of the property, but it conveys along with it. Liens differ from other encumbrances, however, because they are financial or monetary in nature and attach to the property because of a debt. Other encumbrances may be physical in nature (such as the easements and encroachments discussed in Chapter 7).

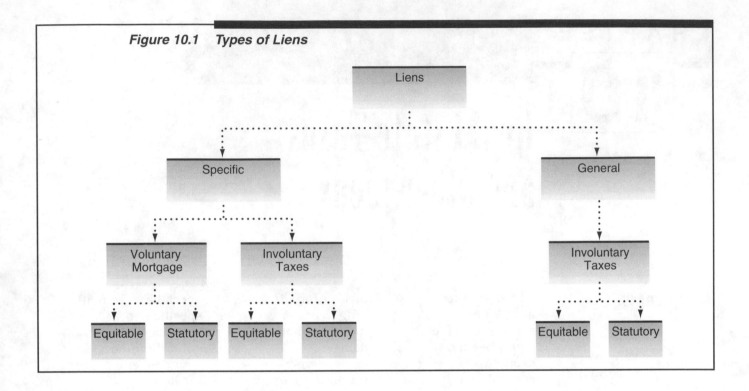

Figure 10.1 Types of Liens

Generally, a lienholder must institute a legal action to force the sale of the property or acquire title. The debt is then paid out of the proceeds of the sale.

There are many different types of liens. (See Figure 10.1.) One way liens are classified is by how they are created. A **voluntary lien** is created intentionally by the property owner's action, such as when someone takes out a mortgage loan. An **involuntary lien,** on the other hand, is not a matter of choice: it is created by law. It may be either statutory or equitable. A **statutory lien** is created by statute. A real estate tax lien, for example, is an involuntary, statutory lien. It is created by statute without any action by the property owner. An **equitable lien** is created when parties agree in writing that a certain property will be held as security for a debt or other obligation. A **judgment lien** applies to all the real and personal property of a debtor, and is created by a court to ensure the payment of a judgment.

Liens also may be classified according to the type of property involved. **General liens** affect all the property, both real and personal, of a debtor. This includes judgments, estate and inheritance taxes, decedent's debts, corporate franchise taxes and Internal Revenue Service taxes. A lien on real estate differs from a lien on personal property, however. A lien attaches to real property *at the moment it is filed.* In contrast, a lien does not attach to personal property until the personal property actually is levied on or seized by the sheriff. **Specific liens** are secured by specific property and affect only that particular property. Specific liens on real estate include mechanics' liens, mortgage liens, real estate tax liens and liens for special assessments and utilities. (Specific liens can also secure personal property, as when a lien is placed on a car to secure payment of a car loan.)

> **MEMORY TIP**
>
> The four ways of creating a lien may be remembered by the acronym **VISE:** *Voluntary, Involuntary, Statutory* and *Equitable.*

Effects of Liens on Title

The existence of a lien does not necessarily prevent a property owner from conveying title to someone else. The lien might reduce the value of the title holder's equity in the real estate, however, because few buyers will take on the risk of a burdened property. Because the lien attaches to the property, not the property owner, a new owner could lose the property if the creditors take court action to enforce payment. Once properly established, a lien runs with the land and will bind all successive owners until the lien is cleared. Future resales could also be jeopardized if the debt is not satisfied.

 Priority of liens. *Priority of liens* refers to the order in which claims against the property will be satisfied. In general, the rule for priority of liens is "first come, first served" (or, in more legalistic terms, "first in time, first in right"). Liens take priority from the date they are recorded in the public records of the county in which the property is located.

There are some notable exceptions to this rule. For instance, real estate taxes and special assessments generally take priority over all other liens, regardless of the order in which the liens are recorded. This means that outstanding real estate taxes and special assessments are paid from the proceeds of a court-ordered sale first. The remainder of the proceeds is used to pay other outstanding liens in the order of their priority. Mechanics' liens take priority as provided by state law but never over tax and special assessment liens.

FOR EXAMPLE Mottley Mansion is ordered sold by the court to satisfy Barry's debts. The property is subject to a $50,000 judgment lien, incurred as a result of a suit to recover a mechanic's lien. $295,000 in interest and principal remains to be paid on Mottley Mansion's mortgage. This year's unpaid real estate taxes amount to $5,000. The judgment lien was entered in the public record on February 7, 1998, and the mortgage lien was recorded January 22, 1996. If Mottley Mansion is sold at the tax sale for $375,000, the proceeds of the sale will be distributed in the following order:

1. $5,000 to the taxing bodies for this year's real estate taxes
2. $295,000 to the mortgage lender (the entire amount of the mortgage loan outstanding as of the date of sale)
3. $50,000 to the creditor named in the judgment lien
4. $25,000 to Barry (the proceeds remaining after paying the first three items)

However, if Mottley Mansion sold for $325,000, the proceeds would be distributed as follows:

1. $5,000 to the taxing bodies for this year's real estate taxes
2. $295,000 to the mortgage lender (the entire amount of the mortgage loan outstanding as of the date of sale)
3. $25,000 to the creditor named in the judgment lien
4. $0 to Barry

Although the creditor is not repaid in full, this outcome is considered fair for two reasons:

1. The creditor's interest arose later than the others, so the others' interests took priority.
2. The creditor knew (or should have known) about the creditors ahead of it when it extended credit to Barry, so it was aware (or should have been aware) of the risk involved.

Subordination agreements are written agreements between lienholders to change the priority of mortgage, judgment and other liens. Under a subordination agreement, the holder of a superior or prior lien agrees to permit a junior lienholder's interest to move ahead of his or her lien. Priority and recording of liens are discussed further in Chapter 15. For now, just keep in mind that the priority of liens is generally determined by the order in which they were recorded: the first lien has priority, and subsequent liens are subject to it. That is, junior liens are paid from what's left over after the first lien has been satisfied.

REAL ESTATE TAX LIENS

As discussed previously, the ownership of real estate is subject to certain government powers. One of these is the right of state and local governments to impose (levy) taxes to pay for their functions. Because the location of real estate is permanently fixed, the government can levy taxes with a high degree of certainty that the taxes will be collected. The annual taxes levied on real estate usually have priority over previously recorded liens, so they may be enforced by a court-ordered sale.

There are two types of real estate taxes: *general real estate taxes* (also called *ad valorem taxes*) and *special assessments* (or *improvement taxes*). Both are levied against specific parcels of property and automatically become liens on those properties.

General Tax (Ad Valorem Tax)

The **general real estate tax,** or **ad valorem tax,** is made up of the taxes levied on real estate by various governmental agencies and municipalities. These taxing bodies include

- states;
- counties;
- cities, towns and villages;
- school districts (local elementary and high schools, publicly funded junior colleges and community colleges);
- drainage districts;
- water districts;
- sanitary districts; and
- parks, forest preserves and recreation and other districts.

Ad valorem is Latin for "according to value." Ad valorem taxes are based on the value of the property being taxed. They are specific, involuntary, statutory liens. General real estate taxes are levied to fund the operation of the governmental agency that imposes the taxes.

Exemptions from general taxes.   Most state laws exempt certain real estate from taxation. Such property must be used for tax-exempt purposes, as defined in the statutes. The most common exempt properties are owned by

- various municipal organizations (such as schools, parks and playgrounds),
- cities and counties,
- state and federal governments,
- religious and charitable organizations,
- hospitals, and
- educational institutions.

Many state laws also allow special exemptions to reduce real estate tax bills for certain property owners or land uses. For instance, senior citizens frequently are granted reductions in the assessed values of their homes. Some state and local governments offer real estate tax reductions to attract industries and sports franchises. Many states also offer tax reductions for agricultural land.

In Illinois . . .

Properties in Illinois that are totally exempt from paying general real estate taxes include those used as schools, religious institutions, cemeteries and charitable institutions, as well as those owned by federal, state, county and local governments. Taxing districts may elect to exempt certain other properties (with some limits), such as commercial and industrial properties.

Illinois property taxes are adjusted to reflect certain concessions given on owner-occupied residences. These properties are designated as *homesteads*. The homestead exemption (not to be confused with the homestead *estate*) reduces the assessed value of a property subject to taxes. There are two exemptions. The *Homeowner's Exemption* applies to owners of single-family homes, condominiums, cooperatives and one- to six-unit apartment buildings. Owners must apply to the assessor for the exemption each year. The *Senior Citizen's Homestead Exemption* is available to homeowners over the age of 65. Once an individual has demonstrated that he or she qualifies for this exemption by age and ownership, it is applied automatically as long as he or she owns the property as a primary residence. These exemption amounts are subtracted from the property's equalized assessed value before the tax rate is applied.

THESE TWO EXEMPTION ARE SUBSTRACTED FROM EQUALIZED VALUE

Property owners may qualify for other tax concessions based on their status as disabled veterans or on improvements to the property, certain maintenance and repair expenses, solar heating, airport land, farmland, rehabilitation of historic buildings and location within enterprise zones or tax concession districts. ■

Assessment. Real estate is valued for tax purposes by county or township assessors or appraisers. This official valuation process is called *assessment*. A property's *assessed value* generally is based on the sales prices of comparable properties, although practices may vary. Land values may be assessed separately from buildings or other improvements, and different valuation methods may be used for different types of property. State laws may provide for property to be reassessed periodically.

In Illinois . . .

Counties with populations in excess of one million may divide the county into three geographic areas. Each area will be assessed once every three years, as in Cook County. All assessments are published in full in a newspaper of general circulation serving the area of the property, and a written notice is sent to the taxpayer of record. The assessment official may adjust the assessed value yearly on those parcels whose use has changed during the intervening years.

In all counties except Cook, real property is assessed at 33⅓ percent of fair market value. (Depending on how the property is classified, real property in Cook County is assessed based on a sliding scale of percentages of fair market value, from 16 to 36 percent.) *Real property* is defined by the Illinois Revenue Act as including land, buildings, structures, improvements and any other permanent fixtures *attached to land*. A mobile home, for instance, probably would be considered personal property if it was simply resting on a foundation with its wheels removed; if it was somehow permanently affixed to the foundation, it would be more likely to be considered real property.

Taxpayers who believe that errors were made in their property's assessment may file a complaint directly with the assessment official (in Cook County, the official is called the *county assessor;* in other counties, he or she usually is called the *supervisor of assessments*). If the taxpayer's complaint is denied, the decision may be appealed to an administrative board of review (in Cook County, this body is called the Board of Appeals). Alternatively, the taxpayer can bypass the county official and go directly to the board of review. If the taxpayer is dissatisfied with the board's decision, he or she may file an administrative appeal or request a review of the decision by the circuit court of the county in which the property is located. ■

Equalization. In some jurisdictions, when it is necessary to correct inequalities in statewide tax assessments, an **equalization factor** is used to achieve uniformity. An equalization factor may be applied to raise or lower assessments in a particular district or county. The equalization issue is important to local governments, because state funding of programs (such as aid to education) is often based on the assessed value of local real estate. The assessed value of each property in the area is multiplied by the equalization factor, and the tax rate is then applied to the equalized assessment.

FOR EXAMPLE The assessments in Laslo County are 20 percent lower than the average assessments throughout the rest of the state. This underassessment can be corrected by requiring the application of an equalization factor of 125 percent to each assessment in Laslo County. Therefore, a parcel of land assessed for tax purposes at $98,000 would be taxed on an equalized value of $122,500 ($98,000 × 1.25 = $122,500). $122,500 is 20 percent greater than $98,000 ($122,500 × 20% = $24,500; $98,000 + $24,500 = $122,500).

In Illinois . . .

The assessed valuation of all real estate is adjusted yearly in each county by applying an equalization factor determined by the Property Tax Administration Bureau of the Department of Revenue. Assessed values are compared with selling prices to arrive at an equalization factor, and each county is assigned a multiplier to be used for equalization purposes. The equalizer is applied before any applicable homeowner's exemptions are deducted. ■

Tax rates. The process of arriving at a real estate tax rate begins with the adoption of a *budget* by each taxing district. Each budget covers the financial requirements of the taxing body for the coming fiscal year. The fiscal year may be the January through December calendar year or some other 12-month period designated by statute. The budget must include an estimate of all expenditures for the year. In addition, the budget must indicate the amount of income expected from all fees, revenue sharing and other sources. The net amount remaining to be raised from real estate taxes is then determined by the difference between these figures.

The next step is *appropriation.* Appropriation is the way a taxing body authorizes the expenditure of funds and provides for the sources of the funding. Appropriation generally involves the adoption of an ordinance or the passage of a law that states the specific terms of the proposed taxation.

The amount to be raised from the general real estate tax then is imposed on property owners through a tax levy. A *tax levy* is the formal action taken to impose the tax, usually a vote of the taxing district's governing body.

The *tax rate* for each taxing body is computed separately. To arrive at a tax rate, the total monies needed for the coming fiscal year are divided by the total assessments of all real estate located within the taxing body's jurisdiction.

FOR EXAMPLE A taxing district's budget indicates that $300,000 must be raised from real estate tax revenues. The assessment roll (assessor's record) of all taxable real estate within the district equals $10 million. The tax rate is computed as follows:

$$\$300,000 \div \$10,000,000 = .03, \text{ or } 3\%$$

The tax rate may be stated in a number of ways. In many areas, it is expressed in mills. A **mill** is 1/1,000 of a dollar, or $.001. The tax rate may be expressed as a mill ratio, in dollars per hundred or in dollars per thousand. A tax rate of .03, or 3 percent, could be expressed as 30 mills or $3 per $100 of assessed value or $30 per $1,000 of assessed value.

Tax bills. A property owner's tax bill is computed by applying the tax rate to the assessed valuation of the property.

Generally, one tax bill that incorporates all real estate taxes levied by the various taxing districts is prepared for each property. In some areas, however, separate bills are prepared by each taxing body. Sometimes, the real estate taxing bodies may operate on different budget years so that the taxpayer receives separate bills for various taxes at different times during the year.

In Illinois . . . The county collector prepares and issues only one combined tax bill to each parcel of property. ■

FOR EXAMPLE IIf a property is assessed for tax purposes at $90,000, at a tax rate of 3 percent, or 30 mills, the tax will be $2,700 ($90,000 × .03). If an equalization factor is used, the computation with an equalization factor of 120 percent will be $3,240 ($108,000 × .03 = $3,240)..

In Illinois . . . General real estate taxes are levied annually for the calendar year and become a prior first lien, superior to all other liens, on January 1 of that tax year. However, they are not due and payable until the following year.

General real estate taxes are payable in two equal installments in the year after they are levied: one-half by June 1 and the second half by September 1, except in Cook County as discussed below. These payment dates are called *penalty dates*, after which a 1.5 percent-per-month penalty is added to any unpaid amount. Because bills must be issued 30 days prior to a penalty date, the penalty date for an installment may be delayed if the county collector is late in preparing the bills.

Penalty dates of March 1 and August 1 have been authorized for Cook County taxes under an accelerated billing procedure. With this accelerated procedure, the billing for the installment due March 1 is sent before the actual tax has been determined. The amount of this first accelerated installment is one-half the amount of the tax bill for the previous year. The second installment then is billed after the tax has been determined and is for the actual tax less the amount billed as the first installment. ∎

Enforcement of tax liens. Real estate taxes must be valid to be enforceable. That means they must be levied properly, must be used for a legal purpose and must be applied equitably to all property. Real estate taxes that have remained delinquent for the statutory period can be collected through a **tax sale.**

In Illinois . . .

The statutory requirements for enforcement of tax liens are complex. When a property owner fails to pay taxes on real estate in this state, the property ultimately may be sold in one of three ways:

1. At an *annual tax sale*
2. At a *forfeiture sale*
3. At a *scavenger sale*

Annual sale. If the taxes on a property have not been paid by the due date of the second installment, the county collector can enforce the tax lien and request that the circuit court order a tax sale. The county has strict notification requirements, which are prescribed by statute. These requirements include publication in a newspaper of general circulation within the community and a certified or registered mailing to the last known address of the taxpayer. The court will render judgment in favor of the county if the taxes are shown to be delinquent and proper notice has been given. *The court order allows only the sale of the tax lien, not the property itself.*

Prior to the time of sale, the owner and any other party with a legal interest (except undisclosed beneficiaries of a land trust) may redeem the property and stop the sale by paying the delinquent taxes, interest and publication costs. Successful purchasers at the sale are those who offer to pay all outstanding taxes, interest, publication costs, processing charges and the county treasurer's indemnity fund fee.

If competitive bidding results, the bid is for the rate of interest that will be accepted by the bidder in case of redemption during the first six months of the redemption period. The only persons not allowed to bid at the sale are owners, persons with legal interest and/or their agents. The successful bidder must pay with cash, cashier's check or certified check. Upon payment, the purchaser receives a *certificate of purchase*. The certificate will ripen into a *tax deed* if no redemption is made within the statutorily prescribed period.

The statutory time period allowed for redemption is two years. If the property is not redeemed by the owner within the period allowed, the tax sale purchaser is required to give notice to the delinquent owner and other parties who hold any interest in the property before applying for a tax deed. A tax deed must be recorded within one year after the expiration of the redemption period, or it becomes null and void.

Forfeiture sale. If there are no bids on a property at the annual tax sale, the property is forfeited to the state, although title does not really change. The owner may redeem the property any time after forfeiture by paying delinquencies, publication costs and interest. On the other hand, anyone who wants to purchase the property for the outstanding taxes may make application to the county. If the owner does not claim the property within 30 days of notification, the applicant will be issued a certificate of purchase once he or she pays the outstanding taxes, interest and other fees. If redemption is made, the owner of the certificate will automatically receive 12 percent interest for each six-month period.

Scavenger sale. If the taxes have not been paid on a property for two years or more, the property may be sold at a *scavenger sale.* The county must go through the same court process as it would for tax sales and receive an order of sale. The successful bidder at these sales is the one who is willing to pay the highest cash price for the property. The buyer is not required to pay the tax lien but must pay current taxes. Former owners may not bid on their delinquent properties, either in person or through an agent, nor may people who own property that is two or more years delinquent.

Redemption rights apply, except that the redemption period for vacant non-farm real estate, commercial or industrial property or property improved with seven or more residential units is only six months. If redemption is made, all past-due taxes plus interest and penalties must be paid by the redeemer. In addition, the owner of the certificate of purchase must be paid back his or her bid price plus interest.

Cook County generally holds scavenger sales. Other counties, such as Kane and Du Page, redeem the properties and sell them to return them to the tax rolls. ■

Special Assessments (Improvement Taxes)

Special assessments are taxes levied on real estate to fund public improvements to the property. Property owners in the area of the improvements are required to pay for them because their properties benefit directly from the improvements. For example, the installation of paved streets, curbs, gutters, sidewalks, storm sewers or street lighting increases the values of the affected properties. The owners, in effect, reimburse the levying authority. However, dollar-for-dollar increases in value are rarely the result.

Special assessments are always specific and statutory, but they can be either involuntary or voluntary liens. Improvements initiated by a public agency create involuntary liens. However, when property owners petition the local government to install a public improvement for which the owners agree to pay (such as a sidewalk or paved alley), the assessment lien is voluntary.

Whether the lien is voluntary or involuntary, each property in the improvement district is charged a prorated share of the total amount of the assessment. The share is determined either on a fractional basis (four houses may equally share the cost of one streetlight) or on a cost-per-front-foot basis (wider lots incur a greater cost than narrower lots for street paving and curb and sidewalk installation).

Special assessments generally are paid in equal annual installments over a period of years. The first installment usually is due during the year following the public authority's approval of the assessment. The first bill includes one year's interest on the property owner's share of the entire assessment. Subsequent bills include one year's interest on the unpaid balance. Property owners have the right to prepay any or all installments to avoid future interest charges.

Strict subdivision regulations have almost eliminated special assessments in some parts of the country. Most items for which assessments traditionally have been levied are now required to be installed as a condition of a subdivision's approval.

In Illinois . . .

Special assessments usually are due in equal annual installments over a period of five to ten years, with the first installment usually due during the year following the public authority's approval of the assessment. The first bill includes one year's interest on the property owner's share of the entire assessment; subsequent bills include one year's interest on the unpaid balance. Property owners have the right to prepay any or all installments to avoid future interest charges. The annual due date for assessment payments in Illinois is generally January 1. ■

OTHER LIENS ON REAL PROPERTY

In addition to real estate tax and special assessment liens, a variety of other liens may be charged against real property.

Mortgage Liens (Deed of Trust Liens)

A **mortgage lien,** or a deed of trust lien, is a voluntary lien on real estate given to a lender by a borrower as security for a real estate loan. It becomes a lien on real property when the lender records the documents in the county where the property is located. Lenders generally require a preferred lien, referred to as a *first mortgage lien.* This means that no other liens against the property (aside from real estate taxes) would take priority over the mortgage lien. Subsequent liens are referred to as *junior liens.*

Mechanics' Liens

A **mechanic's lien** is a specific, involuntary lien that gives security to persons or companies that perform labor or furnish material to improve real property. A mechanic's lien is available to contractors, subcontractors, architects, equipment lessors, surveyors, laborers and other providers. This type of lien is filed when the owner has not fully paid for the work or when the general contractor has been compensated but has not paid the subcontractors or suppliers of materials. However, statutes in some states prohibit subcontractors from placing liens directly on certain types of property, such as owner-occupied residences. The basic theory underlying mechanics' liens is that the lien is on the value added to the property by the lienholder's labor.

In Illinois . . .

To be entitled to a mechanic's lien, the person who did the work must have had a contract (express or implied) with the owner or the owner's authorized representative. If improvements that were not ordered by the property owner have commenced, the property owner should execute a document called a *notice of nonresponsibility* to relieve himself or herself from possible mechanics' liens. By posting this notice in some conspicuous place on the property and recording a verified copy of it in the public record, the owner gives notice that he or she is not responsible for the work done.

In Illinois, contractors whose bills have not been paid and who wish to enforce their lien rights against a lender, other lienholders and any subsequent purchasers must file their lien notices within four months after the work is completed. Subcontractors working on a large construction job must file within four months after completion of their particular work. Subcontractors have the right in Illinois to file for their unpaid claim, even when the general contractor has been paid in full.

In Illinois, property managers are allowed to place a mechanic's lien on the client-owner's property to ensure payment of a commission.

Priority.   In Illinois, mechanics' liens can take priority over a previously recorded lien if the work done has enhanced the value of the property. *The lien attaches as of the date when the work was ordered or the contract was signed by the owner.* The date of attachment establishes the lien's priority over other liens. From the point of view of the public or a prospective purchaser, an unpaid contractor has a "secret lien" until the notice is recorded. A prospective purchaser of property that has been recently constructed, altered or repaired should therefore be cautious about possible unrecorded mechanics' liens against the property.

Waiver and disclaimer.   The names of all subcontractors must be listed by the general contractor in a sworn statement, which is presented to the landowner who ordered the work. *Waivers of Lien* should be collected by the landowner from each contractor, subcontractor, materials supplier and property manager as each payment is made. This creates a continuing record that all lien claimants have released their lien rights.

Expiration.   In Illinois, the contractor's lien right will expire two years after completion of that contractor's work, unless he or she files suit within that time to foreclose the lien. This suit can force the sale of the real estate through a court order to provide funds to pay the claimant's lien.   ■

Judgments   A **judgment** is an order issued by a court that finally settles and defines the rights and obligations of the parties to a lawsuit. When the judgment establishes the amount a debtor owes and provides for money to be awarded, it is referred to as a *money judgment.*

A judgment is a *general, involuntary, equitable lien* on both real and personal property owned by the debtor. A judgment is not the same as a mortgage because no specific parcel of real estate was given as security at the time the debt was created. A lien usually covers only property located within the county in which the judgment is issued. As a result, a notice of the lien must be filed in any county to which a creditor wishes to extend the lien coverage.

In Illinois . . .

A judgment becomes a general lien on all of the defendant's real and personal property in a county at the time the judgment is recorded in the county recorder's office. For the lien to be effective in another county, a memorandum of judgment must be recorded in that county.

Judgment liens are effective in Illinois for seven years and may be renewed for another seven-year term.

To enforce a judgment, the creditor must obtain a *writ of execution* from the court. A writ of execution directs the sheriff to seize and sell as much of the debtor's property as is necessary to pay both the debt and the expenses of the sale. A judgment does not become a lien against the personal property of a debtor until the creditor orders the sheriff to levy on the property and the levy actually is made. When property is sold, the debtor should demand a *satisfaction of judgment* (or *satisfaction piece*) to clear the record. ■

Lis pendens. There is often a considerable delay between the time a lawsuit is filed and the time final judgment is rendered. When any suit is filed that affects title to real estate, a special notice, known as a **lis pendens** (Latin for "litigation pending") is recorded. A lis pendens is not itself a lien, but rather notice of a possible future lien. Recording a lis pendens notifies prospective purchasers and lenders that there is a potential claim against the property. It also establishes a priority for the later lien: the lien is backdated to the recording date of the lis pendens.

Attachments. Special rules apply to realty that is not mortgaged or similarly encumbered. To prevent a debtor from conveying title to such previously unsecured real estate while a court suit is being decided, a creditor may seek a writ of **attachment.** By this writ, the court retains custody of the property until the suit concludes. First, the creditor must post a surety bond or deposit with the court. The bond must be sufficient to cover any possible loss or damage the debtor may suffer while the court has custody of the property. In the event the judgment is not awarded to the creditor, the debtor will be reimbursed from the bond.

Estate and Inheritance Tax Liens

Federal **estate taxes** and state **inheritance taxes** (as well as the debts of decedents) are *general, statutory, involuntary liens* that encumber a deceased person's real and personal property. These are normally paid or cleared in probate court proceedings.

Liens for Municipal Utilities

Municipalities often have the right to impose a *specific, equitable, involuntary lien* on the property of an owner who refuses to pay bills for municipal utility services.

Bail Bond Lien

A real estate owner who is charged with a crime for which he or she must face trial may post bail in the form of real estate rather than cash. The execution and recording of such a bail bond creates a *specific, statutory, voluntary lien* against the owner's real estate. If the accused fails to appear in court, the lien may be enforced by the sheriff or another court officer.

Corporation Franchise Tax Lien

State governments generally levy a corporation franchise tax on corporations as a condition of allowing them to do business in the state. Such a tax is a *general, statutory, involuntary lien* on all real and personal property owned by the corporation.

IRS Tax Lien

A federal **tax lien,** or Internal Revenue Service (IRS) tax lien, results from a person's failure to pay any portion of federal taxes, such as income and withholding taxes. A federal tax lien is a *general, statutory, involuntary lien* on all real and personal property held by the delinquent taxpayer. Its priority, however, is based on the date of filing or recording; it does not supersede previously recorded liens.

A summary of the real estate–related liens discussed in this chapter appears in Table 10.1.

In Illinois . . .

The *Commercial Real Estate Broker Lien Act* permits *commercial* brokers to place a lien on property in the amount of the commission they are entitled to receive for leasing as well as for sales under a written listing agreement in the event they are not paid for their services. The lien applies to commercial property only, and must be recorded to be enforceable. ■

SUMMARY

Liens are claims of creditors or taxing authorities against the real and personal property of a debtor. A lien is a type of encumbrance. Liens are either general, covering all real and personal property of a debtor-owner, or specific, covering only identified property. They also are either voluntary, arising from an action of the debtor, or involuntary, created by statute (statutory) or based on the concept of fairness (equitable).

With the exception of real estate tax liens and mechanics' liens, the priority of liens generally is determined by the order in which they are placed in the public record of the county in which the property is located.

Real estate taxes are levied annually by local taxing authorities and are generally given priority over other liens. Payments are required before stated dates, after which penalties accrue. An owner may lose title to property for nonpayment of taxes because such tax-delinquent property can be sold at a tax sale. Some states allow a time period during which a defaulted owner can redeem his or her real estate from a tax sale.

Special assessments are levied to allocate the cost of public improvements to the specific parcels of real estate that benefit from them. Assessments usually are payable annually over a five- or ten-year period, together with interest due on the balance of the assessment.

Mortgage liens (deed of trust liens) are voluntary, specific liens given to lenders to secure payment for real estate loans.

Mechanics' liens protect general contractors, subcontractors, property managers and material suppliers whose work enhances the value of real estate.

A judgment is a court decree obtained by a creditor, usually for a monetary award from a debtor. A judgment lien can be enforced by court issuance of a writ of execution and sale by the sheriff to pay the judgment amount and costs.

Attachment is a means of preventing a defendant from conveying property before completion of a suit in which a judgment is sought.

Lis pendens is a recorded notice of a lawsuit that is pending in court and that may result in a judgment affecting title to a parcel of real estate.

Federal estate taxes and state inheritance taxes are general liens against a deceased owner's property.

Liens for water charges or other municipal utilities and bail bond liens are specific liens, while corporation franchise tax liens are general liens against a corporation's assets.

IRS tax liens are general liens against the property of a person who is delinquent in paying IRS taxes.

	General	Specific	Voluntary		Involuntary
Table 10.1 Real Estate Related Liens					
General Real Estate Tax (Ad Valorem Tax) Lien		xx			xx
Special Assessment (Improvement Tax) Lien		xx	xx	or	xx
Mortgage Lien		xx	xx		
Deed of Trust Lien		xx	xx		
Mechanic's Lien		xx			xx
Judgment Lien	xx				xx
Estate Tax Lien	xx				xx
Inheritance Tax Lien	xx				xx
Debts of a Decedent	xx				xx
Municipal Utilities Lien		xx			xx
Bail Bond Lien		xx	xx		
Corporation Franchise Tax Lien	xx				xx
Income Tax Lien					xx

In Illinois . . .

The homeowner's exemption is an annual concession that reduces the assessed value of a property. A senior citizen's homestead exemption is available to a homeowner over age 65.

General real estate taxes are payable in two equal installments in the year after they are levied.

When a property owner fails to pay taxes on his or her real estate, the property may be sold at an annual tax sale, a forfeiture sale or a scavenger sale.

A judgment becomes a lien on all the defendant's real and personal property in a county at the time the judgment is recorded. ■

QUESTIONS

1. Warren was sued and found guilty in a court of law. A judgment was placed against all real and personal property that he owned. This is an example of which of the following types of liens?
   A. Specific
   B. Voluntary
   C. Involuntary
   D. General

2. Priority of liens refers to which of the following?
   A. Order in which a debtor assumes responsibility for payment of obligations
   B. Order in which liens will be paid if property is sold to satisfy a debt
   C. Dates liens are filed for record
   D. Fact that specific liens have greater priority than general liens

3. Joyce purchased a house that was 50 years old. When it rained, the old sewer system could not handle the flow of water, and it caused water to back up in the homes on the street. The city decided to put new lines down the street. The property owners will have to pay a(n):
   A. mechanic's lien.
   B. special assessment.
   C. ad valorem.
   D. utility lien.

4. Which of the following would be classified as a general lien?
   A. Mechanic's lien
   B. Bail bond lien
   C. Judgment
   D. Real estate taxes

5. Which of the following liens would usually be given highest priority?
   A. Mortgage dated last year
   B. Real estate taxes due
   C. Mechanic's lien for work started before the mortgage was made
   D. Judgment rendered yesterday

6. A specific parcel of real estate has a market value of $80,000 and is assessed for tax purposes at 35 percent of market value. The tax rate for the county in which the property is located is 30 mills. The tax bill will be:
   A. $50.   C. $720.
   B. $60.   D. $840.

7. Taxes generally are used to distribute the cost of public services among all taxpayers. Which of the following taxes would target homeowners in particular?
   A. Personal property tax
   B. Sales tax
   C. Real property tax
   D. Luxury tax

8. A home owner decided to add a family room onto his house. An electrician was hired to wire the room and has not been paid. The electrician would have the right to:
   A. tear out his or her work.
   B. record a notice of the lien.
   C. record a notice of the lien and file a court suit within the time required by state law.
   D. have personal property of the owner sold to satisfy the lien.

9. What is the annual real estate tax on a property valued at $135,000 and assessed for tax purposes at $47,250, with an equalization factor of 125 percent, when the tax rate is 25 mills?
   A. $945   C. $1,418
   B. $1,181   D. $1,477

10. Which of the following is a voluntary, specific lien?
    A. IRS tax lien
    B. Mechanic's lien
    C. Mortgage lien
    D. Special assessment

11. In two weeks, a general contractor will file a suit against a homeowner for nonpayment. The contractor just learned that the homeowner has listed the property for sale with a real estate broker. In this situation, which of the following will the contractor's attorney use to protect the contractor's interest?
    A. Seller's lien   C. Assessment
    B. Buyer's lien   D. Lis pendens

12. Which of the following statements BEST describes special assessment liens?
    A. They are general liens.
    B. They are paid on a monthly basis.
    C. They take priority over mechanics' liens.
    D. They cannot be prepaid in full without penalty.

13. Which of the following is a lien on real estate?
    A. Easement running with the land
    B. Unpaid mortgage loan
    C. License
    D. Encroachment

14. Which of the following statements is true of both a mortgage lien and a judgment lien?
    A. They must be entered by the court.
    B. They involve a debtor-creditor relationship.
    C. They are general liens.
    D. They are involuntary liens.

15. A mechanic's lien would be available to all of the following EXCEPT a:
    A. subcontractor.
    B. contractor.
    C. surveyor.
    D. broker.

16. Which of the following is a specific, involuntary, statutory lien?
    A. Real estate tax lien
    B. Income tax lien
    C. Estate tax lien
    D. Judgment lien

17. General real estate taxes levied for the operation of the government are called:
    A. assessment taxes.
    B. ad valorem taxes.
    C. special taxes.
    D. improvement taxes.

18. All of the following probably would be exempt from real estate taxes EXCEPT a(n):
    A. public hospital.
    B. golf course operated by the park district.
    C. community church.
    D. apartment building.

In Illinois . . .

19. In Illinois, a broker's lien would be available to which of the following?
    A. A commercial or residential real estate broker
    B. Any licensed broker or salesperson dealing with residential property valued at more than $50,000
    C. A real estate broker seeking to recover a commission under a written or oral listing agreement
    D. A commercial real estate broker dealing with commercial property

20. The equalization factor used in Illinois taxation is designed to:
    A. increase the tax revenues of the state.
    B. correct discrepancies between the assessed values of similar parcels of land in various counties.
    C. correct inequities in taxes for senior citizens and disabled persons.
    D. decrease taxes for the poor and unemployed.

21. Homeowner Nancy contracted with the Belding Construction Company to add a bedroom to her house on June 17. The job was completed on August 28, but Nancy still had not paid for the work by November 28. The Belding Company records a mechanic's lien against the property. When does this lien take effect?
    A. As of June 17
    B. As of August 28
    C. As of November 28
    D. Four months after the contract date

22. Brett owns a condominium town house in Cook County and a weekend retreat in Sangamon County, Illinois. Brett also owns investment property in Montana. If one of his creditors sues him in a Cook County court and a judgment is issued against him and is recorded in Cook County, which of the following is true?
    A. The judgment becomes a lien on the town house, Brett's two cars and other items of personal property in Cook County.
    B. The judgment becomes a lien on the weekend retreat, Brett's speedboat and all other items of real and personal property in Sangamon and Cook counties.
    C. The judgment becomes a lien on all of Brett's real and personal property, wherever located.
    D. The judgment becomes a lien on the Cook County town house only.

23. Which of the following statements is true of the successful bidder on property offered at an annual tax sale?
    A. He or she owns the property after paying the outstanding taxes.
    B. He or she bids the highest percentage of interest he or she will accept if the property is redeemed.
    C. He or she may obtain a tax deed if the property is not redeemed within the redemption period.
    D. He or she receives a tax deed at the time of the sale.

24. With an accelerated billing procedure, such as that used in Cook County, the first installment of the tax bill:
    A. is one half of the previous year's bill.
    B. is due on April 1.
    C. includes special assessments for the current year.
    D. is billed after the actual amount of the current year's tax is determined.

25. The Valmonts own a home valued at $80,000 that is assessed for tax purposes at 33⅓ percent of market value. The equalization factor for the county in which the residence is located is 0.9500, and the tax rate is $6 per $100. The first half of the Valmonts' real estate tax would be:
    A. $752.40   C. $1,518.
    B. $841.   D. $1,682.

26. Branham owns a primary residence and two apartment buildings. He pays property taxes on two of the three properties. The delinquent taxes will result in a lien on:
    A. all three properties.
    B. all real and personal property that he owns.
    C. his primary residence only.
    D. the property on which he has not paid the taxes.

CHAPTER 11

Real Estate Contracts

KEY TERMS

assignment
bilateral contract
breach of contract
commingling
consideration
contingencies
contract
conversion
counteroffer
earnest money

equitable title
executed contract
executory contract
express contract
implied contract
installment contract
land contract
liquidated damages
novation
offer and acceptance

option
statute of frauds
suit for specific
    performance
time is of the essence
unenforceable
unilateral contract
valid
void
voidable

WHAT IS A CONTRACT?

> A **contract** is a voluntary, legally enforceable promise between two competent parties to perform some legal act in exchange for consideration.

A **contract** is a voluntary agreement or promise between legally competent parties, supported by legal consideration, to perform (or refrain from performing) some legal act. That definition may be easier to understand if we consider its various parts separately. A contract must be

- *voluntary*—no one may be forced into a contract;
- *an agreement or a promise*—a contract is essentially a legally enforceable promise;
- made by *legally competent parties*—the parties must be viewed by the law as capable of making a legally binding promise;
- supported by *legal consideration*—a contract must be supported by some valuable thing that induces a party to enter into the contract, and that "thing" must be legally sufficient to support a contract; and
- about a *legal act*—no one may make a legal contract to do something illegal.

Essentially, a contract is a *legally enforceable promise*—a promise that someone may be compelled by a court to keep. Brokers and salespersons use many types of contracts and agreements to carry out their responsibilities to sellers, buyers and the general public. The general body of law that governs such agreements is known as *contract law.*

Express and Implied Contracts

*STATUTE OF FRAUD
DUE Contract shoud
VL WRITING
ORAL OPEN LISTING ARE
ENFORCEABLE*

A contract may be *express* or *implied*, depending on how it is created. An **express contract** exists when the parties state the terms and show their intentions in *words*. An express contract may be either oral or written. Under the **statute of frauds,** *certain types of contracts (including those for the sale of real property) must be in writing to be enforceable in a court of law.* (Enforceable means that the parties may be forced to comply with the contract's terms and conditions.) In an **implied contract,** the agreement of the parties is demonstrated by their *acts and conduct*.

In Illinois . . .

The Illinois Statute of Frauds requires that contracts for the sale of land and leases that will not be fulfilled within one year from the date they are entered into must be in writing to be enforceable in court. All written contracts in Illinois must be signed either by the parties to be bound by the contract's terms or by some other person the parties have authorized to sign on their behalf. Two exceptions to this exist: oral open listings and oral leases of one year or less can be enforced. ■

FOR EXAMPLE Henry approaches his neighbor, Beatrice, and says, "I will paint your house today for $50." Beatrice replies, "If you paint my house today, I will pay you $50." Henry and Beatrice have entered into an express contract. Ken goes into a restaurant and orders a meal. Ken has entered into an implied contract with the restaurant to pay for the meal, even though payment was not mentioned before the meal was ordered.

ARE LEAC OR SPEAS OR ON Exclusive Contr LISTING

Bilateral and Unilateral Contracts

Contracts may be classified as either *bilateral* or *unilateral*. In a **bilateral contract,** both parties promise to do something; one promise is given in exchange for another. A real estate sales contract is a bilateral contract because the seller promises to sell a parcel of real estate and convey title to the property to the buyer, who promises to pay a certain sum of money for the property.

OPEN LISTing   OPEN Contract

> *Bi-* means "two"—a *bilateral contract* must have two promises. *Uni-* means "one"—a *unilateral contract* has only one promise.

A unilateral contract, on the other hand, is a one-sided agreement. One party makes a promise to induce a second party to do something. The second party is not legally obligated to act. However, if the second party does comply, the first party is obligated to keep the promise. For instance, a law enforcement agency might offer a monetary payment to anyone who can aid in the capture of a criminal. Only if someone does aid in the capture is the reward paid. An option contract, which will be discussed later, is another example of a unilateral contract.

FOR EXAMPLE Beatrice puts up a sign that says, "If you paint my house today, I will pay you $50." If Henry paints Beatrice's house, Beatrice will be legally obligated to pay Henry. Beatrice and Henry have a unilateral contract.

Executed and Executory Contracts

not closed yet

AT Closing TABLE

A contract may be classified as either executed or executory, depending on whether the agreement is performed. An **executed contract** is one in which all parties have fulfilled their promises: the contract has been performed. This should not be confused with the word *execute*, which refers to the signing of a contract. An **executory contract** exists when one or both parties still have an act to perform. A sales contract is an executory contract from the time it is signed until closing: ownership has not yet changed hands, and the seller has not received the sales price. At closing, the sales contract is executed.

FND AT Closing TABLe

EXCLUVE Listing are BILATRAM EXEcutory

Essential Elements of a Valid Contract

A contract must meet certain minimum requirements to be considered legally valid. The following are the basic essential elements of a contract.

Offer and acceptance ("Mutual assent"). There must be an offer by one party that is accepted by the other. The person who makes the offer is the *offeror*. The person who accepts the offer is the *offeree*. This requirement also is called *mutual assent*. It means that there must be a *meeting of the minds*, or complete agreement about the purpose and terms of the contract. Courts look to the objective intent of the parties to determine whether they intended to enter into a binding agreement. In cases where the statute of frauds applies, the **offer and acceptance** must be in writing. The wording of the contract must express all the agreed-on terms and must be clearly understood by the parties.

Elements of a contract:

- Offer and acceptance
- Consideration
- Legally competent parties
- Consent

An *offer* is a promise made by one party, requesting something in exchange for that promise. The offer is made with the intention that the offeror will be bound to the terms if the offer is accepted. The terms of the offer must be definite and specific and must be communicated to the offeree.

An *acceptance* is a promise by the offeree to be bound by the exact terms proposed by the offeror. The acceptance must be communicated to the offeror.

Proposing any deviation from the terms of the offer constitutes a rejection of the original offer and becomes a new offer. This is known as a **counteroffer,** and it must be communicated to the original offering party. The counteroffer must be accepted for a contract to exist.

Besides being terminated by a counteroffer, an offer may be terminated by the offeree's outright rejection of it. Alternatively, an offeree may fail to accept the offer before it expires. The offeror may *revoke* the offer at any time before receiving the acceptance. This revocation must be communicated to the offeree by the offeror, either directly or through the parties' agents. The offer also is revoked if the offeree learns of the revocation and observes the offeror acting in a manner that indicates that the offer no longer exists.

In Practice

The process of negotiating a contract may be easy or difficult. In either case, once the seller has held a property out for sale, the negotiation process usually follows the same basic steps. First, the buyer will make an offer. The seller then has three options: to accept the offer, reject it, or make a counteroffer. If the seller accepts or rejects the offer, the process is over: either there is a contract or there is not. If the seller makes a counteroffer, he or she essentially is starting the process over again, and the buyer now has the same three options. Through this back-and-forth process, the parties hope to come to a meeting of the minds. It's important for the broker to help the parties stay aware of where they are in the negotiating process, to avoid confusion about what offers are (or are not) still in force.

Consideration. The contract must be based on consideration. **Consideration** is something of legal value offered by one party and accepted by another as an inducement to perform or to refrain from some act. There must be a definite statement of consideration in a contract to show that something of value was given (or promised) in exchange for the other party's promise.

Consideration must be "good and valuable" between the parties. The courts do not inquire into the adequacy of consideration. Adequate consideration ranges from as little as a promise of "love and affection" to a substantial sum of money. Anything that has been bargained for and exchanged is legally sufficient to satisfy the requirement for consideration. The only requirements are that the parties agree and that no undue influence or fraud has occurred.

Reality of consent. Under the doctrine of *reality of consent,* a contract must be entered into as the free and voluntary act of each party. Each party must be able to make a prudent and knowledgeable decision without undue influence. A mistake, misrepresentation, fraud, undue influence or duress would deprive a person of that ability. If any of these circumstances is present, the contract is voidable by the injured party. If the other party were to sue for breach, the injured party could use lack of voluntary assent as a defense.

Legally competent parties. All parties to the contract must have legal capacity. That is, they must be of legal age and have enough mental capacity to understand the nature or consequences of their actions in the contract. In most states, 18 is the age of contractual capacity. Under state law, an imprisoned felon or certain mentally ill persons may be legally incompetent to enter into a contract.

In Illinois . . .

Illinois law provides that all persons become of legal age on their 18th birthday. Contracts entered into by a minor in Illinois are voidable until the minor reaches majority and for a reasonable time afterward. *There is no statutory period within which a person may void a contract after reaching majority.* What is considered "reasonable" depends on the circumstances of each case, although the courts tend to allow a maximum of six months.

Contracts made by a minor for what the law terms *necessaries* are generally enforceable. "Necessaries" include items such as food, clothing and shelter. While a real estate sales contract with a minor probably would not be enforceable in Illinois, leases or rental agreements signed by minors generally are enforceable because short-term housing usually is considered a necessity. ■

Validity of Contracts

A contract can be described as *valid, void, voidable* or *unenforceable,* depending on the circumstances.

A contract is **valid** when it meets all the essential elements that make it legally sufficient, or enforceable.

A contract is **void** when it has no legal force or effect because it lacks some or all of the essential elements of a contract.

A contract that is **voidable** appears on the surface to be valid but may be rescinded or disaffirmed by one or both parties based on some legal principle. A voidable contract is considered by the courts to be valid if the party who has the option to disaffirm the agreement does not do so within a period of time prescribed by state law. A contract entered into under duress or as a result of fraud, mistake or misrepresentation is voidable by the compelled or defrauded party. A contract with a minor, for instance, usually is voidable. This is because minors are generally permitted to disaffirm real estate contracts at any time while underage and for a certain period of time after

A contract may be

- **Valid**—has all legal elements; fully enforceable;
- **Void**—lacks one or all legal elements;
- **Voidable**—has all legal elements: may be rescinded or disaffirmed; or
- **Unenforceable**—has all legal elements; enforceable only between the parties.

reaching majority age. A contract entered into by a mentally ill person usually is voidable during the mental illness and for a reasonable period after the person is cured. On the other hand, a contract made by a person who has been adjudicated insane (that is, found to be insane by a court) is void on the theory that the judgment is a matter of public record.

In Practice

Mental capacity to enter into a contract is not the same as medical sanity. The test is whether the individual in question is capable of understanding what he or she is doing. A party may suffer from a mental illness but have a clear understanding of the significance of his or her actions. This is a thorny legal and psychological question that requires consultation with experts.

A contract that is **unenforceable** also seems on the surface to be valid; however, neither party can sue the other to force performance. For example, an oral agreement for the sale of a parcel of real estate would be unenforceable. Because the statute of frauds requires that real estate sales contracts be in writing, the defaulting party could not be taken to court and forced to perform. There is, however, a distinction between a suit to force performance and a suit for damages, which is permissible in an oral agreement. An unenforceable contract is said to be "valid as between the parties." This means that once the agreement is fully executed and both parties are satisfied, neither has reason to initiate a lawsuit to force performance.

In Practice

If a contract contains any ambiguity, the courts generally interpret the agreement against the party who prepared it.

DISCHARGE OF CONTRACTS

A contract is discharged when the agreement is terminated. Obviously, the most desirable case is when a contract terminates because it has been completely performed, with all its terms carried out. However, a contract may be terminated for other reasons, such as a party's breach or default.

Performance of a Contract

Each party has certain rights and duties to fulfill. The question of when a contract must be performed is an important factor. Many contracts call for a specific time by which the agreed-on acts must be completely performed. In addition, many contracts provide that **"time is of the essence."** This means that the contract must be performed within the time limit specified. A party who fails to perform on time is liable for breach of contract.

Assignment = *substitution of parties*

Novation = *substitution of contracts*

When a contract does not specify a date for performance, the acts it requires should be performed within a reasonable time. The interpretation of what constitutes a reasonable time depends on the situation. Generally, unless the parties agree otherwise, if the act can be done immediately, it should be performed immediately. Courts sometimes have declared contracts to be invalid because they did not contain a time or date for performance.

In Illinois . . .

A deed or contract executed on a Sunday or legal holiday is valid and enforceable. However, when the last day on which a deed or contract must be executed is a holiday or a Sunday, the deed or contract may be executed on the next regular business day. ■

Assignment

Assignment is a transfer of rights or duties under a contract. Rights may be assigned to a third party (called the *assignee*) unless the contract forbids it. Obligations also may be assigned (or *delegated*), but the original party remains primarily liable unless specifically released. Many contracts include a clause that either permits or forbids assignment.

Novation

A contract may be performed by **novation**—that is, the substitution of a new contract in place of the original. The new agreement may be between the same parties, or a new party may be substituted for either (this is *novation of the parties*). The parties' intent must be to discharge the old obligation. For instance, when a real estate purchaser assumes the seller's existing mortgage loan, the lender may choose to release the seller and substitute the buyer as the party primarily liable for the mortgage debt.

Breach of Contract

A contract may be terminated if it is *breached* by one of the parties. A **breach of contract** is a violation of any of the terms or conditions of a contract without legal excuse. For instance, a seller who fails to deliver title to the buyer breaches a sales contract. The breaching or defaulting party assumes certain burdens, and the nondefaulting party has certain remedies.

When a contract is signed by both the buyer and the seller, the buyer acquires equitable title. If the seller breaches a real estate sales contract, the buyer can have the seller deliver legal title with a **suit for specific performance** unless the contract specifically states otherwise. In a suit for specific performance, the buyer asks the court to force the seller to go through with the sale and convey the property as previously agreed. The buyer may choose to sue for damages, however, in which case he or she asks that the seller pay for any costs and hardships suffered by the buyer as a result of the seller's breach. Alternatively, the buyer may *rescind,* or cancel, the contract, and the seller must return any earnest money deposit.

If the buyer defaults, the seller can sue for damages or sue for the purchase price. A suit for the purchase price is essentially a suit for specific performance: the seller tenders the deed and asks that the buyer be compelled to pay the agreed price. Or the seller may declare the contract forfeited, in which case the contract usually permits the seller to retain the buyer's earnest money as *liquidated damages.* In addition, the seller may sue for *compensatory damages* if the buyer's breach resulted in further financial losses for the seller.

The contract may limit the remedies available to the parties, however. A *liquidated damages clause* permits the seller to keep the earnest money deposit and any other payments received from the buyer as the seller's sole remedy. The clause may limit the buyer's remedy to a return of the earnest money and other payments should the seller default.

Statute of limitations. The law of every state limits the time within which parties to a contract may bring legal suit to enforce their rights. *The statute of limitations varies for different legal actions.* In Illinois, the statute of limitations for oral contracts is five years; for written contracts, ten years. Any rights not enforced within the applicable time period are lost.

Contracts may also be discharged or terminated when any of the following occurs:

- *Partial performance* of the terms, along with a written acceptance by the other party.
- *Substantial performance*, in which one party has substantially performed on the contract but does not complete all the details exactly as the contract requires. (Such performance may be enough to force payment, with certain adjustments for any damages suffered by the other party.) For instance, where a newly constructed addition to a home is finished except for polishing the brass doorknobs, the contractor is entitled to the final payment.
- *Impossibility of performance*, in which an act required by the contract cannot be legally accomplished.
- *Mutual agreement* of the parties to cancel.
- *Operation of law*—such as in the voiding of a contract by a minor—as a result of fraud, due to the expiration of the statute of limitations or because a contract was altered without the written consent of all parties involved.

CONTRACTS USED IN THE REAL ESTATE BUSINESS

The written agreements most commonly used by brokers and sales-persons are

- listing agreements and buyer agency agreements,
- real estate sales contracts,
- options,
- land contracts or contracts for deed and
- leases and escrow agreements.

Contract forms. Because so many real estate transactions are very similar in nature, preprinted forms are available for most kinds of contracts. The use of preprinted forms raises three problems: (1) what to write in the blanks; (2) what words and phrases should be ruled out by drawing lines through them because they don't apply; and (3) what additional clauses or agreements (called *riders* or *addenda*) should be added. All changes and additions are usually initialed in the margin or on the rider by both parties when a contract is signed.

In Practice   It is essential that both parties to a contract understand exactly what they are agreeing to. Poorly drafted documents, especially those containing extensive legal language, may be subject to various interpretations and lead to litigation. Brokers should inform the parties of their right to have a lawyer review the document. When preprinted forms do not sufficiently address the unique provisions of a transaction, the parties should have an attorney draft appropriate provisions.

In Illinois . . .

The 1966 Illinois Supreme Court decision in the case of *Chicago Bar Association, et al. v. Quinlan and Tyson, Inc.,* placed certain limitations on brokers and salespersons in drafting a contract of sale. The court ruled that brokers and salespersons *who are not lawyers* are authorized *only* to fill in blanks and make appropriate deletions on *printed form contracts that are customarily used in the real estate community.* Real estate sales contracts that fit the "customarily used" requirement typically have been drafted by local bar associations and approved by the local Board of REALTORS®.

A licensee may prepare a preprinted contract to secure the parties' signatures. There are a variety of preprinted forms available that provide blank spaces to be filled in and alternate provisions to be selected or ruled out, depending on the requirements of the transaction. *All insertions and deletions must be based solely on factual information.* Advising a buyer or seller of the legal significance of any part of the contract or suggesting an addition to the form language is prohibited as the unauthorized practice of law: only licensed lawyers are permitted to practice law.

A licensee may not request or encourage a party to sign a contract or document that contains blank spaces to be filled in later, after signing, or make changes to a signed contract without the written consent of the parties. All licensees are required to give each person signing or initialing an original contract a "true copy" of the document within 24 hours of the time of signing.

A licensee also is prevented from preparing or completing any document subsequent to or implementing the sales contract, such as a deed, bill of sale, affidavit of title, note, mortgage or other legal instrument. ■

Listing and Buyer Agency Agreements

Listing and buyer agency agreements are employment contracts. A *listing agreement* establishes the rights and obligations of the broker as agent and the seller as principal. A buyer agency contract establishes the relationship between a buyer as principal and his or her agent.

Customary Terms of Real Estate Sales Contracts

A real estate sales contract contains the complete agreement between a buyer of a parcel of real estate and the seller. Depending on the area, this agreement may be known as an *offer to purchase,* a *contract of purchase and sale,* a *purchase agreement,* an *earnest money agreement* or a *deposit receipt.*

In Illinois . . .

A licensee may not use any form designated "Offer to Purchase" if the form is intended to become a binding real estate contract. Although such forms legally are considered to be only offers until accepted, Illinois law requires that such forms be clearly headed "Real Estate Sales Contract" in bold type. ■

Whatever the contract is called, it is an *offer to purchase* real estate as soon as it has been prepared and signed by the purchaser. If the document is accepted and signed by the seller, it becomes a contract of sale. This transformation is referred to as *ripening.*

The *contract of sale* is the most important document in the sale of real estate. It establishes the legal rights and obligations of the buyer and seller. In effect, it dictates the contents of the deed.

Several details frequently appear in a sales contract in addition to the essential elements of a contract discussed previously. These include

- the sales price and terms;
- a legally acceptable description of the land;
- a statement of the kind and condition of the title and the form of deed to be delivered by the seller;
- the kind of title evidence required, who will provide it and how many defects in the title will be eliminated; and
- a statement of all the terms and conditions of the agreement between the parties, and any contingencies (discussed later in this chapter).

The following paragraphs discuss some of the issues that often arise as an offer to purchase ripens into a contract of sale.

Offer, counteroffer and acceptance. A broker lists an owner's real estate for sale at whatever price and conditions the owner sets. When a prospective buyer is found, the broker helps him or her prepare an offer to purchase. The offer is signed by the prospective buyer and presented by the licensee to the seller.

> A *counteroffer* is a *new offer;* it voids the original offer.

As discussed earlier, any change to the terms proposed by the buyer creates a *counteroffer.* An offer or counteroffer may be revoked at any time before it has been accepted, even if the person making the offer or counteroffer agreed to keep the offer open for a set period of time. (See Figure 11.10)

If the seller agrees to the original offer or a later counteroffer exactly as it was made and signs the document, the offer has been accepted. Acceptance of the offer means that a contract is formed. A duplicate original of the contract must be provided to each party.

An offer is not considered accepted until the person making the offer has been notified of the other party's acceptance. When the parties communicate through an agent or at a distance, questions may arise regarding whether an acceptance, a rejection or a counteroffer has occurred. Current technologies make communication faster: a signed agreement that is faxed, for instance, would constitute adequate communication. The licensee must transmit all offers, acceptances or other responses as soon as possible to avoid questions of proper communication.

Earnest money deposits. It is customary (although not legally required) for a purchaser to provide a deposit when making an offer to purchase real estate. This deposit, usually in the form of a check, is referred to as **earnest money.** The earnest money deposit is evidence of the buyer's intention to carry out the terms of the contract in good faith. The check is given to the broker, who usually holds it for the parties in a special account. In some areas, it is common practice for deposits to be held in escrow by the seller's attorney. If the offer is not accepted, the earnest money deposit is returned immediately to the would-be buyer.

The amount of the deposit is a matter to be agreed on by the parties. Under the terms of most listing agreements, a real estate broker is required to accept a "reasonable amount" as earnest money. As a rule, the deposit should be an amount sufficient to

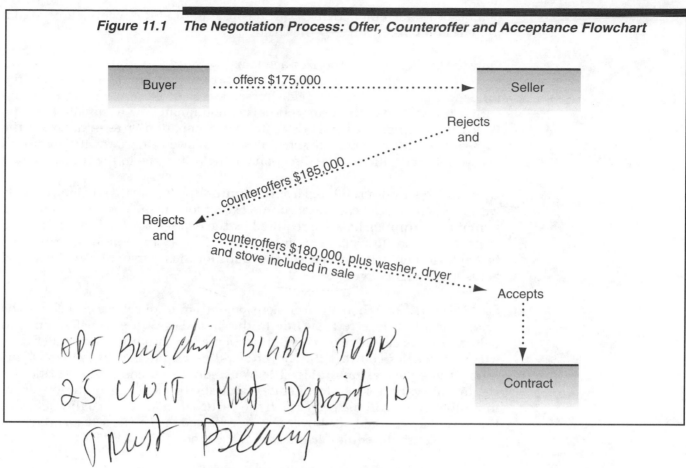

Figure 11.1   The Negotiation Process: Offer, Counteroffer and Acceptance Flowchart

[handwritten notes:] APT Building BIGER THAN 25 UNIT Must Deposit IN Trust BEArIy

- discourage the buyer from defaulting,
- compensate the seller for taking the property off the market and
- cover any expenses the seller might incur if the buyer defaults.

Most contracts provide that the deposit becomes the seller's property as liquidated damages if the buyer defaults. The seller also might claim further damages, however, unless the contract limits recovery to the deposit alone.

In Illinois . . .

[handwritten notes:] BY APT 25 OR BIGAR Should PMLY INTREST ON secuity Deposy

Under the administrative rules established by the Office of Banks and Real Estate (OBRE) for administering the Illinois Real Estate License Act, brokers who are responsible for earnest money deposits in sales and security deposits in leasing must establish special trust (or *escrow*) accounts for the deposit of funds entrusted to them in connection with real estate transactions. A broker need not open a special escrow account for each earnest money deposit received, however, but may deposit all earnest money funds in one account. The rules require that the escrow account be non-interest bearing. There are two exceptions to this: (1) if the parties to the transaction demand in writing that it be placed in an interest-bearing account or (2) if the deposit is required by law to accrue interest. (If interest is paid on the deposit, the disposition of any accrued interest must be designated by the parties in writing.)

Each broker must maintain a complete journal and ledger of all earnest money transactions and notify the OBRE of the name of the federally insured institution where the money is deposited. All funds must be deposited to that account no later than the next business day following the acceptance of the real estate contract. The rules require that brokers make a complete record

[handwritten note:] THE END OF NAXt Busm DAI

of all escrow account activity. Both the account and the records are subject to inspection at any time by the OBRE.

Only the broker or an authorized agent may withdraw funds from the account. Fees and/or commissions earned by the broker that are to be paid from the funds in this account are to be disbursed by the broker from the account no earlier than the day the transaction is consummated or terminated and no later than the next business day after consummation or termination of the transaction. Other payment schedules are allowed, however, if they are in accordance with the written directions of the principals to the transaction.

Brokers are strictly prohibited from **commingling** (or mixing) their own funds with funds in special escrow accounts except for the purpose of maintaining a minimum running balance required by the depository. If a broker uses his or her own funds to avoid incurring service charges, scrupulous records must be kept. Brokers may not use escrow funds for their personal use; this illegal act is known as **conversion.** ■   *THEFT*

Equitable title.   When a buyer signs a contract to purchase real estate, he or she does not receive legal title to the land. Legal title transfers only on delivery and acceptance of a deed. However, after both buyer and seller have executed a sales contract, the buyer acquires an interest in the land. This interest is known as **equitable title.** A person who holds equitable title has rights that vary from state to state. Equitable title may give the buyer an insurable interest in the property. If the parties decide not to go through with the purchase and sale, the buyer may be required to give the seller a quitclaim deed to release the equitable interest in the land.

Destruction of premises.   Under the common law of contracts, the buyer always bore the risk of loss in the event the property was damaged or destroyed prior to closing. A few states still adhere to this common-law principle. The laws and court decisions of most states, however, have placed the risk of loss on the seller. Many of these states have adopted the *Uniform Vendor and Purchaser Risk Act,* which specifically provides that the seller bear any loss that occurs before the title passes or the buyer takes possession.

In Illinois . . . Illinois has adopted the Uniform Vendor and Purchaser Risk Act. If the entire premises or a material part of it is destroyed, the seller cannot enforce the contract against the buyer. Any earnest money must be returned. On the other hand, if title or possession has been transferred to the buyer, he or she must pay the full contract price, even in the event of partially or totally destroyed premises. ■

Liquidated damages.   To avoid a lawsuit if one party breaches the contract, the parties may agree on a certain amount of money that will compensate the nonbreaching party. That money is called **liquidated damages.** If a sales contract specifies that the earnest money deposit is to serve as liquidated damages in case the buyer defaults, the seller will be entitled to keep the deposit if the buyer refuses to perform without good reason. The seller who keeps the deposit as liquidated damages may not sue for any further damages if the contract provides that the deposit is the seller's sole remedy.

In Illinois . . . It is usual to include in the sale of residences some articles of personal property, such as drapes, carpeting and refrigerators, as well as items that are undoubtedly fixtures, such as screens and storm windows. In Illinois, all such fixtures and/or items of personal property are listed specifically in the sales contract. This eliminates possible arguments over which items are to be included and which excluded. Although items of personal property are listed in the sales contract, title to personal property usually is transferred by a *bill of sale.* Real estate contract forms used in Illinois normally provide for the inclusion of personal property. (A typical Illinois residential sales contract is reproduced in Figure 11.2.) ■

Contingencies. Additional conditions that must be satisfied before a sales contract is fully enforceable are called **contingencies.** A contingency includes the following three elements:

1. The actions necessary to satisfy the contingency
2. The time frame within which the actions must be performed
3. Who is responsible for paying any costs involved

The most common contingencies include the following:

- **Mortgage contingency**—A mortgage contingency (sometimes called a financing contingency) protects the buyer's earnest money until a lender commits the mortgage loan funds.
- **Inspection contingency**—A sales contract may be contingent on the buyer's obtaining certain inspections of the property. Inspections may include those for wood-boring insects, lead-based paint, structural and mechanical systems, sewage facilities and radon or other toxic materials.
- **Property sale contingency**—A purchaser may make the sales contract contingent on the sale of his or her current home. This protects the buyer from owning two homes at the same time and also helps ensure the availability of cash for the purchase.

The seller may insist on an escape clause. An escape clause (also called *first right of refusal*) permits the seller to continue to market the property until all the buyer's contingencies have been satisfied or removed. The original buyer should retain the right to eliminate the contingencies if the seller receives a more favorable offer.

Amendments and addendums. An *amendment* is a change to an existing contract. Any time words or provisions are *added to or deleted from the body of the contract,* the contract has been amended. Amendments must be signed or initialed by all parties. For instance, the parties may agree to change a closing date or alter a list of personal property items included in the sale.

On the other hand, an *addendum* is any provision added to an existing contract *without altering the content of the original.* An addendum is essentially a new contract between the parties that includes the original contract's provisions "by reference"; that is, the addendum mentions the original contract. An addendum must be signed by the parties. For example, an addendum might be an agreement to split the cost of repairing certain flaws discovered in a home inspection.

Figure 11.2 **Typical Residential Sales Contract**

MAP MULTIPLE LISTING SERVICE
CONTRACT TO PURCHASE REAL ESTATE

1. **1. PARTIES:** Purchaser _____ agrees to purchase, and
2. Seller, _____ agrees to sell and cause to be conveyed by appropriate deed to Purchaser,
3. the property commonly known as _____
4. **2. PURCHASE PRICE:** The purchase price is $ _____. The payment of the purchase price, including earnest
5. money, subject to applicable prorations, will be paid in cash, cashiers or certified check, or title company check, or mutually agreeable negotiable instrument.
6. **3. EARNEST MONEY:** The Purchaser has paid earnest money in the amount of $ _____ and promises to pay additional earnest money of $_____ on o
7. before _____ 19 _____ . When total earnest money becomes $5,000 or more, such money will be held in an interest bearing account for the
8. benefit of the Parties with interest to be paid to Purchaser. The earnest money and the original of this Contract will be held by the Listing Broker as Escrowee.
9. **4. PERSONAL PROPERTY:** The following is the personal property now located on the premises for which a Bill of Sale is to be given at the closing: (strike inapplicable)

10 Compactor	Dishwasher	Fireplace Screen	Strms/Screens AE	Central Heating &	Built-in or Attd Shelving
11 Disposal	Washer	TV Antenna	Storage Building	Cooling Systems	& Cabinets
12 Built-in Oven/Range	Dryer	Intercom	Gas Grill	Ceiling Fan(s)	Sump Pump(s)
13 Microwave Oven	Water Softener if Owned	Security System	Curtain & Drapery Rods	All Planted Vegetation	Wall-to-Wall & Stair
14 Stove	Humidifier	Smoke Alarm(s)	All Window Treatments &	Electric, Plumbing & Other	Carpeting if any
15 Refrigerator	Electric Air Filter	Electric Garage Door	Coverings, except _____	Attd Fixtures as installed	
16 Central Vacuum	Opener(s) & Transmitter(s)				

17. Other Additions: _____   Exclusions: _____
18. **5. SALE OF EXISTING REAL ESTATE:** (I) This Contract is contingent upon receiving written notice of the occurrence of the following: (strike inapplicable)
19.   A. Execution of a contract for sale of the Purchaser's residence at _____ on or
20. before _____, 19 ____ ; and/or
21.   B. Closing of the sale of the Purchaser's residence at _____ on or before _____ 19 ____ .
22. (II) If the above contingencies have not been met or waived by the Purchaser on or before the specified date, this Contract will become null and void and all earnest money returned
23. to the Purchaser. (III) The parties agree that the Seller's property will remain on the market during the term of each contingency period, and any period allowed for Attorneys' review of
24. this Contract. (IV) In the event Seller accepts another bonafide offer to purchase the subject premises during such period, Seller will notify Purchaser of same upon attorneys approval of
25. said contract. Purchaser will then have _____ hours after Seller gives such notice to waive the above contingencies. If Purchaser does not so waive these contingencies, then this
26. Contract will become null and void, and all earnest money will be returned to the Purchaser.
27. **6. FINANCING:** This Contract is subject to the condition that Purchaser be able to procure on or before _____ 19 ____ an unconditional (except for matters
28. of title or survey) commitment for a _____ type loan to be secured by a mortgage on the real estate in the amount of
29. $ _____, or such lesser amount as Purchaser accepts, with initial interest of not more than _____ % per year plus mortgage insurance,
30. if required, to be amortized over _____ years, with the loan origination and/or service charges to be paid by Purchaser for such loan not to exceed _____ % (including
31. VA funding fees, if any). Purchaser shall make written loan application within 7 business days after acceptance of this Contract. If, after making every reasonable effort, Purchaser
32. is unable to procure such commitment within the time specified herein and so notifies Seller in writing thereof within 3 business days after above date, at Purchaser's option, this
33. Contract will become null and void, and all earnest money will be returned to Purchaser. (IF SELLER IS NOT SO NOTIFIED BY PURCHASER, PURCHASER SHALL BE DEEMED TO HAVE
34. SECURED SUCH COMMITMENT OR AGREED TO PURCHASE THE PROPERTY WITHOUT SUCH MORTGAGE FINANCING.)
35.   Upon Seller receiving notice, however, Purchaser cannot void this Contract, if within 7 calendar days after receipt of Purchaser's notice: (A) Seller grants extension of mortgage
36. commitment date; or (B) Seller notifies Purchaser of their intent to procure for Purchaser such commitment upon the same terms. Purchaser agrees to furnish to Seller and Lender
37. all requested information and will sign all papers necessary to obtain the mortgage commitment and close the loan.
38.   Upon paragraph 5(I)A and/or B being deleted from this Contract or subsequently waived by Purchaser, Purchaser also waives his/her right to cancel this Contract upon receiving a
39. conditional commitment subject to the sale or closing of their residence.
40. **7. TIME AND PLACE OF CLOSING:** (A) Closing or escrow payout will be on _____ , 19 ____ at such time as mutually agreed. Seller will convey by stamped recordable
41. warranty deed (or other appropriate deed if title is vested in trust or in an estate) with release of homestead rights upon payment of the purchase price with appropriate credits
42. for earnest money and other proratable items. (B) This sale will be closed at the title company escrow closing office issuing the owner's title policy situated geographically nearest
43. the property, or the office of the Seller's attorney.
44. **8. POSSESSION:** (check one)
45. _____ Possession will be delivered no later than at closing.
46. _____ Possession will be delivered before 11:59p.m. on _____ , 19 ____ . Seller agrees to pay at closing the sum of $_____ per day to the Purchaser as
47. rent from and including the day after closing to and including the actual date of possession. Seller will deposit in escrow, at closing from the proceeds by separate check, the sum of
48. two percent (2%) of the sale price to guarantee that possession of the property will be delivered to Purchaser on or before the date and time specified in the Contract. If possession
49. is so delivered, the escrow funds will be paid to the Seller. If possession is not so delivered, escrowee will pay to the Purchaser from the escrow funds the sum of 1/15th of the deposit
50. per day for each day possession is withheld from Purchaser after such specified date and time, and will pay the balance of the escrow fund, if any, to the Seller. In the event
51. that possession is not delivered to Purchaser within fifteen (15) days of the date specified herein, Seller shall continue to be liable to Purchaser for a sum of money equal to 1/15th of the
52. possession escrow sum specified herein for each day possession is so withheld from Purchaser, without prejudice to any other rights or remedies to Purchaser. The possession escrow
53. shall also guarantee condition of the property through the date the possession is given.
54.   For purpose of this Contract, possession shall be deemed to have been delivered when the Seller has vacated the premises and delivered the keys to the premises to the Purchaser
55. or to the office of the Listing Broker.
56. **9. PRORATIONS:** (A) Real estate taxes based upon 105% of the most recent real estate yearly tax bill, rents, association dues, accrued interest on mortgage indebtedness for
57. mortgages, which are being assumed, and other proratable items will be prorated to the date of the actual closing. If the current real estate taxes are based on the fact that the Seller
58. qualified for a Homeowners Exemption, Seller agrees that he/she has or will have executed all documents prior to or at the closing necessary to preserve said exemption. Seller is
59. responsible for full payment of any special assessments currently outstanding against the property, except _____ . (B) If applicable, Seller
60. represents that as of the date of acceptance hereof the monthly association dues pertaining to the property are approximately $_____ .
61. Seller will provide to Purchaser, prior to closing if requested, copies of all homeowner association rules and regulations.
62. **10. BROKERAGE FEE AND AGENCY DISCLOSURE:** THE PARTIES TO THIS CONTRACT ACKNOWLEDGE AND UNDERSTAND THAT UNLESS OTHERWISE DISCLOSED IN WRITING, THE
63. LICENSEES WORKING WITH EACH PARTY, ARE THE AGENTS OF THEIR RESPECTIVE PARTIES. IF ANY AGENT IS A DUAL AGENT, THE UNDERSIGNED CLIENT(S) CONFIRM THAT
64. THEY HAVE PREVIOUSLY CONSENTED TO (INSERT NAME(S)) _____ LICENSEE(S), ACTING AS A
65. DUAL AGENT IN PROVIDING BROKERAGE SERVICES ON THEIR BEHALF AND SPECIFICALLY CONSENT TO LICENSEE ACTING AS A DUAL AGENT IN REGARD TO THE TRANSACTION
66. REFERRED TO IN THIS DOCUMENT.
67. (_____)   (_____)   (_____)   (_____) Initials required if any Dual Agents are involved in this transaction.
68.   Buyer(s)   Buyer(s)   Seller(s)   Seller(s)
69. The Seller agrees to compensate the Listing Broker per terms of the listing agreement. The Selling Broker (if any) will be compensated by
70. _____ . Payment of compensation to Selling Broker does not imply Selling Broker is the agent or subagent of the seller.
71. **11. CONDITION REPRESENTATION AND HOME INSPECTION:** Seller will represent as of the date and time of delivering possession: (A) that all systems, equipment, and appliances, if
72. any, to be conveyed by deed or sold by Bill of Sale will be in operating condition including, but not limited to, all mechanical equipment, heating and cooling equipment, water heaters
73. and softeners, septic and plumbing systems, electrical systems, kitchen equipment remaining with the premises, and any miscellaneous mechanical personal property to be transferred to
74. the Purchaser, except _____ and (B) to the best of Seller's knowledge, the roof and foundation are free from leaks.
75. Notwithstanding Seller's representations, Purchaser reserves the right within five (5) business days of contract acceptance by Seller to have, at his/her expense, a professional
76. home inspector inspect and furnish a report on said premises. The inspection will cover but not be limited to the following major components of the real estate as exist: central heating
77. system, central cooling system, interior plumbing system, electrical system, roof and foundation. **PURCHASER AGREES THAT DISCLOSURE OF MINOR REPAIRS AND ROUTINE**
78. **MAINTENANCE ITEMS ARE NOT A PART OF THIS CONTINGENCY UNLESS HABITABILITY IS AFFECTED.** If the inspection reveals any deficiency unacceptable to the Purchaser, the
79. Purchaser will furnish a copy of said report to Seller, and may cancel this Contract upon giving written notice to the Seller of said deficiency within two (2) business days after the five (5)
80. business day inspection period. If Purchaser fails to notify Seller of deficiencies, in said inspection, Purchaser waives his right hereunder as to canceling the Contract and requesting Sellers
81. to repair said deficiencies under paragraph 11 and 22.
82. **12. RIDERS AND GENERAL CONDITIONS:** This Contract is subject to the General Conditions on the back page hereof, and the following riders _____
83. attached hereto, which General Conditions and Riders are made a part of this Contract.

SIGNIFICANCE OF OFFER AND ACCEPTANCE BY PARTIES

84. This offer or any counter offer must be accepted upon presentation or within forty eight (48) hours of the initial counter offer, whichever occurs first or the same shall become null and
85. void. We the undersigned Purchasers and Sellers understand that our signatures and initials (if required) or faxed copies of documents bearing same will constitute a **LEGALLY BINDING**
86. **CONTRACT**, and all parties agree to perform the terms and conditions thereof.

Date of Contract Offer _____ Time: _____   Date of Contract Acceptance ____ __ __ Time: _____

Purchaser's Mailing Address (please print) _____   Seller's Mailing Address _____

City State Zip _____   City State Zip _____

Purchaser/Beneficiary/Agent _____ Social Security # ____   Seller/Beneficiary/Agent _____ Social Security # ____

Purchaser/Beneficiary/Agent _____ Social Security # ____   Seller/Beneficiary/Agent _____ Social Security # ____

FOR INFORMATION ONLY

Name of Selling Agent _____ MAP MLS ID # ____   Name of Listing Agent _____ MAP MLS ID # ____

Company Name ____ MAP MLS ID # ____ Phone # ____   Company Name ____ MAP MLS ID # ____ Phone # ____

Purchaser's Attorney _____ Phone # ____   Seller's Attorney _____ Phone # ____

Name of Mortgage Lender _____   Loan Officer _____ Phone # ____

FORM: C401 8/98

Figure 11.2 Typical Residential Sales Contract (Continued)

GENERAL CONDITIONS

13. ATTORNEYS' REVIEW: The parties agree that their respective attorneys may review and make modifications, other than stated purchase price, mutually acceptable to the parties, within five (5) business days after the acceptance date of the Contract. If the parties do not agree and written notice thereof is given to the other party within the time specified, this Contract will become null and void, and all monies paid by the Purchaser will be refunded. IN THE ABSENCE OF WRITTEN NOTICE WITHIN THE TIME SPECIFIED HEREIN, THIS PROVISION WILL BE DEEMED WAIVED BY ALL PARTIES HERETO AND THIS CONTRACT WILL BE IN FULL FORCE AND EFFECT.

The parties agree that, during the above stated period, the Seller's property will not be shown to prospective purchasers unless conditions stipulated in paragraph 5(I)A or 5(I)B direct that the property remain on the market.

14. PRIOR CONTRACT: In the event a prior contract for sale had been entered into by Seller, this Contract is contingent upon Seller providing Purchaser within four (4) business days hereafter a cancellation or termination of said prior contract.

15. EVIDENCE OF TITLE: Title, when conveyed, will be good and merchantable, subject only to: general real estate taxes not due and payable at the time of closing, covenants, conditions, restrictions of record, building lines and easements if any, so long as they do not interfere with Purchaser's use and enjoyment of the property. Seller will, at his/her expense, deliver or cause to be delivered to Purchaser or Purchaser's attorney within customary time limitations and sufficiently in advance of closing as evidence of title in Seller or Grantor the following: A title commitment for an ALTA title insurance policy with extended coverage by a title company licensed to operate in the State of Illinois, bearing a date on or subsequent to the date of the acceptance of this Contract, but issued not more than 45 days prior to the closing, in the amount of the purchase price, subject only to items herein stated and usual stock objections, together with payment directly or by credit for all customary Seller's charges, including but not limited to; search, insurance, recording charges, and transfer stamps. Delay in delivery by Seller of a commitment for title insurance due to a delay by Purchaser's mortgagee in recording the mortgage and bringing down title, will not cause a default of this Contract.

Commitment for title insurance furnished by Seller will be conclusive evidence of good and merchantable title as therein shown, subject only to the exceptions therein stated. If evidence of title discloses other defects, Seller shall have thirty (30) additional days to cure such defects and notify Purchaser, but Purchaser may take title with such other defects (with the right to deduct from the purchase price liens and encumbrances for a definite or ascertainable amount) by notifying Seller and tendering performance. At closing, if requested, Seller will execute customary form of affidavit of title and sign customary ALTA forms and other forms required by law or custom.

16. CONDOMINIUM: In the event that the subject property is a condominium, Purchaser has, within five(5) business days from the date of acceptance of this Contract, the right to demand from Seller items as stipulated by 30 Ill. Rev. Stat. 322.1 (Illinois Condominium Act). This Contract is subject to the condition that Seller be able to procure and provide to Purchaser, a release or waiver of any option of first refusal or other pre-emptive rights of purchase created by the Declaration of Condominium within the time established by said Declaration. In the event the Condominium Association requires personal appearance of Purchaser and/or additional documentation, Purchaser agrees to comply with same.

17. INSPECTIONS, CERTIFICATIONS, LENDER FEES: If FHA or VA financing is obtained, Seller will pay reasonable costs related to termite inspections, certifications, tax service, and document preparation fees.

18. SURVEY: Prior to closing, Seller, at his/her expense, will provide to Purchaser a Plat of Survey of the Premises acceptable to the Lender and Title Company for extended coverage prepared by an Illinois registered land surveyor, dated not more than six months prior to date of closing provided herein and showing all improvements presently located thereon, including but not limited to, buildings, fences, patios, sidewalks and driveways. In the event the Premises is a condominium unit, no survey shall be required.

In the event the survey discloses encroachments, violations of easements or other violations, this Contract at the option of the Purchaser, will become null and void, unless Seller can obtain Title Insurance over said matters.

19. FLOOD INSURANCE: Purchaser will obtain flood insurance if the premises is located within a designated flood plain as determined by the National Flood Insurance Agency and is required by the Purchaser's lender.

20. SOIL TEST: In the event of vacant land, the Purchaser has the option, at his/her expense, of obtaining a soil boring and percolation test within twenty (20) days of Contract date. If said soil test shows adverse soil conditions; Purchaser, at his/her option, may serve written notice upon Seller within the time specified and this Contract will then become null and void and all earnest monies paid by the Purchaser will be refunded to him/her.

21. WELL AND SEPTIC TEST: In the event the premises has either a well or a septic system, Seller will provide to Purchaser at Seller's expense, prior to closing, test results indicating such system to be in compliance with the applicable governing statutes, ordinances, and health department regulations.

22. CONDITION OF REAL ESTATE: Seller will remove from the premises by the date of possession all debris and personal property not conveyed by Bill of Sale to Purchaser and will leave the premises in broom-clean condition, and further agrees to surrender possession of the real estate in the same condition as it was at the Date of Offer, ordinary wear and tear excepted. Purchaser reserves the right to inspect the premises within seventy-two (72) hours prior to the closing to determine Seller's compliance with the foregoing, as a condition of closing.

23. CODE VIOLATIONS: Seller warrants that he/she has no knowledge of, nor has received any notice from any city, village or other governmental authority of, any dwelling code and/or zoning ordinance violations.

24. WARRANTIES AND REPRESENTATIONS: Any warranties and representations and other similar provisions requiring additional acts after the closing will survive the closing and delivery of the deed and will continue to be binding upon the parties hereto.

25. PAYMENT OF REAL ESTATE TRANSFER TAX: Seller will pay the amount of any stamp tax imposed by State of Illinois law and county law on the transfer of title and any transfer tax imposed by local ordinance, unless otherwise provided by such ordinance. Both parties agree to execute any declarations or any forms required in connection with said transfer taxes.

26. PAYOUTS: Existing mortgage and other lien indebtedness may be paid at closing out of the sale proceeds, unless Purchaser takes title subject thereto.

27. REAL ESTATE PROPERTY TAX ESCROW: If the property has previously not been taxed as improved, the sum of three percent (3%) of the purchase price will be withheld from Seller's proceeds. At closing, a part of the withheld funds, if required, will be deposited with Purchaser's Lender in accordance with their escrow instructions, and the balance if any, with Seller's attorney. When the exact amount of the taxes prorated under this Contract can be ascertained, the taxes will be prorated by the Seller's attorney at the request of either party, and the Seller's share of such tax liability after reproration will be paid to the Purchaser from the escrow funds and the balance, if any, will be paid to the Seller. If the Seller's obligation after such reproration exceeds the amount of the escrow funds, Seller agrees to pay such excess promptly upon demand.

28. ESCROW CLOSING: At the election of either party upon written notice to the other party, this sale will be closed through a deed and money escrow at the office stated in paragraph 7B with such special provisions inserted in the escrow as may be required to conform with this Contract. Upon the creation of such an escrow; anything herein to the contrary notwithstanding, payment of purchase price and delivery of deed, will be made through the escrow; and this Contract along with the earnest money will be deposited in the escrow. The cost of the escrow will be paid by the party requesting it.

29. DEFAULT: In the event either party should breach this agreement, either prior to or subsequent to closing, the other party may pursue any and all remedies provided by law. In addition, upon a finding of a court of competent jurisdiction that one of the parties has breached the Contract, the prevailing party may recover all costs, expenses and reasonable attorney's fees. The parties hereto agree that the Broker may deposit the escrow funds with the Clerk of the Circuit Court; and the parties hereto agree to indemnify and hold the Broker/Agent(s), harmless from any and all claims and demands, including the payment of reasonable attorney's fees, costs and expenses arising out of such claims and demands, said amounts to be shared equally by both Seller and Purchaser.

30. DISBURSEMENT OF EARNEST MONEY: Escrowee may disburse earnest money under one of the following conditions: (A) Seller's failure to accept Purchaser's Offer to Purchase; (B) at Closing (C) Mutual written agreement of Seller and Purchaser; or (D) Court Order.

31. NOTICES: ALL NOTICES REQUIRED WILL BE IN WRITING AND WILL BE SERVED BY ONE PARTY OR THEIR ATTORNEY TO THE OTHER PARTY AT THE MAILING ADDRESS INDICATED HEREIN, WHETHER OR NOT THE OTHER PARTY IS REPRESENTED BY AN ATTORNEY. Notice will be given in the following manner:

(A) By personal delivery of such notice to the other party; or,

(B) By mailing of such notice to the other party by (1) 1ST Class regular mail, or (2) mailgram with confirmation copy. The date of mailing or the mailgram of the notice will be it's effective date. Courtesy copies of all notices will be provided simultaneously to respective attorneys and brokers, by fax, if known.

(C) By Commercial Overnight Provider, the effective date and time of notice shall be the date and time of delivery to the address indicated herein.

32. LOSS: If prior to closing, improvements on the property are destroyed or materially damaged by fire or other casualty, the Contract, at the option of the Purchaser, will become null and void.

33. INTEREST BEARING ACCOUNT AND IRS CERTIFICATION: Seller and Purchaser agree that the earnest money is to be held in a federally insured interest bearing account at a financial institution designated by the Listing Broker with all interest earned to accrue to the Purchaser, to be paid to Purchaser at the time of closing or upon termination of this Contract. Purchaser shall pay any and all service charges and/or costs charged by the financial institution in connection with the earnest money account. Listing Broker shall have no liability for earnest money due to failure of any financial institution. Listing Broker is hereby authorized, on anticipation of closing, to close said interest bearing account and prepare escrow distribution checks within five (5) business days of an anticipated closing. *Certification* - Under penalties of perjury, by affixing my signature to the reverse side of this Contract I certify: (1) The number shown on this form is my correct Taxpayer Identification Number (or I am waiting for a number to be issued to me); and (2) I am not subject to backup withholding either because I have not been notified by the Internal Revenue Service (IRS) that I am subject to backup withholding as a result of failure to report all interest or dividends, or the IRS has notified me that I am no longer subject to backup withholding. *Certification Instructions* - You must cross out item (2) above it if you have been notified by the IRS that you are subject to backup withholding because of under reporting interest or dividends on your tax return. However, if after being notified by the IRS that you were subject to backup withholding you received another notification from the IRS that you are no longer subject to backup withholding, do not cross out item (2).

34. CONSTRUCTION OF TERMS: Wherever appropriate, the singular includes the plural and the masculine or feminine includes the other or the neuter.

35. TIME IS OF THE ESSENCE OF THIS CONTRACT.

FORM: C401 8/98

In Illinois . . .

Illinois requires several mandatory disclosures by sellers and agents, such as disclosure of property conditions and agency relationships. These disclosures may be included in the sales contract by physical attachment or by reference. (See also Chapter 4.) ■

Options

There are various kinds of options used in real estate transactions. An **option** is an agreement to keep open for a set period of time an offer by an *optionor* to an *optionee* to sell, purchase or lease property. One kind is an option to enter into a lease (the prospective tenant has not promised to rent, but the owner has promised to lease). Another is a tenant's option to *renew* a lease. Another is a contract by which an owner gives a prospective purchaser the right to buy the owner's property at a fixed price within a certain period of time. The optionee pays a fee (the agreed-on consideration) for this option right. The optionee has no other obligation until he or she decides to either exercise the option right or allow the option to expire. An option is enforceable by only one party—the optionee.

An option contract is not a sales contract. At the time the option is signed by the parties, the owner does not sell and the optionee does not buy. The parties merely agree that the optionee has the right to buy and the owner is obligated to sell if the optionee decides to exercise his or her right of option. Options must contain all the terms and provisions required for a valid contract.

[handwritten: BEComes EXCUTORY]

[handwritten: UNTIL IT IS EXCERCISED THAN]

The option agreement (which is a unilateral contract) requires that the optionor act only after the optionee gives notice that he or she elects to execute the option. If the option is not exercised within the time specified in the contract, both the optionor's obligation and the optionee's right expire. An option contract may provide for renewal, which often requires additional consideration. The optionee cannot recover the consideration paid for the option right. The contract may state whether the money paid for the option is to be applied to the purchase price of the real estate if the option is exercised.

A common application of an option is a lease that includes an option for the tenant to purchase the property. Options on commercial real estate frequently depend on some specific conditions being fulfilled, such as obtaining a zoning change or a building permit. The optionee may be obligated to exercise the option if the conditions are met. Similar terms could also be included in a sales contract.

Land Contracts

A real estate sale can be made under a common form of seller financing called a **land contract.** A land contract is sometimes called a *contract for deed,* an **installment contract** or *articles of agreement for warranty deed.* Under a typical land contract, the seller (also known as the *vendor*) retains legal title. The buyer (called the *vendee*) takes possession and gets equitable title to the property. The buyer agrees to give the seller a down payment and pay regular monthly installments of principal and interest over a number of years. The buyer also agrees to pay real estate taxes, insurance premiums, repairs and upkeep on the property. Although the buyer obtains possession under the contract, the seller is not obligated to execute and deliver a deed to the buyer until the terms of the contract have been satisfied. This frequently occurs when the buyer has made enough payments to obtain a mortgage loan and pay off the balance due on the contract. Although a land contract usually is assumable by subsequent purchasers, it generally must be approved by the seller.

In Practice   Legislatures and courts have not looked favorably on the harsh provisions of some real estate installment contracts. A seller and buyer contemplating such a sale should first consult an attorney to make sure that the agreement meets all legal requirements. The individual concerns of the parties must be addressed.

In Illinois . . . Installment contracts (or articles of agreement) commonly are used in Illinois when creative seller financing is needed to consummate a sale. Any provision in a contract or an agreement is void if it

- forbids the contract buyer to record the contract,
- provides that recording shall not constitute notice or
- provides any penalty for recording.

Any installment contract for the sale of a dwelling that consists of 12 or fewer units is voidable at the option of the buyer unless a certificate of compliance or an express warranty that no notice of a building code violation has been received within the past ten years is attached to or incorporated into the contract. If any notice has been received within the past ten years *and not complied with*, each notice must be listed with a detailed explanation. Neither buyer nor seller may waive this requirement.

A buyer who, under an installment contract, purchases residential property containing six or fewer units from a land trust must be told the names of all beneficiaries of the trust at the time the contract is executed. The buyer has the option of voiding the contract if the names are not revealed. ■

SUMMARY   A contract is a legally enforceable promise or set of promises that must be performed; if a breach occurs, the law provides a remedy.

Contracts may be classified according to whether the parties' intentions are express or merely implied by their actions. They may also be classified as bilateral (when both parties have obligated themselves to act) or unilateral (when one party is obligated to perform only if the other party acts). In addition, contracts may be classified according to their legal enforceability as valid, void, voidable or unenforceable.

Many contracts specify a time for performance. In any case, all contracts must be performed within a reasonable time. An executed contract is one that has been fully performed. An executory contract is one in which some act remains to be performed.

The essentials of a valid contract are legally competent parties, offer and acceptance, consent and consideration. A valid real estate contract must include a description of the property. It must be in writing and signed by all parties to be enforceable in court.

In many types of contracts, either of the parties may transfer his or her rights and obligations under the agreement by assignment or novation (substitution of a new contract).

Contracts usually provide that the seller has the right to declare a sale canceled if the buyer defaults. If either party suffers a loss because of the other's default, he or she may sue for damages to cover the loss. If one party insists on completing the transaction, he or she may sue the defaulter for specific performance of the terms of the contract; a court can order the other party to comply with the agreement.

Contracts frequently used in the real estate business include listing agreements, sales contracts, options, land contracts (installment contracts) and leases.

A real estate sales contract binds a buyer and a seller to a definite transaction as described in detail in the contract. The buyer is bound to purchase the property for the amount stated in the agreement. The seller is bound to deliver title, free from liens and encumbrances (except those identified in the contract).

Under an option agreement, the optionee purchases from the optionor, for a limited time period, the exclusive right to purchase or lease the optionor's property. A land contract, or installment contract, is a sales/financing agreement under which a buyer purchases a seller's real estate on time. The buyer takes possession of and responsibility for the property, but does not receive the deed immediately.

In Illinois . . .

The Statute of Frauds requires that all contracts for the sale of land that will not be fulfilled within one year must be in writing to be enforceable in court.

Illinois residents become of legal age on their 18th birthday.

Brokers and salespersons may only fill in blanks in preprinted form contracts that are customarily used in the real estate industry.

Earnest money must be deposited in a special escrow account. ■

QUESTIONS

1. A legally enforceable agreement under which two parties agree to do something for each other is known as a(n):
   A. escrow agreement.
   B. legal promise.
   C. valid contract.
   D. option agreement.

2. Doug approaches Betty and says, "I'd like to buy your house." Betty says, "Sure," and they agree on a price. What kind of contract is this?
   A. Implied
   B. Unenforceable
   C. Void
   D. There is no contract.

3. A contract is said to be bilateral if:
   A. one of the parties is a minor.
   B. the contract has yet to be fully performed.
   C. only one party to the agreement is bound to act.
   D. all parties to the contract are bound to act.

4. During the period of time after a real estate sales contract is signed but before title actually passes, the status of the contract is:
   A. voidable.   C. unilateral.
   B. executory.   D. implied.

5. A contract for the sale of real estate that does not state the consideration to be paid for the property and is not signed by the parties is considered to be:
   A. voidable.   C. void.
   B. executory.   D. enforceable.

6. Nick and Keri sign a contract under which Nick will convey Blackacre to Keri. Nick changes his mind, and Keri sues for specific performance. What is Keri seeking in this lawsuit?
   A. Money damages
   B. New contract
   C. Deficiency judgment
   D. Conveyance of the property

7. In a standard sales contract, several words were crossed out; others were inserted. To eliminate future controversy as to whether the changes were made before or after the contract was signed, the usual procedure is to:
   A. write a letter to each party listing the changes.
   B. have each party write a letter to the other approving the changes.
   C. redraw the entire contract.
   D. have both parties initial or sign in the margin near each change.

8. Margaret makes an offer on Diane's house, and Diane accepts. Both parties sign the sales contract. At this point, Margaret has what type of title to the property?
   A. Equitable   C. Escrow
   B. Voidable   D. Contract

9. The sales contract says John will purchase only if his wife approves the sale by the following Saturday. His wife's approval is a:
   A. contingency.   C. warranty.
   B. reservation.   D. consideration.

10. Charles verbally offers to buy Sharon's house for $150,000. No written real estate sales contract is drawn up, but Sharon agrees to the offer. What kind of contract is this?
    A. Unilateral   C. Implied
    B. Option   D. Express

11. Carl's property was listed for $100,000, and he agreed to enter into an option agreement with Keith. They agreed on a sale price of $95,000 and a term of three months. Two weeks later, Carl receives an offer of $100,000 from his neighbor to buy the property. An agent is not involved in the offer. Can he accept the second offer?
    A. Yes, because it is for the full list price.
    B. Yes, because Keith has not yet exercised his option.
    C. No, because an agent was not involved.
    D. No, a seller is bound to an option agreement for the term of the option.

12. Xander and Holly enter into a real estate sales contract. Under the contract's terms, Xander will pay Holly $500 a month for ten years. Holly will continue to hold legal title to Blueacre. Xander will live on Blueacre and pay all real estate taxes, insurance premiums and regular upkeep costs. What kind of contract do Xander and Holly have?
    A. Option contract
    B. Contract for mortgage
    C. Unilateral contract
    D. Land, or installment, contract

13. The purchaser of real estate under an installment contract:
    A. generally pays no interest charge.
    B. receives title immediately.
    C. is not required to pay property taxes for the duration of the contract.
    D. is called a *vendee.*

14. Under the statute of frauds, all contracts for the sale of real estate must be:
    A. originated by a real estate broker.
    B. on preprinted forms.
    C. in writing to be enforceable.
    D. accompanied by earnest money deposits.

15. The Froneks offer in writing to purchase a house for $120,000, including its draperies, with the offer to expire on Saturday at noon. The Whitmores reply in writing on Thursday, accepting the $120,000 offer but excluding the draperies. On Friday, while the Froneks consider this counteroffer, the Whitmores decide to accept the original offer, draperies included, and state that in writing. At this point, which of the following statements is true?
    A. The Froneks are legally bound to buy the house although they have the right to insist that the draperies be included.
    B. The Froneks are not bound to buy.
    C. The Froneks must buy the house and are not entitled to the draperies.
    D. The Froneks must buy the house, but may deduct the value of the draperies from the $120,000.

16. Between June 5 and September 23, Martin suffered from a mental illness that caused delusions, hallucinations and loss of memory. On July 1, Martin signed a contract to purchase Blueacre, with the closing set for October 31. On September 24, Martin began psychiatric treatment. He was declared completely cured by October 15. Which of the following statements is true regarding Martin's contract to purchase Blueacre?
    A. The contract is voidable.
    B. The contract is void.
    C. The contract lacks reality of consent.
    D. The contract is fully valid and enforceable.

17. A broker has found a buyer for a seller's home. The buyer has indicated in writing his willingness to buy the property for $1,000 less than the asking price and has deposited $5,000 in earnest money with the broker. The seller is out of town for the weekend, and the broker has been unable to inform him of the signed document. At this point, the buyer has signed a(n):
    A. voidable contract.
    B. offer.
    C. executory agreement.
    D. implied contract.

18. A buyer and seller agree to the purchase of a house for $200,000. The contract contains a clause stating that "time is of the essence." Which of the following statements is true?
    A. The closing may take place within a reasonable period after the stated date.
    B. A "time is of the essence" clause is not binding on either party.
    C. The closing date must be stated as a particular calendar date, and not simply as a formula, such as "two weeks after loan approval."
    D. If the closing date passes and no closing takes place, the contract may have been breached.

19. Cathy signs a contract under which she may purchase Yellowacre for $30,000 any time in the next three months. Cathy pays Yellowacre's current owner $500 at the time the contract is signed. Which of the following best describes this contract?
    A. Contingency   C. Installment
    B. Option   D. Sales

In Illinois . . .

20. In preparing a sales contract, an Illinois broker who is not a lawyer may:
    A. fill in factual and business details in the blank spaces of a customary preprinted form.
    B. draft riders to alter a preprinted contract to fit the transaction.
    C. fill out and sign an offer to purchase for the customer.
    D. advise a buyer or seller of the legal significance of certain parts of the contract.

21. On Tuesday, broker Loren received a $750 earnest money deposit from Gus. The seller accepted the offer on Thursday. Where and when must Loren deposit Gus's money?
    A. In Loren's personal checking account by Wednesday
    B. In a special trust account no later than midnight on Tuesday
    C. In a special interest-bearing trust account by Friday
    D. In a special non–interest-bearing trust account by Wednesday

22. An Illinois broker does not need written consent of both parties to a transaction to do which of the following?
    A. Disburse interest accrued on an earnest money account
    B. Fill in the blanks on a sales offer
    C. Make changes in the terms of a signed sales contract
    D. Change the commission payment terms designated in the listing agreement

23. The unauthorized practice of law was dealt with in which Illinois Supreme Court case?
    A. *Illinois State Bar Association v. Illinois Board of REALTORS®*
    B. *Chicago Bar Association v. Quinlan and Tyson, Inc.*
    C. *Attorney Registration and Disciplinary Commission v. Illinois State Department of Professional Regulation*
    D. *Quinlan Associates, Inc. v. Illinois Real Estate Commission*

24. All of the following provisions would be void in an Illinois installment contract EXCEPT:
    A. "Buyer may not record this contract."
    B. "Seller will retain legal title."
    C. "Recording shall not constitute notice."
    D. "Buyer will forfeit $1,000 for recording."

25. Sam made an offer on Pam's property. For this contract to be valid, it must contain:
    A. a contingency clause that allows Sam to secure financing.
    B. the date when the listing expires.
    C. a rescission clause.
    D. the consideration Sam is willing to pay.

26. A buyer made an offer of $350,000 offer on a property with no contingencies. The buyer intends to build a shopping center on the property, but no mention was made of this. The seller accepted the offer but before the closing, the buyer discovered he could not build a shopping center on the property. What is the status of the contract?
    A. Valid   C. Voidable
    B. Void   D. Unenforceable

CHAPTER 12

Transfer of Title

KEY TERMS

acknowledgment
adverse possession
bargain and sale deed
deed
deed in trust
devise
general warranty deed
grantee
granting clause

grantor
habendum clause
heir
intestate
involuntary alienation
probate
quitclaim deed
reconveyance deed

special warranty deed
testate
testator
title
transfer tax
trustee's deed
voluntary alienation
will

TITLE

The term *title* has two meanings. **Title** to real estate means the right to or ownership of the land; it represents the owner's bundle of rights. Title also serves as *evidence of that ownership.* A person who holds the title would, if challenged in court, be able to recover or retain ownership or possession of a parcel of real estate. "Title" is just a way of referring to ownership; it is not an actual printed document. The document that shows who holds title to real property is the deed. The deed must be recorded to give public notice of the holder's ownership.

Real estate may be transferred *voluntarily* by sale or gift. Alternatively, it may be transferred *involuntarily* by operation of law. Real estate may be transferred while the owner lives or by will or descent after the owner dies. In any case, it is the title that is transferred as a symbol of ownership.

VOLUNTARY ALIENATION

EQUEL SALES OR   DUE IN CLAUSE IP [handwritten]

> A **grantor** conveys property to a grantee.
>
> A **grantee** receives property from a grantor.
>
> A **deed** is the instrument that conveys property from a grantor to a grantee.

Voluntary alienation is the legal term for the voluntary transfer of title. The owner may voluntarily transfer title by either making a gift or selling the property. To transfer during one's lifetime, the owner must use some form of deed of conveyance.

A **deed** is the written instrument by which an owner of real estate *intentionally* conveys the right, title or interest in the parcel of real estate to someone else. The statute of frauds requires that all deeds be in writing. The owner who

Deed = GRANT = CONVEN'CE = GRANTER [handwritten]

transfers the title is referred to as the **grantor.** The person who acquires the title is called the **grantee.** A deed is executed (that is, *signed*) only by the grantor.

Requirements for a Valid Deed

The formal requirements for a deed are established by state law and thus vary from state to state.

In Illinois . . .

The following are the minimum requirements for a valid deed in Illinois:

- *Grantor,* who has the legal capacity to execute (sign) the deed
- *Grantee* named with reasonable certainty, sufficient to be identifiable
- Recital of *consideration*
- *Granting clause* (words of conveyance, together with any words of limitation)
- Accurate *legal description* of the property conveyed
- *Signature of the grantor,* sometimes with a seal, witness or acknowledgment
- *Delivery* of the deed and *acceptance* by the grantee to pass title

A deed also may include other information that is not necessary for its validity in Illinois, such as a description of any *limitations* on the conveyance of a full fee simple estate and a recital of any *exceptions and reservations* (also known as *"subject to"* clauses) that affect title to the property. Some states require a **habendum clause** (literally, "to have and to hold") to define ownership taken by the grantee. *Acknowledgment and notarization are not required in Illinois. Except in the case of tax deeds, recording is not required.* ■

Grantor. A grantor must be of lawful age, usually at least 18 years old. A deed executed by a minor is generally voidable.

A grantor also must be of sound mind. Generally, any grantor who can understand the action is viewed as mentally capable of executing a valid deed. A deed executed by someone who was mentally impaired at the time is voidable but not void. If, however, the grantor has been judged legally incompetent, the deed will be void. Real estate owned by someone who is legally incompetent can be conveyed only with a court's approval.

The grantor's name must be spelled correctly and consistently throughout the deed. If the grantor's name has been changed since the title was acquired (for instance, a woman who changes her name when she is married), both names should be shown—for example, "Mary Smith, formerly Mary Jones."

Grantee. To be valid, a deed must name a grantee. The grantee must be specifically named so that the person to whom the property is being conveyed can be readily identified from the deed itself.

FOR EXAMPLE Thomas wanted to convey Whiteacre to his nephew, Jack Jackson. In the deed, Thomas wrote the following words of conveyance: "I, Thomas, hereby convey to Jack all my interest in Whiteacre." The only problem was that Thomas also had a son named Jack, a cousin Jack and a neighbor Jack. The grantee's identity could not be discerned from the deed itself. Thomas should have conveyed Whiteacre "to my nephew, Jack Jackson."

The grantee's *present address* is required in Illinois as an element of a valid deed. ■

If more than one grantee is involved, the granting clause should specify their rights in the property. The clause might state, for instance, that the grantees will take title as joint tenants or tenants in common. This is especially important when specific wording is necessary to create a joint tenancy.

Consideration. A valid deed must contain a clause acknowledging that the grantor has received consideration. Generally, the amount of consideration is stated in dollars. When a deed conveys real estate as a gift to a relative, "love and affection" may be sufficient consideration. In most states, however, it is customary to recite a *nominal consideration,* such as "$10 and other good and valuable consideration."

Granting clause (words of conveyance). A deed must contain a **granting clause** that states the grantor's intention to convey the property. Depending on the type of deed and the obligations agreed to by the grantor (discussed later in this chapter), the wording would be similar to one of the following:

- "I, Kent Long, grant . . ." (creates a deed)
- "I, Kent Long, convey and warrant . . ." (creates a warranty deed)
- "I, Kent Long, grant, bargain and sell . . ." (creates a bargain and sale deed)
- "I, Kent Long, remise, release and quitclaim . . ." (creates a quitclaim deed)

Fee Simple & Absolute

A deed that conveys the grantor's entire fee simple interest usually contains wording such as "to Mary Goode and to her heirs and assigns forever." If the grantor conveys less than his or her complete interest, such as a life estate, the wording must indicate this limitation—for example, "to Mary Goode for the duration of her natural life."

Legal description of real estate. To be valid, a deed must contain an accurate legal description of the real estate conveyed. Land is considered adequately described if a competent surveyor can locate the property using the description.

Signature of grantor. To be valid, a deed must be signed by all grantors named in the deed. Some states also require witnesses to the grantor's signature.

Most states permit an attorney-in-fact to sign for a grantor. The attorney must act under a *power of attorney*—the specific written authority to execute and sign one or more legal instruments for another person. Usually, the power of attorney must be recorded in the county where the property is located. The power of attorney terminates when the person on whose behalf it is exercised dies. As a result, adequate evidence must be submitted that the grantor was alive at the time the attorney-in-fact signed the deed.

In some states, including Illinois, a grantor's spouse is required to sign any deed of conveyance to waive any marital or homestead rights. This requirement varies according to state law and depends on the manner in which title to real estate is held and whether the property is used as a homestead (residence).

Many states still require a seal (or simply the word *seal*) to be written or printed after an individual grantor's signature. The corporate seal may be required of a corporate grantor.

In Illinois . . .

Seals are not required for individual grantors' signatures. Corporations need not affix their official corporate seals to validate a deed when they are grantors. ■

Acknowledgment.   An **acknowledgment** is a formal declaration that the person who signs a written document does so voluntarily and that his or her signature is genuine. The declaration is made before a notary public or an authorized public officer, such as a judge, a justice of the peace or some other person as prescribed by state law. An acknowledgment usually states that the person signing the deed or other document is known to the officer or has produced sufficient identification to prevent a forgery. The form of acknowledgment required by the state where the property is located should be used even if the party signing is a resident of another ("foreign") state.

NOTORIZED

An acknowledgment is not essential to the validity of the deed unless it is required by state statute. However, a deed that is not acknowledged is not a completely satisfactory instrument. In most states, an unacknowledged deed is not eligible for recording.

In Illinois . . .

In Illinois acknowledgment is not essential to the *validity* of the deed, nor is it a requirement for recording. However, unless the deed is acknowledged, it may not be introduced as evidence in a court of law without some further proof of its execution. Therefore, it is customary for most documents conveying title to be acknowledged. The recorder of deeds does not require acknowledgment, but most title insurance companies do for deeds covered by their policies. ■

> Transfer of title requires both delivery and acceptance of the deed.

Delivery and acceptance.   A title is not considered transferred until the deed is actually delivered to and accepted by the grantee. The grantor may deliver the deed to the grantee either personally or through a third party. The third party, commonly known as an *escrow agent* (or *settlement agent*), will deliver the deed to the grantee as soon as certain requirements have been satisfied. In an arm's-length transaction, the title must be delivered during the grantor's lifetime and accepted during the grantee's lifetime. Title is said to "pass" only when a deed is delivered. The effective date of the transfer of title from the grantor to the grantee is the date of delivery of the deed itself. When a deed is delivered in escrow, the date of delivery generally relates back to the date it was deposited with the escrow agent.

Execution of Corporate Deeds

The laws governing a corporation's right to convey real estate vary from state to state. However, two basic rules must be followed. First, a corporation can convey real estate only by authority granted in its bylaws or upon a proper resolution passed by its *board of directors*. If all or a substantial portion of a corporation's real estate is being conveyed, usually a resolution authorizing the sale must be secured from the *shareholders*. Second, deeds to real estate can be signed only by an *authorized officer*.

Rules pertaining to religious corporations and not-for-profit corporations are complex and vary even more widely. Because the legal requirements must be followed exactly, an attorney should be consulted for all corporate conveyances.

Types of Deeds

A deed can take several forms, depending on the extent of the grantor's pledges to the grantee. Regardless of any guarantees the deed offers, however, the grantee will want additional assurance that the grantor has the right to offer what the deed conveys. To obtain this protection, grantees commonly seek evidence of title.

The most common deed forms are the

- general warranty deed,
- special warranty deed,
- bargain and sale deed,
- quitclaim deed,
- deed in trust,
- trustee's deed,
- reconveyance deed and
- deed executed pursuant to a court order.

General warranty deed. A **general warranty deed** provides the greatest protection of any deed. It is called a *general warranty deed* because the grantor is legally bound by certain covenants or warranties (promises). In most states, the warranties are implied by the use of certain words specified by statute. In some states, the grantor's warranties are expressly written into the deed itself. Each state law should be examined, but some of the specific words include "convey and warrant" or "warrant generally." The basic warranties are as follows:

- **Covenant of seisin**—The grantor warrants that he or she owns the property and has the right to convey title to it. (Seisin simply means "possession.") The grantee may recover damages up to the full purchase price if this covenant is broken.
- **Covenant against encumbrances**—The grantor warrants that the property is free from liens or encumbrances, except for any specifically stated in the deed. Encumbrances generally include mortgages, mechanics' liens and easements. If this covenant is breached, the grantee may sue for the cost of removing the encumbrances.
- **Covenant of quiet enjoyment**—The grantor guarantees that the grantee's title will be good against third parties who might bring court actions to establish superior title to the property. If the grantee's title is found to be inferior, the grantor is liable for damages.
- **Covenant of further assurance**—The grantor promises to obtain and deliver any instrument needed to make the title good. For example, if the grantor's spouse has failed to sign away dower rights, the grantor must deliver a quitclaim deed (discussed later) to clear the title.
- **Covenant of warranty forever**—The grantor promises to compensate the grantee for the loss sustained if the title fails at any time in the future.

General Warranty Deed

Five covenants:

1. Covenant of seisin
2. Covenant against encumbrances
3. Covenant of quiet enjoyment
4. Covenant of further assurance
5. Covenant of warranty forever

These covenants in a general warranty deed are not limited to matters that occurred during the time the grantor owned the property; they extend back to its origins. The grantor defends the title against both himself or herself and all those who previously held title.

[handwritten: IF PROVIDE THE LIABILITIES TO GRANTOR & MORE PROTECTION GO BUYER]

In Illinois . . .

Illinois law provides that a deed using the words "convey and warrant" implies and includes all covenants of general warranty, which are as binding on the grantor, his or her heirs and personal representatives as if written at length in the deed. These covenants in a general warranty deed are not limited to matters that occurred during the time the grantor owned the property; they extend back to its origins. The grantor defends the title against himself and against all others as predecessors in title.

In addition, it is sufficient for a general warranty deed to recite only nominal consideration. ■

Special warranty deed. A **special warranty deed** contains two basic warranties:

1. That the grantor received title
2. That the property was not encumbered *during the time the grantor held title,* except as otherwise noted in the deed

**Special
Warranty
Deed**

Two warranties:

1. Warranty that grantor
   received title
2. Warranty that property
   was unencumbered by
   grantor

In effect, the grantor defends the title against himself or herself, but not against previous encumbrances. The granting clause generally contains the words "Grantor remises, releases, alienates and conveys." The grantor may include additional warranties, but they must be specifically stated in the deed. In areas where a special warranty deed is more commonly used, the purchase of title insurance is viewed as providing adequate protection to the grantee.

A special warranty deed may be used by fiduciaries such as trustees, executors and corporations. A special warranty deed is appropriate for a fiduciary because he or she lacks the authority to warrant against acts of predecessors in title. A fiduciary may hold title for a limited time without having a personal interest in the proceeds. Sometimes, a special warranty deed may be used by a grantor who has acquired title at a tax sale.

[handwritten: IN SOME STATES IT AFTER OWNERSHIP]

Bargain and sale deed. In some states, a **bargain and sale deed** contains no express warranties against encumbrances. It does, however, *imply* that the grantor holds title and possession of the property. The words in the granting clause are usually "John Smith grants and releases" or "Anne Green grants, bargains and sells." Because the warranty is not specifically stated, the grantee has little legal recourse if title defects appear later. In some areas, this deed is used in foreclosures and tax sales. The buyer should purchase title insurance for protection.

**Bargain and
Sale Deed**

No express warranties:

• Implication that grantor
   holds title and
   possession

A covenant against encumbrances initiated by the grantor may be added to a standard bargain and sale deed to create a *bargain and sale deed with covenant against the grantor's acts.* This deed is roughly equivalent to a special warranty deed. Warranties used in general warranty deeds may be inserted into a bargain and sale deed to give the grantee similar protection.

In Illinois . . .

The words in the granting clause are "grant, bargain and sell." A grant, bargain and sale deed conveys a fee simple title with the following covenants: (1) the grantor holds a fee simple estate, (2) the title is free from encumbrances made by the grantor except those listed in the deed and (3) the grantor warrants quiet enjoyment. Therefore, an Illinois bargain and sale deed is similar to a warranty deed but less complete in its warranties. ■

Quitclaim deed. A **quitclaim deed** provides the grantee with the least protection of any deed. It carries no covenants or warranties and generally conveys only whatever interest the grantor may have when the deed is delivered. If the grantor has no interest, the grantee will acquire nothing. Nor will the grantee acquire any right of warranty claim against the grantor. A quitclaim deed can convey title as effectively as a warranty deed if the grantor has good title when he or she delivers the deed, but it provides none of the guarantees that a warranty deed does. Through a quitclaim deed, the grantor only "remises, releases and quitclaims" his or her interest in the property, if any.

A quitclaim deed may convey less than a fee simple estate. This is because a quitclaim deed conveys only the grantor's right, title or interest.

A quitclaim deed frequently is used to cure a defect, called *a cloud on the title.* For example, if the name of the grantee is misspelled on a warranty deed filed in the public record, a quitclaim deed with the correct spelling may be executed to the grantee to perfect the title.

A quitclaim deed also is used when a grantor allegedly inherits property but is not certain that the decedent's title was valid. A warranty deed in such an instance could carry with it obligations of warranty, while a quitclaim deed would convey only the grantor's interest, whatever it might be.

A quitclaim deed uses the words "convey and quit claim," and conveys in fee all the grantor's existing legal and equitable rights held at the time of delivery. ■

Deed in trust. A deed in trust is the means by which a trustor conveys real estate to a trustee for the benefit of a beneficiary. The real estate is held by the trustee to fulfill the purpose of the trust. (See Figure 12.1.)

Trustee's deed. A deed executed by a trustee is a **trustee's deed.** It is used when a trustee conveys real estate held in the trust to anyone other than the trustor. The trustee's deed must state that the trustee is executing the instrument in accordance with the powers and authority granted by the trust instrument.

Reconveyance deed. A **reconveyance deed** is used by a trustee to return title to the trustor. For example, when a loan secured by a deed of trust has been fully paid, the beneficiary notifies the trustee. The trustee then reconveys the property to the trustor. As with any document of title, a reconveyance deed should be recorded to prevent title problems in the future.

Deed executed pursuant to court order. Executors' and administrators' deeds, masters' deeds, sheriffs' deeds and many other types are all deeds executed pursuant to a court order. These deeds are established by state statute and are used to convey title to property that is transferred by court order or by will. The form of such a deed must conform to the laws of the state in which the property is located.

One common characteristic of deeds executed pursuant to court order is that the full consideration is usually stated in the deed. Instead of "$10 and other valuable consideration," for example, the deed lists the actual sales price.

Quitclaim Deed

No express or implied covenants or warranties:

- Used primarily to convey less than fee simple or to cure a title defect

---

In Illinois . . .

Deed in Trust

Conveyance from trustor to trustee

Trustee's Deed

Conveyance from trustee to third party

Reconveyance Deed

Conveyance from trustee back to trustor

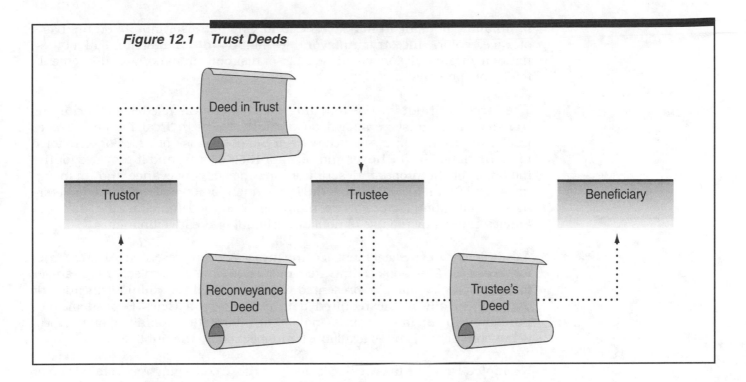

Figure 12.1 **Trust Deeds**

**Transfer
Tax Stamps**

Many states have enacted laws providing for a state transfer tax on conveyances of real estate.

In Illinois . . .

The *Illinois Real Estate Transfer Tax Act* imposes a tax on the privilege of conveying title to real estate. The tax is computed in units of $500, at the rate of $.50 for each $500 (or fraction of $500) of *taxable consideration.* When the real estate is transferred "subject to" an existing mortgage made by the seller before the time of transfer or when an existing mortgage is assumed by the buyer, the amount of the mortgage remaining unpaid is deducted from the full consideration to determine the taxable consideration. Fifty percent of the tax collected is deposited into the Illinois Affordable Housing Trust Fund; 35 percent is deposited into the Open Space Land Acquisition and Development Fund; the remaining 15 percent goes to the Natural Areas Acquisition Fund.

The **transfer tax** must be paid before the recording of the deed (or before transferring the beneficial interest in a land trust) by purchase of transfer tax stamps from the county recorder. Stamps may be affixed to the deed either before or after recording. Currently, all Illinois counties have enacted real estate transfer tax ordinances that are similar to the state act and call for a tax of $.25 for each $500 or fraction thereof of taxable consideration.

Under the *Illinois Affordable Housing Act of 1989,* part of the funds collected by the Illinois Department of Revenue pursuant to the Real Estate Transfer Tax Act are used to fund affordable housing. The statute defines *affordable housing* as residential housing occupied by low-income and very-low-income families, requiring no more than 30 percent of income for housing costs and utilities. (A *low-income family* is one earning less than 80 percent of the median area income for the family size; a *very-low-income family* earns less than 50 percent of the median area family income.) A trust fund has been created within the state treasury to finance programs under the act, such as grants, mortgages or no- and below-market-rate loans for the acquisition, construction, rehabilitation and development of affordable single-family and multifamily housing in Illinois. The fund may not discriminate on the basis of race, color, ancestry, unfavorable military discharge, familial status, national origin, religion, creed, sex, age or disability in making disbursements to eligible persons.

The "Green Sheet." The amount of consideration used for determining transfer taxes must be shown on the form entitled "Real Estate Transfer Declaration," also known as the *Green Sheet* because of its color. The form must be signed by the buyer and seller or their agents, and it provides for the inclusion of the property description, manner of conveyance and financing used. The financing data helps the Department of Revenue accurately determine equalization factors between different counties and eliminate inconsistencies caused by the use of nonconventional or creative financing.

A completed Green Sheet must accompany every deed presented to the recorder for recording. (The Cook County Recorder's office has its own separate transfer form, which also must be presented with every deed.) A willful falsification or omission of any of the required data constitutes a Class B misdemeanor punishable by up to six months in jail. The information contained on the form is not confidential and is available for inspection by the public.

Exempted from the tax are deeds such as those conveying real estate from or between any governmental bodies; those held by charitable, religious or educational institutions; those securing debts or releasing property as security for a debt; partitions; tax deeds; deeds pursuant to mergers of corporations; deeds from subsidiary to parent corporations for cancellation of stock; and deeds subject to federal documentary stamp tax. When the actual consideration for conveyance is less than $100, the transfer is considered a gift and is exempt from tax. An Exemption Statement is usually typed on an exempted deed and signed before the deed is recorded.

Tax formula. The formula used in Illinois to determine the taxable consideration is as follows:

Full actual consideration (sales price)	$ _____
Less value of personal property included in purchase	– _____
Less amount of mortgage to which property remains subject	– _____
Equals net taxable consideration to be covered by stamps	= _____
Amount of state of Illinois tax stamps ($.50 per $500 or part thereof of net taxable consideration)	$ _____
Amount of county tax stamps ($.25 per $500 or part thereof)	$ _____

Rules for calculating transfer tax stamps. The following summary of rules should help you work out stamp tax problems based on Illinois tax requirements:

- No tax is required if the total actual consideration is less than $100. Such deeds usually bear a notation at the bottom: "Consideration less than $100."
- The state of Illinois transfer tax is assessed at the rate of $.50 for each $500 or fractional part of $500.
- The county transfer tax is assessed at the rate of $.25 for each $500 or fractional part of $500.
- The tax is paid by the seller and is based on the sales price of the property.
- The value of personal property included is subtracted from the purchase price.

- Where a new mortgage is being secured by the purchaser and the proceeds are to be used by the purchaser in buying the property, the seller will pay a tax on the full sales price. (In this case, the property is not being conveyed subject to an existing mortgage, and thus the amount of this mortgage is not deducted from the sales price.)
- Where the seller takes back a purchase-money mortgage from the purchaser as part of the purchase price, the seller is required to pay a tax on the full sales price. (As in the preceding rule, the property is not being sold subject to an existing mortgage; the tax authorities consider the mortgage note given to the seller part of the total consideration.)

- Where the purchaser takes the property subject to an existing mortgage or assumes an existing mortgage on the property, that mortgage amount is subtracted from the sales price.

In summary, the tax is almost always based on the sales price. The only two circumstances in which that is not the case are (1) when the sales price includes personal property (then subtract that value) and (2) when the buyers are assuming or taking "subject to" the seller's old mortgage (then subtract the loan balance from the selling price). All other information is irrelevant.

Other transaction taxes. Chicago (and a growing number of other municipalities) have instituted their own transfer taxes in addition to those of the state and county. Most of these ordinances require that tax stamps be purchased from the municipality and that an accompanying form with proof of tax payment be presented to the recorder before recording is permitted. Local municipal regulations should be examined to determine if an amount is owed and by whom.

Land trusts. Under the *Land Trust Recordation and Transfer Tax Act*, a land trustee has the obligation to record a facsimile of the assignment of beneficial interest. The names of the beneficiaries need not be disclosed, and privacy is maintained. The tax rate and the exemptions are the same for the assignment as for the transfer of real property. ■

INVOLUNTARY ALIENATION

Title to property may be transferred without the owner's consent by **involuntary alienation.** (See Figure 12.2.) Involuntary transfers are usually carried out by operation of law—such as by condemnation or a sale to satisfy delinquent tax or mortgage liens. Condemnation occurs under two kinds of government powers: (1) under police powers to protect the public, such as hazardous buildings, and (2) under eminent domain. When a person dies intestate and leaves no heirs, the title to the real estate passes to the state by the state's power of escheat. As discussed earlier, additional land may be acquired through the process of accretion or actually lost through erosion.

Other acts of nature, such as earthquakes, hurricanes, sinkholes and mudslides, may create or eliminate a landowner's holdings.

Transfer by
Adverse
Possession

Adverse possession (sometimes referred to as *squatter's rights*) is another means of involuntary transfer. An individual who makes a claim to certain property, takes possession of it and, most important, uses it may take title away from an owner who fails to use or inspect the property for a period of

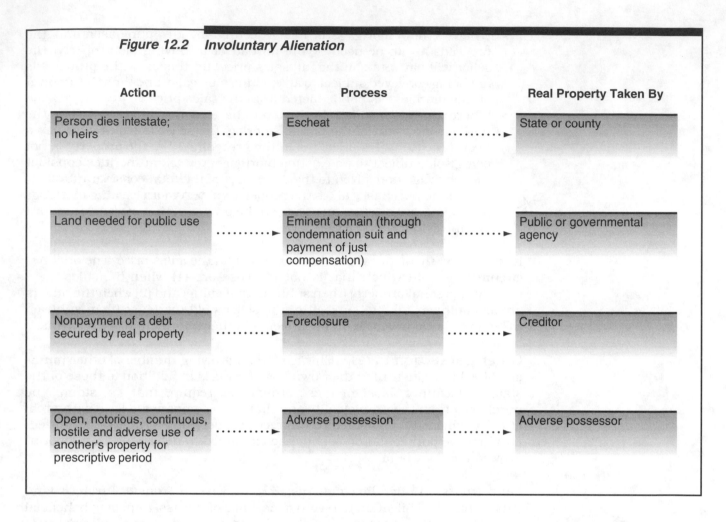

Figure 12.2   *Involuntary Alienation*

Action	Process	Real Property Taken By
Person dies intestate; no heirs	Escheat	State or county
Land needed for public use	Eminent domain (through condemnation suit and payment of just compensation)	Public or governmental agency
Nonpayment of a debt secured by real property	Foreclosure	Creditor
Open, notorious, continuous, hostile and adverse use of another's property for prescriptive period	Adverse possession	Adverse possessor

years. The law recognizes that the use of land is an important function of its ownership. Usually, the possession by the claimant must be

- open,
- notorious,
- continuous and uninterrupted,
- hostile and
- adverse to the true owner's possession.

The necessary period of uninterrupted possession is a matter of state law. The statutory periods range from as few as 5 years in some states to as many as 30 years in others. Through the principle of *tacking,* successive periods of different adverse possession by different adverse possessors can be combined, enabling a person who is not in possession for the entire required time to establish a claim. For instance, if Janet held a property in adverse possession for five years, then her daughter Erin held the same property for ten years, then Janet's other daughter Victoria held the property for five more years, Victoria would be able to claim the property by adverse possession even though she had not *personally* possessed the property for the full statutory 20 years.

In Illinois . . .

The period of uninterrupted possession required to claim title by adverse possession is 20 years. However, if the claimant under adverse possession has color of title (that is, if his or her apparently good title actually is

[handwritten margin note:] ADVERSE POSSESSION need suit to QUIET TITLE or get TITLE BY PRESCRIPTION

invalidated by some flaw) and pays the real estate taxes on the property, while satisfying the other statutory requirements, the possessory period may be shortened to seven years. ■

The difference between an *easement by prescription* and title by adverse possession lies in how the property is used. An easement by prescription is for a limited use of another's property, such as driving across someone else's land to gain access to one's own. On the other hand, if the trespasser builds a fence around the land and plants an orchard there, he or she is exerting a more *comprehensive possessory claim.* Once the statutory requirements are met, that claim will ripen into full title to the property (or ownership), rather than merely an easement (a usage right).

To claim title, the adverse possessor normally files an action in court to receive undisputed title. A claimant who acquires an easement by prescription does not receive title.

In Practice

The right of adverse possession is a statutory right. State requirements must be followed carefully to ensure the successful transfer of title. The parties to a transaction that might involve adverse possession should seek legal counsel because claims of adverse possession often must be resolved in court.

TRANSFER OF A DECEASED PERSON'S PROPERTY

A person who dies **testate** has prepared a will indicating how his or her property will be disposed of. In contrast, when a person dies **intestate** (without a will), real estate and personal property pass to the decedent's heirs according to the state's statute of descent and distribution. In effect, the state makes a will for an intestate decedent.

Legally, when a person dies, ownership of real estate immediately passes either to the heirs by descent or to the persons named in the will. Before these individuals can take full title and possession of the property, however, the estate must go through a judicial process called *probate,* and all claims against the estate must be satisfied.

In Illinois . . .

When the owner of real estate dies, how title to the property was held, rather than the laws of descent and distribution or the presence of a will, may dictate who the new owners will be.

- If the property was owned by a husband and wife in tenancy by the entirety or was held in joint tenancy, the surviving spouse (or other owner) will automatically be the new owner. If the property was held as a life estate, it automatically reverts to the former owner. In any case, no probate is required.
- If the property was not held in joint tenancy, tenancy by the entirety or a life estate, and the owner left a valid will (died testate), the devisees named will own the real estate.

TESTATOR ⟶ *DEVISEE*

PROE

BEQUEATH   *Legacy*

- If the owner died without a will (intestate), relatives will inherit the property according to the Illinois Law of Descent. (In effect, the state makes a will for such decedents.)
- If the owner died without a will (intestate) and left no heirs, the real property will escheat to the Illinois county it lies in. ∎

Transfer of Title by Will

A **will** is an instrument made by an owner to convey title to real or personal property after the owner's death. A will is a testamentary instrument; that is, it takes effect only after death. This differs from a deed, which must be delivered during the lifetime of the grantor and which conveys a present interest in property. While the **testator** (the person who makes a will) is alive, any property included in the will can still be conveyed by the owner. The parties named in a will have no rights or interests as long as the party who made the will lives; they acquire interest or title only after the owner's death.

Only property owned by the testator at the time of his or her death may be transferred by will. The gift of real property by will is known as a **devise,** and a person who receives property by will is known as a *devisee.*

For title to pass to the devisees, state laws require that on the death of a testator, the will must be filed with the court and probated. Probate is a legal procedure for verifying the validity of a will and accounting for the decedent's assets. The process can take several months to complete.

In Illinois . . .

Legal requirements for making a will.   Any person 18 or older, who is of sound mind and memory, may make a will. A will must be in writing and signed and declared by the maker (the testator) in the presence of two or more witnesses to be his or her last will and testament. Witnesses cannot be beneficiaries under the will, because their gifts may be voided by the probate court.

A modification of, an amendment of or an addition to a previously executed will may be set forth in a separate document called a *codicil.*

A *holographic will* is written in the testator's own handwriting and has not been witnessed. A *nuncupative will,* such as a deathbed bequest, is given orally by a testator. *Illinois courts do not recognize nuncupative or holographic wills.*

On the death of a testator, his or her will must be filed and a petition for probate initiated in the circuit court of the county in which the decedent resided. For six months after the executor has been appointed and the decedent's property has been inventoried, claims may be presented to the executor for debts owed by the deceased. Payment of approved claims and estate taxes is made, and the remaining assets are distributed. On completion of this probate process, the executor's final account is filed with the court and the executor is discharged. The real estate is considered free from debts, claims or taxes of the decedent.

While a decedent may freely disinherit children or other previously named heirs, *a surviving spouse may not be disinherited by the decedent spouse.* A surviving spouse who is disinherited by the decedent has a statutory right to renounce the will and claim a share of the estate, as follows:

- If the deceased left no child or descendant(s) of a child, *one-half of the personal estate* and *one-half of each parcel of real estate* goes to the spouse.
- If the deceased left spouse and descendants, *one-third of the personal estate* and *one-third of each parcel of real estate* goes to the spouse.
- The will remains operative with respect to the balance of the estate, but *all provisions in favor of the renouncing spouse are inoperative.* ∎

Transfer of Title by Descent

When a person dies intestate (without leaving a valid will) his or her state's law of descent governs how and to whom his or her property will be distributed.

In Illinois . . .

The *Illinois Law of Descent and Distribution* (in the Illinois Probate Act of 1975) provides that real estate located in Illinois owned by a deceased resident or nonresident *who did not leave a valid will* is distributed as indicated in Figure 12.3.

The estate of an intestate decedent must be probated to determine which statutory heirs will inherit, as well as to inventory the assets of and claims against the estate. Any **heir** or other interested person may petition the circuit court of the county in which the decedent last resided to probate the estate. Proof of heirship must be presented to the court. Probate generally proceeds as if the decedent had left a valid will. (Probate is discussed further below.) ∎

Probate Proceedings

Probate is a formal judicial process that

- proves or confirms the validity of a will,
- determines the precise assets of the deceased person and
- identifies the persons to whom the assets are to pass.

The purpose of probate is to see that the assets are distributed correctly. All assets must be accounted for and the decedent's debts must be satisfied before any property is distributed to the heirs. In addition, estate taxes must be paid before any distribution. The laws of each state govern the probate proceedings and the functions of the individuals appointed to administer the decedent's affairs.

Assets that are distributed through probate are those that do not otherwise distribute themselves. For instance, property held in joint tenancy or tenancy by the entirety passes immediately. Probate proceedings take place *in the county in which the decedent resided.* If the decedent owned real estate in another county, probate would occur in that county as well.

The person who has possession of the will—normally the person designated in the will as *executor*—presents it for filing with the court. The court is responsible for determining that the will meets the statutory requirements for its form and execution. If a codicil or more than one will exists, the court will decide how these documents should be probated.

The court must rule on a challenge if a will is contested. Once the will is upheld, the assets can be distributed according to its provisions. Probate courts distribute assets according to statute only when no other reasonable alternative exists.

[Handwritten note in left margin: IF THE Deseand Left the spanse & Children, No other relitives will get anything]

Figure 12.3	Statutory Distributions under the Illinois Law of Descent and Distribution		
Decedent Status	**Family Status**	**Property Passes . . .**	
Married, with surviving spouse	No children No other relatives	100% to surviving spouse	
	Children	50% to surviving spouse; 50% shared by children or descendants of deceased child	
Married, no surviving spouse	Children	Children share equally, with descendants of a deceased child taking their parent's share	
Unmarried, no children	Other relatives	100% to parents, brothers or sisters equally; however, if there is one surviving parent, that parent takes two shares and all others share equal portions; if no parents or brothers or sisters survive, the estate passes to other relatives as determined by the probate court.	
	No other relatives	100% to the county in which the real estate is located, by escheat	

When a person dies intestate, the court determines who inherits the assets by reviewing proof from relatives of the decedent and their entitlement under the statute of descent and distribution. Once the heirs have been determined, the court appoints an *administrator* or a personal representative to administer the affairs of the estate—the role usually taken by an executor.

Whether or not a will is involved, the administrator or executor is responsible for having the estate's assets appraised and for ensuring that all the decedent's debts are satisfied. He or she is also responsible for paying federal estate taxes and state inheritance taxes out of the assets. Once all obligations have been satisfied, the representative distributes the remaining property according to the terms of the will or the state's law of descent.

[Handwritten note: DIES TESTATE   DIES INTESTATE]

In Practice   A broker entering into a listing agreement with the executor or administrator of an estate in probate should be aware that the amount of commission is fixed by the court and that the commission is payable only from the proceeds of the sale. The broker will not be able to collect a commission unless the court approves the sale.

SUMMARY

Title to real estate is the right to and evidence of ownership of the land. It may be transferred by voluntary alienation, involuntary alienation, will and descent.

The voluntary transfer of an owner's title is made by a deed, executed (signed) by the owner as grantor to the purchaser or donee as grantee.

Among the most common requirements for a valid deed are a grantor with legal capacity to contract, a readily identifiable grantee, a granting clause, a legal description of the property, a recital of consideration, exceptions and reservations on the title and the signature of the grantor. In addition, the deed should be properly witnessed and acknowledged before a notary public or another officer to provide evidence that the signature is genuine and to allow recording. Title to the property passes when the grantor delivers a deed to the grantee and it is accepted. The obligation of a grantor is determined by the form of the deed. The words of conveyance in the granting clause are important in determining the form of deed.

A general warranty deed provides the greatest protection of any deed by binding the grantor to certain covenants or warranties. A special warranty deed warrants only that the real estate is not encumbered except as stated in the deed. A bargain and sale deed carries with it no warranties but implies that the grantor holds title to the property. A quitclaim deed carries with it no warranties whatsoever and conveys only the interest, if any, the grantor possesses in the property.

An owner's title may be transferred without his or her permission by a court action, such as a foreclosure or judgment sale, a tax sale, condemnation under the right of eminent domain, adverse possession or escheat. Land may also be transferred by the natural forces of water and wind, which either increase property by accretion or decrease it through erosion or avulsion.

The real estate of an owner who makes a valid will (who dies testate) passes to the devisees through the probating of the will. The title of an owner who dies without a will (intestate) passes according to the provisions of the law of descent and distribution of the state in which the real estate is located.

In Illinois . . .

In Illinois, the requirements for a valid deed are a grantor with legal capacity to contract, a readily identifiable grantee, a granting clause, a legal description of the property, a recital of consideration and the signature of the grantor. Title to the property passes when the grantor delivers a deed to the grantee and it is accepted. The obligation of a grantor is determined by the form of the deed. The words of conveyance in the granting clause are important in determining the form of deed.

Acknowledgment and notarization are not required. Except for tax deeds, recording is not required.

In Illinois, a bargain and sale deed includes covenants that make it similar to a special warranty deed. A quitclaim deed carries with it no warranties whatsoever and conveys only the interest, if any, the grantor possesses in the property.

The title of an owner who dies without a will (intestate) passes to the decedent's statutory heirs, according to the provisions of the Illinois Law of Descent and Distribution. Where a decedent leaves no statutory heirs, the real property escheats to the county in which it is located. ■

QUESTIONS

1. The basic requirements for a valid conveyance are governed by:
   A. state law.
   B. local custom.
   C. national law.
   D. the law of descent.

2. All of the following are true regarding deeds EXCEPT that a deed must:
   A. be signed by the grantee to be valid.
   B. contain consideration.
   C. be accepted by the grantee.
   D. contain a granting clause.

3. Hal, age 15, recently inherited many parcels of real estate from his late father and has decided to sell one of them. If Hal entered into a deed conveying his interest in the property to a purchaser, such a conveyance would be:
   A. valid.
   B. void.
   C. invalid.
   D. voidable.

4. A husband who works for an international corporation has already moved to Germany. To authorize his wife to act on his behalf, he signed a(n):
   A. power of attorney.
   B. release deed.
   C. quitclaim deed.
   D. acknowledgment.

5. What is the major difference between a general warranty deed and a quitclaim deed?

   A. A general warranty deed provides the least protection for the buyer; a quitclaim deed provides the most protection for the buyer.
   B. A general warranty deed can be used only in foreclosure sales; a quitclaim deed is used only in residential sales.
   C. A general warranty deed provides the most protection for the buyer; a quitclaim deed provides the least protection for the buyer.
   D. A general warranty deed creates an indefeasible title; a quitclaim deed creates a defeasible title.

6. Lou receives a deed from Gary. The granting clause of the deed states, "I, Gary, hereby remise, release, alienate and convey to Lou the property known as Yellowacre." What type of deed has Lou received?
   A. Special warranty
   B. Quitclaim
   C. General warranty
   D. Bargain and sale

7. Which of the following best describes the covenant of quiet enjoyment?
   A. The grantor promises to obtain and deliver any instrument needed to make the title good.
   B. The grantor guarantees that if the title fails in the future, he or she will compensate the grantee.
   C. The grantor warrants that he or she is the owner and has the right to convey title to the property.
   D. The grantor guarantees that the title will be good against the title claims of third parties.

8. A deed includes the following statement: "The full consideration for this conveyance is $125,480." Which type of deed is this most likely to be?
   A. Gift deed
   B. Trustee's deed
   C. Deed in trust
   D. Deed executed pursuant to court order

9. Which of the following types of deeds merely implies, but does not specifically warrant, that the grantor holds good title to the property?
   A. Special warranty
   B. Bargain and sale
   C. Quitclaim
   D. Trustee's

10. Step 1: Herbert decided to convey Blueacre to James. Step 2: Herbert signed a deed transferring title to James. Step 3: Herbert gave the signed deed to James, who accepted it. Step 4: James took the deed to the county recorder's office and had it recorded. At which step did title to Blueacre actually transfer or pass to James?
    A. Step 1   C. Step 3
    B. Step 2   D. Step 4

11. Andrea conveys property to Kurt by deed. The deed contains the following: (1) Kurt's name, spelled out in full; (2) a statement that Andrea has received $10 and Kurt's love and affection; and (3) a statement that the property is conveyed to Kurt "to have and to hold." Which of the following correctly identifies, in order, these three elements of the deed?
    A. Grantee; consideration; granting clause
    B. Grantee; consideration; habendum clause
    C. Grantor; habendum clause; legal description
    D. Grantee; acknowledgment; habendum clause

12. Teresa signed a deed transferring ownership of Whiteacre to Lynn. To provide evidence that Teresa's signature was genuine, Teresa executed a declaration before a notary. This declaration is known as an:
    A. affidavit.
    B. acknowledgment.
    C. affirmation.
    D. estoppel.

13. Roland executes a deed to Philip as grantee, has it acknowledged and receives payment from the buyer. Roland holds the deed, however, and arranges to meet Philip the next morning at the courthouse to give the deed to him. In this situation at this time:
    A. Philip owns the property because he has paid for it.
    B. Legal title to the property will not officially pass until Philip has been given the deed the next morning.
    C. Legal title to the property will not pass until Philip has received the deed and records it the next morning.
    D. Philip will own the property when he signs the deed the next morning.

14. Title to real estate may be transferred during a person's lifetime by:
    A. devise.
    B. descent.
    C. involuntary alienation.
    D. escheat.

15. Fran bought acreage in a distant county, never went to see the acreage and did not use the ground. Harry moved his mobile home onto the land, had a water well drilled and lived there for 22 years. Harry may become the owner of the land if he has complied with the state law regarding:
    A. requirements for a valid conveyance.
    B. adverse possession.
    C. avulsion.
    D. voluntary alienation.

16. What do the terms *condemnation* and *escheat* have in common?
    A. They are examples of voluntary alienation.
    B. They are processes used in adverse possession claims.
    C. They are methods of transferring title by descent.
    D. They are examples of involuntary alienation.

17. A seller lists her property for $99,000 and provides a quitclaim deed to the buyer. A buyer offers $99,000 for the property contingent on the seller's providing a general warranty deed. The seller accepts. Three months after the closing, a relative of the seller claims to have an interest in the property, and sues. Does the seller have to protect the buyer?
    A. No, a general warranty deed does not provide protection to the buyer.
    B. No, because when the property was listed the seller only offered to give a quitclaim deed.
    C. Yes, the covenant of seisin promises the seller will protect the buyer from third parties.
    D. Yes, the covenant of quiet enjoyment guarantees that the seller will protect the buyer from third parties.

18. A deed contains a guarantee that the grantor will compensate the grantee for any loss resulting from the title's failure in the future. This is an example of which type of covenant?
    A. Warranty forever
    B. Further assurance
    C. Quiet enjoyment
    D. Seisin

19. A person who has died leaving a valid will is called a(n):
    A. devisee.   C. legatee.
    B. testator.   D. intestate.

20. Title to real estate can be transferred at death by which of the following documents?
    A. Warranty deed
    B. Special warranty deed
    C. Trustee's deed
    D. Will

21. Jameson, a bachelor, died owning real estate that he devised by his will to his niece, Karen. At what point does full title pass to his niece?
    A. Immediately on Jameson's death
    B. After his will has been probated
    C. After Karen has paid all inheritance taxes
    D. When Karen executes a new deed to the property

In Illinois . . .

22. What does the statement "Illinois courts do not recognize holographic wills" mean?
    A. Wills may not be handwritten.
    B. Deathbed bequests are invalid.
    C. Unwitnessed, handwritten wills are invalid.
    D. Wills modified by codicil are invalid.

23. In Illinois, how many years are required to acquire title by adverse possession?
    A. 5   C. 20
    B. 7   D. 30

24. Which of the following statements is true regarding the execution of a valid will in Illinois?
    A. The testator must be at least 21 years old and of sound mind.
    B. The will must be in writing, signed and witnessed by two people.
    C. The will must be witnessed by three persons.
    D. The will must be notarized.

25. Which of the following statements is true regarding a bargain and sale deed in Illinois?
    A. It warrants that the grantor has fee simple title.
    B. It warrants that the grantor will defend all suits against title.
    C. It conveys to the grantee any future title the grantor may acquire.
    D. It warrants that the premises are free from all encumbrances.

26. In Illinois, the transfer tax is:
    A. customarily paid by the buyer.
    B. computed on the sales price less the amount of any existing mortgage to which the property remains subject.
    C. not required if the actual total consideration is less than $500.
    D. assessed at the rate of $1 per $1,000 of sales price.

27. All of the following deeds are exempt from the Illinois transfer tax, EXCEPT:
    A. a deed conveying a property owned by a charitable institution.
    B. a deed conveying a property owned by a government body.
    C. deeds for property valued at less than $100.
    D. deeds between relatives.

28. Samuel, a longtime Illinois resident who owned considerable real and personal property, died testate, leaving only $1 to his wife, Marianne, who was his sole survivor. The balance of his estate was left to his trusted real estate broker. Marianne renounced the will. Which of the following is true?
    A. The entire will is invalid.
    B. Marianne is entitled to a one-quarter share of all property.
    C. Marianne is entitled to one-half of the personal estate and one-half of each parcel of real estate.
    D. Because Samuel left no descendants, Marianne is entitled to the entire estate by the law of descent.

29. Robert, an Illinois resident, died intestate. Robert was survived by a mother and brother. Under these facts, which of the following correctly states how Robert's estate will be distributed?
    A. Robert's estate will be left entirely to his mother.
    B. The estate will be divided equally between the mother and brother.
    C. The estate will be divided so that Robert's mother receives two-thirds and Robert's brother receives one-third.
    D. Robert's mother receives one-third and Robert's brother receives two-thirds.

30. Jim owned Illinois real estate as a sole owner and died intestate, survived by a spouse and their one child. After Jim's debts and taxes are paid, the child will own:
    A. two-thirds in fee simple.
    B. one-third in fee simple.
    C. one-half in fee simple.
    D. the entire estate in fee simple.

31. A parcel of Illinois real estate encumbered with a mortgage is being sold for $100,000. The purchaser agrees to assume this mortgage with a present balance of $48,000 and to pay $52,000 in cash upon receipt of the seller's deed. What amount of county and state stamps must the seller affix to the deed?
    A. $52   C. $100
    — B. $78   D. $150

32. Millie sells her Springfield condominium to Jane for $80,000. Based on this transaction, which of the following statements is true?
    A. If Millie takes back a purchase-money mortgage of $60,000, her total tax due to the county and state will be $30.
    B. If Millie lets Jane take title subject to Millie's $50,000 mortgage, Millie will pay a total tax of $45 to the county and state.
    C. If the purchase price includes $10,000 of personal property, Millie's total tax due to the county and state will be $115.
    D. This transaction is exempt from real property taxation in Illinois.

33. A seller agreed to sell her home for $127,000. There is an existing mortgage on the property with an unpaid balance of $95,000. This mortgage has a prepayment option, and the seller will pay the $95,000 balance with the proceeds she receives from the sale. The purchaser, who has arranged for a mortgage loan of $100,000, will pay the remaining $27,000 in cash. Because of the two loan transactions, it is necessary to close the sale through an escrow. What amount of Illinois state and county transfer tax stamps is the seller required to affix to her deed conveying this property?
    A. $40.50   C. $140.50
    B. $48.00   D. $190.50

34. Karl has a deed prepared conveying a farm near Champaign to his son as a gift. The deed contains a statement that the farm was given in "consideration of ten dollars and love and affection." The farm has a market value of $73,000. Karl is required to attach what amount of transfer stamps to his executed deed?
    A. $0.00   C. $109.00
    B. $73.00   D. $109.50

13

Title Records

KEY TERMS

abstract of title
actual notice
attorney's opinion of
   title

certificate of title
chain of title
constructive notice
marketable title

priority recording
suit to quite title
title insurance
title search

PUBLIC RECORDS

Public records contain detailed information about each parcel of real estate in a city or county. These records are crucial in establishing ownership, giving notice of encumbrances and establishing priority of liens. They protect the interests of real estate owners, taxing bodies, creditors and the general public. The real estate recording system includes written documents that affect title, such as deeds and mortgages. Public records regarding taxes, judgments, probate and marriage also may offer important information about the title to a particular property.

Public records are maintained by

- recorders of deeds,
- county clerks,
- county treasurers,
- city clerks,
- collectors and
- clerks of court.

In Illinois . . .

The recorder of deeds, county clerk, county treasurer, city clerk and collector, and clerks of various courts maintain these records. In Illinois, a recorder of deeds must be elected in each county with a population of 60,000 or more. In counties with a population of fewer than 60,000, the county clerk serves as the recorder of deeds. ■

Public records are just that: open to the public. This means that anyone interested in a particular property can review the records to learn about the documents, claims and other issues that affect its ownership. A prospective purchaser, for example, needs to be sure that the seller can convey title to the property. If the property is subject to any liens or other encumbrances, a prospective buyer or lender will want to know.

In Practice

Although we speak of prospective purchasers conducting title searches, purchasers themselves rarely search the public records for evidence of title or encumbrances. Instead, title companies conduct searches before providing title insurance. An attorney also may search the title. A growing number of lending institutions require title insurance as part of the mortgage loan commitment.

Recording

> In most states, written documents that affect land *must be recorded in the county where the land is located.*

Recording is the act of placing documents in the public record. The specific rules for recording documents are a matter of state law. However, although the details may vary, all recording acts essentially provide that any written document that affects any estate, right, title or interest in land must be recorded in the county where the land is located to serve as public notice. That way, anyone interested in the title to a parcel of property will know where to look to discover the various interests of all other parties. Recording acts also generally give legal priority to those interests recorded first (the "first in time, first in right" or "first come, first served" principle).

To be eligible for recording, a document must be drawn and executed as stipulated in the recording acts of the state in which the real estate is located.

In Illinois . . .

Illinois law does not require that most documents be filed or recorded within a specified period of time. However, when creditors and subsequent purchasers do not actually know the content of the documents affecting certain real estate interests, the courts will hold these creditors and purchasers responsible for discovering that information only as of the date on which the documents are recorded. Tax deeds, by law, must be recorded within one year after the redemption period expires. A tax deed that is not recorded or filed within this period becomes null and void.

Deeds, mortgages and other instruments that affect title to real estate must be recorded in the Illinois county in which the real estate is located. *No instrument affecting title to real property may include any provision prohibiting recording. Any such prohibiting provision is void as a matter of law.*

The original document must be filed with the county recorder of deeds, and must meet specific requirements (in addition to the eight requirements of a valid deed):

- Grantor's name typed or printed below his or her signature
- Full address of the grantee
- Name and address of the person who prepared the deed
- Permanent tax index number (required only in some counties)
- Common address of the property (required only in some counties)
- 3½" × 3½" blank space for use by the recorder
- Completed state real estate transfer declaration or Green Sheet (for properties in Cook County, the recorder also requires completion of a county transfer declaration)
- Proof of payment of the state and county transfer taxes or indication of an applicable exemption
- Proof of payment of the municipal transfer tax (if applicable)

When the parcel of land being transferred is (1) a division of a larger parcel and (2) smaller than five acres, the recording provisions of the Illinois Plat Act apply. If the conveyance is exempt, an affidavit stating the reason for the exemption may be required by the recorder.

In some municipalities, including Chicago, the water department must declare, by way of an endorsement stamp on the municipal transfer declaration, that all outstanding water bills have been paid.

A deed in any language other than English, although valid between the parties, does not give constructive notice unless an official English translation of the document is attached at the time of recording. The translation must be prepared by a credible source, such as the local consulate of a country in which the language is used. ∎

Notice

Anyone who has an interest in a parcel of real estate can take certain steps, called *giving notice,* to ensure that others know about the individual's interest. There are two basic types of notice: constructive notice and actual notice.

Constructive notice is the legal presumption that information may be obtained by an individual through diligent inquiry. Properly recording documents in the public record serves as constructive notice to the world of an individual's rights or interest. So does the physical possession of a property. Because the information or evidence is readily available to the world, a prospective purchaser or lender is responsible for discovering the interest.

In contrast, **actual notice** means not only that the information is available, but that someone has been given the information and actually knows it. An individual who has searched the public records and inspected the property has actual notice. Actual notice is also known as *direct knowledge.* If an individual can be proved to have had actual notice of information, he or she cannot use a lack of constructive notice (such as an unrecorded deed) to justify a claim.

Priority. Priority refers to the order of rights in time. Many complicated situations can affect the priority of rights in a parcel of real estate—who recorded first; which party was in possession first; who had actual or constructive notice. How the courts rule in any situation depends, of course, on the specific facts of the case. These are strictly legal questions that should be referred to the parties' attorneys.

FOR EXAMPLE In May, Burt purchased Grayacre from Arthur and received a deed. Burt never recorded the deed but began farming operations on the property in June. In November, Arthur (who was forgetful) again sold Grayacre, this time to Carl. Carl accepted the deed and promptly recorded it. However, because Carl never inspected Grayacre to see whether someone was in possession, Burt has the superior right to the property even though Burt never recorded the deed. By taking possession, a purchaser gives constructive notice of his or her interest in the land.

Unrecorded Documents

Certain types of liens are not recorded. Real estate taxes and special assessments are liens on specific parcels of real estate and usually are not recorded until some time after the taxes or assessments are past due. Inheritance taxes and franchise taxes are statutory liens. They are placed against all real estate owned by a decedent at the time of death or by a corporation at the time the franchise taxes became a lien. Like real estate taxes, they are not recorded.

Notice of these liens must be gained from sources other than the recorder's office. Evidence of the payment of real estate taxes, special assessments, municipal utilities and other taxes can be gathered from paid tax receipts and letters from municipalities. Creative measures are often required to get information about these "off the record" liens.

In Illinois . . .

A mechanic's lien that has not been recorded may nonetheless still have priority over other liens that have been recorded. ■

Chain of Title

Chain of title is the record of a property's ownership. Beginning with the earliest owner, title may pass to many individuals. Each owner is linked to the next so that a chain is formed. An unbroken chain of title can be traced through linking conveyances from the present owner back to the earliest recorded owner.

If ownership cannot be traced through an unbroken chain, it is said that there is a *gap* in the chain. In these cases, the cloud on the title makes it necessary to establish ownership by a court action called a **suit to quiet title.** A suit might be required, for instance, when a grantor acquired title under one name and conveyed it under another. Or there may be a forged deed in the chain, after which no subsequent grantee acquired legal title. All possible claimants are allowed to present evidence during a court proceeding; then the court's judgment is filed. Often, the simple procedure of obtaining any relevant quitclaim deeds is used to establish ownership.

Title Search and Abstract of Title

A **title search** is an examination of all of the public records to determine whether any defects exist in the chain of title. The records of the conveyances of ownership are examined, beginning with the present owner. Then the title is traced backward to its origin (or 40 to 60 years, depending on local custom). The time beyond which the title must be searched is limited in states that have adopted the Marketable Title Act. This law extinguishes certain interests and cures certain defects arising before the *root of the title*—the conveyance that establishes the source of the chain of title. Normally, the root is considered to be 40 years or more. Under most circumstances, then, it is necessary to search only from the current owner to the root.

In Illinois . . .

For normal title searches in Illinois, the search goes back 40 years. When the possibility of litigation exists, the search must go back 75 years. Interestingly, in Cook and Du Page counties title searches cannot go back beyond 1871, when most of the records were destroyed in the Great Chicago Fire.

Other public records are examined to identify wills, judicial proceedings and other encumbrances that may affect title. These include a variety of taxes, special assessments and other recorded liens.

A title search usually is not ordered until after the major contingencies in a sales contract have been cleared—for instance, after a loan commitment has been secured. Before providing money for a loan, a lender generally orders a title search to ensure that no lien is superior to its mortgage lien. In most cases, the cost of the title search is paid by the buyer. ■

An **abstract of title** is a summary report of what the title search found in the public record. The person who prepares this report is called an *abstractor.* The abstractor searches all the public records, then summarizes the various events and proceedings that affected the title throughout its history. The report begins with the original grant (or root), then provides a chronological list of recorded instruments. All recorded liens and encumbrances are included, along with their current statuses. A list of all of the public records examined is also provided as evidence of the scope of the search.

In Practice   An abstract of title is a condensed history of those items that can be found in public records. It does not reveal such items as encroachments or forgeries or any interests or conveyances that have not been recorded.

Marketable Title   Under the terms of the typical real estate sales contract, the seller is required to deliver **marketable title** to the buyer at the closing. To be marketable, a title must

- disclose no serious defects and not depend on doubtful questions of law or fact to prove its validity;
- not expose a purchaser to the hazard of litigation or threaten the quiet enjoyment of the property;
- convince a reasonably well-informed and prudent purchaser, acting on business principles and with knowledge of the facts and their legal significance, that he or she could sell or mortgage the property at a later time.

Although a title that does not meet these requirements still could be transferred, it contains certain defects that may limit or restrict its ownership. A buyer cannot be forced to accept a conveyance that is materially different from the one bargained for in the sales contract. However, questions of marketable title must be raised by a buyer before acceptance of the deed. Once a buyer has accepted a deed with an unmarketable title, the only available legal recourse is to sue the seller under any covenants of warranty contained in the deed.

PROOF OF OWNERSHIP

Proof of ownership is evidence that title is marketable. *A deed by itself is not considered sufficient evidence of ownership.* Even though a warranty deed conveys the grantor's interest, it contains no proof of the condition of the grantor's title at the time of the conveyance. The grantee needs some assurance that he or she actually is acquiring ownership and that the title is marketable. A certificate of title and title insurance commonly are used to prove ownership.

Certificate of Title   A **certificate of title** is a statement of opinion of the title's status on the date the certificate is issued. *A certificate of title is not a guarantee of ownership.* Rather, it certifies the condition of the title based on an examination of the public records—a title search. The certificate may be prepared by a title company, a licensed abstractor or an attorney. An owner, a mortgage lender or a buyer may request the certificate.

Although a certificate of title is used as evidence of ownership, it is not perfect. Unrecorded liens or rights of parties in possession cannot be discovered by a search of the public records. Hidden defects, such as transfers involving forged documents, incorrect marital information, incompetent parties, minors or fraud, cannot be detected. A certificate offers no defense against these defects because they are unknown. The person who prepares the certificate is liable only for negligence in preparing the certificate.

An abstract and **attorney's opinion of title** are used in some areas as evidence of title. It is an opinion of the status of the title based on a review of the abstract. Similar to a certificate of title, the opinion of title does not protect against defects that cannot be discovered from the public records. Many buyers purchase title insurance to defend the title from these defects.

Title Insurance

Title insurance is a contract under which the policyholder is protected from losses arising from defects in the title. A title insurance company determines whether the title is insurable based on a review of the public records. If so, a policy is issued. Unlike other insurance policies that insure against future losses, title insurance protects the insured from an event that occurred *before* the policy was issued. Title insurance is considered the best defense of title: the title insurance company will defend any lawsuit based on an insurable defect and pay claims if the title proves to be defective.

After examining the public records, the title company usually issues what may be called a *preliminary report of title* or a *commitment to issue a title policy.* This describes the type of policy that will be issued and includes

- the name of the insured party;
- the legal description of the real estate;
- the estate or interest covered;
- conditions and stipulations under which the policy is issued; and
- a schedule of all exceptions, including encumbrances and defects found in the public records and any known unrecorded defects.

The *premium* for the policy is paid once, at closing. The maximum loss for which the company may be liable cannot exceed the face amount of the policy (unless the amount of coverage has been extended by use of an *inflation rider*). When a title company makes a payment to settle a claim covered by a policy, the company generally acquires the right to any remedy or damages available to the insured. This right is called *subrogation.*

In Illinois . . .

A title insurance policy is the most commonly used evidence that an owner of Illinois real property tenders to a prospective purchaser or lender as proof of good title.

The *Illinois Title Insurance Act of 1990* requires that all producers of title insurance who own a part interest in a title company disclose this fact to clients. *Producers of title insurance* include lawyers and real estate brokers and salespeople, because every time a sale is made, a new title insurance policy must be produced. These producers are permitted to recommend their own title companies, but they must be registered as title agents and must fill out mandatory disclosure forms for the buyer and seller. Failure to comply with the disclosure rules can result in loss of the privilege of doing business in the state. ■

Coverage. Exactly which defects the title company will defend depends on the type of policy. (See Table 13.1.) A *standard coverage policy* normally insures the title as it is known from the public records. In addition, the standard policy insures against such hidden defects as forged documents, conveyances by incompetent grantors, incorrect marital statements and improperly delivered deeds.

Extended coverage, as provided by an *American Land Title Association* (ALTA) policy, includes the protections of a standard policy plus additional protections. An extended policy protects a homeowner against defects that may be discovered by inspection of the property: rights of parties in possession, examination of a survey and certain unrecorded liens. Most lenders require extended coverage title policies.

Title insurance does not offer guaranteed protection against all defects. A title company will not insure a bad title or offer protection against defects that clearly appear in a title search. The policy generally names certain uninsurable losses, called *exclusions.* These include zoning ordinances, restrictive covenants, easements, certain water rights and current taxes and special assessments.

Types of policies. The different types of policies depend on who is named as the insured. An owner's policy is issued for the benefit of the owner and his or her heirs or devisees. This policy is almost always paid for by the seller at the closing. A lender's policy is issued for the benefit of the mortgage company. This policy is almost always paid for by the buyer at the closing. The amount of the coverage depends on the amount of the mortgage loan. As the loan balance is reduced, the coverage decreases.

A lessee's interest can be insured with a leasehold policy. Certificate of sale policies are available to insure the title to property purchased in a court sale.

In Illinois . . .

An extended title insurance policy would offer buyer protection against "secret liens," such as unrecorded mechanics' liens. ■

Table 13.1   *Owner's Title Insurance Policy*

Standard Coverage	Extended Coverage	Not Covered by Either Policy
1. Defects found in public records	Standard coverage plus defects discoverable through the following:	1. Defects and liens listed in policy
2. Forged documents		2. Defects known to buyer
3. Incompetent grantors	1. Property inspection, including unrecorded rights of persons in possession	3. Changes in land use brought about by zoning ordinances
4. Incorrect marital statements	2. Examination of survey	
5. Improperly delivered deeds	3. Unrecorded liens not known of by policyholder	

SUMMARY

The purpose of the recording acts is to give legal, public and constructive notice to the world of parties' interests in real estate. The recording provisions have been adopted to create system and order in the transfer of real estate. Without them, it would be virtually impossible to transfer real estate from one party to another. The interests and rights of the various parties in a particular parcel of land must be recorded so that such rights are legally effective against third parties who do not have knowledge or notice of the rights.

Possession of real estate is generally interpreted as constructive notice of the rights of the person in possession. Actual notice is knowledge acquired directly and personally.

Title evidence shows whether a seller conveys marketable title. A deed of conveyance is evidence that a grantor has conveyed his or her interest in land, but it is not evidence of the title's kind or condition. A marketable title is generally one that is so free from significant defects that the purchaser can be insured against having to defend the title.

Three forms of providing title evidence are commonly used throughout the United States: abstract and attorney's opinion of title, certificate of title, and title insurance policy. Each form reveals the history of a title. Each must be later dated, or continued or reissued, to cover a more recent date.

UNIFORM COMMERCIAL CODE :—

QUESTIONS

1. A title search in the public records may be conducted by:
   A. anyone.
   B. attorneys and abstractors only.
   C. attorneys, abstractors and real estate licensees only.
   D. anyone who obtains a court order under the Freedom of Information Act.

2. Which of the following statements best explains why instruments affecting real estate are recorded?
   A. Recording gives constructive notice to the world of the rights and interests of a party in a particular parcel of real estate.
   B. Failing to record will void the transfer.
   C. The instruments must be recorded to comply with the terms of the statute of frauds.
   D. Recording proves the execution of the instrument.

3. A purchaser went to the county building to check the recorder's records. She found that the seller was the grantee in the last recorded deed and that no mortgage was on record against the property. The purchaser may assume which of the following?
   A. All taxes are paid, and no judgments are outstanding.
   B. The seller has good title.
   C. The seller did not mortgage the property.
   D. No one else is occupying the property.

4. The date and time a document was recorded establish which of the following?
   A. Priority
   B. Abstract of title
   C. Subrogation
   D. Marketable title

5. Pam bought Laura's house, received a deed and moved into the residence but neglected to record the document. One week later, Laura died, and her heirs in another city, unaware that the property had been sold, conveyed title to Michael, who recorded the deed. Who owns the property?
   A. Pam
   B. Michael
   C. Laura's heirs
   D. Both Pam and Michael

6. A property has encumbrances. Can it be sold?
   A. No, a property cannot be sold if it has any encumbrances.
   B. No, not unless the seller secures title insurance.
   C. Yes, if title insurance can be purchased by the buyer covering the encumbrances.
   D. Yes, if the buyer agrees to buy it subject to the encumbrances.

7. All of the following are acceptable proof of ownership EXCEPT a(n):
   A. ALTA policy.
   B. title insurance policy.
   C. abstract and attorney's opinion.
   D. deed signed by the last seller.

8. Chain of title refers to which of the following?
   A. Summary or history of all documents and legal proceedings affecting a specific parcel of land
   B. Report of the contents of the public record regarding a particular property
   C. Instrument or document that protects the insured parties (subject to specific exceptions) against defects in the examination of the record and hidden risks such as forgeries, undisclosed heirs and errors in the public records
   D. Record of a property's ownership

9. Bill, the seller, delivered a deed to the buyer at the closing. A title search disclosed no serious defects, and the title did not appear to be based on doubtful questions of law or fact or to expose the buyer to possible litigation. Bill's title did not appear to present a threat to the buyer's quiet enjoyment, and the title policy was sufficient to convince a reasonably well-informed person that the property could be resold. The title conveyed would commonly be referred to as a(n):
   A. certificate of title.
   B. abstract of title.
   C. marketable title.
   D. attorney's opinion of title.

10. The person who prepares an abstract of title for a parcel of real estate:
   A. searches the public records and then summarizes the events and proceedings that affect title.
   B. insures the condition of the title.
   C. inspects the property.
   D. issues a certificate of title.

11. Susan is frantic because she cannot find her deed and now wants to sell the property. She:
   A. may need a suit to quiet title.
   B. must buy title insurance.
   C. does not need the deed to sell if it was recorded.
   D. should execute a replacement deed to herself.

12. Which of the following is NOT true regarding the lender's title insurance?
   A. The lender's protection decreases with each principal payment that is made.
   B. The buyer is usually required to purchase the lender's policy.
   C. The mortgagee's policy covers both the mortgagor and mortgagee.
   D. The mortgagee's premium is paid once, at the closing.

13. Which of the following are traditionally covered by a standard title insurance policy?
   A. Unrecorded rights of persons in possession
   B. Improperly delivered deeds
   C. Changes in land use due to zoning ordinances
   D. Unrecorded liens not known of by the policyholder

14. General Title Company settled a claim against its insured, Robert. General Title made a substantial payment to the person who sued Robert. Now, General Title may seek damages from Sam, who originally gave Robert a general warranty deed. Through what right can General Title recover the amount it paid out in the settlement?
   A. Escrow
   B. Encumbrance
   C. Subordination
   D. Subrogation

15. A title insurance policy with standard coverage generally covers all of the following EXCEPT:
   A. forged documents.
   B. incorrect marital statements.
   C. unrecorded rights of parties in possession.
   D. incompetent grantors.

16. The documents referred to as title evidence include:
   A. title insurance.
   B. warranty deeds.
   C. security agreements.
   D. a deed.

17. The legal presumption that information can be obtained through diligent inquiry is referred to as:
   A. actual notice.
   B. constructive notice.
   C. priority.
   D. subrogation.

18. Karen sells a portion of her property to Linda. Linda promptly records the deed in the appropriate county office. If Karen tries to sell the same portion of her property to Mark, which of the following statements is true?
   A. Mark has been given constructive notice of the prior sale because Linda promptly recorded it.
   B. Mark has been given actual notice of the prior sale because Linda promptly recorded it.
   C. Because Mark's purchase of the portion of Karen's property is the more recent, it will have priority over Linda's interest, regardless of when Linda recorded the deed.
   D. Because Linda recorded the deed, Mark is presumed by law to have actual knowledge of Linda's interest.

19. Adam sold a house to Brian, who immediately occupied it. Brian neglected to have the deed recorded. Adam, who is somewhat absentminded but of sound mind, later sold the same house to Candace, who recorded the deed but did not make any prior inspection of the property. Based on these facts, which of the following would be the most likely finding of a court in this case?
    A. Brian owns the house, because Candace had constructive notice of Brian's interest.
    B. Candace owns the property, because Brian failed to record his interest.
    C. Adam is still the owner of the property until such time as Brian records; the conveyance to Candace is invalid due to Brian's possessory interest.
    D. Brian and Candace own the property as tenants in common.

In Illinois . . .

20. For a deed to be recorded in Illinois, all of the following are always necessary EXCEPT:
    A. the name of the grantor typed or printed below his or her signature.
    B. the address of the grantee.
    C. a completed state real estate transfer declaration.
    D. proof that the property is exempt from the Illinois Plat Act.

21. Which of the following statements correctly describes the requirements for recording a tax deed?
    A. A tax deed must be recorded within 30 days after expiration of the redemption period.
    B. A tax deed may be recorded at any time before or after the redemption period.
    C. Tax deeds are specifically exempted from recording deadlines and are effective regardless of whether or not they have been recorded.
    D. A tax deed must be recorded within one year after expiration of the redemption period or it will become null and void.

22. Seth, a Chicago resident, purchases farmland in southern Illinois as an investment. The deed to Seth should be recorded:
    A. in the county recorder's office of Cook County, where Seth's permanent residence is located.
    B. in the statewide land registry located in Springfield.
    C. in the recorder's office of the county in which the farm is located.
    D. in the tax records of the city of Chicago.

23. The population of Outlet County is 54,000. In Outlet County, the recorder of deeds:
    A. must be elected.
    B. is the county clerk.
    C. is the county treasurer.
    D. is appointed by the secretary of state.

24. Nathan conveyed Halfacre Farm to Marlon. While both Nathan and Marlon are Illinois residents, the transfer was conducted entirely in their native Urdu language. The deed was written in Urdu so that both parties could read and understand it. Based on these facts, which of the following statements is true of this deed?
    A. The deed is invalid between the parties, because deeds in Illinois must be in English.
    B. The deed gives constructive notice by its existence in the public records, regardless of whether the details of the conveyance can be immediately read by non-Urdu-speakers.
    C. The deed does not give constructive notice unless an English translation is attached at the time of recording.
    D. The deed may not be recorded, because Illinois law prohibits deeds in foreign languages.

25. All of the following would be found in a title insurance policy EXCEPT:
    A. a schedule of all exceptions.
    B. a plat map with a spot survey.
    C. a legal description of the real estate.
    D. the form of ownership being conveyed.

Illinois Real Estate License Laws

KEY TERMS

branch office license
broker
inoperative status

leasing agent license
license
pocket card

salesperson
sponsor car

At the time of printing, the License Act is under revision. A copy of the updated Act should be obtained when it becomes available by contacting the Office of Banks and Real Estate, 500 East Monroe, Suite 200, Springfield, Illinois 62701-1509.

Since 1921, Illinois has had a real estate license law intended to ensure the competency and honesty of persons engaged in the real estate business and to regulate the real estate industry for the protection of the public. Today, the law is called the *Real Estate License Act of 1983*, last amended in 1996. In this chapter, it is referred to as the "license act" or "license law." The license act may be found in the Illinois Compiled Statutes, at 255 ILCS 455/1 through 455/3865. However, for your convenience, the license act is reprinted in this book following the index. The Office of Banks and Real Estate also promulgates rules for the license law's implementation and enforcement. This chapter provides an analysis of the act's most significant provisions, along with relevant rules.

ADMINISTRATION OF THE ILLINOIS REAL ESTATE LICENSE ACT

The Illinois *Office of Banks and Real Estate* (OBRE), pursuant to the powers and duties prescribed to it by the Civil Administration Code of Illinois (Illinois Compiled Statutes, 20 5/1 et seq.), has the authority to administer the Illinois Real Estate License Act as well as other licensing acts of the state. The OBRE is empowered to issue rules and regulations that implement and interpret the act. These rules are referenced throughout this chapter.

The OBRE is also responsible for

- *conducting license examinations;*
- *issuing and renewing licenses;*
- *preparing all forms,* including applications, licenses and sponsor cards; and
- *collecting fees* from applicants and licensees.

The OBRE has the following additional functions, which may be exercised only on the initiative and approval of the Real Estate Administration and

Disciplinary Board (discussed in the following section):

- *Conducting hearings* that may result in the revocation or suspension of licenses or in refusal to issue or renew licenses
- *Imposing penalties* for violations of the act
- *Restoring* suspended or revoked licenses

Real Estate Administration and Disciplinary Board (Section 9)

The *Real Estate Administration and Disciplinary Board* ("the board") acts in an advisory capacity to the Commissioner of Banks and Real Estate regarding matters involving standards of professional conduct, discipline and examination. In addition to its advisory functions, the board conducts hearings on disciplinary actions against persons accused of violating the act or the administrative rules.

Composition of the board. The board is made up of *nine members* appointed by the governor, all of whom must have been residents and citizens of Illinois for at least six years before their appointment date. Six of the nine must have been active brokers or salespeople for at least ten years. The remaining three must be unlicensed, unconnected with the real estate profession and clearly represent the interests of consumers. The board itself should reasonably reflect representation from all the various geographic areas of Illinois.

Members are appointed to terms of four years, staggered so that no more than two terms expire in the same year. Appointments to fill vacancies are for the unexpired portion of the replaced member's term. Board members may be reappointed, but no individual may serve more than a total of eight years. The *Commissioner of Banks and Real Estate* is the ex-officio board chairperson but has no vote.

Director of Real Estate (Section 10)

The commissioner appoints a licensed broker to the position of Director of Real Estate after considering the recommendations of real estate professionals and organizations. The director's license is surrendered to the OBRE during the director's term.

The director's duties include

- acting as ex-officio chairperson of the Real Estate Administration and Disciplinary Board (without a vote);
- being the direct liaison among the OBRE, the real estate profession and real estate organizations and associations;
- preparing and circulating educational material for licensees;
- appointing any committees necessary to assist the OBRE in carrying out its duties; and
- supervising the real estate unit of the OBRE, subject to the administrative approval of the commissioner, to whom the director reports.

REAL ESTATE LICENSING (SECTIONS 3 AND 4)

It is illegal for anyone to act as a broker or salesperson, or to advertise as one, without a properly issued sponsor card or real estate license issued by the OBRE. Any person (or business entity) who performs any of the following services (1) for someone else and (2) for compensation must have a license:

- Sells, exchanges, purchases, rents or leases real estate, or offers to do so

- Negotiates, offers, attempts or agrees to negotiate the sale, exchange, purchase, rental or leasing of real estate
- Lists, offers, attempts or agrees to list real estate for sale, lease or exchange
- Buys, sells, offers to buy or sell or otherwise deals in options on real estate or improvements
- Collects, offers, attempts or agrees to collect rent for the use of real estate
- Advertises or represents himself or herself as being engaged in the business of buying, selling, exchanging, renting or leasing real estate
- Assists in or directs the procuring of prospects intended to result in the sale, exchange, lease or rental of real estate
- Assists in or directs the negotiation of any transaction intended to result in the sale, exchange, lease or rental of real estate
- Employs or supervises a leasing agent or agents

Exempt Persons (Section 6)   The provisions of the act *do not apply* to the following:

- Owners or lessors (whether individuals or business entities) or their regular employees who sell, lease or otherwise deal with their own property in the ways described under Section 4 in the course of the management, the sale or another disposition of their or their employer's property (The exemption does not apply to employees who perform such acts in connection with a real estate business that deals with property not owned by their employers.)
- Attorneys-in-fact acting under duly executed and recorded powers of attorney to convey real estate from the owner or lessor or performing their duties as attorneys-in-fact
- Any person acting as receiver, trustee in bankruptcy, administrator, executor or guardian or while acting under a court order or under the authority of a will or a testamentary trust
- A resident apartment manager working for an owner or working for a broker employed to lease the property, if the apartment is his or her primary residence
- Any officer or employee of a federal agency, state government or other political subdivision performing his or her official duties
- Any multiple-listing service wholly owned by a not-for-profit organization or association of real estate brokers
- Any not-for-profit real estate referral system
- Railroads and other public utilities regulated by the state of Illinois or their subsidiaries or affiliates and the employees of such organizations (This exemption applies only to the portions of the organization's business that are regulated.)
- Any newspaper of general circulation that routinely sells real estate advertising but provides no other related services
- Any resident lessee of a residential dwelling unit who refers no more than three prospective tenants in any 12-month period, and who receives no more than $1,000 or one month's rent (whichever is less) in compensation (or finder's fees), if the lessee's activities are limited to referring prospective tenants to the owner (An exempt resident lessee may not show a residential dwelling to a prospective lessee, discuss terms or conditions or leasing a dwelling unit with a prospective lessee or otherwise participate in the negotiation of the leasing of a dwelling unit.)

Civil Penalty for the Unlicensed Practice of Real Estate (Section 3.5)

It is illegal in Illinois for any person to practice, offer or attempt to practice, or to hold himself or herself out to practice as a real estate broker or salesperson without being licensed. Anyone who does so is subject to a civil penalty (in addition to any other penalties provided by law) of up to $5,000 for each offense. The penalty is assessed by and payable to the OBRE after a disciplinary hearing (discussed later in this chapter). The OBRE has the authority to investigate any alleged unlicensed activity. The civil penalty must be paid within 60 days after the effective date of the judgment order.

Commissions (Section 7)

No person or business entity may bring a court action in Illinois to collect compensation for the performance of any real estate activity, unless the person or entity is a licensed real estate broker and the license was in effect before the agreement for compensation was negotiated or an offer of services was made. For example, a salesperson or broker-associate may not sue a buyer or seller for a commission. The reason is logical: A salesperson or broker-associate may be paid by the employing broker, but never directly by a consumer.

Real Estate Defined (Section 4)

For purposes of the Illinois license act, both leasing and selling come under the license act rules and regulations. Therefore, the term *real estate* includes leaseholds as well as any other interest or estate in land, whether located in this state or elsewhere. That means that an Illinois resident selling property in another state for compensation still is required to hold an Illinois real estate license.

License Categories and Requirements

The license act designates three categories of real estate licensees: *brokers*, *salespeople* and *leasing agents*. The law provides general requirements for each type of license applicant as well as requirements and limitations specific to each type of licensee.

General Requirements (Section 12)

All individual license applicants must pass a written examination authorized by the OBRE and administered by an independent testing service, Applied Measurement Professionals, Inc. (AMP). Anyone who wants to take the exam must apply to AMP. AMP acts as the agent of the OBRE and is empowered to screen potential license candidates to ensure that they meet the statutory requirements of brokers and salespersons as established in the license act and the rules. For a detailed content outline of the AMP examination, see the section on Sample Illinois Real Estate Licensing Examinations on page 420.

Brokers (Sections 4 and 11)

A **broker** is defined as any individual, partnership, limited liability company or corporation, other than a salesperson, that performs any of the services for which a real estate license is required.

Broker Requirements. Individual applicants for a broker's license must meet the following six requirements:

1. Be at least 21 years of age
2. Be of good moral character

3. Have graduated from high school or obtained the equivalent of a high school diploma
4. Have successfully completed 90 hours of approved real estate courses, correspondence courses or college or university courses
5. Have been actively engaged as a licensed salesperson for at least one out of the last three years
6. Satisfactorily pass a written examination

If an applicant for a broker's license is currently an attorney admitted to the practice of law by the Illinois Supreme Court, he or she is exempt from the education and experience requirements of items 4 and 5.

Salespersons (Sections 4 and 11)

A **salesperson** is defined as anyone, other than a broker, who engages in the activities for which a license is required but who is employed by or associated with a broker by written contract.

Salesperson requirements. All applicants for a salesperson's license must meet the following four requirements:

1. Be at least 21 years of age (Applicants who are at least 18 years old also may qualify if they can provide evidence of the successful completion of at least four semesters of post–secondary school study as a full-time student, or the equivalent, with major emphasis on real estate courses, in an approved school.)
2. Be of good moral character
3. Have graduated from high school or obtained the equivalent of a high school diploma
4. Have successfully completed at least 30 class hours of instruction in real estate transactions at an approved school or home-study/correspondence school or have a bachelor's degree with a minor of 30 credit hours in real estate–related courses from an approved college or university

If an applicant for a salesperson's license is an attorney admitted to the practice of law by the Illinois Supreme Court, he or she is exempt from the educational requirement of item 4.

Five-year eligibility. The real estate educational requirements are valid for the purposes of licensure for a period of *five years from the date of completion.*

Corporations, Limited Liability Companies and Partnerships (Section 3)

A corporation, partnership or limited liability company (LLC) may receive a broker's license under the following conditions:

- In a *corporation*, every corporate officer who actively participates in the organization's real estate activities must hold a broker's license. In addition, every employee of the corporation who acts as a salesperson on the corporation's behalf also must hold a license as a real estate broker or salesperson.
- In a *partnership*, every general partner must hold a broker's license. Every employee of the partnership who acts as a salesperson on the partnership's behalf also must hold a license as a real estate broker or salesperson.
- In a *limited liability company* (LLC), every managing member must hold a real estate broker's license, and every employee of the LLC who acts as

a salesperson on the LLC's behalf also must hold a license as a broker or salesperson.

No corporation, partnership or LLC may be licensed to conduct a brokerage business if any individual salesperson or group of salespeople owns, or directly or indirectly controls, more than 49 percent of the shares of stocks or ownership interest in the business entity. This provision does not prohibit a salesperson from owning stock in a company; rather, it is designed to prevent salespersons from dictating company policy—a responsibility limited to brokers.

Appraisers (Real Estate Appraiser Licensing Act)

Under the Illinois Real Estate Appraiser Licensing Act, Illinois provides for voluntary state appraiser licensing and certification regulated by the OBRE for appraisals conducted in the course of federally related transactions. The licensing and certification provisions bring Illinois law into compliance with the requirements of Title XI of the federal Financial Institutions Reform, Recovery and Enforcement Act of 1989 (FIRREA); Title VIII of the Civil Rights Act of 1968 (Fair Housing Act); and the Illinois Human Rights Act.

The license act establishes a fee structure and disciplinary and enforcement mechanism for appraisers, as well as education, qualification, examination and experience requirements. Real estate appraisal is discussed in more detail in Chapter 19.

Leasing Agent License (Sections 6.1 to 6.4)

The real estate license act provides for a limited **leasing agent license** for persons who wish to engage only in activities related to the leasing of residential real property for which a license is required. An applicant must be at least 18 years of age, of good moral character and have a high school diploma or its equivalent. Applicants must successfully complete 15 hours of instruction and pass a written competency examination. Persons who hold leasing agent licenses must comply with qualification requirements, standards of practice and disciplinary guidelines established and enforced by the Real Estate Administration and Disciplinary Board and the OBRE. The licensed leasing agent must be employed and supervised by a licensed real estate broker. A leasing agent may engage in residential leasing activities for up to 120 days without a license, if during that time he or she is engaged in satisfying the educational, testing and fee requirements for obtaining a license and has been registered with the OBRE by the supervising broker.

THE LICENSING EXAMINATION (SECTION 12)

Anyone applying for an original broker's or salesperson's license must receive a passing score on a written exam administered by AMP at established test centers throughout Illinois. The questions are designed to demonstrate "the good moral character of the applicant, and the applicant's competency to transact the business of broker or salesperson, as the case may be, in such a manner as to safeguard the interests of the public" (Section 12 (a)).

Candidates call, fax or mail their registration forms to the testing service, along with any fees to be paid, and make a reservation for one of the frequent exam dates at a convenient site. *All candidates must bring to the testing center two pieces of current identification, including either a driver's license with photograph, a passport or military identifcation with photograph, or an official state identification card with photograph.* The second form of identification must display the name and signature of the candidate for signature verification. All examinations are given on a computer that displays all the test questions on a screen and records all the answers. *No special knowledge of computers is necessary: candidates are given time before the test to practice.*

After completing the test, candidates are immediately informed of their results. Passing candidates will be given a score report, a licensure application, including directions for applying for a real estate license; and an applicant sponsor card. Passing candidates have one year in which to apply for a license, after which time a new examination will be required. Candidates who fail the examination will be told their score and be given diagnostic information in addition to directions on how to apply for a future test. Candidates who fail only one portion (either the state or the national portion) of the exam are only required to retake that failed portion.

If an applicant fails the examination three times, he or she must successfully complete an approved *refresher course* before being admitted to sit for another examination. An applicant's fourth attempt to pass the exam is treated by the OBRE as if it were the first attempt.

THE REAL ESTATE LICENSE (SECTIONS 12.1 AND 13)

Applicants who have met all the requirements will receive a **license** from the OBRE. The license will specify whether the individual is authorized to act as a broker or as a salesperson. *This license is to be displayed conspicuously in the licensee's place of business.* In addition to the license, the OBRE will issue a **pocket card** to each licensee. This card authorizes the bearer to engage in brokerage or sales activity for the current license period. *Licensees must carry this card when engaging in any of the activities for which a license is required by Illinois law.*

Sponsor Cards (Sections 12.1 and 13)

Illinois brokers are required to prepare **sponsor cards** for salespeople and other brokers they have employed or are associated with. The sponsor card certifies the bearer's relationship with the broker and serves as a temporary permit to engage in the practice of real estate. Recipients of sponsor cards must carry them until they receive their pocket cards and display the sponsor card on demand when engaging in activities for which a license is required. Sponsor cards are valid for a maximum of 45 days or until the licensee receives his or her license and pocket card from the OBRE. It is illegal for a salesperson or broker to engage in the real estate business without a valid sponsor card or a current license and pocket card.

A person who has just passed the licensing exam will receive a *sponsor card* with his or her picture on it at the testing site. He or she then has one year to be *sponsored* by a broker. The sponsoring broker signs the card, makes a copy for the new salesperson and for the broker's records and sends the original to the OBRE within 24 hours. The sponsor card remains the property of the broker, and it must be returned by the employee on receipt of his or her pocket card or on termination of employment, whichever comes first.

Termination of salesperson's employment; new broker-salesperson relationship. If a salesperson or broker terminates employment with a broker for any reason, the salesperson or broker associate must obtain his or her original license from the employing broker. The employing broker endorses the license, indicating that the relationship has been terminated, and sends the OBRE a copy of the signed license within two days. The endorsed license automatically becomes inoperative, unless the licensee accepts employment from a new broker. The new broker prepares and sends a sponsor card to the OBRE, along with the endorsed license.

Commissions (Section 7)

It is unlawful for a licensed salesperson to accept a commission *or any other valuable consideration* from anyone except his or her sponsoring broker.

Inoperative Status (Section 13)

Inoperative status means a licensee who holds a current, valid license is prohibited from engaging in the real estate business because he or she is unsponsored (for instance, when a licensee terminates employment with a broker and fails to become employed by a new broker). Inoperative status is also created when the license of the employing broker/licensee becomes expired (lapsed), revoked, suspended or otherwise invalid or if the licensee fails to pay renewal fees or meet continuing education requirements.

Nonresidents and License by Reciprocity (Section 14)

A broker or salesperson who lives in a state that has a reciprocal licensing agreement with Illinois may be issued an Illinois license *without examination* if the following conditions are met:

For a reciprocal broker's license:

- The broker holds an *active license* in his or her home state.
- The licensing standards of that state are *substantially equivalent* to the minimum standards required in Illinois.
- The broker maintains a *definite place of business* in his or her home state.
- The broker has been active in the real estate business for *at least two years immediately preceding the application.*
- The broker furnishes the OBRE with an official statement from his or her home state's licensing authority that the broker has an active license, is in good standing and has no complaints pending.
- The broker's home state grants reciprocal privileges to Illinois licensees.

The issuance of a nonresident salesperson's license is in the discretion of the OBRE. For a nonresident salesperson to qualify for a nonresident license to practice real estate in Illinois under a nonresident broker, the following conditions must be met:

- The salesperson's home state must have entered into a *reciprocal licensing agreement* with the OBRE.
- The salesperson must maintain an *active license* in his or her home state.
- The salesperson must *reside in the same state as the nonresident broker* with whom he or she is associated. (The nonresident broker must issue a sponsor card to the salesperson in compliance with Illinois law.)

The following states have current reciprocal licensing agreements with Illinois: Connecticut, Indiana, Iowa, Kansas, Kentucky, Minnesota, Mississippi, Missouri, Nebraska, North Dakota, Oklahoma and South Dakota.

Before a nonresident broker or salesperson will be issued a license, the applicant must designate, in writing, that he or she appoints the commissioner to act as his or her agent in Illinois and that all judicial or other process or legal notices directed to the nonresident may be served on the commissioner. Service of notice or process on the commissioner is equivalent to personal service upon the nonresident licensee.

Nonresidents applying for licenses must furnish the OBRE with proof of active licensure in their home state. They also must pay the same license fees that are required of resident brokers and salespeople. Prospective nonresident licensees must agree in writing to abide by all provisions of the act and to submit to the OBRE's jurisdiction.

If a nonresident broker or salesperson moves to Illinois or opens an office in Illinois (or relocates to any other state), his or her reciprocal license is automatically invalidated. The broker or salesperson must meet all the licensing requirements of Illinois if he or she desires to participate in the real estate sales profession.

LICENSE FEES (SECTION 15)

Initial Licensing Fees   Applicants for real estate licenses are subject to certain fees in addition to the testing fee paid to AMP when applying for the examination. When applying for a broker or salesperson license, the applicant must submit an *initial license fee* of $100.

The initial broker's license fee for a partnership, LLC or corporation is $100. The fee for an initial license for a real estate branch office is $100. The initial license fee for a real estate school is $1,000, plus $150 for each branch and $50 for each instructor. *Continuing education (CE) sponsors* must pay an initial license fee of $2,000; the initial license fee for a CE instructor is $15.

The initial license fees (except for school's fees) include a *Real Estate Recovery Fund fee* of $10 and a *Real Estate Research and Education fee* of $5 ($1 of this fee is earmarked for real estate education scholarships). The branch office fee includes $5 for deposit in the Research and Education Fund.

Other Fees   Certain miscellaneous fees are imposed in various situations. These include the following:

- Furnishing a duplicate license or pocket card, replacing a lost or stolen license or pocket card or issuing a new card due to a change of address: $25
- Certifying a licensee's records: $25
- Requesting a waiver of continuing education requirements: $25
- Processing a sponsor card other than at the time of initial licensure: $25
- Furnishing a printed record of legal proceedings: $1 per page
- Furnishing a diskette roster of all licensees in the state: $50
- Furnishing a decorative wall license showing the licensee's registration: $10

Other fees are set according to the actual cost incurred by the OBRE and may vary.

Returned check penalties (Section 15.1).   Anyone who delivers a check or other payment to the OBRE that is returned for insufficient funds must pay a returned check fine of $50, plus the amount originally owed. If the check was for a renewal or issuance fee, and the licensee continues to practice real estate without paying the renewal or issuance fee, an additional fine of $100 will be imposed. If the licensee fails to make full payment of all fees and fines owed within 30 days of notification that payment is due, the OBRE will automatically terminate his or her license without a hearing. The licensee may apply for reinstatement of the license and pay all amounts owed, accrued fines and any other fees the OBRE may impose. The commissioner is empowered to waive the fine if he or she finds, in individual cases, that the fine would be unreasonable or unnecessarily burdensome to the licensee.

Expiration and Renewal of Current Licenses (Sections 13 and 15)

Every *salesperson's license* in Illinois expires on March 31 of each odd-numbered year. Licensees may renew their licenses during the month preceding the expiration date by paying the renewal fee of $50 ($25 per year, imposed biennially).

Broker's licenses expire on January 31 of every even-numbered year. Licensees may renew their licenses during the month preceding the expiration date by paying the renewal fee of $100 ($50 per year, imposed biennially).

Licenses issued to *business entities or branch offices* expire on October 31 of every even-numbered year. Holders of such licenses may renew by paying the renewal fee of $100 during the month preceding the expiration date ($50 per year, imposed biennially). In addition, partnerships, corporations, LLCs or branch offices seeking renewal of current licenses must also submit a written consent permitting the OBRE to audit and examine their special accounts and (except for branch offices) a properly completed corporation, LLC or partnership information form.

Real estate schools are required to pay an annual renewal fee of $500, plus $75 for each branch school and $25 for each instructor. Approved *continuing education sponsors* must pay a renewal fee of $2,000; the fee for renewing approval as a CE instructor is $15.

Change of Address and Renewal Notification (Section 13)

It is the licensee's responsibility to notify the OBRE of any change in his or her mailing address. In addition, licensees are responsible for keeping track of their license status: not having received a renewal form from the OBRE does not constitute an excuse for failing to pay the renewal fee and renew a license. When a broker receives a renewal application from the OBRE for another licensee, he or she must notify the licensee within seven days of receipt. If the licensee does not respond to the broker, the broker must return the renewal form to the OBRE ten days after notification of the licensee.

Renewal of Expired Licenses (Sections 13.1, 13.2 and 15)

Broker's and salesperson's licenses that have been expired for less than five years may be renewed by paying all lapsed renewal fees plus a $50 reinstatement fee. However, if the license has been expired for one to three years, the holder must take a 12-hour continuing education class. If the license has been expired for more than three years, the holder must first take a 15-hour real estate *refresher course* approved by the OBRE. A license that has lapsed for five years or more cannot be renewed or reinstated.

The fee for renewing a partnership, LLC, corporation or branch office license that has expired is $50, plus all lapsed renewal fees. To renew an expired approval, continuing education sponsors are required to pay all lapsed fees plus $50. The fee for renewing an expired CE instructor approval is also $50 plus lapsed fees.

Renewal Without Fee (Section 13.1) Licensees whose licenses have expired may renew without paying any lapsed renewal or reinstatement fees if the license expired while the licensee was performing any of the following functions:

- On active duty with any branch of the U.S. armed services or called into the service or training of the United States
- Engaged in training or education prior to induction into military service
- Serving as Director of Real Estate in Illinois
- Employed by the OBRE

An eligible licensee may renew his or her license without fee for two years after terminating his or her service or employment (provided that the termination was by other than dishonorable discharge) on providing the OBRE with an affidavit describing the activity and its termination.

PLACE OF BUSINESS (SECTION 13)

Each real estate broker actively engaged in the real estate business must maintain a definite office or place of business within Illinois. The broker must display a visible, conspicuous identification sign on the outside of his or her office. Inside, the broker must conspicuously display his or her own license certificate along with those of any licensees he or she may employ or be associated with. "Secret" real estate practice is not permitted.

The broker's office or place of business may not be located in any retail or financial business establishment (such as a department store or a bank), unless it is set apart from the surrounding business as a separate and distinct area within that establishment. The OBRE must be notified in writing within 24 hours of any change of principal or branch business location.

If the broker changes the location of his or her office or place of business, the OBRE must be immediately notified, in writing, of the change.

Exceptions. A broker licensed in Illinois, whether by examination or reciprocity, may be exempt from the requirement of maintaining a definite place of business in Illinois if

- the broker maintains an active broker's license in his or her home state;
- the broker maintains an office in his or her home state; and
- the broker has filed a written statement with the OBRE appointing the commissioner as his or her agent for service of process and other legal notices, agreeing to abide by all the provisions of the Illinois license act and submitting to the jurisdiction of the OBRE.

Branch Offices (Section 13) Only a real estate broker may supervise or have control of a real estate office or *branch office*. The broker who wants to establish branch offices (the *employing broker*) must apply for a **branch office license** for each branch office he or she maintains. However, a broker may be in direct operational control of only one office or branch. The *managing broker* of a branch, who oversees the branch's day-to-day operations, must be a licensed broker, closely supervised by the employing broker.

The name of any branch office must be the same as that of the main office or else clearly describe the branch office's relationship with the main office. The employing broker must inform the OBRE of the name and license number of the manager of each branch office and complete a consent form permitting the OBRE to examine and audit the branch's special accounts.

Loss of a Branch Office's Manager or Death of a Sole Proprietor (Section 13)

In the event of the loss of a managing broker (for whatever reason) or the death of a sole proprietor, the OBRE may issue a written authorization allowing the continued operation of the office. A written request for such authorization must be submitted to the OBRE within ten days of the loss or death. In the case of death or adjudicated disability of a sole proprietor, the authorization must be requested by the representative of the sole proprietor's estate, who agrees to personally supervise the operation of the office. No written authorization is valid for more than 30 days, unless extended by the OBRE on written request showing good cause for the extension.

Employment Contracts (Section 13; Rule 1450.60)

A broker must have a written agreement with any salespersons or brokers he or she employs or with any other licensees with whom he or she is associated as independent contractors. The agreement must describe the significant aspects of their professional relationship, such as supervision, duties, compensation and grounds for termination.

If it is an employed broker's responsibility to supervise a branch office, the written agreement must include the address of the branch and the supervisory duties of the broker.

REFUSAL, SUSPENSION OR REVOCATION OF LICENSE OR CIVIL PENALTIES (SECTION 18)

The license act lists a number of specific violations for which licensees may be subject to discipline. The OBRE is authorized to impose the following disciplinary penalties:

- Refuse to issue or renew any license
- Suspend or revoke any license
- Reprimand a licensee
- Place a licensee on probation
- Impose a civil penalty of not more than $10,000

Causes for Discipline (Section 18)

The OBRE may take disciplinary action against a licensee for any one or a combination of causes. Specifically, a licensee may be subject to disciplinary action by the OBRE if the licensee

- makes a false or fraudulent representation in attempting to obtain a license;
- has been convicted of a felony or of a crime involving dishonesty, fraud, larceny, embezzlement, obtaining money, property or credit by false pretenses or by means of a confidence game;
- has been convicted in Illinois or any other state of a crime that constitutes a felony under Illinois law;
- has been convicted of a felony in a federal court;
- has been found by a court to be a person under legal disability or subject to voluntary or judicial admission under the Illinois Mental Health and Developmental Disabilities Code;
- performs or attempts to perform any act as a broker or salesperson in a retail sales establishment from an office, desk or space that is not separated from the main retail business by a separate and distinct area;

- has been subjected to disciplinary action by another state (or the District of Columbia, territory or foreign nation), if at least one of the grounds for that discipline is the same as or equivalent to a cause for discipline in Illinois;
- has engaged in real estate activity without a license or with an expired or inoperative license (an additional civil penalty of up to $5,000 may be imposed for this violation); and
- attempts to subvert or cheat on the licensing exam or assists someone else in doing so.

A licensee also is subject to disciplinary action by the OBRE if, in performing, attempting or pretending to perform any act as a broker or salesperson, *or in handling his or her own property,* whether held by deed, option or otherwise, the licensee is found guilty of any of the following activities:

- Making any substantial misrepresentation or untruthful advertising
- Making any false promises of a character likely to influence, persuade or induce
- Pursuing a continued and flagrant course of misrepresentation or making false promises through agents, salespeople, advertising or otherwise
- Using any misleading or untruthful advertising
- Using any trade name or insignia of membership in any real estate organization of which the licensee is not a member
- Acting for more than one party in a transaction without providing written notice to all parties for whom the licensee acts
- Representing or attempting to represent a broker other than the sponsoring broker
- Failing to account for or to remit any monies or documents belonging to others that come into the licensee's possession
- Failing to maintain and deposit in a special non–interest-bearing account, separate and apart from personal or other business accounts, all escrow monies belonging to others entrusted to the licensee while acting as a broker, escrow agent or temporary custodian until the transaction is consummated or terminated (However, all or part of such monies may be disbursed earlier, and the account itself may be interest-bearing, if required by law or in accordance with the written instructions of the principals.)
- Failing to make all escrow records and related real estate business documents available to the OBRE's real estate enforcement personnel during normal business hours
- Failing to furnish upon request copies of all documents relating to a real estate transaction to all parties executing them
- Paying a commission or valuable consideration to any person for acts or services performed in violation of the license act
- Demonstrating unworthiness or incompetency to act as a broker or salesperson in a manner that endangers the public interest
- Commingling the money or property of others with his or her own
- Employing any person on a purely temporary or single-deal basis as a means of evading the law regarding payment of commission to nonlicensees on some contemplated transactions
- Permitting the use of his or her license as a broker to enable a salesperson or an unlicensed person to operate a real estate business, without actually participating in and controlling the business
- Engaging in any conduct, whether or not specified in the license act, that constitutes dishonest dealing

- Displaying a For Rent or For Sale sign on any property without the written consent of an owner (or his or her duly authorized agent) or advertising by any means that any property is for sale or for rent without the consent of the owner or his or her authorized agent
- Failing to provide information requested by the OBRE within 30 days of the request, either as the result of a formal or an informal complaint to the OBRE or as a result of a random audit conducted by the OBRE, that would indicate a violation of the license act
- Disregarding or violating any provision of this act or the published rules or regulations promulgated by the OBRE to enforce the license act
- Assisting any individual or business entity in disregarding the license act or the OBRE's published rules and regulations
- Advertising any property for sale, or advertising any transaction of any kind relating to the sale of property by whatever means, whether by the broker or by any salesperson or broker employed by the broker, without clearly disclosing the name of the firm with which the licensee is associated; *or* if a sole broker, evidence of the broker's occupation; *or* a name with respect to which the broker has complied with the requirements of the Illinois Assumed Name Act
- Influencing or attempting to influence a prospective seller, purchaser, occupant, landlord or tenant by any words or acts in connection with viewing, buying or leasing real estate, so as to promote, or tend to promote, the continuance or maintenance of racially and religiously segregated housing or so as to retard, obstruct or discourage racially integrated housing on any street or block or in any neighborhood or community
- Engaging in any act that constitutes a violation of the Illinois Human Rights Act's prohibitions against unlawful discrimination in housing (including discrimination on the basis of familial status or disability, blockbusting, exclusion of children and enforcement of unlawful restrictive covenants), regardless of whether a complaint has been filed with or adjudicated by the Illinois Human Rights Commission
- Inducing any party to a contract of sale or listing agreement to break the contract for the purpose of substituting a new contract or listing agreement with a third party
- Negotiating a sale, exchange or a lease of real property directly with an owner or lessor without authority from the listing broker if the licensee knows that the owner or lessor has a written exclusive listing agreement with another broker
- Where the licensee is an attorney, acting as both the lawyer and the broker or salesperson for either the buyer or the seller in the same transaction
- Advertising or offering free merchandise, awards, prizes or services if any necessary conditions or obligations, such as attending a promotional presentation or visiting a site, are not disclosed in the same advertisement or offer
- Recruiting at testing facilities where the licensing examination is being conducted, whether before, during or after the examination
- Failing to make timely child support payments or to repay Illinois student loans
- Disregarding or violating any provision of the Illinois Real Estate Time-Share Act or the rules or regulations promulgated by the OBRE to enforce it
- Violating the terms of a disciplinary order issued by the OBRE
- Paying fees or commissions directly to a licensee employed by another broker

Offering guaranteed sales plans (Section 18 (h)(21)). A licensee is subject to disciplinary action by the OBRE if he or she offers a guaranteed sales plan without complying with the license act's strict requirements for such agreements. A *guaranteed sales plan* is any real estate purchase or sales plan in which a broker enters into an unconditional written contract with a seller, promising to purchase the seller's property for a specified price if the property has not sold within an agreed period of time on terms acceptable to the seller. A broker who offers a guaranteed sales plan must

- provide the details and conditions of the plan in writing to the seller,
- offer evidence of sufficient financial resources to satisfy the agreement's purchase commitment and
- market the listing in the same manner in which he or she would market any other property, unless the agreement with the seller provides otherwise.

A broker who fails to perform on a guaranteed sales plan in strict accordance with its terms is subject to all the penalties provided for violations of the act, plus a civil penalty of up to $~~10,000~~ 25000, payable to the injured party.

Failure to pay Illinois income taxes (Section 18.1). The OBRE may take disciplinary action against any person who fails to file a return or to pay any tax, penalty, interest or final assessment required by the Illinois Department of Revenue.

Licensee guilty of discrimination (Section 18.3). If there has been a civil or criminal trial in which a licensee has been found to have engaged in illegal discrimination in the course of a licensed activity, the OBRE must suspend or revoke the licensee's license unless the adjudication is in appeal. If an administrative agency finds that a licensee has engaged in illegal discriminatory activities, the OBRE must take some disciplinary action against the licensee unless the administrative order is in appeal.

Index of Decisions (Sections 8.2 and 21)

The OBRE is required to maintain an index of its decisions regarding all issuances or refusals to issue, all renewals or refusals to renew, all revocations or suspensions of licenses and all probationary and other disciplinary actions. The decisions must be indexed according to the relevant sections of statutes and rules that form the basis for each. The index is available for public inspection.

In addition, the OBRE is required to prepare a summary report, at least every other month, of all final disciplinary actions it has taken since the last report. The summary must include a brief description of the facts of each case and the final disciplinary action taken. This report is also available for public inspection.

Exemptions

Exclusive representation (Section 18.2a). A broker who enters into any agreement for the listing of property or for the representation of a party in the buying, selling, exchanging, renting or leasing of real estate may specifically designate the salespersons employed by or affiliated with the broker who will be acting as legal agents for the represented party to the exclusion of all other salespersons employed by or affiliated with the broker. A broker who enters into such an agreement is not considered to be acting for more than one party in a transaction if the salespersons designated as legal agents are not representing more than one party in any single transaction.

No licensee will be considered a dual agent, or be liable for acting as an undisclosed dual agent, merely for performing the services described in Section 18.2a.

Unlawful action by employees or associates (Section 20 (f)).

A broker will not have his or her license revoked because of an unlawful act or violation of any salesperson or broker employed by or associated with the broker, or by any unlicensed employee, unless the broker had knowledge of the unlawful act or violation.

Nondisclosure of certain property information (Section 31.1).

No disciplinary or other civil action may be taken by the OBRE against a licensee for his or her failure to disclose to prospective buyers that an occupant of a property was afflicted with the human immunodeficiency virus (HIV) or that it was the site of an act or occurrence (such as a murder or suicide) that had no effect on the physical condition of the property.

Procedure for Disciplinary Hearings (Section 20)

The Real Estate Administration and Disciplinary Board of the OBRE will initiate an investigation of anyone regulated by the license act based on (1) its own initiative; (2) the motion of the OBRE; or (3) on a written, verified complaint that would constitute grounds for disciplinary action submitted by any person.

Prior to any disciplinary hearing, the matter must be reviewed by a subcommittee of the board. If the complaint has merit and is not frivolous, the subcommittee will make a recommendation of its validity, and the board will schedule a hearing. The accused must be notified of the charges in writing at least 30 days prior to the hearing. If the accused fails to file an answer, the board will enter a judgment by default against the accused, and his or her license may be suspended or revoked in addition to other disciplinary actions deemed appropriate by the OBRE. The OBRE is specifically permitted to take any disciplinary action it deems proper, including limiting the scope, nature or extent of the accused's practice.

At the hearing, the accused and the complainant are given the opportunity to appear before the board in person or by counsel to present statements, testimony, evidence and argument. The OBRE and board have the power to subpoena witnesses, documents and evidence and to administer oaths. A record of the proceedings must be kept, and both the OBRE and the accused are entitled to have a court reporter present to transcribe the proceeding or prehearing conference at their own expense. If a transcript is produced, a copy must be provided to the other party at no cost.

At the conclusion of the hearing, the board will present to the commissioner a written report of its findings and recommendations. Within 20 days after receiving a copy of the report, the accused may request a rehearing by submitting a written motion describing the grounds for the request.

If the commissioner is not satisfied that substantial justice has been done, he or she may order a rehearing. The commissioner is required to give the board and the secretary of state a written statement detailing his or her reasons for disagreeing with the findings within 30 days of the board's recommendations and prior to any contrary action. After the 30-day period has passed, the commissioner has the right to take the action recommended by the board.

The OBRE is entitled to seize the license of any person whose license has been suspended or revoked and who has failed to surrender his or her license to the OBRE. At any time after the suspension or revocation of a license, the OBRE may reinstate the license, without examination, upon the written recommendation of the board.

Disciplinary Consent Orders (Section 20 (m))

The OBRE may bypass the hearing process and negotiate a *disciplinary consent order* directly with the accused. A disciplinary consent order may provide for any of the permitted forms of disciplinary action. The order must include a statement that it was not entered into as a result of any coercion by the OBRE against the accused. The order is filed with the commissioner along with the board's disciplinary recommendation. The commissioner may accept or reject the order.

Judicial Review (Section 21)

All final administrative decisions of the OBRE are subject to judicial review under the provisions of the Administrative Review Law. The accused may request a judicial review by petitioning the circuit court of the county of his or her residence. The circuit court's decision may in turn be appealed directly to the Illinois Supreme Court.

Criminal Prosecution and Penalties (Section 22)

In addition to the administrative penalties and procedures, the license act permits criminal prosecution of individuals and business entities as well. Violations are prosecuted by the state's attorney of the county in which the offense was committed. (The act specifically excludes violations of Section 18 (h)(4), misleading and untruthful advertising and improper use of trade names or insignia, from the criminal prosecution specified for other offenses.)

General violations. Any person convicted by a court of violating the license act (and particularly of failing to account for or remit others' money or commingling others' money with his or her own) is guilty of a Class C misdemeanor for a first offense and a Class A misdemeanor for any second or subsequent offense. An LLC or corporation convicted of a first-time violation is guilty of a business offense, and subject to a fine not to exceed $2,000. A second or subsequent business offense results in a fine of not less than $2,000 and not more than $5,000.

Officers, members and agents of corporations, partnerships or LLCs who personally participate in or were accessories to the business entity's violation may be prosecuted as individuals and are subject to the prescribed criminal penalties for individuals.

Violations of Section 3 (license requirement). Individuals, LLCs or corporations who violate any provision of Section 3 (that is, who engage in real estate business activities without a license) are singled out for harsher penalties. For an individual, conviction for a first offense constitutes a Class A misdemeanor (a fine of up to $1,000 and imprisonment for up to one year). For a corporation or LLC, a Section 3 violation constitutes a business offense and carries a fine of up to $10,000.

A second or subsequent violation of Section 3 is a Class 4 felony for individuals. A Class 4 felony carries a fine of up to $10,000 and imprisonment for one to three years. LLCs and corporations convicted of a second or subsequent violation of Section 3 must pay a fine of between $10,000 and $25,000.

**Injunctions
(Sections 22 and 32)**

In addition to criminal prosecutions, the OBRE has the duty and authority to originate an injunction to prevent or stop a violation or to prevent an unlicensed person from acting as a broker or salesperson.

A violation of the license act is specifically declared to be harmful to the public welfare and a public nuisance. The attorney general of Illinois, a county state's attorney, the OBRE and even private citizens may seek an injunction to stop or prevent a violation.

There is, however, no private right of action for Illinois citizens to seek damages or enforce the act or its rules and regulations. Administration and enforcement of the licensing act is the sole responsibility of the OBRE.

**Disciplinary Statute
of Limitations
(Section 31.2)**

The OBRE may not take disciplinary action against any licensee for a violation of the license act or its rules unless the action is commenced within five years after the alleged violation occurred. A violation that is continuing will be deemed to have occurred on the date when the circumstances that gave rise to the violation first existed.

**Advertising
Regulations
(Rule 1450.90)**

A broker must include his or her business name and franchise affiliation (if any) in all advertisements. *Blind ads* (that is, those using only a box number, street address or telephone number) are prohibited. No blind advertisements may be used by a licensee regarding the sale or lease of any real estate, including his or her own, or regarding other real estate activities or the hiring of other licensees.

Advertising may not be fraudulent, deceptive, inherently misleading or proven to be misleading in practice. Advertising is considered misleading or untruthful if, taken as a whole, there is a distinct and reasonable possibility that it will be misunderstood by or will deceive the ordinary purchaser, seller, renter or owner. *Advertising must contain all the information necessary to communicate to the public in an accurate, direct and readily comprehensible manner.*

A sponsored licensee cannot advertise under his or her own name. All advertising must be in the name of the employing broker and prepared under the employing broker's direct supervision. Licensees selling or leasing their own property cannot use the words "For Sale/Lease by Owner." They must, instead, list the employing broker's name on any signs or in any print advertisements and indicate that the owner is licensed.

Licensees may not list their names under the heading "Real Estate" in a telephone directory or otherwise advertise their services to the public through any media without listing the business name of the broker with whom they are affiliated. Printed information relating to the licensees and their names cannot be larger in size than the broker's business name.

**Advertising Signs
(Section 18 (h)(17))**

Real estate brokers cannot place an advertising sign on any property without the *written* consent of the owner or the owner's authorized agent.

THE REAL ESTATE RECOVERY FUND (SECTIONS 23 TO 30)

The *Real Estate Recovery Fund* provides a means of compensation for actual monetary losses (as opposed to losses in market value) suffered by any person as a result of

- a violation of the license act, rules or regulations; or
- an act of embezzlement of money or property, obtaining money or property by false pretenses, artifice, trickery, forgery, fraud, misrepresentation, deceit or discrimination by a licensee or a licensee's unlicensed employee.

Aggrieved persons may recover from the fund only for damages resulting from the act or omission of a licensed broker, salesperson or unlicensed employee who was, at the time of the act or omission, apparently acting in a professional capacity.

An aggrieved person may recover up to $10,000 in actual damages together with court costs and attorney's fees, not to exceed 15 percent of the amount recovered from the fund. The maximum total amount that will be paid for any single act is $10,000, to be spread equitably among all co-owners and aggrieved persons. The maximum liability against the fund arising from the acts of any single licensee or unlicensed employee is $50,000. The circuit court of the county in which the violation occurred has jurisdiction to order recovery of damages from the fund.

Statute of Limitations (Section 25(a))

A suit that may ultimately result in collection from the fund must be commenced within two years after the date the alleged violation occurred.

Collection from the Recovery Fund (Sections 25 and 28)

When a lawsuit may result in a claim against the Real Estate Recovery Fund, the OBRE must be notified in writing by the aggrieved person at the time the action is commenced. Failure to notify the OBRE of the potential liability precludes any recovery from the fund. If the plaintiff is unable to serve the defendant with a summons, the director of the OBRE may be served instead, and this service will be valid and binding on the defendant.

If a claimant recovers a valid judgment in any court against any licensee or unlicensed employee for damages resulting from an act or omission qualifying for coverage under the fund, the OBRE must receive written notice of the judgment within 30 days. The OBRE is also entitled to 20 days' written notice of any supplementary proceedings, to permit it to participate in all efforts to collect on the judgment other than through payment from the Recovery Fund.

For a claimant to obtain recovery from the fund, all proceedings (including all reviews and appeals) must be completed. In addition, the claimant must show that he or she has attempted to recover the judgment amount from the licensee or unlicensed employee's real or personal property or other assets and was either unable to do so or the amount recovered was insufficient to satisfy the judgment. The aggrieved person must also demonstrate that he or she has diligently pursued all alternative remedies against the licensee or unlicensed employee. Finally, he or she must show that the amount of attorney's fees sought to be recovered is reasonable.

When a judgment amount is paid from the Recovery Fund, the OBRE is subrogated to all the rights of the aggrieved person. He or she is required to assign all right, title and interest in the judgment to the OBRE. Any amount and interest subsequently recovered by the OBRE on the judgment is deposited back in the Recovery Fund.

Disciplinary Action Against the Licensee (Section 25)

When payment is made from the Recovery Fund to settle a claim or satisfy a judgment against a licensed broker, salesperson or unlicensed employee, the license of the offending broker or salesperson is automatically terminated. The broker or salesperson may not petition for the restoration of his or her license until he or she has made repayment in full plus interest at the statutory annual rate. A discharge in bankruptcy does not relieve a person from the liabilities and penalties provided for in the act.

Financing of the Recovery Fund (Sections 15 and 24)

All applicants for original broker's and salesperson's licenses, as well as those reinstating lapsed or inactive licenses, must pay $10 to the Recovery Fund. If, on December 31 of any year, the balance in the fund is less than $1,250,000, every licensee must pay an additional fee of $10 to replenish the fund, payable at the time his or her license is renewed.

Management of the Recovery Fund (Section 26)

All Recovery Fund monies received from applications, renewals and other sources is deposited into the state treasury in a specially designated trust account. This account is called the Real Estate Recovery Fund, and its sums may be invested and reinvested. Any interest or dividends returned from the investment of the fund are deposited into the Real Estate Research and Education Fund.

CONTINUING EDUCATION (SECTION 37)

Each broker and salesperson who applies for renewal of his or her license must successfully complete 6 hours per year (or its equivalent) of real estate continuing education (CE) courses approved by the Real Estate Education Advisory Council. That is, licensees must complete 12 hours of CE in any license renewal period.

Real Estate Education Advisory Council (Section 37.2)

The purpose of the Real Estate Education Advisory Council is to approve and regulate schools, curricula, sponsors and programs and to recommend administrative rules to the OBRE. The council is composed of five members appointed by the governor. Three members must be current members of the Real Estate Administration and Disciplinary Board, one must be a representative of an Illinois real estate trade organization (who is not a member of the disciplinary board) and one must be a representative of an approved real estate school or CE sponsor. The Director of Real Estate serves as the ex officio chair of the council, without a vote.

Only sponsors approved by the Advisory Council may provide real estate CE courses. Instructors and course materials also must be approved. The license law includes strict criteria for obtaining and renewing approvals.

Course Content (Section 37.4)

The CE requirement may be satisfied by successfully completing a minimum of six hours of course work in any one or more of the following mandatory topic areas:

- License law and escrow
- Antitrust
- Fair housing
- Agency

A maximum of six hours of course work also must be completed in the following elective topics:

- Appraisal
- Property management
- Residential brokerage
- Farm property management
- Rights and duties of sellers, buyers and brokers
- Commercial brokerage and leasing
- Financing
- Other approved CE courses

Some course offerings are specifically excluded from approval, for instance, exam-prep courses or courses concerning mechanical office and business skills, such as typing, speed reading, memory improvement, advertising or sales psychology. Sales promotion or other meetings held in conjunction with the general business of the attendee or his or her broker are not approved for CE credit, nor is normal in-house staff or employee training.

A maximum of six hours of Real Estate Continuing Education credit may be earned by serving as an approved instructor in an approved course or in prelicense instruction. Credit may also be earned for approved self-study programs.

For purposes of CE credit, one course hour must include at least 50 minutes of classroom instruction exclusive of time spent taking an examination. Courses must be for a minimum of three CE credit-hours and must be offered in three-hour increments. For both on-site and home study courses, the examination must be proctored and given at the sponsor's site. A score of at least 70 percent correct on the final exam is required for the successful completion of a CE course and the crediting of CE hours.

All CE courses must somehow contribute to the advancement, integrity, extension and enhancement of a licensee's professional skills. Courses must provide relevant experiences and be developed and presented by qualified instructors with expertise in the field being taught.

Exemptions and Waivers (Sections 37.1, 37.6 and 37.8)

Licensees who have held their licenses for more than 15 years as of January 31, 1992 (that is, who received their licenses on or before April 1, 1977), are exempt from Illinois's CE requirement. Similarly, licensees who have completed a course of study to obtain their broker's licenses during the renewal period also are exempt. (That is, a broker is not required to fulfill the CE requirement during the first two-year renewal period following his or her initial licensing; the broker's prelicense course qualifies as "continuing education.") A licensee whose prerenewal period is less than one year is also exempt for that renewal period.

Also exempt from the CE requirement are licensees who, during the renewal period, served in the armed services of the United States or as elected state or federal officials. Full-time employees of the OBRE and licensees who are licensed attorneys admitted to practice law in Illinois are also exempt. Licensees whose prerenewal period is less than one year are not required to satisfy the CE requirement for that period.

If a renewal applicant has earned CE hours in another state, the credit may be approved by the Advisory Council.

A licensee who has not complied with the CE requirements may nonetheless seek renewal of his or her license by submitting an application, the renewal fee and an affidavit stating the reasons for his or her failure to comply along with a request for waiver. If the Advisory Council finds that the applicant has shown good cause for a waiver, the OBRE may waive enforcement of the requirement for the renewal period.

Good cause for purposes of obtaining a CE waiver is determined on an individual basis and is limited to full-time service in the armed services of the United States during a substantial part of the prerenewal period or extreme hardship (that is, an incapacitating illness, physical inability to travel to course sites, or other extenuating circumstances).

SUMMARY

The Illinois Real Estate License Act and the relevant rules established by the Office of Banks and Real Estate govern the practice of real estate in the state of Illinois. It is vital that all licensees and prospective licensees have a clear understanding of the law and rules to ensure that their activities are ethical, legal and efficient.

At the time of printing, the License Act is under revision. A copy of the updated Act should be obtained when it becomes available by contacting the Office of Banks and Real Estate, 500 East Monroe, Suite 200, Springfield, Illinois 62701-1509.

QUESTIONS

1. In Illinois, which of the following would need to be a licensed real estate broker or salesperson?
   A. A person who employs fewer than three apartment leasing agents
   B. A licensed attorney acting under a power of attorney to convey real estate
   C. A resident apartment manager working for an owner, if the manager's primary residence is the apartment building being managed
   D. A partnership selling a building owned by the partners

2. An unlicensed individual who engages in activities for which a real estate license is required is subject to which of the following penalties?
   A. A fine not to exceed $1,000
   B. A fine not to exceed $1,000 and one year imprisonment
   C. A civil penalty of $5,000 in addition to other penalties provided by law
   D. A civil penalty not to exceed $5,000 and a mandatory prison term not to exceed five years

3. All of the following statements are true of a corporation that wishes to receive a broker's license in Illinois EXCEPT:
   A. every officer actively engaged in the real estate business must hold a broker's certificate.
   B. no more than 49 percent of the shares of the company may be held by salespeople.
   C. the business must submit a $55 license processing fee.
   D. the initial license fee is $100.

4. To meet the continuing education requirement in Illinois, licensees must obtain how many hours of continuing education per year?
   A. Four
   B. Six
   C. Ten
   D. Twelve

5. The Office of Banks and Real Estate has revoked broker Barry's license for commingling earnest money with his own personal funds. Based on these facts, which of the following is a correct statement?
   A. Barry may appeal the license revocation to the local circuit court.
   B. Barry may have the license reinstated by signing an irrevocable release of liability and filing it with the OBRE within 60 days of the disciplinary action.
   C. Barry may continue to conduct business for 90 days after the revocation by posting a bond with the Recovery Fund.
   D. Barry's employees may continue in business for 90 days because they were not found guilty of any offense.

6. If an aggrieved person is awarded a judgment against a real estate licensee for violations of the Illinois License Act, which of the following correctly states the aggrieved party's rights regarding the Recovery Fund?
   A. He or she has the right, under the license law, to immediately apply to the OBRE for payment from the Recovery Fund for the full judgment amount, plus court costs and attorney's fees.
   B. He or she has the right to a maximum award amount of $50,000 from the Recovery Fund, including court costs and attorney's fees.
   C. He or she has the right to seek satisfaction from the licensee in a private civil action after being compensated from the Recovery Fund.
   D. He or she has the right to a $10,000 maximum recovery from the Recovery Fund, plus limited court costs and attorney's fees.

7. Tanya's broker's license expired three years ago, but she placed ads in the newspaper seeking listings and continued to act as a broker. If found guilty, Tanya's maximum penalty will be a(n):
   A. prison term of five to ten years.
   B. fine of up to $10,000 plus a civil penalty.
   C. fine of between $10,000 and $25,000 but no civil penalty.
   D. injunction, plus a fine appropriate for a Class A misdemeanor.

8. A broker who holds an Illinois license by reciprocity, but whose home state is Iowa, will be exempt from the requirement that he or she maintain a definite place of business in Illinois if all of the following factors are met, EXCEPT:
   A. the broker maintains an office in Iowa.
   B. the broker maintains an active broker's license in the state of Iowa.
   C. the broker employs at least one Illinois licensee, either as a salesperson or associate broker.
   D. the broker files a written statement appointing the commissioner as his or her Illinois agent for service of process, submits to the OBRE's jurisdiction and agrees to abide by the provisions of the license act.

9. When a salesperson passes his or her license examination, the first proof of his or her eligibility to engage in real estate activities in Illinois is a:
   A. sponsor card.   C. license.
   B. pocket card.   D. pass card.

10. To qualify for a nonresident license without examination, an out-of-state broker must do all the following EXCEPT:
    A. be licensed in a state that has licensing requirements similar to those currently in effect in the state of Illinois.
    B. be licensed in a state that has enacted a reciprocal licensing agreement with Illinois.
    C. have been a practicing real estate broker in his or her home state for at least two years prior to application.
    D. open a definite, permanent and conspicuous place of business within Illinois.

11. The fee to apply to the OBRE for a salesperson's license is:
    A. $15.   C. $100.
    B. $50.   D. $500.

12. If a salesperson is found guilty of violating the act, his or her employing broker also may be disciplined by the OBRE if the:
    A. salesperson was a convicted criminal.
    B. broker had prior knowledge of the violation.
    C. broker failed to conduct the four-step preemployment investigation of the salesperson's background and character required by the license law.
    D. broker failed to keep all local business licenses current.

13. Which of the following activities requires a real estate license?
    A. A resident manager who collects rent on behalf of a building owner
    B. A service that, for a fee (not a commission), matches individuals from different parts of the country who want to exchange properties and that assists them in doing so
    C. A not-for-profit real estate referral service
    D. An executor selling a decedent's building

14. An Illinois real estate broker's license can be revoked for all of the following causes, EXCEPT:
    A. being convicted of a felony in Wisconsin.
    B. advertising in a newspaper that he or she is a member of the Illinois Association of Real Estate Professionals when in fact he or she is not.
    C. depositing escrow money in his or her personal checking account.
    D. agreeing with a seller to accept a listing for more than the normal commission rate.

15. If a broker violates the license law, resulting in monetary damages to a consumer, what is the latest date on which the injured party may file a lawsuit that may result in a collection from the Real Estate Recovery Fund?
    A. One year after the alleged violation occurred
    B. Two years after the alleged violation occurred
    C. Three years after the alleged violation occurred
    D. Three years after the date on which a professional relationship of trust and accountability commenced

16. Broker Norman wants to list a property but is getting a lot of competition from other brokers who also would like to list it. Norman offers the seller the following inducement to sign his listing agreement: "I'll buy your property if it doesn't sell in 90 days." Under these facts, Norman must do all of the following EXCEPT:
    A. buy the property at the agreed figure at any time during the 90 days.
    B. market the property as if no special agreement existed.
    C. show the seller evidence of Norman's financial ability to buy the property.
    D. show the seller written details of the plan before any contract of guaranty is executed.

17. All of the following actions violate the Illinois license law EXCEPT:
    A. encouraging a seller to reject an offer because the prospective buyer is a Methodist.
    B. placing a For Sale sign in front of a house after asking the seller's permission and receiving written permission to go ahead.
    C. advertising that individuals who attend a promotional presentation will receive a prize without mentioning that they will also have to take a day trip to a new subdivision site.
    D. standing in the hallway outside the testing room and offering employment to new licensees as soon as they receive their passing score at the testing center.

18. Salesperson Jana Hall placed the following order with the telephone company: "List my name in the directory under the heading, 'Real Estate,' as 'Jana Hall, Real Estate Salesperson, Residential Property My Specialty.'" Jana is also required to include:
    A. her license number.
    B. the expiration date of her license.
    C. her street address.
    D. the name of her employing broker.

19. In Illinois, all real estate salespersons' licenses expire on the same date. What is that date?
    A. March 31 of every odd-numbered year
    B. March 31 of every even-numbered year
    C. January 31 of every even-numbered year
    D. January 31 of every odd-numbered year

20. Victor owns an apartment building in Chicago. He offers to give existing tenants a "finder's fee" equal to one month's rent if they find a tenant for any vacant apartment. This year, Cindy, a longtime tenant, has helped Victor fill three vacant units. If apartments in Victor's building rent for $1,200 per month, and Cindy is not a real estate licensee, which of the following statements is true?
    A. Under these facts, Cindy must have a valid Illinois real estate license to legally collect any compensation.
    B. In this situation, if Victor fails to pay Cindy the finder's fee, Cindy is entitled to bring a lawsuit as a private citizen under the Illinois Real Estate License Act's provisions for recovering a commission of $3,600.
    C. Cindy is entitled to the finder's fee but only in the amount of $3,000.
    D. If Cindy's activities are limited to finding prospective tenants, and if Cindy finds no more tenants this year, Cindy is entitled to legally collect a finder's fee of $1,000 without having a real estate license.

21. In Illinois, which of the following is true of an individual who wishes to engage only in activities related to the leasing of residential real property?
    A. He or she must obtain a salesperson's license and associate with a broker who specializes in residential leases.
    B. He or she may obtain a certified leasing agent designation by completing a 20-hour training course and passing a written examination.
    C. He or she may obtain a limited leasing agent license by completing 15 hours of instruction and passing a written examination.
    D. He or she may engage in residential leasing activities without obtaining a license or other certification.

22. Luke, Manny and Ned are licensees who obtained their licenses in 1994. Luke takes a 12-hour course on using spreadsheet programs effectively in a real estate office, offered by a local community college. Manny takes a 6-hour course on managing agricultural property, offered by an approved CE sponsor. Ned teaches a prelicense real estate class several evenings a week. Based on these facts, which (if any) of these licensees has satisfied the annual CE requirement in Illinois?
    A. None of them
    B. Manny only
    C. Luke and Ned only
    D. Manny and Ned only

23. What is the purpose of the Illinois Real Estate Recovery Fund?
    A. To ensure that Illinois real estate licensees have adequate funds available to pay their licensing and continuing education fees
    B. To provide a means of compensation for actual monetary losses suffered by individuals as a result of the acts of a licensee in violating the license law or committing other illegal acts related to a real estate transaction
    C. To protect the Office of Banks and Real Estate from claims by individuals that they have suffered a monetary loss as the result of the action of a licensee in violating the license law or committing other illegal acts related to a real estate transaction
    D. To provide an interest-generating source of revenue to fund the activities of the Office of Banks and Real Estate

24. Under what circumstances can a limited liability company obtain a real estate broker's license?
    A. Only if every managing member holds a broker's license
    B. Only if at least 50 percent of the ownership interest in the LLC is controlled by individuals who are licensed real estate salespersons
    C. Only if no licensed salesperson holds stock or any other ownership interest in the entity
    D. Only if the LLC has engaged in real estate sales activities for three of the past five years

Real Estate Financing: Principles

[handwritten margin notes:]
3 WAY TO BORROWER
FOR REAL ESTATE
(1) NOTE + MORTGAGE
(2) NOTE + DEED TRUST
(3) LAND CONTRACT.

[handwritten circle:] R/P

KEY TERMS

acceleration clause	hypothecation	prepayment penalty
alienation clause	interest	promissory note
beneficiary	intermediate theory	release deed
deed in lieu of foreclosure	land contract	satisfaction of mortgage
deed of trust	lien theory	statutory right of redemption
defeasance clause	loan origination fee	
deficiency judgment	mortgage	statutory right of reinstatement
discount point	mortgagee	
equitable right of redemption	mortgagor	title theory
	negotiable instrument	usury
foreclosure	note	

MORTGAGE LAW

[handwritten:] MORTGAGE IS NOT LOAN, IT IS A LIEN
WE ALWAYS GIVE MORTGAGE NOT LOAN

> The *mortgagor* is the *borrower*.
>
> The *mortgagee* is the *lender*.

[handwritten margin notes:] TRUSTER OWNS PROPERTY   Beneficiary

A **mortgage** is a voluntary lien on real estate. That is, a person who borrows money to buy a piece of property voluntarily gives the lender the right to take that property if the borrower fails to repay the loan. The borrower, or **mortgagor,** pledges the land to the lender, or **mortgagee,** as security for the debt. Exactly what rights the mortgagor gives the mortgagee, however, vary from state to state.

In **title-theory** states, the mortgagor actually gives *legal title* to the mortgagee (or some other designated individual) and *retains equitable title*. Legal title is returned to the mortgagor only when the debt is paid in full (or some other obligation is performed). In theory, *the lender actually owns the property until the debt is paid.* The lender allows the borrower all the usual rights of ownership, such as possession and use. In effect, because the lender actually holds legal title, the lender has the right to immediate possession of the real estate and rents from the mortgaged property if the mortgagor defaults.

In **lien-theory** states, the mortgagor retains both legal and equitable title. The mortgagee simply has a *lien on the property as security for the mortgage debt.* The mortgage is nothing more than collateral for the loan. If the mortgagor defaults, the mortgagee must go through a formal foreclosure proceeding to obtain legal title. The property is offered for sale, and the funds from the sale are used to pay all or part of the remaining debt. In some states, a defaulting mortgagor may redeem (buy back) the property during a certain period after the sale. A borrower who fails to redeem the property during that time loses the property irrevocably.

A number of states have adopted an **intermediate-theory** based on the principles of title theory but requiring the mortgagee to foreclose to obtain legal title.

In Illinois . . .

Illinois does not adhere strictly to either the title or lien theory. As a result, Illinois often is referred to as an *intermediate-theory state.* Mortgages and deeds of trust in Illinois convey only qualified title, to be used as security for the credit or during the existence of the debt. The mortgagor remains the owner of the mortgaged property for all beneficial purposes, subject to the lien created by the mortgage or deed of trust. Title is subject to the defeasance clause and must be reconveyed, or released back, to the mortgagor at the time the debt is repaid in full. ■

In reality, the differences between the parties' rights in a lien-theory state and those in a title-theory state are more technical than actual.

SECURITY AND DEBT

A basic principle of property law is that no one can convey more than he or she actually owns. This principle also applies to mortgages. The owner of a fee simple estate can mortgage the fee. The owner of a leasehold or sublease-hold can mortgage that leasehold interest. The owner of a condominium unit can mortgage the fee interest in the condominium apartment. Even the owner of a cooperative interest may be able to offer that personal property interest as collateral for a loan.

There are three ways to borrow money for real estate: a note and mortgage, a note and deed of trust, or a land contract with the seller.

Mortgage Loan Instruments

There are two parts to a mortgage loan: the debt itself and the security for the debt. When a property is to be mortgaged, the owner must execute (sign) two separate instruments:

1. The **promissory note,** also referred to simply as the *note* or *financing instrument,* is the borrower's personal promise to repay a debt according to agreed-on terms. The note exposes all of the borrower's assets to claims by creditors. The mortgagor executes one or more promissory notes to total the amount of the debt.
2. The **mortgage,** also known as the *security instrument,* creates the lien on the property. The mortgage gives the creditor the right to sue for foreclosure in the event the borrower defaults.

Hypothecation is the term used to describe the pledging of property as security for payment of a loan without actually surrendering possession of the property. A pledge of security—a mortgage or deed of trust—cannot be legally effective unless there is a debt to secure. Both a note and mortgage are executed to create a secured loan.

[handwritten margin notes: "It is an evident of Debt a, Mortgate is security for note"]

[handwritten margin note: "PLF"]

Deeds of trust. In some situations, lenders may prefer to use a three-party instrument known as a **deed of trust** rather than a mortgage. A deed of trust conveys naked title or bare legal title—that is, title without the right of possession. The deed is given as security for the loan to a third party, called the *trustee.* The trustee holds title on behalf of the lender, who is known as the **beneficiary.** The beneficiary is the legal owner and holder of the note. The conveyance establishes the actions that the trustee may take if the borrower (the *trustor*) defaults under any of the deed of trust terms. (See Figures 15.1 and 15.2 for a comparison of mortgages and deeds of trust.) In states where deeds of trust are generally preferred, foreclosure procedures for default are usually simpler and faster than for mortgage loans.

In Illinois . . . A deed of trust is treated like a mortgage and is subject to the same rules. In Illinois, the trustor (borrower) owns the title to the real estate. ■

Usually, the lender chooses the trustee and reserves the right to substitute trustees in the event of death or dismissal. State law usually dictates who may serve as trustee. Although the deed of trust is particularly popular in certain states, it is used all over the country. For example, in the financing of a commercial or an industrial real estate venture that involves a large loan and several lenders, the borrower generally executes a single deed of trust to secure as many notes as necessary.

PROVISIONS OF THE NOTE

A promissory note executed by a borrower (known as the *maker* or *payor*) generally states the amount of the debt, the time and method of payment and the rate of interest. If a note is used with a mortgage, it names the lender (mortgagee) as the payee; if it is used with a deed of trust, the note may be made payable to the bearer. The note also may refer to or repeat several of the clauses that appear in the mortgage document or deed of trust. The note, like the mortgage or deed of trust, should be signed by all parties who have an interest in the property. In states where dower and curtesy are in effect or where homestead or community property is involved, both spouses may have interests in the property, and both should sign the note and mortgage.

A **note** is a **negotiable instrument** like a check or bank draft. The individual who holds the note is referred to as the payee. He or she may transfer the right to receive payment to a third party in one of two ways:

1. By signing the instrument over (that is, by *assigning it*) to the third party
2. By *delivering* the instrument to the third party

Interest A charge for using money is called **interest.** Interest may be due at either the end or the beginning of each payment period. When payments are made at the end of a period, it is known as payment in arrears. Payment made at the beginning of each period is payment in advance. Whether interest is charged *in arrears* or *in advance* is specified in the note. This distinction is important if the property is sold before the debt is repaid in full.

Usury. To protect consumers from unscrupulous lenders, many states have enacted laws limiting the interest rate that may be charged on loans. In some

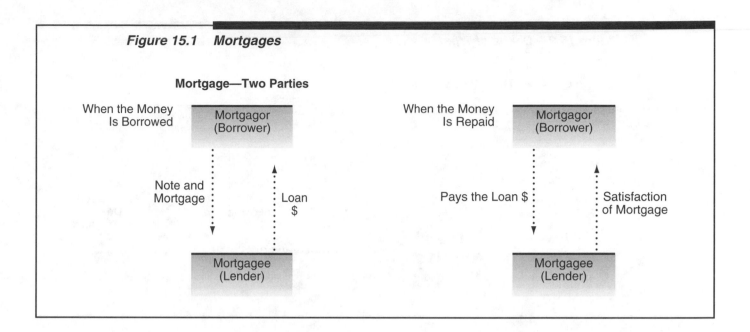

Figure 15.1   Mortgages

Mortgage—Two Parties

When the Money Is Borrowed

Mortgagor (Borrower)

Note and Mortgage

Loan $

Mortgagee (Lender)

When the Money Is Repaid

Mortgagor (Borrower)

Pays the Loan $

Satisfaction of Mortgage

Mortgagee (Lender)

states, the legal maximum rate is a fixed amount. In others, it is a floating interest rate, which is adjusted up or down at specific intervals based on a certain economic standard, such as the prime lending rate or the rate of return on government bonds.

Whichever approach is taken, charging interest in excess of the maximum rate is called usury, and lenders are penalized for making usurious loans. In some states, a lender that makes a usurious loan is permitted to collect the borrowed money but only at the legal rate of interest. In others, a usurious lender may lose the right to collect any interest or may lose the entire amount of the loan in addition to the interest.

In Illinois . . . There is no legal limit on the rate of interest that a lender may charge a borrower when the loan is secured by real estate. ∎

There is, however, a broad exemption from these state laws. Residential first mortgage loans made by federally chartered institutions, or by lenders insured or guaranteed by federal agencies, are exempt from state interest limitations. Included in the federal law's definition of residential loans are loans to buy manufactured housing (mobile homes) and to buy stock in a cooperative. In effect, the federal act limits state usury laws to private lenders. Real estate agents who make third-party loans to buyers to help them afford down payments or closing costs, for instance, are not exempted by the federal law.

Loan origination fee. The processing of a mortgage application is known as *loan origination*. When a mortgage loan is originated, a **loan origination fee,** or *transfer fee,* is charged by most lenders to cover the expenses involved in generating the loan. These include the loan officer's salary, paperwork and the lender's other costs of doing business. A loan origination fee is not prepaid interest; rather, it is a charge that must be paid to the lender. While a loan origination fee serves a different purpose from discount points, both increase the lender's yield. Therefore, the federal government treats the fee like discount points. It is included in the annual percentage rate of Regulation Z

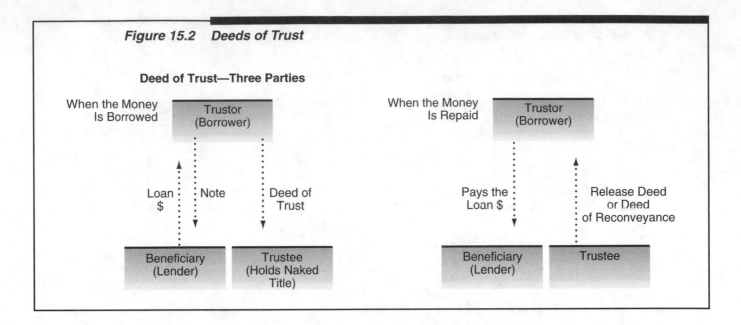

Figure 15.2   Deeds of Trust

(discussed later in Chapter 16), and the IRS lets a buyer deduct the loan origination fee as interest paid up front (as explained in Chapter 3).

> A **point** is *not* 1 percent of the purchase price; a point is 1 percent of the *amount being borrowed.*

Discount points. A lender may sell a mortgage to investors (as discussed later in this chapter). However, the interest rate that a lender charges the borrower for a loan might be less than the yield (true rate of return) an investor demands. To make up the difference, the lender charges the borrower **discount points.** The number of points charged depends on two factors:

1. The difference between the interest rate and the required yield
2. How long the lender expects it will take the borrower to pay off the loan

For the borrowers, one discount point equals 1 percent of the loan amount and is charged as prepaid interest at the closing. For instance, three discount points charged on a $100,000 loan would be $3,000 ($100,000 × 3%, or .03). If a house sells for $100,000 and the borrower seeks an $80,000 loan, each point would be $800, *not* $1,000. In some cases, however, the points in a new acquisition may be paid in cash at closing rather than being financed as part of the total loan amount.

Prepayment   Most mortgage loans are paid in installments over a long period of time. As a result, the total interest paid by the borrower can add up to more than the principal amount of the loan. That does not come as a surprise to the lender; the total amount of accrued interest is carefully calculated during the origination phase to determine the profitability of each loan. If the borrower repays the loan before the end of the term, the lender collects less than the anticipated interest. For this reason, some mortgage notes contain a prepayment clause. This clause requires that the borrower pay a **prepayment penalty** against the unearned portion of the interest for any payments made ahead of schedule.

The penalty may be as little as 1 percent of the balance due at the time of prepayment or as much as all the interest due for the first ten years of the loan. Some lenders allow the borrower to pay off a certain percentage of the original loan without paying a penalty. However, if the loan is paid off in full, the borrower may be charged a percentage of the principal paid in excess of that allowance. Lenders may not charge prepayment penalties on mortgage loans insured or guaranteed by the federal government.

In Illinois . . .

Lenders in Illinois are prohibited from charging a borrower a prepayment penalty on any loan secured by residential real estate when the loan's interest rate is greater than 8 percent per year.   ■

Discount Points and Investor Yield

Lenders use computers or prepared tables to determine the number of discount points that must be paid. However, as a general rule of thumb, each discount point paid to the lender will increase the lender's yield (return) by approximately ⅛ of 1% (.00125). In using the rule of thumb, for each discount point charged by a lender, add ⅛ to the stated (contract) mortgage interest rate to estimate the lender's real return (and cost to the borrower) from the loan.

Note: This rule-of-thumb calculation is designed to estimate the real (or effective) mort-gage interest rate expressed as an annual percentage rate (APR), not as a dollar amount. The stated interest rate, as such, will not change.

To determine the actual cost, in dollars, added by discount points, each discount point is equal to 1% of the mortgage balance (1 point = 1%). The mortgage balance (loan amount) is multiplied by this discount percent to find the dollar amount of the discount being charged.

For example, assume the market rate of interest is 10¾% and the FHA rate of interest is 9½%. The following steps should be used to approximate the discount points required to equal the market rate of interest and determine the amount of discount charged on a $60,000 FHA mortgage:

A. Estimating the discount points required to raise the yield to the lender's required return

   1. Calcuate the difference in the two rates.

      Current market rate − Stated (contract) interest rate = Difference

              10¼% − 9½% = ¾%

   2. Convert the difference to eighths of a percent.

              ¾% = ⁶⁄₈%

   3. Convert the eighths into discount points.

        ⁶⁄₈% ÷ ⅛% = 6 discount points required

B. Amount of discount charged

   1. Convert discount points to discount rate.

        6 points × 1% per point = 6%

   2. Calculate the amount of discount.

      Total loan amount × Discount rate = Amount of discount

        $60,000 × .06 = $3,600 (cost of discount)

With most loans, a borrower usually is not familiar with the above information. The more common experience is for the borrower or his or her agent to be told that a loan will require payment of 4 discount points, or 3, or 5 and so forth. The problem then is not only to calculate the amount of discount cost (step B above) but also to determine the real yield to the lender.

For example, using the same situation as above, assume that the need is to find the amount of yield to the lender if 6 discount points are charged for an FHA loan showing a contract rate of 92% interest.

1. Convert discount points to percent of increase (1 point results in ⅛ of 1% increase)

$$6 \text{ points} \times \tfrac{1}{8}\% \text{ per point} = \tfrac{6}{8}\% \text{ increase}$$

2. Add to the contract rate the percent of increase

$$9\tfrac{1}{2}\% + \tfrac{6}{8}\% = 10\tfrac{1}{4}\% \text{ (approximate yield to lender)}$$

When solving mortgage discount problems, remember that the cost of discount points is figured on the amount of the loan (1 discount point = 1% of the loan amount).

Used with permission: *Real Estate Math,* Fifth Edition, by George Gaines, Jr., David S. Coleman and Linda L. Crawford. Copyright by Dearborn Financial Publishing, Inc.® Published by Real Estate Education Company®, a division of Dearborn Financial Publishing, Inc.®, Chicago, A Kaplan Professional Company. All rights reserved.

PROVISIONS OF THE MORTGAGE DOCUMENT OR DEED OF TRUST

The mortgage document or deed of trust clearly establishes that the property is security for a debt, identifies the lender and the borrower and includes an accurate legal description of the property. Both the mortgage document and deed of trust incorporate the terms of the note by reference. They should be signed by all parties who have an interest in the real estate. Common provisions of both instruments are discussed below.

Duties of the Mortgagor or Trustor

The borrower is required to fulfill certain obligations. These usually include the following:

- Payment of the debt in accordance with the terms of the note
- Payment of all real estate taxes on the property given as security
- Maintenance of adequate insurance to protect the lender if the property is destroyed or damaged by fire, windstorm or other hazard
- Maintenance of the property in good repair at all times
- Receipt of lender authorization before making any major alterations on the property

Failure to meet any of these obligations can result in a borrower's default. The loan documents may, however, provide for a grace period (such as 30 days) during which the borrower can meet the obligation and cure the default. If the borrower does not do so, the lender has the right to foreclose the mortgage or deed of trust and collect on the note.

ENTIRE LOAN IS DUE ON DEFAULT

Provisions for Default

The mortgage or deed of trust typically includes an **acceleration clause** to assist the lender in foreclosure. If a borrower defaults, the lender has the right to accelerate the maturity of the debt. This means the lender may declare the entire debt due and payable immediately. Without an acceleration clause, the lender would have to sue the borrower every time a payment was overdue.

Other clauses in a mortgage or deed of trust enable the lender to take care of the property in the event of the borrower's negligence or default. If the borrower does not pay taxes or insurance premiums or fails to make necessary repairs on the property, the lender may step in and do so. The lender has the power to protect the security (the real estate). Any money advanced by the lender to cure a default may be either added to the unpaid debt or declared immediately due from the borrower.

Assignment of the Mortgage

As mentioned previously, a note may be sold to a third party, such as an investor or another mortgage company. The original mortgagee endorses the note to the third party and executes an assignment of mortgage. The assignee becomes the new owner of the debt and security instrument. When the debt is paid in full (or satisfied), the assignee is required to execute the satisfaction (or release) of the security instrument.

Release of the Mortgage Lien

LAST PAYMENTS

DEFEATS LOAN

When all mortgage loan payments have been made and the note has been paid in full, the mortgagor will want the public record to show that the debt has been satisfied and that the mortgagee is divested of all rights conveyed under the mortgage. By the provisions of the **defeasance clause** in most mortgage documents, the mortgagee is required to execute a **satisfaction of mortgage** (also known as a *release of mortgage* or *mortgage discharge*) when the note has been fully paid. This document returns to the mortgagor all interest in the real estate conveyed to the mortgagee by the original recorded mortgage document. Entering this release in the public record shows that the mortgage lien has been removed from the property.

If a mortgage has been assigned by a recorded assignment, the release must be executed by the assignee or mortgagee.

When a real estate loan secured by a deed of trust has been completely repaid, the beneficiary must make a written request that the trustee convey the property back to the grantor. The trustee executes and delivers a **release deed** (sometimes called a *deed of reconveyance*) to the trustor. The release deed conveys the same rights and powers that the trustee was given under the deed of trust. The release deed should be acknowledged and recorded in the public records of the county in which the property is located.

In Illinois . . .

Any mortgagee, or his or her assigns or agents, who fails to deliver a release to the mortgagor or the grantor of a deed of trust within one month after full payment and satisfaction will be liable to pay the mortgagor or grantor a $200 penalty. The release also must state the following on its face in bold letters: **"FOR THE PROTECTION OF THE OWNER, THIS RELEASE SHALL BE FILED WITH THE RECORDER OR THE REGISTRAR OF TITLES IN WHOSE OFFICE THE MORTGAGE OR DEED OF TRUST WAS FILED."** It is then the mortgagor's responsibility to record the release. ■

87300

Tax and Insurance Reserves

> The basic recurring components of a borrower's monthly loan payment may be remembered as **PITI**: *Principal, Interest, Taxes and Insurance*

Many lenders require that borrowers provide a reserve fund to meet future real estate taxes and property insurance premiums. This fund is called an *impound*, a *trust* or an *escrow account*. When the mortgage or deed of trust loan is made, the borrower starts the reserve by depositing funds to cover the amount of unpaid real estate taxes. If a new insurance policy has just been purchased, the insurance premium reserve will be started with the deposit of one-twelfth of the insurance premium liability. The borrower's monthly loan payments will include principal, interest, tax and insurance reserves and other costs, such as flood insurance or homeowners' association dues. RESPA, the federal Real Estate Settlement Procedures Act, limits the total amount of reserves that a lender may require.

In Illinois . . .

Illinois law prescribes additional guidelines that must be followed by lenders who require escrow accounts for mortgage loans on single-family, owner-occupied residential properties. The *Illinois Mortgage Escrow Account Act* provides that when the principal loan balance has been reduced to 65 percent of its original amount, the borrower may terminate his or her escrow account. *This right does not apply to loans insured, guaranteed, supplemented or assisted by the state of Illinois or the federal government.* Additionally, borrowers have the right to pledge an interest-bearing deposit in an amount sufficient to cover the entire amount of anticipated future tax bills and insurance premiums instead of establishing an escrow account. Except during the first year of the loan, a lender may not require an escrow accumulation of more than 150 percent of the previous year's real estate taxes. Lenders must give borrowers written notice of the act's provisions at closing. ■

Flood insurance reserves. The *National Flood Insurance Reform Act* of 1994 imposes certain mandatory obligations on lenders and loan servicers to set aside (escrow) funds for flood insurance on new loans. However, the act also applies to any loan still outstanding on September 23, 1994. This means that if a lender or servicer discovers that a secured property is in a flood hazard area, it must notify the borrower. The borrower then has 45 days to purchase flood insurance. If the borrower fails to procure flood insurance, the lender must purchase the insurance on the borrower's behalf. The cost of the insurance may be charged to the borrower.

Assignment of Rents

The borrower may provide for rents to be assigned to the lender in the event of the borrower's default. The assignment may be included in the mortgage or deed of trust, or it may be a separate document. In either case, the assignment should clearly indicate that the borrower intends to assign the rents, not merely pledge them as security for the loan. In title-theory states, lenders are automatically entitled to any rents if the borrower defaults.

Buying Subject to or Assuming a Seller's Mortgage or Deed of Trust

When a person purchases real estate that is subject to an outstanding mortgage or deed of trust, the buyer may take the property in one of two ways. The property may be purchased *subject to* the mortgage or the buyer may *assume* the mortgage and agree to pay the debt. This technical distinction becomes important if the buyer defaults and the mortgage or deed of trust is foreclosed.

When the property is sold *subject to* the mortgage, the buyer may not be personally obligated to pay the debt in full. The buyer takes title to the real estate knowing that he or she must make payments on the existing loan. On default, the lender forecloses and the property is sold by court order to pay

[handwritten margin note: IF BUYER ASSUMES THE LOAN CHB]

the debt. If the sale does not pay off the entire debt, the purchaser is not liable for the difference. In some circumstances, however, the original seller might continue to be liable.

In contrast, a buyer who purchases the property and *assumes* the seller's debt becomes *personally* obligated for the payment of the entire debt. If the mortgage is foreclosed and the court sale does not bring enough money to pay the debt in full, a deficiency judgment against the assumer and the original borrower may be obtained for the unpaid balance of the note. If the original borrower has been released by the assumer, only the assumer is liable.

In many cases, a mortgage loan may not be assumed without lender approval. The lending institution requires that the assumer qualify financially, and many lending institutions charge a transfer fee to cover the costs of changing the records. This charge usually is paid by the purchaser.

[handwritten margin note: ALIGN Sale TO ANBALICE ((Due on CLAUSE due on Sales]

Alienation clause. The lender may want to prevent a future purchaser of the property from being able to assume the loan, particularly if the original interest rate is low. For this reason, some lenders include an **alienation clause** (also known as a *resale clause*, *due-on-sale clause* or *call clause*) in the note. An alienation clause provides that when the property is sold, the lender may either declare the entire debt due immediately or permit the buyer to assume the loan at the current market interest rate.

Recording a Mortgage or Deed of Trust

The mortgage document or deed of trust must be recorded in the recorder's office of the county in which the real estate is located. Recording gives constructive notice to the world of the borrower's obligations. Recording also establishes the lien's priority.

Priority of a Mortgage or Deed of Trust

Priority of mortgages and other liens normally is determined by the order in which they were recorded. A mortgage or deed of trust on land that has no prior mortgage lien is a *first mortgage or deed of trust.* If the owner later executes another loan for additional funds, the new loan becomes a *second mortgage* or deed of trust (or a *junior lien*) when it is recorded. The second lien is *subject to* the first lien; the first has prior claim to the value of the land pledged as security. Because second loans represent greater risk to the lender, they are usually issued at higher interest rates.

The priority of mortgage or deed of trust liens may be changed by a *subordination agreement,* in which the first lender subordinates its lien to that of the second lender. To be valid, such an agreement must be signed by both lenders.

PROVISIONS OF LAND CONTRACTS

[handwritten note: SELLER FINANCIANG]

Under a **land contract,** the buyer (called the *vendee*) agrees to make a down payment and a monthly loan payment that includes interest and principal. The payment also may include real estate tax and insurance reserves. The seller (called the *vendor*) retains legal title to the property during the contract term, and the buyer is granted equitable title and possession. At the end of the loan term, the seller delivers clear title. The contract usually permits the seller to evict the buyer in the event of default. In that case, the seller may keep any money the buyer already has paid, which is construed as rent.

FORBEARANCE = PARTIAL PAYMENT
MORATORIUM = FULL PAYMENT
RECAST LOAN = LOWER PAYMENT

FORECLOSURE

When a borrower defaults on the payments or fails to fulfill any of the other obligations set forth in the mortgage or deed of trust, the lender's rights can be enforced through foreclosure. **Foreclosure** is a legal procedure in which property pledged as security is sold to satisfy the debt. The foreclosure procedure brings the rights of the parties and all junior lienholders to a conclusion. It passes title either to the person holding the mortgage document or deed of trust or to a third party who purchases the realty at a *foreclosure sale*. The purchaser could be the mortgagee. The property is sold *free of the foreclosing mortgage and all junior liens.*

Methods of Foreclosure

There are three general types of foreclosure proceedings—judicial, nonjudicial and strict foreclosure. One, two or all three may be available. The specific provisions and procedures for each vary from state to state.

In Illinois . . .

By statute, mortgage foreclosures may be brought about only through a court proceeding. As a result, Illinois is classified as a *judicial foreclosure state*. Under the *Mortgage Foreclosure Law*, the term *mortgage* includes

EXCULPATORY (NON RECOURSE LOAN)

- deeds of trust,
- installment contracts payable over a period in excess of five years (when the unpaid balance is less than 80 percent of the purchase price),
- certain collateral assignments of the beneficial interest in land trusts used as security for lenders and
- traditional mortgage instruments. ■

Judicial foreclosure. Judicial foreclosure allows the property to be sold by court order after the mortgagee has given sufficient public notice. When a borrower defaults, the lender may accelerate the due date of all remaining monthly payments. The lender's attorney then can file a suit to foreclose the lien. After presentation of the facts in court, the property is ordered sold. A public sale is advertised and held, and the real estate is sold to the highest bidder.

TITLE THEORY POWER OF SALES

Nonjudicial foreclosure. Some states allow nonjudicial foreclosure procedures to be used when the security instrument contains a *power-of-sale* clause. In nonjudicial foreclosure, no court action is required. In those states that recognize deed of trust loans, the trustee is generally given the power of sale. Some states allow a similar power of sale to be used with a mortgage loan.

In Illinois . . .

Illinois permits deeds of trust *But* without a power of sale. ■

Strict foreclosure. Although judicial foreclosure is the prevalent practice, it is still possible in some states for a lender to acquire mortgaged property through a strict foreclosure process. First, appropriate notice must be given to the delinquent borrower. Once the proper papers have been prepared and recorded, the court establishes a deadline by which time the balance of the defaulted debt must be paid in full. If the borrower does not pay off the loan by that date, the court simply awards full legal title to the lender. No sale takes place.

Deed in Lieu of Foreclosure

As an alternative to foreclosure, a lender may accept a **deed in lieu of foreclosure** from the borrower. This is sometimes known as a *friendly foreclosure* because it is carried out by mutual agreement, rather than by lawsuit. The major disadvantage of the "deed in lieu" is that the mortgagee takes the real estate subject to all junior liens. In a foreclosure action, all junior liens are eliminated. Also, by accepting a deed in lieu of foreclosure, the lender usually loses any rights pertaining to FHA or private mortgage insurance or VA guarantees. On the positive side, the lender acquires any equity there may be in the property.

Redemption

Most states give defaulting borrowers a chance to redeem their property through the **equitable right of redemption.** If, after default but before the foreclosure sale, the borrower (or any other person who has an interest in the real estate, such as another creditor) pays the lender the amount in default, plus costs, the debt will be reinstated. In some cases, the person who redeems may be required to repay the accelerated loan in full. If some person other than the mortgagor or trustor redeems the real estate, the borrower becomes responsible to that person for the amount of the redemption.

Some states also allow defaulted borrowers a period in which to redeem their real estate after the sale. During this period (which may be as long as one year), the borrower has a **statutory right of redemption.** The mortgagor who can raise the necessary funds to redeem the property within the statutory period pays the redemption money to the court. Because the debt was paid from the proceeds of the sale, the borrower can take possession free and clear of the former defaulted loan. The court may appoint a receiver to take charge of the property, collect rents and pay operating expenses during the redemption period.

In Illinois . . .

There is no statutory right of redemption in Illinois. In Illinois, a mortgagor in default who wishes to exercise the *equitable right of redemption* to avoid loss of the mortgaged real estate may do so *after* the date of judgment of foreclosure is entered. When a property is redeemed, the sale does not occur.

The mortgagor generally has a right to remain in possession of the property from the time of service of summons until the entry of a judgment of foreclosure. After judgment and through the 30th day after confirmation of the sale, the mortgagor can retain possession, but he or she must pay rent to the holder of the certificate of sale. Thirty-one days after judgment, the mortgagor must vacate the property or he or she can be evicted by the owner of the certificate of sale, who receives a sheriff's deed and gains the right to possession.

While Illinois does not offer mortgagors in default a statutory right of redemption, there is another recourse available: the **statutory right of reinstatement,** applicable when the defaulting mortgagor wishes to cure the default and reinstate the loan as if no acceleration had occurred. The mortgagor has the right to exercise this statutory right for a period of 90 days after service of summons. However, the right may be exercised only once every five years. After reinstatement, the suit must be dismissed by the lender, and the mortgage loan remains in effect just as before. ■

Certificate of Sale

In Illinois . . .

When a default is not cured by redemption or reinstatement, the entry of a decree of foreclosure will lead to a *judicial sale* of the property, usually called a *sheriff's sale*. Each defendant to the suit must be given written personal notice of the sale, and public notice of the sale must be published in a newspaper of general circulation. The successful bidder at the sale receives a *certificate of sale*, not a deed. Only after the sale is confirmed by the court will the certificate holder receive a *sheriff's deed* (a quitclaim deed). ■

Deficiency Judgment

The foreclosure sale may not produce enough cash to pay the loan balance in full after deducting expenses and accrued unpaid interest. In some states, the mortgagee may be entitled to a *personal judgment* against the borrower for the unpaid balance. Such a judgment is a **deficiency judgment.** It also may be obtained against any endorsers or guarantors of the note and against any owners of the mortgaged property who assumed the debt by written agreement. However, if any money remains from the foreclosure sale after paying the debt and any other liens (such as a second mortgage or mechanic's lien), expenses and interest, these proceeds are paid to the borrower.

In Illinois . . .

There is no deficiency judgment in Illinois, under the Mortgage Foreclosure Law. ■

SUMMARY

Some states, known as *title-theory states*, recognize the lender as the owner of mortgaged property. Others, known as *lien-theory states*, recognize the borrower as the owner of mortgaged property. A few intermediate-theory states recognize modified versions of these theories.

Mortgage and deed of trust loans provide the principal sources of financing for real estate operations. Mortgage loans involve a borrower (the mortgagor) and a lender (the mortgagee). Deed of trust loans involve a third party (the trustee), in addition to a borrower (the trustor) and a lender (the beneficiary).

After a lending institution has received, investigated and approved a loan application, it issues a commitment to make the mortgage loan. The borrower is required to execute a note agreeing to repay the debt and a mortgage or deed of trust placing a lien on the real estate to secure the note. The security instrument is recorded to give notice to the world of the lender's interest.

The mortgage document or deed of trust secures the debt and sets forth the obligations of the borrower and the rights of the lender. Full payment of the note by its terms entitles the borrower to a satisfaction, or release, which is recorded to clear the lien from the public records. Default by the borrower may result in acceleration of payments, a foreclosure sale and, after the redemption period (if provided by state law), loss of title.

In Illinois . . .

Illinois is an intermediate-theory state. There is no usury limit in Illinois on the rate that may be charged for a loan secured by real estate. The Illinois Mortgage Escrow Account Act gives borrowers certain protections by limiting the size of escrow accounts and permitting alternatives to escrow. Illinois is classified as a judicial foreclosure state (and there is no statutory right of redemption in Illinois). When property is purchased at a sheriff's sale, the successful bidder receives a certificate of sale until the sale is confirmed by a court. After confirmation, the certificate holder receives a quitclaim deed, called a *sheriff's deed.*

QUESTIONS

1. A charge of three discount points on a $120,000 loan equals:
   A. $450.
   C. $4,500.
   B. $3,600.
   D. $116,400.

2. Nancy wants to buy a house but needs to borrow money to do so. She applies for and obtains a real estate loan from the First National Loan Company. Nancy signs a note and a mortgage. In this example, Nancy is referred to as the:
   A. mortgagor.
   C. mortgagee.
   B. beneficiary.
   D. vendor.

3. In the previous question, First National Loan is the:
   A. mortgagor.
   C. mortgagee.
   B. beneficiary.
   D. vendor.

4. The borrower under a deed of trust is known as the:
   A. trustor.
   C. beneficiary.
   B. trustee.
   D. vendee.

5. All of the following are true of the vendee in a land contract EXCEPT that the vendee:
   A. is responsible for the real estate taxes on the property.
   B. must pay interest and principal.
   C. obtains possession at closing.
   D. obtains legal title at closing.

6. The law of the state of New Carolina provides that lenders cannot charge more than 18 percent interest on any loan. This kind of law is called:
   A. a Truth-in-Lending Law.
   B. a usury law.
   C. the statute of frauds.
   D. RESPA.

7. In some states, a borrower who has defaulted on a loan may seek to pay off the debt plus any accrued interest and costs after the foreclosure sale under what right?
   A. Equitable redemption
   B. Defeasance
   C. Usury
   D. Statutory redemption

8. A borrower defaulted on a loan. Which of the following would best describe the rights of the lender in this situation?
   A. The escalation clause in the note allows the lender to collect all future interest due on the loan should a buyer default.
   B. The defeasance clause in the note stipulates that the lender may begin foreclosure proceedings to collect the remaining mortgage balance.
   C. The alienation clause in the note allows the lender to convey the mortgage to a buyer at the foreclosure sale.
   D. The acceleration clause in the note gives the lender the right to have all future installments due and payable on default.

9. A mortgagor has just made her final payment to the mortgagee. Which of the following would MOST LIKELY occur?
   A. The mortgagee would give the mortgagor a satisfaction of mortgage.
   B. The mortgagee would give the mortgagor a release deed.
   C. The mortgagee would give the mortgagor a deed of trust.
   D. The mortgagee would give the mortgagor a mortgage estoppel.

10. Under a typical land contract, when does the vendor give the deed to the vendee?
    A. When the contract is fulfilled
    B. At the closing
    C. When the contract for deed is approved by the parties
    D. After the first year's real estate taxes are paid

11. If a borrower must pay $2,700 for points on a $90,000 loan, how many points is the lender charging for this loan?
    A. 2
    C. 5
    B. 3
    D. 6

12. Paul buys property from Renee in a transaction involving a land contract. The vendor would do all of the following, EXCEPT:
    A. provide financing for the vendee.
    B. be liable for any senior financing.
    C. retain legal title.
    D. retain possession of the property.

13. Which of the following allows a mortgagee to proceed to a foreclosure sale without having to go to court first?
    A. Waiver of redemption right
    B. Power of sale
    C. Alienation clause
    D. Hypothecation

14. Pledging property for a loan without giving up possession of the property itself is referred to as:
    A. hypothecation.   C. alienation.
    B. defeasance.   D. novation.

15. Discount points on a mortgage are computed as a percentage of the:
    A. selling price.
    B. amount borrowed.
    C. closing costs.
    D. down payment.

16. What do the terms *alienation clause, resale clause, due-on-sale clause* or *call clause* have in common?
    A. They are all names for clauses found in mortgages that stipulate that should the borrower default, the lender may declare the entire unpaid balance on the note due and payable.
    B. They are all names for clauses found in mortgages that stipulate that a note may be prepaid at any time without penalty.
    C. They are all names for clauses found in land contracts that stipulate that the vendor must convey the title to the vendee when the final payment is made.
    D. They are all names for clauses found in mortgages that stipulate that when a property is sold, the lender may either declare the entire debt due immediately or permit the buyer to assume the loan at the current market interest rate.

In Illinois. . .

17. In Illinois, mortgage foreclosures may be obtained only through a court proceeding. This means Illinois is characterized as a:
    A. strict foreclosure state.
    B. judicial foreclosure state.
    C. foreclosure-by-lawsuit state.
    D. sheriff's foreclosure state.

18. Hal purchased a home in Cairo, Illinois, and financed the purchase with a loan secured by a deed of trust. If Hal defaults on the loan, what must the lender do?
    A. It need not file a foreclosure suit but need only direct the trustee to sell the property.
    B. It must wait for the statutory reinstatement period to expire before proceeding with any legal action.
    C. It must proceed with a foreclosure action just as if the security were a mortgage.
    D. It need not notify Hal of any legal action because the breach of the loan agreement waives all notification rights.

19. Illinois real estate subject to a mortgage loan that is in default may be redeemed by the mortgagor:
    A. at any time between the entry of a judgment of foreclosure and the foreclosure sale.
    B. up to six months after the property is sold at the foreclosure sale.
    C. by notifying the mortgagee in writing of his or her intent to pay the current market value of the property, and doing so within 90 days of notification.
    D. by paying the current market value to the highest bidder at the sale.

20. In Illinois, a mortgagor in default may exercise his or her right of reinstatement:
    A. at any time prior to the foreclosure sale.
    B. up to six months after the foreclosure sale.
    C. up to 90 days after service of summons.
    D. up to 90 days after the payments become delinquent.

21. In Illinois, when must a release be delivered to a mortgagor or trustor once the mortgage or deed of trust has been fully satisfied?
    A. Within 48 hours of full payment and satisfaction
    B. Within 5 business days after full payment and satisfaction
    C. Within one month after full payment and satisfaction
    D. Within 90 days after full payment and satisfaction

22. The successful bidder at a foreclosure sale in Illinois immediately receives a:
    A. sheriff's deed.
    B. certificate of sale.
    C. deed of foreclosure.
    D. certificate of foreclosure.

23. According to the Illinois Mortgage Escrow Act, an individual who has owned his or her home for 12 years and reduced his or her mortgage balance to 65 percent of its original amount may:
    A. receive a 50 percent rebate from the lender on his or her escrow account.
    B. earn the statutory interest rate on his or her escrow account deposit.
    C. terminate his or her escrow account.
    D. obtain a second loan with only a token down payment.

24. What is the Illinois usury ceiling for loans secured by real property?
    A. 8 percent
    B. 9½ percent
    C. A fluctuating rate based on the quarterly federal reserve rate
    D. There is no usury ceiling for such loans in Illinois.

25. Which of the following is *not* included in the definition of "mortgage" contained in the Illinois Mortgage Foreclosure Law?
    A. Installment contracts payable over at least five years, with a 20 percent down payment
    B. Assignments of beneficial interests in land trusts
    C. Deeds of trust
    D. Installment contracts payable over a maximum of five years

26. Which of the following describes the theory of the mortgagor/mortgagee relationship in Illinois?
    A. Title theory
    B. Lien theory
    C. Intermediate theory
    D. Conventional theory

CHAPTER

16

Real Estate Financing: Practice

[handwritten notes: MORTGATOR = BORROWER / MORTGAGEE = LENDER]

KEY TERMS

[handwritten notes in left margin: LIEN THEORY / MORTGATOR DEED MORTGAGEE / LIENS THEORY / MORTGATOR LIEN MORTGAGEE]

adjustable-rate
   mortgage
amortized loan
balloon payment
blanket loan
buydown
Community
   Reinvestment Act
   of 1977
construction loan
conventional loan
Equal Credit
   Opportunity Act
Fannie Mae
Farm Service Agency
Federal Deposit
   Insurance
   Corporation

Federal Home Loan
   Mortgage
   Corporation
Federal Reserve
   System
FHA loan
Ginnie Mae
growing-equity
   mortgage
home equity loan
loan-to-value ratio
Office of Thrift
   Supervision
open-end loan
package loan
primary mortgage
   market

private mortgage
   insurance
purchase-money
   mortgage
Real Estate
   Settlement
   Procedures Act
Regulation Z
reverse-annuity
   mortgage
sale-leaseback
secondary mortgage
   market
straight loan
Truth-in-Lending Act
VA loan
wraparound loan

INTRODUCTION TO THE REAL ESTATE FINANCING MARKET

[handwritten notes in left margin: ICL / INFORMATION / BORROWER OWN Real Estate]

Most real estate transactions require some sort of financing. Few people have the cash in hand necessary to buy a house or another large property. Also, as economic conditions change, the forces of supply and demand reshape the real estate market. Both of these factors have combined to create a complex and rapidly evolving mortgage market. One of the greatest challenges today's real estate licensees face is how to maintain a working knowledge of all the financing techniques available.

Although it has never been easier to buy a house, it has never been more challenging to keep up with the financing alternatives. By altering the terms of the basic mortgage or deed of trust and note, a borrower and a lender can tailor financing instruments to suit the type of transaction and the financial needs of both parties. Having an overview of current financing techniques and sources of financing can help salespeople direct buyers to the mortgage loans that will help the buyers reach their real estate goals.

The Federal Reserve System

The role of the **Federal Reserve System** (also known as "the Fed") is to maintain sound credit conditions, help counteract inflationary and deflationary trends and create a favorable economic climate. The Federal Reserve System divides the country into 12 federal reserve districts, each served by a federal reserve bank. All nationally chartered banks must join the Fed and purchase stock in its district reserve banks.

The Federal Reserve System regulates the flow of money and interest rates in the marketplace indirectly through its member banks by controlling their *reserve requirements* and *discount rates.*

Reserve requirements. The Federal Reserve System requires that each member bank keep a certain amount of assets on hand as reserve funds. These reserves are unavailable for loans or any other use. This requirement not only protects customer deposits but also provides a means of manipulating the flow of cash in the money market.

By increasing its reserve requirements, the Federal Reserve System in effect limits the amount of money that member banks can use to make loans. When the amount of money available for lending decreases, interest rates (the amount lenders charge for the use of their money) rise. By causing interest rates to rise, the government can slow down an overactive economy by limiting the number of loans that would have been directed toward major purchases of goods and services. The opposite is also true: by decreasing the reserve requirements, the Fed can encourage more lending. Increased lending causes the amount of money circulated in the marketplace to rise while simultaneously causing interest rates to drop.

Discount rates. Federal Reserve System member banks are permitted to borrow money from the district reserve banks to expand their lending operations. The interest rate that the district banks charge for the use of this money is called the *discount rate.* This rate is the basis on which the banks determine the percentage rate of interest they will charge their loan customers. The *prime rate* (the short-term interest rate charged to a bank's largest, most creditworthy customers) is strongly influenced by the Fed's discount rate. In turn, the prime rate is often the basis for determining a bank's interest rate on other loans, including mortgages. In theory, when the Federal Reserve System discount rate is high, bank interest rates are high. When bank interest rates are high, fewer loans are made and less money circulates in the marketplace. On the other hand, a lower discount rate results in lower interest rates, more bank loans and more money in circulation.

The Primary Mortgage Market

The **primary mortgage market** is made up of the lenders that originate mortgage loans. These lenders make money available directly to borrowers. From a borrower's point of view, a loan is a means of financing an expenditure; from a lender's point of view, a loan is an investment. All investors look for profitable returns on their investments. For a lender, a loan must generate enough income to be attractive as an investment. Income on the loan is realized from two sources:

1. *Finance charges*—collected at closing, such as loan origination fees and discount points
2. *Recurring income*—that is, the interest collected during the term of the loan

(3) SERVICE THE LOAN

An increasing number of lenders look at the income generated from the fees charged in originating loans as their primary investment objective. Once the loans are made, they are sold to investors. By selling loans to investors in the secondary mortgage market, lenders generate funds with which to originate additional loans.

In addition to the income directly related to loans, some lenders derive income from *servicing* loans for other mortgage lenders or the investors who have purchased the loans. Servicing involves such activities as

- collecting payments (including insurance and taxes),
- accounting,
- bookkeeping,
- preparing insurance and tax records,
- processing payments of taxes and insurance and
- following up on loan payment and delinquency.

The terms of the servicing agreement stipulate the responsibilities and fees for the service.

Some of the major lenders in the primary market include the following:

Primary Mortgage Market

- Thrifts
- Savings associations
- Commercial banks
- Insurance companies
- Credit unions
- Pension funds
- Endowment funds
- Investment group financing
- Mortgage banking companies
- Mortgage brokers

- *Thrifts, savings associations and commercial banks:* These institutions are known as *fiduciary lenders* because of their fiduciary obligations to protect and preserve their depositors' funds. Mortgage loans are perceived as secure investments for generating income and enable these institutions to pay interest to their depositors. Fiduciary lenders are subject to standards and regulations established by government agencies, intended to protect depositors against the reckless lending that characterized the savings and loan industry in the 1980s.
- *Insurance companies:* Insurance companies accumulate large sums of money from the premiums paid by their policyholders. While part of this money is held in reserve to satisfy claims and cover operating expenses, much of it is free to be invested in profit-earning enterprises, such as long-term real estate loans. Although insurance companies are considered primary lenders, they tend to invest their money in large, long-term loans that finance commercial and industrial properties rather than single-family home mortgages.
- *Credit unions:* Credit unions are cooperative organizations whose members place money in savings accounts. In the past, credit unions made only short-term consumer and home improvement loans. Recently, however, they have branched out to originating longer-term first and second mortgage and deed of trust loans.
- *Pension funds:* Pension funds usually have large amounts of money available for investment. Because of the comparatively high yields and low risks offered by mortgages, pension funds have begun to participate actively in financing real estate projects. Most real estate activity for pension funds is handled through mortgage bankers and mortgage brokers.
- *Endowment funds:* Many commercial banks and mortgage bankers handle investments for endowment funds. The endowments of hospitals, universities, colleges, charitable foundations and other institutions provide a good source of financing for low-risk commercial and industrial properties.
- *Investment group financing:* Large real estate projects, such as highrise apartment buildings, office complexes and shopping centers, are often

financed as joint ventures through group financing arrangements like syndicates, limited partnerships and real estate investment trusts. These complex investment agreements are discussed in the appendix.

- *Mortgage banking companies:* Mortgage banking companies originate mortgage loans with money belonging to insurance companies, pension funds and individuals and with funds of their own. They make real estate loans with the intention of selling them to investors and receiving a fee for servicing the loans. Mortgage banking companies generally are organized as stock companies. As a source of real estate financing, they are subject to fewer lending restrictions than are commercial banks or savings associations. Mortgage banking companies often are involved in all types of real estate loan activities and often serve as intermediaries between investors and borrowers. They are not mortgage brokers.
- *Mortgage brokers:* Mortgage brokers are not lenders. They are intermediaries who bring borrowers and lenders together. Mortgage brokers locate potential borrowers, process preliminary loan applications and submit the applications to lenders for final approval. Frequently, they work with or for mortgage banking companies. They do not service loans once they are made. Mortgage brokers also may be real estate brokers who offer these financing services in addition to their regular brokerage activities. Many state governments are establishing separate licensure requirements for mortgage brokers to regulate their activities.

In Illinois, the majority of residential financing is accomplished with mortgage banking companies and mortgage brokers.

The Secondary Mortgage Market

In addition to the primary mortgage market, where loans are originated, there is a **secondary mortgage market.** Here, loans are bought and sold only after they have been funded. Lenders routinely sell loans to avoid interest rate risks and to realize profits on the sales. This secondary market activity helps lenders raise capital to continue making mortgage loans. Secondary market activity is especially desirable when money is in short supply; it stimulates both the housing construction market and the mortgage market by expanding the types of loans available.

When a loan is sold, the original lender may continue to collect the payments from the borrower. The lender then passes the payments along to the investor who purchased the loan. The investor is charged a fee for servicing the loan.

Warehousing agencies purchase a number of mortgage loans and assemble them into packages (called *pools*). Securities that represent shares in these pooled mortgages are then sold to investors. Loans are eligible for sale to the secondary market only when the collateral, borrower and documentation meet certain requirements to provide a degree of safety for the investors. The major warehousing agencies are discussed in the following paragraphs.

Fannie Mae. Fannie Mae (formerly called the Federal National Mortgage Association, or FNMA) is a quasi-governmental agency. It is organized as a privately owned corporation that issues its own common stock and provides a secondary market for mortgage loans. Fannie Mae deals in conventional, FHA and VA loans. Fannie Mae buys a block or pool of mortgages from a lender in exchange for *mortgage-backed securities,* which the lender may keep or sell. Fannie Mae guarantees payment of all interest and principal to the holder of the securities.

Ginnie Mae. Unlike Fannie Mae, **Ginnie Mae** (the Government National Mortgage Association) is entirely a governmental agency. Ginnie Mae is a division of the Department of Housing and Urban Development (HUD), organized as a corporation without capital stock. Ginnie Mae administers special-assistance programs and works with Fannie Mae in secondary market activities.

In times of tight money and high interest rates, Fannie Mae and Ginnie Mae can join forces through their *tandem plan.* The tandem plan provides that Fannie Mae can purchase high-risk, low-yield (usually FHA) loans at full market rates, with Ginnie Mae guaranteeing payment and absorbing the difference between the low yield and current market prices.

Ginnie Mae also guarantees investment securities issued by private offerors (such as banks, mortgage companies and savings and loan associations) and backed by pools of FHA and VA mortgage loans. The Ginnie Mae *pass-through certificate* is a security interest in a pool of mortgages that provides for a monthly pass-through of principal and interest payments directly to the certificate holder. Such certificates are guaranteed by Ginnie Mae.

Federal Home Loan Mortgage Corporation. The **Federal Home Loan Mortgage Corporation** (FHLMC, or Freddie Mac) provides a secondary market for mortgage loans, primarily conventional loans. Freddie Mac has the authority to purchase mortgages, pool them and sell bonds in the open market with the mortgages as security. However, FHLMC does not guarantee payment of Freddie Mac mortgages.

Many lenders use the standardized forms and follow the guidelines issued by Fannie Mae and Freddie Mac. In fact, the use of such forms is mandatory for lenders that wish to sell mortgages in the agencies' secondary mortgage market. The standardized documents include loan applications, credit reports and appraisal forms.

In Practice	Because Fannie Mae's and FHLMC's involvement in the secondary market is so pervasive, many underwriting guidelines are written to comply with their regulations. Bank statements, tax returns, verifications of employment and child support—most of the paperwork a potential borrower must deal with—may be tied to Fannie Mae and FHLMC requirements.

FINANCING TECHNIQUES

Now that you understand *where* real estate financing comes from, we'll turn to the *what:* the types of financing available. As mentioned at the beginning of this chapter, real estate financing comes in a wide variety of forms. While the payment plans described in the following sections are commonly referred to as *mortgages,* they are really loans secured by either a mortgage or a deed of trust.

STRAIGHT LOANS

A **straight loan** (also known as a *term loan*) essentially divides the loan into two amounts, to be paid off separately. The borrower makes periodic interest payments, followed by the payment of the principal in full at the end of the term. Straight loans were once the only form of mortgage available. Today, they are generally used for home improvements and second mortgages rather than for residential first mortgage loans.

AMORTIZED LOANS

The word *amortize* literally means "to kill off slowly, over time." Most mortgage and deed of trust loans are **amortized loans.** That is, they are paid off slowly, over time. Regular periodic payments are made over a term of years. The most common periods are 15 or 30 years, although 20-year and 40-year mortgages are also available. Unlike a straight loan payment, an amortized loan payment partially pays off both principal and interest. Each payment is applied first to the interest owed; the balance is applied to the principal amount.

MATH CONCEPTS

Interest and Principal Credited from Amortized Payments
Lenders charge borrowers a certain percentage of the principal as interest for each year a debt is outstanding. The amount of interest due on any one payment date is calculated by computing the total yearly interest (based on unpaid balance) and dividing that figure by the number of payments made each year.

For example, assume the current outstanding balance of a loan is $70,000. The interest rate is 7½ percent per year, and the monthly payment is $489.30. Based on these facts, the interest and principal due on the next payment would be computed as shown:

$70,000 loan balance	× .075 annual interest rate	= $5,250 annual interest
$5,250 annual interest	÷ 12 months	= $437.50 monthly interest
$489.30 monthly payment	− $437.50 monthly interest	= $51.80 monthly principal
$70,000 loan balance	− $51.80 monthly principal	= $69,948.20

This process is followed with each payment over the term of the loan. The same calculations are made each month, starting with the declining new balance figure from the previous month.

At the end of the term, the full amount of the principal and all interest due is reduced to zero. Such loans are also called *direct reduction loans.* Most amortized mortgage and deed of trust loans are paid in monthly installments. However, some are payable quarterly (four times a year) or semiannually (twice a year).

Different payment plans tend alternately to gain and lose favor with lenders and borrowers as the cost and availability of mortgage money fluctuate. The most frequently used plan is the *fully amortized loan,* or *level-payment loan.* The mortgagor pays a constant amount, usually monthly. The lender credits each payment first to the interest due, then to the principal amount of the loan. As a result, while each payment remains the same, the portion applied to repayment of the principal grows and the interest due declines as the unpaid balance of the loan is reduced. (See Figure 16.1.) If the borrower pays additional amounts that are applied directly to the principal, the loan will

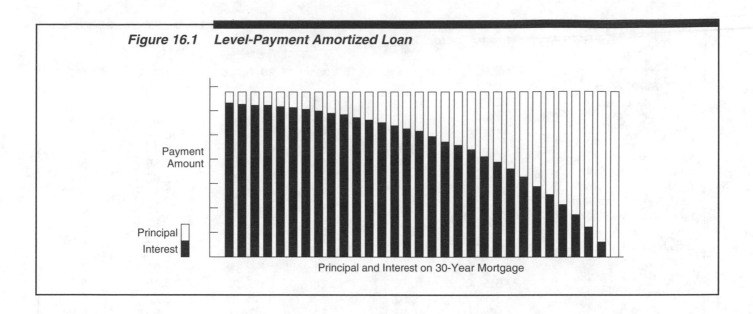

Figure 16.1   *Level-Payment Amortized Loan*

Payment Amount

Principal

Interest

Principal and Interest on 30-Year Mortgage

amortize more quickly. This benefits the borrower because he or she will pay less interest if the loan is paid off before the end of its term. Of course, lenders are aware of this, too, and may guard against unprofitable loans by including penalties for early payment.

The amount of the constant payment is determined from a prepared mortgage payment book or a mortgage factor chart. (See Table 16.1.) The mortgage factor chart indicates the amount of monthly payment per $1,000 of loan, depending on the term and interest rate. The factor is multiplied by the number of thousands (and fractions of thousands) of the amount borrowed.

Adjustable-Rate Mortgages (ARMs)

An **adjustable-rate mortgage** (ARM) is generally originated at one rate of interest. That rate then fluctuates up or down during the loan term, based on some objective economic indicator. Because the interest rate may change, the mortgagor's loan repayments also may change. Details of how and when the interest rate will change are included in the note. Common components of an ARM include the following:

- The interest rate is tied to the movement of an objective economic indicator called an *index*. Most indexes are tied to U.S. Treasury securities.
- Usually, the interest rate is the index rate plus a premium, called the *margin*. The margin represents the lender's cost of doing business. For example, the loan rate may be 2 percent over the U.S. Treasury bill rate.
- *Rate caps* limit the amount the interest rate may change. Most ARMs have two types of rate caps—periodic and aggregate. A *periodic rate cap* limits the amount the rate may increase at any one time. An *aggregate rate cap* limits the amount the rate may increase over the entire life of the loan.
- The mortgagor is protected from unaffordable individual payments by the payment cap. The *payment cap* sets a maximum amount for payments. With a cap, a rate increase could result in *negative amortization*—that is, an increase in the loan balance.
- The adjustment period establishes how often the rate may be changed. For instance, the adjustment period may be monthly, quarterly or annually.

Table 16.1   *Mortgage Factor Chart*

How To Use This Chart

To use this chart, start by finding the appropriate interest rate. Then follow that row over to the column for the appropriate loan term. This number is the *interest rate factor* required each month to amortize a $1,000 loan. To calculate the principal and interest (PI) payment, multiply the interest rate factor by the number of 1,000s in the total loan.

For example, if the interest rate is 10 percent for a term of 30 years, the interest rate factor is 8.78. If the total loan is $100,000, the loan contains 100 1,000s. Therefore

$$100 \times 8.78 = \$878$$
PI only

To estimate a mortgage loan amount using the amortization chart, divide the PI payment by the appropriate interest rate factor. Using the same facts as in the first example:

$$\$878 \div 8.78 = \$100$$
1,000s, or $100,000

Term Rate	10 Years	15 Years	20 Years	25 Years	30 Years
4	10.13	7.40	6.06	5.28	4.78
4⅛	10.19	7.46	6.13	5.35	4.85
4¼	10.25	7.53	6.20	5.42	4.92
4⅜	10.31	7.59	6.26	5.49	5.00
4½	10.37	7.65	6.33	5.56	5.07
4⅝	10.43	7.72	6.40	5.63	5.15
4¾	10.49	7.78	6.47	5.71	5.22
4⅞	10.55	7.85	6.54	5.78	5.30
5⅛	10.61	7.91	6.60	5.85	5.37
5⅛	10.67	7.98	6.67	5.92	5.45
5¼	10.73	8.04	6.74	6.00	5.53
5⅜	10.80	8.11	6.81	6.07	5.60
5½	10.86	8.18	6.88	6.15	5.68
5⅝	10.92	8.24	6.95	6.22	5.76
5¾	10.98	8.31	7.03	6.30	5.84
5⅞	11.04	8.38	7.10	6.37	5.92
6	11.10	8.44	7.16	6.44	6.00
6⅛	11.16	8.51	7.24	6.52	6.08
6¼	11.23	8.57	7.31	6.60	6.16
6⅜	11.29	8.64	7.38	6.67	6.24
6½	11.35	8.71	7.46	6.75	6.32
6⅝	11.42	8.78	7.53	6.83	6.40
6¾	11.48	8.85	7.60	6.91	6.49
6⅞	11.55	8.92	7.68	6.99	6.57
7	11.61	8.98	7.75	7.06	6.65
7⅛	11.68	9.06	7.83	7.15	6.74
7¼	11.74	9.12	7.90	7.22	6.82
7⅜	11.81	9.20	7.98	7.31	6.91
7½	11.87	9.27	8.05	7.38	6.99
7⅝	11.94	9.34	8.13	7.47	7.08
7¾	12.00	9.41	8.20	7.55	7.16
7⅞	12.07	9.48	8.29	7.64	7.25
8	12.14	9.56	8.37	7.72	7.34
8⅛	12.20	9.63	8.45	7.81	7.43
8¼	12.27	9.71	8.53	7.89	7.52
8⅜	12.34	9.78	8.60	7.97	7.61
8½	12.40	9.85	8.68	8.06	7.69
8⅝	12.47	9.93	8.76	8.14	7.78
8¾	12.54	10.00	8.84	8.23	7.87
8⅞	12.61	10.07	8.92	8.31	7.96
9	12.67	10.15	9.00	8.40	8.05
9⅛	12.74	10.22	9.08	8.48	8.14
9¼	12.81	10.30	9.16	8.57	8.23
9⅜	12.88	10.37	9.24	8.66	8.32
9½	12.94	10.45	9.33	8.74	8.41
9⅝	13.01	10.52	9.41	8.83	8.50
9¾	13.08	10.60	9.49	8.92	8.60
9⅞	13.15	10.67	9.57	9.00	8.69
10	13.22	10.75	9.66	9.09	8.78
10⅛	13.29	10.83	9.74	9.18	8.87
10¼	13.36	10.90	9.82	9.27	8.97
10⅜	13.43	10.98	9.90	9.36	9.06
10½	13.50	11.06	9.99	9.45	9.15
10⅝	13.57	11.14	10.07	9.54	9.25
10¾	13.64	11.21	10.16	9.63	9.34

- Lenders may offer a conversion option, which permits the mortgagor to convert from an adjustable-rate to a fixed-rate loan at certain intervals during the life of the mortgage. The option is subject to certain terms and conditions for the conversion.

Figure 16.2 illustrates the effect interest rate fluctuations and periodic caps have on an adjustable-rate mortgage. Obviously, without rate caps and payment caps, a single mortgage's interest rate could fluctuate wildly over several adjustment periods, depending on the behavior of the index to which it is tied. In Figure 16.2, the borrower's rate changes from a low of 5.9 percent to a high of 9.5 percent. Such unpredictability makes personal financial planning difficult. On the other hand, if the loan had a periodic rate cap of 7.5 percent, the borrower's rate would never go above that level, regardless of the index's behavior. Similarly, a lender would want a floor to keep the rate from falling below a certain rate (here, 6.5 percent). The shaded area in the figure shows how caps and floors protect against dramatic changes in interest rates.

Balloon Payment Loan

When the periodic payments are not enough to fully amortize the loan by the time the final payment is due, the final payment is larger than the others. This is called a **balloon payment.** It is a *partially amortized loan* because principal is still owed at the end of the term. It is frequently assumed that if payments are made promptly, the lender will extend the balloon payment for another limited term. The lender, however, is not legally obligated to grant this extension and can require payment in full when the note is due.

Growing-Equity Mortgage (GEM)

A **growing-equity mortgage** (GEM) is also known as a *rapid-payoff mortgage.* The GEM uses a fixed interest rate, but payments of principal are increased according to an index or a schedule. Thus, the total payment increases, and the loan is paid off more quickly. A GEM is most frequently used when the borrower's income is expected to keep pace with the increasing loan payments.

Reverse-Annuity Mortgage (RAM)

A **reverse-annuity mortgage** (RAM) is one in which regular monthly payments are made by the lender to the borrower. The payments are based on the equity the homeowner has invested in the property given as security for the loan. This loan allows senior citizens on fixed incomes to realize the equity they have built up in their homes without having to sell. The borrower is charged a fixed rate of interest, and the loan eventually is repaid from the sale of the property or from the borrower's estate upon his or her death.

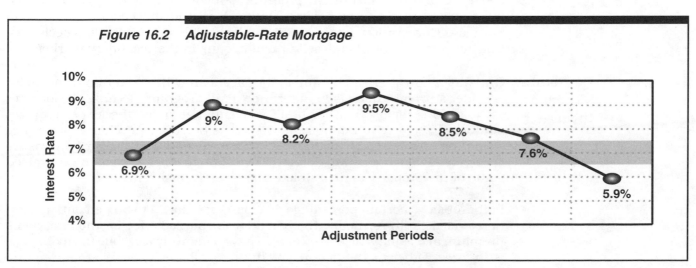

Figure 16.2   Adjustable-Rate Mortgage

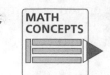

Determining LTV

If a property has an appraised value of $100,000, secured by a $90,000 loan, the LTV is 90 percent:

$$\$90,000 \div \$100,000 = 90\%$$

Nonrecourse Loan

A *nonrecourse loan* is one in which the borrower is not held personally responsible for the loan. That is, the lender has no recourse against the borrower personally in the event of a default. Nonrecourse loans are common in those situations in which the lender is highly confident that the value of the property involved is itself sufficient security. Nonrecourse loans are more common in commercial and investment real estate transactions than in residential situations.

LOAN PROGRAMS

Mortgage loans are generally classified based on their **loan-to-value ratios,** or *LTVs.* The LTV is the ratio of debt to value of the property. *Value* is the sale price or the appraisal value, whichever is less. The *lower* the ratio of debt to value, the *higher* the down payment by the borrower. For the lender, the higher down payment means a more secure loan, which minimizes the lender's risk.

Conventional Loans

Low LTV = *High* down payment

High down payment = *Low* lender risk

Conventional loans are viewed as the most secure loans because their loan-to-value ratios are lowest. Usually, the ratio is 80 percent of the value of the property or less, because the borrower makes a down payment of at least 20 percent. The security for the loan is provided solely by the mortgage; the payment of the debt rests on the ability of the borrower to pay. In making such a loan, the lender relies primarily on its appraisal of the security (the real estate). Information from credit reports that indicates the reliability of the prospective borrower is also important. No additional insurance or guarantee on the loan is necessary to protect the lender's interest.

Lenders can set criteria by which a borrower and the collateral are evaluated to qualify for a loan. However, in recent years the secondary mortgage market has had a significant impact on the borrower qualifications, standards for the collateral and documentation procedures followed by lenders. Loans must meet strict criteria to be sold to Fannie Mae and the Federal Home Loan Mortgage Corporation. Lenders still can be flexible in their lending decisions, but they may not be able to sell unusual loans in the secondary market.

Private Mortgage Insurance

One way a borrower can obtain a mortgage loan with a lower down payment is under a **private mortgage insurance** (PMI) program. Because the loan-to-value ratio is higher than for other conventional loans, the lender requires additional security to minimize its risk. The borrower purchases insurance from a private mortgage insurance company as additional security to insure the lender against borrower default. LTVs of up to 95 percent of the appraised value of the property are possible with mortgage insurance.

PMI protects a certain percentage of a loan, usually 25 to 30 percent, against borrower default. Normally, the borrower is charged a fee for the first year's premium at closing. The borrower also pays a monthly fee while the insurance is in force. Other methods of payment are available, however: the premium may be financed, or the fee at closing may be waived in exchange for slightly

Interna

higher monthly payments. When a borrower has limited funds for investment, these alternative methods of reducing closing costs are very important. Because only a portion of the loan is insured, once the loan is repaid to a certain level, the lender may agree to allow the borrower to terminate the coverage. Practices for termination vary from lender to lender.

FHA-Insured Loans

The Federal Housing Administration (FHA), which operates under HUD, neither builds homes nor lends money itself. The common term **FHA loan** refers to a loan that is insured by the agency. These loans must be made by FHA-approved lending institutions. The FHA insurance provides security to the lender in addition to the real estate. As with private mortgage insurance, the FHA insures lenders against loss from borrower default.

203B—Must Be owner occupied

The most popular FHA program is Title II, Section 203(b), fixed–interest rate loans for 10- to 30-year loans on one- to four-family residences. (Other FHA programs include loans for condominium purchases, ARMs, Graduated Payment Mortgages (GPMs), and rehabilitation programs.) Rates are competitive with other types of loans, even though they are high-LTV loans. Certain technical requirements must be met before the FHA will insure the loans. These requirements include the following:

- The borrower is charged a percentage of the loan as a premium for the FHA insurance. The *upfront premium* is paid at closing by the borrower or some other party. It may also be financed along with the total loan amount. A monthly premium also may be charged. Insurance premiums vary for new loans, refinancing and condominiums.
- FHA regulations set standards for type and construction of buildings, quality of neighborhood and credit requirements for borrowers.
- The mortgaged real estate must be appraised by an approved FHA appraiser. The loan amount generally cannot exceed either of the following: (1) 97 percent on the first $25,000 of appraised value or purchase price, whichever is less; 95 percent up to $125,000; and 90 percent of any amount exceeding $125,000 (including the allowable amount for closing costs); or (2) 97.75 percent of the sales price or appraised value, whichever is less. If the purchase price exceeds the FHA-appraised value, the buyer may pay the difference in cash as part of the down payment.
- In addition, the FHA has set maximum loan amounts for various regions of the country.

Other types of FHA loans are available, including one-year adjustable-rate mortgages, home improvement and rehabilitation loans and loans for the purchase of condominiums. Specific standards for condominium complexes and the ratio of owner-occupants to renters must be met for a loan on a condominium unit to be financed through the FHA insurance programs.

In Practice   FHA-insured mortgages generally offer borrowers greater borrowing power than conventional mortgages. While conventional lenders use the 28/36 "rule of thumb" formula, the FHA uses a more lenient 29/41 formula in determining eligibility.

In Practice   The FHA sets lending limits for single-unit and multiple-unit properties. The limits vary significantly depending on the average cost of housing in different regions of the country. In addition, the FHA changes its regulations for various programs from time to time. Contact your local FHA office or mortgage lender for loan amounts in your area and for specific loan requirements.

Prepayment privileges. A borrower may prepay an FHA-insured loan on a one- to four-family residence without penalty. For loans made before August 2, 1985, the borrower must give the lender written notice of intention to exercise the prepayment privilege at least 30 days before prepayment. If the borrower fails to provide the required notice, the lender has the option of charging up to 30 days' interest. For loans initiated after August 2, 1985, no written notice of prepayment is required.

Assumption rules. The assumption rules for FHA-insured loans vary, depending on the dates the loans were originated.

Under Assumption Seller is not liable

- FHA loans originated before December 1986 generally have no restrictions on their assumptions.
- For an FHA loan originated between December 1, 1986, and December 15, 1989, a creditworthiness review of the prospective assumer is required. If the original loan was for the purchase of a principal residence, this review is required during the first 12 months of the loan's existence. If the original loan was for the purchase of an investment property, the review is required during the first 24 months of the loan.
- For FHA loans originated on December 15, 1989, and later, no assumptions are permitted without complete buyer qualification.

Discount points. The lender of an FHA-insured loan may charge discount points in addition to a loan origination fee. The payment of points is a matter of negotiation between the seller and the buyer. However, if the seller pays more than 6 percent of the costs normally paid by the buyer (such as discount points, the loan origination fee, the mortgage insurance premium, buydown fees, prepaid items and impound or escrow amounts), the lender will treat the payments as a reduction in sales price and recalculate the mortgage amount accordingly. Points are tax deductible to the buyer regardless of which party pays them.

VA-Guaranteed Loans

The Department of Veterans Affairs (VA) is authorized to guarantee loans to purchase or construct homes for eligible veterans and their spouses (including unremarried spouses of veterans whose deaths were service-related). The VA also guarantees loans to purchase mobile homes and plots on which to place them. A veteran who meets any of the following time-in-service criteria is eligible for a VA loan:

- 90 days of active service for veterans of World War II, the Korean War, the Vietnam conflict and the Persian Gulf War
- A minimum of 181 days of active service during interconflict periods between July 26, 1947, and September 6, 1980
- Two full years of service during any peacetime period after September 7, 1980
- Six or more years of continuous duty as a reservist in the U.S. Army, Navy, Air Force, Marine Corps or Coast Guard or as a member of the Army or Air National Guard (eligibility expires on October 28, 1999)

The VA assists veterans in financing the purchase of homes with little or no down payments, at comparatively low interest rates. The VA issues rules and regulations that set forth the qualifications, limitations and conditions under which a loan may be guaranteed.

Like the term *FHA loan, VA loan* is something of a misnomer. The VA does not normally lend money; it guarantees loans made by lending institutions approved by the agency. The term **VA loan** refers to a loan that is not made by the agency but is guaranteed by it.

There is no VA limit on the amount of the loan a veteran can obtain; this is determined by the lender. The VA limits the amount of the loan it will guarantee. (See Table 16.2.)

To determine what portion of a mortgage loan the VA will guarantee, the veteran must apply for a *certificate of eligibility*. This certificate does not mean that the veteran automatically receives a mortgage. It merely sets forth the maximum guarantee to which the veteran is entitled. For individuals with full eligibility, no down payment is required for a loan up to the maximum guarantee limit.

The VA also issues a *certificate of reasonable value (CRV)* for the property being purchased. The CRV states the property's current market value based on a VA-approved appraisal. The CRV places a ceiling on the amount of a VA loan allowed for the property. If the purchase price is greater than the amount cited in the CRV, the veteran may pay the difference in cash.

The VA purchaser pays a loan origination fee to the lender, as well as a funding fee (1.25 to 2 percent, depending on the down payment amount) to the Department of Veterans Affairs. Reasonable discount points may be charged on a VA-guaranteed loan, and either the veteran or the seller may pay them.

Prepayment privileges. As with an FHA loan, the borrower under a VA loan can prepay the debt at any time without penalty.

Assumption rules. VA loans made before March 1, 1988, are freely assumable, although an assumption processing fee will be charged. The fee is 2 percent of the loan balance. For loans made on or after March 1, 1988, the VA must approve the buyer and assumption agreement. The original veteran borrower remains personally liable for the repayment of the loan unless the VA approves a *release of liability*. The release of liability will be issued by the VA only if

- the buyer assumes all of the veteran's liabilities on the loan and
- the VA or the lender approves both the buyer and the assumption agreement.

Table 16.2	**VA Schedule of Guarantees**	
Loan Amount	**Maximum Guarantee Amount**	
Up to $45,000	50%	
$45,001 to $144,000	$22,500 minimum; lesser of $36,000 or 40% of loan maximum	
$144,000 to $203,000	The lesser of $50,750 or 25% of loan	

A release also would be possible if another veteran used his or her own entitlement in assuming the loan.

In Practice

A release of liability issued by the VA does not release the veteran's liability to the lender. This must be obtained separately from the lender. Real estate licensees should contact their local VA offices or mortgage lenders for specific requirements for obtaining or assuming VA-insured loans. The programs change from time to time.

[handwritten margin note: No limit on VA loan thru insura loan guarantee]

Farm Service Agency

The **Farm Service Agency** (FSA), formerly the Federal Agricultural Mortgage Corporation (FAMC, or *Farmer Mac*), is a federal agency of the Department of Agriculture. The FSA offers programs to help families purchase or operate family farms. Through the Rural Housing and Community Development Service, it also provides loans to help families purchase or improve single-family homes in rural areas. Loans are made to low- and moderate-income families, and the interest rate charged can be as low as 1 percent, depending on the borrower's income. The FSA provides assistance to rural and agricultural businesses and industry through the Rural Business and Cooperative Development Service.

FSA loan programs fall into two categories: guaranteed loans, made and serviced by private lenders and guaranteed for a specific percentage by the FSA, and loans made directly by the FSA.

OTHER FINANCING TECHNIQUES

Because borrowers often have different needs, a variety of other financing techniques have been created. Other techniques apply to various types of collateral. The following pages consider some of the loans that do not fit into the categories previously discussed.

Purchase-Money Mortgages

A **purchase-money mortgage** is a note and mortgage created at the time of purchase. Its purpose is to make the sale possible. The term is used in two ways. First, it may refer to any security instrument that originates at the time of sale. More often, it refers to seller financing where the seller receives a note and mortgage at closing instead of money. This is referred to as the "seller takes back paper." A purchase-money mortgage can be for part or all of the purchase price; it can be a first or second mortgage, depending on whether prior liens exist. In a purchase-money mortgage, the seller is the mortgagee.

FOR EXAMPLE Bill wants to buy Brownacre for $200,000. He has a $40,000 down payment and agrees to assume an existing mortgage of $80,000. Because Bill might not qualify for a new mortgage under the circumstances, the owner agrees to take back a purchase-money second mortgage in the amount of $80,000. At the closing, Bill will execute a mortgage and note in favor of the owner, who will convey title to Bill.

Package Loans

A **package loan** includes not only the real estate but also all personal property and appliances installed on the premises. In recent years, this kind of loan has been used extensively to finance furnished condominium units. Package loans usually include furniture, drapes and carpets and the kitchen range, refrigerator, dishwasher, garbage disposal, washer, dryer, food freezer and other appliances as part of the sales price of the home.

Blanket Loans A **blanket loan** covers more than one parcel or lot. It is usually used to finance subdivision developments. However, it can finance the purchase of improved properties or consolidate loans as well. A blanket loan usually includes a provision known as a *partial release clause*. This clause permits the borrower to obtain the release of any one lot or parcel from the lien by repaying a certain amount of the loan. The lender issues a partial release for each parcel released from the mortgage lien. The release form includes a provision that the lien will continue to cover all other unreleased lots.

Wraparound Loans A **wraparound loan** enables a borrower with an existing mortgage or deed of trust loan to obtain additional financing from a second lender *without paying off the first loan*. The second lender gives the borrower a new, increased loan at a higher interest rate and assumes payment of the existing loan. The total amount of the new loan includes the existing loan as well as the additional funds needed by the borrower. The borrower makes payments to the new lender on the larger loan. The new lender makes payments on the original loan out of the borrower's payments.

A wraparound mortgage can be used to refinance real property or to finance the purchase of real property when an existing mortgage cannot be prepaid. The buyer executes a wraparound mortgage to the seller, who collects payments on the new loan and continues to make payments on the old loan. It also can finance the sale of real estate when the buyer wishes to invest a minimum amount of initial cash. A wraparound loan is possible only if the original loan permits it. For instance, an acceleration and alienation or a due-on-sale clause in the original loan documents may prevent a sale under a wraparound loan.

In Practice To protect themselves against a seller's default on a previous loan, buyers should require protective clauses to be included in any wraparound document to grant buyers the right to make payments directly to the original lender.

Open-End Loans An **open-end loan** secures a *note* executed by the borrower to the lender. It also secures any *future advances of funds* made by the lender to the borrower. The interest rate on the initial amount borrowed is fixed, but interest on future advances may be charged at the market rate in effect. An open-end loan is often a less costly alternative to a home improvement loan. It allows the borrower to "open" the mortgage or deed of trust to increase the debt to its original amount, or the amount stated in the note, after the debt has been reduced by payments over a period of time. The mortgage usually states the maximum amount that can be secured, the terms and conditions under which the loan can be opened and the provisions for repayment.

Construction Loans (Interim Financing) A **construction loan** is made to finance the construction of improvements on real estate such as homes, apartments and office buildings. The lender commits to the full amount of the loan but disburses the funds in payments during construction. These payments also are known as *draws*. Draws are made to the general contractor or the owner for that part of the construction work that has been completed since the previous payment. Before each payment, the lender inspects the work. The general contractor must provide the lender with adequate waivers that release all mechanic's lien rights for the work covered by the payment.

This kind of loan generally bears a higher-than-market interest rate because of the risks assumed by the lender. These risks include the inadequate releasing of mechanics' liens, possible delays in completing the construction or the financial failure of the contractor or subcontractors. Construction loans are generally short-term or interim financing. The borrower pays interest only on the monies that have actually been disbursed. The borrower is expected to arrange for a permanent loan, also known as an *end loan* or *take-out loan,* that will repay or "take out" the construction financing lender when the work is completed. Some lenders now offer construction-to-permanent programs. Under these plans, a single loan is used to carry through the construction; it automatically becomes a mortgage loan when the work is finished. *Participation financing* is when a lender demands an equity position in the project as a requirement for making the loan.

Sale-Leaseback

Sale-leaseback arrangements are used to finance large commercial or industrial properties. The land and building, usually used by the seller for business purposes, are sold to an investor. The real estate is then leased back by the investor to the seller, who continues to conduct business on the property as a tenant. The buyer becomes the lessor, and the original owner becomes the lessee. This enables a business to free money tied up in real estate to be used as working capital.

Sale-leaseback arrangements involve complicated legal procedures, and their success is usually related to the effects the transaction has on the firm's tax situation. Legal and tax experts should be involved in this type of transaction.

Buydowns

A **buydown** is a way to temporarily lower the initial interest rate on a mortgage or deed of trust loan. Perhaps a homebuilder wishes to stimulate sales by offering a lower-than-market rate. Or a first-time residential buyer may have trouble qualifying for a loan at the prevailing rates; relatives or the sellers might want to help the buyer qualify. In any case, a lump sum is paid in cash to the lender at the closing. The payment offsets (and so reduces) the interest rate and monthly payments during the mortgage's first few years. Typical buydown arrangements reduce the interest rate by 1 to 3 percent over the first one to three years of the loan term, after which it rises to a fixed (or adjustable) rate. The assumption is that the borrower's income also will increase and that the borrower will be more able to absorb the increased monthly payments.

Home Equity Loans

Using the equity buildup in a home to finance purchases is an alternative to refinancing. **Home equity loans** are a source of funds for homeowners to use for a variety of financial needs:

- To finance the purchase of expensive items
- To consolidate existing installment loans on credit card debt
- To pay medical, education, home improvement or other expenses

The original mortgage loan remains in place; the home equity loan is junior to the original lien. If the homeowner refinances, the original mortgage loan is paid off and replaced by a new loan. (This is an alternative way to borrow the equity; it's not really a home equity loan.)

A home equity loan can be taken out as a fixed loan amount or as an equity line of credit. With the home equity line of credit, the lender extends a line of credit that the borrower can use whenever he or she wants. The borrower receives his or her money by a check sent to him or her, deposits made in a checking or savings account or a book of drafts the borrower can use up to his or her credit limit.

Use of this type of financing has increased in recent years, partly because interest on consumer loans is no longer deductible under IRS rules. Home equity loans are secured by a borrower's residence, and the interest charged is deductible up to a loan limit of $100,000.

In Practice

The homeowner must consider a number of factors before deciding on a home equity loan. The costs involved in obtaining a new mortgage loan or a home equity loan, current interest rates, total monthly payments and income tax consequences are all important issues to be examined.

FINANCING LEGISLATION

The federal government regulates the lending practices of mortgage lenders through the Truth-in-Lending Act, the Equal Credit Opportunity Act, the Community Reinvestment Act of 1977 and the Real Estate Settlement Procedures Act.

Truth-in-Lending Act and Regulation Z

TO KNOW THE TRUE APR

Regulation Z, which was promulgated pursuant to the **Truth-in-Lending Act,** requires that credit institutions inform borrowers of the true cost of obtaining credit. Its purpose is to permit borrowers to compare the costs of various lenders and avoid the uninformed use of credit. Regulation Z applies when credit is extended to individuals for *personal, family or household uses.* The amount of credit sought must be $25,000 or less. Regardless of the amount, however, *Regulation Z always applies when a credit transaction is secured by a residence.* The regulation does not apply to business or commercial loans or to agricultural loans of more than $25,000.

Under Regulation Z, a consumer must be fully informed of all finance charges and the true interest rate before a transaction is completed. The finance charge disclosure must include any loan fees, finder's fees, service charges and points, as well as interest. In the case of a mortgage loan made to finance the purchase of a dwelling, the lender must compute and disclose the *annual percentage rate (APR).* However, the lender does not have to indicate the total interest payable during the term of the loan. Also, the lender does not have to include actual costs such as title fees, legal fees, appraisal fees, credit reports, survey fees and closing expenses as part of the finance charge.

Creditor. A *creditor,* for purposes of Regulation Z, is any person who extends consumer credit more than 25 times each year or more than 5 times each year if the transactions involve dwellings as security. The credit must be subject to a finance charge or payable in more than four installments by written agreement.

Three-day right of rescission. In the case of most consumer credit transactions covered by Regulation Z, the borrower has three days in which to rescind the transaction by merely notifying the lender. *This right of rescission does not apply to residential purchase-money or first mortgage or deed of trust* *loans.* There is a three-day waiting period for equity loans or refinance loans during which time the borrower can cancel the agreement and the lender cannot file a lien on the house. In an emergency, the right to rescind may be waived in writing to prevent a delay in funding.

Advertising. Regulation Z provides strict regulation of real estate advertisements that include mortgage financing terms. General phrases like "liberal terms available" may be used, but if details are given, they must comply with the act. For example, "$6,000 down and you can own this lovely condominium" *triggers* all the rules of Regulation Z. In addition, the annual percentage rate (APR)—which is calculated based on all charges rather than the interest rate alone—must be stated.

Advertisements for buydowns or reduced–interest rate mortgages must show both the limited term to which the interest rate applies and the annual percentage rate. If a variable-rate mortgage is advertised, the advertisement must include

- the number and timing of payments;
- the amount of the largest and smallest payments; and
- a statement of the fact that the actual payments will vary between these two extremes.

Specific credit terms, such as down payment, monthly payment, dollar amount of the finance charge or term of the loan, may not be advertised unless the advertisement includes the following information:

- Cash price
- Required down payment
- Number, amounts and due dates of all payments
- Annual percentage rate
- Total of all payments to be made over the term of the mortgage (unless the advertised credit refers to a first mortgage or deed of trust to finance the acquisition of a dwelling)

Penalties. Regulation Z provides penalties for noncompliance. The penalty for violation of an administrative order enforcing Regulation Z is $10,000 for each day the violation continues. A fine of up to $10,000 may be imposed for engaging in an unfair or a deceptive practice. In addition, a creditor may be liable to a consumer for twice the amount of the finance charge, for a minimum of $100 and a maximum of $1,000, plus court costs, attorney's fees and any actual damages. Willful violation is a misdemeanor punishable by a fine of up to $5,000, one year's imprisonment or both.

Equal Credit Opportunity Act (ECOA)

The federal **Equal Credit Opportunity Act** (ECOA) prohibits lenders and others who grant or arrange credit to consumers from discriminating against credit applicants on the basis of

- race,
- color,
- religion,
- national origin,
- sex,
- marital status,
- age (provided the applicant is of legal age) or

• dependence on public assistance.

In addition, lenders and other creditors must inform all rejected credit applicants of the principal reasons for the denial or termination of credit. The notice must be provided in writing, within 30 days. The federal Equal Credit Opportunity Act also provides that a borrower is entitled to a copy of the appraisal report if the borrower paid for the appraisal.

Community Reinvestment Act of 1977 (CRA)

Community reinvestment refers to the responsibility of financial institutions to help meet their communities' needs for low- and moderate-income housing. In 1977, Congress passed the **Community Reinvestment Act of 1977** (CRA). Under the CRA, financial institutions are expected to meet the deposit and credit needs of their communities; participate and invest in local community development and rehabilitation projects; and participate in loan programs for housing, small businesses and small farms.

The law requires any federally supervised financial institution to prepare a statement containing

• a definition of the geographic boundaries of its community,
• an identification of the types of community reinvestment credit offered (such as residential housing loans, housing rehabilitation loans, small-business loans, commercial loans and consumer loans) and
• comments from the public about the institution's performance in meeting its community's needs.

Financial institutions are periodically reviewed by one of four federal financial supervisory agencies: the Comptroller of the Currency, the Federal Reserve's Board of Governors, the **Federal Deposit Insurance Corporation** and the **Office of Thrift Supervision.** The institutions must post a public notice that their community reinvestment activities are subject to federal review, and they must make the results of these reviews public.

Real Estate Settlement Procedures Act

The federal **Real Estate Settlement Procedures Act** (RESPA) applies to any residential real estate transaction involving a new first mortgage loan. RESPA is designed to ensure that buyer and seller are both fully informed of all settlement costs.

COMPUTERIZED LOAN ORIGINATION AND AUTOMATED UNDERWRITING

A *computerized loan origination* (CLO) system is an electronic network for handling loan applications through remote computer terminals linked to several lenders' computers. With a CLO system, a real estate broker or salesperson can call up a menu of mortgage lenders, interest rates and loan terms, then help a buyer select a lender and apply for a loan right from the brokerage office.

Under federal regulations, licensees may assist applicants in answering the on-screen questions and in understanding the services offered. The broker in whose office the terminal is located may earn fees of up to one half point of the loan amount. The borrower, not the mortgage broker or lender, must pay the fee. The fee amount may be financed, however. While multiple lenders may be represented on an office's CLO computer, consumers must be informed that other lenders are available. An applicant's ability to comparison shop for a loan may be enhanced by a CLO system; the range of options may not be limited.

On the lenders' side, new automated underwriting procedures can shorten loan approvals from weeks to minutes. Automated underwriting also tends to lower the cost of loan application and approval by reducing lenders' time spent on the approval process by as much as 60 percent. The Federal Home Loan Mortgage Corporation uses a system called *Loan Prospector.* Fannie Mae has a system called *Desktop Underwriter* that reduces approval time to minutes, based on the borrower's credit report, a paycheck stub and a drive-by appraisal of the property. Complex or difficult mortgages can be processed in less than 72 hours. Through automated underwriting, one of a borrower's biggest headaches in buying a home—waiting for loan approval—is eliminated. In addition, a prospective buyer can strengthen his or her purchase offer by including proof of loan approval.

SUMMARY

The federal government affects real estate financing money and interest rates through the Federal Reserve Board's discount rate and reserve requirements; it also participates in the secondary mortgage market. The secondary market generally is composed of the investors who ultimately purchase and hold the loans as investments. These include insurance companies, investment funds and pension plans.

Types of loans include fully amortized and straight loans as well as adjustable-rate mortgages, growing-equity mortgages, balloon payment mortgages and reverse-annuity mortgages.

Many mortgage and deed of trust loan programs exist, including conventional loans and those insured by the FHA or private mortgage insurance companies or guaranteed by the VA. FHA and VA loans must meet certain requirements for the borrower to obtain the benefits of government backing, which induces the lender to lend its funds. The interest rates for these loans may be lower than those charged for conventional loans. Lenders also may charge points.

Other types of real estate financing include seller-financed purchase-money mortgages or deeds of trust, blanket mortgages, package mortgages, wrap-around mortgages, open-end mortgages, construction loans, sale-leaseback agreements and home equity loans.

Regulation Z, implementing the federal Truth-in-Lending Act, requires that lenders inform prospective borrowers who use their homes as security for credit of all finance charges involved in such loans. Severe penalties are provided for noncompliance. The federal Equal Credit Opportunity Act prohibits creditors from discriminating against credit applicants on the basis of race, color, religion, national origin, sex, marital status, age or dependence on public assistance. The Real Estate Settlement Procedures Act requires that lenders inform both buyers and sellers in advance of all fees and charges required for the settlement or closing of residential real estate transactions.

QUESTIONS

1. The buyers purchased a residence for $95,000. They made a down payment of $15,000 and agreed to assume the seller's existing mortgage, which had a current balance of $23,000. The buyers financed the remaining $57,000 of the purchase price by executing a mortgage and note to the seller. This type of loan, by which the seller becomes the mortgagee, is called a:
   A. wraparound mortgage.
   B. package mortgage.
   C. balloon note.
   D. purchase-money mortgage.

2. Tammy purchased a new residence for $175,000. She made a down payment of $15,000 and obtained a $160,000 mortgage loan. The builder of Tammy's house paid the lender 3 percent of the loan balance for the first year and 2 percent for the second year. This represented a total savings for Tammy of $8,000. What type of arrangement does this represent?
   A. Wraparound mortgage
   B. Package mortgage
   C. Blanket mortgage
   D. Buydown mortgage

3. Which of the following is not a participant in the secondary market?
   A. Fannie Mae   C. RESPA
   B. GNMA   D. FHLMC

4. Fatima purchased her home for cash 30 years ago. Today, Fatima receives monthly checks from the bank that supplement her income. Fatima most likely has obtained a(n):
   A. shared-appreciation mortgage.
   B. adjustable-rate mortgage.
   C. reverse-annuity mortgage.
   D. overriding deed of trust.

5. If buyers seek a mortgage on a single-family house, they would be likely to obtain the mortgage from any of the following, EXCEPT:
   A. mutual savings bank.
   B. life insurance company.
   C. credit union.
   D. commercial bank.

6. A purchaser obtains a fixed-rate loan to finance a home. Which of the following characteristics is true of this type of loan?
   A. The amount of interest to be paid is predetermined.
   B. The loan cannot be sold in the secondary market.
   C. The monthly payment amount will fluctuate each month.
   D. The interest rate change may be based on an index.

7. When the Federal Reserve Board raises its discount rate, all of the following are likely to happen EXCEPT:
   A. buyer's points will increase.
   B. interest rates will fall.
   C. mortgage money will become scarce.
   D. the percentage of ARMs will increase.

8. In a loan that requires periodic payments that do not fully amortize the loan balance by the final payment, what term best describes the final payment?
   A. Adjustment   C. Balloon
   B. Acceleration   D. Variable

9. A developer received a loan that covers five parcels of real estate and provides for the release of the mortgage lien on each parcel when certain payments are made on the loan. This type of loan arrangement is called a:
   A. purchase-money loan.
   B. blanket loan.
   C. package loan.
   D. wraparound loan.

10. Funds for Federal Housing Administration loans are usually provided by:
   A. the Federal Housing Administration.
   B. the Federal Reserve System.
   C. qualified lenders.
   D. the seller.

11. Under the provisions of the Truth-in-Lending Act (Regulation Z), the annual percentage rate (APR) of a finance charge includes all of the following components EXCEPT:
    A. discount points.
    B. a broker's commission.
    C. a loan origination fee.
    D. a loan interest rate.

12. A home is purchased using a fixed-rate, fully amortized mortgage loan. Which of the following statements is true regarding this mortgage?
    A. A balloon payment will be made at the end of the loan.
    B. Each payment amount is the same.
    C. Each payment reduces the principal by the same amount.
    D. The principal amount in each payment is greater than the interest amount.

13. Which of the following best defines the secondary market?
    A. Lenders who deal exclusively in second mortgages
    B. Where loans are bought and sold after they have been originated
    C. The major lender of residential mortgages and deeds of trust
    D. The major lender of FHA and VA loans

14. With a fully amortized mortgage or deed of trust loan:
    A. interest may be charged in arrears—that is, at the end of each period for which interest is due.
    B. the interest portion of each payment increases throughout the term of the loan.
    C. interest only is paid each period.
    D. a portion of the principal will be owed after the last payment is made.

15. What does Freddie Mac do?
    A. Guarantees mortgages by the full faith and credit of the federal government
    B. Buys and pools blocks of conventional mortgages, selling bonds with such mortgages as security
    C. Acts in tandem with Ginnie Mae to provide special assistance in times of tight money
    D. Buys and sells VA and FHA mortgages

16. The federal Equal Credit Opportunity Act prohibits lenders from discriminating against potential borrowers on the basis of all of the following EXCEPT:
    A. race.
    B. sex.
    C. source of income.
    D. amount of income.

17. A borrower obtains a $100,000 mortgage loan for 30 years at 7½ percent interest. If the monthly payments of $902.77 are credited first to interest and then to principal, what will be the balance of the principal after the borrower makes the first payment?
    A. $99,772.00
    B. $99,722.23
    C. $99,097.32
    D. $100,000.00

18. Using Table 16.1, what is the monthly interest rate factor required to amortize a loan at 8⅛ percent over a term of 25 years?
    A. 7.72
    B. 7.81
    C. 7.89
    D. 8.06

19. Using Table 16.1, calculate the principal and interest payment necessary to amortize a loan of $135,000 at 7¾ percent interest over 15 years.
    A. $1,111.85
    B. $1,270.35
    C. $1,279.80
    D. $1,639.16

20. Henry borrowed $85,000, to be repaid in monthly installments of $823.76 at 11½ percent annual interest. How much of Henry's first month's payment was applied to reducing the principal amount of the loan?
    A. $8.15
    B. $9.18
    C. $91.80
    D. $814.58

21. If a lender agrees to make a loan based on an 80 percent LTV, what is the amount of the loan if the property appraises for $114,500 and the sales price is $116,900?
    A. $83,200
    B. $91,300
    C. $91,600
    D. $92,900

22. A lender has agreed to negotiate a loan on the following terms: 90% of the first $50,000 of the appraised value, 95% of the next $25,000 and 97% of the remaining amount. If a property is appraised for $129,000, how much can he borrow?
    A. $118,750
    B. $120,121
    C. $120,380
    D. $121,130

23. A borrower wanted to negotiate a $113,000 loan. Different lenders in his town offered him the following loans. Which loan would he need to accept to pay the least amount of interest over the life of the loan?
    A. 7 percent amortized over a period of 30 years
    B. 8 percent amortized over a period of 20 years
    C. 9 percent amortized over a period of 15 years
    D. 10 percent amortized over a period of 25 years

24. A borrower negotiated an adjustable rate mortgage at 9 percent with a prepayment penalty of 1 percent and the following terms: monthly payment the first year of $649.33, due on the first of the month, and a ½ percent interest adjustment for the next year. After she made her sixth payment on the first of the month, her loan balance was $75,279.89. She made her seventh payment and on that same day paid the note in full. How much did she pay the lender for the prepayment penalty?
    A. $564.60   C. $751.95
    B. $84.73   D. $376.39

25. The difference between the market value and any mortgages the borrower has on the property is best described by the word:
    A. equity.
    B. equitable interest.
    C. equitable title.
    D. equitable lien.

26. All of the following are true regarding VA-guaranteed loans EXCEPT:
    A. a veteran can secure more than one VA-guaranteed loan during his or her lifetime.
    B. if a veteran agrees to pay $90,000 for a property and the certificate of reasonable value states a market value of $85,000, the veteran cannot buy the property.
    C. the lender will determine the maximum loan a veteran can obtain, and the veteran must pay a funding fee on the loan amount.
    D. the VA will issue a certificate of eligibility and sets the limits on the amount of the loan it will guarantee.

27. Which of the following is NOT associated with a mortgage/note?
    A. Alienation clause/acceleration clause
    B. Pledge of property/evidence of debt
    C. Hypothecation/annual percentage rate
    D. Defeasible fee/indefeasible fee

28. All of the following are true regarding Truth-in-lending (Regulation Z) EXCEPT:
    A. finance charges that must be disclosed include loan fees, insurance premiums for mortgage protection insurance, finder's fees and title insurance premiums.
    B. if a borrower is refinancing, Regulation Z states that the borrower has three days to rescind the transaction by merely notifying the lender.
    C. if an advertisement discloses the APR, then it has met Truth-in-Lending requirements.
    D. for the purposes of Regulation Z, a creditor is a person who extends consumer credit more than 25 times each year or more than 5 times each year if the transactions involve dwellings as security.

29. Which of the following does NOT act as a warehousing agency?
    A. Federal National Mortgage Association
    B. Federal Housing Administration
    C. Federal Home Loan Mortgage Corporation
    D. Government National Mortgage Association

30. Interest rates are 18 percent. To sell their property, Mr. and Mrs. Seller agreed to "take back paper" at the closing for a part of the purchase price. The document MOST LIKELY used would be a:
    A. reverse annuity mortgage.
    B. package mortgage.
    C. purchase-money mortgage.
    D. shared appreciation mortgage.

Leases

LeaseHold Estates
DIFF: Net & Gross Lea
ILL Law

KEY TERMS

actual eviction
assignment
cash rent
constructive eviction
estate at sufferance
estate at will
estate for years
estate from period to
   period
gross lease

ground lease
holdover tenancy
lease
leasehold estate
lease purchase
lessee
lessor
month-to-month
   tenancy

net lease
percentage lease
rental-finding service
reversionary right
security deposit
sharecropping
sublease
triple-net leaset

LEASING REAL ESTATE

A **lease** is a contract between an owner of real estate (the **lessor**) and a tenant (the **lessee**). It is a contract to transfer the lessor's rights to exclusive possession and use of the property to the tenant for a specified period of time. The lease establishes the length of time the contract is to run and the amount the lessee is to pay for use of the property. Other rights and obligations of the parties may be set forth as well.

In effect, the lease agreement combines two contracts. It is a conveyance of an interest in the real estate and a contract to pay rent and assume other obligations. The lessor grants the lessee the right to occupy the real estate and use it for purposes stated in the lease. In return, the landlord receives payment for use of the premises and retains a **reversionary right** to possession after the lease term expires. The lessor's interest is called a *leased fee estate plus reversionary right.*

In Illinois . . .

The statute of frauds in Illinois (and most other states) requires that lease agreements be in writing to be enforceable if they are for *more than one year* or are leases for one year or less that *cannot be performed within one year* of the date on which they are made. Verbal leases for one year or less that can be performed within a year of their making are enforceable. Written leases always should be signed by both lessor and lessee. ■

LEASEHOLD ESTATES

A tenant's right to possess real estate for the term of the lease is called a **leasehold** (less-than-freehold) **estate.** A leasehold is generally considered personal property. Just as there are several types of freehold (ownership) estates, there are different kinds of leasehold estates. (See Figure 17.1.)

Estate for Years

An **estate** (tenancy) **for years** is a leasehold estate that continues for a *definite period of time.* That period may be years, months, weeks or even days. An estate for years (sometimes referred to as an *estate for term*) always has specific starting and ending dates. When the estate expires, the lessee is required to vacate the premises and surrender possession to the lessor. No notice is required to terminate the estate for years. This is because the lease agreement states a specific expiration date. When the date comes, the lease expires, and the tenant's rights are extinguished.

> **Tenancy for years =**
> *Any definite period*

If both parties agree, the lease for years may be terminated before the expiration date. Otherwise, neither party may terminate without showing that the lease agreement has been breached. Any extension of the tenancy requires that a new contract be negotiated.

As is characteristic of all leases, a tenancy for years gives the lessee the right to occupy and use the leased property according to the terms and covenants contained in the lease agreement. It must be remembered that a lessee has the right to use the premises for the entire lease term. That right is unaffected by the original lessor's death or sale of the property unless the lease states otherwise. If the original lease provides for an option to renew, no further negotiation is required; the tenant merely exercises his or her option.

Estate from Period to Period

An **estate from period to period,** *or periodic tenancy,* is created when the landlord and tenant enter into an agreement for an indefinite time. That is, the lease does not contain a specific expiration date. Such a tenancy is created for a specific payment period—for instance, month to month, week to week or year to year—but continues indefinitely until proper notice of termination is given. Rent is payable at definite intervals. A periodic tenancy is characterized by continuity because it is <u>automatically renewable under the original terms</u> of the agreement until one of the parties gives notice to terminate. In effect, the payment and acceptance of rent extend the lease for another period. A **month-to-month tenancy,** for example, is created when a tenant takes possession with no definite termination date and pays monthly rent. Periodic tenancy is commonly used in residential leases.

> **Periodic Tenancy =**
> *Indefinite term;*
> *automatically renewing*

If the original agreement provides for the conversion from an estate for years to a periodic tenancy, no negotiations are necessary; the tenant simply exercises his or her option.

An estate from period to period also might be created when a tenant with an estate for years remains in possession, or holds over, after the lease term expires. If no new lease agreement has been made, a **holdover tenancy** is created. The landlord may evict the tenant or treat the holdover tenant as one who holds a periodic tenancy. The landlord's acceptance of rent usually is considered conclusive proof of acceptance of the periodic tenancy. The courts customarily rule that a tenant who holds over can do so for a term equal to the term of the original lease, provided the period is for one year or less. For example, a tenant with a lease for six months would be entitled to a new six-

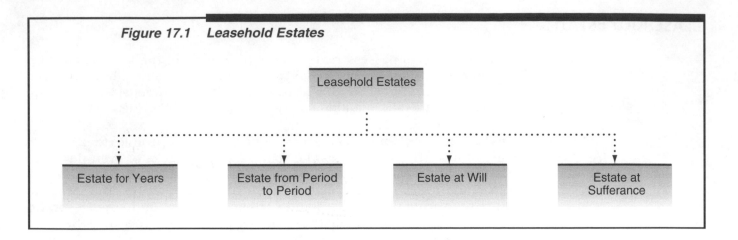

Figure 17.1   **Leasehold Estates**

month tenancy. However, if the original lease were for five years, the holdover tenancy could not exceed one year. Some leases stipulate that in the absence of a renewal agreement, a tenant who holds over does so as a month-to-month tenant. In some states, a holdover tenancy is considered a tenancy at will (discussed below).

In Illinois . . .

In Illinois, a holdover tenancy is for the same term as the estate from period to period. ■

To terminate a periodic estate, either the landlord or the tenant must give proper notice. The form and timing of the notice are usually established by state statute. Normally, the notice must be given *one period in advance.* That is, to terminate an estate from week to week, one week's notice is required; to terminate an estate from month to month, one month's notice is required. For an estate from year to year, however, the requirements vary from two to six months' notice.

In Illinois . . .

The following notices are required by Illinois statute:

- *Tenancy from year to year*—The landlord must give the tenant at least *60 days' written notice at any time within the four-month period prior to the last 60 days of the lease period.*
- *Tenancy from month to month*—In any periodic estate having a term of less than year to year but greater than week to week, the landlord must give the tenant *30 days' written notice.*
- *Tenancy from week to week*—The landlord must give the tenant *seven days' written notice.*
- *Farm tenancies from year to year*—The landlord must give the tenant farmer at least *four months' written notice* to terminate and may terminate *only at the end of the period.* ■

> **Tenancy at will =**
> *Indefinite term; possession with landlord's consent*

Estate at Will   An **estate** (tenancy) **at will** gives the tenant the right to possess property *with the landlord's consent* for an unspecified or uncertain term. An estate at will is a tenancy of indefinite duration. It continues until it is terminated by either party's giving proper notice. No definite initial period is specified, as is the case in a periodic tenancy. An estate at will is automatically terminated by the death of either the landlord or the tenant. It may be created by express agreement or by operation of law During the existence of a tenancy at will, the tenant has all the rights and obligations of a lessor-lessee relationship, including the duty to pay rent at regular intervals.

As a practical matter, tenancy at will is rarely used in a written agreement and is viewed skeptically by the courts. It is usually interpreted as a periodic tenancy, with the period being defined by the interval of rental payments.

Estate at Sufferance

Tenancy at Sufferance
Tenant's previously lawful possession continued without landlord's consent.

An **estate** (tenancy) **at sufferance** arises when a tenant who lawfully possessed real property continues in possession of the premises *without the landlord's consent* after the rights expire. This estate can arise when a tenant for years fails to surrender possession at the lease's expiration. A tenancy at sufferance also can occur by operation of law when a borrower continues in possession after a foreclosure sale and beyond the redemption period's expiration.

In Illinois . . .

A landlord has the option of considering a holdover tenant's action as being a *willful withholding of possession,* in which case the landlord is entitled to charge double rent. ■

LEASE AGREEMENTS

Most states require no special wording to establish the landlord-tenant relationship. The lease may be written, oral or implied, depending on the circumstances and the requirements of the statute of frauds. The law of the state where the real estate is located must be followed to ensure the validity of the lease. Figure 17.2 is an example of a typical residential lease.

Requirements of a Valid Lease

The elements of a valid lease can be remembered by the acronym **CLOAC**: *Capacity, Legal objective, Offer and Acceptance, and Consideration.*

A lease is a form of contract. To be valid, a lease must meet essentially the same requirements as any other contract:

- *Capacity to contract*—The parties must have the legal capacity to contract.
- *Legal objectives*—The objectives of the lease must be legal.
- *Offer and acceptance*—The parties must reach a mutual agreement on all the terms of the contract.
- *Consideration*—The lease must be supported by valid consideration. Rent is the normal consideration given for the right to occupy the leased premises. However, the payment of rent is not essential as long as consideration was granted in creating the lease itself. Sometimes, for instance, this consideration is labor performed on the property. Because a lease is a contract, it is not subject to subsequent changes in the rent or other terms unless these changes are in writing and executed in the same manner as the original lease.

The leased premises should be clearly described. The legal description of the real estate should be used if the lease covers land, such as a ground lease. If the lease is for a part of a building, such as an apartment, the space itself or the apartment designation should be described specifically. If supplemental space is to be included, the lease should clearly identify it.

Figure 17.2   Sample Residential Lease

RESIDENTIAL LEASE

DATE OF LEASE	LEASE TERM		RENT PER MONTH	SECURITY DEPOSIT
	BEGINNING DATE	ENDING DATE		

THIS RESIDENTIAL LEASE AGREEMENT ("Lease") is made between the following parties:

NAME:_____   NAME:_____

ADDRESS OF   *BUSINESS*
PREMISES: *ADDRESS:*

       "LESSEE"   **"LESSOR"**

SECTION ONE. RENT

1. Lessee will pay Lessor (or Lessor's authorized agent) the amount of _____Dollars ($_____) per month, in advance, as monthly rental for the Premises for the term of this Lease. Total rental for the initial term of this Lease shall be _____ Dollars. Lessee's first monthly rental payment is due on or before _____, 19__, and each subsequent payment will be due on the _____ day of each month following for the term of this Lease. Payments will be made at the Lessor's address as stated in this Lease, or at any other address Lessor may specify in writing to Lessee.

2. Installments of rent that are not received by Lessor as required by this Lease are considered late. Late payment of rent constitutes default under the terms of this lease. If full payment is not received by the Lessor within _____ days of the date of default, Lessee agrees to pay to Lessor an administrative fee of _____Dollars ($_____). Lessee will pay Lessor a charge of _____ Dollars ($_____) for any check returned to Lessor for insufficient funds. Lessor may require that any rent payment be made in the form of a certified check, money order or cashier's check.

3. Failure by Lessee to make any payment of rent, or any other fee or charge, under this Lease constitutes a default. In the event that Lessee fails to make any payment within _____ days after receiving written notice of Lessor's intention to terminate this Lease, Lessor may terminate this Lease and any and all unpaid rent for the full remaining term of this Lease shall then become due and payable. In the event of termination, Lessor shall be entitled to:
    A. Immediate possession of the Premises.
    B. Immediate payment of any unpaid rent or other charges.
    C. Recovery of any damages incurred due to Lessee's default, including but not limited
       to the cost of reletting the Premises, lost rental under this Lease and the cost of collections.
    D. Court costs and reasonable attorney's fees as permitted by law, arising due to Lessee's default.
    E. Any other remedy as provided by the law of the State of _____.

4. Lessor's rights and duties under the terms of this Lease are cumulative, and the exercise of any one or more of them does not prohibit Lessor from the exercise or use of any other right or remedy provided by this Lease or by law.

SECTION TWO. SECURITY DEPOSIT

1. Lessee has paid Lessor a Security Deposit in the amount of _____ Dollars ($_____) as set forth above, to secure his or her performance of all the covenants, agreements and terms of this Lease. The Security Deposit is subject to the following conditions:

    A. Lessor may use, apply or retain any or all of the amount of the Security Deposit for the payment of any rent due from Lessee; for any administrative, maintenance or other charges set forth in this Lease; any damages or expenses incurred by Lessor arising from Lessee's failure to comply with any of the terms of this Lease (including but not limited to expenses incurred in reletting the Premises).

    B. If, during the term (or any extension of the term) of this Lease, Lessor is obligated to use all or any part of the Security Deposit in accordance with the terms and conditions of this Lease or any other law or agreement, Lessor shall notify Lessor of the expenditure, in writing, within _____ days of its being incurred, and provide along with such notice an itemized list of the charges and expenses, including the reasonable cost of Lessor's own time and labor. Lessee shall have _____ days in which to deposit with Lessor a sum equal to the amount used, to ensure that the full amount of the Security Deposit is maintained with the Lessor at all times during the term of this Lease.

    C. The use of all or any part of the Security Deposit by Lessor shall not be Lessor's sole remedy in the event of Lessee's default. If the costs of Lessor's expenses and/or damages incurred exceed the total amount of the Security Deposit, Lessee shall pay any excess. LESSEE MAY NOT APPLY THE SECURITY DEPOSIT AS RENT.

    E. During the term of this Lease, and during any extensions of this Lease agreement, the Security Deposit shall be held in a/an:☐ interest-bearing ☐ non-interest-bearing [*check one*] account. *Parties initial here:* _____ _____

    F. When Lessee has performed all obligations required under this Lease, has paid all rent and any other charges, and has surrendered the Premises, its keys, passes and any other documents or fixtures in the same condition as they were provided at the beginning of the term of this Lease, reasonable wear and tear excepted, Lessor shall return to Lessee any remaining amount of the Security Deposit, together with a fully itemized list of all charges deducted from it, with documentation, within _____ days of the termination of this Lease and the surrender of the Premises.

    G. In the event Lessor's interest in the Premises are sold, transferred or assigned, Lessor shall notify Lessee of the change in ownership and the name and business address of the new lessor. Lessor shall transfer the Security Deposit to the new lessor or owner and be released from all liability to Lessee.

Figure 17.2   Sample Residential Lease (Continued)

SECTION THREE. TERM OF LEASE AND EXTENSIONS

The term of this Lease shall be _____ year(s). This Lease will be automatically extended on a month to month basis, on the same terms and conditions as agreed to in this Lease, unless either party gives the other _____ days written notice of his or her intent not to extend the Lease at the end of the term. In the event that this Lease is extended, _____ days prior notice shall be required to terminate it. Such notice must be received by the non-terminating party no later than the _____ day of the month, and Lessee's tenancy shall terminate on the last day of that month.

SECTION FOUR. CONDITION OF PREMISES

Lessee has examined the condition of the Premises, and acknowledges that the Premises are received in good condition and repair except as otherwise specified in this Lease. Lessee is responsible for all day-to-day maintenance of the Premises as defined in the Rules and Regulations, including maintaining all devices and appliances in working order.

SECTION FIVE. USE OF PREMISES

1. The Premises are leased to Lessee exclusively, and shall be used strictly as a residence and for no other purpose. The Premises shall be occupied only by Lessee and any children born to, adopted by or placed under Lessee's legal care and/or guardianship. A violation of any condition of this lease by any guest of Lessee shall be construed as a violation by Lessee.

2. The Premises may not be assigned or sublet by Lessee without the prior written consent of Lessor. Lessee shall not undertake any modification or structural change to the Premises without the written consent of Lessor.

3. Lessee shall not use or allow the Premises to be used for any unlawful or disorderly purpose. The Premises may not be used in any way that represents a material detriment to the health or safety of others. Lessee shall comply with all applicable laws and any Rules and Regulations established by Lessor. Lessee shall be provided with a printed copy of the applicable Rules and Regulations at the time this Lease is signed. Lessor has the right to immediately terminate this lease based on any such violation.

SECTION SIX. ACCESS

Lessee shall permit Lessor, or Lessor's duly authorized agent or representatives, unrestricted access to the Premises at all reasonable times for any necessary purpose, including but not limited to inspection, maintenance and exhibition.

SECTION SEVEN. PETS

No pets of any kind may be kept in or around the Premises for any purpose. This provision does not apply to companion animals trained and certified to assist a person with a disability.

SECTION EIGHT. UTILITIES AND MAINTENANCE

1. Lessor will ensure that hot and cold running water are supplied to the Premises for Lessee's use at all times. Lessor will provide reasonable heating of the Premises at all times between the months of _____ and _____, as required by law. Lessor shall provide reasonable air conditioning to the Premises between the months of _____ and _____, or as provided by law. Lessor shall not be responsible to Lessee for any failure to provide water, heat or air conditioning due to causes beyond Lessor's control or for periods when any necessary systems are under repair.

2. Lessor covenants to maintain the Premises and all grounds and public areas appurtenant to the Premises, in good repair and tenantable condition. Lessor certifies that the Premises contains all smoke detectors and other devices required by law, and that all such detectors or other devices are in good working order. Lessee is responsible for maintaining such systems.

4. Should the Premises be damaged by fire or other casualty, Lessor may either (A) repair the damage within a reasonable time, not to exceed _____ days from the date Lessor is notified in writing of such damage, or (B) terminate this Lease by providing Lessee with written notice. Should such fire or other casualty impair Lessee's occupancy, Lessee may vacate the premises and provide Lessor with written notice, within _____ days of so vacating, of the intent to terminate this Lease. Such termination will be without penalty to Lessee. If such damage is caused by Lessee's own fault or negligence, or that of Lessee's agents, guests, visitors, servants or licensees, Lessee shall continue to be liable for all rent and charges during the remaining unexpired term of this Lease unless specifically released by Lessor.

SECTION NINE. SUBORDINATION, SEVERABILITY AND LAW

1. This Lease is subordinate to all mortgages, deeds of trust or other instruments now or later affecting the Premises.

2. If any provision of this Lease is or should become prohibited under any law, that provision shall be made ineffective, without invalidating any remaining provisions. The governing law of the jurisdiction in which the Premises are located is incorporated into and supersedes this Lease by reference, and the parties agree to be bound by such law.

SECTION TEN. MISCELLANEOUS

The words "Lessor" and "Lessee," as used in this Lease, are construed as including more than one lessor. All terms and conditions of this Lease are binding on and may be enforced by the parties, their heirs, assigns, executors, administrators and successors. This Lease represents the entire agreement between Lessor and Lessee. Neither party is bound by any representations made by any party that are not included in this Lease, except that the Rules and Regulations of the Premises and Lessee's Application are included by reference.

ADDITIONAL COVENANTS, TERMS, CONDITIONS AND AGREEMENTS: [*if none, write "NONE"*]

LESSEE:_____ (SEAL)   LESSOR:_____ (SEAL)

Date: _____   Date: _____

In Practice

Preprinted lease agreements are usually better suited to residential leases. Commercial leases are generally more complex, have different legal requirements and may include complicated calculations of rent and maintenance costs. Drafting a commercial lease—or a complex residential lease, for that matter—may constitute practicing law.

Possession of Premises

The lessor, as the owner of the real estate, is usually bound by the implied covenant of quiet enjoyment. Quiet enjoyment does not have anything to do with barking dogs or late-night motorcycles. The covenant of quiet enjoyment is a presumed promise by the lessor that the lessee may take possession of the premises. The landlord further guarantees that he or she will not interfere in the tenant's possession or use of the property.

The lease may allow the landlord to enter the property to perform maintenance, to make repairs or for other stated purposes. The tenant's permission is usually required.

If the premises are occupied by a holdover tenant or an adverse claimant at the beginning of the new lease period, most states require that the landlord take whatever measures are necessary to recover actual possession. In a few states, however, the landlord is bound to give the tenant only the right of possession; it is the tenant who must bring a court action to secure actual possession.

Use of Premises

A lessor may restrict a lessee's use of the premises through provisions included in the lease.

Use restrictions are particularly common in leases for stores or commercial space. For example, a lease may provide that the leased premises are to be used "only as a real estate office and for no other purpose." In the absence of such clear limitations, a lessee may use the premises for any lawful purpose.

Term of Lease

The term of a lease is the period for which the lease will run. It should be stated precisely, including the beginning and ending dates, together with a statement of the total period of the lease. For instance, a lease might run "for a term of 30 years beginning June 1, 1996, and ending May 31, 2026." A perpetual lease for an inordinate amount of time or an indefinite term usually will be ruled invalid. However, if the language of the lease and the surrounding circumstances clearly indicate that the parties intended such a term, the lease will be binding on the parties. Some states prohibit leases that run for 100 years or more.

Security Deposit

Most leases require that the tenant provide some form of **security deposit** to be held by the landlord during the lease term. If the tenant defaults on payment of rent or destroys the premises, the lessor may keep all or part of the deposit to compensate for the loss. Some state laws set maximum amounts for security deposits and specify how they must be handled. Some prohibit security deposits from being used for both nonpayment of rent and property damage. Some require that lessees receive annual interest on their security deposits.

Other safeguards against nonpayment of rent may include an advance rental payment, contracting for a lien on the tenant's property or requiring that the tenant have a third person guarantee payment.

In Illinois . . . Landlords who receive security deposits on residential leases of units in properties containing *five or more units* may not withhold any part of a security deposit as compensation for property damage unless they give the tenant an itemized statement listing the alleged damage. This statement must be delivered within 30 days of the date on which the premises are vacated, and copies of repair receipts must be furnished 30 days after the statement is delivered. If the statement or receipts are not furnished, the landlord must return the entire security deposit within 45 days of the premises being vacated. Any landlord who is found by a court to have failed to comply with these requirements, or who has done so in bad faith, must pay the tenant double the security deposit due plus court costs and attorney's fees.

Illinois lessees are entitled to receive annual interest on their security deposits. Landlords who receive security deposits on residential leases of units in properties of 25 or more units, on deposits held for more than six months, are required to pay interest from the date of the deposit at a rate equal to the interest paid on a minimum deposit passbook savings account of the state's largest commercial bank (measured by total assets) with its main banking facilities located in Illinois. Any landlord who is found by a court to have willfully withheld interest on a tenant's security deposit must pay the tenant an amount equal to the security deposit plus the tenant's court costs and attorney's fees. Professional property managers must put security deposits in special escrow accounts. ∎

In Practice

A lease should specify whether a payment is a security deposit or an advance rental. If it is a security deposit, the tenant is usually not entitled to apply it to the final month's rent. If it is an advance rental, the landlord must treat it as income for tax purposes.

Improvements

Neither the landlord nor the tenant is required to make any improvements to the leased property. The tenant may, however, make improvements with the landlord's permission. Any alterations generally become the landlord's property; that is, they become fixtures. However, the lease may give the tenant the right to install trade fixtures. Trade fixtures may be removed before the lease expires, provided the tenant restores the premises to their previous condition, with allowance for the wear and tear of normal use.

Accessibility. The federal Fair Housing Act makes it illegal to discriminate against prospective tenants on the basis of physical disability. Tenants with disabilities must be permitted to make reasonable modifications to a property at their own expense. However, if the modifications would interfere with a future tenant's use, the landlord may require that the premises be restored to their original condition at the end of the lease term.

In Practice

The Americans with Disabilities Act (ADA) applies to commercial, nonresidential property in which public goods or services are provided. The ADA requires that such properties either be free of architectural barriers or provide reasonable accommodations for people with disabilities.

Maintenance of Premises

Many states require that a residential lessor maintain dwelling units in a habitable condition. Landlords must make any necessary repairs to common areas such as hallways, stairs and elevators, and they must maintain safety features such as fire sprinklers and smoke alarms. The tenant does not have to make any repairs but must return the premises in the same condition they were received, with allowances for ordinary wear and tear.

In Illinois . . .

The Illinois Supreme Court first confirmed the concept of an implied warranty of habitability in residential tenancies in 1972. Since then, Illinois courts have repeatedly confirmed and amplified the warranty. A landlord must deliver and maintain any residential leasehold free from defects that would render the use of the dwelling "unsafe or unsanitary" and unfit for human occupancy. Nothing may be present on the premises that could seriously endanger the life, health or safety of the tenant.

There are no precisely defined standards; each alleged breach is considered on a case-by-case basis. Not every little defect constitutes a breach of the implied warranty of habitability. A tenant must give the landlord notice of the defect and reasonable time in which to cure it. As a remedy, the tenant may choose to

- move out,
- stay and repair the problem himself or herself or
- terminate the tenancy and claim *constructive eviction* (discussed later in this chapter).

The tenant may sue for any damages resulting from the defective condition. Damages are measured by the decreased rental value of the premises due to the defect or by the reasonable cost incurred to repair the deficiency. The tenant also may use the breach as a defense to a *suit for possession* brought by the landlord. ■

Destruction of Premises

In leases involving agricultural land, the courts have held that when improvements are damaged or destroyed, the tenant is obligated to pay rent to the end of the term. The tenant's liability does not depend on whether the damage was his or her fault. This ruling has been extended in most states to include ground leases for land on which the tenant has constructed a building. In many instances, it also includes leases that give possession of an entire building to the tenant. In this case, the tenant leases the land on which that building is located, as well as the structure itself. Insurance is available to cover such contingencies.

A tenant who leases only part of a building, such as office or commercial space or a residential apartment, however, is not required to continue to pay rent after the leased premises are destroyed. In some states, if the property was destroyed as a result of the landlord's negligence, the tenant can even recover damages.

Assignment and Subleasing

When a tenant transfers all of his or her leasehold interests to another person, the lease has been *assigned*. On the other hand, when a tenant transfers less than all the leasehold interests by leasing them to a new tenant, he or she has **subleased** (or sublet) the property. **Assignment** and subleasing are permitted whenever a lease does not prohibit them.

In most cases, the sublease or assignment of a lease does not relieve the original lessee of the obligation to pay rent. The landlord may, however, agree to waive the former tenant's liability. Most leases prohibit a lessee from assigning or subletting without the lessor's consent. This permits the lessor to retain control over the occupancy of the leased premises. As a rule, the lessor must not unreasonably withhold consent. The sublessor's (original lessee's) interest in the real estate is known as a *sandwich lease.* (See Figure 17.3.)

Recording a Lease

Possession of leased premises is considered constructive notice to the world of the lessee's leasehold interests. Anyone who inspects the property receives actual notice. For these reasons, it is usually considered unnecessary to record a lease. However, most states do allow a lease to be recorded in the county in which the property is located. Furthermore, leases of three years or longer often are recorded as a matter of course. Some states require that long-term leases be recorded, especially when the lessees intend to mortgage the leasehold interests.

In some states, only a memorandum of lease is filed. A *memorandum of lease* gives notice of the interest but does not disclose the terms of the lease. Only the names of the parties and a description of the property are included.

In Illinois . . .

Creditors of the property owner and purchasers who do not have actual notice of a leasehold interest are considered to have legal notice of a lease if the lease, or a memorandum of it, is recorded with the recorder or registrar of the county in which the property is located. ∎

Options

A lease may contain an *option* that grants the lessee the privilege of renewing the lease. The lessee must, however, give notice of his or her intention to exercise the option. Some leases grant the lessees the option to purchase the leased premises. This option normally allows the tenant the right to purchase the property at a predetermined price within a certain time period, possibly the lease term. Although it is not required, the owner may give the tenant credit toward the purchase price for some percentage of the rent paid. The lease agreement is a primary contract over the option to purchase.

In Practice

All of these general statements concerning provisions of a lease are controlled largely by the terms of the agreement and state law. Great care must be exercised in reading the entire lease document before signing it because every clause in the lease has an economic and a legal impact on either the landlord or the tenant. While preprinted lease forms are available, there is no such thing as a standard lease. When complicated lease situations arise, legal counsel should be sought.

TYPES OF LEASES

The manner in which rent is determined indicates the type of lease that exists. (See Figure 17.4.)   STRAIGHT lease

Gross Lease

In a **gross lease,** the tenant pays a *fixed rent,* and the landlord pays all taxes, insurance, repairs, utilities and the like connected with the property (usually called *property charges* or *operating expenses*). This is typically the type of rent structure involved in residential leasing.

APT OR ~~Houses~~ offices

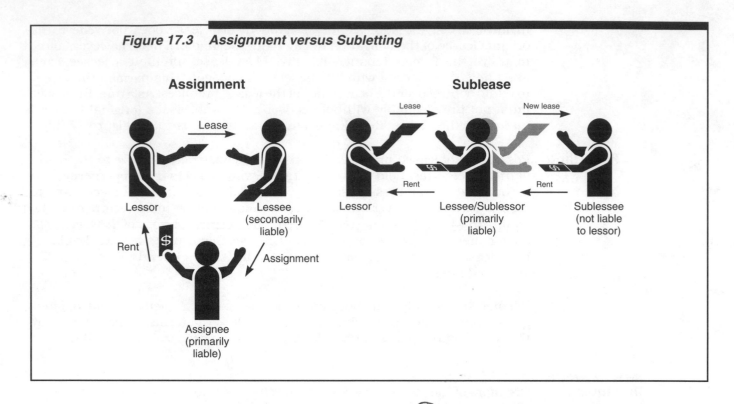

Figure 17.3 **Assignment versus Subletting**

Net Lease

In a **net lease,** the tenant pays all or *some of the property charges* in addition to the rent. The monthly rent is net income for the landlord after operating costs have been paid. Leases for entire commercial or industrial buildings and the land on which they are located, ground leases and long-term leases are usually net leases.

In a **triple-net lease,** or *net-net-net lease,* the tenant pays *all operating and other expenses* in addition to a periodic rent. These expenses include taxes, insurance, assessments, maintenance, utilities and other charges related to the premises.

Percentage Lease

Either a gross lease or a net lease may be a **percentage lease.** The rent is based on a minimum fixed rental fee plus a *percentage of the gross income received by the tenant doing business on the leased property.* This type of lease is usually used for retail businesses and restaurants. The percentage charged is negotiable and varies depending on the nature of the business, the location of the property and general economic conditions.

MATH CONCEPTS

Calculating Percentage Lease Rents

Percentage leases usually call for a minimum monthly rent plus a percentage of gross sales income exceeding a stated annual amount. For example, a lease might require minimum rent of $1,300 per month plus 5 percent of the business's sales exceeding $160,000. On an annual sales volume of $250,000, the annual rent would be calculated as follows:

$1,300 per month	× 12 months	=	$15,600
$250,000	− $160,000	=	$90,000
$90,000	× .05 (5%)	=	$4,500
$15,600 base rent	+ $4,500 percentage rent	=	$20,100 total rent

Other Types of Leases

Variable lease. Several types of leases allow for increases in the rental charges during the lease periods. One of the more common is the *graduated lease.* A graduated lease provides for specified rent increases at set future dates. Another is the *index lease,* which allows rent to be increased or decreased periodically, based on changes in the consumer price index or some other indicator.

Ground lease. When a landowner leases unimproved land to a tenant who agrees to erect a building on the land, the lease is usually referred to as a **ground lease.** Ground leases usually involve *separate ownership of the land and buildings.* These leases must be for a long enough term to make the transaction desirable to the tenant investing in the building. They often run for terms of 50 up to 99 years. Ground leases are generally net leases: the lessee must pay rent on the ground, as well as real estate taxes, insurance, upkeep and repairs.

Oil and gas lease. When an oil company leases land to explore for oil and gas, a special lease agreement must be negotiated. Usually, the landowner receives a cash payment for executing the lease. If no well is drilled within the period stated in the lease, the lease expires. However, most oil and gas leases permit the oil company to continue its rights for another year by paying another flat rental fee. Such rentals may be paid annually until a well is produced. If oil or gas is found, the landowner usually receives a percentage of its value as a royalty. As long as oil or gas is obtained in significant quantities, the lease continues indefinitely.

A **lease purchase** is used when a tenant wants to purchase the property, but is unable to do so. Perhaps the tenant cannot obtain favorable financing or clear title, or the tax consequences of a current purchase would be unfavorable. In this arrangement, the purchase agreement is the primary consideration, and the lease is secondary. Part of the periodic rent is applied toward the purchase price of the property until that price is reduced to an amount for which the tenant can obtain financing or purchase the property outright, depending on the terms of the lease purchase agreement.

Agricultural landowners often lease their land to tenant farmers, who provide the labor to produce and bring in the crop. An owner can be paid by a tenant in one of two ways: as an agreed-on rental amount in cash in advance (**cash rents**) or as a percentage of the profits from the sale of the crop when it is sold (**sharecropping**).

DISCHARGE OF LEASES

As with any contract, a lease is discharged when the contract terminates. Termination can occur when all parties have fully performed their obligations under the agreement. In addition, the parties may agree to cancel the lease. If the tenant, for instance, offers to surrender the leasehold interest and the landlord accepts the tenant's offer, the lease is terminated. A tenant who simply abandons leased property, however, remains liable for the terms of the lease—including the rent. The terms of the lease will usually indicate whether the landlord is obligated to try to rerent the space. If the landlord intends to sue for unpaid rent, however, most states require an attempt to mitigate damages by rerenting the premises to limit the amount owed.

Figure 17.4	Types of Leases		
Type of Lease		**Lessee**	**Lessor**
Gross lease		Pays basic rent	Pays property charges (taxes, repairs, insurance, etc.)
Net lease		Pays basic rent plus all or most property charges	May pay some property charges
Percentage lease (commercial or industrial)		Pays basic rent plus percent of gross sales (may pay property costs)	

The lease does not terminate if the parties die or if the property is sold. *There are two exceptions to this general rule:*

1. A lease from the owner of a *life estate* ends when the life tenant dies.
2. The death of either party terminates a *tenancy at will.* In all other cases, the heirs of a deceased landlord are bound by the terms of existing valid leases.

If leased real estate is sold or otherwise conveyed, the new landlord takes the property subject to the rights of the tenants. A lease agreement may, however, contain language that permits a new landlord to terminate existing leases. The clause, commonly known as a *sale clause,* requires that the tenants be given some period of notice before the termination. Because the new owner has taken title subject to the rights of the tenants, the sale clause enables the new landlord to claim possession and negotiate new leases under his or her own terms and conditions.

A tenancy may also be terminated by operation of law, as in a bankruptcy or condemnation proceeding.

Breach of Lease

When a tenant breaches any lease provision, the landlord may sue the tenant to obtain a judgment to cover past-due rent, damages to the premises or other defaults. Likewise, when a landlord breaches any lease provision, the tenant is entitled to certain remedies. The rights and responsibilities of the landlord-tenant relationship are usually governed by state law.

In Illinois . . .

If a tenant defaults on the payment of rent, the landlord has two options:

1. He or she may elect to serve the tenant with five days' written notice, demanding payment of the delinquent rent within five days after the notice is received. If the tenant fails to pay the rent, the landlord may terminate the lease automatically and sue for possession without further notice. *If the tenant pays the past-due rent, the lease continues in full force.*
2. Alternatively (and in cases in which the tenant's breach is other than nonpayment of rent), the landlord may terminate the tenancy by serving the tenant with ten days' written notice, including a demand for possession. After the ten-day period expires, the landlord may sue

for possession without further notice, *even if the default is cured.* (However, if the default is only nonpayment of rent and the landlord accepts any payment, he or she has waived the right to proceed with a lawsuit.) ■

Suit for possession—actual eviction.

When a tenant breaches a lease or improperly retains leased premises, the landlord may regain possession through a legal process known as **actual eviction.** The landlord must serve notice on the tenant before commencing the lawsuit. Most lease terms require at least a ten-day notice in the case of default. In many states, however, only a five-day notice is necessary when the tenant defaults in the payment of rent. When a court issues a judgment for possession to a landlord, the tenant must vacate the property. If the tenant fails to leave, the landlord can have the judgment enforced by a court officer, who forcibly removes the tenant and the tenant's possessions. The landlord then has the right to reenter and regain possession of the property.

In Illinois . . .

In Illinois, a landlord seeking actual eviction of a tenant must file an action called a *forcible entry and detainer.* It can be used when a tenancy has expired by default, by its terms, by operation of law or by proper notice. The suit should be filed in the circuit court of the county in which the property is located.

If the court rules in favor of the landlord, a *judgment for possession* (and money damages) will be entered, and an *order of possession* will be issued by the clerk of the court. The tenant must then leave peaceably, removing all his or her property from the premises. Traditionally, however, if a residential tenant personally appears in court and the landlord prevails, the court will delay issuing the order for a reasonable period of time, to allow the tenant to find alternative housing.

When a tenant refuses to vacate peaceably after a judgment for possession has been entered, the landlord must deliver the order to the sheriff, who will forcibly evict the tenant. The landlord then has the right to reenter and regain possession of the property.

Until a judgment for possession is issued, the landlord must be careful not to harass the tenant in any manner, such as locking the tenant out of the property, impounding the tenant's possessions or disconnecting the unit's utilities (such as electricity and natural gas). Illinois landlords have no right to *self-help;* that is, they may not forcibly remove a tenant without following the proper legal procedures. ■

Tenants' remedies—constructive eviction.

If a landlord breaches any clause of a lease agreement, the tenant has the right to sue and recover damages against the landlord. If the leased premises become unusable for the purpose stated in the lease, the tenant may have the right to abandon them. This action, called **constructive eviction,** terminates the lease agreement. The tenant must prove that the premises have become unusable because of the conscious neglect of the landlord. To claim constructive eviction, the tenant must leave the premises while the conditions that made the premises uninhabitable exist.

CIVIL RIGHTS LAWS

The fair housing laws affect landlords and tenants just as they do sellers and purchasers. All persons must have access to housing of their choice without any differentiation in the terms and conditions because of their race, color, religion, national origin, sex, handicap or familial status. State and local municipalities may have their own fair housing laws that add protected classes such as age and sexual orientation. Withholding an apartment that is available for rent, segregating certain persons in separate sections of an apartment complex or parts of a building and charging different amounts for rent or security deposits to persons in the protected classes all constitute violations of the law.

It is important that landlords realize that changes in the laws stemming from the federal Fair Housing Amendments Act of 1988 significantly alter past practices, particularly as they affect individuals with disabilities (discussed previously) and families with children. The fair housing laws require that the same tenant criteria be applied to families with children that are applied to adults. A landlord cannot charge a different amount of rent or security deposit because one of the tenants is a child. While landlords have historically argued that children are noisy and destructive, the fact is that many adults are noisy and destructive as well.

In Illinois . . .

The *Illinois Lead Poisoning Prevention Act* requires that the owner of any residential building cited by the state as a lead paint hazard give prospective tenants written notice of the danger unless the owners have a certificate of compliance. When the state issues a *mitigation order* to an owner of a building containing lead hazards, the owner has 90 days in which to eliminate the hazard in a manner prescribed by state law. Owners of residential rentals built before 1978 also must give tenants a brochure prepared by the Department of Public Health concerning lead paint. ■

REGULATION OF THE RENTAL INDUSTRY

Rental-Finding Services

Because of the nationwide demand for rental housing, caused in part by the increased mobility of the U.S. population, there has been a rapid growth in the rental-finding service industry.

In Illinois . . .

A **rental-finding service** is any business that finds, attempts to find or offers to find for any person for consideration a unit of rental real estate or a lessee for a unit of rental real estate not owned or leased by the business (Rules, Section 1450.170). Any person or business entity that operates a rental-finding service must obtain a real estate license and comply with all provisions of the Illinois Real Estate License Act. General-circulation newspapers that advertise rental property and listing contracts between owners or lessors of real estate and registrants are exempt from this requirement.

Rental-finding services are required to enter into written contracts with the parties for whom their services are to be performed. The contract must clearly disclose

- the term of the contract;
- the total amount to be paid for the services;

- the service's policy regarding the refunding of fees paid in advance, and the conditions under which refunds may or may not be paid (printed in a larger typeface than the rest of the contract);
- the type of rental unit, geographic area and price range the prospective tenant desires;
- a detailed statement of the services to be performed;
- a statement that the contract shall be void, and all fees paid in advance shall be refunded, if the information provided regarding possible rental units available is not current or accurate (that is, if a rental unit is listed that has not been available for more than two days); and
- a disclosure that information regarding possible rental units may be up to two days old.

With regard to any individual rental unit, a prospective tenant must be provided with the name, address and telephone number of the owner; a description of the unit, monthly rent and security deposit required; a description of the utilities available and included in the rent; the occupancy date and lease term; a statement describing the source of the information; and any other information the prospective tenant may reasonably be expected to need.

A rental-finding service may not list or advertise any rental unit without the express written authority of the unit's owner or agent.

A licensee who violates any of these requirements will be construed to have demonstrated unworthiness or incompetence and be subject to the appropriate disciplinary measures. ■

Leasing Agents

In Illinois . . .  The Illinois Real Estate License Act (Sections 6.1–6.4) provides for a special, limited-scope license for individuals who wish to engage *solely* in activities related to the leasing of residential real property. For instance, the following activities would appropriately fall under this limited license, if the licensee did not engage in any other real estate activities (such as marketing single-family homes):

- Leasing or renting residential real property
- Collecting rent for residential real property
- Attempting, offering, or negotiating to lease, rent or collect rent for the use of residential real property

The license act establishes specific qualifications and educational requirements for leasing agents, including a written examination. Special standards of practice and disciplinary procedures apply to licensed leasing agents.

Referral Fees

In Illinois . . . 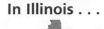 The Illinois Real Estate License Act [Section 6 (11)] allows landlords to pay a referral fee to tenants. A resident tenant of a unit who refers a prospective tenant for a unit in the same building or complex may be paid a referral fee if he or she

1. refers no more than three prospective lessees in any 12-month period;
2. receives compensation of no more than $1,000 or the equivalent of one month's rent, whichever is less, for any 12-month period; and

3. limits his or her activities to referring prospective lessees to the owner (or the owner's agent) and does not show units, discuss lease terms or otherwise participate in the negotiation of a lease. ∎

SUMMARY

A lease is an agreement that grants one person the right to use the property of another in return for consideration.

A leasehold estate that runs for a specific length of time creates an estate for years; one that runs for an indefinite period creates an estate from period to period (year to year, month to month). An estate at will runs as long as the landlord permits; and an estate at sufferance is possession without the consent of the landlord. A leasehold estate is classified as personal property.

The requirements of a valid lease include capacity to contract, legal objectives, offer and acceptance and consideration. In addition, state statutes of frauds generally require that any lease that will not be completed within one year of the date of its making must be in writing to be enforceable in court. Most leases also include clauses relating to rights and obligations of the landlord and tenant, such as the use of the premises, subletting, judgments, maintenance of the premises and termination of the lease period.

A lease may be terminated by the expiration of the lease period, the mutual agreement of the parties or a breach of the lease by either the landlord or tenant. In most cases, neither the death of the tenant nor the landlord's sale of the rental property terminates a lease.

If a tenant defaults on any lease provision, the landlord may sue for a money judgment, actual eviction or both. If the premises have become uninhabitable due to the landlord's negligence or failure to correct within a reasonable time, the tenant may have the remedy of constructive eviction—that is, the right to abandon the premises and refuse to pay rent until the premises are repaired.

The rental industry is highly regulated. The fair housing laws protect the rights of tenants. Besides prohibiting discrimination based on race, color, religion, familial status, national origin and sex, the laws address the rights of individuals with disabilities and families with children.

In Illinois . . .

The Illinois Statute of Frauds requires that leases for more than one year or that cannot be performed within one year be in writing to be enforceable. Oral leases for less than one year are enforceable.

Illinois law establishes certain notice requirements for termination of leases and for the withholding or payment of interest on security deposits. ∎

QUESTIONS

1. A ground lease is usually:
   A. short term.
   B. for 100 years or longer.
   C. long term.
   D. a gross lease.

2. Jane and Yolanda enter into a commercial lease that requires a monthly rent based on a minimum set amount plus an additional amount determined by the tenant's gross receipts exceeding $5,000. This type of lease is called a:
   A. standard lease.
   B. gross lease.
   C. percentage lease.
   D. net lease.

3. If a tenant moved out of a rented store building because access to the building was blocked as a result of the landlord's negligence:
   A. the tenant would have no legal recourse against the landlord.
   B. the landlord would be liable for the rent until the expiration date of the lease.
   C. the landlord would have to provide substitute space.
   D. the tenant would be entitled to recover damages from the landlord.

4. In June, Vince signs a one-year lease and moves into Streetview Apartments. Vince deposits the required security deposit with the landlord. Six months later, Vince pays the January rent and mysteriously moves out. Vince does not arrange for a sublease or an assignment and makes no further rent payments. The apartment is still in good condition. What is Vince's liability to the landlord in these circumstances?
   A. Because half the rental amount has been paid and the apartment is in good condition, Vince has no further liability.
   B. Vince is liable for the balance of the rent, plus forfeiture of the security deposit.
   C. Vince is liable for the balance of the rent only.
   D. Vince is liable for the balance of the rent, plus the security deposit and any marketing costs the landlord incurs.

5. Katy still has five months remaining on a one-year apartment lease. When Katy moves to another city, she transfers possession of the apartment to Lynn for the entire remaining term of the lease. Lynn pays rent directly to Katy. Under these facts, Katy is a(n):
   A. assignor.   C. sublessee.
   B. sublessor.   D. lessor.

6. A tenant's lease has expired. The tenant has neither vacated nor negotiated a renewal lease, and the landlord has declared that she does not want the tenant to remain in the building. This form of possession is called a(n):
   A. estate for years.
   B. periodic estate.
   C. estate at will.
   D. estate at sufferance.

7. Phil's tenancy for years will expire in two weeks. Phil plans to move to a larger apartment across town when the current tenancy expires. What must Phil do to terminate this agreement?
   A. Phil must give the landlord two weeks' prior notice.
   B. Phil must give the landlord one week's prior notice.
   C. Phil needs to do nothing; the agreement will terminate automatically.
   D. The agreement will terminate only after Phil signs a lease for the new apartment.

8. When a tenant holds possession of a landlord's property without a current lease agreement and without the landlord's approval:
   A. the tenant is maintaining a gross lease.
   B. the landlord can file suit for possession.
   C. the tenant has no obligation to pay rent.
   D. the landlord may be subject to a constructive eviction.

9. Under the terms of a residential lease, the lessor is required to maintain the water heater. If a lessee is unable to get hot water because of a faulty water heater that the lessor has failed to repair, all of the following remedies would be available to the lessee EXCEPT:
   A. suing the lessor for damages.
   B. suing the lessor for back rent.
   C. abandoning the premises under constructive eviction.
   D. terminating the lease agreement.

10. Jon has a one-year leasehold interest in Blackacre. The interest automatically renews itself at the end of each year. Jon's interest is referred to as a tenancy:
    A. for years.
    B. from period to period.
    C. at will.
    D. at sufferance.

11. Which of the following describes a net lease?
    A. An agreement in which the tenant pays a fixed rent and the landlord pays all taxes, insurance and other charges on the property
    B. A lease in which the tenant pays rent plus maintenance and property charges
    C. A lease in which the tenant pays the landlord a percentage of the monthly profits derived from the tenant's commercial use of the property
    D. A lease-to-purchase agreement in which the landlord agrees to apply part of the monthly rent toward the ultimate purchase price of the property

12. A tenancy in which the tenant continues in possession after the lease has expired, with the landlord's permission, is a tenancy:
    A. for years.
    B. by the entireties.
    C. at will.
    D. at sufferance.

13. A commercial lease calls for a minimum rent of $1,200 per month plus 4 percent of the annual gross business exceeding $150,000. If the total rent paid at the end of one year was $19,200, how much business did the tenant do during the year?
    A. $159,800   C. $270,000
    B. $250,200   D. $279,200

14. Which of the following would NOT be associated with leases?
    A. Tenancy at sufferance
    B. Tenancy at will
    C. Tenancy in common
    D. Periodic tenancy

15. All of the following are true regarding leases EXCEPT:
    A. an estate for years is a leasehold estate that continues for a definite period of time.
    B. a leasehold estate is also known as a freehold estate.
    C. if a tenant has entered into a periodic tenancy, the lease will automatically renew unless proper notice is given.
    D. for a lease to be valid it must be entered into by a person with the authority to perform, have a legal objective, contain consideration and be offered and accepted.

In Illinois . . .

16. In Illinois, which of the following statements is true regarding a lease for more than one year?
    A. The lease must be in writing and signed to be enforceable in court.
    B. The lease must include a provision for interest to be paid on all security deposits.
    C. The lease must be recorded to give actual notice of the resident tenant's right of possession.
    D. The lease may be terminated only by written notice to the tenant, even if it contains a definite expiration date.

17. Tami rents an apartment in a 100-unit highrise in Chicago for $900 per month. Tami decides to move when she learns that her rent will be raised by 25 percent at the expiration of her one-year lease. When she moved in, Tami deposited $1,200 as a security deposit. How will the interest paid on Tami's deposit be determined?
    A. The interest paid should be based on prime rate as of December 31 of the calendar year preceding the rental agreement.
    B. The interest paid should be 5 percent per year, from the date of deposit.
    C. The interest rate should be computed at a rate equal to that paid on a minimum deposit passbook savings account at Illinois's largest commercial bank.
    D. Under these facts, Tami is not entitled to receive interest on her security deposit.

18. How many days' advance notice is required to terminate a month-to-month tenancy in Illinois?
    A. 5   C. 30
    B. 15   D. 60

19. Ursula, who owns a 20-unit apartment building in Decatur, Illinois, has held tenant Jerry's security deposit for three months. Jerry, who is on a month-to-month lease, informs Ursula that he will be vacating the apartment in 30 days. Based on these facts, which of the following statements is true?
    A. Ursula must pay Jerry four months' interest on the security deposit.
    B. Ursula owes Jerry no interest on the security deposit.
    C. Jerry is entitled to three months' interest on the security deposit.
    D. If Jerry vacates the premises in these circumstances, Ursula is entitled to retain the security deposit as statutory damages.

20. Chuck has a one-year lease on an apartment in Chicago. If Chuck fails to pay his rent when it is due, the landlord may:
    A. serve notice on Chuck to pay the delinquent rent within five days.
    B. terminate Chuck's lease without notice when the rent is more than ten days past due.
    C. hire a moving company to remove Chuck's furniture and personal property from the premises.
    D. serve notice on Chuck to pay the rent within five days and proceed with a suit for possession regardless of whether or not Chuck pays the past-due rent.

21. In Illinois, a landlord must give a tenant at least 60 days' written notice to terminate which of the following tenancies?
    A. Tenancy at will
    B. Tenancy for years
    C. Tenancy from year to year
    D. Tenancy at sufferance

22. Efficient Efficiencies is a rental-finding service specializing in efficiency apartments in Champaign-Urbana. Before entering into a service relationship with a prospective tenant, Efficient Efficiencies must provide her or him with a written contract that discloses all of the following information, EXCEPT:

A. the total amount to be paid in advance.

B. a statement that the contract will be invalid if information about a rental unit is provided when the unit has been unavailable for more than two days.

C. a statement that information about rental units may be up to one week old.

D. a description of the type of unit and geographic area in which the prospective tenant would like to live.

Part Two

PRACTICES

CHAPTER 18

Property Management

KEY TERMS

life-cycle costing
management
  agreement
multiperil policy

property manager
risk management
surety bond

tenant improvement
workers'
  compensation act

THE PROPERTY MANAGER

> A *property manager*
>
> • maintains the owner's investment and
> • ensures that the property produces income

Property management is a real estate specialization. It involves the leasing, managing, marketing and overall maintenance of real estate owned by others, usually rental property. The **property manager** has three principal responsibilities:

1. Financial management
2. Physical management (structure and grounds)
3. Administrative management (files and records)

The property manager is responsible for maintaining the owner's investment and making sure the property earns income. This can be done in several ways. The physical property must be maintained in good condition. Suitable tenants must be found, rent must be collected and employees must be hired and supervised. The property manager is responsible for budgeting and controlling expenses, keeping proper accounts and making periodic reports to the owner. In all of these activities, the manager's primary goal is to operate and maintain the physical property in such a way as to preserve and enhance the owner's capital investment.

Some property managers work for property management companies. These firms manage properties for a number of owners under management agreements (discussed later). Other property managers are independent. The property manager has an agency relationship with the owner, which involves greater authority and discretion over management decisions than an employee would have. A property manager or an owner may employ building managers to supervise the daily operations of a building. In some cases, these individuals may be residents of the building.

In Illinois . . .

As in most states, Illinois property managers must be licensed real estate brokers because they engage in collecting rent, negotiating leases and rentals and procuring tenants, among other functions. However, the Illinois Real Estate License Act specifically exempts resident managers of apartment buildings, duplexes and apartment complexes from licensure requirements when their primary residence is on the premises being managed.

Illinois permits individuals whose real estate practice is limited to leasing or renting residential property, collecting rent, negotiating leases and similar activities to obtain a special leasing agent license instead of the broader-scope broker or salesperson license. An individual with a limited license must be affiliated with a licensed real estate broker. Licensed brokers, however, are not required to obtain an additional leasing agent license in order to engage in rental-related activities. ■

The Management Agreement

The first step in taking over the management of any property is to enter into a **management agreement** with the owner. This agreement creates an *agency relationship* between the owner and the property manager. The property manager usually is considered to be the owner's *general agent.* After entering into an agreement with a property owner, a manager handles the property the same way the owner would. In all activities, the manager's first responsibility is to realize the highest return on the property in a manner consistent with the owner's instructions.

Like any other contract involving real estate, the management agreement should be in writing. It should include the following points:

- *Description* of the property.
- *Time period* the agreement covers.
- Definition of the management's responsibilities. All the manager's duties should be specifically stated in the contract. Any limitations or restrictions on what the manager may do should be included.
- Statement of the *owner's purpose.* The owner should state clearly what he or she wants the manager to accomplish. One owner may want to maximize net income, while another will want to increase the capital value of the investment. What the manager does depends on the owner's long-term goals for the property.
- Extent of the *manager's authority.* This provision should state what authority the manager is to have in matters such as hiring, firing and supervising employees; fixing rental rates for space; and making expenditures and authorizing repairs. Repairs that exceed a certain expense limit may require the owner's written approval.
- *Reporting.* The frequency and detail of the manager's periodic reports on operations and financial position should be agreed on. These reports serve as a means for the owner to monitor the manager's work. They also form a basis for both the owner and manager to spot trends that are important in shaping management policy.
- *Management fee.* The fee may be based on a percentage of gross or net income, a fixed fee or some combination of these and other factors. Management fees are subject to the same antitrust considerations as sales commissions. That is, they cannot be standardized in the marketplace; standardization would be viewed as price-fixing. The fee must be negotiated between the agent and the principal. In addition, the property manager may be entitled to a commission on new rentals and renewed leases.

KEEP & Build Reserve

- *Allocation of costs.* The agreement should state which of the property manager's expenses—such as office rent, office help, telephone, advertising and association fees—will be paid by the manager. Other costs will be paid by the owner.

Rental Commissions

Residential property managers often earn commissions when they find tenants for a property. Rental commissions usually are based on the annual rent from a property. For example, if an apartment unit rents for $475 per month and the commission payable is 8 percent, the commission is calculated as follows:

$475 per month × 12 months = $5,700
$5,700 × .08 (8%) = $456

MANAGEMENT FUNCTIONS

A property manager's specific responsibilities are determined by the management agreement. Certain duties, however, are found in most agreements. These include budgeting, capital expenditures, setting rental rates, selecting tenants, collecting rent, maintaining the property and complying with legal requirements.

Budgeting Expenses

Before attempting to rent any property, the property manager should develop an operating budget. The budget should be based on anticipated revenues and expenses. In addition, it must reflect the owner's long-term goals. In preparing a budget, the manager should allocate money for continuous, fixed expenses such as employees' salaries, property taxes and insurance premiums.

Next, the manager should establish a cash reserve fund for variable expenses such as repairs, decorating and supplies. The amount allocated for the reserve fund can be computed from the previous yearly costs of the variable expenses.

Capital expenditures. The owner and the property manager may decide that modernization or renovation of a property will enhance its value. In this case, the manager should budget money to cover the costs of remodeling. The property manager should either be thoroughly familiar with the *principle of contribution* or seek expert advice when estimating any expected increase in value. In the case of large-scale construction, the expenses charged against the property's income should be spread over several years.

The cost of equipment to be installed in a modernization or renovation must be evaluated over its entire useful life. This is called **life-cycle costing.** This term simply means that both the initial and the operating costs of equipment over its expected life must be measured to compare the total cost of one type of equipment with that of another.

Renting the Property

Effective rental of the property is essential. However, the role of the property manager in managing a property should not be confused with that of a broker who acts as a leasing agent. The manager must be concerned with the long-term financial health of the property; the broker is concerned solely with renting space. The property manager may use the services of a leasing agent, but that agent does not undertake the full responsibility of maintaining and managing the property.

Setting rental rates. Rental rates are influenced primarily by supply and demand. The property manager should conduct a detailed survey of the competitive space available in the neighborhood, emphasizing similar properties. In establishing rental rates, the property manager has four long-term considerations:

1. The rental income must be *sufficient to cover the property's fixed charges and operating expenses.*
2. The rental income must *provide a fair return on the owner's investment.*
3. The rental rate should be *in line with prevailing rates in comparable buildings.* It may be slightly higher or slightly lower, depending on the strength of the property.
4. The *current vacancy rate in the property* is a good indicator of how much of a rent increase is advisable. A building with a low vacancy rate (that is, few vacant units) is a better candidate for an increase than one with a high vacancy rate.

A rental rate for residential space is usually stated as the monthly rate *per unit.* Commercial leases—including office, retail and industrial space rentals—are usually stated according to either annual or monthly rates *per square foot.*

If the vacancy level is high, the manager should attempt to determine why. An elevated level of vacancy does not necessarily indicate that rents are too high. Instead, the problem may be poor management or a defective or an undesirable property. The manager should attempt to identify and correct the problems first rather than immediately lower rents. On the other hand, a high occupancy rate may mean that rental rates are too low. Whenever the occupancy level of an apartment house or office building exceeds 95 percent, serious consideration should be given to raising rents. First, however, the manager should investigate the rental market to determine whether a rent increase is warranted.

Selecting Tenants   A building manager's success depends on establishing and maintaining sound, long-term relationships with his or her tenants. The first and most important step is selection. The manager should be sure that the premises are suitable for a tenant in size, location and amenities. Most important, the manager should be sure that the tenant is able to pay for the space.

A commercial tenant's business should be compatible with the building and the other tenants. The manager must consider the business interests of his or her current tenants as well as the interests of the potential tenant. The types of businesses or services should be complementary, and the introduction of competitors into the same property should be undertaken with care. This not only pleases existing tenants but helps diversify the owner's investment and makes profitability more likely. Some commercial leases bar the introduction of similar businesses.

If a commercial tenant is likely to expand in the future, the manager should consider the property's potential for expansion.

The residential property manager must be sure to comply with all federal, state and local fair housing laws in selecting tenants. Although fair housing laws do not apply to commercial properties, commercial property managers need to be aware of federal, state and local antidiscrimination and equal opportunity laws that may govern industrial or retail properties.

Calculating Monthly Rent per Square Foot

1. Determine the total square footage of the rental premises (generally floorspace only).

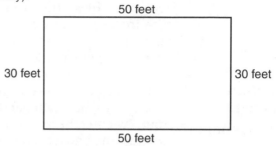

50 feet × 30 feet = 1,500 square feet

2. Find the total annual rent.

$1,850 per month × 12 months = $22,200 per year

3. Divide the total annual rent by the total square feet to determine the annual rate per square foot.

$22,200 ÷ 1,500 square feet = $14.80 per square foot per year

4. Convert the annual rate to a monthly rate.

$14.80 ÷ 12 months = $1.23 per square foot per month

Collecting rents. A property manager should accept only those tenants who can be expected to meet their financial obligations. The manager should investigate financial references, check with local credit bureaus and, when possible, interview a prospective tenant's former landlord.

The terms of rental payment should be spelled out in the lease agreement, including

- time and place of payment
- provisions and penalties for late payment and
- provisions for cancellation and damages in case of nonpayment.

The property manager should establish a firm and consistent collection plan. The plan should include a system of notices and records that complies with state and local law.

Every attempt must be made to collect rent without resorting to legal action. Legal action is costly and time-consuming and does not contribute to good tenant relations. In some cases, however, legal action is unavoidable. In these instances, a property manager must be prepared to initiate and follow through with the necessary legal steps. Obviously, legal action must be taken in cooperation with the property owner's or management firm's legal counsel.

In Illinois . . .

Specific legal procedures must be followed in taking legal action against a tenant. In addition, Illinois law has specific provisions regarding the maintenance and payment of interest on security deposits. Property managers (who must have brokers' licenses) must put security deposits in a special escrow account, in the same wasy that brokers must handle earnest money. The security deposits must be deposited in the escrow account by the next business day after a lease is signed. The deposit must be recorded in the journal and the ledger. The escrow account must be a non–interest–bearing account, unless the property is residential with 25 or more units, in which case interest must be paid to the tenants. Owners of income property do *not* have to have escrow accounts for their tenants' security deposits, even if the owner happens to have a broker's license. ■

Maintaining Good Relations with Tenants

The ultimate success of a property manager depends on the ability of the manager to maintain good relations with tenants. Dissatisfied tenants eventually vacate the property. A high tenant turnover rate results in greater expenses for advertising and redecorating. It also means less profit for the owner due to uncollected rents.

An effective property manager establishes a good communication system with tenants. Regular newsletters or posted memoranda help keep tenants informed and involved. Maintenance and service requests must be attended to promptly, and all lease terms and building rules must be enforced consistently and fairly. A good manager is tactful and decisive and acts to the benefit of both owner and occupants.

The property manager must be able to handle residents who do not pay their rents on time or who break building regulations. When one tenant fails to follow the rules, the other tenants often become frustrated and dissatisfied. Careful record keeping shows whether rent is remitted promptly and in the proper amount. Records of all lease renewal dates should be kept so that the manager can anticipate expiration and retain good tenants who otherwise might move when their leases end.

Maintaining the Property

One of the most important functions of a property manager is the supervision of property maintenance. A manager must learn to balance the services provided with their costs—that is, to satisfy tenants' needs while minimizing operating expenses.

To maintain the property efficiently, the manager must be able to assess the building's needs and how best to meet them. Staffing and scheduling requirements vary with the type, size and geographic location of the property, so the owner and manager usually agree in advance on maintenance objectives. In some cases, the best plan may be to operate a low-rental property, with minimal expenditures for services and maintenance. Another property may be more lucrative if kept in top condition and operated with all possible tenant services. A well-maintained, high-service property can command premium rental rates.

A primary maintenance objective is to protect the physical integrity of the property over the long term. For example, preserving the property by repainting the exterior or replacing the heating system helps decrease long-term maintenance costs. Keeping the property in good condition involves four types of maintenance:

1. Preventive maintenance
2. Repair or corrective maintenance
3. Routine maintenance
4. Construction

Preventive maintenance helps prevent problems and expenses.

Corrective maintenance corrects problems after they've occurred.

Routine maintenance keeps up with everyday wear and tear.

Preventive maintenance includes regularly scheduled activities such as painting and seasonal servicing of appliances and systems. Preventive maintenance preserves the long-range value and physical integrity of the building. This is both the most critical and the most neglected maintenance responsibility. Failure to perform preventive maintenance invariably leads to greater expense in other areas of maintenance.

Repair or *corrective maintenance* involves the actual repairs that keep the building's equipment, utilities and amenities functioning. Repairing a boiler, fixing a leaky faucet and mending a broken air-conditioning unit are acts of corrective maintenance.

A property manager must also supervise the *routine maintenance* of the building. Routine maintenance includes such day-to-day duties as cleaning common areas, performing minor carpentry and plumbing adjustments and providing regularly scheduled upkeep of heating, air-conditioning and landscaping. Good routine maintenance is similar to good preventive maintenance. Both head off problems before they become expensive.

In Practice

One of the major decisions a property manager faces is whether to contract for maintenance services from an outside firm or hire on-site employees to perform such tasks. This decision should be based on a number of factors, including the

- size of the building
- complexity of the tenants' requirements and
- availability of suitable labor.

Construction involves making a prorperty meet a tenant's needs.

A commercial or an industrial property manager often is called on to make **tenant improvements.** These are alterations to the interior of the building to meet a tenant's particular space needs. Such *construction* alterations range from simply repainting or recarpeting to completely gutting the interior and redesigning the space by erecting new walls, partitions and electrical systems. Tenant improvements are especially important when renting new buildings. In new construction, the interiors are usually left incomplete so that they can be adapted to the needs of individual tenants. One matter that must be clarified is which improvements will be considered *trade fixtures* (personal property belonging to the tenant) and which will belong to the owner of the real estate.

Modernization or renovation of buildings that have become functionally obsolete and thus unsuited to today's building needs is also important. The renovation of a building often enhances the building's marketability and increases its potential income.

Handling Environmental Concerns

The environment is an increasingly important property management issue. A variety of environmental issues, from waste disposal to air quality, must be addressed by the property manager. Tenant concerns, as well as federal, state and local regulations, determine the extent of the manager's environmental responsibilities. While property managers are not expected to be experts in all of the disciplines necessary to operate a modern building, they are expected to be knowledgeable in many diverse subjects, most of which are technical in nature. Environmental concerns are one such subject.

Property managers must be able to respond to a variety of environmental problems. Managers may manage structures containing asbestos or radon or be called on to arrange an environmental audit of a property. Managers must see that any hazardous wastes produced by their employers or tenants are properly disposed of. Even the normally nonhazardous waste of an office building must be controlled to avoid violation of laws requiring segregation and recycling of types of wastes. Of course, property managers may want to provide recycling facilities for tenants even if they are not required by law to do so. On-site recycling creates an image of good citizenship that enhances the reputation (and value) of a commercial or residential property.

The Americans with Disabilities Act

The *Americans with Disabilities Act (ADA)* has had a significant impact on the responsibilities of the property manager, both in building amenities and in employment issues.

Title I of the ADA provides for the employment of qualified job applicants regardless of their disability. Any employer with 15 or more employees must adopt nondiscriminatory employment procedures. In addition, employers must make reasonable accommodations to enable individuals with disabilities to perform essential job functions.

[handwritten margin note: To Remove opstad/ For Bmploymano or To Enjoy the facl for Public]

Property managers must also be familiar with Title III of the ADA, which prohibits discrimination in commercial properties. The ADA requires that managers ensure that people with disabilities have full and equal access to facilities and services. The property manager typically is responsible for determining whether a building meets the ADA's accessibility requirements. The property manager must also prepare and execute a plan for restructuring or retrofitting a building that is not in compliance. ADA experts may be consulted, as may architectural designers who specialize in accessibility issues.

To protect owners of existing structures from the massive expense of extensive remodeling, the ADA recommends *reasonably achievable accommodations* to provide access to the facilities and services. New construction and remodeling, however, must meet higher standards of accessibility and usability because it costs less to incorporate accessible features in the design than to retrofit. Though the law intends to provide for people with disabilities, many of the accessible design features and accommodations benefit everyone.

In Practice

The U.S. Department of Justice has ADA specialists available to answer general information questions about compliance issues. The ADA Information Line is at 1-800-514-0301 (TDD 1-800-514-0383). The ADA e-mail address for information is http://www.usdoj.gov/crt/ada/adahom1.htm.

Existing barriers must be removed when this can be accomplished in a readily achievable manner—that is, with little difficulty and at low cost. (See Figure 18.1.) The following are typical examples of readily achievable modifications:

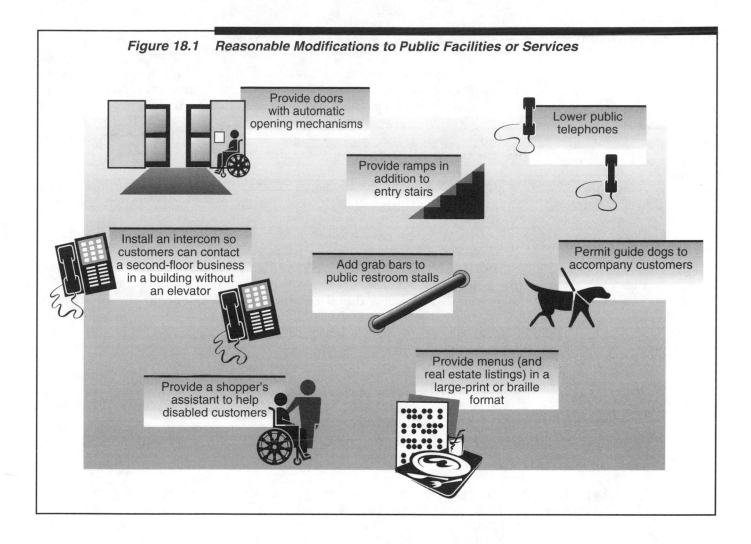

Figure 18.1   Reasonable Modifications to Public Facilities or Services

Provide doors with automatic opening mechanisms

Lower public telephones

Provide ramps in addition to entry stairs

Install an intercom so customers can contact a second-floor business in a building without an elevator

Add grab bars to public restroom stalls

Permit guide dogs to accompany customers

Provide a shopper's assistant to help disabled customers

Provide menus (and real estate listings) in a large-print or braille format

- Ramping or removing an obstacle from an otherwise accessible entrance
- Lowering wall-mounted public telephones
- Adding raised letters and braille markings on elevator buttons
- Installing auditory signals in elevators
- Reversing the direction in which doors open
- Providing doors that have mechanisms that will open and close the doors automatically

Alternative methods can be used to provide reasonable accommodations if extensive restructuring is impractical or if retrofitting is unduly expensive. For instance, installing a cup dispenser at a water fountain that is too high for an individual in a wheelchair may be more practical than installing a lower unit.

In Practice   Federal, state and local laws may provide additional requirements for accommodating people with disabilities. Licensees should be aware of the full range of laws to ensure that their practices are in compliance.

RISK MANAGEMENT

> The four alternative risk management techniques may be remembered by the acronym **ACTOR:** *A*void, *C*ontrol, *T*ransfer or *R*etain.

Enormous monetary losses can result from certain unexpected or catastrophic events. As a result, one of the most critical areas of responsibility for a property manager is risk management. **Risk management** involves answering the question, "What happens if something goes wrong?" The perils of any risk must be evaluated in terms of options. In considering the possibility of a loss, the property manager must decide whether it is better to

- *avoid* it, by removing the source of risk (for instance, a swimming pool may pose an unacceptable risk if a day-care center is located in the building);
- *control* it, by preparing for an emergency before it happens (by installing sprinklers, fire doors and security systems, for example);
- *transfer* it, by shifting the risk onto another party (that is, by taking out an insurance policy); or
- *retain* it, by deciding that the chances of the event occurring are too small to justify the expense of any other response (an alternative might be to take out an insurance policy with a large deductible, which is usually considerably less expensive).

Security of Tenants

The physical safety of tenants of the leased premises is an important issue for property managers and owners. Recent court decisions in several parts of the country have held owners and their agents responsible for physical harm that was inflicted on tenants by intruders. These decisions have prompted property managers and owners to think about how to protect tenants and secure apartments from intruders.

Types of Insurance

Insurance is one way to protect against losses. Many types of insurance are available. An *insurance audit* should be performed by a competent, reliable insurance agent who is familiar with insurance issues for the type of property involved. The audit will indicate areas in which greater or lesser coverage is recommended and will highlight particular risks. The final decision, however, must be made by the property owner.

Some common types of coverage available to income property owners and managers include the following:

- *Fire and hazard:* Fire insurance policies provide coverage against direct loss or damage to property from a fire on the premises. Standard fire coverage can be extended to include other hazards such as windstorm, hail, smoke damage or civil insurrection.
- *Consequential loss, use and occupancy:* Consequential loss insurance covers the results, or consequences, of a disaster. Consequential loss can include the loss of rent or revenue to a business that occurs if the business's property cannot be used.
- *Contents and personal property:* This type of insurance covers building contents and personal property during periods when they are not actually located on the business premises.
- *Liability:* Public liability insurance covers the risks an owner assumes whenever the public enters the building. A claim paid under this coverage is used for medical expenses by a person who is injured in the building as a result of the owner's negligence. Claims for medical or hospital payments for injuries sustained by building employees hurt in the course of their employment are covered by state laws known as **workers'**

compensation acts. These laws require that a building owner who is an employer obtain a workers' compensation policy from a private insurance company.

- *Casualty:* Casualty insurance policies include coverage against theft, burglary, vandalism and machinery damage as well as health and accident insurance. Casualty policies are usually written on specific risks, such as theft, rather than being all-inclusive.
- *Surety bonds:* **Surety bonds** cover an owner against financial losses resulting from an employee's criminal acts or negligence while performing assigned duties.

Many insurance companies offer **multiperil policies** for apartment and commercial buildings. Such a policy offers the property manager an insurance package that includes standard types of commercial coverage, such as fire, hazard, public liability and casualty. Special coverage for earthquakes and floods is also available.

Claims Two possible methods can be used to determine the amount of a claim under an insurance policy. One is the *depreciated,* or *actual cash value* of the damaged property. That is, the property is not insured for what it would cost to replace it, but rather for what it was originally worth, less the depreciation in value that results from use and the passage of time. The other method is *current replacement cost.* In this sort of policy, the building or property is insured for what it would cost to rebuild or replace it today.

When purchasing insurance, a manager must decide whether a property should be insured at full replacement cost or at a depreciated cost. Full replacement cost coverage is generally more expensive than depreciated cost. As with the homeowner's policies, commercial policies include coinsurance clauses that require the insured to carry fire coverage, usually in an amount equal to 80 percent of a building's replacement value.

THE MANAGEMENT PROFESSION

Most metropolitan areas have local associations of building and property owners and managers that are affiliates of regional and national associations. The Institute of Real Estate Management (IREM) is one of the affiliates of the National Association of REALTORS®. It awards the Certified Property Manager (CPM) designation. The Building Owners and Managers Association (BOMA) International is a federation of local associations of building owners and managers. The Building Owners and Managers Institute (BOMI) International, an independent institute affiliated with BOMA, offers training courses leading to several designations: Real Property Administrator (RPA), Systems Maintenance Administrator (SMA) and Facilities Management Administrator (FMA). In addition, many specialized professional organizations provide information and contacts for apartment and condominium association managers, shopping center managers and others.

SUMMARY Property management is a specialized service provided to owners of income-producing properties. The owner's managerial function may be delegated to an individual or a firm with particular expertise in the field. The manager, as agent of the owner, becomes the administrator of the project and assumes the executive functions required for the care and operation of the property.

A management agreement establishes the agency relationship between owner and manager. It must be prepared carefully to define and authorize the manager's duties and responsibilities.

Projected expenses, the manager's analysis of the building's condition and local rent patterns form the basis for determining rental rates for the property. Once a rent schedule is established, the property manager is responsible for soliciting tenants whose needs are suited to the available space. The tenants must be financially capable of meeting the proposed rents. The manager collects rents, maintains the building, hires necessary employees, pays taxes for the building and deals with tenant problems.

Maintenance includes safeguarding the physical integrity of the property and performing routine cleaning and repairs. It also includes making tenant improvements, such as adapting the interior space and overall design of the property to suit tenants' needs.

The manager is expected to secure adequate insurance coverage for the premises. Fire and hazard insurance covers the property and fixtures against catastrophes. Consequential loss, use and occupancy insurance protects the owner against revenue losses. Casualty insurance provides coverage against losses such as theft, vandalism and destruction of machinery. The manager should also secure public liability insurance to insure the owner against claims made by people injured on the premises. Workers' compensation policies cover the claims of employees injured on the job.

This growing real estate specialty is supported by many regional and national organizations that help property managers maintain high professional standards.

In Illinois . . .

Property managers must be licensed real estate brokers. Resident managers are exempt under certain circumstances. ■

QUESTIONS

1. Ken is an employee who is injured on the job. Which of the following types of insurance coverage insures Ken's employer against most claims for job-related injuries?
   A. Consequential loss
   B. Workers' compensation
   C. Casualty
   D. Surety bond

2. Apartment rental rates are usually expressed in what way?
   A. In monthly amounts
   B. On a per-room basis
   C. In square feet per month
   D. In square feet per year

3. From a management point of view, apartment building occupancy that reaches as high as 98 percent would tend to indicate that:
   A. the building is poorly managed.
   B. the building has reached its maximum potential.
   C. the building is a desirable place to live.
   D. rents could be raised.

4. A guest slips on an icy apartment building stair and is hospitalized. A claim against the building owner for medical expenses may be paid under which of the following policies held by the owner?
   A. Workers' compensation
   B. Casualty
   C. Liability
   D. Fire and hazard

5. When a property manager is establishing a budget for the building, all of the following should be included as operating expenses, EXCEPT:
   A. heating oil.
   B. cleaning supplies.
   C. replacement of the gutters.
   D. management fees.

6. A property manager is offered a choice of three insurance policies: one has a $500 deductible, one has a $1,000 deductible and the third has a $5,000 deductible. If the property manager selects the policy with the highest deductible, which risk management technique is he or she using?
   A. Avoiding risk
   B. Retaining risk
   C. Controlling risk
   D. Transferring risk

7. Contaminated groundwater, toxic fumes from paint and carpeting and lack of proper ventilation are all examples of:
   A. issues beyond the scope of a property manager's job description.
   B. problems faced only in newly constructed properties.
   C. issues that arise under the ADA.
   D. environmental concerns that a property manager may have to address.

8. Tenant improvements are:
   A. always construed to be fixtures.
   B. adaptations of space to suit tenants' needs.
   C. removable by the tenant.
   D. paid for by the landlord.

9. In preparing a budget, a property manager should set up which of the following for variable expenses?
   A. Control account
   B. Floating allocation
   C. Cash reserve fund
   D. Asset account

10. Rents should be determined by:
   A. supply-and-demand factors.
   B. the local apartment owners' association.
   C. HUD's annually published rental guidelines.
   D. a tenants' union.

11. Whittaker Towers, a highrise apartment building, burns to the ground. What type of insurance covers the landlord against the resulting loss of rent?
   A. Fire and hazard
   B. Liability
   C. Consequential loss, use and occupancy
   D. Casualty

12. Property manager Janet hires Walter as the full-time maintenance person for one of the buildings she manages. While repairing a faucet in one of the apartments, Walter steals a television set. Janet could protect the owner against this type of loss by obtaining:
    A. liability insurance.
    B. workers' compensation insurance.
    C. a surety bond.
    D. casualty insurance.

13. Which of the following might indicate rents are too low?
    A. A poorly maintained building
    B. Many For Lease signs in the area
    C. High building occupancy
    D. High tenant turnover rates

14. Marilyn repairs a malfunctioning boiler in the building she manages. This is classified as which type of maintenance?
    A. Preventive
    B. Corrective
    C. Routine
    D. Construction

15. An owner has just entered into a property management agreement with a licensee. In regards to this situation, has an agency relationship been formed, and if so, which of the following would BEST describe the relationship?
    A. Yes, an agency relationship has been created and the licensee would be best described as a special agent.
    B. Yes, an agency relationship has been created and the licensee would be best described as a general agent.
    C. No, an agency relationship cannot be created between owners and property managers.
    D. No, an agency relationship can only be created by an executed power of attorney between the property manager and the licensee.

16. Which of the following actions by a property manager would NOT be a breach of her or his fiduciary relationship to the owner?
    A. Placing security deposits in an escrow account
    B. Checking the credit history of minority applicants only
    C. Generating a high net operating income by not maintaining the property
    D. Failing to maintain good relations with the tenants

In Illinois . . .

17. Fred is the manager of an apartment building in central Illinois. Fred's total compensation consists of a monthly salary, a 12 percent commission based on annual rental for each vacant unit Fred fills and the free use of one of the apartments as Fred's personal primary residence. Based on these facts, is Fred required by Illinois law to obtain a real estate broker's license?
    A. Yes. Any person who is compensated for performing real estate activities for a commission must have a broker's license, regardless of any other form of compensation.
    B. Yes. Because Fred's compensation is based in part on recruiting new tenants, rather than simply collecting rents, Fred must have a broker's license.
    C. No. Property managers are not required to have real estate licenses in Illinois.
    D. No. Persons acting as resident managers, who live in the managed property, are specifically exempt from the general licensing requirements.

CHAPTER

19

Real Estate Appraisal

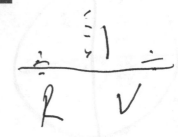

I = Net OPERATING INC
R = RATE OF RETURN (CAP RATE) LEV/BKVOWER
V = MARKET VALUE

KEY TERMS

anticipation
appraisal
appraiser
assemblage
capitalization rate
change
competition
conformity
contribution
cost approach
depreciation
economic life
external obsolescence
functional
   obsolescence

gross income
   multiplier
gross rent multiplier
highest and best use
income approach
index method
law of diminishing
   returns
law of increasing
   returns
market value
physical deterioration
plottage
progression

quantity-survey
   method
reconciliation
regression
replacement cost
reproduction cost
sales comparison
   approach
square-foot method
straight-line method
substitution
supply and demand
unit-in-place method
value

APPRAISING

An **appraisal** is an estimate or opinion of value based on supportable evidence and approved methods. In essence, an appraisal is a "snapshot" of a property's value at a single moment in time. (In fact, an appraisal report often will qualify its conclusions by stating that the valuation is "as of this date"; an appraisal is not a predictor of future value.) An **appraiser** is an independent person trained to provide an *unbiased* estimate of value. Appraising is a professional service performed for a fee.

Regulation of Appraisal Activities

Title XI of the Financial Institutions Reform, Recovery, and Enforcement Act of 1989 (FIRREA) requires that any appraisal used in connection with a federally related transaction must be performed by someone licensed or certified by his or her state. Appraisers conducting business in a federally related transaction must be licensed or certified according to federal law. Each state adopts its own appraiser regulations. These laws must conform to the federal requirements, which in turn follow the criteria for certification established by the Appraiser Qualifications Board of the Appraisal Foundation. The Appraisal Foundation is a national body composed of representatives of the major appraisal and related organizations. Appraisers are also expected to

321

follow the Uniform Standards of Professional Appraisal Practice established by the foundation's Appraisal Standards Board.

A *federally related transaction* is any real estate–related financial transaction in which a federal financial institution or regulatory agency participates. This includes transactions involving the sale, lease, purchase, investment or exchange of real property. It also includes the financing, refinancing or use of real property as security for a loan or an investment, including mortgage-backed securities. Appraisals of residential property valued at $250,000 or less and commercial property valued at $1 million or less in federally related transactions are exempt and need not be performed by licensed or certified appraisers.

In Illinois . . .

The *Illinois Real Estate Appraiser Licensing Act,* effective July 1, 1998, provides for the voluntary licensure and certification of Illinois appraisers in federally related transactions.

The law creates three categories of appraisers:

1. *Licensed real estate appraisers*—qualified to appraise residential properties
2. *Certified residential real estate appraisers*—qualified to appraise residential property of one to six units
3. *Certified general real estate appraisers*—qualified to appraise all types of property, with an emphasis on commercial and income property

Only individuals may be licensed or certified as appraisers. No corporation, partnership, firm or group may be certified or licensed as an appraiser or use the terms "state certified real estate appraiser" or "state licensed real estate appraiser" in connection with its name. A certified or licensed appraiser may, however, sign appraisal reports on behalf of a business entity.

No individual appraiser may use the title "state certified" or "state licensed" unless he or she is in fact licensed or certified by the state. On the other hand, nothing in the appraiser licensing act prohibits a nonlicensed or noncertified individual from appraising real estate for compensation.

In addition, the license act establishes a fee structure and disciplinary and enforcement mechanism for appraisers. Appraisal certification and licensing candidates also must meet strict educational, qualification, examination and experience requirements. ■

Competitive Market Analysis

Not all estimates of value are made by professional appraisers. A salesperson often must help a seller arrive at a listing price or a buyer determine an offering price for property without the aid of a formal appraisal report. In such a case, the salesperson prepares a report compiled from research of the marketplace, primarily similar properties that have been sold, known as a *competitive market analysis* (CMA). The salesperson must be knowledgeable about the fundamentals of valuation to compile the market data. The competitive market analysis is not as comprehensive or technical as an appraisal and may be biased by a salesperson's anticipated agency relationship. A competitive market analysis should not be represented as an appraisal.

[handwritten: VALUE COST ≠ (Does not) Value]

VALUE

To have **value** in the real estate market—that is, to have monetary worth based on desirability—a property must have the following characteristics:

- *Demand*—The need or desire for possession or ownership backed by the financial means to satisfy that need
- *Utility*—The property's usefulness for its intended purposes
- *Scarcity*—A finite supply
- *Transferability*—The relative ease with which ownership rights are transferred from one person to another

Market Value

Generally, the goal of an appraiser is to estimate market value.

The **market value** of real estate is the most probable price that a property should bring in a fair sale. This definition makes three assumptions. First, it presumes a competitive and open market. Second, the buyer and seller are both assumed to be acting prudently and knowledgeably. Finally, market value depends on the price not affected by unusual circumstances.

The following are essential factors in determining market value:

[handwritten: MARKET VALUE PRESUMES :- AN ARM LENGTH TRANSACTION]

- The transaction is an arm's-length transaction; that is, it's fair, honest and the parties are acting in their own best interests.
- The most probable price is *not* the average or the highest price.
- The buyer and seller must be unrelated and acting without undue pressure.
- Both buyer and seller must be well informed about the property's use and potential, including both its defects and its advantages.
- A reasonable time must be allowed for exposure in the open market.
- Payment must be made in cash or its equivalent.
- The price must represent a normal consideration for the property sold, unaffected by special financing amounts or terms, services, fees, costs or credits incurred in the market transaction.

Market value versus market price. *Market value* is an opinion of value based on an analysis of data. The data may include not only an analysis of comparable sales but also an analysis of potential income, expenses and replacement costs (less any depreciation). *Market price,* on the other hand, is what a property *actually* sells for—its sales price. In theory, market price should be the same as market value. Market price can be taken as accurate evidence of current market value, however, only if the conditions essential to market value exist. Sometimes, property may be sold below market value— for instance, when the seller is forced to sell quickly or when a sale is arranged between relatives.

Market value versus cost. An important distinction can be made between market value and *cost.* One of the most common misconceptions about valuing property is that cost represents market value. Cost and market value may be the same. In fact, when the improvements on a property are new, cost and value are likely to be equal. But more often, cost does not equal market value. For example, a homeowner may install a swimming pool for $15,000; however, the cost of the improvement may not add $15,000 to the value of the property.

Basic Principles of Value

A number of economic principles can affect the value of real estate. The most important are defined in the text that follows.

Anticipation. According to the principle of **anticipation** value is created by the expectation that certain events will occur. Value can increase or decrease in anticipation of some future benefit or detriment. For instance, the value of a house may be affected if rumors circulate that an adjacent property may be converted to commercial use in the near future. If the property has been a vacant eyesore, it is possible that the neighboring home's value will increase. On the other hand, if the vacant property is perceived as a park or playground that added to the neighborhood's quiet atmosphere, the news might cause the house's value to decline.

Change. No physical or economic condition remains constant. This is the principle of **change.** Real estate is subject to natural phenomena such as tornadoes, fires and routine wear and tear. The real estate business is subject to market demands, like any other business. An appraiser must be knowledgeable about both the past (and the possibly predictable future) effects of natural phenomena and the changeable behavior of the marketplace.

Competition. **Competition** is the *interaction* of supply and demand. Excess profits tend to attract competition. For example, the success of a retail store may cause investors to open similar stores in the area. This tends to mean less profit for all stores concerned unless the purchasing power in the area increases substantially.

Conformity. The principle of **conformity** says that maximum value is realized when a property is in harmony with its surroundings. Maximum value is realized if the use of land conforms to existing neighborhood standards. In single-family residential neighborhoods, for instance, buildings should be similar in design, construction, size and age.

Contribution. Under the principle of **contribution,** the value of any part of a property is measured by its effect on the value of the whole. Installing a swimming pool, greenhouse or private bowling alley may not add value to the property equal to the cost. On the other hand, remodeling an outdated kitchen or bathroom probably would.

Highest and best use. The most profitable single use to which a property may be put, or the use that is most likely to be in demand in the near future, is the property's **highest and best use.** The use must be

- legally permitted,
- financially feasible,
- physically possible and
- maximally productive.

The highest and best use of a site can change with social, political and economic forces. For instance, a parking lot in a busy downtown area may not maximize the land's profitability to the same extent an office building might. Highest and best use is noted in every appraisal.

Increasing and diminishing returns. The addition of more improvements to land and structures increases value only to the assets' maximum value. Beyond that point, additional improvements no longer affect a property's

Weight is Best Method

value. As long as money spent on improvements produces an increase in income or value, the **law of increasing returns** applies. At the point where additional improvements do not increase income or value, the **law of diminishing returns** applies. No matter how much money is spent on the property, the property's value will not keep pace with the expenditures.

> *Plottage:* The total value of two adjacent properties may be greater if they are combined than the sum of their individual values if each is sold separately.

Plottage. The principle of **plottage** holds that merging or consolidating adjacent lots into a single larger one produces a greater total land value than the sum of the two sites valued separately. For example, two adjacent lots valued at $35,000 each might have a combined value of $90,000 if consolidated. The process of merging two separately owned lots under one owner is known as **assemblage.**

 Regression and progression. In general, the worth of a better-quality property is adversely affected by the presence of a lesser-quality property. This is known as the principle of **regression.** Thus, in a neighborhood of modest homes, a structure that is larger, better maintained or more luxurious would tend to be valued in the same range as the less-lavish homes. Conversely, under the principle of **progression,** the value of a modest home would be higher if it were located among larger, fancier properties.

> *Regression:* the lowering of a property's value due to its neighbors.
>
> *Progression:* the increasing of a property's value due to its neighbors.

Substitution. Under the principle of substitution, the maximum value of a property tends to be set by how much it would cost to purchase an equally desirable and valuable substitute property.

Supply and demand. The principle of **supply and demand** holds that the value of a property depends on the number of properties available in the marketplace—the supply of the product. Other factors include the prices of other properties, the number of prospective purchasers and the price buyers will pay.

Environmental Issues Affecting Real Estate Valuation

Concerns about the existence of possible environmental hazards have intensified in recent years. While residential real estate appraisers are not expected to be environmental risk experts, they must be able to identify the existence of environmental problems and be aware of the impact of various environmental hazards on a property's value. This includes not only the immediate decrease in value due to contamination, but the additional costs of abatement and disposal. (Environmental issues are discussed in detail in Chapter 22.)

THE THREE APPROACHES TO VALUE

To arrive at an accurate estimate of value, appraisers traditionally use three basic valuation techniques: the sales comparison approach, the cost approach and the income approach. The three methods serve as checks against each other. Using them narrows the range within which the final estimate of value falls. Each method is generally considered most reliable for specific types of property.

The Sales Comparison Approach

In the **sales comparison approach** (also known as the *market data or direct market comparison* approach), an estimate of value is obtained by comparing the property being appraised (the *subject property*) with recently sold *comparable properties* (properties similar to the subject, called "comps"). Because no two parcels of real estate are exactly alike, each comparable property must be analyzed for differences and similarities between it and the subject

Best METHOD FOR USED HOUSE & CONDOS

MEMORY TIP

Take the selling price of the comp and add or subtract for any differences, one at a time, from the subject property. The rules are *CBS* and *CPA*. *CBS* = if the **C**omp is **B**etter, **S**ubtract. **CPA** = if the **C**omp is **P**oorer, **A**dd.

---

property. This approach is a good example of the principle of substitution, discussed previously. The sales prices *of the comparables* must be adjusted for any dissimilarities.

FOR EXAMPLE   Two houses in the same neighborhood, one that sold and one that is the subject of an appraisal, are very similar. The comp sold for $145,000 and has a garage valued at $9,000. The subject property has no garage, but it has a fireplace valued at $5,000. What is the indicated value of the property?

$145,000	The comp sale price	
− 9,000	(The Comp is Better, Subtract–CBS)	
+ 5,000	(The Comp is Poorer, Add–CPA)	
$141,000	The indicated value of subject property	

The principal factors for which adjustments must be made include the following:

- *Property rights:* An adjustment must be made when less than fee simple, the full legal bundle of rights, is involved. This includes land leases, ground rents, life estates, easements, deed restrictions and encroachments.
- *Financing concessions:* The financing terms must be considered, including adjustments for differences such as mortgage loan terms and owner financing.
- *Conditions of sale:* Adjustments must be made for motivational factors that would affect the sale, such as foreclosure, a sale between family members or some nonmonetary incentive.
- *Date of sale:* An adjustment must be made if economic changes occur between the date of sale of the comparable property and the date of the appraisal.
- *Location:* Similar properties might differ in price from neighborhood to neighborhood or even between locations within the same neighborhood.
- *Physical features and amenities:* Physical features, such as the structure's age, size and condition, may require adjustments.

The sales comparison approach is essential in almost every appraisal of real estate. It is considered the most reliable of the three approaches in appraising single-family homes, where the intangible benefits may be difficult to measure otherwise. Most appraisals include a minimum of three comparable sales reflective of the subject property. An example of the sales comparison approach is shown in Table 19.1.

The Cost Approach

The **cost approach** to value also is based on the principle of substitution. The cost approach consists of five steps:

THIS IS GOOD ONLY FOR NEW OR FOR UNIQUE

1. Estimate the *current cost* of constructing the existing buildings and improvements.
2. Estimate the amount of *accrued depreciation* resulting from the property's physical deterioration, functional obsolescence and external depreciation.
3. *Deduct* the accrued depreciation (Step 2) from the construction cost (Step 1).
4. Estimate the *value of the land* as if it were vacant and available to be put to its highest and best use.

Table 19.1   Sales Comparison Approach to Value

	Subject Property: 155 Potter Dr.	Comparables				
		A	B	C	D	E
Sales price		$118,000	$112,000	$121,000	$116,500	$110,000
Financing concessions		none	none	none	none	none
Date of sale	none	current	current	current	current	current
Location	good	same	poorer +6,500	same	same	same
Age	6 years	same	same	same	same	same
Size of lot	60′ × 135′	same	same	larger −5,000	same	larger −5,000
Landscaping	good	same	same	same	same	same
Construction	brick	same	same	same	same	same
Style	ranch	same	same	same	same	same
No. of rooms	6	same	same	same	same	same
No. of bedrooms	3	same	same	same	same	same
No. of baths	1½	same	same	same	same	same
Sq. ft. of living space	1,500	same	same	same	same	same
Other space (basement)	full basement	same	same	same	same	same
Condition—exterior	average	better −1,500	poorer +1,000	better −1,500	same	poorer +2,000
Condition—interior	good	same	same	better −500	same	same
Garage	2-car attached	same	same	same	same	none +5,000
Other improvements	none	none	none	none	none	none
Net adjustments		−1,500	+7,500	−7,000	-0-	+2,000
Adjusted value		$116,500	$119,500	$114,000	$116,500	$112,000

Note: The value of a feature that is present in the subject but not in the comparable property is *added* to the sales price of the comparable. Likewise, the value of a feature that is present in the comparable but not in the subject property is *subtracted.* The adjusted sales prices of the comparables represent the probable range of value of the subject property. From this range, a single market value estimate can be selected. Because the value range of the properties in the comparison chart (excluding comparables B and E) is close, and comparable D required no adjustment, an appraiser might conclude that the indicated market value of the subject is $116,500. However, appraisers use a complex process of evaluating adjustment percentages and may consider other objective factors or subjective judgments based on research.

5. *Add* the estimated land value (Step 4) to the depreciated cost of the building and site improvements (Step 3) to arrive at the total property value.

FOR EXAMPLE
Current cost of construction	= $85,000
Accrued depreciation	= $10,000
$85,000 − $10,000	= $75,000
Value of the land	= $25,000
$25,000 + $75,000	= $100,000

In this example, the total property value is $100,000.

There are two ways to look at the construction cost of a building for appraisal purposes: reproduction cost and replacement cost. **Reproduction cost** is the construction cost at current prices of an exact duplicate of the subject improvement, including both the benefits and the drawbacks of the property. **Replacement cost** new is the cost to construct an improvement similar to the subject property using current construction methods and materials, but not necessarily an exact duplicate. Replacement cost new is more frequently used in appraising older structures because it eliminates obsolete features and takes advantage of current construction materials and techniques.

An example of the cost approach to value, applied to the same property as in Table 19.1, is shown in Table 19.2.

Determining reproduction or replacement cost new. An appraiser using the cost approach computes the reproduction or replacement cost of a building using one of the following four methods:

1. **Square-foot method.** The cost per square foot of a recently built comparable structure is multiplied by the number of square feet (using exterior dimensions) in the subject building. This is the most common and easiest method of cost estimation. Table 19.2 uses the square-foot method, which is also referred to as the *comparison method*. For some properties, the cost per cubic foot of a recently built comparable structure is multiplied by the number of cubic feet in the subject structure.
2. **Unit-in-place method.** In the unit-in-place method, the replacement cost of a structure is estimated based on the construction cost per unit of measure of individual building components, including material, labor, overhead and builder's profit. Most components are measured in square feet, although items such as plumbing fixtures are estimated by cost. The sum of the components is the cost of the new structure.
3. **Quantity-survey method.** The quantity and quality of all materials (such as lumber, brick and plaster) and the labor are estimated on a unit cost basis. These factors are added to indirect costs (for example, building permit, survey, payroll, taxes and builder's profit) to arrive at the total cost of the structure. Because it is so detailed and time-consuming, this method is usually used only in appraising historical properties. It is, however, the most accurate method of appraising new construction.
4. **Index method.** A factor representing the percentage increase of construction costs up to the present time is applied to the original cost of the subject property. Because it fails to take into account individual property variables, this method is useful only as a check of the estimate reached by one of the other methods.

Depreciation. In a real estate appraisal, **depreciation** is a loss in value due to any cause. It refers to a condition that adversely affects the value of an improvement to real property. *Land does not depreciate*—it retains its value indefinitely, except in such rare cases as downzoned urban parcels, improperly developed land or misused farmland.

Depreciation is considered to be *curable* or *incurable*, depending on the contribution of the expenditure to the value of the property. For appraisal purposes (as opposed to depreciation for tax purposes, discussed in the appendix), depreciation is divided into three classes, according to its cause:

[handwritten margin note: Loss in value compared with Today Repairs Cost.]

Table 19.2   *Cost Approach to Value*

Subject Property: 155 Potter Dr.

Building Valuation: Replacement Cost
  1,500 sq. ft. @ $65 per sq. ft.   = $97,500

Less Depreciation:
Physical depreciation
  Curable
    (items of deferred maintenance)
     exterior painting $ 4,000
  Incurable (structural deterioration)   9,750
Functional obsolescence   2,000
External depreciation   -0-
    Total   −$15,750

Depreciated Value of Building $ 81,750

Land Valuation: Size 60′ × 135′ @ $450 per front foot $ 27,000
  Plus site improvements: driveway, walks, landscaping, etc.   8,000
    Total $ 35,000

Indicated Value by Cost Approach $116,750

---

1. **Physical deterioration.** *Curable:* An item in need of repair, such as painting (deferred maintenance), that is economically feasible and would result in an increase in value equal to or exceeding the cost. *Incurable:* A defect caused by physical wear and tear if its correction would not be economically feasible or contribute a comparable value to the building. The cost of a major repair may not warrant the financial investment.

2. **Functional obsolescence.** *Curable:* Outmoded or unacceptable physical or design features that are no longer considered desirable by purchasers. Such features, however, could be replaced or redesigned at a cost that would be offset by the anticipated increase in ultimate value. Outmoded plumbing, for instance, is usually easily replaced. Room function may be redefined at no cost if the basic room layout allows for it. A bedroom adjacent to a kitchen, for example, may be converted to a family room. *Incurable:* Currently undesirable physical or design features that could not be easily remedied because the cost of cure would be greater than its resulting increase in value. An office building that cannot be economically air-conditioned, for example, suffers from incurable functional obsolescence if the cost of adding air-conditioning is greater than its contribution to the building's value.

3. **External obsolescence.** *Incurable:* Caused by negative factors not on the subject property, such as environmental, social or economic forces. This type of depreciation is always incurable. The loss in value cannot be reversed by spending money on the property. For example, proximity to a nuisance, such as a polluting factory or a deteriorating neighborhood, is one factor that could not be cured by the owner of the subject property.

The easiest but least-precise way to determine depreciation is the **straight-line method,** also called the *economic age-life method.* Depreciation is assumed to occur at an even rate over a structure's **economic life,** the period during which it is expected to remain useful for its original intended purpose. The property's cost is divided by the number of years of its expected economic life to derive the amount of annual depreciation.

For instance, a $120,000 property may have a land value of $30,000 and an improvement value of $90,000. If the improvement is expected to last 60 years, the annual straight-line depreciation would be $1,500 ($90,000 divided by 60 years). Such depreciation can be calculated as an annual dollar amount or as a percentage of a property's improvements.

The cost approach is most helpful in the appraisal of newer or special-purpose buildings such as schools, churches and public buildings. Such properties are difficult to appraise using other methods because there are seldom enough local sales to use as comparables and because the properties do not ordinarily generate income.

Much of the functional obsolescence and all of the external depreciation can be evaluated by considering the actions of buyers in the marketplace.

The Income Approach

THIS IS Good
For Rental Income

The **income approach** to value is based on the present value of the rights to future income. It assumes that the income generated by a property will determine the property's value. The income approach is used for valuation of income-producing properties such as apartment buildings, office buildings and shopping centers. In estimating value using the income approach, an appraiser must take five steps, illustrated in Table 19.3.

1. Estimate annual *potential gross income.* An estimate of economic rental income must be made based on market studies. Current rental income may not reflect the current market rental rates, especially in the case of short-term leases or leases about to terminate. Potential income includes other income to the property from such sources as vending machines, parking fees and laundry machines.
2. Deduct an appropriate allowance for vacancy and rent loss, based on the appraiser's experience, and arrive at *effective gross income.*
3. Deduct the annual operating expenses, enumerated in Table 19.3, from the effective gross income to arrive at the annual *net operating income* (NOI). Management costs are always included, even if the current owner manages the property. Mortgage payments (principal and interest) are *debt service* and not considered operating expenses.
4. Estimate the price a typical investor would pay for the income produced by this particular type and class of property. This is done by estimating the rate of return (or yield) that an investor will demand for the investment of capital in this type of building. This rate of return is called the **capitalization** (or "cap") **rate** and is determined by comparing the relationship of net operating income to the sales prices of similar properties that have sold in the current market. For example, a comparable property that is producing an annual net income of $15,000 is sold for $187,500. The capitalization rate is $15,000 divided by $187,500, or 8 percent. If other comparable properties sold at prices that yielded substantially the same rate, it may be concluded that 8 percent is the rate that the appraiser should apply to the subject property.
5. Apply the capitalization rate to the property's annual net operating income to arrive at the estimate of the property's value.

With the appropriate capitalization rate and the projected annual net operating income, the appraiser can obtain an indication of value by the income approach.

This formula and its variations are important in dealing with income property:

Income ÷ Rate = Value   Income ÷ Value = Rate   Value × Rate = Income

These formulas may be illustrated graphically as

Net operating income ÷ Capitalization rate = Value

Example: $18,000 income ÷ 9% cap rate = $200,000 value or
$18,000 income ÷ 8% cap rate = $225,000 value

Note the relationship between the rate and value. As the rate goes down, the value increases.

A very simplified version of the computations used in applying the income approach is illustrated in Table 19.3.

*THIS CAN BE
USED Houses &
OFFICES, BUT THIS IS
not Good METHOD
Just Check & Bal*

Gross rent or gross income multipliers. Certain properties, such as single-family homes and two-unit buildings, are not purchased primarily for income. As a substitute for a more elaborate income capitalization analysis, the **gross rent multiplier** (GRM) and **gross income multiplier** (GIM) are often used in the appraisal process. Each relates the sales price of a property to its rental income.

Because single-family residences usually produce only rental incomes, the gross rent multiplier is used. This relates a sales price to monthly rental income. However, commercial and industrial properties generate income from many other sources (rent, concessions, escalator clause income and so forth), and they are valued using their annual income from all sources.

The formulas are as follows:

For five or more residential units, commercial or industrial property:

Sales Price ÷ Gross Annual Income = Gross Income Multiplier (GIM)

or

For one to four residential units:

Sales Price ÷ Gross Monthly Rent = Gross Rent Multiplier (GRM)

For example, if a home recently sold for $82,000 and its monthly rental income was $650, the GRM for the property would be computed

$82,000 ÷ $650 = 126.2 GRM

Table 19.3	Income Capitalization Approach to Value		

Potential Gross Annual Income $60,000
  Market rent (100% capacity)
  Income from other sources   + 600
  (vending machines and pay phones) $60,600

Less vacancy and collection losses (estimated) @ 4%   −2,424
Effective Gross Income $58,176

Expenses:
Real estate taxes	$9,000	
Insurance	1,000	
Heat	2,800	
Maintenance	6,400	
Utilities, electricity, water, gas	800	
Repairs	1,200	
Decorating	1,400	
Replacement of equipment	800	
Legal and accounting	600	
Management	3,000	
Total		$27,000
Annual Net Operating Income		$31,176

Capitalization rate = 10% (overall rate)

Capitalization of annual net income: $$\frac{\$31.176}{.10}$$

Indicated Value by Income Approach = $311,760

To establish an accurate GRM, an appraiser must have recent sales and rental data from at least four properties that are similar to the subject property. The resulting GRM then can be applied to the estimated fair market rental of the subject property to arrive at its market value. The formula would be

Rental Income × GRM = Estimated Market Value

Table 19.4 shows some examples of GRM comparisons.

Reconciliation   When the three approaches to value are applied to the same property, they normally produce three separate indications of value. (For instance, compare Table 19.1 with Table 19.2.) **Reconciliation** is the art of analyzing and effectively weighing the findings from the three approaches.

The process of reconciliation is more complicated than simply taking the average of the three estimates of value. An average implies that the data and logic applied in each of the approaches are equally valid and reliable and should therefore be given equal weight. In fact, however, certain approaches are more valid and reliable with some kinds of properties than with others.

For example, in appraising a home, the income approach is rarely valid, and the cost approach is of limited value unless the home is relatively new. Therefore, the sales comparison approach is usually given greatest weight in valuing single-family residences. In the appraisal of income or investment

Table 19.4   *Gross Rent Multiplier*

Comparable No.	Sales Price	Monthly Rent	GRM
1	$93,600	$650	144
2	78,500	450	174
3	95,500	675	141
4	82,000	565	145
Subject	?	625	?

Note: Based on an analysis of these comparisons, a GRM of 145 seems reasonable for homes in this area. In the opinion of an appraiser, then, the estimated value of the subject property would be $625 × 145, or $90,625.

property, the income approach normally is given the greatest weight. In the appraisal of churches, libraries, museums, schools and other special-use properties, where little or no income or sales revenue is generated, the cost approach usually is assigned the greatest weight. From this analysis, or reconciliation, a single estimate of market value is produced.

THE APPRAISAL PROCESS

Although appraising is not an exact or a precise science, the key to an accurate appraisal lies in the methodical collection and analysis of data. The appraisal process is an orderly set of procedures used to collect and analyze data to arrive at an ultimate value conclusion. The data are divided into two basic classes:

1. *General data,* covering the nation, region, city and neighborhood. Of particular importance is the neighborhood, where an appraiser finds the physical, economic, social and political influences that directly affect the value and potential of the subject property.
2. *Specific data,* covering details of the subject property as well as comparative data relating to costs, sales, and income and expenses of properties similar to and competitive with the subject property.

Figure 19.1 outlines the steps an appraiser takes in carrying out an appraisal assignment.

Once the approaches have been reconciled and an opinion of value has been reached, the appraiser prepares a report for the client. The report should

- identify the real estate and real property interest being appraised;
- state the purpose and intended use of the appraisal;
- define the value to be estimated;
- state the effective date of the value and the date of the report;
- state the extent of the process of collecting, confirming and reporting the data;
- list all assumptions and limiting conditions that affect the analysis, opinion and conclusions of value;
- describe the information considered, the appraisal procedures followed and the reasoning that supports the report's conclusions; if an approach was excluded, the report should explain why;

Figure 19.1   The Appraisal Process

1 State the problem.

2 List the data needed and the sources.

3 Gather, record and verify the necessary data.

General data	Specific Data	Data for Each Approach
• Nation	• Subject site	• Sales data
• Region	• Improvements	• Cost data
• City		• Income and expense data
• Neighborhood		

4 Determine the highest and best use.

5 Estimate the land value.

6 Estimate value by each of the three approaches.

7 Reconcile the estimated values for the final value estimate.

8 Report the final value estimate.

- describe (if necessary or appropriate) the appraiser's opinion of the highest and best use of the real estate;
- describe any additional information that may be appropriate to show compliance with the specific guidelines established in the Uniform Standards of Professional Appraisal Practice (USPAP) or to clearly identify and explain any departures from these guidelines; and
- include signed certification, as required by the Uniform Standards.

Figure 19.2 shows the Uniform Residential Appraisal Report, the form required by many government agencies. It illustrates the types of detailed information required of an appraisal of residential property.

In Practice

The role of an appraiser is not to determine value. Rather, an appraiser develops a supportable and objective report about the value of the subject property. The appraiser relies on experience and expertise in valuation theories to evaluate market data. The appraiser does not establish the property's worth; instead, he or she verifies what the market indicates. This is important to remember, particularly when dealing with a property owner who may lack objectivity about the realistic value of his or her property. The lack of objectivity also can complicate a salesperson's ability to list the property within the most probable range of market value.

SUMMARY

To appraise real estate means to estimate its value. Although many types of value exist, the most common objective of an appraisal is to estimate market value—the most probable sales price of a property. Basic to appraising are certain underlying economic principles, such as highest and best use, substitution, supply and demand, conformity, anticipation, increasing and diminishing returns, regression, progression, plottage, contribution, competition and change.

Value is an estimate of future benefits, cost represents a measure of past expenditures, and price reflects the actual amount of money paid for a property.

In the sales comparison approach, the value of the subject property is compared with the values of others like it that have sold recently. Because no two properties are exactly alike, adjustments must be made to account for any differences. With the cost approach, an appraiser calculates the cost of building a similar structure on a similar site. The appraiser then subtracts depreciation (losses in value), which reflects the differences between new properties of this type and the present condition of the subject property. The income approach is an analysis based on the relationship between the rate of return that an investor requires and the net income that a property produces.

An informal version of the income approach, called the *gross rent multiplier* (GRM), may be used to estimate the value of single-family residential properties that are not usually rented, but could be. The GRM is computed by dividing the sales price of a property by its gross monthly rent. For commercial or industrial property, a gross income multiplier (GIM), based on annual income from all sources, may be used. In the process of reconciliation, the validity and reliability of each approach are weighed objectively to arrive at the single best and most supportable estimate of value.

In Illinois . . .

The Illinois Real Estate Appraiser Licensing Act requires licensure and certification of Illinois appraisers in federally related transactions. Only individuals may be licensed or certified. ■

Figure 19.2 Uniform Residential Appraisal Report

X X

UNIFORM RESIDENTIAL APPRAISAL REPORT File No.

Property Description

SUBJECT

Property Address		City		State	Zip Code
Legal Description				County	

Assessor's Parcel No.　　　　Tax Year　　R.E. Taxes $　　Special Assessments $

Borrower　　Current Owner　　Occupant □ Owner □ Tenant □ Vacant

Property rights appraised □ Fee Simple □ Leasehold　Project Type □ PUD □ Condominium (HUD/VA only)　HOA$ /Mo.

Neighborhood or Project Name　　Map Reference　　Census Tract

Sales Price $　　Date of Sale　　Description and $ amount of loan charges/concessions to be paid by seller

Lender/Client　　Address

Appraiser　　Address

NEIGHBORHOOD

Location	□ Urban	□ Suburban	□ Rural	Predominant occupancy	Single family housing PRICE $ (000)	AGE (yrs)	Present land use %	Land use change
Built up	□ Over 75%	□ 25-75%	□ Under 25%				One family	□ Not likely □ Likely
Growth rate	□ Rapid	□ Stable	□ Slow	□ Owner	Low		2-4 family	□ In process
Property values	□ Increasing	□ Stable	□ Declining	□ Tenant	High		Multi-family	To:
Demand/supply	□ Shortage	□ In balance	□ Over supply	□ Vacant (0-5%)	Predominant		Commercial	
Marketing time	□ Under 3 mos.	□ 3-6 mos.	□ Over 6 mos.	□ Vacant (over 5%)			( )	

Note: Race and the racial composition of the neighborhood are not appraisal factors.

Neighborhood boundaries and characteristics:

Factors that affect the marketability of the properties in the neighborhood (proximity to employment and amenities, employment stability, appeal to market, etc.):

Market conditions in the subject neighborhood (including support for the above conclusions related to the trend of property values, demand/supply, and marketing time -- such as data on competitive properties for sale in the neighborhood, description of the prevalence of sales and financing concessions, etc.):

PUD

Project Information for PUDs (If applicable) -- Is the developer/builder in control of the Home Owners' Association (HOA)? □ Yes □ No

Approximate total number of units in the subject project _____. Approximate total number of units for sale in the subject project _____.

Describe common elements and recreational facilities:

SITE

Dimensions _____ Topography _____

Site area _____ Corner Lot □ Yes □ No　Size _____

Specific zoning classification and description _____ Shape _____

Zoning compliance □ Legal □ Legal nonconforming (Grandfathered use) □ Illegal □ No zoning　Drainage _____

Highest & best use as improved □ Present use □ Other use (explain)　View _____

Utilities	Public	Other	Off-site Improvements	Type	Public	Private	
Electricity			Street				Landscaping _____
Gas			Curb/gutter				Driveway Surface _____
Water			Sidewalk				Apparent easements _____
Sanitary sewer			Street lights				FEMA Special Flood Hazard Area □ Yes □ No
Storm sewer			Alley				FEMA Zone _____ Map Date _____
							FEMA Map No. _____

Comments (apparent adverse easements, encroachments, special assessments, slide areas, illegal or legal nonconforming zoning use, etc.): _____

DESCRIPTION OF IMPROVEMENTS

GENERAL DESCRIPTION	EXTERIOR DESCRIPTION	FOUNDATION	BASEMENT	INSULATION
No. of Units	Foundation	Slab	Area Sq. Ft.	Roof □
No. of Stories	Exterior Walls	Crawl Space	% Finished	Ceiling □
Type (Det./Att.)	Roof Surface	Basement	Ceiling	Walls □
Design (Style)	Gutters & Dwnspts.	Sump Pump	Walls	Floor □
Existing/Proposed	Window Type	Dampness	Floor	None □
Age (Yrs.)	Storm/Screens	Settlement	Outside Entry	Unknown □
Effective Age (Yrs.)	Manufactured House	Infestation		

ROOMS	Foyer	Living	Dining	Kitchen	Den	Family Rm.	Rec. Rm.	Bedrooms	# Baths	Laundry	Other	Area Sq. Ft.
Basement												
Level 1												
Level 2												

Finished area **above grade** contains: _____ Rooms; _____ Bedroom(s); _____ Bath(s); _____ Square Feet of Gross Living Area

INTERIOR	Materials/Condition	HEATING	KITCHEN EQUIP.	ATTIC	AMENITIES	CAR STORAGE:
Floors		Type	Refrigerator	None	Fireplace(s) #	None □
Walls		Fuel	Range/Oven	Stairs	Patio	Garage # of cars
Trim/Finish		Condition	Disposal	Drop Stair	Deck	Attached
Bath Floor		COOLING	Dishwasher	Scuttle	Porch	Detached
Bath Wainscot		Central	Fan/Hood	Floor	Fence	Built-In
Doors		Other	Microwave	Heated	Pool	Carport
		Condition	Washer/Dryer	Finished		Driveway

COMMENTS

Additional features (special energy efficient items, etc.): _____

Condition of the improvements, depreciation (physical, functional, and external), repairs needed, quality of construction, remodeling/additions, etc.: _____

Adverse environmental conditions (such as, but not limited to, hazardous wastes, toxic substances, etc.) present in the improvements, on the site, or in the immediate vicinity of the subject property: _____

Figure 19.2   Uniform Residential Appraisal Report (Continued)

UNIFORM RESIDENTIAL APPRAISAL REPORT   File No. _____

Valuation Section

COST APPROACH

ESTIMATED SITE VALUE. = $ _____

ESTIMATED REPRODUCTION COST-NEW OF IMPROVEMENTS:

Dwelling _____ Sq. Ft @ $ _____ = $ _____

_____ Sq. Ft @ $ _____ = _____

= _____

Garage/Carport _____ Sq. Ft @ $ _____ = _____

Total Estimated Cost-New . . . . = $ _____

Less   Physical | Functional | External

Depreciation _____ = $ _____

Depreciated Value of Improvements . . . . = $ _____

"As-is" Value of Site Improvements . . . . = $ _____

INDICATED VALUE BY COST APPROACH . . . . = $ _____

Comments on Cost Approach (such as, source of cost estimate, site value, square foot calculation and, for HUD, VA and FmHA, the estimated remaining economic life of the property): _____

SALES COMPARISON ANALYSIS

ITEM	SUBJECT	COMPARABLE NO. 1		COMPARABLE NO. 2		COMPARABLE NO. 3	
Address							
Proximity to Subject							
Sales Price	$		$		$		$
Price/Gross Liv. Area	$	$		$		$	
Data and/or Verification Sources							
VALUE ADJUSTMENTS	DESCRIPTION	DESCRIPTION	+ (−) $ Adjustment	DESCRIPTION	+ (−) $ Adjustment	DESCRIPTION	+ (−) $ Adjustment
Sales or Financing Concessions							
Date of Sale/Time							
Location							
Leasehold/Fee Simple							
Site							
View							
Design and Appeal							
Quality of Construction							
Age							
Condition							
Above Grade	Total / Bdrms / Baths	Total / Bdrms / Baths		Total / Bdrms / Baths		Total / Bdrms / Baths	
Room Count							
Gross Living Area	Sq. Ft.	Sq. Ft.		Sq. Ft.		Sq. Ft.	
Basement & Finished Rooms Below Grade							
Functional Utility							
Heating/Cooling							
Energy Efficient Items							
Garage/Carport							
Porch, Patio, Deck, Fireplace(s), etc.							
Fence, Pool, etc.							
Net Adj. (total)		+ / −	$	+ / −	$	+ / −	$
Adjusted Sales Price of Comparable			$		$		$

Comments on Sales Comparison (including the subject property's compatibility to the neighborhood, etc.): _____

ITEM	SUBJECT	COMPARABLE NO. 1	COMPARABLE NO. 2	COMPARABLE NO. 3
Date, Price and Data Source for prior sales within year of appraisal				

Analysis of any current agreement of sale, option, or listing of the subject property and analysis of any prior sales of subject and comparables within one year of the date of appraisal: _____

INDICATED VALUE BY SALES COMPARISON APPROACH . . . . $ _____

INDICATED VALUE BY INCOME APPROACH (If Applicable) Estimated Market Rent $ _____ /Mo. x Gross Rent Multiplier _____ = $ _____

RECONCILIATION

This appraisal is made ☐ "as is" ☐ subject to the repairs, alterations, inspections, or conditions listed below ☐ subject to completion per plans and specifications.

Conditions of Appraisal: _____

Final Reconciliation: _____

The purpose of this appraisal is to estimate the market value of the real property that is the subject of this report, based on the above conditions and the certification, contingent and limiting conditions, and market value definition that are stated in the attached Freddie Mac Form 439/Fannie Mae Form 1004B (Revised _____).

I (WE) ESTIMATE THE MARKET VALUE, AS DEFINED, OF THE REAL PROPERTY THAT IS THE SUBJECT OF THIS REPORT, AS OF _____

(WHICH IS THE DATE OF INSPECTION AND THE EFFECTIVE DATE OF THIS REPORT) TO BE $ _____

APPRAISER: SUPERVISORY APPRAISER (ONLY IF REQUIRED):

Signature _____   Signature _____   ☐ Did   ☐ Did Not

Name _____   Name _____   Inspect Property

Date Report Signed _____   Date Report Signed _____

State Certification # _____ State   State Certification # _____ State

Or State License # _____ State   Or State License # _____ State

Freddie Mac Form 70   6–93   10 CH.   PAGE 2 OF 2   Fannie Mae Form 1004   6–93

QUESTIONS

1. Which of the following appraisal methods uses a rate of investment return?
   A. Sales comparison approach
   B. Cost approach
   C. Income approach
   D. Gross income multiplier method

2. The characteristics of value include which of the following?
   A. Competition   C. Anticipation
   B. Scarcity   D. Balance

3. 457 and 459 Tarpepper Street are adjacent vacant lots, each worth approximately $50,000. If their owner sells them as a single lot, however, the combined parcel will be worth $120,000. What principle does this illustrate?
   A. Substitution   C. Regression
   B. Plottage   D. Progression

4. The amount of money a property commands in the marketplace is its:
   A. intrinsic value. C. subjective value.
   B. market value.   D. book value.

5. Evan constructs an eight-bedroom brick house with a tennis court, a greenhouse and an indoor pool in a neighborhood of modest two-bedroom and three-bedroom frame houses on narrow lots. The value of Evan's house is likely to be affected by what principle?
   A. Progression   C. Change
   B. Assemblage   D. Regression

6. In question 5, the owners of the lesser-valued houses in Evan's immediate area may find that the values of their homes are affected by what principle?
   A. Progression
   B. Increasing returns
   C. Competition
   D. Regression

7. For appraisal purposes, depreciation is caused by all of the following EXCEPT:
   A. functional obsolescence.
   B. physical deterioration.
   C. external obsolescence.
   D. accelerated capitalization.

8. Reconciliation refers to which of the following?
   A. Loss of value due to any cause
   B. Separating the value of the land from the total value of the property to compute depreciation
   C. Analyzing the results obtained by the different approaches to value to determine a final estimate of value
   D. The process by which an appraiser determines the highest and best use for a parcel of land

9. If a property's annual net income is $24,000 and it is valued at $300,000, what is its capitalization rate?
   A. 8 percent   C. 12.5 percent
   B. 10.5 percent   D. 15 percent

10. Certain figures must be determined by an appraiser before value can be computed by the income approach. All of the following are required for this process EXCEPT:
    A. annual net operating income.
    B. capitalization rate.
    C. accrued depreciation.
    D. annual gross income.

11. Janet, an appraiser, is asked to determine the value of an existing strip shopping center. To which approach to value will Janet probably give the most weight?
    A. Cost approach
    B. Sales comparison approach
    C. Income approach
    D. Index method

12. The market value of a parcel of real estate is:
    A. an estimate of its future benefits.
    B. the amount of money paid for the property.
    C. an estimate of the most probable price it should bring.
    D. its value without improvements.

13. Capitalization is the process by which annual net operating income is used to:
    A. determine cost.
    B. estimate value.
    C. establish depreciation.
    D. determine potential tax value.

14. From the reproduction or replacement cost of a building, the appraiser deducts depreciation, which represents:
    A. the remaining economic life of the building.
    B. remodeling costs to increase rentals.
    C. loss of value due to any cause.
    D. costs to modernize the building.

15. The effective gross annual income from a property is $112,000. Total expenses for this year are $53,700. What capitalization rate was used to obtain a valuation of $542,325?
    A. 9.75 percent   C. 10.50 percent
    B. 10.25 percent   D. 10.75 percent

16. All of the following factors would be important in comparing properties under the sales comparison approach to value EXCEPT differences in:
    A. dates of sale.
    B. financing terms.
    C. appearance and condition.
    D. original cost.

17. Trendsetter Terrace cost $240,000. The building is currently 5 years old and has an estimated remaining useful life of 60 years. Using straight-line depreciation, what is the property's total depreciation to date?
    A. $14,364   C. $20,000
    B. $18,462   D. $54,000

18. In question 17, what is the current value of Trendsetter Terrace?
    A. $235,636   C. $220,000
    B. $221,538   D. $186,000

19. The appraised value of a residence with four bedrooms and one bathroom would probably be reduced because of:
    A. external obsolescence.
    B. functional obsolescence.
    C. curable physical deterioration.
    D. incurable physical deterioration.

20. Randy, an appraiser, estimates that it would require 4,000 square feet of concrete, 10,000 square feet of lumber and $15,000 worth of copper pipe to replace a structure. Randy also estimates other factors, such as material, labor, overhead and builder's profit. Which method of determining reproduction or replacement cost is Randy using?
    A. Square-foot method
    B. Quantity-survey method
    C. Index method
    D. Unit-in-place method

21. An appraiser has been hired to determine the value of a vacant city lot. Which of the following would he NOT consider in determining the value of the property?
    A. Topography
    B. Physical depreciation
    C. Assemblage
    D. Utilization of the land

22. If a factory opens or closes in a community, the appraiser would MOST LIKELY consider which of the following principles of appraising in determining the value of property in the community?
    A. Substitution
    B. Regression
    C. Progression
    D. Supply and demand

23. All of the following data must be determined by an appraiser in computing value by the income approach EXCEPT:
    A. Appropriate capitalization rate
    B. Potential gross income
    C. Annual operating expenses
    D. Accrued depreciation

24. All of the following are false regarding gross rent multipliers EXCEPT:
    A. an appraiser would use this method to appraise a vacant city lot.
    B. this method of appraising would be used to find the value of a single-family home used for investment purposes.
    C. the first step to computing the gross rent multiplier is to subtract expenses from the rent.
    D. this method of appraising is also known as the sales comparison approach.

25. A 35-year-old property has been maintained over the years. It is LEAST LIKELY to be suffering from:
    A. physical deterioration.
    B. external obsolescence.
    C. functional obsolescence.
    D. highest and best use.

In Illinois . . .

26. Amanda wants to be an appraiser in the northwest suburbs of Chicago. While Amanda would be willing to appraise residential properties, her real interest is in appraising commercial properties. If Amanda wants to be qualified to conduct appraisals under FIRREA, what must she do?
    A. Amanda must become a licensed real estate appraiser.
    B. Amanda must become a certified appraiser.
    C. Amanda must become a certified general appraiser.
    D. Nothing; individuals who wish to conduct appraisals under FIRREA must receive federal appraisal certification rather than state licensing.

Land-Use Controls and Property Development

KEY TERMS

buffer zone
building code
clustering
comprehensive plan
conditional-use
  permit
deed restriction

density zoning
developer
enabling act
Interstate Land Sales
  Full Disclosure Act
nonconforming use
plat

restrictive covenant
subdivider
subdivision
taking
variance
zoning ordinance

LAND-USE CONTROLS

Broad though they may be, the rights of real estate ownership are not absolute. Land use is controlled and regulated through public and private restrictions and through the public ownership of land by federal, state and local governments.

Over the years, the government's policy has been to encourage private ownership of land. Home ownership is often referred to as "the American Dream." It is necessary, however, for a certain amount of land to be owned by the government for such uses as municipal buildings, state legislative houses, schools and military stations. Government ownership also may serve the public interest through urban renewal efforts, public housing and streets and highways. Often, the only way to ensure that enough land is set aside for recreational and conservation purposes is through direct government ownership in the form of national and state parks and forest preserves. Beyond this sort of direct ownership of land, however, most government controls on property occur at the local level.

 The states' police power is their inherent authority to create regulations needed to protect the public health, safety and welfare. The states delegate to counties and local municipalities the authority to enact ordinances in keeping with general laws. The increasing demands placed on finite natural resources have made it necessary for cities, towns and villages to increase their limitations on the private use of real estate. There are now controls over noise, air and water pollution as well as population density.

In Illinois . . .   Article VII of the Illinois Constitution allows for home rule units of government. Any municipality with a population in excess of 25,000 and any county that has a chief executive officer elected by the people are automatically home rule units. However, a home rule unit may elect by referendum *not* to be one. On the other hand, a municipality of fewer than 25,000 people may elect by referendum to become a home rule unit of government. Townships are not allowed to be home rule units.

Constitutionally, a home rule unit of government may exercise any power and perform any function pertaining to its government, including the exercise of police power by way of laws that control the use of land. They also have greater freedom to enforce their laws, including the power to jail offenders for up to six months. (A violation of a land-use control would not ordinarily warrant imprisonment, but home rule units are able to establish an appropriate schedule of fines and injunctive relief.)

Non–home rule units do not have such unlimited powers. Instead, they derive their authority to pass land-use controls from the state government, through *enabling statutes.*

Occasionally, the laws of one unit of government conflict with another's. If any ordinance of a home rule county conflicts with any ordinance of a home rule municipality, *the municipal ordinance prevails.* If a municipality has passed a zoning ordinance, it will supersede any county or township zoning ordinance, home rule notwithstanding. Township zoning ordinances must give way to county zoning ordinances, and townships are not empowered to pass subdivision controls or building codes. ■

THE COMPREHENSIVE PLAN

Local governments establish development goals by creating a **comprehensive plan.** This is also referred to as a *master plan.* Municipalities and counties develop plans to control growth and development. The plan includes the municipality's objectives for the future and the strategies and timing for those objectives to be implemented. For instance, a community may want to ensure that social and economic needs are balanced with environmental and aesthetic concerns. The comprehensive plan usually includes the following basic elements:

- Land use—that is, a determination of how much land may be proposed for residence, industry, business, agriculture, traffic and transit facilities, utilities, community facilities, parks and recreational facilities, floodplains and areas of special hazards
- Housing needs of present and anticipated residents, including rehabilitation of declining neighborhoods as well as new residential developments
- Movement of people and goods, including highways and public transit, parking facilities and pedestrian and bikeway systems
- Community facilities and utilities, such as schools, libraries, hospitals, recreational facilities, fire and police stations, water resources, sewerage and waste treatment and disposal, storm drainage and flood management
- Energy conservation to reduce energy consumption and promote the use of renewable energy sources

The preparation of a comprehensive plan involves surveys, studies and analyses of housing, demographic and economic characteristics and trends. The municipality's planning activities may be coordinated with other government bodies and private interests to achieve orderly growth and development.

FOR EXAMPLE After the Great Chicago Fire of 1871 reduced most of the city's downtown to rubble and ash, the city engaged planner Daniel Burnham to lay out a design for Chicago's future. The resulting Burnham Plan of orderly boulevards linking a park along Lake Michigan with other large parks and public spaces throughout the city established an ideal urban space. The plan is still being implemented today.

ZONING

Zoning ordinances are local laws that implement the comprehensive plan and regulate and control the use of land and structures within designated land-use districts. If the comprehensive plan is the big picture, zoning is the details. Zoning affects such things as

- permitted uses of each parcel of land,
- lot sizes,
- types of structures,
- building heights,
- setbacks (the minimum distance away from streets or sidewalks that structures may be built),
- style and appearance of structures,
- density (the ratio of land area to structure area) and
- protection of natural resources.

Zoning ordinances cannot be static; they must remain flexible to meet the changing needs of society.

FOR EXAMPLE In many cities, factories and warehouses sit empty. Some cities have begun changing the zoning ordinances for such properties to permit new residential or commercial developments in areas once zoned strictly for heavy industrial use. Coupled with tax incentives, the changes lure developers back into the cities. The resulting housing is modern, conveniently located and affordable. Simple zoning changes can help revitalize whole neighborhoods in big cities.

No nationwide or statewide zoning ordinances exist. Rather, zoning powers are conferred on municipal governments by state **enabling acts.** State and federal governments may, however, regulate land use through special legislation, such as scenic easement, coastal management and environmental laws.

Zoning Objectives   Zoning ordinances traditionally have divided land use into residential, commercial, industrial and agricultural classifications. These land-use areas are further divided into subclasses. For example, residential areas may be subdivided to provide for detached single-family dwellings, semidetached structures containing not more than four dwelling units, walk-up apartments, highrise apartments and so forth.

To meet both the growing demand for a variety of housing types and the need for innovative residential and nonresidential development, municipalities are adopting ordinances for subdivisions and planned residential developments. Some municipalities also use **buffer zones,** such as landscaped parks and playgrounds, to screen residential areas from nonresidential zones. Certain types of zoning that focus on special land-use objectives are used in some areas. These include

- *bulk zoning* (or *density zoning*) to control density and avoid overcrowding by imposing restrictions such as setbacks, building heights and percentage of open area or by restricting new construction projects;
- aesthetic zoning to specify certain types of architecture for new buildings; and
- *incentive zoning* to ensure that certain uses are incorporated into developments, such as requiring the street floor of an office building to house retail establishments.

Constitutional issues and zoning ordinances. Zoning can be a highly controversial issue. Among other things, it often raises questions of constitutional law. The preamble of the U.S. Constitution provides for the promotion of the general welfare, but the Fourteenth Amendment prevents the states from depriving "any person of life, liberty, or property, without due process of law." How is a local government to enact zoning ordinances that protect public safety and welfare without violating the constitutional rights of property owners?

Any land-use legislation that is destructive, unreasonable, arbitrary or confiscatory usually is considered void. Furthermore, zoning ordinances must not violate the various provisions of the constitution of the state in which the real estate is located. Tests commonly applied in determining the validity of ordinances require that the

- power be exercised in a reasonable manner;
- provisions be clear and specific;
- ordinances be nondiscriminatory;
- ordinances promote public health, safety and general welfare under the police power concept; and
- ordinances apply to all property in a similar manner.

Taking. The concept of **taking** comes from the takings clause of the Fifth Amendment to the U.S. Constitution. The clause reads, "nor shall private property be taken for public use, without just compensation." This means that when land is taken for public use through the government's power of eminent domain or condemnation, the owner must be compensated. In general, virtually no land is exempt from government seizure for a public use or public purpose. The rule, however, is that the government cannot seize land without paying for it. This payment is referred to as *just compensation*—compensation that is just, or fair.

Of course, it is sometimes very difficult to determine what level of compensation is fair in any particular situation. The compensation may be negotiated between the owner and the government, or the owner may seek a court judgment setting the amount.

| In Practice | One method used to determine just compensation is the before-and-after method. This method is used primarily where a portion of an owner's property is seized for public use. The value of the owner's remaining property after the taking is subtracted from the value of the whole parcel before the taking. The result is the total amount of compensation due to the owner. |

Zoning Permits   Zoning laws are generally enforced through the use of permits. Compliance with zoning can be monitored by requiring that property owners obtain permits before they begin any development. A permit will not be issued unless a proposed development conforms to the permitted zoning, among other requirements. Zoning permits are usually required before building permits can be issued.

Zoning hearing board.   Zoning hearing boards (or zoning boards of appeal) have been established in most communities to hear complaints about the effects a zoning ordinance may have on specific parcels of property. Petitions for variances or exceptions to the zoning law may be presented to an appeal board.

Nonconforming use.   Frequently, a lot or an improvement does not conform to the zoning law because it existed before the enactment or amendment of the zoning ordinance. Such a **nonconforming use** may be allowed to continue legally as long as it complies with the regulations governing nonconformities in the local ordinance or until the improvement is destroyed or torn down or the current use is abandoned. If the nonconforming use is allowed to continue indefinitely, it is grandfathered into the new zoning.

FOR EXAMPLE   Under Pleasantville's old zoning ordinances, the C&E Store was well within a commercial zone. When the zoning map was changed to accommodate an increased need for residential housing in Pleasantville, C&E was grandfathered into the new zoning; that is, it was allowed to continue its successful operations, even though it did not fit the new zoning rules.

Variances and conditional-use permits.   Each time a plan or zoning ordinance is enacted, some property owners are inconvenienced and want to change the use of their property. Generally, these owners may appeal for either a conditional-use permit or a variance to allow a use that does not meet current zoning requirements.

A **conditional-use permit** (also known as a *special-use permit*) is usually granted to a property owner to allow a special use of property that is defined as an allowable conditional use within that zone, such as a house of worship or day-care center in a residential district. For a conditional-use permit to be appropriate, the intended use must meet certain standards set by the municipality.

A **variance,** on the other hand, permits a landowner to use his or her property in a manner that is strictly prohibited by the existing zoning. Variances provide relief if zoning regulations deprive an owner of the reasonable use of his or her property. To qualify for a variance, the owner must demonstrate the unique circumstances that make the variance necessary. In addition, the owner must prove that he or she is harmed and burdened by the regulations. A variance also might be sought to provide relief if existing zoning regulations create a physical hardship for the development of a specific property. For example, if an owner's lot is level next to a road but slopes steeply 30 feet away from the road, the zoning board may allow a variance so the owner can build closer to the road than the setback requirement allows.

Both variances and conditional-use permits are issued by zoning boards only after public hearings. The neighbors of a proposed use must be given an opportunity to voice their opinions.

Conditional-use permits allow nonconforming but related land uses.

Variances permit prohibited land uses to avoid undue hardship.

A property owner also can seek a change in the zoning classification of a parcel of real estate by obtaining an amendment to the district map or a zoning ordinance for that area. That is, the owner can attempt to have the zoning changed to accommodate his or her intended use of the property. The proposed amendment must be brought before a public hearing on the matter and approved by the governing body of the community.

BUILDING CODES

Most municipalities have enacted ordinances to specify construction standards that must be met when repairing or erecting buildings. These are called **building codes,** and they set the requirements for kinds of materials and standards of workmanship, sanitary equipment, electrical wiring, fire prevention and the like.

A property owner who wants to build a structure or alter or repair an existing building usually must obtain a *building permit.* Through the permit requirement, municipal officials are made aware of new construction or alterations and can verify compliance with building codes and zoning ordinances. Inspectors will closely examine the plans and conduct periodic inspections of the work. Once the completed structure has been inspected and found satisfactory, the municipal inspector issues a *certificate of occupancy* or *occupancy permit.*

If the construction of a building or an alteration violates a deed restriction (discussed later in this chapter), the issuance of a building permit will not cure this violation. A building permit is merely evidence of the applicant's compliance with municipal regulations.

Similarly, communities with historic districts, or those that are interested in maintaining a particular "look" or character, may have aesthetic ordinances. These laws require that all new construction or restorations be approved by a special board. The board ensures that the new structures will blend in with existing building styles. Owners of existing properties may need to obtain approval to have their homes painted or remodeled.

In Practice   The subject of planning, zoning and restricting the use of real estate is extremely technical, and the interpretation of the law is not always clear. Questions concerning any of these subjects in relation to real estate transactions should be referred to legal counsel. Furthermore, the landowner should be aware of the costs for various permits.

SUBDIVISION

Subdividers split up land into parcels.

Developers construct improvements on the subdivided parcels.

Most communities have adopted subdivision and land development ordinances as part of their comprehensive plans. An ordinance includes provisions for submitting and processing subdivision plats. A major advantage of subdivision ordinances is that they encourage flexibility, economy and ingenuity in the use of land. A **subdivider** is a person who buys undeveloped acreage and divides it into smaller lots for sale to individuals or developers or for the subdivider's own use. A **developer** (who also may be a subdivider) improves the land, constructs homes or other buildings on the lots and sells them. Developing is generally a much more extensive activity than subdividing.

Regulation of Land Development

Just as no national zoning ordinance exists, no uniform planning and land development legislation affects the entire country. Laws governing subdividing and land planning are controlled by the state and local governing bodies where the land is located. Rules and regulations developed by government agencies have, however, provided certain minimum standards. Many local governments have established standards that are higher than the minimum standards.

Land development plan. Before the actual subdividing can begin, the subdivider must go through the process of *land planning.* The resulting land development plan must comply with the municipality's comprehensive plan. Although comprehensive plans and zoning ordinances are not necessarily inflexible, a plan that requires them to be changed must undergo long, expensive and frequently complicated hearings.

Plats. From the land development and subdivision plans, the subdivider draws plats. A **plat** is a detailed map that illustrates the geographic boundaries of individual lots. It also shows the blocks, sections, streets, public easements and monuments in the prospective subdivision. A plat also may include engineering data and restrictive covenants. The plats must be approved by the municipality before they can be recorded. A developer often is required to submit an environmental impact report with the application for subdivision approval. This report explains what effect the proposed development will have on the surrounding area.

Subdivision Plans

In plotting out a **subdivision** according to local planning and zoning controls, a subdivider usually determines the size as well as the location of the individual lots. The maximum or minimum size of a lot generally is regulated by local ordinances and must be considered carefully.

The land itself must be studied, usually in cooperation with a surveyor, so that the subdivision takes advantage of natural drainage and land contours. A subdivider should provide for utility easements as well as easements for water and sewer mains.

Most subdivisions are laid out by use of *lots and blocks.* An area of land is designated as a block, and the area making up this block is divided into lots.

One negative aspect of subdivision development is the potential for increased tax burdens on all residents, both inside and outside the subdivision. To protect local taxpayers against the costs of a heightened demand for public services, many local governments strictly regulate nearly all aspects of subdivision development.

Subdivision Density

Zoning ordinances control land use. Such control often includes minimum lot sizes and population density requirements for subdivisions and land developments. For example, a typical zoning restriction may set the minimum lot area on which a subdivider can build a single-family housing unit at 10,000 square feet. This means that the subdivider can build four houses per acre. Many zoning authorities now establish special density zoning standards for certain subdivisions. **Density zoning** (or *bulk zoning*) ordinances restrict the average maximum number of houses per acre that may be built within a particular subdivision. If the area is density zoned at an average maximum of four houses per acre, for instance, the subdivider may choose to cluster building lots to achieve an open effect. Regardless of lot size or number of units, the subdivider will be consistent with the ordinance as long as the

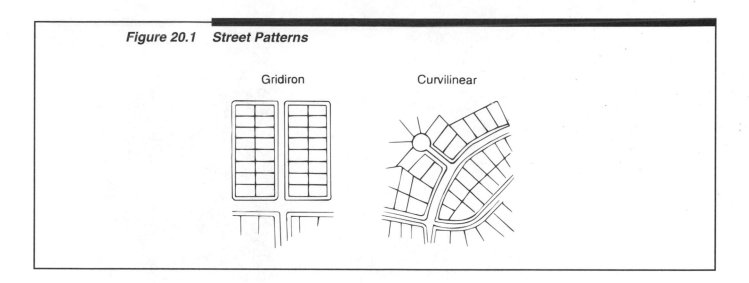

Figure 20.1   Street Patterns

average number of units in the development remains at or below the maximum density. This average is called *gross density.*

Street patterns. By varying street patterns and clustering housing units, a subdivider can dramatically increase the amount of open or recreational space in a development. Two of these patterns are the *gridiron* and *curvilinear* patterns. (See Figure 20.1.)

The gridiron pattern evolved out of the government rectangular survey system. This pattern features large lots, wide streets and limited-use service alleys. Sidewalks are usually adjacent to the streets or separated from the streets by narrow grassy areas. While the gridiron pattern provides for little open space and many lots may front on busy streets, it is an easy system to navigate.

The curvilinear system integrates major arteries of travel with smaller secondary and cul-de-sac streets carrying minor traffic. Curvilinear developments avoid the uniformity of the gridiron, but often lack service alleys. The absence of straight-line travel and the lack of easy access tend to make curvilinear developments quieter and more secure. However, getting from place to place may be more challenging.

Clustering for open space. By slightly reducing lot sizes and **clustering** them around varying street patterns, a subdivider can house as many people in the same area as could be done using traditional subdividing plans but with substantially increased tracts of open space.

For example, compare the two subdivisions illustrated in Figure 20.2. Conventional Gardens is a conventionally designed subdivision containing 368 housing units. It uses 23,200 linear feet of street and leaves only 1.6 acres open for parkland. Contrast this with Cluster Estates. Both subdivisions are equal in size and terrain. But when lots are reduced in size and clustered around limited-access cul-de-sacs, the number of housing units remains nearly the same (366), with less street area (17,700 linear feet) and dramatically increased open space (23.5 acres). In addition, with modern building designs this clustered plan could be modified to accommodate more than 1,000 town houses while retaining the attractive open spaces.

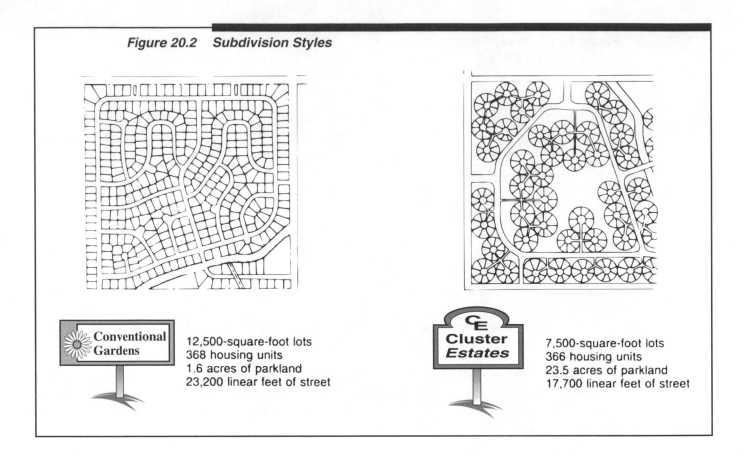

Figure 20.2   Subdivision Styles

Conventional Gardens
12,500-square-foot lots
368 housing units
1.6 acres of parkland
23,200 linear feet of street

Cluster Estates
7,500-square-foot lots
366 housing units
23.5 acres of parkland
17,700 linear feet of street

PRIVATE LAND-USE CONTROLS

Not all restrictions on the use of land are imposed by government bodies. Certain restrictions to control and to maintain the desirable quality and character of a property or subdivision may be created by private entities, including the property owners themselves. These restrictions are separate from, and in addition to, the land-use controls exercised by the government. No private restriction can violate a local, state or federal law.

Restrictive covenants. Restrictive covenants set standards for all the parcels within a defined subdivision. They usually govern the type, height and size of buildings that individual owners can erect, as well as land use, architectural style, construction methods, setbacks and square footage. The deed conveying a particular lot in the subdivision will refer to the plat or declaration of restrictions, thus limiting the title conveyed and binding all grantees. This is known as a **deed restriction** (sometimes also called a *CC&R*). Restrictions may have time limitations. A restriction might state that it is "effective for a period of 25 years from this date." After this time, it becomes inoperative. A time-limited covenant, however, may be extended by agreement.

Restrictive covenants are usually considered valid if they are reasonable restraints that benefit all property owners in the subdivision—for instance, to protect property values or safety. If, however, the terms of the restrictions are too broad, they will be construed as preventing the free transfer of property. If any restrictive covenant or condition is judged unenforceable by a court, the estate will stand free from the invalid covenant or condition. Restrictive covenants cannot be for illegal purposes, such as for the exclusion of members of certain races, nationalities or religions.

In Illinois . . .   Any restrictive covenant that forbids or restricts conveyance, encumbrance, occupancy or lease on the basis of race, color, religion or national origin is void. Exceptions to this section of the Illinois Human Rights Act are allowed for religious and charitable organizations. ■

Private land-use controls may be more restrictive of an owner's use than the local zoning ordinances. The rule is that the more restrictive of the two takes precedence.

Private restrictions can be enforced in court when one lot owner applies to the court for an *injunction* to prevent a neighboring lot owner from violating the recorded restrictions. The court injunction will direct the violator to stop or remove the violation. The court retains the power to punish the violator for failing to obey. If adjoining lot owners stand idly by while a violation is committed, they can lose the right to an injunction by their inaction. The court might claim their right was lost through *laches*—that is, the legal principal that a right may be lost through undue delay or failure to assert it.

REGULATION OF LAND SALES

Just as the sale and use of property within a state are controlled by state and local governments, the sale of property in one state to buyers in another is subject to strict federal and state regulations.

Interstate Land   The federal **Interstate Land Sales Full Disclosure Act** regulates the inter-
Sales Full   state sale of unimproved lots. The act is administered by the Secretary of
Disclosure Act   Housing and Urban Development (HUD), through the office of Interstate Land Sales registration. It is designed to prevent fraudulent marketing schemes that may arise when land is sold without being seen by the purchasers. (You may be familiar with stories about gullible buyers whose land purchases were based on glossy brochures shown by smooth-talking salespersons. When the buyers finally went to visit the "little pieces of paradise" they'd bought, they frequently found worthless swampland or barren desert.)

The act requires that developers file statements of record with HUD before they can offer unimproved lots in interstate commerce by telephone or through the mail. The statements of record must contain numerous disclosures about the properties.

Developers also are required to provide each purchaser or lessee of property with a printed report before the purchaser or lessee signs a purchase contract or lease. The report must disclose specific information about the land, including

- the type of title being transferred to the buyer,
- the number of homes currently occupied on the site,
- the availability of recreation facilities,
- the distance to nearby communities,
- utility services and charges and
- soil conditions and foundation or construction problems.

Under the act, the purchaser has the right to revoke any contract to purchase a regulated lot until midnight on the seventh day after the contract was signed. If the purchaser or lessee does not receive a copy of the property report before signing the purchase contract or lease, he or she may bring an action to void the contract within two years after signing it.

The act provides a number of exemptions. For instance, it does not apply to subdivisions consisting of fewer than 25 lots or to those in which the lots are of 20 acres or more. Lots offered for sale solely to developers also are exempt from the act's requirements, as are lots on which buildings exist or where a seller is obligated to construct a building within two years.

Misrepresentation or failure to comply with the act's requirements subjects a seller to criminal penalties (fines and imprisonment) as well as to civil damages.

State Subdivided-Land Sales Laws

Many state legislatures have enacted their own subdivided-land sales laws. Some affect only the sale of land located outside the state to state residents. Other states' laws regulate sales of land located both inside and outside the states. These state land sales laws tend to be stricter and more detailed than the federal law. Licensees should be aware of the laws in their states and how they compare with federal law.

In Illinois . . .

The sale or promotion within Illinois of subdivided land is regulated by the *Illinois Land Sales Registration Act.* The act regulates the offering, sale, lease or assignment of any improved or unimproved land divided into 25 or more lots and offered as a part of a common promotional plan.

Under the act, subdividers must register with the state and file a full disclosure report containing information on the land, location, tax status, financial arrangements and liens associated with the offering. Similar information must be included in a public property report that must be given to all prospective purchasers. A purchaser who does not receive a copy of this report at least 48 hours before signing a binding contract of sale has the option of voiding the contract within 48 hours after signing.

Every subdivision submitted for registration must be held open for on-site inspection at the expense of the applicant or for searches of records held by other state or federal agencies.

The act does not apply to certain offers or dispositions:

- Those in which the sales promotional costs, including commissions, do not exceed 20 percent of the sales prices
- Offers made by a purchaser for his or her own account in a single isolated transaction
- Offerings in which there is an existing building on the lot or a legal obligation on the part of the seller to construct one within two years
- Offerings involving cemetery lots
- Offerings where the total land is being sold to ten or fewer persons
- Lots of 20 or more unimproved acres or 10 or more acres if each lot has ready access leading to a county-maintained road. ■

SUMMARY

The control of land use is exercised through public controls, private (or nongovernment) controls and direct public ownership of land.

Through power conferred by state enabling acts, local governments exercise public controls based on the states' police powers to protect the public health, safety and welfare.

A comprehensive plan sets forth the development goals and objectives for the community. Zoning ordinances carrying out the provisions of the plan control the use of land and structures within designated land-use districts. Zoning enforcement problems involve zoning hearing boards, conditional-use permits, variances and exceptions, as well as nonconforming uses. Subdivision and land development regulations are adopted to maintain control of the development of expanding community areas so that growth is harmonious with community standards.

Building codes specify standards for construction, plumbing, sewers, electrical wiring and equipment.

Public ownership is a means of land-use control that provides land for such public benefits as parks, highways, schools and municipal buildings.

A subdivider buys undeveloped acreage, divides it into smaller parcels and develops or sells it. A developer builds homes on the lots and sells them through the developer's own sales organization or through local real estate brokerage firms. City planners and land developers, working together, plan whole communities that are later incorporated into cities, towns or villages.

Land development must comply with the master plans adopted by counties, cities, villages or towns. This may entail approval of land-use plans by local planning committees or commissioners.

The process of subdivision includes dividing the tract of land into lots and blocks and providing for utility easements, as well as laying out street patterns and widths. A subdivider generally must record a completed plat of subdivision, with all necessary approvals of public officials, in the county where the land is located. Subdividers usually place restrictions on the use of all lots in a subdivision as a general plan for the benefit of all lot owners.

By varying street patterns and housing density and clustering housing units, a subdivider can dramatically increase the amount of open and recreational space within a development.

Private land-use controls are exercised by owners through deed restrictions and restrictive covenants. These private restrictions may be enforced by obtaining a court injunction to stop a violator.

Subdivided land sales are regulated on the federal level by the Interstate Land Sales Full Disclosure Act. This law requires that developers engaged in certain interstate land sales or leases register the details of the land with HUD. Developers also must provide prospective purchasers or lessees with property reports containing all essential information about the property in any development that exceeds 25 lots.

In Illinois . . .

The Illinois Constitution provides for certain units of government to exercise home rule authority. When a county's ordinance conflicts with a municipality's, the municipal ordinance prevails.

The Illinois Human Rights Act prohibits restrictive covenants that discriminate on the basis of race, color, religion or national origin.

The sale or promotion within Illinois of subdivided land is regulated by the Illinois Land Sales Registration Act.   ■

QUESTIONS

1. A subdivision declaration reads, "No property within this subdivision may be further subdivided for sale or otherwise, and no property may be used for other than single-family housing." This is an example of:
   A. a restrictive covenant.
   B. an illegal reverter clause.
   C. R-1 zoning.
   D. a conditional-use clause.

2. A landowner who wants to use property in a manner that is prohibited by a local zoning ordinance but that would benefit the community can apply for which of the following?
   A. Conditional-use permit
   B. Downzoning
   C. Occupancy permit
   D. Dezoning

3. Public land-use controls include all of the following EXCEPT:
   A. subdivision regulations.
   B. restrictive covenants.
   C. environmental protection laws.
   D. comprehensive plan specifications.

4. Under its zoning, the town of New Pompeii may legally regulate all of the following EXCEPT:
   A. the number of buildings.
   B. the size of buildings.
   C. building ownership.
   D. building occupancy.

5. The purpose of a building permit is to:
   A. override a deed's restrictive covenant.
   B. maintain municipal control over the volume of building.
   C. provide evidence of compliance with municipal regulations.
   D. show compliance with restrictive covenants.

6. Zoning powers would MOST LIKELY be conferred on municipal governments in which of the following ways?
   A. By state enabling acts
   B. Through the master plan
   C. By eminent domain
   D. Through escheat

7. The town of East Westchester enacts a new zoning code. Under the new code, commercial buildings are not permitted within 1,000 feet of Lake Westchester. A commercial building that is permitted to continue in its former use even though it is built on the lakeshore is an example of:
   A. a nonconforming use.
   B. a variance.
   C. a special use.
   D. inverse condemnation.

8. To determine whether a location can be put to future use as a retail store, one would examine the:
   A. building code.
   B. list of permitted nonconforming uses.
   C. housing code.
   D. zoning ordinance.

9. All of the following would properly be included in a list of deed restrictions EXCEPT:
   A. types of buildings that may be constructed.
   B. allowable ethnic origins of purchasers.
   C. activities that are not to be conducted at the site.
   D. minimum size of buildings to be constructed.

10. A restriction in a seller's deed may be enforced by which of the following?
    A. Court injunction
    B. Zoning board of appeal
    C. City building commission
    D. State legislature

11. George owns a large tract of land. After an adequate study of all the relevant facts, George legally divides the land into 30 lots suitable for the construction of residences. George is a(n):
    A. subdivider.   C. land planner.
    B. developer.   D. urban planner.

12. A map illustrating the sizes and locations of streets and lots in a subdivision is called a:
    A. gridiron plan.
    B. survey.
    C. plat of subdivision.
    D. property report.

13. In Glendale, subdivision developers are limited by law to constructing no more than an average of three houses per acre in any subdivision. To what does this restriction refer?
    A. Clustering   C. Out-lots
    B. Density   D. Covenants

14. The city of Northbend is laid out in a pattern of intersecting streets and avenues. All streets run north and south; all avenues run east and west. Northbend is an example of which street pattern style?
    A. Block plan
    B. Gridiron system
    C. Radial streets plan
    D. Intersecting system

15. Permitted land uses and set-asides, housing projections, transportation issues and objectives for implementing future controlled development would all be found in a community's:
    A. zoning ordinance.
    B. comprehensive plan.
    C. enabling act.
    D. land-control law.

16. All of the following items are usually designated on the plat for a new subdivision EXCEPT:
    A. easements for sewer and water mains.
    B. land to be used for streets.
    C. numbered lots and blocks.
    D. prices of residential and commercial lots.

17. Acorn Acres is a subdivision featuring spacious homes grouped on large cul-de-sac blocks connected to a central, winding road and surrounded by large, landscaped common areas. This is an example of which type of subdivision plan?
    A. Cluster plan
    B. Curvilinear system
    C. Rectangular street system
    D. Gridiron system

18. A subdivider can increase the amount of open or recreational space in a development by:
    A. varying street patterns.
    B. meeting local housing standards.
    C. scattering housing units.
    D. eliminating multistory dwellings.

19. Under the federal law designed to protect the public from fraudulent interstate land sales, a developer involved in interstate land sales of 25 or more lots must:
    A. provide each purchaser with a printed report disclosing details of the property.
    B. pay the prospective buyer's expenses to see the property involved.
    C. provide preferential financing.
    D. allow a 30-day cancellation period.

In Illinois . . .

20. Which of the following statements describes enabling statutes in Illinois?
    A. They grant counties, cities and villages the power to make and enforce local zoning ordinances.
    B. They make all counties, cities and villages subject to Illinois state zoning laws.
    C. They require all Illinois counties, cities and villages to adopt the requirements of the federal municipal planning commission.
    D. They set environmental controls on current land use.

21. Sharon lives in River City, Illinois. She thinks that video-game arcades are a bad influence on the city's young people and wants River City zoned to prohibit all arcades and other public video-gaming facilities. Which of the following would be Sharon's best course of action?
    A. Try to get the Illinois legislature to amend the state zoning laws
    B. File suit to force River City to conform with existing Illinois zoning laws
    C. Try to persuade the River City town government to change the local zoning laws
    D. Ask the U.S. Department of Housing and Urban Development to force River City to zone against video arcades under its Fifth Amendment powers

22. A zoning law passed by the Village of Blackhawk conflicts with an existing county zoning law. Both the village and the county are home rule units of government. In this situation, which of the following statements is true?
    A. Under the Illinois constitution, the county law will prevail, because its zoning laws affect a larger geographic area.
    B. The Village of Blackhawk's law will prevail, because municipal ordinances supersede county ordinances under the Illinois Constitution.
    C. The Illinois Constitution provides that a conflict between the laws of two home rule units must be resolved in the appropriate circuit court.
    D. Whichever law is most restrictive will prevail, unless the issue involves a constitutional question, in which case the law least restrictive of private property rights will supersede the more restrictive law.

21

Fair Housing and Ethical Practices

KEY TERMS

Americans with
    Disabilities Act
blockbusting
Civil Rights Act of
    1866
code of ethics

Department of
    Housing and
    Urban
    Development
Equal Credit
    Opportunity Act

ethics
Fair Housing Act
redlining
steering
Title VIII of the Civil
    Rights Act of 1968

EQUAL OPPORTUNITY IN HOUSING

The purpose of civil rights laws that affect the real estate industry is to create a marketplace in which all persons of similar financial means have a similar range of housing choices. The goal is to ensure that everyone has the opportunity to live where he or she chooses. Owners, real estate licensees, apartment management companies, real estate organizations, lending agencies, builders and developers must all take a part in creating this single housing market. Federal, state and local fair housing or equal opportunity laws affect every phase of a real estate transaction, from listing to closing.

> "All citizens of the United States shall have the same right in every state and territory as is enjoyed by white citizens thereof to inherit, purchase, lease, sell, hold, and convey real and personal property."—Civil Rights Act of 1866

The U.S. Congress and the Supreme Court have created a legal framework that preserves the constitutional rights of all citizens. However, while the passage of laws may establish a code for public conduct, centuries of discriminatory practices and attitudes are not so easily changed. Real estate licensees cannot allow their own prejudices to interfere with the ethical and legal conduct of their profession. Similarly, the discriminatory attitudes of property owners or property seekers must not be allowed to affect compliance with the fair housing laws. This is not always easy, and the pressure to avoid offending the person who pays the commission can be intense. However, just remember: Failure to comply with fair housing laws may be a civil or criminal violation, and constitutes grounds for disciplinary action against a licensee.

In Illinois . . .

The Illinois Real Estate License Act and its General Rules require that all licensees in Illinois fully adhere to the principles of equal opportunity in housing. In addition to the provisions contained in the license act, the rules established by the Office of Banks and Real Estate (OBRE) prohibit a licensed broker or salesperson from taking any listing or participating in any transaction in which the owner of the property seeks to apply discriminatory standards based on race, color, creed, religion, national origin, sex, physical handicap or familial status.

Failure to comply with fair housing laws is not only a criminal act but also grounds for disciplinary action against the licensee. Violations of the provisions or restrictions of the Illinois act or the rules can result in the revocation, suspension or nonrenewal of the violator's license or in censure, reprimand or fine imposed by the OBRE.

Section 18.3 of the license act requires that when there has been a judgment in either a civil or criminal proceeding that a licensee has illegally discriminated, his or her license must be suspended or revoked, unless the proceeding is still in the appeals process. Further, if there has been an order by an administrative agency finding discrimination by a licensee, the board must penalize the licensee. However, such penalty needn't be as severe as in the former scenario.

In addition to state and federal laws, many cities and villages in Illinois have their own fair housing laws. These laws are enforced on the local level and may take precedence over federal laws when the local law has been ruled substantially equivalent to the federal statute. Many local fair housing laws are stricter or more broad than state or federal laws. Licensees should be familiar with their local municipal fair housing laws. ■

Federal Laws The federal government's effort to guarantee equal housing opportunities to all U.S. citizens began with the passage of the **Civil Rights Act of 1866.** This law prohibits any type of discrimination based on race.

The U.S. Supreme Court's 1896 decision *Plessy v. Ferguson* established the "separate but equal" doctrine of legalized racial segregation. A series of court decisions and federal laws in the 20 years between 1948 and 1968 attempted to address the inequities in housing that were results of *Plessy.* Those efforts, however, tended to address only certain aspects of the housing market (such as federally funded housing programs). As a result, their impact was limited. Title VIII of the Civil Rights Act of 1968, however, prohibited specific discriminatory practices throughout the real estate industry.

FAIR HOUSING ACT

The *Fair Housing Act* prohibits discrimination based on

1. race,
2. color,
3. religion,
4. sex,
5. handicap,
6. familial status or
7. national origin.

Title VIII of the Civil Rights Act of 1968 prohibited discrimination in housing based on race, color, religion or national origin. In 1974, the Housing and Community Development Act added sex to the list of protected classes. In 1988, the Fair Housing Amendments Act added disability and familial status (that is, the presence of children). Today, these laws are known as the federal **Fair Housing Act.** (See Figure 21.1.) The Fair Housing Act prohibits discrimination on the basis of race, color, religion, sex, handicap, familial status or national origin.

The act also prohibits discrimination against individuals because of their association with persons in the protected classes. This law is administered by the **Department of Housing and Urban Development** (HUD). HUD has established rules and regulations that further interpret the practices affected by the law. In addition, HUD distributes an equal housing opportunity poster. (See Figure 21.2.) The poster declares that the office in which it is displayed promises to adhere to the Fair Housing Act and pledges support for affirmative marketing and advertising programs.

Figure 21.1   Federal Fair Housing Laws

Legislation	Race	Color	Religion	National Origin	Sex	Age	Marital Status	Disability	Discrimination	Familial Status	Public Assistance Income
Civil Rights Act of 1866	●										
Fair Housing Act of 1968 (Title VIII)	●	●	●	●					●		
Housing and Community Development Act of 1974					●				●		
Fair Housing Amendments Act of 1988								●	●	●	
Equal Credit Opportunity Act of 1974 (lending)	●	●	●	●	●	●	●		●		●

Figure 21.2   Equal Housing Opportunity Poster

U.S. Department of Housing and Urban Development

EQUAL HOUSING OPPORTUNITY

We Do Business in Accordance With the Federal Fair Housing Law
(The Fair Housing Amendments Act of 1988)

It is Illegal to Discriminate Against Any Person Because of Race, Color, Religion, Sex, Handicap, Familial Status, or National Origin

- In the sale or rental of housing or residential lots
- In advertising the sale or rental of housing
- In the financing of housing

- In the provision of real estate brokerage services
- In the appraisal of housing
- Blockbusting is also illegal

Anyone who feels he or she has been discriminated against may file a complaint of housing discrimination with the:
1-800-424-8590 (Toll Free)
1-800-424-8529 (TDD)

U.S. Department of Housing and Urban Development
Assistant Secretary for Fair Housing and Equal Opportunity
Washington, D.C. 20410

Previous editions are obsolete

form **HUD-928.1** (3-89)

In Practice	When HUD investigates a broker for discriminatory practices, it may consider failure to prominently display the equal housing opportunity poster in the broker's place of business as evidence of discrimination.

Table 21.1 describes the activities prohibited by the Fair Housing Act.

Definitions   HUD's regulations provide specific definitions that clarify the scope of the Fair Housing Act.

Housing. The regulations define *housing* as a "dwelling," which includes any building or part of a building designed for occupancy as a residence by one or more families. This includes a single-family house, condominium, cooperative or mobile home, as well as vacant land on which any of these structures will be built.

Familial status. Familial status refers to the presence of one or more individuals who have not reached the age of 18 and who live with either a parent or guardian. The term includes a woman who is pregnant. In effect, it means that the Fair Housing Act's protections extend to families with children. Unless a property qualifies as housing for older persons, all properties must be made available to families with children under the same terms and conditions as to anyone else. It is illegal to advertise properties as being for "adults only" or to indicate a preference for a certain number of children. The number of persons permitted to reside in a property (the occupancy standards) must be based on objective factors such as sanitation or safety. Landlords cannot restrict the number of occupants to eliminate families with children.

FOR EXAMPLE Grant owned an apartment building. One of his elderly tenants, Paula, was terminally ill. Paula requested that no children be allowed in the vacant apartment next door because the noise would be difficult for her to bear. Grant agreed and refused to rent to families with children. Even though Grant only wanted to make things easier for a dying tenant, he was nonetheless found to have violated the Fair Housing Act by discriminating on the basis of familial status.

Disability. A *disability* is a physical or mental impairment. The term includes having a history of, or being regarded as having, an impairment that substantially limits one or more of an individual's major life activities. Persons who have AIDS are protected by the fair housing laws under this classification.

In Practice	The federal fair housing law's protection of disabled persons does not include those who are current users of illegal or controlled substances. Nor are individuals who have been convicted of the illegal manufacture or distribution of a controlled substance protected under this law. However, the law does prohibit discrimination against those who are participating in addiction recovery programs. For instance, a landlord could lawfully discriminate against a cocaine addict but not against a member of Alcoholics Anonymous.

Table 21.1 Fair Housing Act Restrictions

Prohibited by Federal Fair Housing Act	Example
• Refusing to sell, rent or negotiate the sale or rental of housing	Kane owns an apartment building with several vacant units. When an Asian family asks to see one of the units, Kane tells them to go away.
• Changing terms, conditions or services for different individuals as a means of discriminating	Sandra, a Roman Catholic, calls on a duplex, and the landlord tells her the rent is $400 per month. When she talks to the other tenants, she learns that all the Lutherans in the complex pay only $325 per month.
• Advertising any discriminatory preference or limitation in housing or making any inquiry or reference that is discriminatory in nature	A real estate agent places the following advertisement in a newspaper: "Just Listed! Perfect home for white family, near excellent parochial school!" A developer places this ad in an urban newspaper: "Sunset River Hollow—Dream Homes Just For You!" The ad is accompanied by a photo of several African-American families.
• Representing that a property is not available for sale or rent when in fact it is	Julie, who uses a wheelchair, is told that the house she wants to rent is no longer available. The next day, however, the For Rent sign is still in the window.
• Profiting by inducing property owners to sell or rent on the basis of the prospective entry into the neighborhood of persons of a protected class	Nadia, a real estate agent, sends brochures to homeowners in the predominantly white Ridgewood neighborhood. The brochures, which feature Nadia's past success selling homes, include photos of racial minorities, population statistics and the caption, "The Changing Face of Ridgewood."
• Altering the terms or conditions of a home loan, or denying a loan, as a means of discrimination	A lender requires Maria, a divorced mother of two young children, to pay for a credit report. In addition, her father must co-sign her application. After talking to a single male friend, Maria learns that he was not required to do either of those things, despite his lower income and poor credit history.
• Denying membership or participation in a multiple-listing service, a real estate organization or another facility related to the sale or rental of housing, as a means of discrimination	The Topper County Real Estate Practitioners' Association meets every week to discuss available properties and buyers. None of Topper County's black or female agents is allowed to be a member of the association.

It is unlawful to discriminate against prospective buyers or tenants on the basis of disability. Landlords must make reasonable accommodations to existing policies, practices or services to permit persons with disabilities to have equal enjoyment of the premises. For instance, it would be reasonable for a landlord to permit support animals (such as guide dogs and service monkeys) in a normally no-pets building or to provide a designated handicapped parking space in a generally unreserved lot.

People with disabilities must be permitted to make reasonable modifications to the premises at their own expense. Such modifications might include lowering door handles or installing bath rails to accommodate a person in a wheelchair. Failure to permit reasonable modification constitutes discrimination. However, the law recognizes that some reasonable modifications might make a rental property undesirable to the general population. In such a case, the landlord is allowed to require that the property be restored to its previous condition when the lease period ends.

The law does not prohibit restricting occupancy exclusively to persons with handicaps in dwellings that are designed specifically for their accommodation.

For new construction of certain multifamily properties, a number of accessibility and usability requirements must be met under federal law. Access is specified for public- and common-use portions of the buildings, and adaptive and accessible design must be implemented for the interior of the dwelling units. Some states have their own laws as well.

Exemptions to the Fair Housing Act

The federal Fair Housing Act provides for certain exemptions. It is important for licensees to know in what situations the exemptions apply. However, licensees should be aware that no exemptions involve race and that no exceptions apply when a real estate licensee is involved in a transaction (including when selling or leasing his or her own property).

The sale or rental of a single-family home is exempt when

- the home is owned by an individual who does not own more than three such homes at one time,
- a real estate broker or salesperson is not involved in the transaction and
- discriminatory advertising is not used.

Only one such sale by an owner who does not live in the dwelling at the time of the transaction, or who is not the most recent occupant, is exempt from the law within any 24-month period.

The rental of rooms or units is exempted in an owner-occupied one- to four-family dwelling.

Dwelling units owned by religious organizations may be restricted to people of the same religion if membership in the organization is not restricted on the basis of race, color or national origin. Similarly, a private club that is not open to the public may restrict the rental or occupancy of lodgings that it owns to its members as long as the lodgings are not operated commercially.

The Fair Housing Act does not require that housing be made available to any individual whose tenancy would constitute a direct threat to the health or safety of other individuals or that would result in substantial physical damage to the property of others.

Housing for older persons. While the Fair Housing Act protects families with children, certain properties can be restricted to occupancy by elderly persons. Housing intended for persons age 62 or older or housing occupied by at least one person 55 years of age or older per unit (where 80 percent of the units are occupied by individuals 55 or older) is exempt from the familial status protection.

Jones v. Mayer. In 1968, the Supreme Court heard the case of *Jones v. Alfred H. Mayer Company*, 392 U.S. 409 (1968). In its decision, the court upheld the Civil Rights Act of 1866. This decision is important because although the federal law exempts individual homeowners and certain groups, the 1866 law prohibits all racial discrimination without exception. A person who is discriminated against on the basis of race may still recover damages under the 1866 law. Where race is involved, no exceptions apply.

The U.S. Supreme Court has expanded the definition of the term *race* to include ancestral and ethnic characteristics, including certain physical, cultural or linguistic characteristics that are commonly shared by a group with a common national origin. These rulings are significant because discrimination on the basis of race, as it is now defined, affords due process of complaints under the provisions of the Civil Rights Act of 1866.

> The *Equal Credit Opportunity Act* prohibits discrimination in granting credit based on
>
> * race,
> * color,
> * religion,
> * national origin,
> * sex,
> * marital status,
> * age or
> * public assistance.

Equal Credit Opportunity Act

The federal **Equal Credit Opportunity Act** (ECOA) prohibits discrimination based on race, color, religion, national origin, sex, marital status or age in the granting of credit. Note that the ECOA protects more classes of persons than the Fair Housing Act: the ECOA also bars discrimination on the basis of marital status and age. It also prevents lenders from discriminating against recipients of public assistance programs such as food stamps and Social Security. As in the Fair Housing Act, the ECOA requires that credit applications be considered only on the bases of income, net worth, job stability and credit rating.

Americans with Disabilities Act

Although the **Americans with Disabilities Act** (ADA) is not a housing or credit law, it still has a significant effect on the real estate industry. The ADA is important to licensees because it addresses the rights of individuals with disabilities in employment and public accommodations. Real estate brokers are often employers, and real estate brokerage offices are public spaces. The ADA's goal is to enable individuals with disabilities to become part of the economic and social mainstream of society.

The ADA requires that employers (including real estate licensees) make reasonable accommodations that enable an individual with a disability to perform essential job functions. *Reasonable accommodations* include making the work site accessible, restructuring a job, providing part-time or flexible work schedules and modifying equipment that is used on the job. The provisions of the ADA apply to any employer with 15 or more employees.

> The *Americans with Disabilities Act* requires *reasonable accommodations* in employment and access to goods, services and public buildings.

Title III of the ADA provides for accessibility to goods and services for individuals with disabilities. While the federal civil rights laws have traditionally been viewed in the real estate industry as housing-related, the practices of licensees who deal with nonresidential property are significantly affected by the ADA. Because people with disabilities have the right to full and equal access to businesses and public services under the ADA, building owners and managers must ensure that any obstacle restricting this right is eliminated. The Americans with Disabilities Act Accessibility Guidelines (ADAAG) contain detailed specifications for designing parking spaces, curb ramps, elevators, drinking fountains, toilet facilities and directional signs to ensure maximum accessibility.

In Practice

Real estate agents need a general knowledge of the ADA's provisions. It is necessary for a broker's workplace and employment policies to comply with the law. Also, licensees who are building managers must ensure that the properties are legally accessible. However, ADA compliance questions may arise with regard to a client's property, too. Unless the agent is a qualified ADA expert, it is best to advise commercial clients to seek the services of an attorney, an architect or a consultant who specializes in ADA issues. It is possible that an appraiser may be liable for failing to identify and account for a property's noncompliance.

FAIR HOUSING PRACTICES

For the civil rights laws to accomplish their goal of eliminating discrimination, licensees must apply them routinely. Of course, compliance also means that licensees avoid violating both the laws and the ethical standards of the profession. The following discussion examines the ethical and legal issues that confront real estate licensees.

Blockbusting

> *Blockbusting:* encouraging the sale or renting of property by claiming that the entry of a protected class of people into the neighborhood will negatively affect property values.

Blockbusting is the act of encouraging people to sell or rent their homes by claiming that the entry of a protected class of people into the neighborhood will have some sort of negative impact on property values. Blockbusting was a common practice during the 1950s and 1960s, as unscrupulous real estate agents profited by fueling "white flight" from cities to suburbs. Any message, however subtle, that property should be sold or rented because the neighborhood is "undergoing changes" is considered blockbusting. It is illegal to assert that the presence of certain persons will cause property values to decline, crime or antisocial behavior to increase and the quality of schools to suffer.

A critical element in blockbusting, according to HUD, is the profit motive. A property owner may be intimidated into selling his or her property at a depressed price to the blockbuster, who in turn sells the property to another person at a higher price. Another term for this activity is panic selling. To avoid accusations of blockbusting, licensees should use good judgment when choosing locations and methods for marketing their services and soliciting listings.

Steering

> *Steering:* channeling home seekers to particular neighborhoods based on race, religion, national origin or some other consideration.

Steering is the channeling of home seekers to particular neighborhoods. It also includes discouraging potential buyers from considering some areas. In either case, it is an illegal limitation of a purchaser's options.

Steering may be done either to preserve the character of a neighborhood or to change its character intentionally. Many cases of steering are subtle, motivated by assumptions or perceptions about a home seeker's preferences, based on some stereotype. Assumptions are not only dangerous—they are often wrong. The licensee cannot assume that a prospective home seeker expects to be directed to certain neighborhoods or properties. Steering anyone is illegal.

In Illinois . . . Section 18(h) 22 of the Illinois Real Estate License Act (255 ILCS 455/18(h) 22) expressly prohibits "Influencing or attempting to influence by any words or acts a prospective seller, purchaser, occupant, landlord or tenant of real estate, in connection with viewing, buying or leasing of real estate, so as to promote, or tend to promote, the continuance or maintenance of racially and religiously segregated housing, or so as to retard, obstruct or discourage racially integrated housing on or in any street, block, neighborhood or community." ■

Advertising No advertisement of property for sale or rent may include language indicating a preference or limitation. No exception to this rule exists, regardless of how subtle the choice of words. HUD's regulations cite examples that are considered discriminatory. (See Figure 21.3.) The media used for promoting property or real estate services cannot target one population to the exclusion of others. The selective use of media, whether by language or geography, may have discriminatory impact. For instance, advertising property only in a Korean-language newspaper tends to discriminate against non-Koreans. Similarly, limiting advertising to a cable television channel available only to white suburbanites may be construed as a discriminatory act. However, if an advertisement appears in general-circulation media as well, it may be legal.

Appraising Those who prepare appraisals or any statements of valuation, whether they are formal or informal, oral or written (including a competitive market analysis), may consider any factors that affect value. However, race, color, religion, national origin, sex, handicap and familial status are not factors that may be considered.

Redlining The practice of refusing to make mortgage loans or issue insurance policies in specific areas for reasons other than the economic qualifications of the applicants is known as **redlining.** Redlining refers to literally drawing a line around particular areas. This practice is often a major contributor to the deterioration of older neighborhoods. Redlining is frequently based on racial grounds rather than on any real objection to an applicant's creditworthiness. That is, the lender makes a policy decision that no property in a certain area is qualified for a loan, no matter who wants to buy it, because of the neighborhood's ethnic character. The federal Fair Housing Act prohibits discrimination in mortgage lending and covers not only the actions of primary lenders but also activities in the secondary mortgage market. A lending institution, however, can refuse a loan solely on sound economic grounds.

The Home Mortgage Disclosure Act requires that all institutional mortgage lenders with assets in excess of $10 million and one or more offices in a given geographic area make annual reports. The reports must detail all mortgage loans the institution has made or purchased, broken down by census tract. This law enables the government to detect patterns of lending behavior that might constitute redlining.

Intent and Effect If an owner or real estate licensee *purposely* sets out to engage in blockbusting, steering or other unfair activities, the *intent* to discriminate is obvious. However, owners and licensees must examine their activities and policies carefully to determine whether they have unintentional discriminatory, effects. Whenever policies or practices result in unequal treatment of persons in the protected classes, they are considered discriminatory regardless of any innocent intent. This *effects test* is applied by regulatory agencies to determine whether an individual has been discriminated against.

Figure 21.3	**HUD's Advertising Guidelines**		
CATEGORY	**RULE**	**PERMITTED**	**NOT PERMITTED**
Race Color National Origin	No discriminatory limitation/preference may be expressed	"master bedroom" "good neighborhood"	"white neighborhood" "no French"
Religion	No religious preference/limitation	"chapel on premises" "kosher meals available" "Merry Christmas"	"no Muslims" "nice Christian family" "near great Catholic school"
Sex	No explicit preference based on sex	"mother-in-law suite" "master bedroom"	"great house for a man" "wife's dream kitchen"
Handicap	No exclusions or limitations based on handicap	"wheelchair ramp" "walk to shopping"	"no wheelchairs" "able-bodied tenants only"
Familial Status	No preference or limitation based on family size or nature	"two-bedroom" "family room" "quiet neighborhood"	"married couple only" "no more than two children" "retiree's dream house"
Photographs or Illustrations of People	People should be clearly representative and nonexclusive	Illustrations showing mixtures of ethnic groups, family groups, singles, etc.	Illustrations showing *only* singles, African American families, elderly white adults, etc.

ENFORCEMENT OF THE FAIR HOUSING ACT

The federal Fair Housing Act is administered by the Office of Fair Housing and Equal Opportunity (OFHEO) under the direction of the secretary of HUD. Any aggrieved person who believes illegal discrimination has occurred may file a complaint with HUD within one year of the alleged act. HUD may also initiate its own complaint. Complaints may be reported to the Office of Fair Housing and Equal Opportunity, Department of Housing and Urban Development, Washington, DC 20410, or to the Office of Fair Housing and Equal Opportunity in care of the nearest HUD regional office.

On receiving a complaint, HUD initiates an investigation. Within 100 days of the filing of the complaint, HUD either determines that reasonable cause exists to bring a charge of illegal discrimination or dismisses the complaint. During this investigation period, HUD can attempt to resolve the dispute informally through conciliation. *Conciliation* is the resolution of a complaint by obtaining assurance that the person against whom the complaint was filed (the respondent) will remedy any violation that may have occurred. The respondent further agrees to take steps to eliminate or prevent discriminatory practices in the future. If necessary, these agreements can be enforced through civil action.

The aggrieved person has the right to seek relief through administrative proceedings. *Administrative proceedings* are hearings held before administrative law judges (ALJs). An ALJ has the authority to award actual damages to the aggrieved person or persons and, if it is believed the public interest will be served, to impose monetary penalties. The penalties range from up to $10,000 for the first offense to $25,000 for a second violation within five years and $50,000 for further violations within seven years. The ALJ also has the authority to issue an injunction to order the offender to either do something (such as rent an apartment to the complaining party) or refrain from doing something (such as acting in a discriminatory manner).

The parties may elect civil action in federal court at any time within two years of the discriminatory act. For cases heard in federal court, unlimited punitive damages can be awarded in addition to actual damages. The court also can issue injunctions. Errors and omissions insurance carried by licensees normally does not pay for violations of the fair housing laws.

Whenever the attorney general has reasonable cause to believe that any person or group is engaged in a pattern or practice of resistance to the full enjoyment of any of the rights granted by the federal fair housing laws, he or she may file a civil action in any federal district court. Civil penalties may result in an amount not to exceed $50,000 for a first violation and an amount not to exceed $100,000 for second and subsequent violations.

Complaints brought under the Civil Rights Act of 1866 are taken directly to federal courts. The only time limit for action is a state's statute of limitations for *torts*—injuries one individual inflicts on another.

In Illinois . . .

The Illinois Human Rights Act.   Section 18(h) 23 of the Illinois Real Estate License Act prohibits any act that constitutes a violation of the Illinois Human Rights Act, *regardless of whether a complaint has been filed with or adjudicated by the Human Rights Commission.* The Human Rights Act includes some prohibitions that also are specifically addressed by the license act, such as blockbusting.

Under the Human Rights Act, it is a civil rights violation for an Illinois licensee to engage in *any of the following acts*, based on discrimination on the basis of race, color, religion, national origin, ancestry, age, sex, marital status, physical disability, military service or unfavorable discharge from military service, or on the basis of familial status:

- Refuse to engage in a real estate transaction with a person
- Alter the terms, conditions or privileges of a real estate transaction
- Refuse to receive or fail to transmit an offer
- Refuse to negotiate
- Represent that real property is not available for inspection, sale, rental or lease when in fact it is available, or fail to bring a property listing to an individual's attention, or refuse to permit him or her to inspect real estate
- Publicize, through any means or use, an application form that indicates an intent to engage in unlawful discrimination
- Offer, solicit, accept, use or retain a listing of real property with knowledge that unlawful discrimination is intended

It is a civil rights violation for the owner or agent of any housing accommodation to engage in any of the following discriminatory acts *against children:*

- Require, as a condition to the rental of a housing accommodation, that the prospective tenant shall not have one or more children under 18 residing in his or her family at the time the application for rental is made
- Insert in any lease a condition that terminates the lease if one or more children younger than age 18 are ever in the family occupying the housing

Any agreement or lease that contains a condition such as these is void as to that condition. That is, a lease will still be in force regardless of the fact that it may contain an invalid discriminatory clause; only the clause is void.

It is also a civil rights violation in Illinois to discriminate against any blind, hearing-impaired or physically handicapped person in the terms, conditions or privileges of sale or rental property. Similarly, it is a civil rights violation to refuse to sell or rent to a prospective buyer or tenant because he or she has a guide, hearing or support dog. Neither may a seller or landlord require the inclusion of any additional charge in a lease, rental agreement or contract of purchase or sale because a blind, hearing-impaired or physically handicapped person has a guide, hearing or support dog. Of course, the tenant or purchaser may be liable for any actual damage done to the premises by the animal.

The Illinois Human Rights Act defines an *elderly person* as anyone over the age of 40.

Exemptions. Certain individuals, property types and transactions are exempt from the antidiscriminatory provisions of the Human Rights Act:

- Private owners of single-family homes are exempt if (1) they own *fewer than three single-family homes* (including beneficial interests); (2) they were (or a member of their family was) the *last current resident of the home;* (3) the home was sold *without the use of a real estate salesperson or broker;* and (4) the home was sold *without the use of discriminatory advertising.*
- Owner-occupied apartment buildings of five units or less are exempt.
- Private rooms in a private home occupied by an owner or owner's family member are exempt.
- Reasonable local, state or federal restrictions limiting the maximum number of occupants permitted to occupy a dwelling are permitted.
- A religious organization, association or society (or any nonprofit institution or organization operated, controlled or supervised by or in conjunction with a religious organization, association or society) may limit the sale, rental or occupancy of dwellings owned or operated by it (for other than commercial reasons) to persons of the same religion or give preference to persons of the same religion. This exemption is limited: it does not apply if membership in the religion is restricted on account of race, color or national origin.
- Rental of rooms in a housing accommodation may be restricted to persons of one sex.
- Individuals who have been convicted by any court of illegally manufacturing or distributing controlled substances are not protected by the Human Rights Act's antidiscrimination provisions.

- Appraisers may take into consideration any factors *other than those based on unlawful discrimination or familial status* in furnishing appraisals.
- Housing for older persons is exempt from the act's provisions regarding nondiscrimination against individuals on the basis of familial status. "Housing for older persons" means housing that is (1) intended for and occupied solely by persons 62 years of age or older or (2) intended and operated for occupancy by persons 55 years of age or older and at least 80 percent of the occupied units are occupied by at least one person who is 55 or older. ∎

Threats or Acts of Violence

Being a real estate agent is not generally considered a dangerous occupation. However, some licensees may find themselves the targets of threats or violence merely for complying with fair housing laws. The federal Fair Housing Act of 1968 protects the rights of those who seek the benefits of the open housing law. It also protects owners, brokers and salespersons who aid or encourage the enjoyment of open housing rights. Threats, coercion and intimidation are punishable by criminal action. In such a case, the victim should report the incident immediately to the local police and to the nearest office of the Federal Bureau of Investigation.

IMPLICATIONS FOR BROKERS AND SALESPEOPLE

The real estate industry is largely responsible for creating and maintaining an open housing market. Brokers and salespersons are a community's real estate experts. Along with the privilege of profiting from real estate transactions come the social and legal responsibilities to ensure that everyone's civil rights are protected. The reputation of the industry cannot afford any appearance that its licensees are not committed to the principles of fair housing. Licensees and the industry must be publicly conspicuous in their equal opportunity efforts. Establishing relationships with community and fair housing groups to discuss common concerns and develop solutions to problems is a constructive activity. Moreover, a licensee who is active in helping to improve his or her community will earn a reputation for being a concerned citizen, which may well translate into a larger client base.

Fair housing is the law. The consequences for anyone who violates the law are serious. In addition to the financial penalties, a real estate broker's or salesperson's livelihood will be in danger if his or her license is suspended or revoked. That the offense was unintentional is no defense. Licensees must scrutinize their practices and be particularly careful not to fall victim to clients or customers who expect to discriminate.

All parties deserve the same standard of service. Everyone has the right to expect equal treatment, within his or her property requirements, financial ability and experience in the marketplace. A good test is to answer the question, "Are we doing this for everyone?" If an act is not performed consistently, or if an act affects some individuals differently from others, it could be construed as discriminatory. Standardized inventories of property listings, standardized criteria for financial qualification and written documentation of all conversations are three effective means of self-protection for licensees.

HUD requires that its fair housing posters be displayed in any place of business where real estate is offered for sale or rent. Following HUD's advertising procedures and using the fair housing slogan and logo keep the public aware of the broker's commitment to equal opportunity.

Beyond being the law, fair housing is good business. It ensures the greatest number of properties available for sale and rent and the largest possible pool of potential purchasers and tenants.

PROFESSIONAL ETHICS

Professional conduct involves more than just complying with the law. In real estate, state licensing laws establish those activities that are illegal and therefore prohibited. However, merely complying with the letter of the law may not be enough: licensees may perform legally yet not ethically. **Ethics** refers to a system of moral principles, rules and standards of conduct. The ethical system of a profession establishes conduct that goes beyond merely complying with the law. These moral principles address two sides of a profession:

1. They establish standards for integrity and competence in dealing with consumers of an industry's services.
2. They define a code of conduct for relations within the industry and among its professionals.

Code of Ethics

One way that many organizations address ethics among their members or in their respective businesses is by adopting codes of professional conduct. A **code of ethics** is a written system of standards for ethical conduct. The code contains statements designed to advise, guide and regulate job behavior. To be effective, a code of ethics must be specific by dictating rules that either prohibit or demand certain behavior. Lofty statements of positive goals are not especially helpful. By including sanctions for violators, a code of ethics becomes more effective.

The National Association of REALTORS® (NAR), the largest trade association in the country, adopted a Code of Ethics and Standards of Practice for its members in 1913. The code is reproduced in the Appendix. REALTORS® are expected to subscribe to this strict code of conduct. Not all licensees are REALTORS®—only those who are members of NAR. NAR has established procedures for professional standards committees at the local, state and national levels of the organization to administer compliance. Interpretations of the code are known as Standards of Practice. The Code of Ethics has proved helpful because it contains practical applications of business ethics. Many other professional organizations in the real estate industry also have codes of ethics. In addition, many state real estate commissions are required by law to establish codes or canons of ethical behavior for the states' licensees.

> A copy of the Code of Ethics and Standards of Practice may be obtained by writing the National Association of REALTORS® at 410 North Michigan Avenue, Chicago, Illinois 60811, or on the Internet at http://www.realtor.com.

In addition to having an established code of ethics, NAR and HUD have created "A Fair Housing Partnership Resolution" agreement that outlines their commitment to furthering the fair housing rights of all Americans. Contact your local REALTOR® chapter for more information.

SUMMARY

The federal regulations regarding equal opportunity in housing are contained principally in two laws. The Civil Rights Act of 1866 prohibits all racial discrimination, and the Fair Housing Act (Title VIII of the Civil Rights Act of 1968), as amended, prohibits discrimination on the basis of race, color, religion, sex, handicap, familial status or national origin in the sale, rental or financing of residential property. Discriminatory actions include refusing to deal with an individual or a specific group, changing any terms of a real estate or loan transaction, changing the services offered for any individual or group, creating statements or advertisements that indicate discriminatory restrictions or otherwise attempting to make a dwelling unavailable to any person or group because of race, color, religion, sex, handicap, familial status or national origin. The law also prohibits steering, blockbusting and redlining.

Complaints under the Fair Housing Act may be reported to and investigated by the Department of Housing and Urban Development (HUD). Such complaints also may be taken directly to U.S. district courts. In states and localities that have enacted fair housing legislation that is substantially equivalent to the federal law, complaints are handled by state and local agencies and state courts. Complaints under the Civil Rights Act of 1866 must be taken to federal courts.

A real estate business is only as good as its reputation. Real estate licensees can maintain good reputations by demonstrating good business ability and adhering to ethical standards of business practices. Many licensees subscribe to a code of ethics as members of professional real estate organizations.

In Illinois . . .

Licensees are required by law to adhere to the principles of equal opportunity in housing. Failure to comply with state and federal equal housing laws is grounds for license revocation in addition to other civil or criminal penalties.

The Illinois Human Rights Act bars discrimination on the basis of race, color, religion, national origin, ancestry, age, sex, marital status, physical disability, military service or unfavorable discharge, or familial status. ■

QUESTIONS

1. Which of the following actions is legally permitted?
   A. Advertising property for sale only to a special group
   B. Altering the terms of a loan for a member of a minority group
   C. Refusing to make a mortgage loan to a minority individual because of a poor credit history
   D. Telling a minority individual that an apartment has been rented when in fact it has not

2. Which of the following statements is true of complaints relating to the Civil Rights Act of 1866?
   A. They must be taken directly to federal courts.
   B. They are no longer reviewed in the courts.
   C. They are handled by HUD.
   D. They are handled by state enforcement agencies.

3. Why is the Civil Rights Act of 1866 unique?
   A. It has been broadened to protect the aged.
   B. It adds welfare recipients as a protected class.
   C. It contains "choose your neighbor" provisions.
   D. It provides no exceptions that would permit racial discrimination.

4. On a listing presentation a real estate agent said to the seller, who owned two residential properties, "I hear they are moving in and you'd better put your house on the market before values drop!" Has the agent violated fair housing law?
   A. Yes, and this example represents steering.
   B. Yes, and this example represents blockbusting.
   C. No, because the seller owns fewer than three houses.
   D. No, because the agent does not intend to publicly advertise the property.

5. A licensee entered into a buyer agency agreement with a person from Japan who was moving to America. The agent only showed him properties where it was obvious that other Japanese people lived. Has the agent violated fair housing law?
   A. Yes, and this example represents blockbusting.
   B. Yes, and this example represents steering.
   C. No, because a buyer from Japan would want to live in a Japanese neighborhood.
   D. No, because as a buyer agent it is the agent's responsibility to make decisions for the buyer.

6. A lender's refusal to lend money to potential homeowners attempting to purchase properties located in predominantly African American neighborhoods is known as:
   A. redlining.   C. steering.
   B. blockbusing.   D. qualifying.

7. Which of the following would NOT be permitted under the federal Fair Housing Act?
   A. The Harvard Club in New York rents rooms only to graduates of Harvard who belong to the club.
   B. The owner of a 20-unit residential apartment building rents to white men only.
   C. A Catholic convent refuses to furnish housing for a Jewish man.
   D. An owner refuses to rent the other side of her duplex to a family with children.

8. Nathan, a real estate broker, wants to end racial segregation. As an office policy, Nathan requires that salespersons show prospective buyers from racial or ethnic minority groups only properties that are in certain areas of town where few members of their groups currently live. Nathan prepares a map illustrating the appropriate neighborhoods for each racial or ethnic group. Through this

policy, Nathan hopes to achieve racial balance in residential housing. Which of the following statements is true regarding Nathan's policy?

A. While Nathan's policy may appear to constitute blockbusting, application of the effects test proves its legality.

B. Because the effect of Nathan's policy is discriminatory, it constitutes illegal steering regardless of his intentions.

C. Nathan's policy clearly shows the intent to discriminate.

D. While Nathan's policy may appear to constitute steering, application of the intent test proves its legality.

9. If a mortgage lender discriminates against a loan applicant on the basis of marital status, it violates what law?

A. ADA

B. Civil Rights Act of 1866

C. ECOA

D. Fair Housing Act

10. A Lithuanian American real estate broker offers a special discount to Lithuanian American clients. This practice is:

A. legal in certain circumstances.

B. illegal.

C. legal but ill-advised.

D. an example of steering.

11. Which of the following statements describes the Supreme Court's decision in the case of *Jones v. Alfred H. Mayer Company?*

A. Racial discrimination is prohibited by any party in the sale or rental of real estate.

B. Sales by individual residential homeowners are exempted, provided the owners do not use brokers.

C. Laws against discrimination apply only to federally related transactions.

D. Persons with disabilities are a protected class.

12. After a broker takes a listing of a residence, the owner specifies that he will not sell his home to any Asian family. The broker should do which of the following?

A. Advertise the property exclusively in Asian-language newspapers

B. Explain to the owner that the instruction violates federal law and that the broker cannot comply with it

C. Abide by the principal's directions despite the fact that they conflict with the fair housing laws

D. Require that the owner sign a separate legal document stating the additional instruction as an amendment to the listing agreement

13. The fine for a first violation of the federal Fair Housing Act could be as much as:

A. $500.   C. $5,000.

B. $1,000.   D. $10,000.

14. A single man with two small children has been told by a real estate salesperson that homes for sale in a condominium complex are available only to married couples with no children. Which of the following statements is true?

A. Because a single-parent family can be disruptive if the parent provides little supervision of the children, the condominium is permitted to discriminate against the family under the principle of rational basis.

B. Condominium complexes are exempt from the fair housing laws and can therefore restrict children.

C. The man may file a complaint alleging discrimination on the basis of familial status.

D. Restrictive covenants in a condominium take precedence over the fair housing laws.

15. The following ad appeared in the newspaper: "For sale: 4 BR brick home; Redwood School District; excellent Elm Street location; next door to St. John's Church and right on the bus line. Move-in condition; priced to sell."

Which of the following statements is true?

A. The ad describes the property for sale and is very appropriate.

B. The fair housing laws do not apply to newspaper advertising.

C. The ad should state that the property is available to families with children.

D. The ad should not mention St. John's Church.

16. A landlord rented an apartment to a handicapped person. With the landlord's permission, the tenant made changes to the unit. When the tenant moves, which of the following will the tenant LEAST LIKELY be required to return to its original condition?

A. Return the doors, which have been widened, to their original condition.

B. Return the kitchen cabinets, which have been lowered, to their original condition.

C. Return the light switches to their original position on the wall.

D. Remove the handrails in the bathroom.

In Illinois . . .

17. The Illinois Human Rights Act defines an elderly person as being how old?

A. 40   C. 68

B. 65   D. 70

18. When landlord Robert rented an apartment in his six-unit building to Charlotte and Len, he didn't notice that Charlotte was pregnant. After the baby was born, Robert canceled their lease, citing the no-children clause that had been inserted in it. Based on these facts, which of the following statements is true?

A. Robert is violating the Illinois Human Rights Act regarding the exclusion of children.

B. Robert is acting legally under an exemption to the Illinois Human Rights Act.

C. Robert must give Charlotte and Len 60 days in which to find a new apartment.

D. Robert may refuse to rent to families with children only if he lives in the building.

19. Lydia owns two multiunit apartment buildings: a two-flat on Oak Street and a 12-unit building on Main Street. She lives in an apartment in the Main Street property. Which of Lydia's properties, if any, is exempt from the Illinois Human Rights Act?

A. The Oak Street property only

B. The Main Street property only

C. Neither property

D. Both properties

Environmental Issues and the Real Estate Transaction

KEY TERMS

asbestos	electromagnetic field	retroactive liability
capping	encapsulation	strict liability
carbon monoxide	groundwater	underground storage
Comprehensive	joint and several	tank
Environmental	liability	UFFI
Response,	landfill	urea-formaldehyde
Compensation, and	lead	water table
Liability Act	radon	

ENVIRONMENTAL ISSUES

Most states, including Illinois, have recognized the need to balance the legitimate commercial use of land with the need to preserve vital resources and protect the quality of the states' air, water and soil. A growing number of homebuyers base their decisions in part on the desire for fresh air, clean water and outdoor recreational opportunities. Preservation of a state's environment both enhances the quality of life and helps strengthen property values. The prevention and cleanup of pollutants and toxic wastes not only revitalize the land, but create greater opportunities for responsible development.

In Illinois . . .

The Illinois Environmental Protection Agency (IEPA) is charged with maintaining and enhancing the state's air, land and water quality through education, inspection, regulation, enforcement, recycling and prevention activities. The Pollution Control Board and Hazardous Waste Advisory Council are two of the many bodies created to assist the IEPA in specific areas. State agricultural, transportation and energy agencies (among others) also have specific environmental protection responsibilities. Most Illinois environmental regulations are required by statute to be "identical in substance" to environmental protection regulations established by the U.S. Environmental Protection Agency (EPA). ■

Environmental issues have become an important factor in the practice of real estate. Consumers are becoming more health conscious and safety concerned and are enforcing their rights to make informed decisions. Scientists are learning more about our environment, and consumers are reacting by demanding that their surroundings be free of chemical hazards. These developments affect not only sales transactions but also appraisers, developers, lending institutions and property managers.

Real estate licensees must be alert to the existence of environmental hazards. Although it is important to ensure the health and safety of a property's user, the burden for disclosure or elimination of hazards seems to arise at the time the ownership of property transfers. This creates added liability for real estate practitioners if the presence of a toxic substance causes a health problem. If a property buyer suffers physical harm because of the substance, the licensee can be vulnerable to a personal injury suit in addition to other legal liability. Environmental issues are health issues, and health issues based on environmental hazards have become real estate issues. For this reason, it is extremely important that licensees not only make property disclosures but also see that prospective purchasers get authoritative information about hazardous substances so that they can make informed decisions.

Licensees should be familiar with state and federal environmental laws and the regulatory agencies that enforce them. Licensees are not expected to have the technical expertise necessary to determine whether a hazardous substance is present. However, they must be aware of environmental issues and take steps to ensure that the interests of all parties involved in real estate transactions are protected.

HAZARDOUS SUBSTANCES

Pollution and hazardous substances in the environment are of interest to real estate licensees because they affect the attractiveness, desirability and market value of cities, neighborhoods and backyards. A toxic environment is not a place where anyone would want to live. (See Figure 22.1.)

Asbestos   **Asbestos** is a mineral that once was used as insulation because it was resistant to fire and contained heat effectively. Before 1978 (the year when the use of asbestos insulation was banned), asbestos was found in most residential construction. It was a component of more than 3,000 types of building materials. The EPA estimates that about 20 percent of the nation's commercial and public buildings contain asbestos.

Today, we know that inhaling microscopic asbestos fibers can result in a variety of respiratory diseases. The presence of asbestos insulation alone is not necessarily a health hazard. Asbestos is harmful only if it is disturbed or exposed, as often occurs during renovation or remodeling. Asbestos is highly friable. This means that as it ages, asbestos fibers break down easily into tiny filaments and particles. When these particles become airborne, they pose a risk to humans. Airborne asbestos contamination is most prevalent in public and commercial buildings, including schools. If the asbestos fibers in the indoor air of a building reach a dangerous level, the building becomes difficult to lease, finance or insure. No safe level of asbestos exposure has been determined.

Asbestos insulation can create airborne contaminants that may result in respiratory diseases.

Asbestos contamination also can be found in residential properties. It was used to cover pipes, ducts and heating and hot water units. Its fire-resistant properties made it a popular material for use in floor tile, exterior siding and roofing products. Though it may be easy to identify asbestos when it is visible

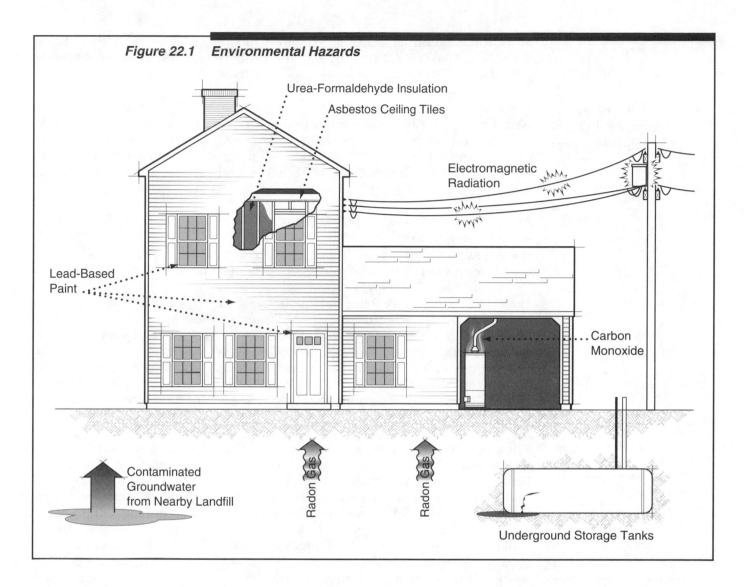

Figure 22.1   Environmental Hazards

(for instance, when it is wrapped around heating and water pipes), identification may be more difficult when it is behind walls or under floors.

Asbestos is costly to remove because the process requires state-licensed technicians and specially sealed environments. In addition, removal itself may be dangerous: improper removal procedures may further contaminate the air within the structure. The waste generated should be disposed of at a licensed facility, which further adds to the cost of removal. **Encapsulation,** or the sealing off of disintegrating asbestos, is an alternate method of asbestos control that may be preferable to removal in certain circumstances. However, an owner must periodically monitor the condition of the encapsulated asbestos to make sure it is not disintegrating.

Tests can be conducted to determine the level of airborne asbestos to provide an accurate disclosure in a sales transaction. A more thorough analysis of a building can be performed by an engineer skilled in identifying the presence of materials that contain asbestos. Either of these approaches can satisfy the concerns of a consumer. Appraisers also should be aware of the possible presence of asbestos.

More information on asbestos-related issues is available from the EPA at 202-554-1404. In addition, the EPA has numerous publications that provide guidance, information and assistance with asbestos issues.

Lead-Based Paint and Other Lead Hazards

Lead was used as a pigment and drying agent in alkyd oil-based paint. Lead-based paint may be on any interior or exterior surface, but it is particularly common on doors, windows and other woodwork. The federal government estimates that lead is present in about 75 percent of all private housing built before 1978; that's approximately 57 million homes, ranging from low-income apartments to million-dollar mansions.

An elevated level of lead in the body can cause serious damage to the brain, kidneys, nervous system and red blood cells. The degree of harm is related to the amount of exposure and the age at which a person is exposed. The blood lead levels of as many as one in six children may be dangerously high.

Lead dust can be ingested from the hands by a crawling infant, inhaled by any occupant of a structure or ingested from the water supply because of lead pipes or lead solder. In fact, lead particles can be present elsewhere, too. Soil and groundwater may be contaminated by everything from lead plumbing in leaking landfills to discarded skeet and bullets from an old shooting range. High levels of lead have been found in the soil near waste-to-energy incinerators. The air may be contaminated by leaded gasoline fumes from gas stations or automobile exhausts.

> *Lead* from paint or other sources can result in damage to the brain, nervous system, kidneys and blood.

The use of lead-based paint was banned in 1978. Licensees who are involved in the sale, management, financing or appraisal of properties constructed before 1978 face potential liability for any personal injury that might be suffered by an occupant. Numerous legislative efforts affect licensees, sellers and landlords. There is considerable controversy about practical approaches for handling the presence of lead-based paint. Some suggest that it should be removed; others argue that it should be encapsulated; still others advocate testing to determine the amount of lead present, which then would be disclosed to a prospective owner or resident. In many states, only licensed lead inspectors, abatement contractors, risk assessors, abatement project designers and abatement workers may deal with the removal or encapsulation of lead in a structure.

In Illinois . . .

Anyone who performs lead abatement or mitigation activities without a license is guilty of a Class A misdemeanor. The Department of Public Health (DPH) oversees the qualifying, training and licensing of lead abatement contractors and lead abatement workers in Illinois. ■

No federal law requires that homeowners test for the presence of lead-based paint. However, known lead-based paint hazards must be disclosed. In 1996, the EPA and the Department of Housing and Urban Development (HUD) issued final regulations requiring disclosure of the presence of any known lead-based paint hazards to potential buyers or renters. Under the *Lead-Based Paint Hazard Reduction Act,* persons selling or leasing residential housing constructed before 1978 must disclose the presence of known lead-based paint and provide purchasers or tenants with any relevant records or reports. A lead-based paint disclosure statement must be attached to all sales contracts and leases regarding residential properties built before 1978, and a lead hazard pamphlet must be distributed to all buyers and tenants. (See Figure 22.2.)

Figure 22.2   Disclosure of Lead-Based Paint and Lead-Based Paint Hazards

LEAD-BASED PAINT OR LEAD-BASED PAINT HAZARD ADDENDUM

It is a condition of this contract that, until midnight of _____ , Buyer shall have the right to obtain a risk assessment or inspection of the Property for the presence of lead-based paint and/or lead-based paint hazards* at Buyer's expense. This contingency will terminate at that time unless Buyer or Buyer's agent delivers to the Seller or Seller's agent a written inspection and/or risk assessment report listing the specific existing deficiencies and corrections needed, if any. If any corrections are necessary, Seller shall have the option of (i) completing them, (ii) providing for their completion, or (iii) refusing to complete them. If Seller elects not to complete or provide for completion of the corrections, then Buyer shall have the option of (iv) accepting the Property in its present condition, or (v) terminating this contract, in which case all earnest monies shall be refunded to Buyer. Buyer may waive the right to obtain a risk assessment or inspection of the Property for the presence of lead-based paint and/or lead based paint hazards at any time without cause.

*Intact lead-based paint that is in good condition is not necessarily a hazard. See EPA pamphlet "Protect Your Family From Lead in Your Home" for more information.

Disclosure of Information on Lead-Based Paint and Lead-Based Paint Hazards

Lead Warning Statement
Every Buyer of any interest in residential real property on which a residential dwelling was built prior to 1978 is notified that such property may present exposure to lead from lead-based paint that may place young children at risk of developing lead poisoning. Lead poisoning in young children may produce permanent neurological damage, including learning disabilities, reduced intelligence quotient, behavioral problems, and impaired memory. Lead poisoning also poses a particular risk to pregnant women. The Seller of any interest in residential real property is required to provide the Buyer with any information on lead-based paint hazards from risk assessments or inspections in the Seller's possession and notify the Buyer of any known lead-based paint hazards. A risk assessment or inspection for possible lead-based paint hazards is recommended prior to purchase.

Seller's Disclosure (initial)
_____ (a) Presence of lead-based paint and/or lead-based paint hazards (check one below):
❑ Known lead-based paint and/or lead-based paint hazards are present in the housing (explain).

_____

❑ Seller has no knowledge of lead-based paint and/or lead-based paint hazards in the housing.
_____ (b) Records and reports available to the Seller (check one below):
❑ Seller has provided the Buyer with all available records and reports pertaining to lead-based paint and/or lead-based paint hazards in the housing (list documents below).

_____

❑ Seller has no reports or records pertaining to lead-based paint and/or lead-based paint hazards in the housing.

Buyer's Acknowledgment (initial)
_____ (c) Buyer has received copies of all information listed above.
_____ (d) Buyer has received the pamphlet *Protect Your Family from Lead in Your Home.*
_____ (e) Buyer has (check one below):
❑ Received a 10-day opportunity (or mutually agreed upon period) to conduct a risk assessment or inspection for the presence of lead-based paint and/or lead-based paint hazards; or
❑ Waived the opportunity to conduct a risk assessment or inspection for the presence of lead-based paint and/or lead-based paint hazards.

Agent's Acknowledgment (initial)
_____ (f) Agent has informed the Seller of the Seller's obligations under 42 U.S.C. 4582(d) and is aware of his/her responsibility to ensure compliance.

Certification of Accuracy
The following parties have reviewed the information above and certify, to the best of their knowledge, that the information provided by the signatory is true and accurate.
Buyer: _____ (SEAL) Date _____
Buyer: _____ (SEAL) Date _____
Agent: _____ Date _____
Seller: _____ (SEAL) Date _____
Seller: _____ (SEAL) Date _____
Agent: _____ Date _____

Purchasers must be given ten days in which to conduct risk assessments or inspections for lead-based paint or lead-based paint hazards. Purchasers are not bound by any real estate contract until the ten-day period has expired. The regulations specifically require that real estate agents ensure that all parties comply with the law.

EPA guidance pamphlets and other information about lead-based hazards are available from the National Lead Information Center at 800-424-5323.

In Illinois . . .

The *Illinois Lead Poisoning Prevention Act* (410 ILCS 45) requires that physicians screen children younger than six years old for lead poisoning when the child lives in an area considered by the state to be at "high risk" for lead exposure. *High-risk areas* include slum and blighted housing, proximity to highway or heavy local traffic, proximity to a lead-using or lead-generating industry, incidence of elevated blood lead levels, poverty and the number of young children in the area.

When a child (or any other person who lives in a high-risk area) is diagnosed as having an elevated level of lead in his or her bloodstream, the physician must report the condition to the DPH. After notification, the DPH may inspect the child's residence for the existence of exposed lead-bearing substances (including dust, paint and metal). If the inspection identifies a lead hazard, the property owner is required to mitigate the condition within 90 days (30 days if the blood report is from, or the dwelling unit is occupied by, a child under six or a pregnant woman). Mitigation activities involving the destruction or disturbance of a leaded surface must be conducted by a licensed lead abatement contractor using licensed lead abatement workers. The owner will receive a certificate of compliance once the DPH is satisfied that the lead hazard has been removed.

An owner who has received a lead mitigation notice must provide any prospective lessees for the affected unit with a written notice of the existence of an identified lead hazard. In addition, all owners of residential buildings or units must give current and prospective lessees information on the potential health hazards posed by lead and a copy of an informational brochure. ■

Radon

Radon is a radioactive gas produced by the natural decay of other radioactive substances. Although radon can occur anywhere, some areas are known to have abnormally high amounts. The eastern United States is especially rich in radon. If radon dissipates into the atmosphere, it is not likely to cause harm. However, when radon enters buildings and is trapped in high concentrations (usually in basements with inadequate ventilation), it can cause health problems.

Opinions differ as to minimum safe levels. But growing evidence suggests that radon may be the most underestimated cause of lung cancer, particularly for children, individuals who smoke and those who spend considerable time indoors.

Because radon is odorless and tasteless, it is impossible to detect without testing. Care should be exercised in the manner in which tests are conducted to ensure that the results are accurate. Radon levels vary, depending on the amount of fresh air that circulates through a house, the weather conditions and the time of year. It is relatively easy to reduce levels of radon by installing ventilation systems or exhaust fans.

Interestingly, the modern practice of creating energy-efficient homes and buildings with practically airtight walls and windows may increase the potential for radon gas accumulation. Once radon accumulates in a basement, efficient heating and ventilation systems can rapidly spread the gas throughout the building.

Radon is a naturally occurring gas that is a suspected cause of lung cancer.

Home radon-detection kits are available, although more accurate testing can be conducted by radon-detection professionals. The EPA's pamphlet, "A Citizen's Guide to Radon," is available from your local EPA office.

Urea-Formaldehyde

Urea-formaldehyde was first used in building materials, particularly insulation, in the 1970s. Gases leak out of the urea-formaldehyde foam insulation (**UFFI**) as it hardens and become trapped in the interior of a building. In 1982, the Consumer Product Safety Commission banned the use of UFFI. The ban was reduced to a warning after courts determined that there was insufficient evidence to support a ban. Urea-formaldehyde is known to cause cancer in animals, though the evidence of its effect on humans is inconclusive.

UFFI is an insulating foam that can release harmful formaldehyde gases.

Formaldehyde does cause some individuals to suffer respiratory problems as well as eye and skin irritations. Consumers are becoming increasingly wary of the presence of formaldehyde, particularly if they are sensitive to it.

Because UFFI has received considerable adverse publicity, many buyers express concern about purchasing properties in which it was installed. Tests can be conducted to determine the level of formaldehyde gas in a house. Again, however, care should be exercised to ensure that the results of the tests are accurate and that the source of the gases is properly identified. Elevated levels could be due to a source other than the insulation.

Licensees should be careful that any conditions in an agreement of sale that require tests for formaldehyde are worded properly to identify the purpose for which the tests are being conducted, such as to determine the presence of the insulation or to identify some other source. Appraisers should also be aware of the presence of UFFI.

Carbon Monoxide

Carbon monoxide (CO) is a colorless, odorless gas that occurs due to incomplete combustion as a by-product of burning such fuels as wood, oil and natural gas. Furnaces, water heaters, space heaters, fireplaces and wood stoves all produce CO as a natural result of combustion. When these appliances function properly and are properly ventilated, their CO emissions are not a problem. However, when improper ventilation or equipment malfunctions permit large quantities of CO to be released into a residence or commercial structure, it poses a significant health hazard. Its effects are compounded by the fact that CO is so difficult to detect. CO is quickly absorbed by the body. It inhibits the blood's ability to transport oxygen and results in dizziness and nausea. As the concentrations of CO increase, the symptoms become more severe. More than 200 deaths from carbon monoxide poisoning occur each year.

Carbon monoxide is a by-product of fuel combustion that may result in death in poorly ventilated areas.

Carbon monoxide detectors are available, and their use is mandatory in some areas. Annual maintenance of heating systems also helps avoid CO exposure.

In Illinois . . .

The city of Chicago (and other municipalities throughout the state) requires that all residences be equipped with working carbon monoxide detectors. ■

Electromagnetic Fields

EMFs are produced by electrical currents and may be related to a variety of health complaints.

Electromagnetic fields (EMFs) are generated by the movement of electrical currents. The use of any electrical appliance creates a small field of electromagnetic radiation; clock radios, blow-driers, televisions and computers all produce EMFs. The major concern regarding EMFs involves high-tension power lines. The EMFs produced by these high-voltage lines, as well as by secondary distribution lines and transformers, are suspected of causing cancer, hormonal changes and behavioral abnormalities. There is considerable controversy (and much conflicting evidence) about whether EMFs pose a health hazard. The most recent studies suggest that only very high levels pose any possible danger. However, buyers who are aware of the controversy may be unwilling to purchase property near power lines or transformers. As research into EMFs continues, real estate licensees should stay informed about current findings.

GROUNDWATER CONTAMINATION

Groundwater is the water that exists under the earth's surface within the tiny spaces or crevices in geological formations. Groundwater forms the **water table,** the natural level at which the ground is saturated. This may be near the surface (in areas where the water table is very high) or several hundred feet underground. Surface water also can be absorbed into the groundwater.

Any contamination of the underground water can threaten the supply of pure, clean water for private wells or public water systems. If groundwater is not protected from contamination, the earth's natural filtering systems may be inadequate to ensure the availability of pure water. Numerous state and federal laws have been enacted to preserve and protect the water supply.

Water can be contaminated from a number of sources. Runoff from waste disposal sites, leaking underground storage tanks and pesticides and herbicides are some of the main culprits. Because water flows from one place to another, contamination can spread far from its source. Numerous regulations are designed to protect against water contamination. Once contamination has been identified, its source can be eliminated. The water may eventually become clean. However, the process can be time-consuming and extremely expensive.

In Practice

Real estate agents need to be aware of potential groundwater contamination sources both on and off a property. These include underground storage tanks, septic systems, holding ponds, drywells, buried materials and surface spills. Remember, because groundwater flows over wide areas, the source of contamination may not be nearby.

UNDERGROUND STORAGE TANKS

Approximately 3 million to 5 million **underground storage tanks** (USTs) exist in the United States. Underground storage tanks are commonly found on sites where petroleum products are used or where gas stations and auto repair shops are located. They also may be found in a number of other commercial and industrial establishments—including printing and chemical plants, wood treatment plants, paper mills, paint manufacturers, dry cleaners and food processing plants—for storing chemical or other process waste. Military bases and airports are also common sites for underground tanks. In residential areas, they are used to store heating oil.

Some tanks are currently in use, but many are long forgotten. It is an unfortunate fact that it was once common to dispose of toxic wastes by simple burial: out of sight, out of mind. Over time, however, neglected tanks may leak hazardous substances into the environment. This permits contaminants to pollute not only the soil around the tank but also adjacent parcels and groundwater. Licensees should be particularly alert to the presence of fill pipes, vent lines, stained soil and fumes or odors, any of which may indicate the presence of a UST. Detection, removal and cleanup of surrounding contaminated soil can be an expensive operation.

FOR EXAMPLE In the 1940s, a gas station in a small town in northeastern Illinois went out of business. The building fell into disrepair and was torn down. The site was vacant for several years, and its former use was forgotten. A series of commercial ventures were built on the land: a grocery store, a drive-in restaurant, a convenience store. In the late 1980s, residents of the town began noticing strong gasoline fumes in their basements, particularly after a rainstorm. Government investigators concluded that the gasoline tanks buried beneath the former gas station had broken down with age and leaked their contents into the soil. Because the town was located over a large subsurface rock slab, the gasoline could not leach down into the soil but rather was forced to spread out under the entire town and surrounding farmland. Because the water table floated on the rock slab and the gasoline floated on the water, rains that raised the water table forced the gasoline into the soil near the residents' basements and crawlspaces, resulting in the unpleasant and potentially unhealthy fumes. When the gasoline fumes ignited and destroyed a local manufacturing plant, the residents learned that the problem was not only unpleasant but dangerous as well.

Recent state and federal laws impose very strict requirements on landowners to detect and correct leaks in an effort to protect the groundwater. The federal UST program is regulated by the EPA. The regulations apply to tanks that contain hazardous substances or liquid petroleum products and that store at least 10 percent of their volume underground. UST owners are required to register their tanks and adhere to strict technical and administrative requirements that govern

- installation,
- maintenance,
- corrosion prevention,
- overspill prevention,
- monitoring and
- record keeping.

Owners also are required to demonstrate that they have sufficient financial resources to cover any damage that might result from leaks.

The following types of tanks are among those that are exempt from the federal regulations:

- Tanks that hold less than 110 gallons
- Farm and residential tanks that hold 1,100 gallons or less of motor fuel used for noncommercial purposes
- Tanks that store heating oil burned on the premises

- Tanks on or above the floor of underground areas such as basements or tunnels
- Septic tanks and systems for collecting stormwater and wastewater

Some states have adopted laws regulating underground storage tanks that are more stringent than the federal laws.

In addition to being aware of possible noncompliance with state and federal regulations, the parties to a real estate transaction should be aware that many older tanks have never been registered. There may be no visible sign of their presence.

In Illinois . . .

The Leaking Underground Storage Tank (LUST) program governs the detection, identification, monitoring, mitigation and removal of buried underground storage tanks (particularly those containing petroleum products). The program is administered by the state fire marshal and the IEPA and is authorized to disburse money from a special fund to assist property owners in complying with mandatory remediation activities. The fund derives from permit fees, fines and payments required under such acts as the *Motor Fuel Tax Law* and the *Environmental Impact Fee Law*. ■

WASTE DISPOSAL SITES

Americans produce vast quantities of garbage every day. Despite public and private recycling and composting efforts, huge piles of waste materials—from beer cans, junk mail and diapers to food, paint and toxic chemicals—must be disposed of. Landfill operations have become the main receptacles for garbage and refuse. Special hazardous waste disposal sites have been established to contain radioactive waste from nuclear power plants, toxic chemicals and waste materials produced by medical, scientific and industrial processes.

Perhaps the most prevalent method of common waste disposal is simply to bury it. A **landfill** is an enormous hole, either excavated for the purpose of waste disposal or left over from surface mining operations. The hole is lined with clay or a synthetic liner to prevent leakage of waste material into the water supply. A system of underground drainage pipes permits monitoring of leaks and leaching. Waste is laid on the liner at the bottom of the excavation, and a layer of topsoil is then compacted onto the waste. The layering procedure is repeated again and again until the landfill is full, the layers mounded up sometimes as high as several hundred feet over the surrounding landscape. **Capping** is the process of laying two to four feet of soil over the top of the site and then planting grass or some other vegetation to enhance the landfill's aesthetic value and to prevent erosion. A ventilation pipe runs from the landfill's base through the cap to vent off accumulated natural gases created by the decomposing waste.

Federal, state and local regulations govern the location, construction, content and maintenance of landfill sites. Test wells around landfill operations are installed to constantly monitor the groundwater in the surrounding area, and soil analyses can be used to test for contamination. Completed landfills have been used for such purposes as parks and golf courses. Rapid suburban growth has resulted in many housing developments and office campuses being built on landfill sites. However, problems can arise from these uses.

FOR EXAMPLE A suburban office building constructed on an old landfill site was very popular until its parking lot began to sink. While the structure itself was supported by pilings driven deep into the ground, the parking lot was unsupported. As the landfill beneath it compacted, the wide concrete lot sank lower and lower around the building. Each year, the building's management had to relandscape to cover the exposed foundations. The sinking parking lot eventually severed underground phone and power lines and water mains, causing the tenants considerable inconvenience. Computers were offline for hours, and flooding was frequent on the ground floor. Finally, leaking gases from the landfill began causing unpleasant odors. The tenants moved out, and the building was left vacant, a victim of poorly conceived landfill design.

Hazardous and radioactive waste disposal sites are subject to strict state and federal regulation to prevent the escape of toxic substances into the surrounding environment. Some materials, such as radioactive waste, are sealed in containers and placed in "tombs" buried deep underground. The tombs are designed to last thousands of years and are built according to strict federal and state regulations. These disposal sites are usually limited to extremely remote locations, well away from populated areas or farmland.

The Midwest Interstate Compact on Low-Level Radioactive Waste is one example of a regional approach to the disposal of hazardous materials. The states of Delaware, Illinois, Indiana, Iowa, Kansas, Kentucky, Maryland, Michigan, Minnesota, Missouri, Nebraska, North Dakota, Ohio, South Dakota, Virginia and Wisconsin have agreed to cooperate in establishing and managing regional low-level radioactive waste sites. This approach allows the participants to share the costs, benefits, obligations and inconveniences of radioactive waste disposal in a fair and reasonable way.

In Illinois . . .

The construction and maintenance of waste disposal sites are regulated by statute (415 ILCS 5/20 et seq.). In establishing regulations, the legislature stated that the purpose of the law is

> to prevent the pollution or misuse of land, to promote the conservation of natural resources and minimize environmental damage by reducing the difficulty of disposal of wastes and encouraging and effecting the recycling and reuse of waste materials, and upgrading waste collection, treatment, storage and disposal practices. . . . ■

In Practice

Environmental issues have a significant impact on the real estate industry. In 1995, a jury awarded $6.7 million to homeowners whose property values had been lowered because of the defendant tire company's negligent operation and maintenance of a hazardous waste dump site. The 1,713 plaintiffs relied on testimony from economists and a real estate appraiser to demonstrate how news stories about the site had lowered the market values of their homes. Nationwide, some landfill operators now offer price guarantees to purchasers of homes near waste disposal sites. Similarly, a recent university study found that a home's value increases by more than $6,000 for each mile of its distance from a garbage incinerator.

CERCLA AND ENVIRONMENTAL PROTECTION

The majority of legislation dealing with environmental problems has been instituted within the past two decades. Although the EPA was created at the federal level to oversee such problems, several other federal agencies' areas of concern generally overlap. The federal laws were created to encourage state and local governments to enact their own legislation.

Comprehensive Environmental Response, Compensation, and Liability Act

The ***Comprehensive Environmental Response, Compensation, and Liability Act** (CERCLA) was created in 1980. It established a fund of $9 billion, called the Superfund,* to clean up uncontrolled hazardous waste sites and to respond to spills. It created a process for identifying potential responsible parties (PRPs) and ordering them to take responsibility for the cleanup action. CERCLA is administered and enforced by the EPA.

Liability. A landowner is liable under CERCLA when a release or a threat of release of a hazardous substance has occurred on his or her property. Regardless of whether the contamination is the result of the landowner's actions or those of others, the owner can be held responsible for the cleanup. This liability includes the cleanup not only of the landowner's property but also of any neighboring property that has been contaminated. A landowner who is not responsible for the contamination can seek recovery reimbursement for the cleanup cost from previous landowners, any other responsible party or the Superfund. However, if other parties are not available, even a landowner who did not cause the problem could be solely responsible for the costs.

Once the EPA determines that hazardous material has been released into the environment, it is authorized to begin remedial action. First, it attempts to identify the PRPs. If the PRPs agree to cooperate in the cleanup, they must agree about how to divide the cost. If the PRPs do not voluntarily undertake the cleanup, the EPA may hire its own contractors to do the necessary work. The EPA then bills the PRPs for the cost. If the PRPs refuse to pay, the EPA can seek damages in court for up to three times the actual cost of the cleanup.

Liability under the Superfund is considered to be strict, joint and several, and retroactive. **Strict liability** means that the owner is responsible to the injured party without excuse. **Joint and several liability** means that each of the individual owners is personally responsible for the total damages. If only one of the owners is financially able to handle the total damages, that owner must pay the total and collect the proportionate shares from the other owners whenever possible. **Retroactive liability** means that the liability is not limited to the current owner but includes people who have owned the site in the past.

Superfund Amendments and Reauthorization Act

In 1986, the U.S. Congress reauthorized the *Superfund Amendments and Reauthorization Act* (SARA). The amended statute contains stronger cleanup standards for contaminated sites and five times the funding of the original Superfund, which expired in September 1985.

The amended act also sought to clarify the obligations of lenders. As mentioned, liability under the Superfund extends to both the present and all previous owners of the contaminated site. Real estate lenders found themselves either as present owners or somewhere in the chain of ownership through foreclosure proceedings.

The amendments created a concept called innocent landowner immunity. It was recognized that in certain cases, a landowner in the chain of ownership was completely innocent of all wrongdoing and therefore should not be held liable. The innocent landowner immunity clause established the criteria by which to judge whether a person or business could be exempted from liability. The criteria included the following:

- The pollution was caused by a third party.
- The property was acquired after the fact.
- The landowner had no actual or constructive knowledge of the damage.
- Due care was exercised when the property was purchased (the landowner made a reasonable search, called an *environmental site assessment*) to determine that no damage to the property existed.
- Reasonable precautions were taken in the exercise of ownership rights.

LIABILITY OF REAL ESTATE PROFESSIONALS

Environmental law is a relatively new phenomenon. Although federal and state laws have defined many of the liabilities involved, common law is being used for further interpretation. The real estate professional and all others involved in a real estate transaction must be aware of both actual and potential liability.

Sellers, as mentioned earlier, often carry the most exposure. Innocent landowners might be held responsible, even though they did not know about the presence of environmental hazards. Purchasers may be held liable, even if they didn't cause the contamination. Lenders may end up owning worthless assets if owners default on the loans rather than undertaking expensive cleanup efforts. Real estate licensees could be held liable for improper disclosure; therefore, it is necessary to be aware of the potential environmental risks from neighboring properties, such as gas stations, manufacturing plants or even funeral homes.

Additional exposure is created for individuals involved in other aspects of real estate transactions. For example, real estate appraisers must identify and adjust for environmental problems. Adjustments to market value typically reflect the cleanup cost plus a factor of the degree of panic and suspicion that exist in the current market. Although the sales price can be affected dramatically, it is possible that the underlying market value would remain relatively equal to others in the neighborhood. The real estate appraiser's greatest responsibility is to the lender, who depends on the appraiser to identify environmental hazards. Although the lender may be protected under certain conditions through the 1986 amendments to the Superfund Act, the lender must be aware of any potential problems and may require additional environmental reports.

Insurance carriers also might be affected in the transactions. Mortgage insurance companies protect lenders' mortgage investments and might be required to carry part of the ultimate responsibility in cases of loss. More important, hazard insurance carriers might be directly responsible for damages if such coverage was included in the initial policy.

Discovery of Environmental Hazards

Real estate licensees are not expected to have the technical expertise necessary to discover the presence of environmental hazards. However, because they are presumed by the public to have special knowledge about real estate, licensees must be aware both of possible hazards and of where to seek professional help.

Obviously, the first step for a licensee is to ask the owner. He or she already may have conducted tests for carbon monoxide or radon. The owner also may be aware of a potential hazardous condition. An environmental hazard actually can be turned into a marketing plus if the owner has already done the detection and abatement work. Potential buyers can be assured that an older home is no longer a lead paint or an asbestos risk.

The most appropriate people on whom a licensee can rely for sound environmental information are scientific or technical experts. Environmental auditors can provide the most comprehensive studies. Their services usually are relied on by developers and purchasers of commercial and industrial properties. An environmental audit includes the property's history of use and the results of extensive and complex tests of the soil, water, air and structures. Trained inspectors conduct air-sampling tests to detect radon, asbestos or EMFs. They can test soil and water quality and can inspect for lead-based paints (lead inspections required by the Residential Lead-Based Paint Hazard Reduction Act must be conducted by certified inspectors). While environmental auditors may be called on at any stage in a transaction, they are most frequently brought in as a condition of closing. Not only can such experts detect environmental problems, they usually can offer guidance about how best to resolve the conditions.

Disclosure of Environmental Hazards

State laws address the issue of disclosure of known material facts regarding a property's condition. These same rules apply to the presence of environmental hazards. A real estate licensee may be liable if he or she should have known of a condition, even if the seller neglected to disclose it.

In Illinois . . .

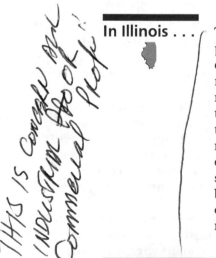

THIS IS concern on INDUSTRIAL property of Commercial Prop

The *Illinois Responsible Property Transfer Act* is intended to ensure that all parties involved in certain real estate transactions are aware of the existence of specific environmental conditions and liabilities associated with contaminated property. The act does not apply to single family or multiple-unit residences, residential condominiums or other residential property, unless the property has underground storage tanks. Specifically, this act requires the seller to deliver to the buyer not later than 30 days prior to the transfer of real property a disclosure statement that reveals any knowledge of a release or substantial threat of a release of a hazardous substance. If the disclosure statement reveals environmental defects that previously were unknown to the buyer or seller, or if the seller does not deliver a disclosure statement, then either party may renegotiate the contract within 10 days after demand for or receipt of the disclosure statement. ■

SUMMARY

Environmental issues are important to real estate licensees because they may affect real estate transactions by raising issues of health risks or cleanup costs. Some of the principal environmental toxins include asbestos, lead, radon and urea-formaldehyde insulation.

Licensees who are involved with the sale, management, financing or appraisal of properties constructed before 1978 should be aware of potential lead-based paint in the structures, as well as other environmental hazards.

Landfills are the most common method of disposing of solid waste materials by layering them between several feet of soil. Improperly constructed or maintained landfills may present a danger to groundwater.

CERCLA established the Superfund to finance the cleanup of hazardous waste disposal sites. Under the Superfund, liability for those found to have created unlawful hazardous waste sites is strict, joint and several, and retroactive.

QUESTIONS

1. Asbestos is most dangerous when it:
   A. is used as insulation.
   B. crumbles and becomes airborne.
   C. gets wet.
   D. is wrapped around heating and water pipes.

2. *Encapsulation* refers to the:
   A. process of sealing a landfill with three to four feet of topsoil.
   B. way in which asbestos insulation is applied to pipes and wiring systems.
   C. method of sealing disintegrating asbestos.
   D. way in which asbestos becomes airborne.

3. Jerry is a real estate salesman. He shows a pre–World War I house to Theresa, a prospective buyer. Theresa has two toddlers and is worried about potential health hazards. Which of the following is true?
   A. There is a risk that urea-foam insulation was used in the original construction.
   B. Because Jerry is a licensed real estate salesman, he can offer to inspect for lead and remove any lead risks.
   C. Because the house was built before 1978, there is a good likelihood of the presence of lead-based paint.
   D. Lead poisoning occurs only when lead paint chips are chewed and swallowed.

4. Which of the following is true regarding asbestos?
   A. The removal of asbestos can cause further contamination of a building.
   B. Asbestos causes health problems only when it is eaten.
   C. The level of asbestos in a building is affected by weather conditions.
   D. HUD requires all asbestos-containing materials to be removed from all residential buildings.

5. Which of the following best describes the water table?
   A. Natural level at which the ground is saturated
   B. Level at which underground storage tanks may be safely buried
   C. Measuring device used by specialists to measure groundwater contamination
   D. Always underground

6. All of the following are true of electromagnetic fields EXCEPT that electromagnetic fields are:
   A. a suspected but unproven cause of cancer, hormonal abnormalities and behavioral disorders.
   B. generated by all electrical appliances.
   C. present only near high-tension wires or large electrical transformers.
   D. caused by the movement of electricity.

7. Which of the following describes the process of creating a landfill site?
   A. Waste is liquefied, treated and pumped through pipes to "tombs" under the water table.
   B. Waste and topsoil are layered in a pit, mounded up, then covered with dirt and plants.
   C. Waste is compacted and sealed into a container, then placed in a "tomb" designed to last several thousand years.
   D. Waste is buried in an underground concrete vault.

8. Liability under the Superfund is:
   A. limited to the owner of record.
   B. joint and several and retroactive, but not strict.
   C. voluntary.
   D. strict, joint and several, and retroactive.

9. All of the following have been proven to pose health hazards EXCEPT:
   A. asbestos fibers.
   B. carbon monoxide.
   C. electromagnetic fields.
   D. lead-based paint.

10. Which of the following environmental hazards poses a risk due to particles or fibers in the air?
    A. Carbon monoxide
    B. Radon
    C. UFFI
    D. Asbestos

In Illinois . . .

11. The agency primarily responsible for protecting Illinois's natural resources against pollution and other hazards is the:
    A. Pollution Control Board of Illinois (PCB).
    B. Illinois Department of Environmental Affairs (IDEA).
    C. Illinois Environmental Protection Agency (IEPA).
    D. Illinois Department of Environmental Regulation (IDER).

12. Environmental regulations in Illinois are:
    A. all more stringent than federal regulations.
    B. substantially equivalent to federal regulations.
    C. less restrictive than federal regulations.
    D. not subject to federal regulations.

Closing the Real Estate Transaction

PRECLOSING PROCEDURES

> *Closing* is the point at which ownership of a property is transferred in exchange for the selling price.

Everything a licensee does in the course of a real estate transaction, from soliciting clients to presenting offers and coordinating inspections, leads to one final event—closing. Closing is the consummation of the real estate transaction. Closing actually involves two events: the promises made in the sales contract are fulfilled, and the mortgage loan funds (if any) are distributed to the buyer. It is the time when the title to the real estate is transferred in exchange for payment of the purchase price. Closing marks the end of any real estate transaction. Before the property changes hands, however, important issues must be resolved.

Buyer's Issues
The buyer wants to be sure that the seller delivers title. The buyer also should ensure that the property is in the promised condition. This involves inspecting

- the title evidence;
- the seller's deed;
- any documents demonstrating the removal of undesired liens and encumbrances;
- the survey;
- the results of any required inspections, such as termite or structural inspections, or required repairs; and
- any leases if tenants reside on the premises.

In Practice
One of the most frequent causes of lawsuits against licensees is inaccurate lot lines. Buyers want to be confident that the properties they purchase are in fact what they believe they are paying for. Relying on old surveys is not necessarily a good idea;

the property should be resurveyed by a competent surveyor, whether or not the title company or lender requires it.

Final property inspection. Shortly before the closing takes place, the buyer usually makes a final inspection of the property with the broker (often called the *walk-through*). Through this inspection, the buyer makes sure that necessary repairs have been made, that the property has been well maintained, that all fixtures are in place and that there has been no unauthorized removal or alteration of any part of the improvements.

Survey. A survey gives information about the exact location and size of the property. The sales contract specifies who will pay for the survey. It is usual for the survey to "spot" the location of all buildings, driveways, fences and other improvements located primarily on the premises being purchased. Any improvements located on adjoining property that may encroach on the premises being bought also will be noted. The survey should set out, in full, any existing easements and encroachments. Whether or not the sales contract calls for a survey, lenders frequently require one.

Seller's Issues

Obviously, the seller's main interest is in receiving payment for the property. She or he will want to be sure that the buyer has obtained the necessary financing and has sufficient funds to complete the sale. The seller also will want to be certain that he or she has complied with all the buyer's requirements so the transaction will be completed.

Both parties will want to inspect the closing statement to make sure that all monies involved in the transaction have been accounted for properly. The parties may be accompanied by their attorneys.

In Practice

Licensees often assist in preclosing arrangements as part of their service to clients. In some states, licensees are required to advise the parties of the approximate expenses involved in closing at the time that the sales contract is signed. In other states, it is the licensees' statutory duty to coordinate and supervise closing activities.

Title Procedures

Both the buyer and the buyer's lender will want assurance that the seller's title complies with the requirements of the sales contract. The seller usually is required to produce a current abstract of title or title commitment from the title insurance company. When an abstract of title is used, the purchaser's attorney examines it and issues an opinion of title. This opinion, like the title commitment, is a statement of the status of the seller's title. It discloses all liens, encumbrances, easements, conditions or restrictions that appear on the record and to which the seller's title is subject.

On the date when the sale is actually completed (the date of delivery of the deed), the buyer has a title commitment or an abstract that was issued several days or weeks before the closing. For this reason, there usually are two searches of the public records. The first shows the status of the seller's title on the date of the first search. Usually, the seller pays for this search. The second search, known as a *bring-down*, is made after the closing and generally paid for by the purchaser. The abstract should be reviewed before closing to resolve any problems that might cause delays or threaten the transaction.

When the purchaser pays cash or obtains a new loan to purchase the property, the seller's existing loan is paid in full and satisfied on record. The exact amount required to pay the existing loan is provided in a current payoff statement from the lender, effective on the date of closing. This payoff statement notes the unpaid amount of principal, the interest due through the date of payment, the fee for issuing the certificate of satisfaction or release deed, credits (if any) for tax and insurance reserves and the amount of any prepayment penalties. The same procedure would be followed for any other liens that must be released before the buyer takes title.

In a transaction in which the buyer assumes the seller's existing mortgage loan, the buyer will want to know the exact balance of the loan as of the closing date. In some areas, it is customary for the buyer to obtain a mortgage reduction certificate from the lender that certifies the amount owed on the mortgage loan, the interest rate and the last interest payment made.

As part of this later search, the seller may be required to execute an *affidavit of title.* This is a sworn statement in which the seller assures the title insurance company (and the buyer) that there have been no judgments, bankruptcies or divorces involving the seller since the date of the title examination. The affidavit promises that no unrecorded deeds or contracts have been made, no repairs or improvements have gone unpaid and no defects in the title have arisen that the seller knows of. The seller also affirms that he or she is in possession of the premises. In some areas, this form is required before the title insurance company will issue an owner's policy to the buyer. The affidavit gives the title insurance company the right to sue the seller if his or her statements in the affidavit are incorrect.

In some areas, real estate sales transactions customarily are closed through an escrow (discussed below). In these areas, the escrow instructions usually provide for an extended coverage policy to be issued to the buyer as of the date of closing. The seller has no need to execute an affidavit of title.

CONDUCTING THE CLOSING

Closing is known by many names. For instance, in some areas closing is called *settlement* and *transfer.* In other parts of the country, the parties to the transaction sit around a single table and exchange copies of documents, a process known as *passing papers.* ("We passed papers on the new house Wednesday morning.") In still other regions, the buyer and seller may never meet at all; the paperwork is handled by an escrow agent. This process is known as *closing escrow.* ("We'll close escrow on our house next week.") Whether the closing occurs face-to-face or through escrow, the main concerns are that the buyer receives marketable title, the seller receives the purchase price and certain other items are adjusted properly between the two.

In Illinois . . .

In Illinois, the closing statement is customarily prepared by the buyer's lender, the lender's agent (usually a title insurance company) or the seller's lawyer. Although real estate licensees are prohibited by the Illinois Supreme Court's decision in *Chicago Bar Association, et al., v. Quinlan and Tyson, Inc.* from completing formal closing statements, estimated statements are often needed when preparing a CMA, when filling out an offer for a buyer or when presenting an offer to a seller. For this reason, licensees must understand the preparation of a closing statement, which includes the expenses and prorations of costs to close the transaction. In addition, the Illinois licensing examination for broker candidates includes specific questions regarding closing statement calculations. ■

Face-to-Face Closing

A face-to-face closing involves the resolution of two issues. First, the promises made in the sales contract are fulfilled. Second, the buyer's loan is finalized, and the mortgage lender disburses the loan funds. The difference between a face-to-face closing and an escrow closing is that in a face-to-face closing, these two issues are resolved during a single meeting of all the parties and their attorneys. As discussed earlier, the parties in an escrow closing may never meet. The phrase "passing papers" vividly describes a face-to-face closing.

In a *face-to-face closing,* the parties meet face-to-face.

Face-to-face closings may be held at a number of locations, including the offices of the title company, the lending institution, one of the parties' attorneys, the broker, the county recorder or the escrow company. Those attending a closing may include

- the buyer;
- the seller;
- the real estate salespersons or brokers (both the buyer's and the seller's agents);
- the seller's and the buyer's attorneys;
- representatives of the lending institutions involved with the buyer's new mortgage loan, the buyer's assumption of the seller's existing loan or the seller's payoff of an existing loan; and
- a representative of the title insurance company.

Closing agent or closing officer. One person usually conducts the proceedings at a closing and calculates the division of income and expenses between the parties (called *settlement*). In some areas, real estate brokers preside. In others, the closing agent is the buyer's or seller's attorney, a representative of the lender or a representative of the title company. Some title companies and law firms employ paralegal assistants who conduct closings for their firms.

Preparation for closing involves ordering and reviewing an array of documents, such as the title insurance policy or title certificate, surveys, property insurance policies, and other items. Arrangements must be made with the parties for the time and place of closing. Closing statements and other documents must be prepared.

The exchange. When the parties are satisfied that everything is in order, the exchange is made. All pertinent documents are then recorded in the correct order to ensure continuity of title. For instance, if the seller pays off an existing loan and the buyer obtains a new loan, the seller's satisfaction of mortgage must be recorded before the seller's deed to the buyer. The buyer's new mortgage or deed of trust must be recorded *after* the deed because the buyer cannot pledge the property as security for the loan until he or she owns it.

Closing in Escrow

Although a few states prohibit transactions that are closed in escrow, escrow closings are used to some extent in most states.

An **escrow** is a method of closing in which a disinterested third party is authorized to act as escrow agent and to coordinate the closing activities. The escrow agent also may be called the *escrow holder*. The escrow agent may be an attorney, a title company, a trust company, an escrow company or the escrow department of a lending institution. Many real estate firms offer escrow services. However, a broker cannot be a disinterested party in a transaction from which he or she expects to collect a commission. Because the escrow agent is placed in a position of great trust, many states have laws regulating escrow agents and limiting who may serve in this capacity.

> In an *escrow closing,* a third party coordinates the closing activities on behalf of the buyer and seller.

Escrow procedure. When a transaction will close in escrow, the buyer and seller execute escrow instructions to the escrow agent after the sales contract is signed. One of the parties selects an escrow agent. Which party selects the agent is determined either by negotiation or by state law. Once the contract is signed, the broker turns over the earnest money to the escrow agent, who deposits it in a special trust, or escrow, account.

The escrow agent has the authority to examine the title evidence. When marketable title is shown in the name of the buyer and all other conditions of the escrow agreement have been met, the agent is authorized to disburse the purchase price to the seller, minus all charges and expenses. The agent then records the deed and mortgage or deed of trust (if a new loan has been obtained by the purchaser).

If the escrow agent's examination of the title discloses liens, a portion of the purchase price can be withheld from the seller. The withheld portion is used to pay the liens to clear the title.

If the seller cannot clear the title, or if for any reason the sale cannot be consummated, the escrow instructions usually provide that the parties be returned to their former statuses, as if no sale occurred. The escrow agent reconveys title to the seller and returns the purchase money to the buyer. If the seller dies prior to the closing date, but after having given a signed deed to the escrow agent, the closing still may proceed, with the escrow agent transferring title to the buyer and turning the purchase price over to the seller's estate.

IRS Reporting Requirements

Every real estate transaction must be reported to the IRS by the closing agent on a Form 1099-S. Information includes the sales price, the amount of property tax reimbursement credited to the seller and the seller's Social Security number. If the closing agent does not notify the IRS, the responsibility for filing the form falls on the mortgage lender, although the brokers or the parties to the transaction ultimately could be held liable.

Broker's Role at Closing

Depending on local practice, the broker's role at closing can vary from simply collecting the commission to conducting the proceedings. Real estate brokers are not authorized to give legal advice or otherwise engage in the practice of law. This means that in some states, a broker's job is essentially finished as soon as the sales contract is signed. After the contract is signed, the attorneys take over. Even so, a broker's service generally continues all the way through closing. The broker makes sure all the details are taken care of so that the closing can proceed smoothly. This means making arrangements for title evidence, surveys, appraisals, inspections or repairs for structural conditions, water supplies, sewage facilities or toxic substances.

Though real estate licensees do not always conduct closing proceedings, they usually attend. Often, the parties look to their agents for guidance, assistance and information during what can be a stressful experience. Licensees need to be thoroughly familiar with the process and procedures involved in preparing a closing statement, which includes the expenses and prorations of costs to close the transaction. It is also in the brokers' best interests that the transactions they worked so hard to bring about move successfully and smoothly to a conclusion. Of course, a broker's (and a salesperson's) commission is generally paid out of the proceeds at closing.

In Practice   Licensees should avoid recommending sources for any inspection or testing services. If a buyer suffers any injury as a result of a provider's negligence, the licensee also may be liable. The better practice is to give clients the names of several professionals who offer high-quality services.

Lender's Interest in Closing   Whether a buyer obtains new financing or assumes the seller's existing loan, the lender wants to protect its security interest in the property. The lender has an interest in making sure the buyer gets good, marketable title and that tax and insurance payments are maintained. Lenders want their mortgage lien to have priority over other liens. They also want to ensure that insurance is kept up-to-date in case property is damaged or destroyed. For this reason, a lender generally requires a title insurance policy and a fire and hazard insurance policy (along with a receipt for the premium). In addition, a lender may require other information: a survey, a termite or another inspection report, or a certificate of occupancy (for a newly constructed building). A lender also may request that a reserve account be established for tax and insurance payments. Lenders sometimes even require representation by their own attorneys at closings.

RESPA REQUIREMENTS

The federal **Real Estate Settlement Procedures Act** (RESPA) was enacted to protect consumers from abusive lending practices. RESPA also aids consumers during the mortgage loan settlement process. It ensures that consumers are provided with important, accurate and timely information about the actual costs of settling or closing a transaction. It also eliminates kickbacks and other referral fees that tend to inflate the costs of settlement unnecessarily. RESPA prohibits lenders from requiring excessive escrow account deposits.

RESPA requirements apply when a purchase is financed by a federally related mortgage loan. *Federally related loans* means loans made by banks, savings and loan associations or other lenders whose deposits are insured by federal agencies. It also includes loans insured by the FHA and guaranteed by the VA; loans administered by HUD; and loans intended to be sold by the lenders to Fannie Mae, Ginnie Mae or Freddie Mac. RESPA is administered by HUD.

RESPA regulations apply to first-lien residential mortgage loans made to finance the purchases of one- to four-family homes, cooperatives and condominiums, for either investment or occupancy. RESPA also governs second or subordinate liens for home equity loans. A transaction financed solely by a purchase-money mortgage taken back by the seller, an installment contract (contract for deed) and a buyer's assumption of a seller's existing loan are not covered by RESPA. However, if the terms of the assumed loan are modified, or if the lender charges more than $50 for the assumption, the transaction is subject to RESPA regulations.

In Practice

While RESPA's requirements are aimed primarily at lenders, some provisions of the act affect real estate brokers and agents as well. Real estate licensees fall under RESPA when they refer buyers to particular lenders, title companies, attorneys or other providers of settlement services. Licensees who offer computerized loan origination (CLO) services also are subject to regulation. Remember: Buyers have the right to select their own providers of settlement services.

Controlled Business Arrangements

A consumer service that is increasing in popularity is one-stop shopping for real estate services. A real estate firm, title insurance company, mortgage broker, home inspection company or even moving company may agree to offer a package of services to consumers. RESPA permits such a **controlled business arrangement** (CBA), as long as a consumer is clearly informed of the relationship among the service providers and that other providers are available. Fees may not be exchanged among the affiliated companies simply for referring business to one another. This may be a particularly important issue for licensees who offer *computerized loan origination (CLO) services*. While a borrower's ability to comparison shop for a loan may be enhanced by a CLO system, his or her range of choices may not be limited. Consumers must be informed of the availability of other lenders.

Disclosure Requirements

Lenders and settlement agents have certain disclosure obligations at the time of loan application and loan closing:

- *Special information booklet*—Lenders must provide a copy of a special informational HUD booklet to every person from whom they receive or for whom they prepare a loan application (except for refinancing). The HUD booklet must be given at the time the application is received or within three days afterward. The booklet provides the borrower with general information about settlement (closing) costs. It also explains the various provisions of RESPA, including a line-by-line description of the Uniform Settlement Statement.
- *Good-faith estimate of settlement costs*—No later than three business days after receiving a loan application, the lender must provide to the borrower a good-faith estimate of the settlement costs the borrower is likely to incur. This estimate may be either a specific figure or a range of costs based on comparable past transactions in the area. In addition, if the lender requires use of a particular attorney or title company to conduct the closing, the lender must state whether it has any business relationship with that firm and must estimate the charges for this service.
- Uniform Settlement Statement (HUD Form 1)—RESPA requires that a special HUD form be completed to itemize all charges to be paid by a borrower and seller in connection with settlement. The **Uniform Settle-**

ment Statement includes all charges that will be collected at closing, whether required by the lender or a third party. Items paid by the borrower and seller outside closing, not required by the lender, are not included on HUD-1. Charges required by the lender that are paid for before closing are indicated as "paid outside of closing" (POC). RESPA prohibits lenders from requiring that borrowers deposit amounts in escrow accounts for taxes and insurance that exceed certain limits, thus preventing the lenders from taking advantage of the borrowers. Sellers are also prohibited from requiring, as a condition of a sale, that the buyer purchase title insurance from a particular company. A copy of the HUD-1 form is illustrated later in this chapter. (See Figure 23.3.)

The settlement statement must be made available for inspection by the borrower at or before settlement. Borrowers have the right to inspect a completed HUD-1, to the extent that the figures are available, one business day before the closing. (Sellers are not entitled to this privilege.)

Lenders must retain these statements for two years after the dates of closing. In addition, state laws generally require that licensees retain all records of a transaction for a specific period. The Uniform Settlement Statement may be altered to allow for local custom, and certain lines may be deleted if they do not apply in an area.

Kickbacks and referral fees. RESPA prohibits the payment of kickbacks, or unearned fees, in any real estate settlement service. It prohibits referral fees when no services are actually rendered. The payment or receipt of a fee, a kickback or anything of value for referrals for settlement services includes activities such as mortgage loans, title searches, title insurance, attorney services, surveys, credit reports and appraisals.

In Practice   Under HUD regulations, employers may not pay referral fees to employees who steer customers to the brokerage's ancillary businesses. However, employees who generate business *for the brokerage itself* (not for any ancillary) may be paid a referral fee. Management-level employees may be paid bonuses for performance but may not be paid individual referral fees.

PREPARATION OF CLOSING STATEMENTS

The purpose of a closing statement is to determine how much money the buyer must bring to the closing and how much the seller will net after the closing. A typical real estate transaction involves, in addition to the purchase price, expenses for both parties. These include items prepaid by the seller for which he or she must be reimbursed (such as taxes) and items of expense the seller has incurred but for which the buyer will be billed (such as mortgage interest paid in arrears when a loan is assumed). The financial responsibility for these items must be prorated (or divided) between the buyer and the seller. All expenses and prorated items are accounted for on the settlement statement. This is how the exact amount of cash required from the buyer and the net proceeds to the seller are determined. (See Figure 23.1.)

Item	Paid by Seller	Paid by Buyer
Broker's commission	✗ by agreement	✗ by agreement
Attorney's fees	✗ by agreement	✗ by agreement
Recording expenses	✗ to clear title	✗ record deed and mortgage
Transfer tax	✗ state, county and some municipal taxes	✗ some municipal taxes
Title expenses	✗ title search	✗ lender's title policy
Loan fees	✗ prepayment penalty	✗ origination fee and/or discount points
Tax and insurance reserves (escrow or impound accounts)		✗
Appraisal fees		✗ if required by lender
Survey fees	✗ if required to pay by sales contract	✗ new mortgage financing

Figure 23.1   **Allocation of Expenses**

How the Closing Statement Works

The completion of a **closing statement** involves an accounting of the parties' debits and credits. A **debit** is a charge. That is, it is an amount that a party owes and must pay at closing. A **credit** is an amount entered in a person's favor—an amount that has already been paid, an amount being reimbursed or an amount the buyer promises to pay in the form of a loan.

To determine the amount a buyer needs at closing, the buyer's debits are totaled. Any expenses and prorated amounts for items prepaid by the seller are added to the purchase price. Then the buyer's credits are totaled. These include the earnest money (already paid), the balance of the loan the buyer obtains or assumes and the seller's share of any prorated items the buyer will pay in the future. (See Figure 23.2.) Finally, the total of the buyer's credits is subtracted from the total debits to arrive at the actual amount of cash the buyer must bring to closing. Usually, the buyer brings a cashier's or certified check.

A *debit* is an amount *to be paid by* the buyer or seller; a *credit* is an amount *payable to* the buyer or seller.

A similar procedure is followed to determine how much money the seller actually will receive. The seller's debits and credits are each totaled. The credits include the purchase price plus the buyer's share of any prorated items that the seller has prepaid. The seller's debits include expenses, the seller's share of prorated items to be paid later by the buyer and the balance of any mortgage loan or other lien that the seller pays off. Finally, the total of the seller's debits is subtracted from the total credits to arrive at the amount the seller will receive.

Broker's commission. The responsibility for paying the broker's commission will have been determined by previous agreement. If the broker is the

Figure 23.2	Credits and Debits				
Item	Credit to Buyer	Debit to Buyer	Credit to Seller	Debit to Seller	Prorated
Principal amount of new mortgage	X				
Payoff of existing mortgage				X	
Unpaid principal balance if assumed mortgage	X			X	
Accrued interest on existing assumed mortgage	X			X	X
Tenants' security deposit	X			X	
Purchase-money mortgage	X			X	
Unpaid water and other utility bills	X			X	X
Buyer's earnest money	X				
Selling price of property		X	X		
Fuel oil on hand (valued at current market price)		X	X		X
Prepaid insurance and tax reserve for mortgage assumed by buyer		X	X		X
Refund to seller of prepaid water charges and similar utility expenses		X	X		X
Accrued general real estate taxes	X			X	X

agent for the seller, the seller normally is responsible for paying the commission. If an agency agreement exists between a broker and the buyer, or if two agents are involved, one for the seller and one for the buyer, the commission may be apportioned as an expense between both parties or according to some other arrangement.

Attorney's fees. If either of the parties' attorneys will be paid from the closing proceeds, that party will be charged with the expense in the closing statement. This expense may include fees for the preparation or review of documents or for representing the parties at settlement.

Recording expenses. The seller usually pays for recording charges (filing fees) necessary to clear all defects and furnish the purchaser with a marketable title. Items customarily charged to the seller include the recording of release deeds or satisfaction of mortgages, quitclaim deeds, affidavits and satisfaction of mechanics' liens. The purchaser pays for recording charges that arise from the actual transfer of title. Usually, such items include recording the deed that conveys title to the purchaser and a mortgage or deed of trust executed by the purchaser.

Transfer tax. Most states require some form of transfer tax, conveyance fee or tax stamps on real estate conveyances. This expense is most often borne by the seller, although customs vary. In addition, many cities and local municipalities charge transfer taxes. Responsibility for these charges varies according to local practice.

In Illinois . . .

State and county transfer taxes are usually paid by the seller, in accordance with most sales contracts. On the other hand, local ordinances usually establish which party is responsible for paying municipal transfer taxes. If there is no ordinance, then payment of local transfer taxes must be negotiated between the parties. ■

Title expenses. Responsibility for title expenses varies according to local custom. In most areas, the seller is required to furnish evidence of good title and pay for the title search. If the buyer's attorney inspects the evidence or if the buyer purchases title insurance policies, the buyer is charged for the expense.

In Illinois . . .

Because the seller usually is required by the contract to furnish evidence of good title, the seller customarily pays for the owner's title insurance policy. The buyer customarily pays for the lender's policy, which ensures that the lender has a valid first lien. ■

Loan fees. When the buyer secures a new loan to finance the purchase, the lender ordinarily charges a loan origination fee of 1 to 2 percent of the loan. The fee is usually paid by the purchaser at the time the transaction closes. The lender also may charge discount points. If the buyer assumes the seller's existing financing, the buyer may pay an assumption fee. Also, under the terms of some mortgage loans, the seller may be required to pay a prepayment charge or penalty for paying off the mortgage loan before its due date.

Tax reserves and insurance reserves (escrow or impound accounts). Most mortgage lenders require that borrowers provide reserve funds or escrow accounts to pay future real estate taxes and insurance premiums. A borrower starts the account at closing by depositing funds to cover at least the amount of unpaid real estate taxes from the date of lien to the end of the current month. (The buyer receives a credit from the seller at closing for any unpaid taxes.) Afterward, an amount equal to one month's portion of the estimated taxes is included in the borrower's monthly mortgage payment.

The borrower is responsible for maintaining adequate fire or hazard insurance as a condition of the mortgage loan. Generally, the first year's premium is paid in full at closing. An amount equal to one month's premium is paid after that. The borrower's monthly loan payment includes the principal and interest on the loan, plus one-twelfth of the estimated taxes and insurance (PITI). The taxes and insurance are held by the lender in the escrow or impound account until the bills are due.

Appraisal fees. Either the seller or the purchaser pays the appraisal fees, depending on who orders the appraisal. When the buyer obtains a mortgage, it is customary for the lender to require an appraisal. In this case, the buyer bears the cost. If the fee is paid at the time of the loan application, it is reflected on the closing statement as already having been paid.

Survey fees. The purchaser who obtains new mortgage financing customarily pays the survey fees. The sales contract may require the seller to furnish a survey.

In Illinois . . . Most real estate contracts require that the seller furnish a current survey to the buyer. As a result, the expense of preparing a survey usually is borne by the seller. ■

Additional fees. An FHA borrower owes a lump sum for payment of the mortgage insurance premium (MIP) if it is not financed as part of the loan. A VA mortgagor pays a funding fee directly to the VA at closing. If a conventional loan carries private mortgage insurance, the buyer prepays one year's insurance premium at closing.

Accounting for Expenses

Expenses paid out of the closing proceeds are debited only to the party making the payment. Occasionally, an expense item, such as an escrow fee, a settlement fee or a transfer tax, may be shared by the buyer and the seller. In this case, each party is debited for his or her share of the expense.

PRORATIONS

Most closings involve the division of financial responsibility between the buyer and seller for such items as loan interest, taxes, rents, fuel and utility bills. These allowances are called **prorations.** Prorations are necessary to ensure that expenses are divided fairly between the seller and the buyer. For example, the seller may owe current taxes that have not been billed; the buyer would want this settled at the closing. Where taxes must be paid in advance, the seller is entitled to a rebate at the closing. If the buyer assumes the seller's existing mortgage or deed of trust, the seller usually owes the buyer an allowance for accrued interest through the date of closing.

Accrued items = buyer credits

Prepaid items = seller credits

Accrued items, such as water bills, Illinois real estate taxes and interest on an assumed mortgage that is paid in arrears, are expenses to be prorated that are owed by the seller but later will be paid by the buyer. The seller therefore pays for these items by giving the buyer credits for them at closing.

Prepaid items, such as fuel oil in a tank, are expenses to be prorated that have been prepaid by the seller but not fully used up. They are therefore credits to the seller.

The Arithmetic of Prorating

Accurate prorating involves four considerations:

1. Nature of the item being prorated

2. Whether it is an accrued item that requires the determination of an earned amount
3. Whether it is a prepaid item that requires the determination of an unearned amount (that is, a refund to the seller)
4. What arithmetic processes must be used

The computation of a proration involves identifying a yearly charge for the item to be prorated, then dividing by 12 to determine a monthly charge for the item. Usually, it is also necessary to identify a daily charge for the item by dividing the monthly charge by the number of days in the month. These smaller portions then are multiplied by the number of months or days in the prorated time period to determine the accrued or unearned amount that will be figured in the settlement.

Using this general principle, there are two methods of calculating prorations:

1. The yearly charge is divided by a *360-day year* (commonly called a *statutory,* or *banking, year*), or 12 months of 30 days each.
2. The yearly charge is divided by *365* (366 in a leap year) to determine the daily charge. Then the actual number of days in the proration period is determined, and this number is multiplied by the daily charge.

In Illinois . . .

A third method, the *statutory month variation*, is also acceptable in Illinois. In this method, the yearly charge is divided by 12 to determine a monthly amount. The monthly charge then is divided by the actual number of days in the month in which the closing occurs. This final number is the daily charge for that month. ■

The final proration figure will vary slightly, depending on which computation method is used. The final figure also varies according to the number of decimal places to which the division is carried. All of the computations in this chapter are computed by carrying the division to three decimal places. The third decimal place is rounded off to cents only after the final proration figure is determined.

Accrued Items

When the real estate tax is levied for the calendar year and is payable during that year or in the following year, the accrued portion is for the period from January 1 to the date of closing (or to the day before the closing in states where the sale date is excluded). If the current tax bill has not yet been issued, the parties must agree on an estimated amount based on the previous year's bill and any known changes in assessment or tax levy for the current year.

Sample proration calculation. Assume a sale is to be closed on September 17. Current real estate taxes of $1,200 are to be prorated. A 360-day year is used. The accrued period, then, is 8 months and 17 days. First determine the prorated cost of the real estate tax per month and day:

$$\frac{\$100 \text{ per month}}{12\overline{)\$1,200}} \qquad \frac{\$3.333 \text{ per day}}{30\overline{)\$100.000}}$$
$$\text{months} \qquad\qquad\qquad \text{days}$$

Next, multiply these figures by the accrued period, and add the totals to determine the prorated real estate tax:

$100	$ 3.333	$800.000
× 8 months	× 17 days	+ 56.661
$800	$56.661	$856.661

Thus, the accrued real estate tax for 8 months and 17 days is $856.66 (rounded off to two decimal places after the final computation). This amount represents the seller's accrued earned tax. It will be a credit to the buyer and a debit to the seller on the closing statement.

To compute this proration using the actual number of days in the accrued period, the following method is used: The accrued period from January 1 to September 17 runs 260 days (January's 31 days plus February's 28 days and so on, plus the 17 days of September).

$$\text{\$1,200 tax bill} \div 365 \text{ days} = \$3.288 \text{ per day}$$
$$\$3.288 \times 260 \text{ days} = \$854.880, \text{ or } \$854.88$$

While these examples show proration as of the date of settlement, the agreement of sale may require otherwise. For instance, a buyer's possession date may not coincide with the settlement date. In this case, the parties could prorate according to the date of possession.

In Practice   On state licensing examinations, tax prorations are usually based on a 30-day month (360-day year), unless specified otherwise. This may differ from local customs regarding tax prorations. Many title insurance companies provide proration charts that detail tax factors for each day in the year. To determine a tax proration using one of these charts, multiply the factor given for the closing date by the annual real estate tax.

Prepaid Items   A tax proration could be a prepaid item. Because real estate tax may be paid in the early part of the year, a tax proration calculated for a closing taking place later in the year must reflect the fact that the seller has already paid the tax. For example, in the preceding problem, suppose that all taxes had been paid. The buyer, then, would have to reimburse the seller; the proration would be credited to the seller and debited to the buyer.

In figuring the tax proration, it is necessary to ascertain the number of future days, months and years for which taxes have been paid. The formula commonly used for this purpose is as follows:

	Years	Months	Days
Taxes paid to (Dec. 31, end of tax year)	1999	12	30
Date of closing (Sept. 17, 2000)	2000	−9	−17
Period for which tax must be paid		3	13

With this formula (using the statutory-month method), we can find the amount the buyer will reimburse the seller for the unearned portion of the real estate tax. The prepaid period, as determined using the formula for prepaid items, is 3 months and 13 days. Three months at $100 per month equals $300, and 13 days at $3.333 per day equals $43.329. Add this to determine that the proration is $343.329, or $343.33 credited to the seller and debited to the buyer.

Sample prepaid item calculation. One example of a prepaid item is a water bill. Assume that the water is billed in advance by the city without using a meter. The six months' billing is $60 for the period ending October 31. The sale is to be closed on August 3. Because the water bill is paid to October 31, the prepaid time must be computed. Using a 30-day basis, the time period is the 27 days left in August plus 2 full months: $60 ÷ 6 = $10 per month. For one day, divide $10 by 30, which equals $0.333 per day. The prepaid period is 2 months and 27 days, so

$$
\begin{array}{lll}
27\ \text{days} & \times\ \$\ 0.333\ \text{per day} & =\ \$\ 8.991 \\
2\ \text{months} & \times\ \$10 & =\ \underline{\$20} \\
& & \$28.991,\ \text{or}\ \$28.99
\end{array}
$$

This is a prepaid item; it is credited to the seller and debited to the buyer on the closing statement.

To figure this based on the actual days in the month of closing, the following process would be used:

$$
\begin{array}{lll}
\$10\ \text{per month} \div 31\ \text{days in August} & = & \$0.323\ \text{per day} \\
\text{August 4 through August 31} & = & 28\ \text{days} \\
28\ \text{days} \times \$0.323 & = & \$9.044 \\
2\ \text{months} \times \$10 & = & \$20 \\
\$9.044 + \$20 & = & \$29.044,\ \text{or}\ \$29.04
\end{array}
$$

General Rules for Prorating

The rules or customs governing the computation of prorations for the closing of a real estate sale vary widely from state to state. The following are some general guidelines for preparing the closing statement:

- In most states, the seller owns the property on the day of closing, and prorations or apportionments usually are made to and including the day of closing. In a few states, however, it is provided specifically that the buyer owns the property on the closing date. In that case, adjustments are made as of the day preceding the day on which title is closed.
- Mortgage interest, general real estate taxes, water taxes, insurance premiums and similar expenses usually are computed by using 360 days in a year and 30 days in a month. However, the rules in some areas provide for computing prorations on the basis of the actual number of days in the calendar month of closing. The agreement of sale should specify which method will be used.
- Accrued general real estate taxes usually are prorated at the closing. When the amount of the current real estate tax cannot be determined definitely, the proration is usually based on the last obtainable tax bill.
- Special assessments for municipal improvements such as sewers, water mains or streets usually are paid in annual installments over several years, with annual interest charged on the outstanding balance of future installments. The seller normally pays the current installment, and the buyer assumes all future installments. The special assessment installment generally is not prorated at the closing. A buyer may insist that the seller allow the buyer a credit for the seller's share of the interest to the closing date. The agreement of sale may address the manner in which special assessments will be handled at settlement.

- Rents are usually adjusted on the basis of the actual number of days in the month of closing. It is customary for the seller to receive the rents for the day of closing and to pay all expenses for that day. If any rents for the current month are uncollected when the sale is closed, the buyer often agrees by a separate letter to collect the rents if possible and remit the pro rata share to the seller.
- Security deposits made by tenants to cover the last month's rent of the lease or to cover the cost of repairing damage caused by the tenant generally are transferred by the seller to the buyer.

Real estate taxes. Proration of real estate taxes varies widely, depending on how the taxes are paid in the area where the real estate is located. In some states, real estate taxes are paid in advance; that is, if the tax year runs from January 1 to December 31, taxes for the coming year are due on January 1. In this case, the seller, who has prepaid a year's taxes, should be reimbursed for the portion of the year remaining after the buyer takes ownership of the property. In other areas, taxes are paid in arrears, on December 31 for the year just ended. In this case, the buyer should be credited by the seller for the time the seller occupied the property. Sometimes, taxes are due during the tax year, partly in arrears and partly in advance; sometimes they are payable in installments. It gets even more complicated: city, state, school and other property taxes may start their tax years in different months. Whatever the case may be in a particular transaction, the licensee should understand how the taxes will be prorated.

In Illinois . . .

Taxes in Illinois are paid *in the year after they become a lien*. If an unpaid installment has been billed, this amount is credited to the buyer and debited to the seller—no proration is necessary. The buyer must be credited with the current year's taxes, and the seller debited accordingly; a proration is necessary for this figure, however.

The following formula may be used:

(Last annual tax bill ÷ 360) × number of days (January 1 to closing) = proration ■

Mortgage loan interest. On almost every mortgage loan the interest is paid in arrears, so buyer and seller must understand that the mortgage payment due on June 1, for example, includes interest due for the month of May. Thus, the buyer who assumes a mortgage on May 31 and makes the June payment pays for the time the seller occupied the property and should be credited with a month's interest. On the other hand, the buyer who places a new mortgage loan on May 31 may be pleasantly surprised to hear that he or she will not need to make a mortgage payment until a month later.

In Illinois . . .

The terms of some assumed mortgage loans provide that interest is charged at the beginning of the month (in advance); without this provision, interest is always charged at the end of the month (in arrears). When the interest on the existing mortgage to be assumed by the buyer is charged at the beginning of the month, the *unearned portion* (that is, the part that is prepaid from the date of closing to the end of the month) must be credited to the seller and debited to the buyer. When the mortgage interest is charged at the end of the month, the *earned* portion of the mortgage interest through the date of closing is an accrued expense, debited to the seller and credited to the buyer. ■

SAMPLE CLOSING STATEMENT

Settlement computations take many possible formats. The remaining portion of this chapter illustrates a sample transaction using the Uniform Settlement Statement in Figure 23.3.

Basic Information of Offer and Sale

John and Joanne Iuro list their home at 3045 North Racine Avenue in Riverdale with the Open Door Real Estate Company. The listing price is $118,500, and possession can be given within two weeks after all parties have signed the contract. Under the terms of the listing agreement, the sellers agree to pay the broker a commission of 6 percent of the sales price.

On May 18, the Open Door Real Estate Company submits a contract offer to the Iuros from Brook Redemann, a bachelor residing at 22 King Court, Riverdale. Redemann offers $115,000, with earnest money and down payment of $23,000 and the remaining $92,000 of the purchase price to be obtained through a new conventional loan. No private mortgage insurance is necessary because the loan-to-value ratio does not exceed 80 percent. The Iuros sign the contract on May 29. Closing is set for June 15 at the office of the Open Door Real Estate Company, 720 Main Street, Riverdale.

The unpaid balance of the Iuros' mortgage as of June 1, 2000, will be $57,700. Payments are $680 per month, with interest at 11 percent per annum on the unpaid balance.

The sellers submit evidence of title in the form of a title insurance binder at a cost of $10. The title insurance policy, to be paid by the sellers at the time of closing, costs an additional $540, including $395 for lender's coverage and $145 for homeowner's coverage. Recording charges of $20 are paid for the recording of two instruments to clear defects in the sellers' title. State transfer tax stamps in the amount of $115 ($.50 per $500 of the sales price or fraction thereof) are affixed to the deed. In addition, the sellers must pay an attorney's fee of $400 for preparing the deed and for legal representation. This amount will be paid from the closing proceeds.

The buyer must pay an attorney's fee of $300 for examining the title evidence and for legal representation. He also must pay $10 to record the deed. These amounts also will be paid from the closing proceeds.

Real estate taxes in Riverdale are paid in arrears. Taxes for this year, estimated at last year's figure of $1,725, have not been paid. According to the contract, prorations will be made on the basis of 30 days in a month.

Computing the prorations and charges. The following list illustrates the various steps in computing the prorations and other amounts to be included in the settlement to this point:

- Closing date: June 15, 2000
- Commission: 6% (.06) × $115,000 sales price = $6,900
- Seller's mortgage interest: 11% (.11) × $57,700 principal due after June 1 payment = $6,347 interest per year; $6,347 ÷ 360 days = $17.631 interest per day; 15 days of accrued interest to be paid by the seller × $17.631 = $264.465 interest owed by the seller; $57,700 + $264.465 = $57,964.465, or $57,964.47 payoff of seller's mortgage

Figure 23.3   RESPA Uniform Settlement Statement

U.S. DEPARTMENT OF HOUSING AND URBAN DEVELOPMENT   OMB No. 2502-0265(Exp. 12-31-86)

A. Settlement Statement	B. Type of Loan
	1. ☐ FHA 2. ☐ FMHA 3. ☒ CONV. UNINS. 4. ☐ VA 5. ☐ CONV. INS. 6. File Number 7. Loan Number 8. Mortgage Insurance Case Number

C. Note: This form is furnished to give you a statement of actual settlement costs. Amounts paid to and by the settlement agent are shown. Items marked '(p.o.c)' were paid outside the closing; they are shown here for informational purposes and are not included in the totals.

D. Name of Borrower: Brook Redemann

E. Name of Seller: John Iuro and Joanne Iuro

F. Name of Lender: Thrift Federal Savings

G. Property Location: 3045 N. Racine Ave., Riverdale IL

H. Settlement Agent: Open Door Real Estate Company
Address: 720 Main Street, Riverdale

I. Settlement Date: June 15, 19--

Place of Settlement: Open Door Real Estate Company
Address: 720 Main Street, Riverdale

J. Summary of Borrower's Transaction		K. Summary of Seller's Transaction	
100. Gross Amount Due From Borrower		**400. Gross Amount Due To Seller**	
101. Contract Sales Price	$115,000.00	401. Contract Sales Price	$115,000.00
102. Personal Property		402. Personal Property	
103. Settlement charges to borrower (line 1400)	4,900.84	403.	
104.		404.	
105.		405.	
Adjustments for items paid by seller in advance		**Adjustments for items paid by seller in advance**	
106. City/town taxes to		406. City/town taxes to	
107. County taxes to		407. County taxes to	
108. Assessments to		408. Assessments to	
109.		409.	
110.		410.	
111.		411.	
112.		412.	
113.		413.	
114.		414.	
115.		415.	
120. Gross Amount Due From Borrower	$119,900.84	**420. Gross Amount Due To Seller**	$115,000.00
200. Amounts Paid By Or In Behalf Of Borrower		**500. Reductions In Amount Due To Seller**	
201. Deposit or earnest money	23,000.00	501. Excess deposit (see instructions)	
202. Principal amount of new loan(s)	92,000.00	502. Settlement charges (line 1400)	8,255.00
203. Existing loan(s) taken subject to		503. Existing loan(s) taken subject to	
204.		504. Payoff of first mortgage loan	57,964.47
205.		505. Payoff of second mortgage loan	
206.		506.	
207.		507.	
208.		508.	
209.		509.	
Adjustments for items unpaid by seller		**Adjustments for items unpaid by seller**	
210. City/town taxes to		510. City/town taxes to	
211. County taxes 1/1 to 6/15	790.63	511. County taxes 1/1 to 6/15	790.63
212. Assessments to		512. Assessments to	
213.		513.	
214.		514.	
215.		515.	
216.		516.	
217.		517.	
218.		518.	
219.		519.	
220. Total Paid By/For Borrower	$115,790.63	**520. Total Reductions Amount Due Seller**	$ 67,009.47
300. Cash At Settlement From/To Borrower		**600. Cash At Settlement To/From Seller**	
301. Gross amount due from borrower (line 120)	$119,900.84	601. Gross amount due to seller (line 420)	$115,000.00
302. Less amounts paid by/for borrower (line 220)	(115,790.63)	602. Less reductions in amount due to seller (line 520)	(67,009.47)
303. Cash (☒ From) (☐ To) Borrower	$ 4,110.21	603. Cash (☒ To) (☐ From) Seller	$ 47,990.53

Figure 23.3   **RESPA Uniform Settlement Statement (Continued)**

OBM No. 2502-0265 (Exp. 12-31-86)

L. Settlement Charges

			Paid From Borrower's Funds at Settlement	Paid From Seller's Funds at Settlement
700. Total Sales/Broker's Commission based on price $115,000 @ 6 % = 6,900.00				
Division of Commission (line 700) as follows				
701. $	to			
702. $	to			
703. Commission paid at Settlement				$6,900.00
704.				
800. Items Payable In Connection With Loan				
801. Loan Origination Fee %			$ 920.00	
802. Loan Discount 2 %			$1,840.00	
803. Appraisal Fee to Swift Appraisal		$125.00	POC	
804. Credit Report to Acme Credit Bureau		$ 60.00	POC	
805. Lender's Inspection Fee				
806. Mortgage Insurance Application Fee to				
807. Assumption Fee				
808.				
809.				
810.				
811.				
900. Items Required By Lender To Be Paid In Advance				
901. Interest from 6/16 to 6/30 @ $ 25.556 /day			$ 383.34	
902. Mortgage Insurance Premium for months to				
903. Hazard Insurance Premium for 1 years to Hite Insurance Company			$ 345.00	
904.				
905.				
1000. Reserves Deposited With Lender				
1001. Hazard Insurance 3 months @ $ 28.75 per month			$ 86.25	
1002. Mortgage Insurance months @ $ per month				
1003. City property taxes months @ $ per month				
1004. County property taxes 7 months @ $ 143.75 per month			$1,006.25	
1005. Annual assessments months @ $ per month				
1006. months @ $ per month				
1007. months @ $ per month				
1008. months @ $ per month				
1100. Title Charges				
1101. Settlement or closing fee to				
1102. Abstract or title search to				
1103. Title examination to				
1104. Title insurance binder to				$ 10.00
1105. Document preparation to				
1106. Notary fees to				
1107. Attorney's fee to			$ 300.00	$ 400.00
(includes above items numbers:)				
1108. Title insurance to				$ 540.00
(includes above items numbers: 1102-1103-1104)				
1109. Lender's coverage $ 395.00				
1110. Owner's coverage $ 145.00				
1111.				
1112.				
1113.				
1200. Government Recording And Transfer Charges				
1201. Recording fees: Deed $ 10.00 Mortgage $ 10.00 Release $ 10.00			$ 20.00	$ 10.00
1202. City/county tax/stamps: Deed $;Mortgage $				
1203. State tax/stamps: Deed $ 115.00 ;Mortgage $				$ 115.00
1204. Record 2 documents to clear title				$ 20.00
1205.				
1300. Additional Settlement Charges				
1301. Survey to				$ 175.00
1302. Pest inspection to				$ 85.00
1303.				
1304.				
1305.				
1400. Total Settlement Charges (enter on lines 103, Section J and 502, Section K)			$4,900.84	$8,255.00

I have carefully reviewed the HUD-1 Settlement Statement and to the best of my knowledge and belief, it is a true and accurate statement of all receipts and distributions made on my account or by me in this transaction. I further certify that I have received a copy of HUD-1 Settlement Statement.

_____   _____

Borrowers   Sellers

The HUD-1 Settlement Statement which I have prepared is a true and accurate account of this transaction. I have caused or will cause the funds to be disbursed in accordance with this statement.

_____   _____

Settlement Agent   Date

WARNING: It is a crime to knowingly make false statements to the United States on this or any other similar form. Penalties upon conviction can include a fine or imprisonment. For details see Title 18 U.S. Code Section 1001 and Section 1010.

- Real estate taxes (estimated at $1,725): $1,725 ÷ 12 months = $143.75 per month; $143.75 ÷ 30 days = $ 4.792 per day
- The earned period, from January 1 to and including June 15, equals 5 months and 15 days: $143.75 × 5 months = $718.75; $4.792 × 15 days = $71.88; $718.75 + $71.88 = $790.63 seller owes buyer
- Transfer tax ($.50 per $500 of consideration or fraction thereof): $115,000 ÷ $500 = $230; $230 × $.50 = $115 transfer tax owed by seller

The sellers' loan payoff is $57,964.47. They must pay an additional $10 to record the mortgage release, as well as $85 for a pest inspection. The buyer's new loan is from Thrift Federal Savings, 1100 Fountain Plaza, Riverdale, in the amount of $92,000 at 10 percent interest. In connection with this loan, Redemann will be charged $125 to have the property appraised by Swift Appraisal. Acme Credit Bureau will charge $60 for a credit report. (Because appraisal and credit reports are performed before loan approval, they are paid at the time of loan application, whether or not the transaction eventually closes. These items are noted as POC—paid outside closing—on the settlement statement.) In addition, Redemann will pay for interest on his loan for the remainder of the month of closing: 15 days at $25.556 per day, or $383.34. His first full payment (including July's interest) will be due on August 1. He must deposit $1,006.25 into a tax reserve account. That's seven-twelfths of the anticipated county real estate tax of $1,725. A one-year hazard insurance premium at $3 per $1,000 of appraised value ($115,000 ÷ 1,000 × 3 = $345) is paid in advance to Hite Insurance Company. An insurance reserve to cover the premium for three months is deposited with the lender. Redemann will have to pay an additional $10 to record the mortgage, a loan origination fee of $920 and two discount points. The sellers will pay $175 for a survey.

The Uniform Settlement Statement

The Uniform Settlement Statement is divided into 12 sections. Sections J, K and L contain particularly important information. The borrower's and seller's summaries (J and K) are very similar. In Section J, the buyer-borrower's debits are listed on lines 100 through 112. They are totaled on line 120 (gross amount due from borrower). The total of the settlement costs itemized in Section L of the statement is entered on line 103 as one of the buyer's charges. The buyer's credits are listed on lines 201 through 219 and totaled on line 220 (total paid by or for borrower). Then the buyer's credits are subtracted from the charges to arrive at the cash due from the borrower to close (line 303).

In Section K, the seller's credits are entered on lines 400 through 412 and totaled on line 420 (gross amount due to seller). The seller's debits are entered on lines 501 through 519 and totaled on line 520 (total reductions in amount due seller). The total of the seller's settlement charges is on line 502. Then the debits are subtracted from the credits to arrive at the cash due to the seller at closing (line 603).

Section L summarizes all the settlement charges for the transaction; the buyer's expenses are listed in one column and the seller's expenses in the other. If an attorney's fee is listed as a lump sum in line 1107, the settlement should list by line number the services that were included in that total fee.

SUMMARY

Closing a real estate sale involves both title procedures and financial matters. The real estate salesperson or broker is often present at the closing to see that the sale is actually concluded and to account for the earnest money deposit.

Closings must be reported to the IRS on Form 1099-S.

The federal Real Estate Settlement Procedures Act (RESPA) requires disclosure of all settlement costs when a residential real estate purchase is financed by a federally related mortgage loan. RESPA requires lenders to use a Uniform Settlement Statement to detail the financial particulars of a transaction.

The actual amount to be paid by a buyer at closing is computed on a closing, or settlement, statement. This lists the sales price, earnest money deposit and all adjustments and prorations due between buyer and seller. The purpose of this statement is to determine the net amount due the seller at closing. The buyer reimburses the seller for prepaid items like unused taxes or fuel oil. The seller credits the buyer for bills the seller owes, but the buyer will have to pay accrued items such as unpaid water bills.

In Illinois . . .

The closing statement is customarily prepared by the buyer's lender, the lender's agent or the seller's lawyer. State and county transfer taxes are usually paid by the seller, who also customarily pays for the survey and the owner's title insurance policy. The buyer usually pays for the lender's policy.

Illinois permits proration by the statutory month variation.

Taxes in Illinois are paid in the year after they become a lien. ■

QUESTIONS

1. Which of the following statements is true of real estate closings in most states?
   A. Closings are generally conducted by real estate salespersons.
   B. The buyer usually receives the rents for the day of closing.
   C. The buyer must reimburse the seller for any title evidence provided by the seller.
   D. The seller usually pays the expenses for the day of closing.

2. All encumbrances and liens shown on the report of title other than those waived or agreed to by the purchaser and listed in the contract must be removed so that the title can be delivered free and clear. The removal of such encumbrances is the duty of the:
   A. buyer.   C. broker.
   B. seller.   D. title company.

3. Legal title always passes from seller to buyer:
   A. on the date of execution of the deed.
   B. when the closing statement has been signed.
   C. when the deed is placed in escrow.
   D. when the deed is delivered.

4. Which of the following would a lender generally require at the closing?
   A. Title insurance binder
   B. Market value appraisal
   C. Application
   D. Credit report

5. Walter is buying a house. In Walter's area, closings are traditionally conducted in escrow. Which of the following items will Walter deposit with the escrow agent before the closing date?
   A. Deed to the property
   B. Title evidence
   C. Estoppel certificate
   D. Cash needed to complete the purchase

6. The RESPA Uniform Settlement Statement must be used to illustrate all settlement charges for:
   A. every real estate transaction.
   B. transactions financed by VA and FHA loans only.
   C. residential transactions financed by federally related mortgage loans.
   D. all transactions involving commercial property.

7. A mortgage reduction certificate is executed by a(n):
   A. abstract company.
   B. attorney.
   C. lending institution.
   D. grantor.

8. The principal amount of a purchaser's new mortgage loan is a:
   A. credit to the seller.
   B. credit to the buyer.
   C. debit to the seller.
   D. debit to the buyer.

9. The earnest money left on deposit with the broker is a:
   A. credit to the seller.
   B. credit to the buyer.
   C. balancing factor.
   D. debit to the buyer.

10. The annual real estate taxes on a property amount to $1,800. The seller has paid the taxes in advance for the calendar year. If closing is set for June 15, which of the following is true?
    A. Credit seller $825; debit buyer $975
    B. Credit seller $1,800; debit buyer $825
    C. Credit buyer $975; debit seller $975
    D. Credit seller $975; debit buyer $975

11. If a seller collected rent of $400, payable in advance, from an attic tenant on August 1, which of the following is true at the closing on August 15?
    A. Seller owes buyer $400
    B. Buyer owes seller $400
    C. Seller owes buyer $200
    D. Buyer owes seller $200

12. Security deposits should be listed on a closing statement as a credit to the:
    A. buyer.   C. lender.
    B. seller.   D. broker.

13. A building was purchased for $85,000, with 10 percent down and a loan for the balance. If the lender charged the buyer two discount points, how much cash did the buyer need to come up with at closing if the buyer incurred no other costs?
    A. $1,700   C. $10,030
    B. $8,500   D. $10,200

14. A buyer of a $100,000 home has paid $12,000 as earnest money and has a loan commitment for 70 percent of the purchase price. How much more cash does the buyer need to bring to the closing, provided the buyer has no closing costs?
    A. $18,000   C. $58,000
    B. $30,000   D. $61,600

15. At closing, the listing broker's commission usually is shown as a:
    A. credit to the seller.
    B. credit to the buyer.
    C. debit to the seller.
    D. debit to the buyer.

16. At the closing of a real estate transaction, the seller's attorney gave the buyer a credit for certain accrued items. These items were:
    A. bills relating to the property that have already been paid by the seller.
    B. bills relating to the property that will have to be paid by the buyer.
    C. all of the seller's real estate bills.
    D. all of the buyer's real estate bills.

17. The Real Estate Settlement Procedures Act (RESPA) applies to the activities of:
    A. brokers selling commercial and office buildings.
    B. security salespersons selling limited partnerships.
    C. Ginnie Mae or Fannie Mae when purchasing mortgages.
    D. lenders financing the purchases of borrowers' residences.

18. The purpose of RESPA is to:
    A. make sure buyers do not borrow more than they can repay.
    B. make real estate brokers more responsive to buyers' needs.
    C. help buyers know how much money is required.
    D. see that buyers know all settlement costs.

19. The document that provides borrowers with general information about settlement costs, RESPA provisions and the Uniform Settlement Statement is the:
    A. HUD Form 1.
    B. special information booklet.
    C. good-faith estimate of settlement costs.
    D. closing statement.

20. Which of the following statements is true of a computerized loan origination (CLO) system?
    A. The mortgage broker or lender may pay any fee charged by the real estate broker in whose office the CLO terminal is located.
    B. The borrower must pay any fee charged by the real estate broker in whose office the CLO terminal is located.
    C. The real estate broker in whose office the CLO terminal is located may charge a fee of up to two points for the use of the system.
    D. The fee charged by the real estate broker for using the CLO terminal may not be financed as part of the loan.

21. All of the following are false regarding the Real Estate Settlement Procedures Act (RESPA) EXCEPT:
    A. the purpose of RESPA is to assist lenders in determining their settlement charges on a local level.
    B. if a borrower is negotiating a loan on a six- unit apartment building, RESPA regulations must be followed.
    C. RESPA is a federal law enacted so buyers and sellers will be informed of settlement costs in residential real estate transactions.
    D. RESPA is a federal law enacted to regulate the settlement procedures on agricultural properties.

22. A real estate agent negotiated a contract for deed for a buyer and seller on a single-family residential property. A HUD-1 settlement sheet was not used in the transaction. Must the agent use a HUD-1 settlement sheet in this transaction?
    A. Yes; because it is a single-family residential property, a HUD-1 settlement sheet must be used.
    B. Yes; if a real estate agent is involved in a transaction, RESPA requires a HUD-1 settlement sheet.
    C. No, because RESPA does not regulate contract for deeds.
    D. No, because RESPA regulates only commercial properties.

In Illinois . . .

23. If the annual real estate taxes on a property were $2,129 last year, what would be the per diem amount for prorations this year using the actual-number-of-days method?
    A. $4.90
    B. $5.83
    C. $5.86
    D. $5.98

24. In Illinois, the closing statement is customarily prepared by which party?
    A. Buyer's attorney
    B. Listing broker
    C. Buyer's lender
    D. Seller's lender

25. Which of the following formulas best expresses the statutory month variation method of calculating a daily prorated charge for an annual prepaid expense?
    A. (Total Charge ÷ 12) ÷ Actual Days in Month of Closing = Daily Prorated Charge
    B. (Total Charge ÷ 360) × 12 = Daily Prorated Charge
    C. (Total Charge ÷ 360) × Actual Days in the Month of Closing = Daily Prorated Charge
    D. (Total Charge ÷ 365 = y) (y ÷ 12) × actual Days in Closing Month = Daily Prorated Charge

26. In Illinois, which party usually pays the state and county transfer taxes?
    A. Buyer
    B. Buyer pays state taxes; seller pays county sand municipal taxes
    C. Whichever party is specified in the local ordinance
    D. Seller

Appendix One
Real Estate Investment: An Overview

The decisions to invest in real estate and in what sort of property to invest involve a number of important considerations for a prospective investor. Not least among these are the issues discussed below.

LEVERAGE

Leverage is the use of borrowed money to finance an investment. As a rule, an investor can receive a maximum return from the initial investment (the down payment and closing and other costs) by making a small down payment, paying a low interest rate and spreading mortgage payments over as long a period as possible.

The effect of leveraging is to provide a return that reflects the impact of market forces on the entire original purchase price but that is measured against only the actual cash invested. For example, if an investor spends $100,000 for rental property and makes a $20,000 down payment, then sells the property five years later for $125,000, the return over five years is $25,000. Disregarding ownership expenses, the return is not 25 percent ($25,000 compared with $100,000) but 125 percent on the original amount invested ($25,000 compared with $20,000).

Risks are directly proportional to leverage. A high degree of leverage translates into greater risk for the investor and lender because of the high ratio of borrowed money to the value of the real estate. Lower leverage results in less risk. When values drop in an area or vacancy rates rise, the highly leveraged investor may be unable to pay even the financing costs of the property.

EQUITY BUILDUP

Equity buildup is that portion of the loan payment directed toward the principal rather than the interest, *plus* any gain in property value due to appreciation. In a sense, equity buildup is like money in the investor's bank account. This accumulated equity is not realized as cash unless the property is sold or refinanced. However, the equity interest may be sold, exchanged or mortgaged (refinanced) to be used as leverage for other investments.

PYRAMIDING THROUGH REFINANCING

An effective method for a real estate investor to increase his or her holdings without investing additional capital is through *pyramiding*. **Pyramiding** is simply the process of using one property to drive the acquisition of additional properties. Two methods of pyramiding can be used: *pyramiding through sale* and *pyramiding through refinance*.

In pyramiding through selling, an investor first acquires a property. He or she then improves the property for resale at a substantially higher price. The profit from the sale of the first property is used to purchase additional properties. Thus, the proceeds from a single investment (the point of the pyramid) provide the means for acquiring other properties. These properties also are improved and sold, and the proceeds are reinvested, until the investor is satisfied with his or her return.

The goal of pyramiding through refinancing, on the other hand, is to use the value of the original property to drive the acquisition of additional properties while retaining all the properties acquired. The investor refinances the original property and uses the proceeds of the refinance to purchase additional properties. These properties are refinanced in turn to enable the investor to acquire further properties, and so on. By holding on to the properties, the investor increases his or her income–producing property holdings.

Appendix Two

Sample Illinois Real Estate Licensing Examinations

Modern Real Estate Practice in Illinois, Third Edition, is designed to prepare you for a career in real estate. However, before you can become a broker or salesperson, you must obtain a license. Passing the real estate licensing examination plays a large part in determining your eligibility to become licensed. The exam is designed to test your knowledge of real estate laws, principles and practices.

The Illinois Real Estate Licensing Examination is currently prepared and administered by Applied Measurement Professionals, Inc. (AMP), an independent testing company.

WHAT TO EXPECT FROM THE EXAM

Salesperson and broker candidates are given separate examinations. The broker's examination includes greater emphasis on brokerage, escrow accounts, record keeping, business entities and commercial brokerage. Both exams consist of 140 questions in two parts: 100 questions in the general section (national real estate practice and principles) and 40 questions in the state section (Illinois-specific practice and licensing issues). At least 10 percent of the questions involve some sort of mathematical calculations. *You must pass both parts of the exam in order to qualify for your real estate license.* Candidates who fail one part of the exam have to retake only the section they failed. Candidates may take the examination a total of three times before they must retake a real estate course. The questions are entirely multiple-choice in format, with four alternative answer choices for each question. Only silent, hand-held, solar- or battery-operated, paperless calculators are permitted while taking the exam, and scratch paper is provided. The exam must be completed within the allotted time, but ample time is provided if the test taker is prepared adequately.

Salesperson Examination Approximately 70 percent of the questions in the Illinois real estate salesperson's exam are devoted to national real estate topics and the remainder to Illinois real estate topics. Like the broker's exam, it includes questions based on closing statement prorations and computations. However, salesperson candidates are also expected to solve basic problems in real estate mathematics related to such topics as commissions, interest and square footage. Just about anything that you have studied in this book may be included in the exam—all subject matter is "fair game." When you receive your *AMP Illinois Candidate Handbook*, it will include an outline of the subject areas that are tested on the National Section and the approximate number of questions coming from each area.

The following is the most recent AMP Detailed Content Outline, along with the chapters of *Modern Real Estate Practice in Illinois*, Third Edition, in which the subjects are covered:

Topic Headings	Chapter

1. Listing Property

A. Listing

	Chapter
1. Hidden defects	6
2. Listing agreement signatures by all parties	6
3. Tax assessment and tax rate	10
4. Deed restrictions and covenants	7
5. Legal description	6, 9
6. Lot size	9
7. Physical dimensions of structure	9
8. Appurtenances	7
9. Utilities	7
10. Type of construction	8
11. Encumbrances	6, 7
12. Compliance with health and safety building codes	20
13. Ownership of record	13
14. Homeowners' association bylaws and fees	8
15. Brokerage fee	5

B. Assessment of Property Value

	Chapter
1. Location	2
2. Anticipated changes	2
3. Depreciation	2
4. Deterioration	2
5. Obsolescence	2
6. Improvements	2
7. Economic trends	2

C. Property Valuation

	Chapter
1. Sales comparison approach	19
2. Income approach	19
3. Replacement cost estimate	19
4. Appropriate listing price recommendations for the seller	19
5. Need for independent appraisal	19

D. Nature of Real Property

	Chapter
1. Property subdivision and selling of parcels	20
2. Real and personal property included in, or excluded from, the sale	2
3. Differences between personal and real property	2
4. Forms of ownership interests in real estate and issues related to conveyance of real property	8

5.   Methods of land description   9
6.   Interests in real property   7
7.   Planning and zoning, including special study zones 20

E.   Services Provided in the Agency Relationship with the Seller

1.   Agency, responsibility of an agency and
services the agency will provide   4
2.   Net proceeds estimation   4
3.   Listing agreements, documents provided
to the seller   4, 6
4.   Safeguarding property   4
5.   Methods of improving marketability   5
6.   Property marketing, keeping seller informed   5
7.   Property files   5
8.   Civil rights and fair housing policy   21

2.   Selling Property

A.   Contracts and Offers

1.   Sales contract forms and provisions   11
2.   Offers and counteroffers   11

B.   Characteristics of Real Property

1.   Rights of ownership   8
2.   Characteristics of residential property   2
3.   Characteristics of commercial property   2
4.   Characteristics of industrial property   2
5.   Right of property subdivision   20
6.   Planning and zoning, including special study zones 20

C.   Agency

1.   Agency relationship to buyers   4
2.   Material facts   4
3.   Physical condition of property   4
4.   Psychological impact related to property   4

D.   Advising Buyers of Outside Services

1.   Income tax implications of home ownership   10
2.   Income tax implications for real estate investments 10
3.   Need for buyer to seek legal counsel   4
4.   Home protection plans   13
5.   Insurance   13
6.   Inspection reports   23
7.   Surveys   13
8.   Appraisals   19

E.   Services Provided to the Buyer

1.   Information needed to assess prospective
buyer's price range and eligibility for financing   4, 11
2.   Qualify prospective buyers   11
3.   Preview and choose property to show buyer   4
4.   Current market conditions   1
5.   Show properties and note amenities   4
6.   Affirmative marketing to ensure equal
opportunity   14, 21
7.   Civil rights and fair housing laws   21

3. **Property Management**

   A. Services to Landlords

      1. Advertising property   18
      2. Evaluating rental markets   18
      3. Obtaining tenants   18
      4. Screening applicants according to appropriate
         laws and regulations   18
      5. Tenant complaints and conflicts among tenants   18
      6. Maintaining fiduciary responsibilities to owners   18
      7. Income, expenses and rate of return for property   18
      8. Federal reporting requirements   18
      9. Federal fair housing   18, 21
      10. Maintenance   18
      11. Fees, security deposits and rent collection   18

   B. Services to Tenants

      1. Lease agreements used in property management   17, 18
      2. Rental and lease agreements   17, 18
      3. Material facts   17
      4. Showing property to prospective tenants   18
      5. Occupancy terms   17
      6. Proration of rents and leases   17

4. **Settlement/Transfer of Ownership**

   A. Tax Issues

      1. Tax implications of interest expenses   10
      2. Real property taxes   10
      3. Capital gains tax   10
      4. Refinancing   10
      5. Property taxation   10

   B. Titles

      1. Title search   13
      2. Title insurance   13
      3. Title problems   13
      4. Legal procedures   13
      5. Title abstracts   13
      6. Liens, and order of priority   13
      7. Legal proceedings against property   13
      8. Methods of recording   13

   C. Settlement Procedures

      1. Purposes and procedures of settlement   23
      2. Federal statutory requirements   23
      3. Real Estate Settlement Procedures Act (RESPA)   23
      4. Closing statements   23
      5. Rescission clauses   16
      6. Obligations of settlement agent   23
      7. Calculations regarding proration/prepayment   23
      8. Warranties associated with deeds   12
      9. Settlement statement (HUD-1)   23
      10. Other settlement documents   23
      11. Transfer tax   12

D. Characteristics of Real Property

    1. Ways of holding and conveying title and characteristics of the different approaches to tenancy   12

    2. Rights of home ownership   8

    3. Rights of others related to property   8, 9

    4. Nature and types of common interest ownership   8

    5. Eminent domain proceedings   20

E. Additional Services

    1. Negotiations between buyers and sellers leading to agreement   11, 23

    2. Contract requirements and fulfillment of contingencies leading to closing   11, 23

    3. Fair housing laws   21

    4. Securities laws, providing appropriate referrals   4, 14

    5. Other situations where experts are required   4, 10, 14

5. Financing

A. Sources of Financing

    1. Institutional   16

    2. Seller financing   16

    3. Assumption of existing financing   16

    4. Other sources of financing   16

B. Types of Loans

    1. Security for loans   16

    2. Repayment methods   16

    3. Forms of financing   16

    4. Secondary mortgage markets   16

    5. Other types of mortgage loans   16

C. Terms and Conditions

    1. Loan application requirements   15

    2. Loan origination costs   15

    3. Lender requirements   15

    4. Conditional approval   15

    5. Provisions of federal regulations   15, 23

D. Common Clauses and Terms in Mortgage Instruments

    1. Prepayment   15

    2. Interest rates   15

    3. Release   15

    4. Due-on-sale   15

    5. Subordination   15

    6. Escalation   15

    7. Acceleration   15

    8. Default   15

    9. Foreclosure and redemption rights   15

    10. Nonrecourse provision   15

6. Professional Responsibilities/Fair Practice/Administration

A. Professional Responsibilities and Fair Practice

    1. Legal responsibilities of a licensee under the law of agency   4, 14

2.   Laws, rules and regulations pertaining to real estate practice, including fair housing and civil rights 14, 21

3.   Market trends, availability of financing, rates and conditions of obtaining rent 16, 17

4.   Resolving misunderstandings among parties to real estate transactions 23

B.   Administration

1.   Terms of contract between licensee and broker 5

2.   Complete and accurate records of all business transactions 5

3.   Required notifications and reports of the real estate regulatory agency 5

4.   Company policies, procedures and standards 5

5.   Determining commissions for brokerage agreements and closing statements 5

Illinois-Specific Topics   The following is the most recent AMP Detailed Content Outline for the Illinois-specific portion of the examination, along with the chapters of *Modern Real Estate Practice in Illinois*, Third Edition, in which the subjects are covered:

Topic Headings	Chapter
1. Licensing Requirements	**14**
A. License Exemptions	14
B. Activities Requiring a License	14
C. Types of Licenses	14
1. Salesperson	14
2. Broker	14
3. Leasing agent	14
D. Personal Assistants	5, 14
E. Eligibility for Licensing, Including Sponsor Card	14
F. Examination	14
G. License Renewal	14
H. Continuing Education	14
I. Change in Licensee Information	14
J. Reciprocity	14
K. Real Estate Recovery Fund	14
2. Laws and Rules Regulating Real Estate Practice	**14**
A. Purpose of License Law	14
B. Advertising	14
C. Broker/Salesperson Relationship	4, 14
D. Commissions	5, 6, 14
1. Finder's fee/referral fee	14
2. Rental finding services	14, 17

Broker Examination

Approximately 70 percent of the questions in the Illinois real estate broker's exam are devoted to national real estate topics and the remainder to Illinois real estate topics. The broker candidate must answer questions on the state section that require knowledge of closing statement prorations and computations. Candidates also should be familiar with the mathematics and terminology of prorations. They must know, based on the four-column format, whether items shown at closing are debits or credits to the buyer or the seller. The broker's outline is different from the salesperson's. The areas of contract law, zoning and land use, deeds, rights and interests and agency law, as well as closing and proration, are tested more heavily on the broker's exam.

Broker candidates are expected to be familiar with all areas of Illinois real estate law and practice covered in this book. For study purposes, brokers should be particularly aware of the following topics, in addition to those listed for the salesperson's exam:

- Broker responsibilities
- Escrow accounts
- Examination of records
- Corporation/partnership/limited liability company licensure
- Commercial Broker Lien Act
- Services to landlords
- Effect of capital improvements on tax basis
- Administration

MULTIPLE-CHOICE QUESTIONS: TEST-TAKING STRATEGIES

There are as many different ways to prepare for and take multiple-choice examinations as there are test takers. Before you try the following sample exams, take some time to read this brief overview of test-taking strategies. While no one can tell you which method will work best for you, it's always a good idea to think about what you're going to do before you do it.

One of the most important things to remember about multiple-choice test questions is this: they always give you the correct answer. You don't have to remember how things are spelled, and you don't have to try to guess what the question is about. The answer is always there, right in front of you.

Of course, if it were as easy as that, it wouldn't be much of a test. The key to success in taking multiple-choice examinations is actually two keys: first, *know the correct answer.* You do that by going to class, paying attention, taking good notes and studying the material. Then, if you don't know the correct answer, be able to analyze the questions and answers effectively, so you can apply the second key: *be able to make a reasonable guess.* Even if you don't know the answer, you will probably know which answers are clearly wrong and which ones are more likely than the others to be right.

If you can eliminate one answer as wrong, you have improved your odds of "guessing correctly" by 25 percent, from 4-to-1 to 3-to-1. If you can eliminate two wrong answers, you have a 50/50 shot at a correct guess. Of course, if you can eliminate *three* wrong answers, your chance of a correct response is 100 percent. In any case, there is no secret formula: *the only sure way to improve your odds of a correct answer is to study and learn the material.*

Structure of the Question

A multiple-choice question has a basic structure. It starts with what test writers call the *stem.* That's the text of the question that sets up the need for an answer. The stem may be an incomplete statement that is finished by the correct answer; it may be a story problem or hypothetical example (called a *fact-pattern*) about which you will be asked a question. Or it may be a math problem, in which you are given basic information and asked to solve a mathematical issue, such as the amount of a commission or capital gain.

The stem is always followed by *options:* four possible answers to the question presented by the stem. Depending on the structure and content of the stem, the options may be single words or numbers, phrases or complete sentences.

Three of the options are *distractors:* incorrect answers intended to "distract" you from the correct choice. One of the options is the correct answer, called the *key.*

Reading a Multiple-Choice Question

Here are three suggestions for how to read a multiple-choice test question.

1. The Traditional Method. Read the question through from start to finish, then read the options. When you get to the correct answer, mark it and move on. This method works best for short questions, such as those that require completion or simply define a term. For long, more complicated questions or those that are not quite so clear, however, you may miss important information.

2. The Focus Method. As we've seen, multiple-choice questions have different parts. In longer math or story-type questions, the last line of the stem will contain the question's *focus:* the basic issue the item asks you to address. That is, *the question is always in the last line of the stem.* In the focus method, when you come to a longer item, read the last line of the stem first. This will clue you in to what the question is about. Then go back and read the stem from beginning to end. The advantage is this: while you are reading the complicated facts or math elements, you know what to look for. You can watch for important items and disregard unnecessary information. It's a sad fact of multiple-choice exams that sometimes test writers include distracting elements in the stem itself. If you check for the question's focus first, you'll spot the test-writer's tricks right away.

3. The Upside-Down Method. This technique takes the focus method one step further. Here, you do just what the name implies: you start reading the question from the bottom up. By reading the four options first, you can learn exactly what the test writer wants you to focus on. For instance, a fact-pattern problem might include several dollar values in the stem, leading you to believe you're going to have to do a math calculation. You'll be trying to recall all the equations you've memorized, only to find at the end of the stem that you're only expected to define a term. If you've read the options first, you would have known what to look for.

TAKING THE SAMPLE EXAMINATIONS

The following two sample examinations have been designed to help you prepare for the actual licensing exam. Each of the sample exams is in two parts: 85 questions on general real estate principles and 55 covering Illinois-specific law and practice. On your exam, 5 questions in each section are "pretest" items, used for statistical purposes only. They do not factor into your final score. For our review purposes here, however, there are no pretest-type items: every question counts. Note that proration calculations are based on a 30-day month unless otherwise specified.

EXAM ONE

Part One
General Real Estate Practice and Principles

1. Which of the following is a lien on real estate?
   A. Recorded easement
   B. Recorded mortgage
   C. Encroachment
   D. Deed restriction

2. A sales contract was signed under duress. Which of the following describes this contract?
   A. Voidable   C. Discharged
   B. Breached   D. Void

3. A broker receives a check for earnest money from a buyer and deposits the money in the broker's personal interest-bearing checking account over the weekend. This action exposes the broker to a charge of:
   A. commingling.   C. subrogation.
   B. novation.   D. accretion.

4. A borrower takes out a mortgage loan that requires monthly payments of $875.70 for 20 years and a final payment of $24,095. This is what type of loan?
   A. Wraparound   C. Balloon
   B. Accelerated   D. Variable

5. If a borrower computed the interest charged for the previous month on his $60,000 loan balance as $412.50, what is the borrower's interest rate?
   A. 7.5 percent   C. 8.25 percent
   B. 7.75 percent   D. 8.5 percent

6. A broker signs a contract with a buyer. Under the contract, the broker agrees to help the buyer find a suitable property and to represent the buyer in negotiations with the seller. Although the buyer may not sign an agreement with any other broker, she may look for properties on her own. The broker is entitled to payment only if the broker locates the property that is purchased. What kind of agreement has this broker signed?
   A. Exclusive buyer agency agreement
   B. Exclusive-agency buyer agency agreement
   C. Open buyer agency agreement
   D. Option contract

7. Talia conveys property to Nicholas by delivering a deed. The deed contains five covenants. This is most likely a:
   A. warranty deed.   C. grant deed.
   B. quitclaim deed.   D. deed in trust.

8. Pamela, a real estate broker, does not show non-Asian clients any properties in several traditionally Asian neighborhoods. She bases this practice on the need to preserve the valuable cultural integrity of Asian immigrant communities. Which of the following statements is true regarding Pamela's policy?
   A. Pamela's policy is steering and violates the fair housing laws regardless of her motivation.
   B. Because Pamela is not attempting to restrict the rights of any single minority group, the practice does not constitute steering.
   C. Pamela's policy is steering, but it does not violate the fair housing laws because she is motivated by cultural preservation, not by exclusion or discrimination.
   D. Pamela's policy has the effect, but not the intent, of steering.

9. Helene grants a life estate to her grandson and stipulates that upon the grandson's death, the title to the property will pass to her son-in-law. This second estate is known as a(n):
   A. remainder.
   B. reversion.
   C. estate at sufferance.
   D. estate for years.

10. When property is held in joint tenancy:
    A. a maximum of two people can own the real estate.
    B. the fractional interests of the owners can be different.
    C. additional owners may be added later.
    D. there is always the right of survivorship.

11. A real estate salesperson who has a written contract with his broker that specifies that he will not be treated as an employee, and whose entire income is from sales commissions rather than an hourly wage, is probably a(n):
    A. real estate assistant.
    B. employee.
    C. subagent.
    D. independent contractor.

12. The states in which the lender holds title of mortgaged real estate are known as:
    A. title-theory states.
    B. lien-theory states.
    C. statutory title states.
    D. strict title forfeiture states.

13. The form of tenancy that expires on a specific date is a:
    A. joint tenancy.
    B. tenancy for years.
    C. tenancy in common.
    D. tenancy by the entirety.

14. A suburban home that lacks indoor plumbing suffers from which of the following?
    A. Functional obsolescence
    B. Curable physical deterioration
    C. Incurable physical deterioration
    D. External obsolescence

15. If a developer wants to build a commercial building closer to the street than is permitted by the local zoning ordinance because the shape of the lot makes a standard setback impossible, she or he should seek a:
    A. variance.
    B. nonconforming use permit.
    C. conditional use permit.
    D. density zoning permit.

16. Assuming that the listing broker and the selling broker in a transaction split their commission equally, what was the sales price of the property if the commission rate was 6.5 percent and the listing broker, after paying the selling broker, kept $2,593.50?
    A. $39,900   C. $79,800
    B. $56,200   D. $88,400

17. Karl, a real estate broker, specializes in helping both buyers and sellers with the necessary paperwork involved in transferring property. While Karl is not an agent of either party, he may not disclose either party's confidential information to the other. Karl is a(n):
    A. buyer's agent.
    B. independent contractor.
    C. dual agent.
    D. transactional broker.

18. A mortgage lender intends to lend money at 9¾ percent on a 30-year loan. If the loan yields 10⅜ percent, how many discount points must be charged on this loan?
    A. ½   C. 5
    B. 4   D. 8

19. The listing and selling brokers agree to split a 7 percent commission 50/50 on a $95,900 sale. The listing broker gives the listing salesperson 30 percent of his commission, and the selling broker gives the selling salesperson 35 percent of his commission. How much does the selling salesperson earn from the sale after deducting expenses of $35?
    A. $1,139.78   C. $1,183.95
    B. $1,174.78   D. $1,971.95

20. Police powers include all of the following EXCEPT:
    A. zoning.
    B. deed restrictions.
    C. building codes.
    D. subdivision regulations.

21. A seller wants to net $65,000 from the sale of her house after paying the broker's fee of 6 percent. The seller's gross sales price will be:
    A. $61,100.   C. $68,900.
    B. $64,752.   D. $69,149.

22. How many square feet are in three acres?
    A. 43,560   C. 156,840
    B. 130,680   D. 27,878,400

23. Wendy is purchasing a condominium unit in a subdivision and obtains financing from a local savings and loan association. In this situation, which of the following best describes Wendy?
    A. Vendor   C. Grantor
    B. Mortgagor   D. Lessor

24. The current value of a property is $40,000. The property is assessed at 40 percent of its current value for real estate tax purposes, with an equalization factor of 1.5 applied to the assessed value. If the tax rate is $4 per $100 of assessed valuation, what is the amount of tax due on the property?
    A. $640   C. $1,600
    B. $960   D. $2,400

25. A building was sold for $60,000, with the purchaser putting 10 percent down and obtaining a loan for the balance. The lending institution charged a 1 percent loan origination fee. What was the total cash used for the purchase?
    A. $540   C. $6,540
    B. $6,000   D. $6,600

26. A parcel of vacant land has an assessed valuation of $274,550. If the assessment is 85 percent of market value, what is the market value?
    A. $315,732.50   C. $323,000.00
    B. $320,000.00   D. $830,333.33

27. What is a capitalization rate?
    A. Amount determined by the gross rent multiplier
    B. Rate of return a property will produce
    C. Mathematical value determined by a sales price
    D. Rate at which the amount of depreciation in a property is measured

28. A parcel of land described as "the NW¼ and the SW¼ of Section 6, T4N, R8W of the Third Principal Meridian" was sold for $875 per acre. The listing broker will receive a 5 percent commission on the total sales price. How much will the broker receive?
    A. $1,750   C. $14,000
    B. $5,040   D. $15,040

29. If a house was sold for $40,000 and the buyer obtained an FHA-insured mortgage loan for $38,500, how much money would the buyer pay in discount points if the lender charged four points?
    A. $385   C. $1,540
    B. $1,500   D. $1,600

30. The commission rate is 7¾ percent on a sale of $50,000. What is the dollar amount of the commission?
    A. $3,500   C. $4,085
    B. $3,875   D. $4,585

31. An offer would be terminated by all of the following events EXCEPT:
    A. Wyatt signed a written offer to buy a house but called the seller and revoked the offer just after his agent presented it and before it was formally accepted.
    B. Charles signed a written offer to buy a house and then died.
    C. Yolanda signed a written offer to buy a house, and the seller made a counteroffer.
    D. Zoa signed a written offer to buy a house, but another buyer submitted an offer at the same time.

home under a land
contract is paid in full,
...s of Garrett's interest in the

...ds legal title to the premises.

...is no legal interest in the

... possesses a legal life estate in the
...ses.

D. Garrett has equitable title in the property.

33. Fred and Karen enter into an agreement. Karen will mow Fred's lawn every week during the summer. Later, Karen decides to go into a different business. Valerie would like to assume Karen's obligation to mow Fred's lawn. Fred agrees and enters into a new contract with Valerie. Fred and Karen tear up their original agreement. This is known as:
    A. assignment.   C. substitution.
    B. novation.   D. rescission.

34. Using the services of a mortgage broker, Gerald borrowed $4,000 from a private lender. After deducting the loan costs, Gerald received $3,747. What is the face amount of the note?
    A. $3,747   C. $4,253
    B. $4,000   D. $7,747

35. Whose signature is necessary for an offer to purchase real estate to become a contract?
    A. Buyer's only
    B. Buyer's and seller's
    C. Seller's only
    D. Seller's and seller's broker's

36. A borrower has just made the final payment on a mortgage loan. Regardless of this fact, the records will still show a lien on the mortgaged property until which of the following events occurs?
    A. A satisfaction of the mortgage document is recorded.
    B. A reconveyance of the mortgage document is delivered to the mortgage holder.
    C. A novation of the mortgage document takes place.
    D. An estoppel of the mortgage document is filed with the clerk of the county in which the mortgagee is located.

37. If the annual net income from a commercial property is $22,000 and the capitalization rate is 8 percent, what is the value of the property using the income approach?
    A. $176,000   C. $200,000
    B. $183,000   D. $275,000

38. A broker enters into a listing agreement with a seller in which the seller will receive $120,000 from the sale of a vacant lot and the broker will receive any sale proceeds exceeding that amount. This is what type of listing?
    A. Exclusive-agency
    B. Net
    C. Exclusive-right-to-sell
    D. Multiple

39. An individual sold her house and moved into a cooperative apartment. Under the cooperative form of ownership, the individual will:
    A. become a shareholder in the corporation.
    B. not lose her apartment if she pays her share of the expenses.
    C. have to take out a new mortgage loan on her unit.
    D. receive a fixed-term lease for her unit.

40. A defect or a cloud on title to property may be cured by:
    A. obtaining quitclaim deeds from all appropriate parties.
    B. bringing an action to register the title.
    C. paying cash for the property at the settlement.
    D. bringing an action to repudiate the title.

41. A buyer signed an exclusive-agency buyer agency agreement with a broker. If the buyer finds a suitable property with no assistance from any broker, the broker is entitled to:
    A. full compensation from the buyer, regardless of who found the property.
    B. full compensation from the seller.
    C. partial compensation as generally required under this type of agreement.
    D. no compensation under the terms of this type of agreement.

42. Under the terms of a net lease, a commercial tenant usually would be responsible for paying all of the following EXCEPT:
    A. maintenance expenses.
    B. mortgage debt service.
    C. fire and extended-coverage insurance.
    D. real estate taxes.

43. The Civil Rights Act of 1866 prohibits discrimination based on:
    A. sex.   C. race.
    B. religion.   D. familial status.

44. If a borrower must pay $6,000 for points on a $150,000 loan, how many points is the lender charging for this loan?
    A. 3   C. 5
    B. 4   D. 6

45. What is the difference between a general lien and a specific lien?
    A. A general lien cannot be enforced in court, while a specific lien can.
    B. A specific lien is held by only one person, while a general lien must be held by two or more.
    C. A general lien is a lien against personal property, while a specific lien is a lien against real estate.
    D. A specific lien is a lien against a certain parcel of real estate, while a general lien covers all of a debtor's property.

46. In an option to purchase real estate, which of the following statements is true of the optionee?
    A. The optionee must purchase the property but may do so at any time within the option period.
    B. The optionee is limited to a refund of the option consideration if the option is exercised.
    C. The optionee cannot obtain third-party financing on the property until after the option has expired.
    D. The optionee has no obligation to purchase the property during the option period.

47. In 1974, an owner constructed a building that was eight stories high. In 1997, the municipality changed the zoning ordinance and prohibited buildings taller than six stories. Which of the following statements is true regarding the existing eight-story building?
    A. The building must be demolished.
    B. The building is a conditional use.
    C. The building is a nonconforming use.
    D. The owner must obtain a variance.

48. How many acres are there in the N½ of the SW¼ and the NE¼ of the SE¼ of a section?
    A. 20   C. 80
    B. 40   D. 120

49. Branca's home is the smallest in a neighborhood of large, expensive houses. The effect of the other houses on the value of Branca's home is known as:
    A. regression.   C. substitution.
    B. progression.   D. contribution.

50. A lien that arises as a result of a judgment, estate or inheritance taxes, the decedent's debts or federal taxes is what sort of lien?
    A. Specific   C. Voluntary
    B. General   D. Equitable

51. A broker received a deposit, along with a written offer from a buyer. The offer stated: "The offeror will leave this offer open for the seller's acceptance for a period of ten days." On the fifth day, and before acceptance by the seller, the offeror notified the broker that the offer was withdrawn and demanded the return of the deposit. Which of the following statements is true in this situation?
    A. The offeror cannot withdraw the offer; it must be held open for the full ten-day period, as promised.
    B. The offeror has the right to withdraw the offer and secure the return of the deposit any time before being notified of the seller's acceptance.
    C. The offeror can withdraw the offer, and the seller and the broker will each retain one-half of the forfeited deposit.
    D. While the offeror can withdraw the offer, the broker is legally entitled to declare the deposit forfeited and retain all of it in lieu of the lost commission.

52. Charles and Linda are joint tenants. Linda sells her interest to Francine. What is the relationship between Charles and Francine regarding the property?
    A. Joint tenants
    B. Tenants in common
    C. Tenants by the entirety
    D. No relationship exists because Linda cannot sell her joint tenancy interest.

53. Sam and Wally orally enter into a six-month lease. If Wally defaults, which of the following statements is true?
    A. Sam may not bring a court action because six-month leases must be in writing under the parol evidence rule.
    B. Sam may not bring a court action because the statute of frauds governs six-month leases.
    C. Sam may bring a court action because six-month leases need not be in writing to be enforceable.
    D. Sam may bring a court action because the statute of limitations does not apply to oral leases, regardless of their term.

54. On Monday, Tom offers to sell his vacant lot to Kent for $12,000. On Tuesday, Kent counteroffers to buy the lot for $10,500. On Friday, Kent withdraws his counteroffer and accepts Tom's original price of $12,000. Under these circumstances:
    A. a valid agreement exists because Kent accepted Tom's offer exactly as it was made, regardless of the fact that it was not accepted immediately.
    B. a valid agreement exists because Kent accepted before Tom advised him that the offer was withdrawn.
    C. no valid agreement exists because Tom's offer was not accepted within 72 hours of its having been made.
    D. no valid agreement exists because Kent's counteroffer was a rejection of Tom's offer, and once rejected, it cannot be accepted later.

55. Yvette's neighbors use her driveway to reach their garage, which is on their property. Yvette's attorney explains that the neighbors have an easement appurtenant that gives them the right to use her driveway. Yvette's property is the:
    A. dominant tenement.
    B. servient tenement.
    C. prescriptive tenement.
    D. appurtenant tenement.

56. If the quarterly interest at 7.5 percent is $562.50, what is the principal amount of the loan?
    A. $7,500
    B. $15,000
    C. $30,000
    D. $75,000

57. A deed conveys ownership to the grantee "as long as the existing building is not torn down." What type of estate does this deed create?
    A. Determinable fee estate
    B. Fee simple absolute estate
    C. Nondestructible estate
    D. Life estate pur autre vie, with the measuring life being the building's

58. If the mortgage loan is 80 percent of the appraised value of a house and the interest rate of 8 percent amounts to $460 for the first month, what is the appraised value of the house?
    A. $69,000
    B. $71,875
    C. $86,250
    D. $92,875

59. Local zoning ordinances may regulate all of the following EXCEPT the:
    A. height of buildings in an area.
    B. density of population.
    C. appropriate use of buildings in an area.
    D. market value of a property.

60. A broker took a listing and later discovered that the client had been declared incompetent by a court. What is the current status of the listing?
    A. The listing is unaffected because the broker acted in good faith as the owner's agent.
    B. The listing is of no value to the broker because the contract is void.
    C. The listing is the basis for recovery of a commission from the client's guardian or trustee if the broker produces a buyer.
    D. The listing may be renegotiated between the broker and the client, based on the new information.

61. A borrower defaulted on his home mortgage loan payments, and the lender obtained a court order to foreclose on the property. At the foreclosure sale, the property sold for $64,000; the unpaid balance on the loan at the time of foreclosure was $78,000. What must the lender do to recover the $14,000 that the borrower still owes?
    A. Sue for specific performance
    B. Sue for damages
    C. Seek a deficiency judgment
    D. Seek a judgment by default

62. All of the following are exemptions to the federal Fair Housing Act of 1968 EXCEPT:
    A. the sale of a single-family home where the listing broker does not advertise the property.
    B. the restriction of noncommercial lodgings by a private club to members of the club.
    C. the rental of a unit in an owner-occupied three-family dwelling where an advertisement is placed in the paper.
    D. the restriction of noncommercial housing in a convent where a certified statement has not been filed with the government.

63. Greg purchases a $37,000 property, depositing $3,000 as earnest money. If Greg obtains a 75 percent loan-to-value loan on the property, no additional items are prorated and there are no closing costs to Greg, how much more cash will Greg need at the settlement?
    A. $3,250   C. $5,250
    B. $3,500   D. $6,250

64. Broker Kyra arrives to present a purchase offer to Don, who is seriously ill, and finds Don's son and daughter-in-law also present. The son and daughter-in-law angrily urge Don to accept the offer, even though it is much less than the asking price for the property. If Don accepts the offer, Don may later claim that:
    A. Kyra improperly presented an offer that was less than the asking price.
    B. Kyra's failure to protect Don from the son and daughter-in-law constituted a violation of Kyra's fiduciary duties.
    C. Don's rights under the ADA have been violated by the son and daughter-in-law.
    D. Don was under undue influence from the son and daughter-in-law, so the contract is voidable.

65. Pat sold his property to Wallace. The deed of conveyance contained only the following guarantee: "This property was not encumbered during the time Pat owned it except as noted in this deed." What type of deed did Pat give to Wallace?
    A. General warranty
    B. Special warranty
    C. Bargain and sale
    D. Quitclaim

66. Steve and Teri, who are not married, own a parcel of real estate. Each owns an undivided interest, with Steve owning one-third and Teri owning two-thirds. The form of ownership under which Steve and Teri own their property is:
    A. severalty.
    B. joint tenancy.
    C. tenancy at will.
    D. tenancy in common.

67. Tyrone agrees to purchase a house for $84,500. Tyrone pays $2,000 as earnest money and obtains a new mortgage loan for $67,600. The purchase contract provides for a March 15 settlement. Tyrone and the sellers prorate the present year's real estate taxes of $1,880.96, which have been prepaid. Tyrone has additional closing costs of $1,250, and the sellers have other closing costs of $850. Using the actual number of days method, how much cash must Tyrone bring to the settlement?
    A. $16,389   C. $17,839
    B. $17,641   D. $19,639

68. A broker advertised a house he had listed for sale at the price of $47,900. Jon, a member of a racial minority group, saw the house and was interested in it. When Jon asked the broker the price of the house, the broker told Jon $53,000. Under the federal Fair Housing Act of 1968, such a statement is:
    A. legal because the law requires only that Jon be given the opportunity to buy the house.
    B. legal because the representation was made by the broker and not directly by the owner.
    C. illegal because the difference in the offering price and the quoted price was greater than 10 percent.
    D. illegal because the terms of the potential sale were changed for Jon.

69. Linda placed Blackacre in a trust, naming herself as the beneficiary. When Linda died, her will directed the trustee to sell Blackacre and distribute the proceeds of the sale to her heirs. The trustee sold Blackacre in accordance with the will. What type of deed was delivered at settlement?
    A. Trustee's deed
    B. Trustor's deed
    C. Deed in trust
    D. Reconveyance deed

70. An appraiser has been hired to prepare an appraisal report of a property for loan purposes. The property is an elegant old mansion that is now leased out as a restaurant. To which approach to value should the appraiser probably give the greatest weight when making this appraisal?
    A. Income
    B. Sales comparison
    C. Replacement cost
    D. Reproduction cost

71. Catherine applies for a mortgage, and the loan officer suggests that she might consider a term mortgage loan. Which of the following statements best explains what the loan officer means?
    A. All of the interest is paid at the end of the term.
    B. The debt is partially amortized over the life of the loan.
    C. The length of the term is limited by state law.
    D. The entire principal amount is due at the end of the term.

72. Valley Place is a condominium community with a swimming pool, tennis courts and biking trail. These facilities are most likely owned by the:
    A. Valley Place condominium board.
    B. corporation in which the unit owners hold stock.
    C. unit owners in the form of proportional divided interests.
    D. unit owners in the form of percentage undivided interests.

73. On a closing statement in a typical real estate transaction, the buyer's earnest money deposit is reflected as a:
    A. credit to buyer only.
    B. credit to seller, debit to buyer.
    C. credit to buyer and seller.
    D. debit to buyer only.

74. Prepaid insurance and tax reserves, where the buyer assumes the mortgage, will appear on a typical closing statement as a:
    A. credit to buyer, debit to seller.
    B. credit to seller only.
    C. debit to seller only.
    D. debit to buyer, credit to seller.

75. Real property can become personal property by the process known as:
    A. attachment.   C. hypothecation.
    B. severance.   D. accretion.

76. Jack and Sal are next-door neighbors. Sal gives Jack permission to park a camper in Sal's yard for a few weeks. Sal does not charge Jack rent for the use of the yard. Sal has given Jack a(n):
    A. easement.
    B. estate for years.
    C. license.
    D. permissive encroachment.

77. What is the cost of constructing a fence 6 feet, 6 inches high around a lot measuring 90 feet by 175 feet if the cost of erecting the fence is $1.25 per linear foot and the cost of materials is $.825 per square foot of fence?
    A. $1,752   C. $2,084
    B. $2,054   D. $3,505

78. Ken signs a listing agreement with broker Elaine. Broker Nancy obtains a buyer for the house, and Elaine does not receive a commission. *Elaine does not sue Ken.* The listing agreement between Ken and Elaine was probably which of the following?
    A. Exclusive-right-to-sell
    B. Open
    C. Exclusive-agency
    D. Dual agency

79. Antitrust laws prohibit all of the following EXCEPT:
    A. real estate companies agreeing on fees charged to sellers.
    B. real estate brokers allocating markets based on the value of homes.
    C. real estate companies allocating markets based on the location of commercial buildings.
    D. real estate salespersons within the same office recommending the same commission rate.

80. Tina leased an apartment from Lou. Because Lou failed to perform routine maintenance, the apartment building's central heating plant broke down in the fall. Lou neglected to have the heating system repaired, and Tina had no heat in her apartment for the first six weeks of winter. Although eight months remained on Tina's lease, she moved out of the apartment and refused to pay any rent. If Lou sues to recover the outstanding rent, which of the following would be Tina's best defense?
    A. Because Tina lived in the apartment for more than 25 percent of the lease term, she was entitled to move out at any time without penalty.
    B. Tina was entitled to vacate the premises because the landlord's failure to repair the heating system constituted abandonment.
    C. Because the apartment was made uninhabitable, the landlord's actions constituted actual eviction.
    D. The landlord's actions constituted constructive eviction.

81. The right to control one's property includes all of the following EXCEPT the right to:
    A. invite people on the property for a political fund-raiser.
    B. exclude the utilities meter reader.
    C. erect "No Trespassing" signs.
    D. leave the property undeveloped.

82. Legally, the term *improvements* refers to all of the following EXCEPT:
    A. sidewalks.
    B. a natural grove of trees.
    C. sewers.
    D. a rusty tin tool shed.

83. What is the maximum capital gains tax exclusion allowable for a married couple who have lived in their home for the past 3½ years?
    A. $100,000　　　C. $500,000
    B. $250,000　　　D. $750,000

84. Statements by a real estate licensee exaggerating the benefits of a property are called:
    A. polishing.　　　C. prospecting.
    B. puffing.　　　　D. marketing.

85. A building sold for $157,000. The broker divided the 6 percent commission as follows: 10 percent to the listing salesperson; one-half of the balance to the selling salesperson. What was the listing salesperson's commission?
    A. $239　　　　C. $1,570
    B. $942　　　　D. $4,239

86. All of the following are true regarding condominiums EXCEPT:
    A. it is a blend of severalty and tenancy in common ownership.
    B. the by-laws define the responsibilities of the owners and declare how the home-owner's association will operate the condo community.
    C. balconies and assigned parking spaces are examples of limited common areas.
    D. if a unit owner does not pay their monthly maintenance fee the entire community will be foreclosed.

87. Which of the following is NOT an unlawful practice?
    A. To refuse to sell, rent or negotiate with a person because of race
    B. As a property manager, to check the credit of females only
    C. To display the Equal Housing Opportunity poster
    D. To refuse to let a handicapped person, at their expense, modify a dwelling

88. All of the following are voidable contracts EXCEPT a contract entered into:
    A. by the guardian of a minor.
    B. under duress.
    C. under fraud.
    D. with contingencies.

89. An owner has entered into a listing agreement in which the broker may NOT collect a commission. The owner negotiated a(n):
    A. exclusive right to sell listing.
    B. private listing.
    C. exclusive listing.
    D. net listing.

90. All of the following would be associated with depreciation EXCEPT:
    A. a neighbor who does not maintain his property.
    B. a house without enough electrical outlets.
    C. shutters that need to be painted.
    D. the square foot method.

EXAM ONE

Part Two
Illinois Real Estate Law and Practice

1. A large manufacturing company agrees to relocate to an economically depressed neighborhood of Chicago if the city can provide suitable property in a short period of time. The property needed is a large vacant lot owned by an investment partnership that refuses to sell. If the city of Chicago wants to relieve unemployment in the neighborhood and improve commercial conditions in the city by bringing in the manufacturer immediately, what can the city legally do?
   A. Nothing: private real property is exempt from the power of eminent domain.
   B. Obtain title to the property by escheat through the provisions of Article I, Section 15, of the Illinois Constitution.
   C. Obtain title to the property through a court action seeking condemnation of the property.
   D. Obtain immediate rights of possession and use by depositing a sum of money that a court preliminarily considers to be just compensation with the county treasurer through a process known as a *quick-take*.

2. Illinois law requires that a preprinted offer to purchase that is intended to become a binding contract have which of the following headings?
   A. REAL ESTATE SALE CONTRACT
   B. OFFER TO PURCHASE
   C. Standard Purchase Offer and Contract
   D. Purchase Offer Form

3. In 1957, James (an Illinois resident) granted Rolling Acre to Brian "so long as no liquor is ever served on the property." The conveyance provided that if liquor was served on Rolling Acre, ownership would immediately revert to James. In 1990, Brian sold Rolling Acre to Charles. Based on these facts, which of the following statements is true?
   A. The sale of Rolling Acre in 1990 extinguished James's right of reverter.
   B. Both James's right of reverter and the limiting condition expired by operation of Illinois statute in 1978; Charles is free to sell Rolling Acre without condition.
   C. While the condition continues forever, James's right of reverter automatically expired in 1997.
   D. Both the condition and James's right of reverter automatically expired in 1997.

4. Chris and Debbie are married Illinois residents. If their co-owned home is sold to satisfy their unpaid credit card debts, how much will the creditors receive if the property sells for $165,000?
   A. Nothing. By statute, an Illinois resident's home may not be sold except to satisfy a mortgage debt or real estate taxes.
   B. $150,000
   C. $157,500
   D. $163,600

5. Which of the following statements in a deed would establish a valid tenancy by the entirety in Illinois?
   A. "To Ken and Helen, a lawfully married couple, as tenants by the entirety"
   B. "To Ken and Helen, husband and wife, not as joint tenants or tenants in common but as tenants by the entirety"
   C. "To Ken and Helen jointly, as married tenants by the entirety"
   D. "To Ken and Helen as tenants by the entirety in accordance with Illinois law"

arrangement in which the
... receives a fee simple ownership in
...perty and the right to use the property
... specific period of less than one year on
...ecurring basis for more than three years is
referred to as a:

A. time-share use.

B. time-share estate.

C. public offering statement.

D. membership camp.

7. Which of the following would be required to be surveyed and have a plat recorded under the Illinois Plat Act?

A. An owner divides a 30-acre parcel into five equal lots.

B. An owner divides a 20-acre parcel into five equal lots.

C. An owner conveys a single 20-acre parcel.

D. An owner divides a single 20-acre parcel into two 6-acre lots and an 8-acre lot.

8. The general datum plane referred to by surveyors throughout Illinois is the:

A. Chicago City Datum.

B. New York Harbor Datum.

C. United States Geological Survey Datum.

D. Centralia Datum.

9. While the identity of the beneficiary of a land trust is not usually disclosed without the beneficiary's written permission, the trustee may be compelled to do so in all the following situations EXCEPT:

A. when the information is demanded by the Internal Revenue Service.

B. during the discovery process of a lawsuit or criminal action involving the property.

C. when applying to a state agency for a license or permit affecting the property.

D. when a private request is filed in the public records office.

10. An owner paid the first installment of her Illinois general real estate tax on July 1. The amount due was $2,380. If the county assessor issued the owner's bill 30 days before the penalty date of June 1, does the owner owe any penalty?

A. No: the penalty date for the payment of all Illinois general real estate taxes is September 1.

B. Yes: the owner will have to pay $35.70 as a penalty in addition to the real estate tax owed.

C. No: the assessor is required by statute to issue tax bills 60 days before any penalty date.

D. Yes: the owner will have to pay $71.40 as a penalty in addition to the real estate tax owed.

11. A judgment issued by an Illinois court is a:

A. general, involuntary legal lien on all of a debtor's real property and an equitable, specific lien on the debtor's personal property.

B. general, involuntary, equitable lien on both real and personal property owned by the debtor.

C. specific lien on the debtor's real and personal property, effective for a nonrenewable period of five years.

D. general, involuntary, equitable lien on both real and personal property, effective for renewable five-year periods.

12. 614 Stevenson Street in Peoria is owned by Walter, who is married to Hanna. Hanna has no ownership interest in the property. Walter and Hanna live in Chicago, and the house in Peoria is occupied by a tenant, Tia. If Walter wants to sell the property, who is required by law to sign the listing agreement?

A. Both Walter and Hanna, because they are a married couple.

B. Walter only, because Walter and Hanna do not live in the house.

C. Walter as owner and Tia as tenant in possession.

D. Walter, Hanna, and Tia.

13. All of the following must appear in a written Illinois listing agreement EXCEPT:
    A. a statement that the property must be shown to all prospective buyers regardless of race, color, religion, national origin, sex, handicap or familial status.
    B. the complete legal description of the property being sold.
    C. the time duration of the listing.
    D. the proposed gross sales price of the property.

14. In Illinois, which agency is responsible for registering title agents?
    A. Department of Professional Regulation
    B. Department of Financial Institutions
    C. Office of Banks and Real Estate
    D. Department of Insurance Registration

15. In Illinois, if a broker is taking a listing and asks the seller to complete a disclosure of property conditions, which of the following statements is true?
    A. The disclosures are optional, and the seller may avoid liability by refusing to make any disclosures about the condition of the property.
    B. The standard disclosures cover a narrow range of structural conditions only.
    C. An agent should not give the seller any advice regarding which property conditions to disclose and which to ignore.
    D. Seller disclosure of known property conditions is required by Illinois statute.

16. How long must a claimant hold adverse, exclusive, continuous and uninterrupted use of a property under claim of right in Illinois in order to obtain a prescriptive easement in Illinois?
    A. 10 years   C. 20 years
    B. 17 years   D. 30 years

17. Keri is an Illinois real estate licensee and the listing agent for a home. After one month of the three-month listing has gone by without any offers on the property, Keri becomes concerned. At the time the listing agreement was signed, Keri and the sellers orally agreed that if no offers were received after one month, the price of the property would be reduced by 10 percent. Because the sellers are out of town, Keri crosses out the old listing price, writes in the new one, and then updates the information on the computerized listing service. Three days later, a prospective buyer comes into Keri's office to make an offer on the property. Based on these facts, which of the following statements is true?
    A. Illinois licensees are prohibited by law from making any addition to, deletion from or other alteration of a written listing agreement without the written consent of the principal.
    B. While alteration of a written listing agreement is usually prohibited by Illinois law, Keri acted properly in this situation because the sellers were out of town.
    C. Changing the listing price of a property is a matter of professional discretion, and Illinois licensees are permitted to make alterations to only that aspect of a listing agreement without the written consent of the principal.
    D. While alteration of a written listing agreement is usually prohibited by Illinois law, Keri acted properly in this situation because of the prior oral agreement with the sellers.

18. Martin, a broker, signs a listing agreement with a seller. The agreement contains the following clause: "If the Property has not been sold after three months from the date of this signing, this agreement will automatically continue for additional three-month periods thereafter until the property is sold." Based on these facts, which of the following statements is true?
    A. The agreement is legal under Illinois law, because it contains a reference to a specific time limit.
    B. This agreement is illegal in Illinois.
    C. Illinois law will automatically apply a statutory six-month listing period to this open listing.
    D. This agreement is legal under Illinois law, because the time periods are for less than six months each.

19. The total initial license fees for a broker, salesperson and corporation in Illinois are (in order):
    A. $85; $50; $50.
    B. $100; $85; $85.
    C. $100; $100; $100.
    D. $150; $100; $100.

20. How are members of the Illinois Real Estate Disciplinary Board selected?
    A. Appointed by the governor
    B. Appointed by the Commissioner of Real Estate
    C. Elected by licensees
    D. Elected in statewide elections every six years

21. Assuming that a reciprocal licensing agreement exists, all of the following are requirements for a non-Illinois resident to obtain an Illinois broker's license by reciprocity EXCEPT:
    A. an active broker's license in her or his home state.
    B. active participation in the real estate business for the two years prior to her or his application.
    C. a sealed statement from her or his home state licensing authority stating that the applicant is active, in good standing and that no complaints are pending.
    D. a reciprocal licensing fee in addition to the license fees required of resident brokers, to cover administrative expenses.

22. An Illinois broker may have his or her license suspended or revoked for all of the following actions EXCEPT:
    A. being declared mentally incompetent.
    B. depositing earnest money into the firm's escrow account.
    C. helping another person cheat on the licensing examination.
    D. displaying a For Sale sign on a property without the owner's consent.

23. In Illinois, all of the following are required elements of a valid deed EXCEPT a(n):
    A. acknowledgment clause.
    B. specifically identified grantee.
    C. granting clause.
    D. statement of consideration.

24. A straight line more or less connecting Rockford and Cairo is the:
    A. Second Principal Meridian.
    B. Third Principal Meridian.
    C. Fourth Principal Meridian.
    D. Centralia Base Line.

25. Broker Greg received an earnest money deposit from a buyer. Under Illinois law, what should Greg do with the money?
    A. Open a special, separate escrow account that will contain funds for this transaction only, separate from funds received in any other transaction
    B. Deposit the money in an existing special non–interest-bearing escrow account in which all earnest money received from buyers may be held at the same time
    C. Immediately (or by the next business day) commingle the funds by depositing the earnest money in Greg's personal interest-bearing checking or savings account
    D. Hold the earnest money deposit in a secure place in Greg's real estate brokerage office until the offer is accepted

26. *Chicago Bar Association, et al. v. Quinlan and Tyson, Inc.* established what principle in Illinois real estate law?
    A. Real estate brokers must establish a special escrow account for earnest money deposits.
    B. The seller must bear any losses that occur before title to property passes or before the buyer takes possession.
    C. Brokers and salespersons who are not lawyers may only fill in blanks and make appropriate deletions on preprinted standard form contracts.
    D. Once a contract is signed, a broker or salesperson may not make any additions, deletions or insertions without the written consent of the parties.

27. In Illinois, what is the statutory usury ceiling on loans secured by real estate?
    A. 10 percent
    B. 15 percent
    C. 22 percent
    D. There is none.

28. Derek, a real estate broker, is aware that certain areas of the city are particularly unfriendly to members of certain minority groups. For these groups' own protection, Derek shows members of such groups homes for sale only in "friendly" neighborhoods into which members of their minority group have moved in the past. Based on these facts, which of the following statements is true?
    A. The Illinois Real Estate License Act would not prohibit Derek's actions, because Derek is being protective rather than discriminatory.
    B. The critical element in this type of activity is profit motive; if Derek's actions are not driven by increased profits, Derek will not be subject to discipline under the Illinois Real Estate License Act.
    C. While Derek's actions are clearly prohibited by Illinois statute, the Illinois Real Estate License Act does not address blockbusting or steering.
    D. Derek's actions are expressly prohibited by the Illinois Real Estate License Act.

29. Ben conveys real property to Chris. The sale price of the property is $250,000. What is the Illinois state transfer tax on this transaction?
    A. $125   C. $500
    B. $250   D. $1,250

30. In the previous question, how much of the transfer tax payable will go to fund affordable housing under the Illinois Affordable Housing Act of 1989?
    A. 10 percent
    B. 25 percent
    C. 50 percent
    D. None

31. In Illinois, how must the real property transfer tax be paid?
    A. By personal check, made out to the Illinois Department of Revenue
    B. By certified check, made out to the Illinois Housing Development Authority
    C. By purchasing transfer tax stamps from the county recorder
    D. By purchasing a "Green Sheet" from the county recorder for the total due

32. In Illinois, all of the following properties are totally exempt from paying general real estate taxes EXCEPT:
    A. cemeteries.
    B. federal government buildings.
    C. housing owned by a disabled veteran.
    D. private schools.

33. Tom, a landlord, has a "no pets" policy in his apartment building. If a visually impaired person wants to rent an apartment from Tom, but owns a guide dog, which of the following statements is true?
    A. If Tom's "no pets" policy is applied uniformly, in a nondiscriminatory manner, it may be legally applied to the guide dog as well.
    B. The Illinois Human Rights Act specifically prohibits Tom from refusing to rent the apartment to the visually impaired person on the basis of Tom's "no pets" policy.
    C. Under the Illinois Human Rights Act, Tom may not discriminate against the visually impaired person on the basis of a "no pets" policy, but Tom may require the tenant to pay an additional damage fee.
    D. The Illinois Human Rights Act does not address the issue of guide, hearing or support dogs.

34. Marta conveys real property to Noelle for $185,000. What amount will have to be paid in county transfer tax?
    A. $37.00   C. $185.00
    B. $92.50   D. $1,850.00

35. Which of the following statements is true of an Illinois county having fewer than 60,000 residents?
    A. The recorder of deeds must be elected.
    B. Deeds are recorded by the elected recorder of deeds in the nearest county having a population over 60,000.
    C. The city clerk of the largest population center acts as recorder of deeds.
    D. The county clerk also serves as recorder of deeds.

36. All of the following are requirements for a deed to be recorded in Illinois EXCEPT:
    A. the name of the grantor must be typed or printed below her or his signature.
    B. the name, address and age of the grantee.
    C. a 32-by-32-inch blank space for use by the recorder.
    D. a "Green Sheet."

37. The purpose of the Real Estate Recovery Fund is to:
    A. permit licensees to reestablish their businesses after a natural or financial disaster.
    B. reward consumers for identifying licensees who are engaged in violations of the real estate license law or other wrongful acts.
    C. compensate individuals who suffer losses due to the wrongful acts of a licensee.
    D. pay for the court costs and legal fees required to defend licensees against accusations of wrongdoing.

38. All of the following services would require an Illinois real estate license if performed for compensation EXCEPT:
    A. selling real estate options.
    B. assisting in the negotiation of a lease.
    C. operating a multiple-listing service wholly owned by a nonprofit real estate brokers' association.
    D. operating a business (as an individual licensee) to assist or direct the procuring of prospects for exchanging real estate.

39. Lynn is an Illinois real estate broker and also a part-owner of LMN Title, a title insurance company. Lynn has registered with the appropriate state agency and has disclosed the relationship to the owner of Blackacre. Under these facts, can Lynn recommend that LMN produce the title insurance policy when Blackacre sells?
    A. Yes: Lynn has fully complied with the requirements of the Illinois Title Insurance Act.
    B. No: Lynn also must obtain the written permission of her client.
    C. Yes: because Lynn is only a part owner of LMN Title, the provisions of the Illinois Title Insurance Act do not apply.
    D. Yes, if Lynn also fills out and provides state disclosure forms to both the buyer and the seller of Blackacre.

40. Why is 1997 a significant year in the history of title recording in Illinois?
    A. The Torrens Act was repealed.
    B. All property registered under the Torrens Act was automatically transferred to the recordation system.
    C. Registration of new conveyances of real property under Torrens ceased.
    D. Individuals may voluntarily change their property's registration from Torrens to the recordation system after that year.

41. In Illinois, if an owner defaults on her or his mortgage loan and the property is ordered sold at a foreclosure sale, the owner may redeem the property:
    A. prior to the sale, under the statutory right of redemption.
    B. prior to the sale, under the equitable right of redemption.
    C. after the sale, under the statutory right of redemption.
    D. after the sale, under the statutory right of reinstatement.

42. For three days, Manuel watched from his kitchen window as a small construction crew built an attractive gazebo in his backyard. Manuel had not contracted with anyone to build a gazebo and in fact had never given much thought to having one. But Manuel liked what he saw. When the contractor presented Manuel with a bill for the work, Manuel refused to pay, pointing out that he'd never signed a contract to have the work done. Can the contractor impose a mechanic's lien on Manuel's property under Illinois law?
    A. No: in Illinois a mechanic's lien attaches on the date the contract is signed or the work is ordered, and neither event occurred here.
    B. No: Manuel cannot be forced to pay for the contractor's mistake.
    C. Yes: where a landowner knows of work being done on his or her property and does not object or disclaim responsibility, a mechanic's lien may be created.
    D. Yes: Manuel should have mailed a notice of nonresponsibility to the contractor's main place of business.

43. Penny's property in Peoria has an assessed value of $175,000. The local tax rate is 30 mills, and no equalization factor is used. If the tax was levied in April 1999, Penny had to pay:
    A. $5,250 on June 1, 1999.
    B. $2,625 on September 1, 1999.
    C. $2,625 on January 1, 2000.
    D. $2,625 on June 1, 2000.

44. In Illinois, brokers and salespeople who are not lawyers may do which of the following?
    A. Complete a bill of sale after a sales contract has been signed
    B. Fill in blanks on preprinted form contracts customarily used in their community
    C. Suggest additional language to be added to a preprinted sales contract by a buyer or seller
    D. Explain the legal significance of specific preprinted contract clauses to a buyer or seller

45. For which of the following acts is the Office of Banks and Real Estate required to suspend or revoke a licensee's license?
    A. Failing to perform as promised in a guaranteed sales plan
    B. Having been found liable in a civil trial for illegal discrimination
    C. Commingling others' money or property with her or his own
    D. Failing to provide information requested by the Office of Banks and Real Estate within 30 days of the request as part of a complaint or audit procedure

46. Three weeks before Nate begins his Illinois real estate prelicense class, he offers to help his neighbor sell her house. The neighbor agrees to pay Nate a 5 percent commission. An offer is accepted while Nate is taking the class and closes the day before Nate passes the examination and receives his salesperson's license. The neighbor refuses to pay Nate the agreed commission. Can Nate sue to recover payment?
    A. Yes: because Nate was formally enrolled in a course of study intended to result in a real estate license at the time an offer was procured and accepted, the commission agreement is binding.
    B. No: in Illinois, a real estate salesperson must have a permanent office in which his or her license is displayed in order to collect a commission from a seller.
    C. Yes: while the statute of frauds forbids recovery on an oral agreement for the conveyance of real property, Illinois law permits enforcement of an oral commission contract under these facts.
    D. No: Illinois law prohibits lawsuits to collect commissions unless the injured party is a licensed broker and the license was in effect before the agreement was reached.

47. An Illinois real estate salesperson may lawfully collect compensation from:
    A. either a buyer or a seller.
    B. her or his sponsoring broker only.
    C. any party to the transaction or the party's representative.
    D. a licensed real estate broker only.

48. Pat has a mortgage loan secured by real property. Under Illinois law, Pat may terminate the loan's escrow account when the remaining balance is equal to or less than what percentage of the original amount?
    A. 35 percent
    B. 50 percent
    C. 65 percent
    D. 75 percent

49. The JKL Partnership was established to buy and sell real estate. Of the three general partners, only Janet and Kallie will be actively involved in real estate transactions. Janet plans to specialize in commercial properties and Kallie in residential. The third general partner, Laura, is responsible only for supervising the partnership's office decor and planning holiday parties. Under these facts, which of the general partners needs to be licensed for JKL to qualify for a broker's license in Illinois?
   A. None: under Illinois law, a partnership is an independent entity that may obtain a broker's license regardless of the status of any individual partner.
   B. Either Janet or Kallie, depending on whether the partnership's emphasis will be residential or commercial properties.
   C. Both Janet and Kallie must be licensed salespersons, but Laura need not be licensed.
   D. Janet, Kallie and Laura must all be licensed real estate brokers.

50. With regard to mortgages, Illinois is most accurately described as a(n):
   A. intermediate-theory state.
   B. lien-theory state.
   C. title-theory state.
   D. equitable-theory state.

51. Broker Jane wants to renew the license for one of her Illinois brokerage's branch offices. She also notices that she's lost her pocket card and needs a replacement immediately. How much will she have to pay for these two things combined?
   A. $100   C. $125
   B. $120   D. $150

52. Theo is the landlord of a 3-unit apartment building. Dane is the landlord of a 30-unit apartment building. Based on these facts, which of the following is true of security deposits under Illinois law?
   A. Both Theo and Dane must give tenants an itemized statement of alleged damages before they can withhold any part of the security deposit as compensation.
   B. Only Dane is required to pay interest on security deposits.
   C. Only Theo is required to give tenants an itemized statement of alleged damages before any part of the security deposit may be withheld as compensation.
   D. Both Theo and Dane are required to pay interest on security deposits at a rate linked to minimum deposit passbook savings accounts at Illinois's largest commercial bank.

53. How many members are on the Illinois Real Estate Administration and Disciplinary Board?
   A. 6   C. 9
   B. 8   D. 12

54. In Illinois, how much written notice is a landlord required to give a tenant to pay overdue rent prior to terminating the lease, when the tenant is in default only for failing to pay rent on time?
   A. 0 days   C. 5 days
   B. 3 days   D. 10 days

55. In Illinois, if a home rule county has an ordinance that conflicts with that of a home rule city, whose ordinance will prevail?
   A. The county's ordinance
   B. The city's ordinance
   C. The relevant township ordinance
   D. The dispute is constitutional in nature and so may be resolved only by the Illinois Supreme Court.

56. Which of the following is NOT a requirement for a valid lease?
    A. An option agreement
    B. Description of the leased premises
    C. Signatures of the parties
    D. Consideration

57. Carol is an agent for XYZ Realty. When Carol is representing her broker, she is MOST LIKELY acting as a(n):
    A. universal agent.
    B. ostensible agent.
    C. general agent.
    D. special agent.

58. Which of the following is NOT necessary to create a fiduciary relationship?
    A. A listing agreement
    B. A buyer agency agreement
    C. A contractual agreement to represent another
    D. The payment of the commission

59. Which of the following statements are true regarding severance and annexation?
    A. Annexation is associated with real property, while severance is associated with personal property.
    B. Annexation means to add to the land, while severance means to separate from the land.
    C. Annexation means to separate from the land, while severance means to add to the land.
    D. Annexation is associated with condominiums, while severance is associated with cooperatives.

60. All of the following are false regarding fee simple absolute estates EXCEPT that it:
    A. is based on calendar time.
    B. is not inheritable.
    C. is the highest amount of ownership recognized by law.
    D. represents a defeasible title.

EXAM TWO

Part One
General Real Estate Practice and Principles

1. Tenant Dennis's landlord has sold the building where Dennis lives to the state so that a freeway can be built. Dennis's lease has expired, but the landlord permits him to stay in the apartment until the building is torn down. Dennis continues to pay the rent as prescribed in the lease. What kind of tenancy does Dennis have?
   A. Holdover tenancy
   B. Month-to-month tenancy
   C. Tenancy at sufferance
   D. Tenancy at will

2. The owner of a house wants to fence the yard for her dog. When the fence is erected, the fencing materials are converted to real estate by:
   A. severance.   C. annexation.
   B. subrogation.   D. attachment.

3. George is interested in selling his house as quickly as possible and believes that the best way to do this is to have several brokers compete against each other for the commission. George's listing agreements with four different brokers specifically promise that if one of them finds a buyer for his property, he will be obligated to pay a commission to that broker. What type of agreement has George entered into?
   A. Executed   C. Unilateral
   B. Discharged   D. Bilateral

4. In some states, by paying the debt after a foreclosure sale, a borrower has the right to regain the property under which of the following?
   A. Novation   C. Reversion
   B. Redemption   D. Recovery

5. Wendy enters into a sale-leaseback agreement with Jerry, under which Jerry will become the owner of Wendy's ranch. Which of the following statements is true of this arrangement?
   A. Wendy retains title to the ranch.
   B. Jerry receives possession of the property.
   C. Jerry is the lessor.
   D. Wendy is the lessor.

6. Tammy is a real estate broker employed by Milos. When Tammy finds a property that Milos might be interested in buying, she is careful to find out as much as possible about the property's owners and why their property is on the market. Tammy's efforts to keep Milos informed of all facts that could affect a transaction is the duty of:
   A. care.   C. obedience.
   B. loyalty.   D. disclosure.

7. A parcel of vacant land 80 feet wide and 200 feet deep was sold for $200 per front foot. How much money would a salesperson receive for her 60 percent share in the 10 percent commission?
   A. $640   C. $1,600
   B. $960   D. $2,400

8. All of the following situations violate the federal Fair Housing Act of 1968 EXCEPT:
   A. the refusal of a property manager to rent an apartment to a Catholic couple who are otherwise qualified.
   B. the general policy of a loan company to avoid granting home improvement loans to individuals living in transitional neighborhoods.
   C. the intentional neglect of a broker to show an Asian family any property listings in all-white neighborhoods.
   D. a widowed woman's insistence on renting her spare bedroom only to another widowed woman.

9. If a storage tank that measures 12 feet by 9 feet by 8 feet is designed to store a gas that costs $1.82 per cubic foot, what does it cost to fill the tank to one-half of its capacity?
   A. $685
   B. $786
   C. $864
   D. $1,572

10. Roland bought a house for $125,000. It appraised for $120,500 and previously sold for $118,250. Based on these facts, if Roland applies for an 80 percent mortgage, what will be the amount of the loan Roland will receive?
    A. $94,600
    B. $96,400
    C. $100,000
    D. $106,750

11. Wesley offers to buy Vance's property by signing a purchase contract. Vance accepts Wesley's offer. What kind of title interest does Wesley have in the property at this point?
    A. Legal
    B. Equitable
    C. Defeasible
    D. Wesley has no title interest at this point.

12. Which of the following federal laws requires that finance charges be stated as an annual percentage rate?
    A. Truth-in-Lending Act
    B. Real Estate Settlement Procedures Act (RESPA)
    C. Equal Credit Opportunity Act (ECOA)
    D. Federal Fair Housing Act

13. Fran signed a 90-day listing agreement with a broker. Two weeks later, Fran was killed in an accident. What is the present status of the listing?
    A. The listing agreement is binding on Fran's estate for the remainder of the 90 days.
    B. Because Fran's intention to sell was clearly defined, the listing agreement is still in effect and the broker may proceed to market the property on behalf of Fran's estate.
    C. The listing agreement is binding on Fran's estate only if the broker can produce an offer to purchase the property within the remainder of the listing period.
    D. The listing agreement was terminated automatically when Fran died.

14. Maria conveys the ownership of an office building to a nursing home. The nursing home agrees that the rental income will pay for the expenses of caring for Maria's parents. When Maria's parents die, ownership of the office building will revert to Maria. The estate held by the nursing home is a:
    A. remainder life estate.
    B. legal life estate.
    C. life estate pur autre vie.
    D. temporary leasehold estate.

15. Henry is a real estate broker. Stan signs a buyer's brokerage agreement under which Henry will help Stan find a three-bedroom house in the $85,000 to $100,000 price range. James comes into Henry's office and signs a listing agreement to sell James's two-bedroom condominium for $70,000. Based on these facts, which of the following statements is true?
    A. Stan is Henry's client; James is Henry's customer.
    B. Stan is Henry's customer; James is Henry's client.
    C. While both Stan and James are clients, Henry owes the fiduciary duties of an agent only to James.
    D. Because both Stan and James are Henry's clients, Henry owes the fiduciary duties of an agent to both.

16. In a township of 36 sections, which of the following statements is true?
    A. Section 31 lies to the east of Section 32.
    B. Section 18 is by law set aside for school purposes.
    C. Section 6 lies in the northeast corner of the township.
    D. Section 16 lies to the north of Section 21.

17. Broker Sara represented the seller in a transaction. Her client informed her that he did not want to recite the actual consideration that was paid for the house. In this situation, which of the following statements is true?
   A. Sara must inform her client that only the actual price of the real estate may appear on the deed.
   B. Sara may ask that a deed be prepared that shows only nominal consideration of $10.
   C. Sara should inform the seller that either the full price should be stated in the deed or all references to consideration should be removed from it.
   D. Sara may show a price on the deed other than the actual price, provided that the variance is not greater than 10 percent of the purchase price.

18. Broker Bess obtained a listing agreement to act as the agent in the sale of Geri's house. A buyer has been found for the property, and all agreements have been signed. As an agent for Geri, the broker is responsible for which of the following?
   A. Completing the buyer's loan application
   B. Making sure that the buyer receives copies of all documents the seller is required to deliver to the buyer
   C. Ensuring that the buyer is qualified for the new mortgage loan
   D. Scheduling the buyer's inspection of the property

19. Jeff is a real estate salesperson employed by broker Tim. What is Jeff's share of the commission when the sales price of a property was $195,000 and Jeff is entitled to 65 percent of the 72 percent commission?
   A. $950.63
   B. $8,872.50
   C. $9,506.25
   D. $95,062.50

20. Quinn, an appraiser, estimates the value of a property using the cost approach. Which of the following describes what Quinn should do?
   A. Estimate the replacement cost of the improvements
   B. Deduct the depreciation of the land and buildings
   C. Determine the original cost and adjust for depreciation
   D. Review the sales prices of comparable properties

21. Tonya is a mortgage lender. Before the closing of a real estate transaction, Tonya provides the buyer and seller with statements of all fees and charges they will incur. In doing this, Tonya complies with the:
   A. Equal Credit Opportunity Act (ECOA).
   B. Truth-in-Lending Act (Regulation Z).
   C. Real Estate Settlement Procedures Act (RESPA).
   D. Fair Housing Act.

22. The landlord of an apartment building neglected to repair the building's plumbing system. As a result, the apartments did not receive water, as provided by the leases. If a tenant's unit becomes uninhabitable, which of the following would most likely result?
   A. Suit for possession
   B. Claim of constructive eviction
   C. Tenancy at sufferance
   D. Suit for negligence

23. Philip conveys a life estate to Mary. Under the terms of Philip's conveyance, the property will pass to Terrence upon Mary's death. Which of the following best describes Terrence's interest in the property during Mary's lifetime?
   A. Remainder
   B. Reversion
   C. Life estate pur autre vie
   D. Redemption

24. On a settlement statement, prorations for real estate taxes paid in arrears are shown as a:
   A. credit to the seller and a debit to the buyer.
   B. debit to the seller and a credit to the buyer.
   C. credit to both the seller and the buyer.
   D. debit to both the seller and the buyer.

25. What type of lease establishes a rental payment and requires that the lessor pay for the taxes, insurance and maintenance on the property?
   A. Percentage
   B. Net
   C. Expense only
   D. Gross

26. A conventional loan was closed on July 1 for $57,200 at 13.5 percent interest amortized over 25 years at $666.75 per month. On August 1, what would the principal amount be after the monthly payment was made?
   A. $56,533.25
   B. $56,556.50
   C. $57,065.35
   D. $57,176.75

27. In the preceding question, what would the interest portion of the payment be?
    A. $610.65   C. $643.50
    B. $620.25   D. $666.75

28. Rebecca listed her home with broker Kent for $90,000. Rebecca told Kent, "I have to sell quickly because of a job transfer. If necessary, I can accept a price as low as $75,000." Kent tells a prospective buyer to offer $80,000 "because Rebecca is desperate to sell." Rebecca accepts the buyer's offer. In this situation, which of the following statements is true?
    A. Kent's action did not violate his agency relationship with Rebecca because Kent did not reveal Rebecca's lowest acceptable price.
    B. Kent violated his agency relationship with Rebecca.
    C. Kent acted properly to obtain a quick offer on Rebecca's property, in accordance with Rebecca's instructions.
    D. Kent violated his common-law duties toward the buyer by failing to disclose that Rebecca would accept a lower price than the buyer offered.

29. Which of the following best describes the capitalization rate under the income approach to estimating the value of real estate?
    A. Rate at which a property increases in value
    B. Rate of return a property earns as an investment
    C. Rate of capital required to keep a property operating most efficiently
    D. Maximum rate of return allowed by law on an investment

30. On a settlement statement, the cost of the lender's title insurance policy required for a new loan is usually shown as which of the following?
    A. Credit to the seller
    B. Credit to the buyer
    C. Debit to the seller
    D. Debit to the buyer

31. An FHA-insured loan in the amount of $57,500 at 82 percent for 30 years was closed on July 17. The first monthly payment is due on September 1. Because interest is paid monthly in arrears, what was the amount of the interest adjustment the buyer had to make at the settlement?
    A. $190.07   C. $407.29
    B. $230.80   D. $4,887.50

32. If a home that originally cost $142,500 three years ago is now valued at 127 percent of its original cost, what is its current market value?
    A. $164,025   C. $174,310
    B. $172,205   D. $180,975

33. Carol has a contract to paint Otto's garage door for $200. Before starting the project, Carol has a skiing accident and breaks both arms. Carol asks another painter, Jamie, to take over the job. Jamie paints Otto's garage door, and Otto pays Jamie $200 for the work. This scenario is an example of:
    A. assignment.   C. acceptance.
    B. novation.   D. revocation.

34. Whitney searches the public record regarding title to Brownacre. Which of the following is Whitney most likely to discover?
    A. Encroachments
    B. Rights of parties in possession
    C. Inaccurate survey
    D. Mechanics' liens

35. A rectangular lot is worth $193,600. This value is the equivalent of $4.40 per square foot. If one lot dimension is 200 feet, what is the other dimension?
    A. 110 feet   C. 400 feet
    B. 220 feet   D. 880 feet

36. Broker Bart listed Kendra's property at an 8 percent commission rate. After the property was sold and the settlement had taken place, Kendra discovered that the broker had been listing similar properties at 6 percent commission rates. Based on this information alone, which of the following statements is true?
    A. Bart has done nothing wrong because a commission rate is always negotiable between the parties.
    B. If Bart inflated the usual commission rate for the area, Bart may be subject to discipline by the state real estate commission.
    C. Kendra is entitled to rescind the transaction based on the principle of lack of reality of consent.
    D. Kendra is entitled to a refund from Bart of 2 percent of the commission.

37. Melanie has six months remaining on her apartment lease. Melanie's monthly rent is $875. Melanie moves out of the apartment, and Teresa moves in. Teresa pays Melanie a monthly rental of $700, and Melanie continues paying the full rental amount under her lease to the landlord. When Melanie's lease term expires, Teresa will either move out or sign a new lease with the landlord. This is an example of:
    A. assignment.
    B. subletting.
    C. rescission and renewal.
    D. surrender.

38. One broker asked another, "Will I have to prove that I was the procuring cause if my seller sells the property himself?" The other broker answers, "No, not if you have an:
    A. option listing."
    B. open listing."
    C. exclusive-agency listing."
    D. exclusive-right-to-sell listing."

39. The capitalization rate on a property reflects (among other things) which of the following factors?
    A. Risk of the investment
    B. Replacement cost of the improvements
    C. Real estate taxes
    D. Debt service

40. An investment property worth $180,000 was purchased seven years ago for $142,000. At the time of the purchase, the land was valued at $18,000. Assuming a 3½-year life for straight-line depreciation purposes, what is the present book value of the property?
    A. $95,071   C. $114,444
    B. $113,071   D. $126,000

41. A person who dies without having made a will is said to be:
    A. a testate.   C. in probate.
    B. a testator.   D. intestate.

42. A farmer owns the W½ of the NW¼ of the NW¼ of a section. The remainder of the NW¼ can be purchased for $300 per acre. Owning all of the NW¼ of the section would cost the farmer:
    A. $6,000.   C. $42,000.
    B. $12,000.   D. $48,000.

43. An offer to purchase real estate may be terminated by all of the following EXCEPT:
    A. failure to accept the offer within a prescribed period.
    B. revocation by the offeror communicated to the offeree after acceptance.
    C. a conditional acceptance of the offer by the offeree.
    D. the death of the offeror or offeree.

44. Pablo is the manager of the Bellevue Terrace apartments. For each new tenant that Pablo signs, the owner pays him an 8½ percent commission, based on the unit's annualized rent. In one year, Pablo signed five new tenants. Three of the apartments rented for $795 per month; one rented for $1,200 per month; and one rented for $900 per month. What was the total amount of Pablo's new-tenant commissions for that year?
    A. $381.23   C. $3,685.47
    B. $2,952.90   D. $4,574.70

45. The monthly rent on a warehouse is $1 per cubic yard. Assuming the warehouse is 36 feet by 200 feet by 12 feet high, what would the annual rent be?
    A. $3,200   C. $38,400
    B. $9,600   D. $115,200

46. A veteran wishes to refinance his home with a VA-guaranteed loan. The lender is willing, but insists on 3½ discount points. In this situation, the veteran can:
   A. refinance with a VA loan, provided the lender charges no discount points.
   B. refinance with a VA loan, provided the lender charges no more than two discount points.
   C. be required to pay a maximum of 1 percent of the loan as an origination fee.
   D. proceed with the refinance loan and pay the discount points.

47. Grant owns two properties: Redacre and Brownacre. He conveys Redacre to Sharon with no restrictions; Sharon holds all rights to Redacre forever. Grant then conveys Brownacre to Tim "so long as no real estate broker or salesperson ever sets foot on the property." If a broker or salesperson visits Brownacre, ownership will revert to Grant. Based on these two conveyances, which of the following statements is true?
   A. Sharon holds Redacre in fee simple; Tim holds Brownacre in fee simple determinable.
   B. Sharon holds Redacre in fee simple absolute; Tim holds Brownacre in fee simple defeasible, subject to a condition subsequent.
   C. Tim may not transfer ownership of Brownacre without Grant's permission.
   D. Grant has retained a right of reentry with regard to Brownacre.

48. A real estate transaction had a closing date of November 15. The seller, who was responsible for costs up to and including the date of settlement, paid the property taxes of $1,116 for the calendar year. On the closing statement, the buyer would be:
   A. debited $139.50.
   B. debited $976.50.
   C. credited $139.50.
   D. credited $976.50.

49. An agreement that ends all future lessor-lessee obligations under a lease is known as a(n):
   A. assumption.   C. novation.
   B. surrender.   D. breach.

50. Aaron buys a house for $234,500. He makes a $25,000 cash down payment and takes out a $209,500 mortgage for 30 years. The lot value is $80,000. If Aaron wants to depreciate the property over a period of 27½ years, how much will the annual depreciation amount be using the straight-line method?
   A. $3,818.18   C. $5,618.18
   B. $4,709.09   D. $8,527.27

51. A property manager leased a store for three years. The first year, the store's rent was $1,000 per month, and the rent was to increase 10 percent per year thereafter. The manager received a 7 percent commission for the first year, 5 percent for the second year and 3 percent for the balance of the lease. The total commission earned by the property manager was:
   A. $840.   C. $1,936.
   B. $1,613.   D. $2,785.

52. Against a recorded deed from the owner of record, the party with the weakest position is a:
   A. person with a prior unrecorded deed who is not in possession.
   B. person in possession with a prior unrecorded deed.
   C. tenant in possession with nine months remaining on the lease.
   D. painter who is half-finished painting the house at the time of the sale and who has not yet been paid.

53. Jon, age 58, bought a home in 1994 for $46,000. Three years later, he sold the home for $74,800 and moved into an apartment. In computing Jon's income tax, what amount of this transaction is taxable?
   A. $11,320
   B. $16,980
   C. $28,800
   D. Nothing is taxable; Jon's capital gain is within the exemption guidelines.

54. Kevin moved into an abandoned home and installed new cabinets in the kitchen. When the owner discovered the occupancy, the owner had Kevin ejected. What is the status of the kitchen cabinets?
  A. Kevin has no right to the cabinets.
  B. The cabinets remain because they are trade fixtures.
  C. Although the cabinets stay, Kevin is entitled to the value of the improvements.
  D. Kevin can keep the cabinets if they can be removed without damaging the real estate.

55. Walter, Frank and Joe are joint tenants. Joe sells his interest to Larry, and then Frank dies. As a result, which of the following statements is true?
  A. Frank's heirs are joint tenants with Larry and Walter.
  B. Frank's heirs and Walter are joint tenants, but Larry is a tenant in common.
  C. Walter is a tenant in common with Larry's and Frank's heirs.
  D. Walter and Larry are tenants in common.

56. In a settlement statement, the selling price always is:
  A. a debit to the buyer.
  B. a debit to the seller.
  C. a credit to the buyer.
  D. greater than the loan amount.

57. The state wants to acquire a strip of farmland to build a highway. Does the state have the right to acquire privately owned land for public use?
  A. Yes: the state's right is called *condemnation.*
  B. Yes: the state's right is called *eminent domain.*
  C. Yes: the state's right is called *escheat.*
  D. No: under the U.S. Constitution, private property may never be taken by state governments or the federal government.

58. Rhonda's estate was distributed according to her will as follows: 54 percent to her husband, 18 percent to her children, 16 percent to her grandchildren and the remainder to her college. The college received $79,000. How much did Rhonda's children receive?
  A. $105,333   C. $355,500
  B. $118,500   D. $658,333

59. Which of the following is an example of external obsolescence?
  A. Numerous pillars supporting the ceiling in a store
  B. Leaks in the roof of a warehouse, making the premises unusable and therefore unrentable
  C. Coal cellar in a house with central heating
  D. Vacant, abandoned and run-down buildings in an area

60. Which of the following phrases, when placed in a print advertisement, would comply with the requirements of the Truth-in-Lending Act (Regulation Z)?
  A. "12 percent interest"
  B. "12 percent rate"
  C. "12 percent annual interest"
  D. "12 percent annual percentage rate"

61. All of the following are true regarding a capitalization rate EXCEPT:
  A. the rate increases when the risk increases.
  B. an increase in rate means a decrease in value.
  C. the net income is divided by the rate to estimate value.
  D. a decrease in rate results in a decrease in value.

62. The Equal Credit Opportunity Act makes it illegal for lenders to refuse credit to or otherwise discriminate against which of the following applicants?
  A. Parent of twins who receives public assistance and who cannot afford the monthly mortgage payments
  B. New homebuyer who does not have a credit history
  C. Single person who receives public assistance
  D. Unemployed person with no job prospects and no identifiable source of income

63. When Polly died, a deed was found in her desk drawer. While the deed had never been recorded, it was signed, dated and acknowledged. The deed gave Polly's house to a local charity. Polly's will, however, provided as follows: "I leave all of the real and personal property that I own to my beloved nephew, Robert." In this situation, the house most likely will go to the:
    A. charity because acknowledgment creates a presumption of delivery.
    B. charity because Polly's intent was clear from the deed.
    C. nephew because Polly still owned the house when she died.
    D. nephew because the deed had not been recorded.

64. If Margaret takes out a $90,000 loan at 7½ percent interest to be repaid at the end of 15 years with interest paid annually, what is the total interest that Margaret will pay over the life of the loan?
    A. $10,125
    B. $80,000
    C. $101,250
    D. $180,000

65. After an offer is accepted, the seller finds that the broker was the undisclosed agent for the buyer as well as the agent for the seller. The seller may:
    A. withdraw without obligation to broker or buyer.
    B. withdraw but would be subject to liquidated damages.
    C. withdraw but only with the concurrence of the buyer.
    D. refuse to sell but would be subject to a suit for specific performance.

66. To net the owner $90,000 after a 6 percent commission is paid, the selling price would have to be:
    A. $95,400.
    B. $95,745.
    C. $95,906.
    D. $96,000.

67. Which of the following would most likely be legal under the provisions of the Civil Rights Act of 1968?
    A. A lender refuses to make loans in areas where more than 25 percent of the population is Hispanic.
    B. A private country club development ties home ownership to club membership, but due to local demographics, all club members are white.
    C. A church excludes African Americans from membership and rents its nonprofit housing to church members only.
    D. A licensee directs prospective buyers away from areas where they are likely to feel uncomfortable because of their race.

68. It is discovered after a sale that the land parcel is 10 percent smaller than the owner represented it to be. The broker who passed this information on to the buyer is:
    A. not liable as long as he only repeated the seller's data.
    B. not liable if the misrepresentation was unintentional.
    C. not liable if the buyer actually inspected what she was getting.
    D. liable if he knew or should have known of the discrepancy.

69. On a residential lot 70 feet square, the side yard building setbacks are 10 feet, the front yard setback is 25 feet, and the rear yard setback is 20 feet. The maximum possible size for a single-story structure would be how many square feet?
    A. 1,000
    B. 1,200
    C. 1,250
    D. 4,900

70. All of the following are violations of the Real Estate Settlement Procedures Act (RESPA) EXCEPT:
    A. providing a completed HUD-1 Uniform Settlement Statement to a borrower one day before the closing.
    B. accepting a kickback on a loan subject to RESPA requirements.
    C. requiring a particular title insurance company.
    D. accepting a fee or charging for services that were not performed.

71. The rescission provisions of the Truth-in-
    Lending Act apply to which of the following
    transactions?
    A. Home purchase loans
    B. Construction lending
    C. Business financing
    D. Consumer credit

72. A property has a net income of $30,000. An
    appraiser decides to use a 12 percent
    capitalization rate rather than a 10 percent
    rate on this property. The use of the higher
    rate results in:
    A. a 2 percent increase in the appraised
       value.
    B. a $50,000 increase in the appraised value.
    C. a $50,000 decrease in the appraised
       value.
    D. no change in the appraised value.

73. The section of a purchase contract that
    provides for the buyer to forfeit any earnest
    money if the buyer fails to complete the
    purchase is known as the provision for:
    A. liquidated damages.
    B. punitive damages.
    C. hypothecation.
    D. subordination.

74. In one commercial building, the tenant
    intends to start a health food shop using her
    life savings. In an identical adjacent building
    is a showroom leased to a major national
    retailing chain. Both tenants have long-term
    leases with identical rents. Which of the
    following statements is correct?
    A. If the values of the buildings were the
       same before the leases, the values will be
       the same after the leases.
    B. An appraiser would most likely use a
       higher capitalization rate for the store
       leased to the national retailing chain.
    C. The most accurate appraisal method an
       appraiser could use would be the sales
       comparison approach to value.
    D. The building with the health food shop
       will probably appraise for less than the
       other building.

75. A first-time homebuyer finds that he is
    unlikely to qualify for a mortgage under
    current interest rates. His parents agree to
    pay a lump sum in cash to the lender at
    closing to offset the high rate. What type of
    loan is this?
    A. Equity   C. Open-end
    B. Participation   D. Buydown

76. A $100,000 loan at 12 percent could be
    amortized with monthly payments of
    $1,200.22 on a 15-year basis or payments of
    $1,028.63 on a 30-year basis. The 30-year
    loan results in total payments of what
    percent of the 15-year loan's total payments?
    A. 146 percent   C. 171 percent
    B. 158 percent   D. 228 percent

77. According to a broker's CMA, a property is
    worth $125,000. The homeowner bought the
    property for $90,000 and added $50,000 in
    improvements, for a total of $140,000. The
    property sold for $122,500. Which of these
    amounts represents the property's market
    price?
    A. $90,000   C. $125,000
    B. $122,500   D. $140,000

78. What will be the amount of tax payable where
    the property's assessed value is $85,000 and
    the tax rate is 40 mills in a community in
    which an equalization factor of 110 percent
    is used?
    A. $2,337.50   C. $3,700.40
    B. $3,090.91   D. $3,740.00

79. In a settlement statement, how will a
    proration of prepaid water, gas and electric
    charges be reflected?
    A. Debit to the seller, credit to the buyer
    B. Debit to the buyer, credit to the seller
    C. Debit to the buyer only
    D. Credit to the seller only

80. An apartment manager decides not to
    purchase flood insurance. Instead, the
    manager installs raised platforms in the
    basement storage areas and has the furnace
    placed on eight-inch legs. This form of risk
    management is known as:
    A. avoiding the risk.
    B. controlling the risk.
    C. retaining the risk.
    D. transferring the risk.

81. A real estate broker was responsible for a chain of events that resulted in the sale of one of his client's properties. The broker is legally referred to as the:
   A. initiating factor.
   B. procuring cause.
   C. responsible party.
   D. compensible cause.

82. A characteristic of a real estate salesperson who is an independent contractor is that he or she commonly receives:
   A. more than 50 percent of her or his income in the form of a monthly salary or hourly wage.
   B. company-provided health insurance and other benefits.
   C. reimbursement for documented travel and business expenses.
   D. more than 90 percent of her or his income based on sales production.

83. In the cost approach to value, the appraiser makes use of:
   A. the owner's original cost of the building.
   B. the estimated current replacement cost of the building.
   C. the sales prices of similar buildings in the area.
   D. the assessed value of the building.

84. Janet enters into an exclusive-agency buyer agency agreement with a real estate broker. Based on these facts, which of the following statements is true?
   A. Janet is obligated to pay the broker's compensation regardless of who finds a suitable property.
   B. If Janet finds a suitable property without the broker's assistance, she is under no obligation to pay the broker.
   C. Janet may enter into other, similar agreements with other brokers.
   D. If Janet finds a suitable property without the broker's assistance, Janet will have to pay the broker's compensation.

85. An owner is usually concerned about how much money she can get when she sells her home. A competitive market analysis may help the seller determine a realistic listing price. Which of the following is true of a CMA?
   A. A competitive market analysis is the same as an appraisal.
   B. A broker, not a salesperson, is permitted to prepare a competitive market analysis.
   C. A competitive market analysis is prepared by a certified real estate appraiser.
   D. A competitive market analysis contains a compilation of other similar properties that have sold.

86. An owner sells his four-plex. In regards to this situation, which of the following is TRUE?
   A. The tenants may void their leases.
   B. The lender may void the leases.
   C. The current leases must be honored by the new landlord.
   D. The current leases may be discharged by the previous landlord.

87. When appraising a single family home, the appraiser would NOT consider which of the following in determining the value of a property?
   A. Date sold
   B. Racial demographics
   C. Square feet of living area
   D. Date of comparable sales

88. Which of the following is NOT an essential element of a contract?
   A. Date
   B. Consideration
   C. Meeting of the minds
   D. Signatures of the parties authorized to perform

89. All of the following would be exempt from Federal Fair Housing laws EXCEPT:
   A. a non-profit private club.
   B. a Baptist retirement home.
   C. any local housing program designed for the elderly.
   D. an owner occupied eight unit apartment building.

90. All of the following are examples of encumbrances EXCEPT a(n):
   A. license.   C. easement.
   B. encroachment.   D. lien.

EXAM TWO

Part Two
Illinois Real Estate Law and Practice

1. A transaction is closing on May 2 in a non-leap year. Which of the following is the correct proration of an annual charge of $560, using the statutory month method?
   A. $188.78   C. $190.78
   B. $189.68   D. $191.98

2. In Illinois, what is the statutory ceiling on the prepayment penalty a lender may charge on loans secured by real estate that bear more than 8 percent annual interest?
   A. 1 percent   C. 8 percent
   B. 3 percent   D. There is none.

3. All of the following are true of leases in Illinois EXCEPT a(n):
   A. lease for 15 months would have to be in writing to be enforceable.
   B. lease for a term that begins one year after the date of signing would have to be in writing to be enforceable.
   C. lease for six months would have to be in writing to be enforceable.
   D. oral lease for 12 months could be enforceable.

4. What principle of landlord-tenant relations was established by the Illinois Supreme Court in 1972?
   A. Interest payments required on certain security deposits
   B. Landlord damages for a tenant's failure to vacate the premises
   C. Implied warranty of habitability in residential tenancies
   D. Landlord may forcibly remove a tenant without court action under the doctrine of "self-help"

5. In Illinois, if a landlord purposefully fails to maintain an apartment building's furnace and plumbing, what option is available to a tenant whose apartment is without heat and water during the first three months of winter?
   A. Suit for constructive eviction
   B. Suit for actual eviction
   C. Suit for forcible detainer
   D. Suit for negligent default

6. Betty pays $1,250 per month for her apartment. If Betty refers three new tenants to the building's owner during the year, how much is she entitled to receive under the Illinois Real Estate License Act if the landlord's normal referral fee is $500 per new tenant?
   A. Nothing, unless Betty is a licensed real estate broker, salesperson or rental-finding agent
   B. $1,000
   C. $1,250
   D. $1,500

7. All of the following properties are exempt from the Illinois Responsible Property Transfer Act EXCEPT:
   A. single-family residences.
   B. multiple-unit residences.
   C. residential condominiums.
   D. commercial property.

8. Under the Illinois Human Rights Act, an "elderly person" is defined as any person who is over:
   A. 40.   C. 62.
   B. 55.   D. 65.

9. The Illinois Human Rights Act specifically exempts all of the following EXCEPT:
   A. gender-based discrimination in housing intended for single-gender occupancy.
   B. religious organizations giving preference in housing to members (unless membership is based on discriminatory factors).
   C. a three-unit apartment building, with the owner living in one of the units.
   D. a five-unit apartment building, in which one of the units is occupied by a resident manager.

10. Many of the residents of Randy's apartment building are elderly, and some are in poor health. To ensure that they are not disturbed, Randy politely declines to rent units to families or individuals who have young children. However, Randy provides such persons with a printed list of nearby apartment buildings that welcome children. Based on these facts, which of the following statements is true?
    A. By providing a printed list of alternative comparable housing, Randy is in full compliance with the Illinois Human Rights Act.
    B. Because Randy's primary intent is to protect existing tenants' quality of life, and not to discriminate against prospective tenants who have young children, the Illinois Human Rights Act does not apply to this situation.
    C. Randy's policy violates the Illinois Human Rights Act.
    D. While Randy's policy, as stated, violates the Illinois Human Rights Act, he could add a "no children" provision to leases offered to new tenants and avoid violating the act.

11. What is the relationship between the Illinois agency statute (the Brokerage Relationships in Real Estate Transaction Law) and the common law of agency?
    A. The Illinois agency statute replaces the common law of agency in Illinois.
    B. The Illinois agency statute and the common law of agency both govern agency relationships in Illinois.
    C. The Illinois agency statute is simply an administrative codification of the common law of agency.
    D. The Illinois agency statute governs broker's relationships with clients, while the common law of agency applies to salesperson-client relationships.

12. Which of the following is an example of a "ministerial act" under the Illinois agency law?
    A. Arguing the merits of an offer on behalf of a prospective buyer
    B. Helping prospective buyers determine an appropriate price range and geographic location for their home search
    C. Responding to general questions about the price and location of a specific property
    D. Assisting a buyer through the closing process

13. Gloria, a real estate broker, commonly names individual salespersons in her brokerage office as the exclusive agents of certain clients, leaving the other salespeople free to represent other parties in a transaction. Which of the following statements is true regarding this practice?
    A. Because it is a common office practice, it is permitted as an exception to the general statutory prohibition against such arrangements.
    B. Designated agency arrangements such as this are specifically permitted by the Illinois agency law.
    C. This is an example of designated agency, which is an illegal relationship under the Illinois agency law.
    D. Gloria will be considered an undisclosed dual agent under these facts and will be in violation of Illinois law.

14. A broker decides to "sweeten" an MLS listing for a property by making a blanket offer of subagency. Is the broker's action acceptable?
    A. Yes, because Illinois law permits the creation of subagency relationships only through multiple-listing services.
    B. Yes, because a subagency relationship may be created by either a blanket offer in an MLS or through a specific agreement between parties.
    C. No, because subagency is illegal under Article IV of the Illinois Real Estate License Act.
    D. No, because subagency relationships in Illinois may be created only by a specific agreement between the parties.

15. Salesperson Donna represents the seller in a transaction. When prospective buyers ask to look at the property, which of the following must Donna do?
    A. Tell them that they must first enter into a buyer representation agreement with another licensee.
    B. Inform them in writing that Donna represents the seller's interests.
    C. Inform them, either orally or in writing, that Donna represents the seller's interests.
    D. Show them the property without making any disclosures about Donna's relationship with the seller, because such disclosure would be a violation of Donna's fiduciary duties.

16. Several years ago, Unit 5B in the Grand Towers condominium was the site of a brutal and highly publicized murder. The unit was sold to an elderly woman who contracted the AIDS virus in a blood transfusion and died in the unit last year. As the agent for the woman's estate, what are your disclosure responsibilities to prospective purchasers of Unit 5B in this situation?
    A. You must disclose both the murder and the AIDS-related death.
    B. You are specifically prohibited by law from disclosing either event.
    C. You are specifically relieved of liability for nondisclosure by the Illinois license law.
    D. You do not need to disclose the murder, but you must disclose the AIDS-related death.

17. In Illinois, an unlicensed real estate assistant may perform all of the following activities, EXCEPT:
    A. compute commission checks.
    B. assemble legal documents required for a closing.
    C. explain simple contract documents to prospective buyers.
    D. prepare and distribute flyers and promotional materials.

18. Which of the following statements is true regarding personal real estate assistants in Illinois?
    A. Real estate assistants must be licensed.
    B. An assistant may insert factual information into form contracts under the employing broker's supervision and approval.
    C. An assistant may host open houses and home show booths.
    D. Only unlicensed individuals may be employed as real estate assistants; licensees must be either salespeople or associate brokers.

19. Broker Kate's unlicensed assistant, Tina, worked late nights and weekends to help ensure the successful closing of a difficult transaction. Tina's extra work included making several phone calls to the prospective buyers, encouraging them to accept the seller's counteroffer. Largely because of Tina's efforts, the sale went through with no problem. Kate wants to pay Tina a percentage of the commission, "because Tina has really earned it." Under Illinois law, what may Kate do?
    A. Illinois law permits Kate to compensate Tina in the form of a commission under the circumstances described here.
    B. While Kate may not pay Tina a cash commission, Kate is permitted to make a gift of tangible personal property.
    C. Kate may not pay a commission to Tina under the facts presented here. They are both in violation of rules regarding unlicensed assistants.
    D. Kate may pay a commission to Tina only if Tina is an independent contractor.

20. If a buyer wants to have a clause included in the sales contract under which the seller offers assurances against the existence of werewolves, vampires and trolls on the property, which of the following statements is true in Illinois?
    A. The broker may include the clause, because such standard supernatural disclosures are in general usage.
    B. Only a licensed attorney may prepare the clause for inclusion in the sales contract.
    C. In Illinois, brokers are permitted to add additional clauses to blank form contracts, such as the clause described here, that do not directly involve the conveyance of title to real property.
    D. Under Illinois law, a frivolous clause, such as the one described here, is not permitted and any contract containing such a clause will be invalid.

21. Broker Rodney enters into a listing agreement with a seller. Under the terms of the agreement, when the property sells, the seller will receive a guaranteed $75,000. Any amount left over after the seller's $75,000 will constitute Rodney's compensation. Based on these facts, which of the following statements is true in Illinois?
    A. This type of arrangement, called a "guaranteed sales agreement," is illegal in Illinois, and Rodney will be disciplined for entering into it.
    B. This type of arrangement, called a "net listing," is illegal in Illinois, and Rodney will be disciplined for entering into it.
    C. This is an example of a "guaranteed sales agreement," which is permissible in Illinois if Rodney provides the seller with the necessary disclosures.
    D. This is an example of a "net listing," which is discouraged (but not illegal) in Illinois.

22. In Illinois, which of the following, in a listing agreement, would result in the suspension or revocation of a licensee's license to practice real estate?
    A. A specified commission rate
    B. No specific termination date
    C. No broker protection clause
    D. A specific termination date

23. All of the following disclosures must be included in a listing contract under Illinois law, EXCEPT:
    A. special compensation.
    B. property condition.
    C. disposition of earnest money in the event of a purchaser default.
    D. seller's net return.

24. Lou and Missy are a married couple living in Springfield, Illinois. Missy is the owner of their home. If Lou and Missy decide to sell their home and move to Wisconsin, who is required to sign the listing agreement?
    A. Both Lou and Missy must sign the listing.
    B. Because Missy is the sole owner of their home, she is the only party legally required to sign the listing.
    C. Because Lou and Missy are married, the signature of either spouse is legally sufficient.
    D. Lou is required to sign the listing only if Missy plans to use the capital gains exclusion.

25. From what source do Illinois local units of government receive their powers of eminent domain?
    A. A grant of authority signed by the governor
    B. Article 5 of the U.S. Constitution
    C. The Illinois Statehood Charter of 1818 and the Code of Administrative Procedure
    D. The Illinois Constitution and Code of Civil Procedure

26. Peg dies without leaving a will. If Peg owns real property in Illinois and has no heirs, what will happen to her real property?
    A. Peg's real property will be taken by the county in which it is located under the power of eminent domain.
    B. Ownership of Peg's real property will go to the state of Illinois through escheat.
    C. Peg's property will escheat to the county in which it is located.
    D. Peg's property will escheat to the county in which she last resided.

27. Is there any limitation on an original grantor's right of reverter in Illinois?
    A. Yes: both an original grantor's right of reverter and the enforceability of the underlying condition expire by law after 20 years.
    B. Yes: the original grantor's right of reverter continues for 40 years, although the underlying condition remains enforceable.
    C. Yes: both the original grantor's right of reverter and the underlying condition automatically expire after 99 years.
    D. No: under Illinois law there is no limitation on an original grantor's future interest.

28. Which of the following legal life estates could be available to a surviving husband in Illinois?
    A. Homestead   C. Curtesy
    B. Dower   D. A marital easement

29. How much of an estate of homestead is an individual entitled to in his or her Illinois residence?
    A. $3,250   C. $7,500
    B. $5,000   D. $10,000

30. Elliot and Diane live in Moline, Illinois. They were married on July 10, 1995. On June 15, 1990, Elliot purchased Maroon Manor. On July 15, 1996, Dinae inherited Riverview Terrace. On August 5, 1997, Elliot purchased Orion Farm. On August 10, Diane sold Riverview Terrace and bought Blackhawk Acres. Based on these facts, which of the following best describes the interests held by Elliot and Diane under Illinois law in the event the marriage is dissolved?
    A. Under Illinois' community property laws, Elliot and Diane are equal co-owners of all three properties.
    B. Maroon Manor and Blackhawk Acres are nonmarital property; Orion Farm is marital property.
    C. Maroon Manor is nonmarital property; Orion Farm is marital property; Blackhawk Acres is marital property by transmutation.
    D. All three properties are considered marital property.

31. Real property locations in Illinois are described by their geographic relation to all of the following, EXCEPT the:
    A. Second Principal Meridian.
    B. Third Principal Meridian.
    C. Fourth Principal Meridian.
    D. Fifth Principal Meridian.

32. How often is the assessed valuation of all real estate in Illinois adjusted by county authorities?
    A. Quarterly   C. Biennially
    B. Annually   D. Every three years

33. Nadia, an Illinois resident, was born on March 6, 1986. When will Nadia become of legal age?
    A. March 6, 2004   C. March 6, 2005
    B. March 7, 2004   D. March 7, 2007

34. If a minor enters into a contract in Illinois, what is the statutory period within which she or he may legally void the contract after reaching the age of majority?
    A. 6 months
    B. 1 year
    C. The contract may be voided only up to the date when the minor reaches the age of majority; after that date, the contract is binding.
    D. There is no statutory period.

35. Which of the following is essential to the validity of a deed in Illinois?
    A. A seal (or the word *seal*)
    B. Acknowledgment
    C. Granting clause
    D. Recording

36. In Illinois, the amount of consideration used to determine transfer taxes must be shown on a special form. What is the popular name of that form?
    A. The "Recording Form"
    B. The "Green Sheet"
    C. The "Blue Sheet"
    D. The "T-Sheet"

37. How far back does a normal Illinois title search go?
    A. 15 years   C. 75 years
    B. 40 years   D. 125 years

38. All of the following are exempt from the provisions of the Illinois Real Estate License Act, EXCEPT a(an):
    A. property owner who sells or leases his or her own property.
    B. individual who receives compensation for procuring prospective buyers or renters of real estate.
    C. individual who is employed as a resident property manager.
    D. resident lessee who receives the equivalent of one month's rent as a "finder's fee" for referring a new tenant to the owner.

39. All of the following are requirements for obtaining an Illinois broker's license EXCEPT:
    A. having successfully completed 90 hours of approved real estate courses
    B. being at least 21 years of age.
    C. having been actively engaged as a licensed salesperson for at least three years.
    D. being of good moral character.

40. If Kayla successfully completed her Illinois real estate education requirement on November 1, 1999, what is the latest date on which she may obtain a salesperson's license?
    A. December 31, 1999
    B. November 1, 2000
    C. October 31, 2002
    D. November 1, 2004

41. What is the expiration date of every salesperson's license in Illinois?
    A. January 31 of every even-numbered year
    B. March 31 of each odd-numbered year
    C. October 31 of each odd-numbered year
    D. Every other anniversary date of the individual salesperson's license

42. Broker Ken, an Illinois licensee, wants to open a branch office in a neighboring town. Ken applies for a branch office license and gives the branch a name that clearly identifies its relationship with his main office. Ken names Tony, a licensed Illinois real estate salesperson, as the branch office manager. Under these facts, will Ken receive approval for the branch office?
    A. Yes: Ken has fully complied with the requirements of the Illinois Real Estate License Act.
    B. No: under the Illinois Real Estate License Act, brokers cannot have branch offices in more than one municipality.
    C. Yes: by naming Tony as the branch's manager, Ken is in compliance with the requirement that a broker may be in direct operational control of only one office or branch.
    D. No: the manager of a branch office must be a licensed real estate broker.

43. Max could tell that a prospective buyer would probably not make an offer if she knew the previous occupant of a property had died from complications due to AIDS and so decided not to disclose that fact. Vince, an Illinois real estate broker, set up a "microbrokerage" real estate services outlet in a convenience store by placing a desk at the end of the snack food aisle. James waited outside an AMP testing facility and handed out brochures to prospective licensees on their way in to take the real estate exam, encouraging them to apply for a job at his office. Which, if any, of these individuals is subject to disciplinary action for violating the Illinois Real Estate License Act?
    A. Max only
    B. James only
    C. Max, Vince and James
    D. Vince and James only

44. The Office of Banks and Real Estate is authorized to take any of the following disciplinary actions against a licensee who violates the license law, EXCEPT:
    A. suspend or revoke his or her real estate license.
    B. impose a criminal penalty in the form of a fine (not to exceed $25,000) or imprisonment (for not more than one year).
    C. impose a civil penalty not to exceed $10,000.
    D. issue a formal reprimand against a licensee without suspending or revoking his or her license for at least 60 days.

45. Salesperson Renee engaged in activities that constitute violations of the Illinois Human Rights Act, including blockbusting and discrimination on the basis of disability. Renee also cashed a $25,000 earnest money check from a prospective buyer and used the proceeds to buy a new car. Renee's employing broker was unaware of all of these activities. When Renee's violations are brought to the attention of the OBRE, which of the following statements is true?
    A. The employing broker will not have his or her license revoked as a result of Renee's violations.
    B. Renee's employing broker will be required to pay any fine imposed against Renee out of her or his own personal funds.
    C. Renee's violations are legally the responsibility of the employing broker, who will be subject to the same disciplinary action as Renee, regardless of whether she or he knew the violations had occurred.
    D. Renee's employing broker will be held liable for the Human Rights Act violations only.

46. The Real Estate Administration and Disciplinary Board of the OBRE may undertake an investigation of a licensee based on all the following grounds, EXCEPT:
    A. its own initiative.
    B. a random selection of licensees.
    C. a motion from the OBRE.
    D. a written complaint submitted by a disgruntled customer.

47. Which of the following accurately describes the review process for a final administrative decision of the OBRE?
    A. The accused may appeal a final administrative decision of the OBRE directly to the Illinois Supreme Court.
    B. The accused may petition the circuit court of the county in which he or she resides. The circuit court's decision may be appealed directly to the Illinois Supreme Court.
    C. The accused may petition the circuit court of the county in which the property involved in the transaction that gave rise to the violation is located. The circuit court's decision may be appealed directly to the federal district court.
    D. The accused may request a rehearing by the OBRE, but administrative decisions may not be appealed to any court.

48. If a limited liability company is convicted for the second time of engaging in real estate business activities without a license, what is the maximum penalty to which it may be subjected?
    A. A fine of no more than $2,000
    B. A fine of no less than $2,000 and no more than $5,000
    C. A fine of up to $10,000
    D. A fine of no less than $10,000 and no more than $25,000

49. Every Illinois broker and salesperson who applies for renewal of his or her license must successfully complete a certain number of hours of continuing education courses in each two-year license renewal period. How many hours are required by Illinois law?
    A. Six   C. Nine
    B. Eight   D. Twelve

50. With regard to mortgage theory, Illinois is usually described as a(n):
    A. title-theory state.
    B. lien-theory state.
    C. intermediate-theory state.
    D. security-theory state.

51. Twenty years ago, Ron obtained a 30-year mortgage loan to purchase a home. The interest rate on the loan was 9.275 percent. Today, Ron is prepared to pay off the loan early. Based on these facts, which of the following statements is true in Illinois?
    A. Ron's lender is entitled by statute to charge Ron a prepayment penalty equal to one year's interest on the current balance of the loan.
    B. Ron's lender is permitted by Illinois statute to charge Ron a prepayment penalty of no more than 8 percent of the current outstanding balance of the loan.
    C. Illinois does not take an official statutory position on the issue of prepayment penalties.
    D. Because Ron's interest rate is greater than 8 percent, the lender may not charge a prepayment penalty under Illinois law.

52. In Illinois, if a landlord wants to terminate a year-to-year tenancy, how much notice must the tenant receive?
    A. 7 days
    B. 30 days
    C. 60 days
    D. 4 months

53. In Illinois, are property managers required to have a real estate license?
    A. Yes, but they may be licensed real estate brokers or salespersons.
    B. Yes, but they must be licensed real estate brokers.
    C. No, but they must hold a limited-scope property management license.
    D. No, if their activities are limited to leasing or renting residential property, collecting rent and negotiating leases.

54. All of the following are exempt from the antidiscriminatory provisions of the Illinois Human Rights Act EXCEPT:
    A. owner-occupied apartment buildings of fewer than ten units.
    B. private rooms in a private home occupied by the home's owner.
    C. rooms rented only to persons of one sex.
    D. private, single-family homes sold by their owners if the owner holds fewer than three properties, the home was last occupied by the owner and it was sold without the assistance of a licensee and without the use of discriminatory advertising.

55. If an annual charge of $560 is prorated in October using the statutory month variation method, which of the following will be the resulting daily charge?
    A. $1.51
    B. $1.53
    C. $1.54
    D. $1.56

56. Which of the following terms is NOT associated with water rights?
    A. Littoral
    B. Ingress
    C. Riparian
    D. Doctrine of prior appropriation

57. Zoning ordinances may regulate all of the following EXCEPT:
    A. density.
    B. floor area ratios.
    C. down zoning.
    D. ownership in severality.

58. Which of the following is NOT true regarding option contracts?
    A. An option contract is classified as a unilateral contract.
    B. An option contract that has been exercised is classified as a bilateral contract.
    C. The option money may or may not be applied toward the purchase price.
    D. The seller is the optionee and the buyer is the optionor.

59. All of the following are assignable contracts EXCEPT a:
    A. note.
    B. mortgage.
    C. lease.
    D. listing contract.

60. Which of the following would NOT terminate a listing contract?
    A. Death of the broker
    B. Destruction of the property
    C. Death of the sales associate
    D. Bankruptcy of the seller

Glossary

abstract of title The condensed history of a title to a particular parcel of real estate, consisting of a summary of the original grant and all subsequent conveyances and encumbrances affecting the property and a certification by the abstractor that the history is complete and accurate.

acceleration clause The clause in a mortgage or deed of trust that can be enforced to make the entire debt due immediately if the borrower defaults on an installment payment or other covenant.

accession Acquiring title to additions or improvements to real property as a result of the annexation of fixtures or the accretion of alluvial deposits along the banks of streams.

accretion The increase or addition of land by the deposit of sand or soil washed up naturally from a river, lake or sea.

accrued items On a closing statement, items of expense that are incurred but not yet payable, such as interest on a mortgage loan or taxes on real property.

acknowledgment A formal declaration made before a duly authorized officer, usually a notary public, by a person who has signed a document.

acre A measure of land equal to 43,560 square feet, 4,840 square yards, 4,047 square meters, 160 square rods or 0.4047 hectares.

actual eviction The legal process that results in the tenant's being physically removed from the leased premises.

actual notice Express information or fact; that which is known; direct knowledge.

adjustable-rate mortgage (ARM) A loan characterized by a fluctuating interest rate, usually one tied to a bank or savings and loan association cost-of-funds index.

adjusted basis *See* basis.

ad valorem tax A tax levied according to value, generally used to refer to real estate tax. Also called the *general tax.*

adverse possession The actual, open, notorious, hostile and continuous possession of another's land under a claim of title. Possession for a statutory period may be a means of acquiring title.

affidavit of title A written statement, made under oath by a seller or grantor of real property and acknowledged by a notary public, in which the grantor (1) identifies himself or herself and indicates marital status, (2) certifies that since the examination of the title on the date of the contract no defects have occurred in the title and (3) certifies that he or she is in possession of the property (if applicable).

agency The relationship between a principal and an agent wherein the agent is authorized to represent the principal in certain transactions.

agency coupled with an interest An agency relationship in which the agent is given an estate or interest in the subject of the agency (the property).

agent One who acts or has the power to act for another. A fiduciary relationship is created under the *law of agency* when a property owner, as the principal, executes a listing agreement or management contract authorizing a licensed real estate broker to be his or her agent.

air lot A designated airspace over a piece of land. An air lot, like surface property, may be transferred.

air rights The right to use the open space above a property, usually allowing the surface to be used for another purpose.

alienation The act of transferring property to another. Alienation may be voluntary, such as by gift or sale, or involuntary, as through eminent domain or adverse possession.

alienation clause The clause in a mortgage or deed of trust that states that the balance of the secured debt becomes immediately due and payable at the lender's option if the property is sold by the borrower. In effect this clause prevents the borrower from assigning the debt without the lender's approval.

allodial system A system of land ownership in which land is held free and clear of any rent or service due to the government; commonly contrasted to the feudal system. Land is held under the allodial system in the United States.

American Land Title Association (ALTA) policy A title insurance policy that protects the interest in a collateral property of a mortgage lender who originates a new real estate loan.

amortized loan A loan in which the principal as well as the interest is payable in monthly or other periodic installments over the term of the loan.

annual percentage rate (APR) The relationship of the total finance charges associated with a loan. This must be disclosed to borrowers by lenders under the Truth-in-Lending Act.

anticipation The appraisal principle that holds that value can increase or decrease based on the expectation of some future benefit or detriment produced by the property.

antitrust laws Laws designed to preserve the free enterprise of the open marketplace by making illegal certain private conspiracies and combinations formed to minimize competition. Most violations of antitrust laws in the real estate business involve either *price-fixing* (brokers conspiring to set fixed compensation rates) or *allocation of customers or markets* (brokers agreeing to limit their areas of trade or dealing to certain areas or properties).

appraisal An estimate of the quantity, quality or value of something. The process through which conclusions of property value are obtained; also refers to the report that sets forth the process of estimation and conclusion of value.

appreciation An increase in the worth or value of a property due to economic or related causes, which may prove to be either temporary or permanent; opposite of depreciation.

appurtenance A right, privilege or improvement belonging to, and passing with, the land.

appurtenant easement An easement that is annexed to the ownership of one parcel and allows the owner the use of the neighbor's land.

asbestos A mineral once used in insulation and other materials that can cause respiratory diseases.

assemblage The combining of two or more adjoining lots into one larger tract to increase their total value.

assessment The imposition of a tax, charge or levy, usually according to established rates.

assignment The transfer in writing of interest in a bond, mortgage, lease or other instrument.

assumption of mortgage Acquiring title to property on which there is an existing mortgage and agreeing to be personally liable for the terms and conditions of the mortgage, including payments.

attachment The act of taking a person's property into legal custody by writ or other judicial order to hold it available for application to that person's debt to a creditor.

attorney's opinion of title An abstract of title that an attorney has examined and has certified to be, in his or her opinion, an accurate statement of the facts concerning the property ownership.

automated underwriting Computer systems that permit lenders to expedite the loan approval process and reduce lending costs.

automatic extension A clause in a listing agreement that states that the agreement will continue automatically for a certain period of time after its expiration date. In many states, use of this clause is discouraged or prohibited.

avulsion The sudden tearing away of land, as by earthquake, flood, volcanic action or the sudden change in the course of a stream.

balance The appraisal principle that states that the greatest value in a property will occur when the type and size of the improvements are proportional to each other as well as to the land.

balloon payment A final payment of a mortgage loan that is considerably larger than the required periodic payments because the loan amount was not fully amortized.

bargain and sale deed A deed that carries with it no warranties against liens or other encumbrances but that does imply that the grantor has the right to convey title. The grantor may add warranties to the deed at his or her discretion.

base line The main imaginary line running east and west and crossing a principal meridian at a definite point, used by surveyors for reference in locating and describing land under the rectangular (government) survey system of legal description.

basis The financial interest that the Internal Revenue Service attributes to an owner of an investment property for the purpose of determining annual depreciation and gain or loss on the sale of the asset. If a property was acquired by purchase, the owner's basis is the cost of the property plus the value of any capital expenditures for improvements to the property, minus any depreciation allowable or actually taken. This new basis is called the *adjusted basis.*

bench mark A permanent reference mark or point established for use by surveyors in measuring differences in elevation.

beneficiary (1) The person for whom a trust operates or in whose behalf the income from a trust estate is drawn. (2) A lender in a deed of trust loan transaction.

bilateral contract *See* contract.

binder An agreement that may accompany an earnest money deposit for the purchase of real property as evidence of the purchaser's good faith and intent to complete the transaction.

blanket loan A mortgage covering more than one parcel of real estate, providing for each parcel's partial release from the mortgage lien on repayment of a definite portion of the debt.

blockbusting The illegal practice of inducing homeowners to sell their properties by making representations regarding the entry or prospective entry of persons of a particular race or national origin into the neighborhood.

blue-sky laws Common name for those state and federal laws that regulate the registration and sale of investment securities.

boot Money or property given to make up any difference in value or equity between two properties in an *exchange.*

branch office A secondary place of business apart from the principal or main office from which real estate business is conducted. A branch office usually must be run by a licensed real estate broker working on behalf of the broker.

branch office license In Illinois, a separate license that must be obtained for each branch office a broker wishes to establish.

breach of contract Violation of any terms or conditions in a contract without legal excuse; for example, failure to make a payment when it is due.

broker One who acts as an intermediary on behalf of others for a fee or commission.

brokerage The bringing together of parties interested in making a real estate transaction.

buffer zone A strip of land, usually used as a park or designated for a similar use, separating land dedicated to one use from land dedicated to another use (e.g., residential from commercial).

building code An ordinance that specifies minimum standards of construction for buildings to protect public safety and health.

building permit Written governmental permission for the construction, alteration or demolition of an improvement, showing compliance with building codes and zoning ordinances.

bulk transfer *See* Uniform Commercial Code.

bundle of legal rights The concept of land ownership that includes ownership of all legal rights to the land—for example, possession, control within the law and enjoyment.

buydown A financing technique used to reduce the monthly payments for the first few years of a loan. Funds in the form of discount points are given to the lender by the builder or seller to buy down or lower the effective interest rate paid by the buyer, thus reducing the monthly payments for a set time.

buyer-agency agreement A principal-agent relationship in which the broker is the agent for the buyer, with fiduciary responsibilities to the buyer. The broker represents the buyer under the law of agency.

buyer's agent A residential real estate broker or salesperson who represents the prospective purchaser in a transaction. The buyer's agent owes the buyer/principal the common-law or statutory agency duties.

buyer's broker A residential real estate broker who represents prospective buyers exclusively. As the *buyer's agent*, the broker owes the buyer/principal the common-law or statutory agency duties.

capital gain Profit earned from the sale of an asset.

capitalization A mathematical process for estimating the value of a property using a proper rate of return on the investment and the annual net operating income expected to be produced by the property. The formula is expressed as

$$\frac{\text{Income}}{\text{Rate}} = \text{Value}$$

capitalization rate The rate of return a property will produce on the owner's investment.

cash flow The net spendable income from an investment, determined by deducting all operating and fixed expenses from the gross income. When expenses exceed income, a *negative cash flow* results.

cash rent In an agricultural lease, the amount of money given as rent to the landowner at the outset of the lease, as opposed to sharecropping.

caveat emptor A Latin phrase meaning "Let the buyer beware."

certificate of reasonable value (CRV) A form indicating the appraised value of a property being financed with a VA loan.

certificate of sale The document generally given to the purchaser at a tax foreclosure sale. A certificate of sale does not convey title; normally it is an instrument certifying that the holder received title to the property after the redemption period passed and that the holder paid the property taxes for that interim period.

certificate of title A statement of opinion on the status of the title to a parcel of real property based on an examination of specified public records.

chain of title The succession of conveyances, from some accepted starting point, whereby the present holder of real property derives title.

change The appraisal principle that holds that no physical or economic condition remains constant.

chattel *See* personal property.

Civil Rights Act of 1866 An act that prohibits racial discrimination in the sale and rental of housing.

closing statement A detailed cash accounting of a real estate transaction showing all cash received, all charges and credits made and all cash paid out in the transaction.

cloud on title Any document, claim, unreleased lien or encumbrance that may impair the title to real property or make the title doubtful; usually revealed by a title search and removed by either a quitclaim deed or suit to quiet title.

clustering The grouping of homesites within a subdivision on smaller lots than normal, with the remaining land used as common areas.

code of ethics A written system of standards for ethical conduct.

codicil A supplement or an addition to a will, executed with the same formalities as a will, that normally does not revoke the entire will.

coinsurance clause A clause in insurance policies covering real property that requires that the policyholder maintain fire insurance coverage generally equal to at least 80 percent of the property's actual replacement cost.

commingling The illegal act by a real estate broker of placing client or customer funds with personal funds. By law, brokers are required to maintain a separate *trust or escrow account* for other parties' funds held temporarily by the broker.

commission Payment to a broker for services rendered, such as in the sale or purchase of real property; usually a percentage of the selling price of the property.

common elements Parts of a property that are necessary or convenient to the existence, maintenance and safety of a condominium or are normally in common use by all of the condominium residents. Each condominium owner has an undivided ownership interest in the common elements.

common law The body of law based on custom, usage and court decisions.

common law of agency The traditional law govering the principal-agent relationship, superseded by statute in Illinois.

community property A system of property ownership based on the theory that each spouse has an equal interest in the property acquired by the efforts of either spouse during marriage. A holdover of Spanish law found predominantly in western states; the system was unknown under English common law.

comparables Properties used in an appraisal report that are substantially equivalent to the subject property.

competition The appraisal principle that states that excess profits generate competition.

competitive market analysis (CMA) A comparison of the prices of recently sold homes that are similar to a listing seller's home in terms of location, style and amenities.

Comprehensive Environmental Response, Compensation, and Liability Act (CERCLA) A federal law administered by the Environmental Protection Agency that establishes a process for identifying parties responsible for creating hazardous waste sites, forcing liable parties to clean up toxic sites, bringing legal action against responsible parties and funding the abatement of toxic sites. *See* Superfund.

comprehensive plan *See* master plan.

computerized loan origination (CLO) system An electronic network for handling loan applications through remote computer terminals linked to various lenders' computers.

condemnation A judicial or administrative proceeding to exercise the power of eminent domain, through which a government agency takes private property for public use and compensates the owner.

conditional-use permit Written governmental permission allowing a use inconsistent with zoning but necessary for the common good, such as locating an emergency medical facility in a predominantly residential area.

condominium The absolute ownership of a unit in a multiunit building based on a legal description of the airspace the unit actually occupies, plus an undivided interest in the ownership of the common elements, which are owned jointly with the other condominium unit owners.

confession of judgment clause Permits judgment to be entered against a debtor without the creditor's having to institute legal proceedings.

conformity The appraisal principle that holds that the greater the similarity among properties in an area, the better they will hold their value.

consideration (1) That received by the grantor in exchange for his or her deed. (2) Something of value that induces a person to enter into a contract.

construction loan *See* interim financing.

constructive eviction Actions of a landlord that so materially disturb or impair a tenant's enjoyment of the leased premises that the tenant is effectively forced to move out and terminate the lease without liability for any further rent.

constructive notice Notice given to the world by recorded documents. All people are charged with knowledge of such documents and their contents, whether or not they have actually examined them. Possession of property is also considered constructive notice that the person in possession has an interest in the property.

contingency A provision in a contract that requires a certain act to be done or a certain event to occur before the contract becomes binding.

contract A legally enforceable promise or set of promises that must be performed and for which, if a breach of the promise occurs, the law provides a remedy. A contract may be either *unilateral*, by which only one party is bound to act, or *bilateral*, by which all parties to the instrument are legally bound to act as prescribed.

contribution The appraisal principle that states that the value of any component of a property is what it gives to the value of the whole or what its absence detracts from that value.

conventional loan A loan that requires no insurance or guarantee.

conversion The wrongful appropriation of property belonging to another; also, the process of changing a property's status from rental to condominium.

conveyance A term used to refer to any document that transfers title to real property. The term is also used in describing the act of transferring.

cooperating broker *See* listing broker.

cooperative A residential multiunit building whose title is held by a trust or corporation that is owned by and operated for the benefit of persons living within the building, who are the beneficial owners of the trust or stockholders of the corporation, each possessing a proprietary lease.

co-ownership Title ownership held by two or more persons.

corporation An entity or organization, created by operation of law, whose rights of doing business are essentially the same as those of an individual. The entity has continuous existence until it is dissolved according to legal procedures.

correction lines Provisions in the rectangular survey (government survey) system made to compensate for the curvature of the earth's surface. Every fourth township line (at 24-mile intervals) is used as a correction line on which the intervals between the north and south range lines are remeasured and corrected to a full six miles.

cost approach The process of estimating the value of a property by adding to the estimated land value the appraiser's estimate of the reproduction or replacement cost of the building, less depreciation.

cost recovery An Internal Revenue Service term for *depreciation.*

counteroffer A new offer made in response to an offer received. It has the effect of rejecting the original offer, which cannot be accepted thereafter unless revived by the offeror.

covenant A written agreement between two or more parties in which a party or parties pledge to perform or not to perform specified acts with regard to property; usually found in such real estate documents as deeds, mortgages, leases and contracts for deed.

covenant of quiet enjoyment The covenant implied by law by which a landlord guarantees that a tenant may take possession of leased premises and that the landlord will not interfere in the tenant's possession or use of the property.

credit On a closing statement, an amount entered in a person's favor—either an amount the party has paid or an amount for which the party must be reimbursed.

curtesy A life estate, usually a fractional interest, given by some states to the surviving husband in real estate owned by his deceased wife. Most states have abolished curtesy.

datum A horizontal plane from which heights and depths are measured.

debit On a closing statement, an amount charged; that is, an amount that the debited party must pay.

decedent A person who has died.

dedication The voluntary transfer of private property by its owner to the public for some public use, such as for streets or schools.

deed A written instrument that, when executed and delivered, conveys title to or an interest in real estate.

deed in lieu of foreclosure A deed given by the mortgagor to the mortgagee when the mortgagor is in default under the terms of the mortgage. This is a way for the mortgagor to avoid foreclosure.

deed in trust An instrument that grants a trustee under a land trust full power to sell, mortgage and subdivide a parcel of real estate. The beneficiary controls the trustee's use of these powers under the provisions of the trust agreement.

deed of trust *See* trust deed.

deed of trust lien *See* trust deed lien.

deed restrictions Clauses in a deed limiting the future uses of the property. Deed restrictions may impose a vast variety of limitations and conditions—for example, they may limit the density of buildings, dictate the types of structures that can be erected or prevent buildings from being used for specific purposes or even from being used at all.

default The nonperformance of a duty, whether arising under a contract or otherwise; failure to meet an obligation when due.

defeasance clause A clause used in leases and mortgages that cancels a specified right upon the occurrence of a certain condition, such as cancellation of a mortgage on repayment of the mortgage loan.

defeasible fee estate An estate in which the holder has a fee simple title that may be divested on the occurrence or nonoccurrence of a specified event. There are two categories of defeasible fee estates: fee simple on condition precedent (fee simple determinable) and fee simple on condition subsequent.

deficiency judgment A personal judgment levied against the borrower when a foreclosure sale does not produce sufficient funds to pay the mortgage debt in full.

demand The amount of goods people are willing and able to buy at a given price; often coupled with *supply.*

density zoning Zoning ordinances that restrict the maximum average number of houses per acre that may be built within a particular area, generally a subdivision.

depreciation (1) In appraisal, a loss of value in property due to any cause, including *physical deterioration, functional obsolescence* and *external obsolescence.* (2) In real estate investment, an expense deduction for tax purposes taken over the period of ownership of income property.

descent Acquisition of an estate by inheritance in which an heir succeeds to the property by operation of law.

designated agent A licensee authorized by a broker to act as the agent for a specific principal in a particular transaction.

developer One who attempts to put land to its most profitable use through the construction of improvements.

devise A gift of real property by will. The donor is the devisor, and the recipient is the devisee.

discount point A unit of measurement used for various loan charges; one point equals 1 percent of the amount of the loan.

dominant tenement A property that includes in its ownership the appurtenant right to use an easement over another person's property for a specific purpose.

dower The legal right or interest, recognized in some states, that a wife acquires in the property her husband held or acquired during their marriage. During the husband's lifetime the right is only a possibility of an interest; on his death it can become an interest in land.

dual agency Representing both parties to a transaction. This is unethical unless both parties agree to it, and it is illegal in many states.

due-on-sale clause A provision in the mortgage that states that the entire balance of the note is immediately due and payable if the mortgagor transfers (sells) the property.

duress Unlawful constraint or action exercised on a person whereby the person is forced to perform an act against his or her will. A contract entered into under duress is voidable.

earnest money Money deposited by a buyer under the terms of a contract, to be forfeited if the buyer defaults but applied to the purchase price if the sale is closed.

easement A right to use the land of another for a specific purpose, such as for a right-of-way or utilities; an incorporeal interest in land.

easement by condemnation An easement created by the government or government agency that has exercised its right under eminent domain.

easement by necessity An easement allowed by law as necessary for the full enjoyment of a parcel of real estate; for example, a right of ingress and egress over a grantor's land.

easement by prescription An easement acquired by continuous, open and hostile use of the property for the period of time prescribed by state law.

easement in gross An easement that is not created for the benefit of any *land* owned by the owner of the easement but that attaches *personally to the easement owner.* For example, a right granted by Eleanor Franks to Joe Fish to use a portion of her property for the rest of his life would be an easement in gross.

economic life The number of years during which an improvement will add value to the land.

emblements Growing crops, such as grapes and corn, that are produced annually through labor and industry; also called *fructus industriales.*

eminent domain The right of a government or municipal quasi-public body to acquire property for public use through a court action called *condemnation,* in which the court decides that the use is a public use and determines the compensation to be paid to the owner.

employee Someone who works as a direct employee of an employer and has employee status. The employer is obligated to withhold income taxes and Social Security taxes from the compensation of employees. *See also* independent contractor.

employment contract A document evidencing formal employment between employer and employee or between principal and agent. In the real estate business this generally takes the form of a listing agreement or management agreement.

enabling acts State legislation that confers zoning powers on municipal governments.

encapsulation A method of controlling environmental contamination by sealing off a dangerous substance.

encroachment A building or some portion of it—a wall or fence, for instance—that extends beyond the land of the owner and illegally intrudes on some land of an adjoining owner or a street or alley.

encumbrance Anything—such as a mortgage, tax or judgment lien; an easement; a restriction on the use of the land; or an outstanding dower right—that may diminish the value or use and enjoyment of a property.

Equal Credit Opportunity Act (ECOA) The federal law that prohibits discrimination in the extension of credit because of race, color, religion, national origin, sex, age or marital status.

equalization The raising or lowering of assessed values for tax purposes in a particular county or taxing district to make them equal to assessments in other counties or districts.

equalization factor A factor (number) by which the assessed value of a property is multiplied to arrive at a value for the property that is in line with statewide tax assessments. The *ad valorem tax* is based on this adjusted value.

equitable lien *See* statutory lien.

equitable right of redemption The right of a defaulted property owner to recover the property prior to its sale by paying the appropriate fees and charges.

equitable title The interest held by a vendee under a contract for deed or an installment contract; the equitable right to obtain absolute ownership to property when legal title is held in another's name.

equity The interest or value that an owner has in property over and above any indebtedness.

erosion The gradual wearing away of land by water, wind and general weather conditions; the diminishing of property by the elements.

escheat The reversion of property to the state or county, as provided by state law, in cases where a decedent dies intestate without heirs capable of inheriting, or when the property is abandoned.

escrow The closing of a transaction through a third party called an *escrow agent,* or *escrowee,* who receives certain funds and documents to be delivered on the performance of certain conditions outlined in the escrow instructions.

escrow account The trust account established by a broker under the provisions of the license law for the purpose of holding funds on behalf of the broker's principal or some other person until the consummation or termination of a transaction.

escrow instructions A document that sets forth the duties of the escrow agent, as well as the requirements and obligations of the parties, when a transaction is closed through an escrow.

estate (tenancy) at sufferance The tenancy of a lessee who lawfully comes into possession of a landlord's real estate but who continues to occupy the premises improperly after his or her lease rights have expired.

estate (tenancy) at will An estate that gives the lessee the right to possession until the estate is terminated by either party; the term of this estate is indefinite.

estate (tenancy) for years An interest for a certain, exact period of time in property leased for a specified consideration.

estate (tenancy) from period to period An interest in leased property that continues from period to period—week to week, month to month or year to year.

estate in land The degree, quantity, nature and extent of interest a person has in real property.

estate taxes Federal taxes on a decedent's real and personal property.

estoppel Method of creating an agency relationship in which someone states incorrectly that another person is his or her agent, and a third person relies on that representation.

estoppel certificate A document in which a borrower certifies the amount owed on a mortgage loan and the rate of interest.

ethics The systems of moral principles and rules that becomes standards for professional conduct.

eviction A legal process to oust a person from possession of real estate.

evidence of title Proof of ownership of property; commonly a certificate of title, an abstract of title with lawyer's opinion, title insurance or a Torrens registration certificate.

exchange A transaction in which all or part of the consideration is the transfer of *like-kind* property (such as real estate for real estate).

exclusive-agency listing A listing contract under which the owner appoints a real estate broker as his or her exclusive agent for a designated period of time to sell the property on the owner's stated terms for a commission. The owner reserves the right to sell without paying anyone a commission if he or she sells to a prospect who has not been introduced or claimed by the broker.

exclusive-right-to-sell listing A listing contract under which the owner appoints a real estate broker as his or her exclusive agent for a designated period of time to sell the property on the owner's stated terms, and agrees to pay the broker a commission when the property is sold, whether by the broker, the owner or another broker.

executed contract A contract in which all parties have fulfilled their promises and thus performed the contract.

execution The signing and delivery of an instrument. Also, a legal order directing an official to enforce a judgment against the property of a debtor.

executory contract A contract under which something remains to be done by one or more of the parties.

express agreement An oral or written contract in which the parties state the contract's terms and express their intentions in words.

express contract *See* express agreement.

external depreciation Reduction in a property's value caused by outside factors (those that are off the property).

facilitator *See* non-agent.

Fair Housing Act The federal law that prohibits discrimination in housing based on race, color, religion, sex, handicap, familial status and national origin.

Fannie Mae A quasi-government agency established to purchase any kind of mortgage loans in the secondary mortgage market from the primary lenders. Formerly called Federal National Mortgage Association (FNMA).

Farmer's Home Administration (FmHA) An agency of the federal government that provides credit assistance to farmers and other individuals who live in rural areas.

Federal Deposit Insurance Corporation (FDIC) An independent federal agency that insures the deposits in commercial banks.

Federal Home Loan Mortgage Corporation (FHLMC) A corporation established to purchase primarily conventional mortgage loans in the secondary mortgage market.

Federal National Mortgage Association (FNMA) *See* Fannie Mae.

Federal Reserve System The country's central banking system, which controls the nation's monetary policy by regulating the supply of money and interest rates.

fee simple absolute The maximum possible estate or right of ownership of real property, continuing forever.

fee simple defeasible *See* defeasible fee estate.

feudal system A system of ownership usually associated with precolonial England, in which the king or other sovereign is the source of all rights. The right to possess real property was granted by the sovereign to an individual as a life estate only. On the death of the individual title passed back to the sovereign, not to the decedent's heirs.

FHA loan A loan insured by the Federal Housing Administration and made by an approved lender in accordance with the FHA's regulations.

fiduciary One in whom trust and confidence is placed; a reference to a broker employed under the terms of a listing contract or buyer agency agreement.

fiduciary relationship A relationship of trust and confidence, as between trustee and beneficiary, attorney and client or principal and agent.

Financial Institutions Reform, Recovery and Enforcement Act (FIRREA) This act restructured the savings and loan association regulatory system; enacted in response to the savings and loan crisis of the 1980s.

financing statement *See* Uniform Commercial Code.

fiscal policy The government's policy in regard to taxation and spending programs. The balance between these two areas determines the amount of money the government will withdraw from or feed into the economy, which can counter economic peaks and slumps.

fixture An item of personal property that has been converted to real property by being permanently affixed to the realty.

foreclosure A legal procedure whereby property used as security for a debt is sold to satisfy the debt in the event of default in payment of the mortgage note or default of other terms in the mortgage document. The foreclosure procedure brings the rights of all parties to a conclusion and passes the title in the mortgaged property to either the holder of the mortgage or a third party, who may purchase the realty at the foreclosure sale, free of all encumbrances affecting the property subsequent to the mortgage.

fractional section A parcel of land less than 160 acres, usually found at the edge of a rectangular survey.

fraud Deception intended to cause a person to give up property or a lawful right.

Freddie Mac *See* Federal Home Loan Mortgage Corporation (FHLMC).

freehold estate An estate in land in which ownership is for an indeterminate length of time, in contrast to a *leasehold estate.*

front footage The measurement of a parcel of land by the number of feet of street or road frontage.

functional obsolescence A loss of value to an improvement to real estate arising from functional problems, often caused by age or poor design.

future interest A person's present right to an interest in real property that will not result in possession or enjoyment until some time in the future, such as a reversion or right of reentry.

gap A defect in the chain of title of a particular parcel of real estate; a missing document or conveyance that raises doubt as to the present ownership of the land.

general agent One who is authorized by a principal to represent the principal in a specific range of matters.

general lien The right of a creditor to have all of a debtor's property—both real and personal— sold to satisfy a debt.

general partnership *See* partnership.

general warranty deed A deed in which the grantor fully warrants good clear title to the premises. Used in most real estate deed transfers, a general warranty deed offers the greatest protection of any deed.

Ginnie Mae *See* Government National Mortgage Association (GNMA).

government check The 24-mile-square parcels composed of 16 townships in the rectangular (government) survey system of legal description.

government lot Fractional sections in the rectangular (government) survey system that are less than one quarter-section in area.

Government National Mortgage Association (GNMA) A government agency that plays an important role in the secondary mortgage market. It sells mortgage-backed securities that are backed by pools of FHA and VA loans.

government survey system *See* rectangular (government) survey system.

graduated-payment mortgage (GPM) A loan in which the monthly principal and interest payments increase by a certain percentage each year for a certain number of years and then level off for the remaining loan term.

grantee A person who receives a conveyance of real property from a grantor.

granting clause Words in a deed of conveyance that state the grantor's intention to convey the property at the present time. This clause is generally worded as "convey and warrant," "grant," "grant, bargain and sell" or the like.

grantor The person transferring title to or an interest in real property to a grantee.

gross income multiplier A figure used as a multiplier of the gross annual income of a property to produce an estimate of the property's value.

gross lease A lease of property according to which a landlord pays all property charges regularly incurred through ownership, such as repairs, taxes, insurance and operating expenses. Most residential leases are gross leases.

gross rent multiplier (GRM) The figure used as a multiplier of the gross monthly income of a property to produce an estimate of the property's value.

ground lease A lease of land only, on which the tenant usually owns a building or is required to build as specified in the lease. Such leases are usually long-term net leases; the tenant's rights and obligations continue until the lease expires or is terminated through default.

growing-equity mortgage (GEM) A loan in which the monthly payments increase annually, with the increased amount being used to reduce directly the principal balance outstanding and thus shorten the overall term of the loan.

habendum clause That part of a deed beginning with the words "to have and to hold," following the granting clause and defining the extent of ownership the grantor is conveying.

heir One who might inherit or succeed to an interest in land under the state law of descent when the owner dies without leaving a valid will.

highest and best use The possible use of a property that would produce the greatest net income and thereby develop the highest value.

holdover tenancy A tenancy whereby a lessee retains possession of leased property after the lease has expired and the landlord, by continuing to accept rent, agrees to the tenant's continued occupancy as defined by state law.

holographic will A will that is written, dated and signed in the testator's handwriting.

home equity loan A loan (sometimes called a *line of credit*) under which a property owner uses his or her residence as collateral and can then draw funds up to a prearranged amount against the property.

homeowner's insurance policy A standardized package insurance policy that covers a residential real estate owner against financial loss from fire, theft, public liability and other common risks.

homestead Land that is owned and occupied as the family home. In many states a portion of the area or value of this land is protected or exempt from judgments for debts.

hypothecate To pledge property as security for an obligation or loan without giving up possession of it.

implied agreement A contract under which the agreement of the parties is demonstrated by their acts and conduct.

implied contract *See* implied agreement.

implied warranty of habitability A theory in landlord/tenant law in which the landlord renting residential property implies that the property is habitable and fit for its intended use.

improvement (1) Any structure, usually privately owned, erected on a site to enhance the value of the property—for example, building a fence or a driveway. (2) A publicly owned structure added to or benefiting land, such as a curb, sidewalk, street or sewer.

income approach The process of estimating the value of an income-producing property through capitalization of the annual net income expected to be produced by the property during its remaining useful life.

incorporeal right A nonpossessory right in real estate; for example, an easement or a right-of-way.

independent contractor Someone who is retained to perform a certain act but who is subject to the control and direction of another only as to the end result and not as to the way in which the act is performed. Unlike an employee, an independent contractor pays for all expenses and Social Security and income taxes and receives no employee benefits. Most real estate salespeople are independent contractors.

index method The appraisal method of estimating building costs by multiplying the original cost of the property by a percentage factor to adjust for current construction costs.

inflation The gradual reduction of the purchasing power of the dollar, usually related directly to the increases in the money supply by the federal government.

inheritance taxes State-imposed taxes on a decedent's real and personal property.

inoperative status In Illinois, a license status that prohibits a licensee from engaging in real estate activities because he or she is unsponsored or his or her license has lapsed or been suspended or revoked.

installment contract A contract for the sale of real estate whereby the purchase price is paid in periodic installments by the purchaser, who is in possession of the property even though title is retained by the seller until a future date, which may be not until final payment. Also called a *contract for deed* or *articles of agreement for warranty deed.*

installment sale A transaction in which the sales price is paid in two or more installments over two or more years. If the sale meets certain requirements, a taxpayer can postpone reporting such income until future years by paying tax each year only on the proceeds received that year.

interest A charge made by a lender for the use of money.

interim financing A short-term loan usually made during the construction phase of a building project (in this case often referred to as a *construction loan*).

Interstate Land Sales Full Disclosure Act A federal law that regulates the sale of certain real estate in interstate commerce.

intestate The condition of a property owner who dies without leaving a valid will. Title to the property will pass to the decedent's heirs as provided in the state law of descent.

intrinsic value An appraisal term referring to the value created by a person's personal preferences for a particular type of property.

investment Money directed toward the purchase, improvement and development of an asset in expectation of income or profits.

involuntary alienation *See* alienation.

involuntary lien A lien placed on property without the consent of the property owner.

joint tenancy Ownership of real estate between two or more parties who have been named in one conveyance as joint tenants. Upon the death of a joint tenant, the decedent's interest passes to the surviving joint tenant or tenants by the *right of survivorship.*

joint venture The joining of two or more people to conduct a specific business enterprise. A joint venture is similar to a partnership in that it must be created by agreement between the parties to share in the losses and profits of the venture. It is unlike a partnership in that the venture is for one specific project only, rather than for a continuing business relationship.

judgment The formal decision of a court on the respective rights and claims of the parties to an action or suit. After a judgment has been entered and recorded with the county recorder, it usually becomes a general lien on the property of the defendant.

judicial precedent In law, the requirements established by prior court decisions.

junior lien An obligation, such as a second mortgage, that is subordinate in right or lien priority to an existing lien on the same realty.

laches An equitable doctrine used by courts to bar a legal claim or prevent the assertion of a right because of undue delay or failure to assert the claim or right.

land The earth's surface, extending downward to the center of the earth and upward infinitely into space, including things permanently attached by nature, such as trees and water.

land contract *See* installment contract.

latent defect A hidden structural defect that could not be discovered by ordinary inspection and that threatens the property's soundness or the safety of its inhabitants. Some states impose on sellers and licensees a duty to inspect for and disclose latent defects.

law of agency *See* agency.

lease A written or oral contract between a landlord (the *lessor*) and a tenant (the *lessee*) that transfers the right to exclusive possession and use of the landlord's real property to the lessee for a specified period of time and for a stated consideration (rent). By state law leases for longer than a certain period of time (generally one year) must be in writing to be enforceable.

leasehold estate A tenant's right to occupy real estate during the term of a lease, generally considered to be a personal property interest.

lease option A lease under which the tenant has the right to purchase the property either during the lease term or at its end.

lease purchase The purchase of real property, the consummation of which is preceded by a lease, usually long-term. Typically done for tax or financing purposes.

leasing agent license In Illinois, a limited license for individuals who wish to engage only in activities related to leasing residential property.

legacy A disposition of money or personal property by will.

legal description A description of a specific parcel of real estate complete enough for an independent surveyor to locate and identify it.

legally competent parties People who are recognized by law as being able to contract with others; those of legal age and sound mind.

lessee *See* lease.

lessor *See* lease.

leverage The use of borrowed money to finance an investment.

levy To assess; to seize or collect. To levy a tax is to assess a property and set the rate of taxation. To levy an execution is to officially seize the property of a person to satisfy an obligation.

license (1) A privilege or right granted to a person by a state to operate as a real estate broker or salesperson. (2) The revocable permission for a temporary use of land—a personal right that cannot be sold.

lien A right given by law to certain creditors to have their debts paid out of the property of a defaulting debtor, usually by means of a court sale.

lien theory Some states interpret a mortgage as being purely a lien on real property. The mortgagee thus has no right of possession but must foreclose the lien and sell the property if the mortgagor defaults.

life cycle costing In property management, comparing one type of equipment with another based on both purchase cost and operating cost over its expected useful lifetime.

life estate An interest in real or personal property that is limited in duration to the lifetime of its owner or some other designated person or persons.

life tenant A person in possession of a life estate.

limited partnership *See* partnership.

liquidated damages An amount predetermined by the parties to a contract as the total compensation to an injured party should the other party breach the contract.

liquidity The ability to sell an asset and convert it into cash, at a price close to its true value, in a short period of time.

lis pendens A recorded legal document giving constructive notice that an action affecting a particular property has been filed in either a state or a federal court.

listing agreement A contract between an owner (as principal) and a real estate broker (as agent) by which the broker is employed as agent to find a buyer for the owner's real estate on the owner's terms, for which service the owner agrees to pay a commission.

listing broker The broker in a multiple-listing situation from whose office a listing agreement is initiated, as opposed to the *cooperating broker,* from whose office negotiations leading up to a sale are initiated. The listing broker and the cooperating broker may be the same person.

littoral rights (1) A landowner's claim to use water in large navigable lakes and oceans adjacent to his or her property. (2) The ownership rights to land bordering these bodies of water up to the high-water mark.

loan origination fee A fee charged to the borrower by the lender for making a mortgage loan. The fee is usually computed as a percentage of the loan amount.

loan-to-value ratio The relationship between the amount of the mortgage loan and the value of the real estate being pledged as collateral.

lot-and-block (recorded plat) system A method of describing real property that identifies a parcel of land by reference to lot and block numbers within a subdivision, as specified on a recorded subdivision plat.

management agreement A contract between the owner of income property and a management firm or individual property manager that outlines the scope of the manager's authority.

market A place where goods can be bought and sold and a price established.

marketable title Good or clear title, reasonably free from the risk of litigation over possible defects.

market value The most probable price property would bring in an arm's-length transaction under normal conditions on the open market.

master plan A comprehensive plan to guide the long-term physical development of a particular area.

mechanic's lien A statutory lien created in favor of contractors, laborers and materialmen who have performed work or furnished materials in the erection or repair of a building.

meridian One of a set of imaginary lines running north and south and crossing a base line at a definite point, used in the rectangular (government) survey system of property description.

metes-and-bounds description A legal description of a parcel of land that begins at a well-marked point and follows the boundaries, using directions and distances around the tract, back to the point of beginning.

mill One-tenth of one cent. Some states use a mill rate to compute real estate taxes; for example, a rate of 52 mills would be $.052 tax for each dollar of assessed valuation of a property.

ministerial acts In Illinois, acts that a licensee may perform for a consumer that are informative and do not constitute active representation.

minor Someone who has not reached the age of majority and therefore does not have legal capacity to transfer title to real property.

monetary policy Governmental regulation of the amount of money in circulation through such institutions as the Federal Reserve Board.

month-to-month tenancy A periodic tenancy under which the tenant rents for one month at a time. In the absence of a rental agreement (oral or written) a tenancy is generally considered to be month to month.

monument A fixed natural or artificial object used to establish real estate boundaries for a metes-and-bounds description.

mortgage A conditional transfer or pledge of real estate as security for the payment of a debt. Also, the document creating a mortgage lien.

mortgage banker Mortgage loan companies that originate, service and sell loans to investors.

mortgage broker An agent of a lender who brings the lender and borrower together. The broker receives a fee for this service.

mortgagee A lender in a mortgage loan transaction.

mortgage lien A lien or charge on the property of a mortgagor that secures the underlying debt obligations.

mortgagor A borrower in a mortgage loan transaction.

multiperil policies Insurance policies that offer protection from a range of potential perils, such as those of a fire, hazard, public liability and casualty.

multiple-listing clause A provision in an exclusive listing for the authority and obligation on the part of the listing broker to distribute the listing to other brokers in the multiple-listing organization.

multiple-listing service (MLS) A marketing organization composed of member brokers who agree to share their listing agreements with one another in the hope of procuring ready, willing and able buyers for their properties more quickly than they could on their own. Most multiple-listing services accept exclusive-right-to-sell or exclusive agency listings from their member brokers.

negotiable instrument A written promise or order to pay a specific sum of money that may be transferred by endorsement or delivery. The transferee then has the original payee's right to payment.

net lease A lease requiring that the tenant pay not only rent but also costs incurred in maintaining the property, including taxes, insurance, utilities and repairs.

net listing A listing based on the net price the seller will receive if the property is sold. Under a net listing the broker can offer the property for sale at the highest price obtainable to increase the commission. This type of listing is illegal in many states.

net operating income (NOI) The income projected for an income-producing property after deducting losses for vacancy and collection and operating expenses.

non-agent An intermediary between a buyer and seller, or landlord and tenant, who assists both parties in a transaction without representing either. Also known as a *facilitator, transaction broker, transaction coordinator* and *contract broker.*

nonconforming use A use of property that is permitted to continue after a zoning ordinance prohibiting it has been established for the area.

nonhomogeneity A lack of uniformity; dissimilarity. Because no two parcels of land are exactly alike, real estate is said to be *nonhomogeneous.*

note *See* promissory note.

novation Substituting a new obligation for an old one or substituting new parties to an existing obligation.

nuncupative will An oral will declared by the testator in his or her final illness, made before witnesses and afterward reduced to writing.

obsolescence The loss of value due to factors that are outmoded or less useful. Obsolescence may be functional or economic.

occupancy permit A permit issued by the appropriate local governing body to establish that the property is suitable for habitation by meeting certain safety and health standards.

offer and acceptance Two essential components of a valid contract; a "meeting of the minds."

offeror/offeree The person who makes the offer is the *offeror.* The person to whom the offer is made is the *offeree.*

Office of Thrift Supervision (OTS) Monitors and regulates the savings and loan industry. OTS was created by FIRREA.

open-end loan A mortgage loan that is expandable by increments up to a maximum dollar amount, the full loan being secured by the same original mortgage.

open listing A listing contract under which the broker's commission is contingent on the broker's producing a ready, willing and able buyer before the property is sold by the seller or another broker.

option An agreement to keep open for a set period an offer to sell or purchase property.

option listing Listing with a provision that gives the listing broker the right to purchase the listed property.

ostensible agency A form of implied agency relationship created by the actions of the parties involved rather than by written agreement or document.

package loan A real estate loan used to finance the purchase of both real property and personal property, such as in the purchase of a new home that includes carpeting, window coverings and major appliances.

parol evidence rule A rule of evidence providing that a written agreement is the final expression of the agreement of the parties, not to be varied or contradicted by prior or contemporaneous oral or written negotiations.

participation mortgage A mortgage loan wherein the lender has a partial equity interest in the property or receives a portion of the income from the property.

partition The division of cotenants' interests in real property when the parties do not all voluntarily agree to terminate the co-ownership; takes place through court procedures.

partnership An association of two or more individuals who carry on a continuing business for profit as co-owners. Under the law a partnership is regarded as a group of individuals rather than as a single entity. A *general partnership* is a typical form of joint venture in which each general partner shares in the administration, profits and losses of the operation. A *limited partnership* is a business arrangement whereby the operation is administered by one or more general partners and funded, by and large, by limited or silent partners, who are by law responsible for losses only to the extent of their investments.

party wall A wall that is located on or at a boundary line between two adjoining parcels of land and is used or is intended to be used by the owners of both properties.

patent A grant or franchise of land from the United States government.

payment cap The limit on the amount the monthly payment can be increased on an adjustable-rate mortgage when the interest rate is adjusted.

payoff statement *See* reduction certificate.

percentage lease A lease, commonly used for commercial property, whose rental is based on the tenant's gross sales at the premises; it usually stipulates a base monthly rental plus a percentage of any gross sales above a certain amount.

percolation test A test of the soil to determine if it will absorb and drain water adequately to use a septic system for sewage disposal.

periodic estate (tenancy) *See* estate (tenancy) from period to period.

personal property Items, called *chattels*, that do not fit into the definition of real property; movable objects.

physical deterioration A reduction in a property's value resulting from a decline in physical condition; can be caused by action of the elements or by ordinary wear and tear.

planned unit development (PUD) A planned combination of diverse land uses, such as housing, recreation and shopping, in one contained development or subdivision.

plat map A map of a town, section or subdivision indicating the location and boundaries of individual properties.

plottage The increase in value or utility resulting from the consolidation (*assemblage*) of two or more adjacent lots into one larger lot.

pocket card In Illinois, a card that must be carried by the licensee when engaging in real estate activities for which a license is required.

point of beginning (POB) In a metes-and-bounds legal description, the starting point of the survey, situated in one corner of the parcel; all metes-and-bounds descriptions must follow the boundaries of the parcel back to the point of beginning.

police power The government's right to impose laws, statutes and ordinances, including zoning ordinances and building codes, to protect the public health, safety and welfare.

power of attorney A written instrument authorizing a person, the *attorney-in-fact*, to act as agent for another person to the extent indicated in the instrument.

prepaid items On a closing statement, items that have been paid in advance by the seller, such as insurance premiums and some real estate taxes, for which he or she must be reimbursed by the buyer.

prepayment penalty A charge imposed on a borrower who pays off the loan principal early. This penalty compensates the lender for interest and other charges that would otherwise be lost.

price-fixing *See* antitrust laws.

primary mortgage market The mortgage market in which loans are originated, consisting of lenders such as commercial banks, savings and loan associations and mutual savings banks.

principal (1) A sum loaned or employed as a fund or an investment, as distinguished from its income or profits. (2) The original amount (as in a loan) of the total due and payable at a certain date. (3) A main party to a transaction—the person for whom the agent works.

principal meridian The main imaginary line running north and south and crossing a base line at a definite point, used by surveyors for reference in locating and describing land under the rectangular (government) survey system of legal description.

prior appropriation A concept of water ownership in which the landowner's right to use available water is based on a government-administered permit system.

priority The order of position or time. The priority of liens is generally determined by the chronological order in which the lien documents are recorded; tax liens, however, have priority even over previously recorded liens.

private mortgage insurance (PMI) Insurance provided by private carrier that protects a lender against a loss in the event of a foreclosure and deficiency.

probate A legal process by which a court determines who will inherit a decedent's property and what the estate's assets are.

procuring cause The effort that brings about the desired result. Under an open listing the broker who is the procuring cause of the sale receives the commission.

progression An appraisal principle that states that, between dissimilar properties. the value of the lesser-quality property is favorably affected by the presence of the better-quality property.

promissory note A financing instrument that states the terms of the underlying obligation, is signed by its maker and is negotiable (transferable to a third party).

property manager Someone who manages real estate for another person for compensation. Duties include collecting rents, maintaining the property and keeping up all accounting.

property reports The mandatory federal and state documents compiled by subdividers and developers to provide potential purchasers with facts about a property prior to their purchase.

proprietary lease A lease given by the corporation that owns a cooperative apartment building to the shareholder for the shareholder's right as a tenant to an individual apartment.

prorations Expenses, either prepaid or paid in arrears, that are divided or distributed between buyer and seller at the closing.

protected class Any group of people designated as such by the Department of Housing and Urban Development (HUD) in consideration of federal and state civil rights legislation. Currently includes ethnic minorities, women, religious groups, the handicapped and others.

puffing Exaggerated or superlative comments or opinions.

pur autre vie "For the life of another." A life estate pur autre vie is a life estate that is measured by the life of a person other than the grantee.

purchase-money mortgage (PMM) A note secured by a mortgage or deed of trust given by a buyer, as borrower, to a seller, as lender, as part of the purchase price of the real estate.

pyramiding The process of acquiring additional properties by refinancing properties already owned and investing the loan proceeds in additional properties.

quantity-survey method The appraisal method of estimating building costs by calculating the cost of all of the physical components in the improvements, adding the cost to assemble them and then including the indirect costs associated with such construction.

quiet title A court action to remove a cloud on the title.

quitclaim deed A conveyance by which the grantor transfers whatever interest he or she has in the real estate, without warranties or obligations.

radon A naturally occurring gas that is suspected of causing lung cancer.

range A strip of land six miles wide, extending north and south and numbered east and west according to its distance from the principal meridian in the rectangular (government) survey system of legal description.

rate cap The limit on the amount the interest rate can be increased at each adjustment period in an adjustable-rate loan. The cap also may set the maximum interest rate that can be charged during the life of the loan.

ratification Method of creating an agency relationship in which the principal accepts the conduct of someone who acted without prior authorization as the principal's agent.

ready, willing and able buyer One who is prepared to buy property on the seller's terms and is ready to take positive steps to consummate the transaction.

real estate Land; a portion of the earth's surface extending downward to the center of the earth and upward infinitely into space, including all things permanently attached to it, whether naturally or artificially.

real estate assistant A licensed or unlicensed individual who assists a broker or salesperson in the real estate business. In Illinois, there are strict limits on the activities in which an unlicensed assistant may engage.

real estate investment syndicate *See* syndicate.

real estate investment trust (REIT) Trust ownership of real estate by a group of individuals who purchase certificates of ownership in the trust, which in turn invests the money in real property and distributes the profits back to the investors free of corporate income tax.

real estate license law State law enacted to protect the public from fraud, dishonesty and incompetence in the purchase and sale of real estate.

real estate mortgage investment conduit (REMIC) A tax entity that issues multiple classes of investor interests (securities) backed by a pool of mortgages.

real estate recovery fund A fund established in some states from real estate license revenues to cover claims of aggrieved parties who have suffered monetary damage through the actions of a real estate licensee.

Real Estate Settlement Procedures Act (RESPA) The federal law that requires certain disclosures to consumers about mortgage loan settlements. The law also prohibits the payment or receipt of kickbacks and certain kinds of referral fees.

real property The interests, benefits and rights inherent in real estate ownership.

REALTOR® A registered trademark term reserved for the sole use of active members of local REALTOR® boards affiliated with the National Association of REALTORS®.

reconciliation The final step in the appraisal process, in which the appraiser combines the estimates of value received from the sales comparison, cost and income approaches to arrive at a final estimate of market value for the subject property.

reconveyance deed A deed used by a trustee under a deed of trust to return title to the trustor.

recording The act of entering or recording documents affecting or conveying interests in real estate in the recorder's office established in each county. Until it is recorded, a deed or mortgage ordinarily is not effective against subsequent purchasers or mortgagees.

rectangular (government) survey system A system established in 1785 by the federal government, providing for surveying and describing land by reference to principal meridians and base lines.

redemption The right of a defaulted property owner to recover his or her property by curing the default.

redemption period A period of time established by state law during which a property owner has the right to redeem his or her real estate from a foreclosure or tax sale by paying the sales price, interest and costs. Many states do not have mortgage redemption laws.

redlining The illegal practice of a lending institution denying loans or restricting their number for certain areas of a community.

reduction certificate (payoff statement) The document signed by a lender indicating the amount required to pay a loan balance in full and satisfy the debt; used in the settlement process to protect both the seller's and the buyer's interests.

regression An appraisal principle that states that, between dissimilar properties, the value of the better-quality property is affected adversely by the presence of the lesser-quality property.

Regulation Z Implements the Truth-in-Lending Act requiring that credit institutions inform borrowers of the true cost of obtaining credit.

reinstatement The activation of a suspended, revoked or inoperative license.

release deed A document, also known as a *deed of reconveyance*, that transfers all rights given a trustee under a deed of trust loan back to the grantor after the loan has been fully repaid.

remainder interest The remnant of an estate that has been conveyed to take effect and be enjoyed after the termination of a prior estate, such as when an owner conveys a life estate to one party and the remainder to another.

rent A fixed, periodic payment made by a tenant of a property to the owner for possession and use, usually by prior agreement of the parties.

rent schedule A statement of proposed rental rates, determined by the owner or the property manager or both, based on a building's estimated expenses, market supply and demand and the owner's long-range goals for the property.

replacement cost The construction cost at current prices of a property that is not necessarily an exact duplicate of the subject property but serves the same purpose or function as the original.

reproduction cost The construction cost at current prices of an exact duplicate of the subject property.

Resolution Trust Corporation The organization created by FIRREA to liquidate the assets of failed savings and loan associations.

restrictive covenants A clause in a deed that limits the way the real estate ownership may be used.

reverse-annuity mortgage (RAM) A loan under which the homeowner receives monthly payments based on his or her accumulated equity rather than a lump sum. The loan must be repaid at a prearranged date or on the death of the owner or the sale of the property.

reversionary interest The remnant of an estate that the grantor holds after granting a life estate to another person.

reversionary right The return of the rights of possession and quiet enjoyment to the lessor at the expiration of a lease.

right of survivorship *See* joint tenancy.

right-of-way The right given by one landowner to another to pass over the land, construct a roadway or use as a pathway, without actually transferring ownership.

riparian rights An owner's rights in land that borders on or includes a stream, river or lake. These rights include access to and use of the water.

risk management Evaluation and selection of appropriate property and other insurance.

rules and regulations Real estate licensing authority orders that govern licensees' activities; they usually have the same force and effect as statutory law.

sale and leaseback A transaction in which an owner sells his or her improved property and, as part of the same transaction, signs a long-term lease to remain in possession of the premises.

sales comparison approach The process of estimating the value of a property by examining and comparing actual sales of comparable properties.

salesperson A person who performs real estate activities while employed by or associated with a licensed real estate broker.

satisfaction of mortgage A document acknowledging the payment of a mortgage debt.

secondary mortgage market A market for the purchase and sale of existing mortgages, designed to provide greater liquidity for mortgages; also called the *secondary money market*. Mortgages are originated in the *primary mortgage market*.

section A portion of a township under the rectangular (government) survey system. A township is divided into 36 sections, numbered 1 through 36. A section is a square with mile-long sides and an area of one square mile, or 640 acres.

security agreement *See* Uniform Commercial Code.

security deposit A payment by a tenant, held by the landlord during the lease term and kept (wholly or partially) on default or destruction of the premises by the tenant.

seisin Possession of real property under claim of freehold estate (fee simple).

separate property Under community property law, property owned solely by either spouse before the marriage, acquired by gift or inheritance after the marriage or purchased with separate funds after the marriage.

servient tenement Land on which an easement exists in favor of an adjacent property (called a *dominant estate*); also called a *servient estate*.

setback The amount of space local zoning regulations require between a lot line and a building line.

severalty Ownership of real property by one person only, also called *sole ownership*.

severance Changing an item of real estate to personal property by detaching it from the land; for example, cutting down a tree.

sharecropping In an agricultural lease, the agreement between the landowner and the tenant farmer to split the crop or the profit from its sale, actually sharing the crop.

shared-appreciation mortgage (SAM) A mortgage loan in which the lender, in exchange for a loan with a favorable interest rate, participates in the profits (if any) the borrower receives when the property is eventually sold.

single agency The representation of a single principal.

situs The personal preference of people for one area over another, not necessarily based on objective facts and knowledge.

special agent One who is authorized by a principal to perform a single act or transaction; a real estate broker is usually a special agent authorized to find a ready, willing and able buyer for a particular property.

special assessment A tax or levy customarily imposed against only those specific parcels of real estate that will benefit from a proposed public improvement like a street or sewer.

special warranty deed A deed in which the grantor warrants, or guarantees, the title only against defects arising during the period of his or her tenure and ownership of the property and not against defects existing before that time, generally using the language, "by, through or under the grantor but not otherwise."

specific lien A lien affecting or attaching only to a certain, specific parcel of land or piece of property.

specific performance A legal action to compel a party to carry out the terms of a contract.

sponsor card In Illinois, a card that certifies a new licensee's relationship with a broker and serves as a temporary permit to practice until a permanent pocket card is received.

square-foot method The appraisal method of estimating building costs by multiplying the number of square feet in the improvements being appraised by the cost per square foot for recently constructed similar improvements.

statute of frauds That part of a state law that requires that certain instruments, such as deeds, real estate sales contracts and certain leases, be in writing to be legally enforceable.

statute of limitations That law pertaining to the period of time within which certain actions must be brought to court.

statutory lien A lien imposed on property by statute—a tax lien, for example—in contrast to an *equitable lien*, which arises out of common law.

statutory redemption The right of a defaulted property owner to recover the property after its sale by paying the appropriate fees and charges.

steering The illegal practice of channeling home seekers to particular areas, either to maintain the homogeneity of an area or to change the character of an area, which limits their choices of where they can live.

stigmatized property A property that has acquired an undesirable reputation due to an event that occurred on or near it, such as violent crime, gang-related activity, illness or personal tragedy. Some states restrict the disclosure of information about stigmatized properties.

straight-line method A method of calculating depreciation for tax purposes, computed by dividing the adjusted basis of a property by the estimated number of years of remaining useful life.

straight (term) loan A loan in which only interest is paid during the term of the loan, with the entire principal amount due with the final interest payment.

subagent One who is employed by a person already acting as an agent. Typically a reference to a salesperson licensed under a broker (agent) who is employed under the terms of a listing agreement.

subdivider One who buys undeveloped land, divides it into smaller, usable lots and sells the lots to potential users.

subdivision A tract of land divided by the owner, known as the *subdivider,* into blocks, building lots and streets according to a recorded subdivision plat, which must comply with local ordinances and regulations.

subdivision and development ordinances Municipal ordinances that establish requirements for subdivisions and development.

subdivision plat *See* plat map.

sublease *See* subletting.

subletting The leasing of premises by a lessee to a third party for part of the lessee's remaining term. *See also* assignment.

subordination Relegation to a lesser position, usually in respect to a right or security.

subordination agreement A written agreement between holders of liens on a property that changes the priority of mortgage, judgment and other liens under certain circumstances.

subrogation The substitution of one creditor for another, with the substituted person succeeding to the legal rights and claims of the original claimant. Subrogation is used by title insurers to acquire from the injured party rights to sue to recover any claims the insurers have paid.

substitution An appraisal principle that states that the maximum value of a property tends to be set by the cost of purchasing an equally desirable and valuable substitute property, assuming that no costly delay is encountered in making the substitution.

subsurface rights Ownership rights in a parcel of real estate to the water, minerals, gas, oil and so forth that lie beneath the surface of the property.

suit for possession A court suit initiated by a landlord to evict a tenant from leased premises after the tenant has breached one of the terms of the lease or has held possession of the property after the lease's expiration.

suit to quiet title A court action intended to establish or settle the title to a particular property, especially when there is a cloud on the title.

Superfund Popular name of the hazardous-waste cleanup fund established by the Comprehensive Environmental Response, Compensation, and Liability Act (CERCLA).

Superfund Amendments and Reauthorization Act (SARA) An amendatory statute that contains stronger cleanup standards for contaminated sites, increased funding for Superfund and clarifications of lender liability and innocent landowner immunity. *See* Comprehensive Environmental Response, Compensation, and Liability Act (CERCLA).

supply The amount of goods available in the market to be sold at a given price. The term is often coupled with *demand.*

supply and demand The appraisal principle that follows the interrelationship of the supply of and demand for real estate. As appraising is based on economic concepts, this principle recognizes that real property is subject to the influences of the marketplace just as is any other commodity.

surety bond An agreement by an insurance or bonding company to be responsible for certain possible defaults, debts or obligations contracted for by an insured party; in essence, a policy insuring one's personal and/or financial integrity. In the real estate business a surety bond is generally used to ensure that a particular project will be completed at a certain date or that a contract will be performed as stated.

surface rights Ownership rights in a parcel of real estate that are limited to the surface of the property and do not include the air above it (*air rights*) or the minerals below the surface (*subsurface rights*).

survey The process by which boundaries are measured and land areas are determined; the on-site measurement of lot lines, dimensions and position of a house on a lot, including the determination of any existing encroachments or easements.

syndicate A combination of people or firms formed to accomplish a business venture of mutual interest by pooling resources. In a *real estate investment syndicate* the parties own and/or develop property, with the main profit generally arising from the sale of the property.

tacking Adding or combining successive periods of continuous occupation of real property by adverse possessors. This concept enables someone who has not been in possession for the entire statutory period to establish a claim of adverse possession.

taxation The process by which a government or municipal quasi-public body raises monies to fund its operation.

tax credit An amount by which tax owed is reduced directly.

tax deed An instrument, similar to a certificate of sale, given to a purchaser at a tax sale. *See also* certificate of sale.

tax lien A charge against property, created by operation of law. Tax liens and assessments take priority over all other liens.

tax sale A court-ordered sale of real property to raise money to cover delinquent taxes.

tenancy by the entirety The joint ownership, recognized in some states, of property acquired by husband and wife during marriage. Upon the death of one spouse the survivor becomes the owner of the property.

tenancy in common A form of co-ownership by which each owner holds an undivided interest in real property as if he or she were sole owner. Each individual owner has the right to partition. Unlike joint tenants, tenants in common have right of inheritance.

tenant One who holds or possesses lands or tenements by any kind of right or title.

tenant improvements Alterations to the interior of a building to meet the functional demands of the tenant.

testate Having made and left a valid will.

testator A person who has made a valid will. A woman often is referred to as a *testatrix,* although testator can be used for either gender.

tier (township strip) A strip of land six miles wide, extending east and west and numbered north and south according to its distance from the base line in the rectangular (government) survey system of legal description.

time is of the essence A phrase in a contract that requires the performance of a certain act within a stated period of time.

time-share A form of ownership interest that may include an estate interest in property and that allows use of the property for a fixed or variable time period.

time-share estate A fee simple interest in a time-share property.

time-share use A right of occupancy in a time-share property, less than a fee simple interest.

title (1) The right to or ownership of land. (2) The evidence of ownership of land.

title insurance A policy insuring the owner or mortgagee against loss by reason of defects in the title to a parcel of real estate, other than encumbrances, defects and matters specifically excluded by the policy.

title search The examination of public records relating to real estate to determine the current state of the ownership.

title theory Some states interpret a mortgage to mean that the lender is the owner of mortgaged land. On full payment of the mortgage debt the borrower becomes the landowner.

Torrens system A method of evidencing title by registration with the proper public authority, generally called the *registrar,* named for its founder, Sir Robert Torrens.

township The principal unit of the rectangular (government) survey system. A township is a square with six-mile sides and an area of 36 square miles.

township strips *See* tier.

trade fixture An article installed by a tenant under the terms of a lease and removable by the tenant before the lease expires.

transfer tax Tax stamps required to be affixed to a deed by state and/or local law.

trust A fiduciary arrangement whereby property is conveyed to a person or institution, called a *trustee,* to be held and administered on behalf of another person, called a *beneficiary.* The one who conveys the trust is called the *trustor.*

trust deed An instrument used to create a mortgage lien by which the borrower conveys title to a trustee, who holds it as security for the benefit of the note holder (the lender); also called a *deed of trust.*

trust deed lien A lien on the property of a trustor that secures a deed of trust loan.

trustee The holder of bare legal title in a deed of trust loan transaction.

trustee's deed A deed executed by a trustee conveying land held in a trust.

trustor A borrower in a deed of trust loan transaction.

undivided interest *See* tenancy in common.

unenforceable contract A contract that has all the elements of a valid contract, yet neither party can sue the other to force performance of it. For example, an unsigned contract is generally unenforceable.

Uniform Commercial Code A codification of commercial law, adopted in most states, that attempts to make uniform all laws relating to commercial transactions, including chattel mortgages and bulk transfers. Security interests in chattels are created by an instrument known as a *security agreement.* To give notice of the security interest, a *financing statement* must be recorded. Article 6 of the code regulates *bulk transfers*—the sale of a business as a whole, including all fixtures, chattels and merchandise.

unilateral contract A one-sided contract wherein one party makes a promise so as to induce a second party to do something. The second party is not legally bound to perform; however, if the second party does comply, the first party is obligated to keep the promise.

unit-in-place method The appraisal method of estimating building costs by calculating the costs of all of the physical components in the structure, with the cost of each item including its proper installation, connection, etc.; also called the *segregated cost method.*

unit of ownership The four unities that are traditionally needed to create a joint tenancy—unity of title, time, interest and possession.

usury Charging interest at a higher rate than the maximum rate established by state law.

valid contract A contract that complies with all the essentials of a contract and is binding and enforceable on all parties to it.

VA loan A mortgage loan on approved property made to a qualified veteran by an authorized lender and guaranteed by the Department of Veterans Affairs to limit the lender's possible loss.

value The power of a good or service to command other goods in exchange for the present worth of future rights to its income or amenities.

variance Permission obtained from zoning authorities to build a structure or conduct a use that is expressly prohibited by the current zoning laws; an exception from the zoning ordinances.

vendee A buyer, usually under the terms of a land contract.

vendor A seller, usually under the terms of a land contract.

voidable contract A contract that seems to be valid on the surface but may be rejected or disaffirmed by one or both of the parties.

void contract A contract that has no legal force or effect because it does not meet the essential elements of a contract.

voluntary alienation *See* alienation.

voluntary lien A lien placed on property with the knowledge and consent of the property owner.

waste An improper use or an abuse of a property by a possessor who holds less than fee ownership, such as a tenant, life tenant, mortgagor or vendee. Such waste ordinarily impairs the value of the land or the interest of the person holding the title or the reversionary rights.

will A written document, properly witnessed, providing for the transfer of title to property owned by the deceased, called the *testator.*

workers' compensation acts Laws that require an employer to obtain insurance coverage to protect his or her employees who are injured in the course of their employment.

wraparound loan A method of refinancing in which the new mortgage is placed in a secondary, or subordinate, position; the new mortgage includes both the unpaid principal balance of the first mortgage and whatever additional sums are advanced by the lender. In essence it is an additional mortgage in which another lender refinances a borrower by lending an amount over the existing first mortgage amount without disturbing the existence of the first mortgage.

zoning ordinance An exercise of police power by a municipality to regulate and control the character and use of property.

Answer Key

Following are the correct answers to the review questions included in each chapter of the text. *In parentheses following the correct answers are references to the pages where the question topics are discussed or explained.* Suggested math calculations for some of the review questions can be found on page 490 amd 491. *If you have answered a question incorrectly, be sure to go back to the page or pages noted and restudy the material until you understand the correct answer.* The references for the Sample Examinations are to chapter numbers.

Chapter 1
Introduction to the
Real Estate Business

1. B (5)
2. B (6)
3. D (7, 8)
4. C (8)
5. B (4)
6. D (5)
7. B (6)
8. A (4)

Chapter 2
Real Property and
the Law

1. A (13)
2. B (15)
3. C (17)
4. B (15)
5. D (16)
6. B (11)
7. A (15)
8. D (16)
9. B (14)
10. A (15)
11. B (13)
12. C (13)
13. D (12)
14. A (16)

Chapter 3
Concepts of Home
Ownership

1. D (24)
2. B (26)
3. A (24)
4. B (24)
5. B (26)
6. D (26)
7. D (26)
8. C (26)
9. C (26)
10. C (27)
11. C (490)
12. C (490)

Chapter 4
Real Estate Agency

1. C (35)
2. A (40)
3. A (34)
4. B (33)
5. C (40)
6. B (39)
7. D (50)
8. C (41)
9. C (41)
10. C (42)
11. B (42)

12. A (35)
13. D (48)
14. B (43)
15. B (49)

Chapter 5
Real Estate
Brokerage

1. B (41)
2. B (59)
3. B (61)
4. B (61)
5. D (58)
6. C (58)
7. A (62)
8. C (64)

Chapter 6
Broker Employment
Contracts

1. A (68)
2. C (62)
3. C (85)
4. A (69)
5. B (73)
6. D (71)
7. A (69)
8. C (72)
9. A (69)

10. D (73)
11. C (69)
12. B (69)
13. A (82)
14. B (82)
15. B (72)
16. A (73)
17. C (73)
18. C (71)
19. B (85)
20. C (82)
21. A (70)
22. D (79)

Chapter 7
Interests in Real
Estate

1. C (92)
2. A (94)
3. C (94)
4. D (100)
5. A (96)
6. D (98)
7. D (101)
8. C (104)
9. A (92)
10. D (94)
11. B (100)
12. A (95)
13. B (96)

14. B (103)
15. A (99)
16. D (103)
17. B (98)
18. A (99)
19. C (101)
20. C (93)
21. D (95)
22. A (97)
23. B (96)
24. B (95)

Chapter 8
Forms of Real Estate
Ownership

1. D (112)
2. D (111)
3. A (112)
4. B (120)
5. B (117)
6. D (115)
7. B (111)
8. A (116)
9. D (122)
10. C (123)
11. C (118)
12. D (110)
13. D (114)
14. B (111)
15. B (111)
16. C (122)
17. B (122)
18. B (112)
19. D (120)
20. A (112)
21. D (124)
22. B (117)
23. A (114)
24. A (111)
25. B (111)
26. D (113)
27. A (120)

Chapter 9
Legal Descriptions

1. B (137)
2. D (137)
3. D (490)
4. B (132)
5. C (138)
6. C (138)
7. A (138)
8. A (138)
9. A (138)
10. D (490)

11. C (134)
12. D (490)
13. C (133)
14. D (140)
15. B (137)
16. B (490)
17. B (490)
18. B (490)
19. B (138)
20. C (135, 136)
21. B (135)
22. A (134)
23. C (140)
24. C (134)
25. B (145)
26. C (145)
27. C (145)

Chapter 10
Real Estate Taxes and
Other Liens

1. D (150)
2. B (151)
3. B (157)
4. C (150)
5. B (149)
6. D (490)
7. C (154)
8. C (158)
9. D (490)
10. C (150)
11. D (160)
12. C (157)
13. B (150)
14. B (149)
15. D (158)
16. A (150)
17. B (152)
18. D (161)
19. D (150)
20. B (154)
21. A (159)
22. A (159)
23. C (160)
24. A (153)
25. A (490)
26. D (156)

Chapter 11
Real Estate Contracts

1. C (167)
2. B (170)
3. D (167)
4. B (167)
5. C (169)

6. D (177)
7. D (177)
8. A (177)
9. A (177)
10. D (167)
11. D (180)
12. D (180)
13. D (180)
14. C (167)
15. B (174)
16. A (169)
17. B (168)
18. D (171)
19. B (180)
20. A (173)
21. C (175)
22. B (173)
23. B (173)
24. C (181)
25. D (174)
26. A (169)

Chapter 12
Transfer of Title

1. A (187)
2. A (188)
3. D (169)
4. A (479)
5. C (190)
6. A (191)
7. D (190)
8. D (192)
9. C (192)
10. C (189)
11. B (187)
12. B (189)
13. B (189)
14. C (195)
15. B (196)
16. D (195)
17. D (190)
18. A (190)
19. D (197)
20. D (198)
21. A (198)
22. C (198)
23. C (196)
24. B (198)
25. A (191)
26. B (195)
27. D (194)
28. C (198)
29. C (200)
30. C (200)
31. B (490)
32. B (490)

33. D (490)
34. A (194)

Chapter 13
Title Records

1. A (207)
2. A (207)
3. C (208)
4. A (208)
5. A (209)
6. D (209)
7. D (210)
8. D (208)
9. C (211)
10. A (210)
11. C (207)
12. C (212)
13. B (213)
14. D (212)
15. C (213)
16. A (212)
17. B (209)
18. A (209)
19. A (209)
20. D (208)
21. D (208)
22. C (207)
23. B (207)
24. C (217)
25. B (212)

Chapter 14
Illinois Real Estate
License Laws

1. A (220)
2. C (221)
3. C (226)
4. B (237)
5. A (234)
6. D (236)
7. B (236)
8. C (225)
9. A (224)
10. D (225)
11. C (226)
12. B (229)
13. B (220)
14. D (230)
15. B (236)
16. A (232)
17. B (231)
18. D (220)
19. A (227)
20. D (220)
21. C (223)

22. D (238)
23. B (235)
24. A (222)

Chapter 15
Real Estate
Financing: Principles

1. B (490)
2. A (244)
3. C (244)
4. A (250)
5. D (253)
6. B (246)
7. D (255)
8. D (251)
9. A (251)
10. A (253)
11. B (490)
12. D (253)
13. B (250)
14. A (245)
15. B (248)
16. D (253)
17. B (254)
18. C (251)
19. A (255)
20. C (255)
21. C (251)
22. B (256)
23. C (256)
24. D (256)
25. D (254)
26. C (245)

Chapter 16
Real Estate
Financing: Practice

1. D (274)
2. D (276)
3. C (264)
4. C (269)
5. B (263)
6. A (266)
7. B (262)
8. C (269)
9. B (275)
10. C (271)
11. B (280)
12. B (266)
13. B (264)
14. A (266)
15. B (265)
16. D (280)
17. B (266)
18. B (268)

19. B (268)
20. B (266)
21. C (270)
22. D (270)
23. C (266, 267)
24. C (267, 269)
25. A (26, 276, 277)
26. B (273)
27. D (251, 253, 245)
28. A (280)
29. B (264)
30. C (274)

Chapter 17
Leases

1. C (295)
2. C (294)
3. D (292)
4. C (290)
5. B (292)
6. D (287)
7. C (285)
8. B (297)
9. B (292)
10. B (285)
11. B (294)
12. C (286)
13. A (294)
14. C (111)
15. B (285)
16. A (284)
17. C (291)
18. C (286)
19. B (291)
20. A (296)
21. C (286)
22. C (299)

Chapter 18
Property
Management

1. B (316)
2. A (310)
3. D (310)
4. C (316)
5. C (312)
6. B (316)
7. D (314)
8. B (313)
9. C (309)
10. A (310)
11. C (316)
12. C (317)
13. C (310)
14. B (313)

15. B (308)
16. A (310)
17. D (308)

Chapter 19
Real Estate Appraisal

1. C (330)
2. B (324)
3. B (325)
4. B (323)
5. D (325)
6. A (325)
7. D (329)
8. C (334)
9. A (490)
10. C (323)
11. C (330)
12. C (323)
13. B (323)
14. C (328)
15. D (490)
16. D (326)
17. B (490)
18. B (490)
19. B (329)
20. B (328)
21. B (329)
22. D (325)
23. D (330)
24. B (339)
25. A (329)
26. C (322)

Chapter 20
Land-Use Controls
and Property
Development

1. A (350)
2. A (346)
3. B (350)
4. C (344)
5. C (397)
6. A (344)
7. A (346)
8. D (346)
9. B (350)
10. A (351)
11. A (347)
12. C (348)
13. B (348)
14. B (349)
15. B (343)
16. D (348)
17. A (349)
18. A (349)

19. A (351)
20. A (352)
21. C (344)
22. B (343)

Chapter 21
Fair Housing and
Ethical Practices

1. C (365)
2. A (359)
3. D (359)
4. B (366)
5. B (366)
6. A (367)
7. B (368)
8. B (367)
9. C (365)
10. B (359)
11. A (365)
12. B (359)
13. D (369)
14. C (362)
15. D (363)
16. A (365)
17. A (370)
18. A (369)
19. C (370)

Chapter 22
Environmental Issues
and the Real Estate
Transaction

1. B (378)
2. C (379)
3. C (381)
4. A (379)
5. A (384)
6. C (379)
7. B (386)
8. D (388)
9. C (379)
10. D (378)
11. C (377)
12. B (377)

Chapter 23
Closing the Real
Estate Transaction

1. D (408)
2. B (395)
3. D (395)
4. A (395)
5. D (398)
6. C (399, 400)
7. C (396)

8. B (403)	13. C (490)	18. D (399)	23. B (491)
9. B (403)	14. A (490)	19. B (400)	24. C (404)
10. D (406-409)	15. C (402, 403)	20. B (400)	25. A (406)
11. C (409)	16. B (405)	21. C (399)	26. D (404)
12. A (403)	17. D (399)	22. C (400)	

MATH CALCULATIONS FOR REVIEW QUESTIONS

Chapter 3

11    $45,000 × .065 = $2,925 + $400 = $3,325
$45,000 − $30,000 − $3,325 = $11,675

12    $9,500 + $800 + $1,000 = $11,300

Chapter 9

3   2 × 4 = 8
640 ÷ 8 = 80

10   43,560 × $21 = $93,654

12   4 × 4 = 16
640 ÷ 16 × $1,500 = $60,000

16   4.5 × 43,560 = 196,020
$78,400 ÷ 196,020 = .40
150 × 100 = 15,000
.40 × 15,000 = 6,000

17   10 × 43,560 − 26,000 ÷ 5,000 = 81.92

18   400 × 640 ÷ 2 = 128,000 ÷ 43,560 = 2.94

Chapter 10

6    $80,000 × .35 × .030 = $840

9    $47,250 × 1.25 × .025 = $1,477

25    $80,000 × .33 × .95 ÷ 100 × 6 ÷ 2 = $752.40

Chapter 12

31    $48,000 or 48 × $1.50 = $72

32    $80,000 − $50,000 = $30,000
30 × $1.50 = $45

33    $127,000 or 127 × 1.50 = $190.50

Chapter 15

1    $120,000 × .03 = $3,600

11    $2,700 ÷ $90,000 = .03 or 3 points

Chapter 19

9    $24,000 ÷ $300,000 = .08 or 8 percent

15    $112,000 − $53,700 ÷ $542,000 = 10.75 percent

17    $240,000 ÷ 65 × 5 = $18,462

18    $240,000 − $18,462 = $221,538

Chapter 23

13 $85,000 × .10 = 8,500
$85,000 − $8,500 = $76,500 × .02 = $1,530
$1,530 + $8,500 = $10,030

14 $100,000 × .30 = $30,000 − $12,000 = $18,000

23 $2,129 ÷ 365 = $5.83

SAMPLE EXAMINATION ONE

(Part One)

1. B (10)	24. B (10)	47. C (20)	70. A (19)
2. A (11)	25. C (math)	48. D (9)	71. D (16)
3. A (11)	26. C (math)	49. B (19)	72. D (8)
4. C (16)	27. B (19)	50. B (10)	73. A (23)
5. C (16)	28. C (9)	51. B (11)	74. D (23)
6. B (6)	29. C (15)	52. B (8)	75. B (2)
7. A (12)	30. B (5)	53. C (17)	76. C (7)
8. A (21)	31. D (11)	54. D (11)	77. D (math)
9. A (7)	32. D (11)	55. B (7)	78. B (6)
10. D (8)	33. B (11)	56. C (math)	79. D (5)
11. D (5)	34. B (16)	57. A (7)	80. D (17)
12. A (16)	35. B (11)	58. C (math)	81. B (2)
13. D (17)	36. A (15)	59. D (20)	82. B (2)
14. A (19)	37. D (19)	60. B (11)	83. C (3)
15. A (20)	38. B (5)	61. C (15)	84. B (5)
16. C (5)	39. A (8)	62. A (21)	85. B (5)
17. D (4)	40. A (12)	63. D (23)	86. D (8)
18. C (15)	41. D (6)	64. D (11)	87. C (21)
19. A (5)	42. B (17)	65. B (12)	88. A (6)
20. B (7, 20)	43. C (21)	66. D (8)	89. C (6)
21. D (6)	44. B (15)	67. B (23)	90. D (19)
22. B (9)	45. D (10)	68. D (21)	
23. B (15)	46. D (11)	69. A (12)	

(Part Two)

1. D (7)	16. C (7)	31. C (12)	46. D (14)
2. A (11)	17. A (6)	32. C (10)	47. B (14)
3. C (7)	18. B (6)	33. B (17, 21)	48. C (15)
4. B (7)	19. C (14)	34. B (12)	49. D (14)
5. B (8)	20. A (14)	35. D (13)	50. A (15)
6. B (8)	21. D (14)	36. B (13)	51. C (14)
7. B (9)	22. B (14)	37. C (14)	52. B (17)
8. C (9)	23. A (12)	38. C (14)	53. C (14)
9. D (8)	24. B (9)	39. D (14)	54. C (17)
10. B (10)	25. B (11)	40. B (13)	55. B (20)
11. B (10)	26. C (11)	41. B (15)	56. A (17)
12. B (6)	27. D (15)	42. C (10)	57. C (4)
13. B (6)	28. D (21)	43. D (10)	58. D (4)
14. C (14)	29. B (12)	44. B (11)	59. B (2)
15. D (6)	30. C (12)	45. B (21)	60. C (8)

SAMPLE EXAMINATION TWO

(Part One)

1. D (17)	24. B (23)	47. A (7)	70. A (23)
2. C (2)	25. D (17)	48. A (23)	71. D (16)
3. C (11)	26. D (16)	49. B (17)	72. C (19)
4. B (15)	27. C (16)	50. C (19)	73. A (11)
5. C (16)	28. B (4)	51. C (18)	74. D (19)
6. D (4)	29. B (19)	52. A (13)	75. D (16)
7. B (math)	30. D (23)	53. D (3)	76. C (16)
8. D (21)	31. A (23)	54. A (2)	77. B (19)
9. B (math)	32. D (19)	55. D (8)	78. D (10)
10. B (15)	33. A (11)	56. A (23)	79. B (23)
11. B (11)	34. D (13)	57. B (7)	80. B (18)
12. A (16, 23)	35. B (math)	58. B (12)	81. B (5, 6)
13. D (6)	36. A (6)	59. D (19)	82. D (5)
14. C (7)	37. B (17)	60. D (16)	83. B (19)
15. D (4)	38. D (6)	61. D (19)	84. B (6)
16. D (9)	39. A (19)	62. C (21)	85. D (6)
17. B (12)	40. C (19)	63. C (12)	86. C (17)
18. B (23)	41. D (12)	64. C (16)	87. B (19)
19. C (6)	42. C (9)	65. A (4)	88. A (6)
20. A (19)	43. B (11)	66. B (6)	89. D (21)
21. C (23)	44. D (18)	67. B (21)	90. A (10)
22. B (17)	45. C (math)	68. D (4)	
23. A (7)	46. D (16)	69. C (math)	

(Part Two)

1. B (23)	16. C (4)	31. D (9)	46. B (14)
2. D (15)	17. C (5)	32. B (10)	47. B (14)
3. C (17)	18. B (5)	33. A (11)	48. D (14)
4. C (17)	19. C (5)	34. D (11)	49. D (14)
5. A (17)	20. B (11)	35. C (12)	50. C (15)
6. B (17)	21. D (6)	36. B (12)	51. D (15)
7. D (20)	22. B (6)	37. B (13)	52. C (17)
8. A (21)	23. D (6)	38. B (14)	53. B (18)
9. D (21)	24. A (6)	39. C (14)	54. A (21)
10. C (21)	25. D (7)	40. D (14)	55. A (23)
11. A (4)	26. C (7)	41. B (14)	56. B (7)
12. C (4)	27. B (7)	42. D (14)	57. D)20)
13. B (4)	28. A (7)	43. D (14)	58. D (11)
14. D (4)	29. C (7)	44. B (14)	59. D (11)
15. B (4)	30. C (8)	45. A (14)	60. C (6)

Index

STATE OF ILLINOIS

ACT

THE REAL ESTATE LICENSE ACT OF 1983

225 Illinois Compiled Statues 1994
455/1 - 455/38.65, Inclusive
(Current through Public Act 89-0340)
Effective June 1, 1996

OFFICE OF BANKS AND REAL ESTATE

(Printed by the Authority of the State of Illinois)

1996

At the time of printing, the License Act is under revision. A copy of the updated Act should be obtained when it becomes available by contacting the Office of Banks and Real Estate, 500 East Monroe, Suite 200, Springfield, Illinois 62701-1509.

THE REAL ESTATE LICENSE ACT OF 1983
Effective January 1, 1984, as amended

CONTENTS

The paragraph numbers in the first column refer to the relevant paragraphs of 225 Illinois Compiled Statutes 1992.
The section numbers in the second column refer to the Sections of the Real Estate License Act of 1983, as amended.

Note: This is a copy of a portion of the Statutes data base maintained by the Legislative Reference Bureau. The data base incorporates public acts through P.A. 89-679.

CHAPTER 225
PROFESSIONS AND OCCUPATIONS

(225 ILCS 455/) (Real Estate License Act of 1983.)
Title: An Act to revise the law in relation to the definition, registration and regulation of real estate brokers, real estate associate brokers and real estate salespersons, and to amend or repeal certain Acts herein named.
Cite: 225 ILCS 455/1 et seq.
Source: P.A. 83-191. This Act is scheduled to be repealed December 31, 1999.
Date: Approved August 31, 1983.
Short title: Real Estate License Act of 1983.

ARTICLE 1. REAL ESTATE LICENSING

(225 ILCS 455/1)
Sec. 1. The intent of the General Assembly in enacting this statute is to evaluate the competency of persons engaged in the real estate business and to regulate such business for the protection of the public.
(Source: P.A. 83-191.)

(225 ILCS 455/2)
Sec. 2. This Act shall be known and may be cited as the Real Estate License Act of 1983, and it shall supersede the Real Estate Brokers and Salesmen License Act repealed by this Act.
(Source: P.A. 83-191.)

(225 ILCS 455/3)
Sec. 3. It is unlawful for any person, corporation, limited liability company, or partnership to act as a real estate broker or real estate salesperson, or to advertise or assume to act as such broker or salesperson, without a properly issued sponsor card or a license issued under this Act by the Office of Banks and Real Estate, either directly or through its authorized designee.
No corporation shall be granted a license, or engage in the business or capacity, either directly or indirectly, of a real estate broker, unless every officer of such corporation who actively participates in the real estate activities of such corporation holds a license as a real estate broker, and unless every employee who acts as a salesperson for such corporation holds a license as a real estate broker or salesperson.
Nothing in this Act shall prohibit the cooperation of, or a division of commission between, a duly licensed broker of this State and a nonresident of this State, licensed as a real estate broker in his resident state, having no office in this State.
No partnership shall be granted a license, or engage in the business or serve in the capacity, either directly or indirectly, of a real estate broker, unless every general partner in such partnership holds a license as a real estate broker, and unless every employee who acts as a salesperson for such partnership holds a license as a real estate broker or salesperson.
No limited liability company shall be granted a license, or engage in the business or serve in the capacity, either directly or indirectly, of a real estate broker, unless every managing member in the limited liability company holds a license as a real estate broker, and unless every employee who acts as a salesperson for the limited liability company holds a license as a real estate broker or salesperson.
No partnership, limited liability company, or corporation shall be licensed to conduct a brokerage business where an individual salesperson or group of salespersons owns or directly or indirectly controls more than 49% of the shares of stock or other ownership in the partnership, limited liability company, or corporation.
(Source: P.A. 88-683, eff. 1-24-95; 89-23, eff. 7-1-95; 89-508, eff. 7-3-96.)

(225 ILCS 455/3.5)
Sec. 3.5. Unlicensed practice; violation; civil penalty.
(a) Any person who practices, offers to practice, attempts to practice, or holds oneself out to practice as a real estate broker or real estate salesperson without being licensed under this Act shall, in addition to any other penalty provided by law, pay a civil penalty to the Office of Banks and Real Estate in an amount not to exceed $5,000 for each offense as determined by the Office of Banks and Real Estate. The civil penalty shall be assessed by the Office of Banks and Real Estate after a hearing is held in accordance with the provisions set forth in this Act regarding the provision of a hearing for the discipline of a licensee.
(b) The Office of Banks and Real Estate has the authority and power to investigate any and all unlicensed activity.
(c) The civil penalty shall be paid within 60 days after the effective date of the order imposing the civil penalty. The order shall constitute a judgment and may be filed and execution had thereon in the same manner as any judgment from any court of record.
(Source: P.A. 89-474, eff. 6-18-96.)

(225 ILCS 455/4)
Sec. 4. As used in this Act, unless the context otherwise requires:
(1) "Applicant" means any person, as defined in subsection (16) of this Section, who applies to the Office of Banks and Real Estate for a valid license as a real estate broker or real estate salesperson.
(2) "Board" means the Real Estate Administration and Disciplinary Board of the Office of Banks and Real Estate.
(3) "Branch office" means a real estate broker's office other than the broker's principal place of business.
(4) "Broker" means an individual, partnership, limited liability company, or corporation, other than a real estate salesperson, who for another and for compensation:
(a) Sells, exchanges, purchases, rents or leases real estate.

(b) Offers to sell, exchange, purchase, rent or lease real estate.
(c) Negotiates, offers, attempts or agrees to negotiate the sale, exchange, purchase, rental or leasing of real estate.
(d) Lists, offers, attempts or agrees to list real estate for sale, lease, or exchange.
(e) Buys, sells, offers to buy or sell or otherwise deals in options on real estate or improvements thereon.
(f) Collects, offers, attempts or agrees to collect rent for the use of real estate.
(g) Advertises or represents himself as being engaged in the business of buying, selling, exchanging, renting, or leasing real estate.
(h) Assists or directs in procuring of prospects, intended to result in the sale, exchange, lease, or rental of real estate.
(i) Assists or directs in the negotiation of any transaction intended to result in the sale, exchange, lease, or rental of real estate.
(j) Employs or supervises a leasing agent or agents.
(5) "Commissioner" means the Commissioner of Banks and Real Estate or a person authorized by the Commissioner, the Office of Banks and Real Estate Act, or this Act to act in the Commissioner's stead.
(6) (Blank).
(7) (Blank).
(8) "Employee" or other derivative of the word "employee" when used to refer to, describe or delineate the relationship between a real estate broker and a real estate salesperson or another real estate broker shall be construed to include an independent contractor relationship provided that there exists a written agreement clearly establishing and stating the relationship. All responsibilities of a broker shall remain.
(9) "Escrow monies" means all monies, promissory notes or any other type or manner of legal tender or financial consideration deposited with any person for the benefit of the parties to the transaction. Escrow monies include, but are not limited to, earnest monies and security deposits, except those security deposits in which the person holding the security deposit is also the sole owner of the property being leased and for which the security deposit is being held.
(10) "Financial institution" means a bank or savings and loan institution or credit union chartered by the federal government or any State of the United States.
(11) "Inoperative" means a status of licensure where the licensee holds a current license under this Act, but that licensee is prohibited from engaging in licensed activities because the licensee is unsponsored or the license of the broker with whom the licensee is associated or by whom he is employed is currently expired, revoked, suspended, or otherwise rendered invalid under this Act.
(11.5) "Leasing agent" means a person who has obtained a license as provided in Section 6.1 of this Act.
(12) "License" means the document issued by the Office of Banks and Real Estate certifying that the person named thereon has fulfilled all requirements prerequisite to registration under this Act.
(13) "Licensee" means any person, as defined in subsection (16) of this Section who holds a valid unexpired license as a real estate broker or real estate salesperson.

(14) "Newspaper" means a publication regularly printed and distributed, usually daily or weekly, containing news, opinions, advertisements, and other items of general interest.
(15) "Office" means a real estate broker's place of business located within a structure used either for residential or commercial purposes, where records may be maintained and licenses displayed, whether or not it is the broker's principal place of business.
(16) "Person" means and includes individuals, corporations, limited liability companies, and partnerships, foreign or domestic, except that when referring to a person licensed under this Act it may mean only an individual.

(17) "Pocket card" means the card issued by the Office of Banks and Real Estate to signify that the person named on the card is currently licensed under this Act.
(18) "Real estate" means and includes leaseholds, as well as any other interest or estate in land, whether corporeal, incorporeal, freehold, or non-freehold, and whether the real estate is situated in this State or elsewhere.
(19) "Real Estate Education Advisory Council" means the Real Estate Education Advisory Council created under Section 37.2 of this Act.
(20) "Real estate school" means a school approved by the Office of Banks and Real Estate offering courses in subjects related to real estate transactions, including the subjects upon which an applicant is examined in determining fitness to receive a license.
(21) "Salesperson" means any individual, other than a real estate broker or leasing agent, who is employed by a real estate broker or leasing agent with a real estate broker as an independent contractor and participates in any activity described in subsection (4) of this Section.
(22) "Sponsor card" means the card issued by a real estate broker certifying that the real estate broker, real estate salesperson, or leasing agent named therein is employed by or associated by written agreement with the real estate broker.
(Source: P.A. 88-683, eff. 1-24-95; 89-23, eff. 7-1-95; 89-340, eff. 1-1-96; 89-508, eff. 7-3-96; 89-626, eff. 8-9-96.)

(225 ILCS 455/5)
Sec. 5. The commission of a single act prohibited by this Act, or a violation of a disciplinary order issued under this Act, constitutes a violation of this Act.
(Source: P.A. 86-925.)

(225 ILCS 455/6)
Sec. 6. The requirement for holding a license under this Act shall not apply to:
(1) Any person, limited liability company, partnership or corporation who as owner or lessor shall perform any of the acts described in subsection (4) of Section 4 of this Act with reference to property owned or leased by them, or to the regular employees thereof with respect to the property so owned or leased, where such acts are performed in the regular course of or as an incident to the management, sale or other disposition of such property and the investment therein provided that such regular employees shall not perform any of the acts described in subsection (4) of Section 4 of this Act in connection with a vocation of selling or leasing any real estate or the improvements thereon not so owned or leased.

(2) An attorney in fact acting under a duly executed and recorded power of attorney to convey real estate from the owner or lessor, or the services rendered by an attorney at law in the performance of the attorney's duty as such attorney at law.

(3) Any person acting as receiver, trustee in bankruptcy, administrator, executor or guardian or while acting under a court order or under the authority of a will or testamentary trust.

(4) Any person acting as a resident manager for the owner or any employee acting as the resident manager for a broker managing an apartment building, duplex, apartment complex, when such resident manager resides on the premises, the premises is his primary residence, and such resident manager is engaged in the leasing of the property of which he or she is the resident manager.

(5) Any officer or employee of a federal agency in the conduct of his official duties.

(6) Any officer or employee of the State government or any political subdivision thereof performing his official duties.

(7) Any multiple listing service wholly owned by a not-for-profit organization or association of real estate brokers.

(8) Any not-for-profit referral system or organization of real estate brokers formed for the purpose of referrals of prospects for the sale or purchase of real estate.

(9) Railroads and other public utilities regulated by the State of Illinois, or their subsidiaries or affiliated corporations, or to the officers or regular employees thereof, unless performance of any of the acts described in subsection (4) of Section 4 of this Act is in connection with the sale, purchase, lease or other disposition of real estate or investment therein unrelated to the regulated business activity of such railroad or other public utility or affiliated or subsidiary corporation thereof.

(10) Any newspaper of general circulation in the routine course of selling advertising along with which no related services are provided.

(11) Any resident lessee of a residential dwelling unit who refers for compensation to the owner of the dwelling unit, or to the owner's agent, prospective lessees of dwelling units in the same building or complex as the resident lessee's unit, but only if the resident lessee (i) refers no more than 3 prospective lessees in any 12-month period, (ii) receives compensation of no more than $1,000 or the equivalent of one month's rent, whichever is less, in any 12-month period, and (iii) limits his or her activities to referring prospective lessees to the owner, or the owner's agent, and does not show a residential dwelling unit to a prospective lessee, discuss terms or conditions of leasing a dwelling unit with a prospective lessee, or otherwise participate in the negotiation of the leasing of a dwelling unit.
(Source: P.A. 88-449; 88-683, eff. 1-24-95.)

(225 ILCS 455/6.1 new)
Sec. 6.1. Leasing agent license.
(a) The purpose of this Section is to provide for a limited scope license to enable persons who wish to engage in activities relating to the leasing of residential real property for which a license is required under this Act, and only those activities, to do so by obtaining the license provided for under this Section.

(b) Notwithstanding the other provisions of this Act, there is hereby created a leasing agent license which shall enable the licensee to engage only in residential leasing activities for which a license is required under this Act. Such activities include, but are not limited to: leasing or renting residential real property; collecting rent for the use of residential real estate; or attempting, offering, or negotiating to lease, rent, or collect rent for the use of residential real property. Nothing in this Section shall be construed to require a licensed real estate broker or salesperson to obtain a leasing agent license in order to perform leasing activities for which a license is required under this Act. Licensed leasing agents must be employed and supervised by a person holding a valid real estate broker's license issued under this Act.

(c) The Department, by rule, with the advice and consent of the Real Estate Administration and Disciplinary Board, shall provide for the licensing of leasing agents including the issuance, renewal, and administration of licenses.

(d) Notwithstanding any other provisions of this Act to the contrary, a person may engage in residential leasing activities for which a license is required under this Act, for a period of 120 consecutive days without being licensed, so long as the person is acting under the supervision of a licensed real estate broker and the broker has notified the Department that the person is pursuing licensure under this Section. During the 120 day period all requirements of Sections 6.2 and 6.3 of this Act with respect to education, successful completion of an examination, and the payment of all required fees must be satisfied. The Department may adopt rules to ensure that the provisions of this subsection are not used in a manner that enables an unlicensed person to repeatedly or continually engage in activities for which a license is required under this Act.
(Source: P.A. 89-340, eff. 1-1-96.)

(225 ILCS 455/6.2)
Sec. 6.2. Application for leasing agent license. Every person who desires to obtain a leasing agent license shall apply to the Department in writing on forms provided by the Department. All application or license fees must accompany the application. Each applicant shall be at least 18 years of age, be of good moral character, have successfully completed a 4-year course of study in a high school or secondary school or an equivalent course of study approved by the Illinois State Board of Education, and must successfully complete a written examination authorized by the Department sufficient to demonstrate the applicant's knowledge of the provisions of this Act relating to leasing agents and the applicant's competence to engage in the activities of a licensed leasing agent.

Applicants must successfully complete 15 hours of instruction in an approved course of study relating to the leasing of residential real property. Successfully completed coursework, completed pursuant to the requirements of this Section, may be applied to the coursework requirements to obtain a real estate broker's or salesperson's license as provided by rule.

The Real Estate Education Advisory Council shall

recommend and the Department shall adopt requirements for approved courses, course content, and the approval of courses, instructors, and schools, as well as school and instructor fees.

The Department, by rule, with the advice and consent of the Real Estate Education Advisory Council may establish continuing education requirements for licensed leasing agents.
(Source: P.A. 89-340, eff. 1-1-96.)

(225 ILCS 455/6.3)
Sec. 6.3. Leasing agent application, license, and renewal fees. The Department by rule may prescribe application, license and renewal fees sufficient to administer the provisions of this amendatory Act of 1995. Fees shall be deposited in the Real Estate License Administration Fund.
(Source: P.A. 89-340, eff. 1-1-96.)

(225 ILCS 455/6.4)
Sec. 6.4. Standards of practice; disciplinary procedures. The Department by rule with the advice and consent of the Real Estate Administration and Disciplinary Board may prescribe standards of practice to be followed by licensed leasing agents. Standards of practice shall include, but not be limited to, acts or omissions that leasing agents are prohibited from engaging in, disciplinary procedures, and penalties for violating provisions of this Act. Disciplinary procedures shall conform with disciplinary procedures for licensed real estate brokers and salespersons. Complaints shall be heard by the Real Estate License Administration Board.
(Source: P.A. 89-340, eff. 1-1-96.)

(225 ILCS 455/7)
Sec. 7. No action or suit shall be instituted, nor recovery therein be had, in any court of this State by any person, partnership, limited liability company, or corporation for compensation for any act done or service performed, the doing or performing of which is prohibited by this Act to other than licensed brokers or salespersons unless such person, partnership, limited liability company, or corporation was duly licensed hereunder as a broker or salesperson under Article 1 of this Act at the time that any such act was done or service performed which would give rise to a cause of action for compensation.
(Source: P.A. 87-795; 88-683, eff. 1-24-95.)

(225 ILCS 455/8)
Sec. 8. The Office of Banks and Real Estate shall exercise the powers and duties prescribed by the Civil Administrative Code of Illinois for the administration of licensing acts, and shall exercise such other powers and duties as are prescribed by this Act.
(Source: P.A. 89-508, eff. 7-3-96.)

(225 ILCS 455/8.1)
Sec. 8.1. Fees for wall certificates. The Office of Banks and Real Estate may, when a fee is payable to it for a wall certificate of registration provided by the Department of Central Management Services, require that a portion of the payment for printing and distribution costs be made, either directly or through the Office of Banks and Real Estate, to the Department of Central Management Services for deposit into the Paper and Printing Revolving Fund; the remainder shall be deposited into the General Revenue Fund.
(Source: P.A. 89-23, eff. 7-1-95; 89-508, eff. 7-3-96.)

(225 ILCS 455/8.2)
Sec. 8.2. Index of decisions. The Office of Banks and Real Estate shall maintain an index of formal decisions regarding the issuance, refusal to issue, renewal, refusal to renew, revocation, and suspension of licenses and probationary or other disciplinary action taken under this Act on or after July 1, 1995. The decisions shall be indexed according to the Sections of statutes and the administrative rules, if any, that are the basis for the decision. The index shall be available to the public during regular business hours.
(Source: P.A. 89-23, eff. 7-1-95; 89-508, eff. 7-3-96.)

(225 ILCS 455/8.3)
Sec. 8.3. Restoration of license or certificate. At any time after the suspension, revocation, placement on probationary status, or other disciplinary action taken under this Act with reference to any license or certificate, the Office of Banks and Real Estate may restore the license or certificate to the licensee or registrant without examination, upon the written recommendation of the appropriate board.
(Source: P.A. 89-23, eff. 7-1-95; 89-508, eff. 7-3-96.)

(225 ILCS 455/9)
Sec. 9. There is created the Real Estate Administration and Disciplinary Board, hereinafter referred to as the "Board". The Board shall be composed of 9 persons appointed by the Governor. Members shall be appointed to the Board subject to the following conditions:

(a) All members shall have been residents and citizens of this State for at least 6 years prior to the date of appointment;

(b) Six members shall have been actively engaged as brokers or salespersons or both for at least the 10 years prior to such appointment;

(c) Three members of the Board shall be public members who clearly represent consumer interests. None of these members shall be a person who is licensed under this Act, the spouse of a person licensed under this Act, or a person who has an ownership interest in a real estate brokerage business.

The members' terms shall be 4 years, but no more than 3 members' terms shall expire in any one year. Appointments to fill vacancies shall be for the unexpired portion of the term.

A member may be reappointed for successive terms but no member shall serve more than 8 years in his lifetime.

Persons holding office as members of the Board immediately prior to the effective date of this Act under the Act repealed herein shall continue as members of the Board until the expiration of the term for which they were appointed and until their successors are appointed and qualified.

The membership of the Board should reasonably reflect representation from the geographic areas in this State. In making such appointments, the Governor shall give due consideration to the recommendations by members and organizations of the profession.

The Governor may terminate the appointment of any member for cause which in the opinion of the Governor reasonably justifies such termination. Cause for termination shall include, but not be limited to, misconduct, incapacity, neglect of duty or missing 4 board meetings during any one calendar year.

Each member of the Board shall receive a per diem stipend in an amount to be determined by the Commissioner. Each member shall be paid his necessary expenses while engaged in the performance of his duties.
Such compensation and expenses shall be paid out of the Real Estate License Administration Fund.

The Commissioner shall consider the recommendations of the Board on questions involving standards of professional conduct, discipline and examination of candidates under this Act.

The Commissioner, on the recommendation of the Board, may issue rules, consistent with the provisions of this Act, for the administration and enforcement thereof and may prescribe forms which shall be used in connection therewith.

None of the functions, powers or duties enumerated in Sections 18 and 31 and paragraphs (a) and (j) of Section 20 of this Act shall be exercised by the Office of Banks and Real Estate except upon the action and report in writing of the Board.
(Source: P.A. 89-508, eff. 7-3-96.)

(225 ILCS 455/10)

Sec. 10. Director of Real Estate. There shall be in the Office of Banks and Real Estate a Director of Real Estate appointed by the Commissioner, who shall hold a currently valid broker's license, which shall be surrendered to the Office of Banks and Real Estate during such appointment. The Director of Real Estate shall report to the Commissioner and shall do the following:

(1) Act as Chairperson of the Board, ex-officio, without vote;

(2) Be the direct liaison between the Office of Banks and Real Estate, the profession, and real estate organizations and associations;

(3) Prepare and circulate to licensees such educational and informational material as the Office of Banks and Real Estate deems necessary for providing guidance or assistance to licensees;

(4) Appoint any necessary committees to assist in the performance of the functions and duties of the Office of Banks and Real Estate under this Act; and

(5) Subject to the administrative approval of the Commissioner, supervise the real estate unit of the Office of Banks and Real Estate.

In designating the Director of Real Estate, the Commissioner shall give due consideration to recommendations by members and organizations of the profession.
(Source: P.A. 89-23, eff. 7-1-95; 89-508, eff. 7-3-96.)

(225 ILCS 455/11)

Sec. 11. License. Every person who desires to obtain a license shall make application to the Office of Banks and Real Estate in writing upon forms prepared and furnished by the Office of Banks and Real Estate. Each applicant shall be at least 21 years of age, be of good moral character and have successfully completed a 4 year course of study in a high school or secondary school approved by the Illinois State Board of Education or an equivalent course of study as determined by an examination conducted by the Illinois State Board of Education and shall be verified under oath by the applicant.

When an applicant has had his license revoked on prior occasion or when an applicant is found to have committed any of the practices enumerated in Section 18 or when an applicant has been convicted of forgery, embezzlement, obtaining money under false pretenses, larceny ,extortion, conspiracy to defraud, or any other similar offense or offenses, or has been convicted of a felony involving moral turpitude in any court of competent jurisdiction in this or any other state, district or territory of the United States, or of a foreign country, the Board may consider such prior revocation, conduct or conviction in its determination of the applicant's moral character and whether to grant the applicant a license. In its consideration of such prior revocation, conduct or conviction, the Board shall take into account the nature of the conduct, any aggravating or extenuating circumstances, the time elapsed since such revocation, conduct or conviction, the rehabilitation or restitution performed by the applicant and such other factors as the Board deems relevant. When an applicant has made a false statement of material fact on his application, such false statement may in itself be sufficient grounds to revoke or refuse to issue a license.

All applicants for a broker's license, except applicants who are currently admitted to practice law by the Supreme Court of Illinois and are currently in active standing, shall have first served actively for one year of the last 3 prior years as a salesperson and give satisfactory evidence of having completed at least 90 classroom hours in real estate courses approved by the Real Estate Education Advisory Council established in Article 3 of this Act or in lieu thereof a correspondence course approved by the Real Estate Education Advisory Council or show evidence of receiving a baccalaureate degree including at least minor courses involving real estate or related material from a college or university approved by the Real Estate Education Advisory Council, and all such applicants shall satisfactorily pass a written examination as provided for in this Act.

All applicants for a salesperson's license, except applicants who are currently admitted to practice law by the Supreme Court of Illinois and are currently in active standing, shall show evidence satisfactory to the Board that they have completed at least 30 hours of instruction in real estate courses approved by the Real Estate Education Advisory Council or in lieu thereof a correspondence course approved by the Real Estate Education Advisory Council, or show evidence of receiving a baccalaureate degree including at least minor courses involving real estate or related materials from a college or university approved by the Real Estate Education Advisory Council, and all such applicants shall satisfactorily pass a written examination as provided for in this Act. The minimum age of 21 years shall be waived for any person

seeking a license as a real estate salesperson who has attained the age of 18 and can provide evidence of the successful completion of at least 4 semesters of post secondary school study as a full-time student or the equivalent, with major emphasis on real estate courses, in a school approved by the Real Estate Education Advisory Council.
(Source: P.A. 89-508, eff. 7-3-96.)

(225 ILCS 455/12)

Sec. 12. (a) Every person who makes application for an original license as a broker or salesperson shall personally take a written examination authorized by the Office of Banks and Real Estate, and answer such questions as may be required to determine the good moral character of the applicant, and the applicant's competency to transact the business of broker or salesperson, as the case may be, in such a manner as to safeguard the interests of the public. In determining such competency, the Office of Banks and Real Estate shall require proof that the applicant has a good understanding and the knowledge to conduct real estate brokerage and of the provisions of this Act. The examination shall be prepared by the Board or by an independent testing service designated by the Board subject to the approval of the examinations by the Board. The Board or its designated independent testing service shall conduct such examinations at such times and places as the Board shall approve. In addition, every person who desires to take such written examination shall make application to do so to the Office of Banks and Real Estate or to the designated independent testing service in writing upon forms approved by the Office of Banks and Real Estate. An applicant shall be eligible to take such examination only after
fulfilling the following requirements:

(1) successfully completing the education requirements,

(2) attaining the minimum age specified in this Act, and

(3) for applicants for a broker's license, having completed one year of experience as a real estate salesperson as provided in this Act.

Each applicant shall be required to establish compliance with such eligibility requirements in the manner provided by the rules and regulations promulgated for the administration of this Act.

(b) If a person who has received a passing score on the written examination hereinbefore described fails to file an application and meet all requirements for a license under this Act within one year after receiving a passing score on such examination, credit for such examination shall terminate. Such person thereafter may make a new application for examination.

(c) If an applicant has failed an examination 3 times, the applicant must successfully complete a refresher course or its equivalent approved by the Board in order to be readmitted to sit for the examination. For the purposes of this Section, the fourth attempt shall be the same as the first. Approved education, as prescribed by this Act for licensure as a salesperson or broker, shall be valid for a period ending on the later of 5 years after the date of satisfactory completion of the education or 5 years after the expiration of the individual's license.

(d) Every valid application for issuance of an initial license shall be accompanied by a sponsor card and the fees specified in Section 15 of this Act.

(e) No applicant shall engage in any of the activities covered bythis Act until a valid sponsor card has been issued to such applicant pursuant to rules promulgated by the Office of Banks and Real Estate. Such sponsor card shall be valid for a maximum period of 45 days from the date of issuance unless extended for good cause as provided by rule.

(f) No licensee employed by a broker shall accept a commission or valuable consideration for the performance of activities under this Act except from the broker by whom the licensee is employed.

(g) The Office of Banks and Real Estate shall issue to each applicant entitled thereto, a license in such form and size as shall be prescribed by the Office of Banks and Real Estate. The person to whom such a license is issued is hereafter designated a "licensee". Each license shall bear the name of the licensee as the person so qualified, shall specify whether such person is qualified to act in a broker or salesperson capacity, and shall contain such other information as shall be recommended by the Board and approved by the Office of Banks and Real Estate. Each person licensed under this Act shall display his own license conspicuously in his place of business.
(Source: P.A. 89-508, eff. 7-3-96.)

(225 ILCS 455/12.1)

Sec. 12.1. (a) The broker shall prepare upon forms provided by the Office of Banks and Real Estate and deliver to each salesperson or broker employed by or associated with the broker a sponsor card certifying that the person whose name appears thereon is in fact employed by or associated with said broker. The broker shall send a duplicate of each sponsor card, along with a valid license or other authorization as provided by rule and the appropriate fee to the Office of Banks and Real Estate within 24 hours of issuance of the sponsor card. It is a violation of this Act for any broker to issue a sponsor card to any salesperson, broker or applicant unless such salesperson, broker or applicant presents in hand a valid license or other authorization as provided by rule.

(b) When a salesperson or broker terminates his employment or association with a broker, or such employment is terminated by such broker, such salesperson or broker shall obtain from that broker his license endorsed by the broker indicating said termination. That broker shall surrender to the Office of Banks and Real Estate a copy of the license of such salesperson or broker within 2 days of said termination or shall notify the Office of Banks and Real Estate in writing of such termination and explain why a copy of such license is not surrendered.

The license of any salesperson whose association with a broker is terminated shall automatically become inoperative immediately upon such termination unless the licensee accepts employment or becomes associated with a new broker pursuant to subsection (c) of this Section.

(c) When a salesperson or broker accepts employment or association with a new broker, the new broker shall send to the Office of Banks and Real Estate by registered or certified mail, return receipt requested, a duplicate sponsor card, along

with the salesperson's or broker's endorsed license, or an explanation of why the endorsed license is not surrendered, and shall pay the appropriate fee prescribed in Section 15 of this Act to the Office of Banks and Real Estate to cover administrative expenses attendant to the changes in the registration of the licensee.
(Source: P.A. 89-508, eff. 7-3-96.)

(225 ILCS 455/13)
Sec. 13. The expiration date and renewal period for each license issued under this Act shall be set by rule. Except as otherwise provided in Sections 13.1 and 13.2 of this Act, the holder of a license may renew such license during the month preceding the expiration date thereof by paying the fees specified in Section 15 of this Act. Within 60 days after the conclusion of each renewal period, the Office of Banks and Real Estate shall prepare and mail to each real estate broker licensed under this Act a listing of licensees under this Act who, according to the records of the Office of Banks and Real Estate, are sponsored by that broker. The sponsoring broker shall provide the Office of Banks and Real Estate with verification of the information on the list or notify the Office of Banks and Real Estate of any discrepancies in the list according to procedures established by rule. Every licensee associated with or employed by a broker whose license is revoked, suspended, terminated, or expired shall be considered as inoperative until such time as the employing broker's license is reinstated or renewed, or the licensee changes employment as set forth in subsection (c) of Section 12.1.

The Office of Banks and Real Estate shall establish and maintain a register of all licensees currently licensed by the State and shall issue and prescribe a form of pocket card. Upon payment by a licensee of an appropriate fee as prescribed in Section 15 of this Act for engagement in the activity for which the licensee is qualified and holds a license for the current period, the Office of Banks and Real Estate shall issue a pocket card to such licensee. The pocket card shall be verification that the required fee for the current period has been paid and shall indicate that the person named thereon is licensed for the current year as a broker or salesperson, as the case may be. The pocket card shall further indicate that the licensee named thereon is authorized by the Office of Banks and Real Estate to engage in the licensed activity appropriate for his status (broker or salesperson). Each licensee shall carry on his person his pocket card or, if such pocket card has not yet been issued, a properly issued sponsor card when engaging in any licensed activity and shall display the same on demand.

Except as provided below, each broker shall maintain a definite office or place of business within this State for the transaction of real estate business, shall conspicuously display an identification sign on the outside of his office of adequate size and visibility and shall conspicuously display his certificate in his office or place of business and also the certificates of all brokers and salespersons associated with or employed by him at that location. The office or place of business shall not be located in any retail or financial business establishment unless it is separated from the other business by a separate and distinct area within such establishment. A broker who is licensed in this State by examination or pursuant to the provisions of Section 14 of this Act shall not be required to maintain a definite office or place of business in this State provided all of the following conditions are met: (1) the broker maintains an active broker's license in his state; (2) the broker maintains an office in his state; and (3) the broker has filed with the Office of Banks and Real Estate written statements appointing the Commissioner to act as his agent upon whom all judicial and other process or legal notices directed to such licensee may be served and agreeing to abide by all of the provisions of this Act with respect to his real estate activities within the State of Illinois and submitting to the jurisdiction of the Office of Banks and Real Estate. Such statements shall be in form and substance the same as those statements required under Section 14 of the Act and shall operate to the same extent.

Upon any change of a principal place of business or branch office, the broker shall immediately notify the Office of Banks and Real Estate in writing of such change.

If a broker maintains more than one place of business within the State, the broker shall apply for a branch office license for each branch office so maintained, and the branch office license shall be displayed conspicuously in each branch office. The name of the branch office shall be the same as that of the main office, or shall clearly delineate the branch office's relationship with the main office. The manager of a branch office shall be a broker and must be closely supervised by the employing broker. However, no broker shall be permitted to be in direct operational control of more than one office or branch office except as provided below.

Upon the loss of the managing broker or in the event of the death or adjudicated disability of the sole proprietor of an office, a written request for authorization allowing the continued operation of the office may be submitted to the Office of Banks and Real Estate within 10 days of such loss. The Office of Banks and Real Estate may issue a written authorization allowing the continued operation; provided that a licensed broker, or in the case of the death or adjudicated disability of a sole proprietor, the representative of the estate, assumes responsibility, in writing, for the operation of the office and agrees to personally supervise the operation of the office. No such written authorization shall be valid for more than 30 days unless extended by the Office of Banks and Real Estate for good cause shown and upon written request by the broker or representative.
(Source: P.A. 89-508, eff. 7-3-96.)

(225 ILCS 455/13.1)
Sec. 13.1. Notwithstanding any other provisions of this Act to the contrary, any licensee whose license under this Act has expired is eligible to renew such license without paying any lapsed renewal fees or reinstatement fee provided that such license expired while the licensee was:

(1) on active duty with the United States Army, United States Navy, United States Marine Corps, United States Air Force, United States Coast Guard, the State Militia called into the service or training of the United States, or

(2) engaged in training or education under the supervision of the United States prior to induction into military service, or

(3) serving as the Director of Real Estate in the State of

Illinois, or as an employee of the Office of Banks and Real Estate.

A licensee shall be eligible to renew a license under the provisions of this Section for a period of 2 years following the termination of such service, education, or training, provided that the termination was by other than dishonorable discharge, and provided that the licensee furnishes the Office of Banks and Real Estate an affidavit specifying that the licensee has been so engaged and that such service, education, or training has been so terminated.
(Source: P.A. 89-508, eff. 7-3-96.)

(225 ILCS 455/13.2)
Sec. 13.2. Any licensee whose license under this Act has expired shall be eligible to renew such license for a period of 5 years following the expiration date provided the licensee pays the fees required by Section 15 of this Act.

A licensee whose license has been expired for more than 3 years but less than 5 years shall be eligible for license renewal under this Section only after providing the Office of Banks and Real Estate with evidence that the licensee has satisfactorily completed at least 15 hours of refresher courses or its equivalent in real estate subjects at a school approved by the Office of Banks and Real Estate as provided by rule.

The Office of Banks and Real Estate shall establish by rule a means for the verification of completion of the refresher courses required by this Section. This verification may be accomplished through audits of records maintained by registrants; by requiring the filing of refresher course certificates with the Office of Banks and Real Estate; or by other means established by the Office of Banks and Real Estate.

Notwithstanding any other provision of this Act, for the period between July 1, 1992, and July 8, 1992, any person whose license has been expired for a period of at least 5, but not more than 6, years and the expiration was caused by the person's failure to receive a renewal notification because of a change of address shall have his or her license renewed by the Office of Banks and Real Estate without examination or the completion of refresher courses upon filing a renewal application and paying the required renewal fees.
(Source: P.A. 89-508, eff. 7-3-96.)

(225 ILCS 455/14)
Sec. 14. A broker's license may be issued by the Office of Banks and Real Estate without examination to a broker licensed under the laws of another state of the United States, such state having entered into a reciprocal agreement with the Office of Banks and Real Estate in regard to issuance of reciprocal licenses, under the following conditions: (1) the broker holds a broker's license in his home state; (2) the standards for that state for registration as a broker are substantially equivalent to the minimum standards in the State of Illinois; (3) the broker has been actively practicing as a broker in the resident state for a period of not less than 2 years, immediately prior to the date of application; (4) the broker furnishes the Office of Banks and Real Estate with a statement under seal of the proper authority in real estate licensure of the state in which the broker is licensed showing that the broker has an active broker's license, is in good standing and no complaints are pending against the broker, in that state.

A nonresident salesperson employed by or associated with a broker holding a broker's license in this State may, in the discretion of the Office of Banks and Real Estate, be issued, without examination, a nonresident salesperson's license under such nonresident broker provided all of the following conditions are met: (1) the state in which the salesperson resides has entered into a reciprocal agreement with the Office of Banks and Real Estate in regard to the issuance of reciprocal licenses; (2) the salesperson maintains an active license in the state in which he resides; and (3) the salesperson resides in the same state as the broker with whom he is associated. The nonresident broker with whom the salesperson is associated shall comply with the provisions of this Act and issue the salesperson a sponsor card upon the form provided by the Office of Banks and Real Estate.

Prior to the issuance of a license to a nonresident broker or salesperson, such broker or salesperson shall file with the Office of Banks and Real Estate a designation in writing that appoints the Commissioner to act as his agent upon whom all judicial and other process or legal notices directed to such licensee may be served. Service upon the agent so designated shall be equivalent to personal service upon the licensee. Copies of such appointment, certified by the Commissioner, shall be deemed sufficient evidence thereof and shall be admitted in evidence with the same force and effect as the original thereof might be admitted. In such written designation, the licensee shall agree that any lawful process against the licensee which is served upon such agent shall be of the same legal force and validity as if served upon the licensee, and that the authority shall continue in force so long as any liability remains outstanding in this State. Upon the receipt of any such process or notice, the Commissioner shall forthwith mail a copy of the same by certified mail to the last known business address of the licensee.

As a condition precedent to the issuance of a license to a nonresident broker or salesperson, such broker or salesperson shall agree in writing to abide by all the provisions of this Act with respect to his real estate activities within the State of Illinois and submit to the jurisdiction of the Office of Banks and Real Estate as provided in this Act. Such agreement shall be filed with the Office of Banks and Real Estate and shall remain in force for so long as the nonresident broker or salesperson is licensed by this State and thereafter with respect to acts or omissions committed while licensed as a broker or salesperson in this State.

Prior to the issuance of any license to any nonresident, verification of active licensure issued for the conduct of such business in any other state must be filed with the Office of Banks and Real Estate by such nonresident, and the same fees must be paid as provided in this Act for the obtaining of a broker's or salesperson's license in this State.

Licenses granted under reciprocal agreements as provided in this Section shall remain in force, unless suspended or revoked or terminated by the Office of Banks and Real Estate for just cause or for failure to pay the required renewal fee, only as long as the reciprocal agreement is in effect between this State and the resident state of the licensee.
(Source: P.A. 89-508, eff. 7-3-96.)

(225 ILCS 455/15)
Sec. 15. The Office of Banks and Real Estate may provide by rule for fees to be paid by applicants and licensees (other than applicants and licensees under Article 2 of this Act) to cover the reasonable costs of the Office of Banks and Real Estate in administering and enforcing the provisions of this Act (other than the provisions of Article 2 of this Act). The Office of Banks and Real Estate may also provide by rule for general fees to cover the reasonable expenses of carrying out other functions and responsibilities under this Act (other than Article 2 of this Act). The rules promulgated hereunder shall include, but need not be limited to the following:

(1) The fee for an initial license and a renewal license for real estate salespersons and real estate brokers shall include a $10 fee for deposit in the Real Estate Recovery Fund as provided in Section 23, and a $5 fee for deposit in the Real Estate Research and Education Fund for use as provided in Section 16.

(2) The fee for an initial license for a partnership or corporation shall include a $10 fee for deposit in the Real Estate Recovery Fund as provided in Section 23, and a $5 fee for deposit in the Real Estate Research and Education Fund for use as provided in Section 16.

(3) The fee for an initial license for a branch office shall include a $5 fee for deposit in the Real Estate Research and Education Fund for use as provided in Section 16.
(Source: P.A. 88-683, eff. 1-24-95; 89-23, eff. 7-1-95; 89-508, eff.
7-3-96.)

(225 ILCS 455/15.1)
Sec. 15.1. Returned checks; fines. Any person who delivers a check or other payment to the Office of Banks and Real Estate that is returned to the Office of Banks and Real Estate unpaid by the financial institution upon which it is drawn shall pay to the Office of Banks and Real Estate, in addition to the amount already owed to the Office of Banks and Real Estate, a fine of $50. If the check or other payment was for a renewal or issuance fee and that person practices without paying the renewal fee or issuance fee and the fine due, an additional fine of $100 shall be imposed. The fines imposed by this Section are in addition to any other discipline provided under this Act for unlicensed practice or practice on a nonrenewed license. The Office of Banks and Real Estate shall notify the person that payment of fees and fines shall be paid to the Office of Banks and Real Estate by certified check or money order within 30 calendar days of the notification. If, after the expiration of 30 days from the date of the notification, the person has failed to submit the necessary remittance, the Office of Banks and Real Estate shall automatically terminate the license or certificate or deny the application, without hearing. If, after termination or denial, the person seeks a license or certificate, he or she shall apply to the Office of Banks and Real Estate for restoration or issuance of the license or certificate and pay all fees and fines due the Office of Banks and Real Estate. The Office of Banks and Real Estate may establish a fee for the processing of an application for restoration of a license or certificate to pay all expenses of processing this application. The Commissioner may waive the fines due under this Section in individual cases where the Commissioner finds that the fines would be unreasonable or unnecessarily burdensome.
(Source: P.A. 89-508, eff. 7-3-96.)

(225 ILCS 455/16)
Sec. 16. A special fund to be known as the Real Estate Research and Education Fund is created in the State Treasury. All money deposited in such special fund shall be used only for the ordinary and contingent expenses of operation of the Office of Real Estate Research or its successor, by whatever name designated, at the University of Illinois.

In addition to any other permitted use of moneys in the Fund, and notwithstanding any restriction on the use of the Fund, moneys in the Real Estate Research and Education Fund may be transferred to the General Revenue Fund as authorized by this amendatory Act of 1992. The General Assembly finds that an excess of moneys exists in the Fund. On February 1, 1992, the Comptroller shall order transferred and the Treasurer shall transfer $140,000 (or such lesser amount as may be on deposit in the Fund and unexpended and unobligated on that date) from the Fund to the General Revenue Fund.

Out of each $5 fee deposited in the Real Estate Research and Education Fund pursuant to Section 15 or Section 36.6, $1 shall be used to fund a scholarship program for persons of minority racial origin who wish to pursue a course of study in the field of real estate. For the purposes of this Section, "course of study" shall mean a course or courses that are part of a program of courses in the field of real estate designed to further an individual's knowledge or expertise in the field of real estate. These courses shall include, but are not limited to, courses that a salesperson licensed under this Act must complete to qualify for a real estate broker's license, courses required to obtain the Graduate Realtors Institute designation, and any other courses or programs offered by accredited colleges, universities, or other institutions of higher education in Illinois. The scholarship program shall be administered by the Office of Real Estate Research.

Moneys in the Real Estate Research and Education Fund may be invested and reinvested in the same manner as funds in the Real Estate Recovery Fund. All earnings received from such investment shall be deposited in the Real Estate Research and Education Fund and may be used for the same purposes as fees deposited in such fund.
(Source: P.A. 86-925; 87-795; 87-838.)

(225 ILCS 455/17)
Sec. 17. All fees received by the Office of Banks and Real Estate under Article 1 and Article 3 of this Act, other than fees which this Act directs to be deposited in the Real Estate Recovery Fund, in the Real Estate Research and Education Fund, or in the Department of Central Management Services Printing Revolving Fund, shall be deposited in a special fund in the State Treasury to be known as the Real Estate License Administration Fund. The moneys deposited in the Real Estate License Administration Fund shall be appropriated to the Office of Banks and Real Estate for expenses of the Office of Banks and Real Estate and the Board in the administration of this Act and for the administration

of any Act administered by the Office of Banks and Real Estate providing revenue to this Fund.

In addition to any other permitted use of moneys in the Fund, and notwithstanding any restriction on the use of the Fund, moneys in the Real Estate License Administration Fund may be transferred to the General Revenue Fund as authorized by this amendatory Act of 1992. The General Assembly finds that an excess of moneys exists in the Fund. On February 1, 1992, the Comptroller shall order transferred and the Treasurer shall transfer $1,500,000 (or such lesser amount as may be on deposit in the Fund and unexpended and unobligated on that date) from the Fund to the General Revenue Fund.

The Commissioner shall employ, in conformity with the Personnel Code, one full time Chief of Real Estate Investigations; and the Commissioner shall also employ, in conformity with the Personnel Code,
or contract for, not less than one full time investigator and one full time auditor for every 15,000 licensees registered under this Act.

The Chief of Real Estate Investigations shall be a college graduate from an accredited 4 year college or university with 3 years' responsible administrative experience and a minimum of 3 years' responsible investigatory experience in law enforcement or a related field.

Moneys in the Real Estate License Administration Fund may be invested and reinvested in the same manner as funds in the Real Estate Recovery Fund. All earnings received from such investment shall be deposited in the Real Estate License Administration Fund and may be used for the same purposes as fees deposited in such fund.

Upon the completion of any audit of the Office of Banks and Real Estate, as prescribed by the Illinois State Auditing Act, which includes an audit of the Real Estate License Administration Fund, the Office of Banks and Real Estate shall make the audit open to inspection by any interested person.
(Source: P.A. 89-23, eff. 7-1-95; 89-204, eff. 1-1-96; 89-508, eff.
7-3-96; 89-626, eff. 8-9-96.)

(225 ILCS 455/18)
Sec. 18. The Office of Banks and Real Estate may refuse to issue or renew a license, may place on probation, suspend or revoke any license, or may reprimand or impose a civil penalty not to exceed $10,000 upon any licensee hereunder for any one or any combination of the following causes:

(a) Where the applicant or licensee has, by false or fraudulent representation, obtained or sought to obtain a license.

(b) Where the applicant or licensee has been convicted of any crime, an essential element of which is dishonesty or fraud or larceny, embezzlement, obtaining money, property or credit by false pretenses or by means of a confidence game, has been convicted in this or another state of a crime which is a felony under the laws of this State or has been convicted of a felony in a federal court.

(c) Where the applicant or licensee has been adjudged to be a person under legal disability or subject to involuntary admission or to meet the standard for judicial admission as provided in the Mental Health and Developmental Disabilities Code, as now or hereafter amended.

(d) Where the licensee performs or attempts to perform any act as a broker or salesperson in a retail sales establishment, from an office, desk or space that is not separated from the main retail business by a separate and distinct area within such establishment.

(e) Discipline by another state, the District of Columbia, territory, or foreign nation of a licensee if at least one of the grounds for that discipline is the same as or the equivalent of one of the grounds for discipline set forth in this Act.

(f) Where the applicant or licensee has engaged in real estate activity without a license, or after the licensee's license was expired, or while the license was inoperative.

(g) Where the applicant or licensee attempts to subvert or cheat on the Real Estate License Exam, or aids and abets an applicant to subvert or cheat on the Real Estate License Exam administered pursuant to this Act.

(h) Where the licensee in performing or attempting to perform or pretending to perform any act as a broker or salesperson, or where such licensee, in handling his own property, whether held by deed, option, or otherwise, is found guilty of:

1. Making any substantial misrepresentation, or untruthful advertising;

2. Making any false promises of a character likely to influence, persuade, or induce;

3. Pursuing a continued and flagrant course of misrepresentation or the making of false promises through agents, salespersons or advertising or otherwise;

4. Any misleading or untruthful advertising, or using any trade name or insignia of membership in any real estate organization of which the licensee is not a member;

5. Acting for more than one party in a transaction without providing written notice to all parties for whom the licensee acts;

6. Representing or attempting to represent a broker other than the employer;

7. Failure to account for or to remit any moneys or documents coming into their possession which belong to others;

8. Failure to maintain and deposit in a special account, separate and apart from personal and other business accounts, all escrow monies belonging to others entrusted to a licensee while acting as a real estate broker, escrow agent, or temporary custodian of the funds of others, or failure to maintain all escrow monies on deposit in such account until the transactions are consummated or terminated, except to the extent that such monies, or any part thereof, shall be disbursed prior to the consummation or termination in accordance with the written direction of the principals to the transaction or their duly authorized agents. Such account shall be noninterest bearing, unless the character of the deposit is such that payment of interest thereon is otherwise required by law or unless the principals to the transaction specifically require, in writing, that the deposit be placed in an interest bearing account;

9. Failure to make available to the real estate enforcement personnel of the Office of Banks and Real Estate during normal business hours all escrow records and

related documents maintained in connection with the practice of real estate;

10. Failing to furnish copies upon request of all documents relating to a real estate transaction to all parties executing them;

11. Paying a commission or valuable consideration to any person for acts or services performed in violation of this Act;

12. Having demonstrated unworthiness or incompetency to act as a broker or salesperson in such manner as to endanger the interest of the public;

13. Commingling the money or property of others with his own;

14. Employing any person on a purely temporary or single deal basis as a means of evading the law regarding payment of commission to nonlicensees on some contemplated transactions;

15. Permitting the use of his license as a broker to enable a salesperson or unlicensed person to operate a real estate business without actual participation therein and control thereof by the broker;

16. Any other conduct, whether of the same or a different character from that specified in this Section which constitutes dishonest dealing;

17. Displaying a "for rent" or "for sale" sign on any property without the written consent of an owner or his duly authorized agent, or advertising by any means that any property is for sale or for rent without the written consent of the owner or his authorized agent;

18. Failing to provide information requested by the Office of Banks and Real Estate, within 30 days of the request, either as the result of a formal or informal complaint to the Office of Banks and Real Estate or as a result of a random audit conducted by the Office of Banks and Real Estate, which would indicate a violation of this Act;

19. Disregarding or violating any provision of this Act, or the published rules or regulations promulgated by the Office of Banks and Real Estate to enforce this Act, or aiding or abetting any individual, partnership, limited liability company, or corporation in disregarding any provision of this Act, or the published rules or regulations promulgated by the Office of Banks and Real Estate to enforce this Act;

20. Advertising any property for sale or advertising any transaction of any kind or character relating to the sale of property by whatsoever means, without clearly disclosing in or on such advertising one of the following: the name of the firm with which the licensee is associated, if a sole broker, evidence of the broker's occupation, or a name with respect to which the broker has complied with the requirements of "An Act in relation to the use of an assumed name in the conduct or transaction of business in this State", approved July 17, 1941, as amended, whether such advertising is done by the broker or by any salesperson or broker employed by the broker;

21. "Offering guaranteed sales plans" as defined in subparagraph (A) except to the extent hereinafter set forth:

(A) A "guaranteed sales plan" is any real estate purchase or sales plan whereby a broker enters into a conditional or unconditional written contract with a seller by the terms of which a broker agrees to purchase a property of the seller within a specified period of time at a specific price in the event the property is not sold in accordance with the terms of a listing contract between the broker and the seller or on other terms acceptable to the seller;

(B) A broker offering a "guaranteed sales plan" shall provide the details and conditions of such plan in writing to the party to whom the plan is offered;

(C) A broker offering a "guaranteed sales plan" shall provide to the party to whom the plan is offered, evidence of sufficient financial resources to satisfy the commitment to purchase undertaken by the broker in the plan;

(D) Any broker offering a "guaranteed sales plan" shall undertake to market the property of the seller subject to the plan in the same manner in which the broker would market any other property, unless such agreement with the seller provides otherwise;

(E) Any broker who fails to perform on a "guaranteed sales plan" in strict accordance with its terms shall be subject to all the penalties provided in this Act for violations thereof, and, in addition, shall be subject to a civil penalty payable to the party injured by the default in an amount of up to $10,000.

22. Influencing or attempting to influence, by any words or acts a prospective seller, purchaser, occupant, landlord or tenant of real estate, in connection with viewing, buying or leasing of real estate, so as to promote, or tend to promote, the continuance or maintenance of racially and religiously segregated housing, or so as to retard, obstruct or discourage racially integrated housing on or in any street, block, neighborhood or community;

23. Engaging in any act which constitutes a violation of Section 3-102, 3-103, 3-104 or 3-105 of the Illinois Human Rights Act, whether or not a complaint has been filed with or adjudicated by the Human Rights Commission;

24. Inducing any party to a contract of sale or listing agreement to break such a contract of sale or listing agreement for the purpose of substituting, in lieu thereof, a new contract for sale or listing agreement with a third party.

25. Negotiating a sale, exchange or lease of real property directly with an owner or lessor without authority from the listing broker if the licensee knows that the owner or lessor has a written exclusive listing agreement covering the property with another broker.

26. Where a licensee is also an attorney, acting as the attorney for either the buyer or the seller in the same transaction in which such licensee is acting or has acted as a broker or salesperson.

27. Advertising or offering merchandise or services as free if any conditions or obligations necessary for receiving such merchandise or services are not disclosed in the same advertisement or offer. Such conditions or obligations include, but are not limited to, the requirement that the recipient attend a promotional activity or visit a real estate site. As used in this paragraph 27, "free" includes terms such as "award", "prize", "no charge," "free of charge," "without charge" and similar words or phrases which reasonably lead a person to believe that he may receive, or has been selected to receive, something of value, without any conditions or obligations on the part of the recipient.

28. Disregarding or violating any provision of the

Illinois Real Estate Time-Share Act, enacted by the 84th General Assembly, or the published rules or regulations promulgated by the Office of Banks and Real Estate to enforce that Act.

29. A finding that the licensee has violated the terms of the disciplinary order issued by the Office of Banks and Real Estate.

30. Paying fees or commissions directly to a licensee employed by another broker.

(Source: P.A. 88-683, eff. 1-24-95; 89-508, eff. 7-3-96.)

(225 ILCS 455/18.1)

Sec. 18.1. The Office of Banks and Real Estate may refuse to issue or renew, or may suspend the license of any person who fails to file a return, or to pay the tax, penalty or interest shown in a filed return, or to pay any final assessment of tax, penalty or interest, as required by any tax Act administered by the Illinois Department of Revenue, until such time as the requirements of any such tax Act are satisfied.

(Source: P.A. 89-508, eff. 7-3-96.)

(225 ILCS 455/18.2)

Sec. 18.2. (Repealed).

(Source: Repealed by P.A. 88-610, eff. 1-1-95.)

(225 ILCS 455/18.2a)

Sec. 18.2a. Exclusive representation. A broker entering into an agreement with any person for the listing of property or for the purpose of representing any person in the buying, selling, exchanging, renting, or leasing of real estate may specifically designate those salespersons employed by or affiliated with the broker who will be acting as legal agents of that person to the exclusion of all other salespersons employed by or affiliated with the broker. A broker entering into an agreement under the provisions of this Section shall not be considered to be acting for more than one party in a transaction if the salespersons specifically designated as legal agents of a person are not representing more than one party in a transaction.

No licensee shall be considered a dual agent nor shall the licensee be liable for acting as an undisclosed dual agent merely by performing licensed services in accordance with the provisions of this Section.

(Source: P.A. 87-1278; 88-535.)

(225 ILCS 455/18.3)

Sec. 18.3. When there has been an adjudication in a civil or criminal proceeding that a licensee has illegally discriminated while engaged in any activity for which a license is required under this Act, the Office of Banks and Real Estate, upon the recommendation of the Board as to the extent of the suspension or revocation, shall suspend or revoke the license of that licensee in a timely manner, unless the adjudication is in the appeal process. When there has been an order in an administrative proceeding finding that a licensee has illegally discriminated while engaged in any activity for which a license is required under this Act, the Office of Banks and Real Estate, upon recommendation of the Board as to the nature and extent of the discipline, shall take one or more of the disciplinary actions provided for in Section 18 in a timely manner, unless the administrative order is in the appeal process.

(Source: P.A. 89-508, eff. 7-3-96.)

(225 ILCS 455/19)

Sec. 19. No licensee shall obtain any written listing contract which does not provide for automatic expiration within a definite period of time. No notice of termination at the final expiration thereof shall be required. Any listing contract not containing a provision for automatic expiration shall be void.

(Source: P.A. 83-191.)

(225 ILCS 455/20)

Sec. 20. Hearings; investigation; notice.

(a) The Office of Banks and Real Estate may conduct hearings on proceedings to suspend, revoke or to refuse to issue or renew licenses of persons applying for licensure or licensed under this Act, or to censure, reprimand or impose a civil penalty not to exceed $10,000 upon any licensee hereunder and may revoke, suspend or refuse to issue or renew such licenses or censure, reprimand or impose a civil penalty not to exceed $10,000 upon any licensee hereunder.

(b) Upon the motion of either the Office of Banks and Real Estate or the Board or upon the verified complaint in writing of any persons setting forth facts which if proven would constitute grounds for suspension or revocation under Section 18 of this Act, the Board shall cause to be investigated the actions of any person so accused who holds or represents to hold a license. Such person is hereinafter called the accused.

(c) Prior to initiating any formal disciplinary proceedings resulting from an investigation conducted pursuant to subsection (b) of this Section, that matter shall be reviewed by a subcommittee of the Board according to procedures established by rule. The subcommittee shall make a recommendation to the full Disciplinary Board as to the validity of the complaint and may recommend that the Board not proceed with formal disciplinary proceedings if the complaint is determined to be frivolous or without merit.

(d) The Office of Banks and Real Estate shall, before suspending, revoking, placing on probationary status, or taking any other disciplinary action as the Office of Banks and Real Estate may deem proper with regard to any license: (1) notify the accused in writing at least 30 days prior to the date set for the hearing of any charges made and the time and place for the hearing of the charges to be heard before the Board under oath; and (2) inform the accused that upon failure to file an answer and request a hearing before the date originally set for such hearing, default will be taken against the accused and his license may be suspended, revoked, placed on probationary status, or other disciplinary action, including limiting the scope, nature or extent of the accused's practice, as the Office of Banks and Real Estate may deem proper, may be taken with regard thereto. In case the person fails to file an answer after receiving notice, his or her license or certificate may, in the discretion of the Office of Banks and Real Estate, be suspended, revoked, or placed on probationary status, or the Office of Banks and Real Estate may take whatever disciplinary action deemed proper, including limiting the scope, nature, or extent of the person's practice or the imposition of a fine, without a hearing, if the act or acts charged constitute sufficient grounds for such action under this Act.

(e) At the time and place fixed in the notice, the Board shall proceed to hearing of the charges and both the accused person and the complainant shall be accorded ample opportunity to present in person or by counsel such statements, testimony, evidence and argument as may be pertinent to the charges or to any defense thereto. The Board may continue such hearing from time to time. If the Board shall not be sitting at the time and place fixed in the notice or at the time and place to which the hearing shall have been continued, the Office of Banks and Real Estate shall continue such hearing for a period not to exceed 30 days.

(f) Any unlawful act or violation of any of the provisions of this Act upon the part of any salesperson, broker employed by a real estate broker or associated by written agreement with such real estate broker, or unlicensed employee of a licensed broker, shall not be cause for the revocation of the license of any such broker, partial or otherwise, unless it appears to the satisfaction of the Office of Banks and Real Estate that the broker had knowledge thereof.

(g) The Office of Banks and Real Estate or Board has power to subpoena and bring before it any person in this State and to take testimony either orally or by deposition, or both, with the same fees and mileage and in the same manner as prescribed by law in judicial procedure in civil cases in courts of this State.

The Commissioner, the Director of Real Estate, and any member of the Board shall each have power to administer oaths to witnesses at any hearing which the Office of Banks and Real Estate is authorized under this Act to conduct.

(h) Any circuit court or any judge thereof, upon the application of the accused person or complainant or the Office of Banks and Real Estate or Board, may, by order entered, require the attendance of witnesses and the production of relevant books and papers before the Board in any hearing relative to the application for or refusal, recall, suspension or revocation of a license, and the court or judge may compel obedience to the court's and the judge's order by proceedings for contempt.

(i) The Office of Banks and Real Estate, at its expense, shall preserve a record of all proceedings at the formal hearing of any case involving the refusal to issue or the revocation, suspension or other discipline of a licensee. The notice of hearing, complaint and all other documents in the nature of pleadings and written motions filed in the proceedings, the transcript of testimony, the report of the Board and the orders of the Office of Banks and Real Estate shall be the record of such proceeding.

At all hearings or pre-hearing conferences, the Office of Banks and Real Estate and the accused shall be entitled to have a court reporter in attendance for purposes of transcribing the proceeding or pre-hearing conference at the expense of the party requesting the court reporter's attendance. A copy of the transcribed proceeding shall be provided to the other party at no cost to that party upon completion of the transcript.

(j) The Board shall present to the Commissioner its written report of its findings and recommendations. A copy of such report shall be served upon the accused person, either personally or by registered mail as provided in this Act for the service of the citation. Within 20 days after such service, the accused person may present to the Commissioner a motion in writing for a rehearing which shall specify the particular grounds therefor. If the accused person shall order and pay for a transcript of the record as provided in this Act, the time elapsing thereafter and before such transcript is ready for delivery to the accused shall not be counted as part of such 20 days.

Whenever the Commissioner is satisfied that substantial justice has not been done, the Commissioner may order a rehearing by the Board or other special committee appointed by the Commissioner. In all instances, under this Act, in which the Board has rendered a recommendation to the Commissioner with respect to a particular registrant, the Commissioner shall, in the event that he disagrees with or takes action contrary to the recommendation of the Board, file with the Board and the Secretary of State his specific written reasons of disagreement with the Board. Such reasons shall be filed within 30 days of the Board's recommendation to the Commissioner and prior to any contrary action. At the expiration of the time specified for filing a motion for a rehearing the Commissioner shall have the right to take the action recommended by the Board. Upon the suspension or revocation of a license, the licensee shall be required to surrender their license to the Office of Banks and Real Estate, and upon failure or refusal so to do, the Office of Banks and Real Estate shall have the right to seize such license.

(k) At any time after the suspension or revocation of any license, the Office of Banks and Real Estate may restore it to the accused person without examination, upon the written recommendation of the Board.

(l) An order or revocation or suspension or a certified copy thereof, over the seal of the Office of Banks and Real Estate and purporting to be signed by the Commissioner, shall be prima facie proof that:

1. Such signature is the genuine signature of the Commissioner;
2. Such Commissioner is duly appointed and qualified;
3. The Board and the members thereof are qualified.

Such proof may be rebutted.

(m) Notwithstanding any provisions concerning the conduct of hearings and recommendations for disciplinary actions, the Office of Banks and Real Estate has the authority to negotiate agreements with licensees and applicants resulting in disciplinary consent orders. Such consent orders may provide for any of the forms of discipline provided in this Act. Such consent orders shall provide that they were not entered into as a result of any coercion by the Office of Banks and Real Estate. Any such consent order shall be filed with the Commissioner along with the Board's recommendation and accepted or rejected by the Commissioner in a timely manner.
(Source: P.A. 89-508, eff. 7-3-96.)

(225 ILCS 455/21)

Sec. 21. All final administrative decisions of the Office of Banks and Real Estate shall be subject to judicial review pursuant to the provisions of the Administrative Review Law, and all amendments and modifications thereof, and the rules adopted pursuant thereto. The term "administrative decision" is defined in Section 3-101 of the Administrative Review Law.

The Office of Banks and Real Estate shall not be required to certify any record or file any answer or otherwise appear unless the party filing the complaint pays to the Office of Banks and Real Estate the certification fee provided for in Section 15 representing costs of such certification. Failure on the part of the plaintiff to make such a deposit shall be grounds for dismissal of the action.

The Office of Banks and Real Estate shall prepare from time to time, but in no event less often than once every other month, a summary report of final disciplinary actions taken since the previous summary report.
The summary report shall contain a brief description of the action which brought about the discipline and the final disciplinary action taken. The summary report shall be made available upon request.
(Source: P.A. 89-508, eff. 7-3-96.)

(225 ILCS 455/22)

Sec. 22. Any person, limited liability company, or corporation violating any provision of this Act other than paragraph 4 of subsection (h) of Section 18, and other than Section 3, or any person, limited liability company, or corporation failing to account for or to remit for any moneys coming into his or its possession which belong to others or commingling the money or other property of his or its principal with his or its own, upon conviction for the first offense, is guilty of a Class C misdemeanor, and if a limited liability company or corporation, is guilty of a business offense and shall be fined not to exceed $2,000.

Upon conviction of a second or subsequent offense the violator, if a person, is guilty of a Class A misdemeanor; and if a limited liability company or corporation, is guilty of a business offense and shall be fined not less than $2,000 nor more than $5,000.

Any person, limited liability company, or corporation violating any provision of Section 3 of this Act, upon conviction for the first offense, is guilty of a Class A misdemeanor, and if a limited liability company or corporation, is guilty of a business offense and shall be fined not to exceed $10,000.

Upon conviction of a second or subsequent offense the violator, if a person, is guilty of a Class 4 felony; and if a limited liability company or corporation, is guilty of a business offense and shall be fined not less than $10,000 nor more than $25,000.

Any officer or agent of a corporation, or member or agent of a partnership or limited liability company who shall personally participate in or be accessory to any violation of this Act by such corporation, limited liability company, or partnership shall be subject to the penalties herein prescribed for individuals; and the State's Attorney of the county where such offense is committed shall prosecute all persons violating the provisions of this Act upon proper complaint being made.

All fines and penalties shall be deposited in the Real Estate Recovery Fund in the State Treasury.

The Office of Banks and Real Estate shall have the duty and the right on behalf of the People of the State of Illinois to originate injunction proceedings against any person acting or purporting to act as a broker or salesperson without a license issued under the provisions of this Act. The Office of Banks and Real Estate shall also have the duty and the right on behalf of the People of the State of Illinois to originate injunction proceedings against any licensee to enjoin acts by the licensee which constitute violations of this Act.
(Source: P.A. 88-683, eff. 1-24-95; 89-508, eff. 7-3-96.)

(225 ILCS 455/23)

Sec. 23. The Office of Banks and Real Estate shall maintain a Real Estate Recovery Fund from which any person aggrieved by an act, representation, transaction or conduct of a duly licensed broker, salesperson or unlicensed employee, which is in violation of Article 1 of this Act or the regulations promulgated pursuant thereto, or which constitutes embezzlement of money or property or results in money or property being unlawfully obtained from any person by false pretenses, artifice, trickery or forgery or by reason of any fraud, misrepresentation, discrimination or deceit by or on the part of any such licensee or the unlicensed employee of any such broker, and which results in a loss of actual cash money as opposed to losses in market value, may recover. Such aggrieved person may recover, by order of the circuit court of the county where the violation occurred, an amount of not more than $10,000 from such fund for damages sustained by the act, representation, transaction, or conduct, together with costs of suit and attorneys' fees incurred in connection therewith of not to exceed 15% of the amount of the recovery ordered paid from the Fund. However, no licensed broker, or salesperson may recover from the Fund unless the court finds that the person suffered a loss resulting from intentional misconduct. Such court order shall not include interest on the judgment.

The maximum liability against the Fund arising out of any one act shall be as provided in this Section and the judgment order shall spread the award equitably among all co-owners or otherwise aggrieved persons, if any. The maximum liability against the Fund arising out of the activities of any single broker, any single salesperson or any single unlicensed employee, since January 1, 1974, shall be $50,000.

Nothing in this Section shall be construed to authorize recovery from the Real Estate Recovery Fund unless the loss of the aggrieved person results from an act or omission of a licensed broker, salesperson or unlicensed employee who was at the time of the act or omission acting in such capacity or was apparently acting in such capacity, and unless the aggrieved person has obtained a valid judgment as provided in Section 25.

No person aggrieved by an act, representation, or transaction which is in violation of the Illinois Real Estate Time-Share Act, the Land Sales Act of 1989, or Article 2 of this Act may recover from the Real Estate Recovery Fund created pursuant to this Section.

The Office of Banks and Real Estate shall from time to

time, upon the written direction of the Governor, transfer from the Real Estate Recovery Fund any amounts the Governor determines are in excess of the amounts required to meet the obligations of the Fund. The amounts transferred to the General Revenue Fund shall not, however, exceed $1,000,000.
(Source: P.A. 89-508, eff. 7-3-96.)

(225 ILCS 455/24)
Sec. 24. If, on December 31 of any year, the balance remaining in the Real Estate Recovery Fund is less than $1,250,000, every broker, when renewing his license, at the next regular renewal time, shall pay, in addition to his renewal fee, a fee of $10 for deposit in the Real Estate Recovery Fund, and every salesperson, when renewing his license, at the next regular renewal time, shall pay, in addition to their renewal fee, a fee of $10 for deposit in the Real Estate Recovery Fund.
(Source: P.A. 84-875.)

(225 ILCS 455/25)
Sec. 25. (a) No action for a judgment which subsequently results in an order for collection from the Real Estate Recovery Fund shall be started later than 2 years after the date on which the aggrieved person knew, or through the use of reasonable diligence should have known, of the acts or omissions giving rise to a right of recovery from the Real Estate Recovery Fund.

(b) When any aggrieved person commences action for a judgment which may result in collection from the Real Estate Recovery Fund, the aggrieved person must name as parties defendant to that action any and all individual real estate brokers, real estate salespersons, or their employees, who allegedly committed or are responsible for acts or omissions giving rise to a right of recovery from the Real Estate Recovery Fund. Failure to name as parties defendant such individual brokers, salespersons, or their employees, shall preclude recovery from the Real Estate Recovery Fund of any portion of any judgment received in such an action. The aggrieved party may also name as additional parties defendant any corporations, limited liability companies, partnerships, or other business associations which may be responsible for acts giving rise to a right of recovery from the Real Estate Recovery Fund.

(c) When any aggrieved person commences action for a judgment which may result in collection from the Real Estate Recovery Fund, the aggrieved person must notify the Office of Banks and Real Estate in writing to this effect at the time of the commencement of such action.
Failure to so notify the Office of Banks and Real Estate shall preclude recovery from the Real Estate Recovery Fund of any portion of any judgment received in such an action. After receiving notice of the commencement of such an action, the Office of Banks and Real Estate, upon timely application, shall be permitted to intervene as a party defendant to that action.

(d) When any aggrieved person commences action for a judgment which may result in collection from the Real Estate Recovery Fund, and the aggrieved person is unable to obtain legal and proper service upon the defendant under the provisions of Illinois law concerning service of process in civil actions, the aggrieved person may petition the court where the action to obtain judgment was begun for an order to allow service of legal process on the Commissioner. Service of process on the Commissioner shall be taken and held in that court to be as valid and binding as if due service had been made upon the defendant. In case any process mentioned in this Section is served upon the Commissioner, the Commissioner shall forward a copy of the process by registered mail to the licensee's last address on record with the Office of Banks and Real Estate. Any judgment obtained after service of process on the Commissioner under this Act shall apply to and be enforceable against the Real Estate Recovery Fund only. The Office of Banks and Real Estate may intervene in and defend any such action.

(e) When an aggrieved party commences action for a judgment which may result in collection from the Real Estate Recovery Fund, and the court before which that action is commenced enters judgment by default against the defendant and in favor of the aggrieved party, the court shall upon motion of the Office of Banks and Real Estate set aside that judgment by default. After such a judgment by default has been set aside, the Office of Banks and Real Estate shall appear as party defendant to that action, and thereafter the court shall require proof of the allegations in the pleadings upon which relief is sought.

(f) The aggrieved person shall give written notice to the Office of Banks and Real Estate within 30 days of the entry of any judgment which may result in collection from the Real Estate Recovery Fund. Such aggrieved person shall provide the Office of Banks and Real Estate with 20 days prior written notice of all supplementary proceedings so as to allow the Office of Banks and Real Estate to participate in all efforts to collect on the judgment.

(g) When any aggrieved person recovers a valid judgment in any court of competent jurisdiction against any licensee, or an unlicensed employee of any broker, upon the grounds of fraud, misrepresentation, discrimination or deceit, the aggrieved person may, upon the termination of all proceedings, including review and appeals in connection with the judgment, file a verified claim in the court in which the judgment was entered and, upon 30 days' written notice to the Office of Banks and Real Estate, and to the person against whom the judgment was obtained, may apply to the court for an order directing payment out of the Real Estate Recovery Fund, of the amount unpaid upon the judgment, not including interest on such judgment, and subject to the limitations stated in Section 23 of this Act. The aggrieved person must set out in that verified claim, and at an evidentiary hearing to be held by the court upon such application the aggrieved party shall be required to show, that such aggrieved person:

(1) is not a spouse of debtor, or the personal representative of such spouse.

(2) has complied with all the requirements of this Section.

(3) has obtained a judgment stating the amount thereof and the amount owing thereon, not including interest thereon, at the date of the application.

(4) has made all reasonable searches and inquiries to ascertain whether the judgment debtor is possessed of real or

personal property or other assets, liable to be sold or applied in satisfaction of the judgment.

(5) by such search has discovered no personal or real property or other assets liable to be sold or applied, or has discovered certain of them, describing them owned by the judgment debtor and liable to be so applied, and has taken all necessary action and proceedings for the realization thereof, and the amount thereby realized was insufficient to satisfy the judgment, stating the amount so realized and the balance remaining due on the judgment after application of the amount realized.

(6) has diligently pursued all remedies against all the judgment debtors and all other persons liable to the aggrieved person in the transaction for which recovery is sought from the Real Estate Recovery Fund.

The aggrieved person shall also be required to prove the amount of attorney's fees sought to be recovered and the reasonableness of those fees up to the maximum allowed pursuant to Section 23 of this Act.

(h) The court shall make an order directed to the Office of Banks and Real Estate requiring payment from the Real Estate Recovery Fund of whatever sum it finds to be payable upon the claim, pursuant to and in accordance with the limitations contained in Section 23, if the court is satisfied, upon the hearing, of the truth of all matters required to be shown by the aggrieved person by subsection (g) of this Section and that the aggrieved person has fully pursued and exhausted all remedies available for recovering the amount awarded by the judgment of the court.

(i) Should the Office of Banks and Real Estate pay from the Real Estate Recovery Fund any amount in settlement of a claim or toward satisfaction of a judgment against a licensed broker or salesperson, or an unlicensed employee of a broker, the license of the broker or salesperson shall be automatically terminated upon the issuance of a court order authorizing payment from the Real Estate Recovery Fund. No petition for restoration of a license shall be heard until repayment has been made in full, plus interest at the rate prescribed in Section 12-109 of the Code of Civil Procedure, as now or hereafter amended, the amount paid from the Real Estate Recovery Fund on their account. A discharge in bankruptcy shall not relieve a person from the penalties and disabilities provided in this subsection.

(j) If, at any time, the money deposited in the Real Estate Recovery Fund is insufficient to satisfy any duly authorized claim or portion thereof, the Office of Banks and Real Estate shall, when sufficient money has been deposited in the Real Estate Recovery Fund, satisfy such unpaid claims or portions thereof, in the order that such claims or portions thereof were originally filed, plus accumulated interest at the rate prescribed in Section 12-109 of the Code of Civil Procedure, as now or hereafter amended.
(Source: P.A. 88-683, eff. 1-24-95; 89-508, eff. 7-3-96.)

(225 ILCS 455/26)
Sec. 26. The sums received by the Office of Banks and Real Estate pursuant to the provisions of Sections 18 and 23 through 30 of this Act shall be deposited into the State Treasury and held in a special fund to be known as the Real Estate Recovery Fund, and except for interest and dividends received from the investment of money in such fund, shall be held by the Office of Banks and Real Estate in trust for carrying out the purposes of this Act. These funds may be invested and reinvested in the same manner as funds of the State Employees' Retirement System. All interest and dividends received from investment of funds in the Real Estate Recovery Fund shall be deposited in a special fund in the StateTreasury to be known as the Real Estate Research and Education Fund and shall be used only for the ordinary and contingent expenses of operation of the Office of Real Estate Research or its successor, by whatever name designated, at the University of Illinois.
(Source: P.A. 89-508, eff. 7-3-96.)

(225 ILCS 455/27)

Sec. 27. When the Office of Banks and Real Estate receives any process, notice, order or other document provided for or required under this Act, it may enter an appearance, file an answer, appear at the court hearing, defend the action, or take whatever other action it deems appropriate on behalf and in the name of the defendant, and take recourse through any appropriate method of review on behalf of, and in the name of, the defendant.
(Source: P.A. 89-508, eff. 7-3-96.)

(225 ILCS 455/28)
Sec. 28. When, upon the order of the court, the Office of Banks and Real Estate has paid from the Real Estate Recovery Fund any sum to the judgment creditor, the Office of Banks and Real Estate shall be subrogated to all of the rights of the judgment creditor and the judgment creditor shall assign all right, title, and interest in the judgment to the Office of Banks and Real Estate and any amount and interest so recovered by the Office of Banks and Real Estate on the judgment shall be deposited in the Real Estate Recovery Fund.
(Source: P.A. 89-508, eff. 7-3-96.)

(225 ILCS 455/29)

Sec. 29. The failure of an aggrieved person to comply with this Act relating to the Real Estate Recovery Fund shall constitute a waiver of any rights under Sections 23 through 28 of this Act.
(Source: P.A. 83-191.)

(225 ILCS 455/30)
Sec. 30. Nothing contained in Sections 23 through 30 of this Act limits the authority of the Office of Banks and Real Estate to take disciplinary action against any licensee for a violation of this Act, or the rules and regulations of the Office of Banks and Real Estate; nor shall the repayment in full of all obligations to the Real Estate Recovery Fund by any licensee nullify or modify the effect of any other disciplinary proceeding brought pursuant to this Act.
(Source: P.A. 89-508, eff. 7-3-96.)

(225 ILCS 455/31)
Sec. 31. The Real Estate Education Advisory Council shall recommend and the Office of Banks and Real Estate approve rules: (1) defining what constitutes a school or a school

ARTICLE 3. CONTINUING EDUCATION

(225 ILCS 455/37.1)

Sec. 37.1. For the prerenewal period ending March 31, 1993 for salespersons, and January 31, 1994 for brokers, and for each prerenewal period thereafter, each person who applies for renewal of his license as a real estate broker or real estate salesman must successfully complete real estate continuing education courses approved by the Real Estate Education Advisory Council at the rate of 6 hours per year or its equivalent. No license may be renewed except upon the successful completion of the required courses or their equivalent or upon a waiver of those requirements as provided in this Article.

The requirements of this Article are applicable to all licensees who have had a license for less than 15 years as of January 1, 1992, except those licensees who, during the prerenewal period:

(a) complete the course of study required in Article 1 of this Act and obtain a license as a real estate broker;

(b) serve in the armed services of the United States;

(c) serve as an elected State or federal official;

(d) serve as a full-time employee of the Office of Banks and Real Estate (or, for a prerenewal period beginning before the effective date of this amendatory Act of 1996, the applicable predecessor regulatory agency); or

(e) are admitted to practice law pursuant to Illinois Supreme Court rule.

In addition, any licensee whose prerenewal period is less than one year is exempt from the continuing education requirements of this Article.

For the purposes of this Section, a licensee shall be deemed to have had a license for 15 years as of January 1, 1992, if the licensee submitted an application to obtain a license under this Act or a predecessor Act on or before December 31, 1976, and the licensee was issued a license under this Act or a predecessor Act on or before April 1, 1977.
(Source: P.A. 89-508, eff. 7-3-96.)

(225 ILCS 455/37.2)

Sec. 37.2. There is hereby created within the Office of Banks and Real Estate a Real Estate Education Advisory Council to be comprised of 5 members appointed by the Governor. Three of the members shall be licensees who are current members of the Real Estate Administration and Disciplinary Board, one member shall be a representative of an Illinois real estate trade organization who is not a member of the Disciplinary Board, and one member shall be a representative of an approved real estate school or continuing education sponsor. The Director of Real Estate shall serve as the chairman of the Advisory Council, ex officio, without vote.

The Real Estate Education Advisory Council shall approve real estate schools and curricula, shall approve real estate continuing education sponsors and programs, and shall make recommendations to the Office of Banks and Real Estate regarding rules to be adopted for the administration of the education provisions of Article 1 and Article 3 of this Act.
(Source: P.A. 89-23, eff. 7-1-95; 89-508, eff. 7-3-96.)

---

branch offering work in subjects relating to real estate transactions which shall include the subjects upon which an applicant is examined in determining fitness to receive a license; (2) providing for the establishment of a uniform and reasonable standard of instruction and maintenance to be observed by such schools; and (3) defining an approved school, college or university, reputable and in good standing.

Every person who desires to operate a real estate school shall make application to the Office of Banks and Real Estate in writing in form and substance satisfactory to the Office of Banks and Real Estate and pay the required fees prescribed in Section 15 of this Act. The Office of Banks and Real Estate may withdraw approval of an approved real estate school or approval of a course offered by a school for good cause.
(Source: P.A. 89-508, eff. 7-3-96.)

(225 ILCS 455/31.1)

Sec. 31.1. No cause of action shall arise against a licensee for the failure to disclose that an occupant of that property was afflicted with Human Immunodeficiency Virus (HIV) or that the property was the site of an act or occurrence which had no effect on the physical condition of the property or its environment or the structures located thereon.
(Source: P.A. 86-925.)

(225 ILCS 455/31.2)

Sec. 31.2. No action may be taken against any licensee for violation of the terms of this Act or its rules unless the action is commenced within 5 years after the occurrence of the alleged violation. A continuing violation will be deemed to have occurred on the date when the circumstances first existed which gave rise to the alleged continuing violation.
(Source: P.A. 86-925.)

(225 ILCS 455/32)

Sec. 32. Engaging in business as a broker or salesperson by any person in violation of this Act is declared to be harmful to the public welfare and to be a public nuisance. An action to enjoin any person from such unlawful activity may be maintained in the name of the People of the State of Illinois by the Attorney General, by the State's Attorney of the county in which the action is brought, by the Office of Banks and Real Estate, or by any resident citizen. This remedy shall be in addition to other remedies provided for violation of this Act.

Nothing in this Act shall be construed to grant to any person a private right of action for damages or to enforce the provisions of this Act or the rules or regulations issued under this Act.
(Source: P.A. 89-508, eff. 7-3-96.)

(225 ILCS 455/33)

Sec. 33. It is declared to be the public policy of this State, pursuant to paragraphs (h) and (i) of Section 6 of Article VII of the Illinois Constitution of 1970, that any power or function set forth in this Act to be exercised by the State is an exclusive State power or function. Such power or function shall not be exercised concurrently, either directly or indirectly, by any unit of local government, including home rule units, except as otherwise provided in this Act.

Nothing in this Section shall be construed to affect or impair the validity of Section 11-11.1-1 of the Illinois Municipal Code, as amended, or to deny to the corporate authorities of any municipality the powers granted in that Act to enact ordinances: prescribing fair housing practices, defining unfair housing practices, establishing Fair Housing or Human Relations Commissions and standards for the operation of such commissions in the administration and enforcement of such ordinances; prohibiting discrimination based on race, color, creed, ancestry, national origin or physical or mental handicap in the listing, sale, assignment, exchange, transfer, lease, rental or financing of real property for the purpose of the residential occupancy thereof; and prescribing penalties for violations of such ordinances.
(Source: P.A. 83-191.)

(225 ILCS 455/34)

Sec. 34. Administrative Procedure Act. The Illinois Administrative Procedure Act is hereby expressly adopted and incorporated herein as if all of the provisions of that Act were included in this Act, except that the provision of subsection (d) of Section 10-65 of the Illinois Administrative Procedure Act that provides that at hearings the licensee has the right to show compliance with all lawful requirements for retention, continuation or renewal of the license is specifically excluded. For the purposes of this Act the notice required under Section 10-15 of the Administrative Procedure Act is deemed sufficient when mailed to the last known address of a party.
(Source: P.A. 88-45.)

(225 ILCS 455/37.3)
Sec. 37.3. As used in this Article:
(a) "Prerenewal period" means the period between the date of issue of a currently valid license and the license expiration date.
(b) "Credit hour" means 50 minutes of classroom instruction in course work which meets the requirements set forth in rules adopted by the Office of Banks and Real Estate.
(c) "Sponsor" means any person approved by the Office of Banks and Real Estate as a sponsor in accordance with Section 37.5.
(Source: P.A. 89-508, eff. 7-3-96.)

(225 ILCS 455/37.4)
Sec. 37.4. The continuing education requirement shall be satisfied by successful completion of the following:
(a) A minimum of 6 hours of course work in any one or more of the following:
(1) license law and escrow;
(2) anti-trust;
(3) fair housing; and
(4) agency.
(b) A maximum of 6 hours of course work in:
(1) appraisal;
(2) property management;
(3) residential brokerage;
(4) farm property management;
(5) rights and duties of sellers, buyers, and brokers;
(6) commercial brokerage and leasing;
(7) financing; and
(8) such other courses as may be designated by rule.
(c) In lieu of credit for those courses listed in subsection (b) of this Section, a maximum of 6 hours of Real Estate Continuing Education credit may be earned for serving as an approved instructor in an approved course of continuing education or pre-license instruction.
(d) Credit hours may be earned for self-study programs approved by the Real Estate Education Advisory Council.
(e) A licensee may earn credit for a specific continuing education course only once during the prerenewal period.
(Source: P.A. 86-1276; 87-795; 87-1278.)

(225 ILCS 455/37.5)
Sec. 37.5. Approval of sponsors and instructors. Only sponsors approved by the Advisory Council may provide real estate continuing education courses which will satisfy the requirements of this Article. Real estate schools approved to offer the courses required by Article 1 of this Act shall be deemed to be approved sponsors of continuing education courses upon completion of an application for approval and the submission of the fee required in this Article. Those entities seeking approval as continuing education sponsors shall provide to the Advisory Council satisfactory proof of:
(a) A sound financial base for establishing, promoting, and delivering the necessary courses. Budget planning for the sponsor's courses should be clearly projected.
(b) A sufficient number of qualified instructors as provided by rule.
(c) Adequate support personnel to assist with administrative matters and technical assistance.

(d) Maintenance and availability of records of participation for licensees.
(e) The ability to provide each participant who successfully completes an approved program with a certificate of completion signed by the sponsor. The sponsor's certificate of completion will contain:
(1) the name and address of the sponsor;
(2) the name and address of the participant;
(3) a detailed statement of the subject matter;
(4) the required number of credit hours, and
(5) the date of the program.
(f) The sponsor must have a written policy dealing with procedures for the management of grievances and fee refunds.
(g) The sponsor shall maintain lesson plans and examinations for each course.
(h) The sponsor shall require a 70% passing grade for successful completion of any continuing education course.
(i) The sponsor shall identify and use instructors who will teach in a planned program. The suggested criteria for presented selections include:
(1) appropriate credentials;
(2) competence as a teacher;
(3) knowledge of content area; and
(4) qualification by experience.
(j) Advertising and promotion of continuing education activities must be carried out in a responsible fashion, clearly showing the educational objectives of the activity, the nature of the audience that may benefit from the activity, the cost of the activity to the participant and the items covered by the cost, the amount of credit that can be earned, and the credentials of the faculty.
(k) Upon the failure of any sponsor to comply with any of the requirements, the Office of Banks and Real Estate, after notice to the sponsor and hearing before the Advisory Council, shall thereafter refuse to accept successful completion of or participation in any such continuing education courses for continuing education credit until such time as the Office of Banks and Real Estate receives satisfactory assurance of compliance with this Section.
(l) All sponsors shall maintain these minimum criteria and pay the required fee in order to retain their sponsor status.
(m) All sponsors shall submit, at the time of initial application and with each sponsor renewal, a list of courses to be offered during the year. The Office of Banks and Real Estate, however, shall establish a mechanism whereby sponsors may apply for and obtain approval to offer courses during the year which are submitted after the time of initial application or renewal.
The Advisory Council shall recommend to the Office of Banks and Real Estate, and the Office of Banks and Real Estate shall promulgate, rules providing for the approval of and fees to be paid by continuing education instructors.
(Source: P.A. 89-23, eff. 7-1-95; 89-508, eff. 7-3-96.)

(225 ILCS 455/37.6)
Sec. 37.6. If a renewal applicant has earned continuing education hours in another state or territory for which he is claiming credit toward full compliance in Illinois, the Advisory Council shall review, approve, or disapprove those

courses, using criteria provided by statute or rule.
(Source: P.A. 86-1276.)

(225 ILCS 455/37.7)
Sec. 37.7. (a) Each renewal applicant shall certify, on his renewal application, full compliance with continuing education requirements set forth in Section 37.1. The approved sponsor shall retain and submit to the Commissioner after the completion of each course evidence of compliance as provided by rule.
(b) The Office of Banks and Real Estate may require additional evidence demonstrating compliance with the continuing education requirements. The renewal applicant shall retain and produce such evidence of compliance upon request of the Office of Banks and Real Estate.
(Source: P.A. 89-23, eff. 7-1-95; 89-508, eff. 7-3-96.)

(225 ILCS 455/37.8)
Sec. 37.8. (a) Any renewal applicant seeking renewal of his license without having fully complied with the continuing education requirements shall file with the Office of Banks and Real Estate a renewal application, the required renewal fee, an affidavit setting forth the facts concerning such non-compliance, and a request for waiver of the continuing education requirements on the basis of those facts along with a waiver processing fee of $25. If the Office of Banks and Real Estate, upon written recommendation of the Advisory Council, finds from the affidavit or any other evidence submitted that good cause has been shown for granting a waiver, the Office of Banks and Real Estate may waive enforcement of the continuing education requirements for the renewal period for which the applicant has applied.
(b) "Good cause" means an inability to devote sufficient hours to fulfilling the continuing education requirements during the applicable prerenewal period because of extreme hardship. Good cause shall be determined on an individual basis by the Advisory Council, is limited to:
(1) full-time service in the armed services of the United States of America during a substantial part of the prerenewal period; or
(2) extreme hardship, which shall be determined on an individual basis by the Advisory Council, is limited to:
(A) an incapacitating illness;
(B) a physical inability to travel to the sites of approved programs, or
(C) any other extenuating circumstances deemed by the Advisory Council to be sufficient.
(c) An interview before the Advisory Council with respect to a request for waiver may be granted by the Council only if the interview is requested at the time the request for the waiver is filed with the Office of Banks and Real Estate.
(Source: P.A. 89-508, eff. 7-3-96.)

(225 ILCS 455/37.9)
Sec. 37.9. The following offerings do not meet the continuing education requirements:
(a) Examination preparation offerings, except as provided in Section 37.1.
(b) Offerings in mechanical office and business skills such as typing, speed reading, memory improvement, advertising,

or salesmanship psychology.
(c) Sales promotion or other meetings held in conjunction with the general business of the attendee or his employer.
(d) Meetings which are a normal part of in-house staff or employee training.
The listings in this Section do not limit the Advisory Council's authority to disapprove any program which fails to meet the standards of this Article or rules adopted by the Office of Banks and Real Estate.
(Source: P.A. 89-508, eff. 7-3-96.)

(225 ILCS 455/37.10)
Sec. 37.10. All applications for sponsor status shall be accompanied by a nonrefundable application fee in an amount established by rule. All sponsors shall be required to submit a renewal application, an annual fee in an amount to be established by rule, and a listing of the courses to be offered during the year to maintain their sponsor status.
The fees collected under this Article shall be deposited in the Real Estate Administration Fund and shall be used to defray the cost of administration of the program and per diem of the Council as determined by the Commissioner.
(Source: P.A. 89-23, eff. 7-1-95; 89-508, eff. 7-3-96.)

(225 ILCS 455/37.11)
Sec. 37.11. The Office of Banks and Real Estate, with the advice of the Board and Advisory Council, is authorized to promulgate and issue such rules as may be necessary for the implementation and enforcement of this Article.
(Source: P.A. 89-508, eff. 7-3-96.)

ARTICLE 4
BROKERAGE RELATIONS

(225 ILCS 455/38.1)
Sec. 38.1. Short title. This Article may be cited as the Brokerage Relationships in Real Estate Transactions Law.
(Source: P.A. 88-610, eff. 1-1-95.)

(225 ILCS 455/38.5)
Sec. 38.5. Legislative intent.
(a) The General Assembly finds that application of the common law of agency to the relationships among real estate brokers and salespersons and consumers of real estate brokerage services has resulted in misunderstandings and consequences that have been contrary to the best interests of the public; the General Assembly further finds that the real estate brokerage industry has a significant impact upon the economy of the State of Illinois and that it is in the best interests of the public to provide codification of the relationships between real estate brokers and salespersons and consumers of real estate brokerage services in order to prevent detrimental misunderstandings and misinterpretations of the relationships by consumers, real estate brokers, and salespersons and thus promote and provide stability in the real estate market. This Article is enacted to govern the relationships between consumers of real estate brokerage services and real estate brokers and salespersons to the extent not governed by individual written agreements. This Article applies to the exclusion of the common law concepts of

principal and agent and be applied to the fiduciary duties, which have to this date been applied to real estate brokers, salespersons, and real estate brokerage services.

(b) The General Assembly further finds that this Article is not intended to prescribe or affect contractual relationships between real estate brokers and the broker's affiliated licensees.

(c) This Article may serve as a basis for private rights of action and defenses by sellers, buyers, landlords, tenants, real estate brokers, and real estate salespersons. The private rights of action, however, do not extend to the provisions of Article 1 of this Act.
(Source: P.A. 88-610, eff. 1-1-95.)

(225 ILCS 455/38.10)
Sec. 38.10. Definitions. In this Article:
"Act" means the Real Estate License Act of 1983.
"Agency" means a relationship in which a real estate broker or licensee, whether directly or through an affiliated licensee, represents a consumer by the consumer's consent, whether express or implied, in a real property transaction.
"Broker" is defined as in Article 1 of this Act.
"Brokerage agreement" means a written or oral agreement for brokerage services to be provided to a consumer in return for compensation or the right to receive compensation from another.
"Brokerage services" means those activities of a broker specified in Section 4 of Article 1 of this Act.
"Client" means a person who is being represented by a licensee.
"Confidential information" means information obtained by a licensee from a client during the term of a brokerage agreement that (a) was made confidential by the written request or written instruction of the client; (b) deals with the negotiating position of the client; or (c) is information the disclosure of which could materially harm the position of the client; unless at any time:
(i) the client permits the disclosure by word or conduct;
(ii) the disclosure is required by law; or
(iii) the information becomes public from a source other than the licensee.
"Confidential information" shall not be considered to include material information about the physical condition of the property.
"Consumer" means a person or entity seeking or receiving real estate brokerage services.
"Customer" means a consumer who is not being represented by a licensee but for whom the licensee is performing ministerial acts.
"Designated agency" means a contractual relationship between a broker and a client under Section 18.2a of this Act in which one or more licensees affiliated with the broker are designated as agent of the client.
"Designated agent" means a licensee named by a broker as the legal agent of a client as provided for in Section 18.2a of this Act.
"Dual agency" means an agency relationship in which a licensee is representing both buyer and seller or both landlord and tenant in the same transaction. When the agency relationship is a designated agency, the question of whether

there is a dual agency shall be determined by the agency relationships of the designated agent of the parties and not of the broker.
"Licensee" means a person or entity licensed as a broker or salesperson under Article 1 of this Act.
"Ministerial acts" means those acts that a licensee may perform for a consumer that are informative in nature and do not rise to the level of active representation on behalf of a consumer. Examples of these acts include, but are not limited to, (i) responding to phone inquiries by consumers as to the availability and pricing of brokerage services; (ii) responding to phone inquiries from a consumer concerning the price or location of property; (iii) attending an open house and responding to questions about the property from a consumer; (iv) setting an appointment to view property; (v) responding to questions of consumers walking into a licensee's office concerning brokerage services offered or particular properties; (vi) accompanying an appraiser, inspector, contractor, or similar third party on a visit to a property; (vii) describing a property or the property's condition in response to a consumer's inquiry; (viii) completing business or factual information for a consumer on an offer or contract to purchase on behalf of a client; (ix) showing a client through a property being sold by an owner on his or her own behalf; or (x) referral to another broker or service provider.
"Person" means and includes individuals, corporations, partnerships, and limited liability companies, foreign or domestic.
"Salesperson" is defined as in Article 1 of this Act.
(Source: P.A. 88-610, eff. 1-1-95; 89-23, eff. 7-1-95; 89-508, eff. 7-3-96.)

(225 ILCS 455/38.15)
Sec. 38.15. Relationships between licensees and consumers.
Licensees shall be considered to be representing the consumer they are working with as a designated agent for the consumer unless:
(1) there is a written agreement between the broker and the consumer providing that there is a different relationship; or
(2) the licensee is performing only ministerial acts on behalf of the consumer.
(Source: P.A. 88-610, eff. 1-1-95.)

(225 ILCS 455/38.20)
Sec. 38.20. Duties of licensees representing clients.
(a) A licensee representing a client shall:
(1) Perform the terms of the brokerage agreement between a broker and the client.
(2) Promote the best interests of the client by:
(A) Seeking a transaction at the price and terms stated in the brokerage agreement or at a price and terms otherwise acceptable to the client.
(B) Timely presenting all offers to and from the client, unless the client has waived this duty.
(C) Disclosing to the client material facts concerning the transaction of which the licensee has actual knowledge, unless that information is confidential information.
(D) Timely accounting for all money and property

---

received in which the client has, may have, or should have had an interest.
(E) Obeying specific directions of the client that are not otherwise contrary to applicable statutes, ordinances, or rules.
(F) Acting in a manner consistent with promoting the client's best interests as opposed to a licensee's or any other person's self-interest.
(3) Exercise reasonable skill and care in the performance of brokerage services.
(4) Keep confidential all confidential information received from the client.
(5) Comply with all requirements of this Article and all applicable statutes and regulations, including but not limited to fair housing and civil rights statutes.
(b) A broker representing a client does not breach a duty or obligation to the client by showing alternative properties to prospective buyers or tenants or by showing properties in which the client is interested to other prospective buyers or tenants.
(c) A licensee representing a buyer or tenant client will not be presumed to have breached a duty or obligation to that client by working on the basis that the licensee will receive a higher fee or compensation based on a higher selling price or lease cost.
(d) A licensee shall not be liable to a client for providing false information to the client if the false information was provided to the licensee by a customer unless the licensee knew or should have know the information was false.
(e) Nothing in this Section shall be construed as changing a licensee's duty under common law as to negligent or fraudulent misrepresentation of material information.
(Source: P.A. 88-610, eff. 1-1-95.)

(225 ILCS 455/38.25)
Sec. 38.25. Licensee's relationship with customers.
(a) Licensees shall treat all customers honestly and shall not negligently or knowingly give them false information. A licensee engaged by a seller client shall timely disclose to customers who are prospective buyers all material adverse facts pertaining to the physical condition of the property that are actually known by the licensee and that could not be discovered by a reasonably diligent inspection of the property by the customer. A licensee shall not be liable to a customer for providing false information to the customer if the false information was provided to the licensee by the licensee's client and the licensee did not have actual knowledge that the information was false. No cause of action shall arise on behalf of any person against a licensee for revealing information in compliance with this Section.
(b) A licensee representing a client in a real estate transaction may provide assistance to a customer by performing ministerial acts.
Performing those ministerial acts shall not be construed in a manner that would violate the brokerage agreement with the client, and performing those ministerial acts for the customer shall not be construed in a manner as to form a brokerage agreement with the customer.
(Source: P.A. 88-610, eff. 1-1-95.)

(225 ILCS 455/38.30)
Sec. 38.30. Termination of brokerage agreement. Except as may be provided in a written agreement between the broker and the client, neither a broker nor any licensee affiliated with the broker owes any further duties to the client after termination, expiration, or completion of performance of the brokerage agreement, except:
(1) to account for all moneys and property relating to the transaction; and
(2) to keep confidential all confidential information received during the course of the brokerage agreement.
(Source: P.A. 88-610, eff. 1-1-95.)

(225 ILCS 455/38.35)
Sec. 38.35. Agency relationship disclosure.
(a) No later than entering into a brokerage agreement with a consumer, a broker shall:
(1) Advise the consumer of the designated agency relationship that will exist unless there is written agreement between the broker and consumer providing for a different brokerage relationship.
(2) Advise the consumer of any other agency relationships available through the broker.
(3) Advise the consumer in writing of the name or names of his or her designated agent or agents.
(4) Advise the consumer as to the broker's compensation and whether the broker will share the compensation with brokers who represent other parties in a transaction.
(b) A licensee shall disclose in writing to a customer that the licensee is not acting as the agent of the customer at a time intended to prevent disclosure of confidential information from a customer to a licensee, but in no event later than the preparation of an offer to purchase or lease real property. This subsection does not apply to residential lease or rental transactions unless the lease or rental agreement includes an option to purchase real estate.
(Source: P.A. 88-610, eff. 1-1-95.)

(225 ILCS 455/38.40)
Sec. 38.40. Compensation does not determine agency relationship.
The payment or promise of payment of compensation to a broker or salesperson is not determinative of whether an agency relationship has been created between any licensee and a consumer.
(Source: P.A. 88-610, eff. 1-1-95.)

(225 ILCS 455/38.45)
Sec. 38.45. Dual agency.
(a) A licensee may act as a dual agent only with the informed written consent of all clients. Informed written consent shall be presumed to have been given by any client who signs a document that includes the following:
"The undersigned (insert name(s)), ("licensee"), may undertake a dual representation (represent both the seller or landlord and the buyer or tenant) for the sale or lease of the property located at (insert address). The undersigned acknowledge they were informed of the possibility of this type of representation. Before signing this document please

read the following:

Representing more than one party to a transaction presents a conflict of interest since both clients may rely upon licensee's advice and the client's respective interests may be adverse to each other.

Licensee will undertake this representation only with the written consent of ALL clients in the transaction.

Any agreement between the clients as to a final contract price and other terms is a result of negotiations between the clients acting in their own best interests and on their own behalf. You acknowledge that licensee has explained the implications of dual representation, including the risks involved, and understand that you have been advised to seek independent advice from your advisors or attorneys before signing any documents in this transaction.

WHAT A LICENSEE CAN DO FOR CLIENTS WHEN ACTING AS A DUAL AGENT

1. Treat all clients honestly.
2. Provide information about the property to the buyer or tenant.
3. Disclose all latent material defects in the property that are known to Licensee.
4. Disclose financial qualification of the buyer or tenant to the seller or landlord.
5. Explain real estate terms.
6. Help the buyer or tenant to arrange for property inspections.
7. Explain closing costs and procedures.
8. Help the buyer compare financing alternatives.
9. Provide information about comparable properties that have sold so both clients may make educated decisions on what price to accept or offer.

WHAT LICENSEE CANNOT DISCLOSE TO CLIENTS WHEN ACTING AS A DUAL AGENT

1. Confidential information that Licensee may know about the clients, without that client's permission.
2. The price the seller or landlord will take other than the listing price without permission of the seller or landlord.
3. The price the buyer or tenant is willing to pay without permission of the buyer or tenant.
4. A recommended or suggested price the buyer or tenant should offer.
5. A recommended or suggested price the seller or landlord should counter with or accept.

If either client is uncomfortable with this disclosure and dual representation, please let Licensee know. You are not required to sign this document unless you want to allow the Licensee to proceed as a Dual Agent in this transaction.

By signing below, you acknowledge that you have read and understand this form and voluntarily consent to the Licensee acting as a Dual Agent (that is, to represent BOTH the seller or landlord and the buyer or tenant) should that become necessary."

(b) The dual agency disclosure language provided for in subsection (a) of this Section must be presented by a licensee, who offers dual representation, to the client at the time the

brokerage agreement is entered into and may be signed by the client at that time or at any time before the licensee acting as a dual agent as to the client.

(c) A licensee acting in a dual agency capacity in a transaction must obtain a written confirmation from the licensee's clients of their consent for the licensee to act as a dual agent in the transaction. This confirmation should be obtained at the time the clients are executing any offer or contract to purchase or lease in a transaction in which the licensee is acting as a dual agent. This confirmation may be included in another document, such as a contract to purchase, in which case the client must not only sign the document but also initial the confirmation of dual agency provision. That confirmation must state, at a minimum, the following:

"The undersigned confirm that they have previously consented to (insert name(s)), ("licensee"), acting as a Dual Agent in providing brokerage services on their behalf and specifically consent to Licensee acting as a Dual Agent in regard to the transaction referred to in this document."

(d) No cause of action shall arise on behalf of any person against a dual agent for making disclosures allowed or required by this Article, and the dual agent does not terminate any agency relationship by making the allowed or required disclosures.

(e) In the case of dual agency, each client and licensee possess only actual knowledge and information. There shall be no imputation of knowledge or information among or between the clients, brokers, or their affiliated licensees.

(f) In any transaction, a licensee may without liability withdraw from representing a client who has not consented to a disclosed dual agency. The withdrawal shall not prejudice the ability of the licensee to continue to represent the other client in the transaction or limit the licensee from representing the client in other transactions. When a withdrawal as contemplated in this subsection occurs, the licensee shall not receive a referral fee for referring a client to another licensee unless written disclosure is made to both the withdrawing client and the client that continues to be represented by the licensee.

(g) The dual agency disclosure language provided for in subsection (a) of this Section may be included in any written brokerage agreement.
(Source: P.A. 88-610, eff. 1-1-95; 89-340, eff. 1-1-96.)

(225 ILCS 455/38.50)
Sec. 38.50. Designated agency.
(a) A broker designating affiliated licensees to act as agents of clients shall take ordinary and necessary care to protect confidential information disclosed by a client to his or her designated agent.

(b) A designated agent may disclose to his or her sponsoring broker, or persons specified by the sponsoring broker, confidential information of a client for the purpose of seeking advice or assistance for the benefit of the client in regard to a possible transaction.

Confidential information shall not be disclosed by the sponsoring broker or other specified representative of the sponsoring broker unless otherwise required by this Article or requested or permitted by the client who originally disclosed the confidential information.

(Source: P.A. 88-610, eff. 1-1-95.)

(225 ILCS 455/38.55)
Sec. 38.55. No subagency. A broker is not considered to be a subagent of a client of another broker solely by reason of membership or other affiliation by the brokers in a multiple listing service or other similar information source, and an offer of subagency may not be made through a multiple listing service or other similar information source.
(Source: P.A. 88-610, eff. 1-1-95.)

(225 ILCS 455/38.60)
Sec. 38.60. Vicarious liability. A consumer shall not be vicariously liable for the acts or omissions of a licensee in providing brokerage services for or on behalf of the consumer.
(Source: P.A. 88-610, eff. 1-1-95.)

(225 ILCS 455/38.65)
Sec. 38.65. Regulatory enforcement. Nothing contained in this Article limits the Office of Banks and Real Estate in its regulation of licensees under Article 1 of this Act and the substantive rules adopted by the Office of Banks and Real Estate. The Office of Banks and Real Estate, with the advice of the Real Estate Administration Disciplinary Board, is authorized to promulgate such rules as may be necessary for the implementation and enforcement of this Article.
(Source: P.A. 88-610, eff. 1-1-95; 89-508, eff. 7-3-96.)

STATE OF ILLINOIS

RULES

RULES FOR THE ADMINISTRATION OF THE
REAL ESTATE LICENSE ACT OF 1983
PART 1450

OFFICE OF BANKS AND REAL ESTATE

(Printed by the Authority of the State of Illinois)

1996

TITLE 68: PROFESSIONS AND OCCUPATIONS

CHAPTER VIII: OFFICE
OF BANKS AND REAL ESTATE

SUBCHAPTER b: PROFESSIONS AND OCCUPATIONS

PART 1450

REAL ESTATE LICENSE ACT OF 1983

SUBPART A: GENERAL RULES

SUBPART B: SCHOOL RULES

AUTHORITY: Subpart A implementing Sections 9 and 15 of the Real Estate License Act of 1983 [225 ILCS 455/9 and 15] (see P.A. 89-23, effective July 1, 1995), and authorized by Section 60(7) of the Civil Administrative Code of Illinois [20 ILCS 2105/60(7)]; Subpart B implementing Sections 4(17) and 11 of the Real Estate License Act of 1983 [225 ILCS 445/4(17) and 11] (see P.A. 89-23) and authorized by Section 60(7) of the Civil Administrative Code of Illinois [20 ILCS 2105/60(7)].

SOURCE: Rules and Regulations for the Administration of the Real Estate Brokers and Salesmen License Act (General Rules), effective December 4, 1974; Rules and Regulations for the Administration of the Real Estate Brokers and Salesmen License Act (School Rules), effective July 29, 1974; amended at 3 Ill. Reg. 885, effective February 2, 1979; amended at 4 Ill. Reg. 195, effective August 12, 1980; amended at 5 Ill. Reg. 5343, effective May 6, 1981; amended at 5 Ill. Reg. 8541, effective August 10, 1981; codified at 5 Ill. Reg. 11064; emergency amendment at 6 Ill. Reg. 916, effective January 6, 1982, for a maximum of 150 days; emergency amendment at 6 Ill. Reg. 2406, effective February 3, 1982, for a maximum of 150 days; amended at 6 Ill. Reg. 8221, effective July 1, 1982; amended at 9 Ill. Reg. 341, effective January 3, 1985; transferred from Chapter I, 68 Ill. Adm. Code 450 (Department of Registration and Education) to Chapter VII, 68 Ill. Adm. Code 1450 Department of Professional Regulation) pursuant to P.A. 85-225, effective January 1, 1988, at 12 Ill. Reg. 2977; amended at 12 Ill. Reg. 8036, effective April 26, 1988; amended at 15 Ill. Reg. 10416, effective July 1, 1991; amended at 16 Ill. Reg. 3204, effective February 14, 1992; emergency amendment at 19 Ill. Reg. 12003, effective August 8, 1995, for a maximum of 150 days; amended at 19 Ill. Reg. 16623, effective December 1, 1995; amended at 20 Ill. Reg. 6492, effective April 30, 1996; recodified from Chapter VII, Department of Professional Regulation to Chapter VIII, Office of Banks and Real Estate, pursuant to PA 89-23 and PA 89-508, at 20 Ill. Reg. 11984.

SUBPART A: GENERAL RULES

Section 1450.10 Definitions

As used in this Part:

"Act" means the Real Estate License Act of 1983 [225 ILCS 455].

"Board" means the Real Estate Administration and Disciplinary Board of the Office of Banks and Real Estate.

"Class hour" means classroom attendance for a minimum of 50 minutes of lecture or its equivalent through correspondence in a program approved by the Office of Banks and Real Estate.

"Commissioner" means the Commissioner of Banks and Real Estate.

"Director" means the Director of Real Estate, Office of Banks and Real Estate.

"License" means "certificate of registration with the Office of Banks and Real Estate."

"Managing broker" means a broker who has supervisory responsibilities for licensees in a branch office or single office real estate brokerage.

"Principal broker" means a managing broker who has active control of a multi-office real estate brokerage.

"Semester hours" shall be converted into quarter hours at the ratio of 2 semester hours to 3 quarter hours.

"Sponsoring broker" means a firm or individual broker (in the case of a sole proprietorship) who employs or contracts for services with the firm's sponsored licensees.

(Source: Amended at 15 Ill. Reg. 10416, effective July 1, 1991)

Section 1450.11 Educational Requirements of Broker Applicant Licensed as an Illinois Real Estate Salesperson (Renumbered)

a) 90 class hours of instruction in approved courses are required for broker applicants. Credit shall be given for class hours successfully completed in the following manner:

1) 30 class hours credit for the Real Estate Transactions Course.

2) 15 class hours credit for the Advanced Real Estate Principles.

3) 15 class hours credit for Contracts and Conveyancing.

4) Credit for the remaining 30 class hours may be obtained by completing at least two of the following courses listed:

A) Appraisal
B) Property Management
C) Financing
D) Sales and Brokerage
E) Farm Property Management
F) Real Property Insurance

b) An applicant for a broker license who is licensed as an Illinois real estate salesperson is presumed to have completed the Real Estate Transactions Course provided that such licensee has not been inactive or nonrenewed for five years or more. Having received 30 class hours credit as a licensed real estate salesperson, an additional 30 class hours credit cannot accrue by taking the Real Estate Transactions Course.

(Source: Section 1450.11 renumbered from Section 1450.230, amended at 15 Ill. Reg. 10416, effective July 1, 1991)

Section 1450.12 Educational Requirements for a Baccalaureate Degree with a Minor in Coursework in Real Estate (Renumbered)

A "minor in courses involving real estate" as set forth in Section 11 of the Act shall consist of the following:

a) 30 semester hours in accounting, law, business law, finance, agriculture, computer science, land economics, real estate principles, and appraisal or related courses.

b) No more than 10 semester hours shall be granted in any one subject listed in subsection (a) above.

c) At least 6 semester hours of the 30 semester hours listed in subsection (a) above shall be in courses listed in subsection (a) above. Thirty (30) class hours in an approved real estate school may be substituted for 6 semester hours in real estate principles.

(Source: Section 1450.12 renumbered from Section 1450.250, amended at 15 Ill. Reg. 10416, effective July 1, 1991)

Section 1450.15 Salesperson and Broker Examinations

a) Each applicant for a salesperson's license shall file an application for examination as determined by the designated testing service. The application shall include:

1) Certification that the applicant is 21 years of age. The minimum age of 21 years shall be waived for any person seeking a license as a real estate salesperson who has attained the age of 18 and can provide evidence of the successful completion of at least 4 semesters of post secondary school study as a full-time student or the equivalent, with major emphasis on real estate courses, in a school approved by the Real Estate Education Advisory Council (Section 11 of the Act). For the purposes of this Section, 48 semester hours shall be determined to meet the requirements of Section 11 of the Act.

2) Certification of graduation from high school or its equivalent (e.g., GED).

3) The required fee as provided in Section 15 of the Act.

4) Proof of one of the following:

A) Currently admitted to practice law by the Supreme Court of Illinois;

B) Completion of at least 30 class hours of instruction in real estate courses approved by the Board in accordance with Section 1450.290(d)(2)(A) of this Part;

C) Completion of a correspondence course approved by the Board in accordance with Section 1450.215 of this Part;

or

D) Evidence of receiving a baccalaureate degree from a college or university with a minor in coursework in real estate as defined in Section 1450.12 of this Part.

b) Each applicant for a broker's license shall file an application for examination as determined by the designated testing service.

The application shall include:

1) Certification that the applicant is 21 years of age;

2) Certification of graduation from high school or its equivalent (e.g., GED);

3) The required fee as provided in Section 15 of the Act;

4) Proof of one of the following:

A) Currently admitted to practice law by the Supreme Court of Illinois;

B) Completion of at least 90 hours of instruction in real estate courses approved by the Board in accordance with Section 1450.11 of this Part;

C) Completion of a correspondence course approved by the Board in accordance with Section 1450.215 of this Part;

or

D) Evidence of receiving a baccalaureate degree from a college or university with a minor in coursework in real estate as defined in Section 1450.12 of this Part.

c) Applicants for licensure based upon proof of either subsection (B), (C), or (D) as outlined in Section 1450.15(c)(4) above shall submit proof of one year of the last three years of active practice as a licensed salesperson.

1) Proof of active practice shall be in the form of a verification of employment/experience certification on a form provided by the Office of Banks and Real Estate.

2) If an applicant sits for the examination prior to meeting the experience requirement, the examination scores shall be null and void and the applicant shall be required to retake the examination.

d) Applicants who complete the instruction described in subsection (a)(4)(B) and (c)(4)(B) above after the final filing date for an examination will be permitted to submit such proof at the time of the examination, subject to the late fee and late proof procedures established by the Office of Banks and Real Estate.

e) If an applicant has failed an examination 3 times, the applicant must successfully complete a refresher course or its equivalent approved by the Board in order to be readmitted to sit for the examination (Section 12 of the Act).

1) The refresher course must be completed after the third failure.

2) For the purposes of this Section, the fourth attempt shall be the same as the first (Section 12 of the Act).

f) Pursuant to Section 12 of the Act, the 5 year time period does not apply to education earned as part of a baccalaureate degree program in accordance with Section 1450.12 of this Part.

(Source: Amended at 15 Ill. Reg. 10416, effective July 1, 1991)

Section 1450.17 Applications for Salespersons and Brokers Licenses by Examination

a) Each applicant for a salesperson's license shall submit to the Office of Banks and Real Estate:

1) An application which is signed by the applicant and on which all questions have been answered;

2) The fee as provided by Section 15 of the Act;

3) Proof of successful completion of the examination authorized by the Office of Banks and Real Estate;

4) A properly completed sponsor card issued in accordance with Section 1450.18(b); and

b) Each applicant for a broker's license shall submit to the Office of Banks and Real Estate:

1) An application which is signed and on which all questions have been answered;

2) The fee as provided by Section 15 of the Act;

3) Proof of successful completion of the examination authorized by the Office of Banks and Real Estate;

4) A properly completed sponsor card form issued in accordance with 1450.18(b); and

5) A properly completed consent to audit and examine special accounts form.

c) An applicant shall have one year from the date of receipt of a passing score on the examination to file an application with the Office of Banks and Real Estate and to meet all of the requirements for licensure.

(Source: Amended at 15 Ill. Reg. 10416, effective July 1, 1991)

Section 1450.18 Sponsor Card

a) Authority

1) A properly issued sponsor card shall serve as a temporary permit allowing the sponsored individual to engage in the practice of real estate.

2) The sponsored individual holding a temporary permit may practice real estate for a maximum of 45 days only under the supervision of the sponsoring broker (or the designated managing broker) named on the sponsor card.

b) Circumstances of Issuance

A licensed real estate broker (or the designated managing broker) shall issue a sponsor card to an individual only in the following instances:

1) Upon presentation of a real estate examination pass score report which states that the broker may issue a sponsor card;

2) Upon presentation of an original license endorsed by the broker by whom the licensee was previously employed or with whom the licensee was previously associated;

3) Upon presentation of a license expired for less than 5 years.

c) Issuance Procedures

Upon issuance of a sponsor card, the issuing broker shall, within 24 hours of issuance, submit the following to the Office of Banks and Real Estate by certified or registered mail return receipt requested:

1) Licensees

A) a copy of the sponsor card; and

B) appropriate sponsor card fee as set forth in Section 15 of the Act; and

C) the properly endorsed real estate license and pocket card of the sponsored licensee; or

D) an expired license of the sponsored licensee along with the fee as provided by Section 15 of the Act and proof of education, if applicable, as required by Section 13.2 of the Act; or

E) the pocket card of the licensee and a sworn statement by the licensee explaining why the license is not submitted. If neither the license nor pocket card is available, the status of the license shall be verified by the Director of Real Estate or his designee.

2) Salesperson Applicant

A) a copy of the sponsor card;

B) a real estate pass score report which states that the broker may issue a sponsor card; and

C) other documentation as required by Section 1450.17(a).

3) Broker Applicant

A) a copy of the sponsor card;

B) a real estate pass score report which states that the broker may issue a sponsor card; and

C) other documentation as required by Section 1450.17(b).

4) Should applicant be found not to have completed all the requirements including experience, his sponsor card shall be void, and he shall be considered to have never been authorized to practice, and he shall be subject to disciplinary action in accordance with Section 18 of the Act and Section 1450.305 of this Part.

5) The broker issuing the sponsor card shall retain a copy of such card until such time as the license is received and properly displayed in the broker's office.

d) The Office of Banks and Real Estate shall, within 30 days of receipt of the sponsor card, appropriate fees and appropriate documentation, issue a license to the sponsored licensee, or notify the applicant why such license cannot be issued.

e) Expiration of the Sponsor Card

A sponsor card shall be valid for a period of 45 days from issue date unless extended for an additional 45 days by the Office of Banks and Real Estate for good cause.

1) Good cause shall be limited to those instances where the Office of Banks and Real Estate has unnecessarily delayed the processing of a license.

2) The request for extension shall be considered granted only upon written notice thereof from the Office of Banks and Real Estate.

f) Broker/Sole Proprietor

1) A licensed real estate salesperson or attorney who has passed the real estate broker examination may practice as a sole proprietor, provided that prior to doing business as a sole proprietor the prospective broker submits to the Office of Banks and Real Estate the following by certified or registered mail return receipt requested:

A) a copy of the sponsor card, issued to himself; and

B) the appropriate licensure fees in accordance with Section 15 of the Act;

C) a real estate examination pass score report, which states that the broker may issue a sponsor card ; and

D) a completed consent to audit and examine special accounts form.

2) Said prospective broker shall not sponsor or employ any licensee, or manage a partnership or corporation until such time as he is issued a real estate broker license.

3) A licensed real estate broker may practice as a sole proprietor or manage a partnership, corporation or branch office provided that prior to doing business the broker complies with the licensing requirements for partnerships, corporations or branch offices set forth in Section 1450.25 or 1450.30 and submits the following to the Office of Banks and Real Estate by certified or registered mail return receipt requested:

A) a copy of the sponsor card issued to himself; and

B) the appropriate sponsor card fee as provided by Section 15 of the Act; and

C) his properly endorsed real estate broker license and pocket card; or

D) an expired broker license along with the fee set forth in Section 15(b)(3) of the Act and proof of education, if applicable, as required by Section 13 of the Act; or

E) the pocket card and a sworn statement by the licensee explaining why the license is not submitted. If neither the license nor the pocket card is available, the status of the license shall be verified by the Director or his designee.

4) The broker shall retain a copy of such sponsor card until such time as the license is received.

5) The Office of Banks and Real Estate shall within 30 days of receipt of the sponsor card, appropriate fees and documents, issue a license to the broker or shall notify the broker why such license cannot be issued (for example, if additional documentation is required or the documents are completed incorrectly).

g) Termination

1) Upon termination of a licensee, a managing broker shall immediately:

A) Endorse the licensee's license as provided for on that document;

B) Submit a photocopy of the endorsed license to the Office of Banks and Real Estate within 24 hours of termination by certified mail return receipt requested;

C) Retain a copy of the endorsed license at least until the expiration date printed on that license; and

D) Give the original endorsed license to the licensee.

2) Once a license has been endorsed, the licensee is prohibited from practicing real estate until such time as he is issued a properly completed sponsor card.

h) Display

Each licensee shall carry either a properly issued sponsor card or valid pocket card at all times and shall display same upon demand.

(Source: Amended at 15 Ill. Reg. 10416, effective July 1, 1991)

Section 1450.19 Inoperative Salespersons and Brokers Licenses

a) "Inoperative" means a status of licensure where the licensee holds a current license under this Act, but that licensee is prohibited from engaging in licensed activities because the licensee is unsponsored or the license of the broker with whom the licensee is associated or by whom he is employed is currently expired, revoked, suspended, or otherwise rendered invalid pursuant to this Act (Section 4(11) of the Act).

b) Pursuant to Section 12.1(b) of the Act, the license of any individual acting as a salesperson whose association with a broker is terminated shall automatically become inoperative immediately upon such termination unless the licensee accepts employment or becomes associated with a new broker or in the case of a broker sponsoring himself.

c) For the purposes of Section 12.1(b) of the Act, salesperson shall be defined as any licensee acting in the capacity of a salesperson whether holding a salesperson or broker's license.

(Source: Added at 15 Ill. Reg. 10416, effective July 1, 1991)

Section 1450.20 Managing Broker Responsibilities

a) The managing broker shall comply with the requirements of Section 13 of the Act.

b) At the time of application for a branch office license, or at the time of renewal of a branch office license, the principal broker shall inform the Office of Banks and Real Estate of the name and certificate number of the manager of the branch office. The name of the branch office shall be the same as that of the main office, or shall clearly delineate the branch office's relationship with the main office (e.g. affiliated with, associated with, subsidiary of). The branch office manager shall have an active license as a broker. The branch office manager's primary occupation shall be the supervisor of that office only. The name of the manager of the branch office shall appear on the branch office license.

Nothing in this Section shall relieve the principal broker of any legal responsibility for the overall supervision of branch offices.

c) The managing broker shall be responsible for issuing sponsor cards.

d) Upon written request within ten days after the loss of a managing broker, the Office of Banks and Real Estate shall issue a written authorization to allow the continuing operation of a licensed office or branch office, provided that the principal broker or representative under a duly executed power of attorney assumes responsibility, in writing, for the operation of the office and agrees to personally supervise the operations. No such authorization shall be valid for more than thirty days unless extended by the Office of Banks and Real Estate for good cause and upon written request by the principal broker. Good cause includes such circumstances as sales under contract pending closing, loss of livelihood for sales associates, and undue hardship caused to sellers.

e) When a managing broker receives a renewal application from the Office of Banks and Real Estate for another licensee, he shall notify the licensee of such receipt, personally within 7 days or by certified or registered mail within 10 days. Such notice shall also inform the licensee that the unprocessed renewal form will be returned to the Office of Banks and Real Estate, by the broker, 10 days after the date of the notice.

f) All managing brokers shall notify the Office of Banks and Real Estate on business letterhead of any change of business address within 24 hours of any change. The Office of Banks and Real Estate shall, upon receipt, issue a change of address application which shall be returned within 10 days to the Office of Banks and Real Estate along with the firm license and the appropriate fees specified in Section 15 of the Act. Change of address is required for licensed corporations, partnerships and/or branch offices. A license returned to the Office of Banks and Real Estate for the reason described in this subsection shall remain in good standing until such time as the new licenses are issued and in the possession of the licensee.

g) The Office of Banks and Real Estate will honor the Order of a court of competent jurisdiction appointing a legal representative for the sole purpose of closing out the affairs of a deceased broker or a broker who has been adjudicated disabled, who was a sole proprietor, until the real estate brokerage is closed but not to actively engage in the brokerage business as defined in Section 4(5) of the Act.

(Source: Amended at 15 Ill. Reg. 10416, effective July 1, 1991)

Section 1450.25 Branch Offices

a) Brokers wanting to operate a real estate branch office shall, in accordance with Section 13 of the Act, file an application with the Office of Banks and Real Estate, on forms provided by the Office of Banks and Real Estate, together with the following:

1) A properly completed Consent to Examine and Audit Special Accounts Form;

2) The name and license number of the manager of the branch office; and

3) The fee as provided by Section 15 of the Act.

b) Upon receipt of the above documents and review of the application, the Office of Banks and Real Estate shall issue a license authorizing the Broker to engage in real estate activities at that branch office or shall notify the applicant of the reason for the denial of such license.

c) The name of the branch office shall be the same as that of the main office, or shall clearly delineate the branch office's relationship with the main office (e.g., affiliated with, associated with, subsidiary of).

d) The broker in charge of a branch office shall submit sponsor cards for himself and brokers and salespersons in his employ only AFTER receipt of the branch office license.

(Source: Added at 15 Ill. Reg. 10416, effective July 1, 1991)

Section 1450.30 Corporations, Partnerships, and Limited Partnerships

a) Persons who desire to practice real estate in this State in the form of a partnership or corporation shall, in accordance with Section 3 of the Act, file an application with the Office of Banks and Real Estate, on forms provided by the Office of Banks and Real Estate, together with the following:

1) If an assumed name is to be used, a copy of the assumed name certificate;

2) A Federal Employer Identification Number (FEIN). If a FEIN has not been issued, a photocopy of the FEIN application;

3) A properly completed consent to examine and audit special accounts form;

4) A properly completed real estate corporation/partnership information form;

5) The fee as provided by Section 15 of the Act.

b) All requirements for a license to practice as a corporation or partnership shall be met within 1 year of the date of original application or the application shall be denied and the fee forfeited. Thereafter, to be considered for licensure, such applicant shall file a new application and fee.

c) Corporations, in addition to the above, shall submit the following:

1) The name of the corporation and its registered address, a list of all officers, and the license number for each officer who is licensed as a real estate broker;

2) A copy of the Articles of Incorporation bearing the seal of the office, in the jurisdiction in which the Corporation is organized, whose duty it is to register corporations under the laws of that jurisdiction. If it is a foreign corporation, a copy of the certificate of authority to transact business in this State is also required; and

3) All unlicensed officers shall submit with the corporation application affidavits of non-participation. Licensed salespersons cannot be officers of the corporation even if they submit an affidavit of non-participation.

d) Partnerships, in addition to the above, shall submit the following:

1) An application containing the name of the partnership and its business address and the names of all general partners, and the license number of each general partner;

2) An affidavit stating that the partnership has been legally formed.

e) Limited Partnerships, in addition to the above, shall submit the following:

(A) A letter of authority from the Secretary of State's Limited Partnership Department; and

(B) A listing of all limited partners and their license numbers.

f) Upon receipt of the above documents and review of the application, the Office of Banks and Real Estate shall issue a license authorizing the partnership or corporation to engage in the practice of real estate or shall notify the applicant of the reason for the denial of such license.

g) No corporation shall be granted a license, or engage in the business or capacity, either directly or indirectly, of a real estate broker, unless every officer of such corporation who actively participates in the real estate activities of such corporation holds a license as a real estate broker and unless every employee who acts as a salesperson for such corporation holds a license as a real estate broker or salesperson.

h) No partnership shall be granted a license, or engage in the business or serve in the capacity, either directly or indirectly, of a real estate broker, unless every general partner in such partnership holds a license as a real estate broker, and unless every employee who acts as a salesperson for such partnership holds a license as a real estate broker or salesperson (Section 3 of the Act). Licensed salespersons who have an ownership interest in a partnership shall only be limited partners.

i) Stenographic, clerical, or office personnel not directly engaged in the practice of real estate brokerage as defined in Section 4(4) of the Act are not required to be licensed.

j) No corporation shall be licensed to conduct a brokerage business where an individual salesperson or group of salespersons owns or directly or indirectly controls more than 49% of the shares of stock or other ownership interest in the corporation or constitutes more than 49% of the directors of the corporation.

(Source: Amended at 15 Ill. Reg. 10416, effective July 1, 1991)

Section 1450.40 Special Accounts (Escrow Accounts)

a) Escrow Monies

1) "Escrow monies" means all monies, promissory notes or any other type or manner of legal tender or financial consideration deposited with any person for the benefit of the parties to the transaction. Escrow monies include, but are not limited to, earnest monies and security deposits except those security deposits in which the person holding the security deposit is also the sole owner of the property being leased and for which the security deposit is being held (Section 4 of the Act).

2) For purposes of this Section, a sole owner shall be a licensee who has a 100% ownership interest held by the licensee alone or ownership as a joint tenant or tenant by the entirety. Ownership of 100% of the beneficial interest of a land trust by a licensee shall be considered as sole ownership by the licensee.

b) Requirements

1) Pursuant to Section 18 of the Act, brokers who accept escrow monies shall maintain and deposit in a special account, separate and apart from his personal or other business accounts, all escrow monies entrusted to him while acting as a real estate broker, escrow agent, or as the temporary custodian of the

funds of others and shall keep same on deposit in such account until the transactions are consummated or terminated, except to the extent that such monies, or any part thereof, shall be disbursed prior to the consummation or termination, in accordance with the written direction of the principals to the transaction or their duly authorized agents.

A) Such account shall be noninterest bearing, unless the character of the deposit is such that payment of interest thereon is otherwise required by law or unless the principals to the transaction specifically require, in writing, that the deposit be placed in an interest bearing account.

B) If an interest bearing account is required, the recipient of the interest shall be specifically indicated, in writing, by the principals of the transaction.

2) A broker may maintain more than one special account.

3) A special account need not be maintained by a broker who does not receive escrow monies entrusted to him while acting as a real estate broker, or as escrow agent, or as temporary custodian of the funds of others.

4) All escrow monies, interest bearing or non-interest bearing, shall be placed in a federally insured depository.

5) All escrow monies collected by a licensee on behalf of owners pursuant to property management activities shall be placed in a special account. The balance in the special account shall not be less than the liability represented by security deposits which are to be held in the account. These requirements may be waived in writing by the tenants. Such waiver, if included in the lease, shall appear in bold print.

c) Disputes

1) In the event of a dispute over the return or forfeiture of any escrow monies held by the broker or if a broker knows there are facts or circumstances which should reasonably cause a broker to know that any party to a transaction contests or disagrees with an anticipated disbursement of escrow monies held by the broker, the broker shall continue to hold the deposit in his special account:

(A) until he has a written release from all parties consenting to its disposition;

(B) until a civil action is filed, by either the broker or one of the parties, to determine its disposition, at which time payment may be made into court;

(C) until the funds are turned over to the Illinois Department of Financial Institutions because of inactivity of the account or inability to locate the parties; or

2) In the event of a dispute over the return of escrow monies a broker is authorized to withdraw from his special account such amounts as may be provided for by contract and which are necessary to reimburse the broker for the handling of the escrow monies, including the participation in or filing of any civil action to determine the appropriate disposition of the monies, or to pay any commissions or fees authorized by subsection (i) below. This subsection applies to an interpleader action only.

d) Notification and Consent

1) Each broker, corporation, and partnership shall, at the time of original application for licensure and at the time of renewal of licensure, on forms provided by the Office of Banks and Real Estate, file with the Office of Banks and Real Estate the name of the bank(s), savings and loan associations, or other recognized depositories in which each special account is maintained, and the name of each account, and the name(s) of the person(s) authorized to withdraw funds from such accounts, and shall consent on such form to the examination and audit of all accounts by the Office of Banks and Real Estate. The bank, savings and loan association or other recognized depository shall certify on the form that the information contained therein is correct. A new form shall be executed by the broker and filed with the Office of Banks and Real Estate within 10 days of the time of a change of depository, method of doing business, person authorized to make withdrawal and/or opening of additional accounts.

2) Any broker who fails to file the required form within the time limit shall be deemed to have endangered the interest of the public and is subject to discipline pursuant to Section 18(h)(12) of the Act.

e) Authorization.

As a condition of licensure, each broker shall authorize the Office of Banks and Real Estate to examine each special account opened by him in connection with the broker's real estate business, shall obtain the certification of the bank or savings and loan association of the special account and shall consent to the examination and audit of special accounts by the Office of Banks and Real Estate. A new authorization shall be filed with the Office of Banks and Real Estate with every license renewal application. The certification and consent shall be furnished on forms prescribed by the Office of Banks and Real Estate.

f) Commingling Prohibited. Each broker shall deposit only funds received in connection with any real estate transaction in a special account designated as a special account and shall not deposit personal funds in a special account, except a broker may deposit from his own personal funds, and keep in any special account, an amount sufficient to avoid incurring service charges relating to the special account. The sum shall be specifically documented as being for service charges and the broker shall have proof available that the

amount of his own funds in the special account does not exceed the minimum amount required by the depository to maintain the account without incurring service charges.

g) Time of Deposit. All funds accepted by a broker on behalf of his principals shall be placed in the broker's special account, of which the Office of Banks and Real Estate has received notice pursuant to subsection (d) above, not later than the next business day following acceptance of the real estate contract. If such funds are received on a day prior to a bank holiday or any other day on which the bank or savings and loan association is closed, such funds shall then be deposited on the next business day upon which the depository is open.

1) Branch Office Special Account. If a broker maintains a special account at a branch office, the Office of Banks and Real Estate shall receive notice pursuant to subsection (d) above and a separate bookkeeping system shall be maintained in the branch office as set forth in subsection (h) below.

2) No Branch Office Special Account. If a broker does not maintain a special account at a branch office, the broker in charge of the branch office shall deliver or mail such funds received at the branch office to the broker's main office not later than the next business day following acceptance of the real estate contract. The funds received at the main office from a branch office shall be placed in the broker's special account of which the Office of Banks and Real Estate has received notice pursuant to subsection (d) above, not later than the next business day following receipt of such funds from the branch office.

h) Bookkeeping System. Each broker shall maintain, in his office or place of business, a bookkeeping system in accordance with sound accounting principles, and without limiting the foregoing, such system, shall consist of at least the following:

1) A record book, called a journal, for each special account.

Such journal shall show the chronological sequence in which funds are received and disbursed by the broker:

A) For funds received such journal shall include the date, the name of the party who delivers such funds to the broker, the name of the person on whose behalf such funds are delivered to the broker and the amount of such funds so delivered.

B) For fund disbursements, such journal shall include the date, the payee, the check number and amount disbursed.

C) A running balance shall be shown after each entry (receipt or disbursement).

2) A ledger or a record book shall show the receipt and the disbursement of funds affecting a single particular transaction such as between buyer and seller, or landlord and tenant, or the respective parties to any other relationship. The ledger shall include the names of both parties to a transaction, the amount of such funds received by such broker and the date of such receipt. The ledger shall show, in connection with the disbursement of such funds, the date thereof, the payee, the check number and the amount disbursed. The ledger shall segregate one transaction from another transaction. There shall be a separate ledger or separate section of each ledger, as the broker shall elect, for each of the various kinds of real estate transactions. (e.g. lease).

3) Each broker shall reconcile, within ten days after receipt of the monthly bank statement, each special account maintained by such broker except where there has been no transactional activity during the previous month. Such reconciliation shall include a written work sheet comparing the balances as shown on the bank or savings and loan association statement, the journal and the ledger, respectively, in order to insure agreement between the special account and the journal and the ledger entries with respect to such special account. Each such reconciliation shall be kept for at least three years from the last day of the month covered by such reconciliation.

4) A broker may employ a more sophisticated bookkeeping system based on sound accounting principles, including a system of electronic data processing equipment that includes information required by the bookkeeping system set forth in subsection(h)(1), (2) and (3) above.

5) A broker may employ a special bookkeeping system for each special account, provided that the special account bookkeeping system is in accordance with an agreement between the broker and the principals. At a minimum, the bookkeeping system set forth in subsection(h)(1), (2) and (3), above shall be required.

6) The Office of Banks and Real Estate shall have available for distribution, on request, samples of approved journal, ledger and reconciliation sheets.

7) Pursuant to Section 18(9) of the Act, the broker shall make available to the real estate enforcement personnel of the Office of Banks and Real Estate during business hours all escrow records and related documents maintained in connection with the practice of real estate.

i) Disbursements of Funds for Commissions and Fees

1) Commissions and/or fees earned by a broker in any transaction shall be disbursed by the broker from the funds deposited in a special account no earlier than

the day the transaction is consummated or terminated and not later than the next business day after the transaction is consummated or terminated, or otherwise in accordance with the written direction of all principals to the transaction.

2) Authorized disbursements are those which are made on behalf of, and at the written direction of, all principals to the transaction.

(Source: Amended at 15 Ill. Reg. 10416, effective July 1, 1991)

Section 1450.45 Fees

a) License of real estate salesperson.

1) The fee for an initial license as a salesperson is $100. The fee must accompany the application to determine the applicant's fitness to receive a license.

2) The fee for renewal of a salesperson's license which has not expired shall be calculated at the rate of $25 per year.

3) The fee for the renewal of a salesperson's license which has been expired for not more than 5 years, as provided for in Section 13.2 of the Act, is the sum of all lapsed renewal fees plus $50.

b) License of Broker.

1) The fee for an initial license as a broker is $100. The fee must accompany the application to determine an applicant's fitness to receive a license.

2) The fee for the renewal of a broker's license which has not expired shall be calculated at the rate of $50 per year.

3) The fee for the renewal of a broker's license which has been expired for not more than 5 years, as provided for in Section 13.2 of the Act, is the sum of all lapsed renewal fees plus $50.

c) License of partnership, limited liability company, or corporation.

1) The fee for an initial license for a partnership, limited liability company, or corporation is $100. The fee must accompany the application to determine an applicant's fitness to receive a license.

2) The fee for the renewal of a license for a partnership, limited liability company, or corporation shall be calculated at the rate of $50 per year.

3) The fee for the renewal of a license for a partnership, limited liability company or corporation which has been expired is the sum of all lapsed renewal fees plus $50.

d) License for Branch Office.

1) The fee for an initial license for a branch office is $100. The fee must accompany the application to determine an applicant's fitness to receive a license.

2) The fee for the renewal of a branch office license shall be calculated at the rate of $50 per year.

3) The fee for the renewal of a branch office license which has been expired is the sum of all lapsed renewal fees plus $50.

e) Real Estate School and Instructor Fees.

1) The fee for an application for initial approval of a private, business, or vocational real estate school is $1,000. The fee must accompany the application to determine an applicant's fitness to receive a license.

2) The fee for renewal of approval of a private, business, or vocational real estate school shall be calculated at the rate of $500 per year.

3) The fee for renewal of approval of a private, business, or vocational real estate school which has been expired is the sum of all lapsed renewal fees plus $50.

4) The fee for an application for initial approval of a branch for a private, business, or vocational real estate school is $150 per branch. The fee must accompany the application to determine an applicant's fitness to receive approval.

5) The fee for renewal of approval of a branch for a private, business, or vocational real estate school shall be calculated at the rate of $75 per branch per year.

6) The fee for the renewal of approval of a private, business, or vocational real estate school which has been expired is the sum of all lapsed renewal fees plus $50.

7) The fee for transferring a branch location shall be $25 per transfer.

8) The fee for application for initial approval of a private, business, or vocational real estate school instructor is $50.

The fee must accompany the application to determine the applicant's fitness for approval.

9) The fee for renewal of approval of a private, business, or vocational real estate school instructor shall be calculated at the rate of $25 per year.

10) The fee for the renewal of approval of a private, business, or vocational real estate school instructor which has been expired is the sum of all lapsed renewal fees plus $50.

f) Continuing Education Sponsor and Instructor Fees.

1) The fee for an application for initial approval as a continuing education sponsor shall be $2,000. The fee must accompany the application to determine an applicant's fitness for approval.

2) The fee for renewal of approval as a continuing education sponsor shall be $2,000.

3) The fee for renewal of approval as a continuing education sponsor which has expired shall be the sum of all lapsed renewal fees plus $50.

4) The fee for an application for initial approval as a continuing education instructor shall be $15. The fee must accompany the application to determine an applicant's fitness to receive approval.

5) The fee for renewal of approval as a continuing education instructor shall be $15.

6) The fee for the renewal of approval as a continuing education instructor which has been expired is the sum of all lapsed renewal fees plus $50.

g) General.

1) All fees paid pursuant to the Act and this Section are non-refundable.

2) The fee for the issuance of a duplicate license or pocket card, for the issuance of a replacement license or pocket card for a license or pocket card which has been lost or destroyed, or for the issuance of a license with a change of name or address other than during the renewal period, or for the issuance of a license with a change of location of business is $25.

3) The fee for a certification of a licensee's record for any purpose is $25.

4) The fee for a wall license showing registration shall be the cost of producing such license.

5) The fee for a roster of persons licensed as brokers or salespersons in this State shall be the cost of producing such a roster.

6) Applicants for an examination as a broker, salesperson, or real estate instructor shall be required to pay a fee covering the cost of providing the examination, such fee shall be paid directly to the designated testing service. Failure to appear for the examination on the scheduled date, at the time and place specified, after the applicant's application for examination has been received and acknowledged, shall result in the forfeiture of the examination fee.

7) The fee for requesting a waiver of continuing education requirements pursuant to Section 37.8 of the Act shall be $25.

8) The fee for processing a sponsor card other than at the time of original licensure is $25.

9) The fee for furnishing a record of proceedings provided for in subsection (h) of Section 20 of this Act or for certifying the record referred to in Section 21 of the Act is $1 per page of the record.

10) Pursuant to Section 15 of the Act, the fee for an initial license and a renewal license for real estate salespersons and real estate brokers shall include a $10 fee for deposit in the Real Estate Recovery Fund and a $5 fee for deposit in the Real Estate Research and Education Fund.

11) Pursuant to Section 15 of the Act, the fee for an initial license for a partnership or corporation shall include a $10 fee for deposit in the Real Estate Recovery Fund and a $5 fee for deposit in the Real Estate Research and Education Fund.

12) Pursuant to Section 15 of the Act, the fee for an initial license for a branch office shall include a $5 fee for deposit in the Real Estate Research and Education Fund.

(Source: Added at 19 Ill. Reg. 16623, effective December 1, 1995)

Section 1450.50 Disclosure

a) No licensee shall withhold material information of which he has knowledge and which is not reasonably discoverable by inspection of the real estate from any party with whom he is doing business under the Act. This Section shall not be construed to require a licensee to violate his duties under the laws of agency.

b) No licensee shall accept any finder fees, commissions, discounts or any other compensation from any financial institution, title insurance company or any other person other than a broker, without full disclosure in writing of such receipt to all parties to the conveyance of the property.

c) A licensee shall disclose, in writing, to all parties in that transaction his status as a licensee and any and all interest he or it does have or may have in the real estate constituting the subject matter thereof or in such transaction, directly or indirectly according to the following guidelines:

1) On broker yard signs, no disclosure of ownership is necessary; however, such ownership shall be indicated on any property data form and disclosed to people responding to the ad or the sign. The term "broker owned" or "agent owned" is sufficient disclosure.

2) Only licensees holding inoperative licenses may advertise by owner. Inoperative licensees shall comply with the following if advertising by owner:

A) On "By Owner" yard signs, inoperative licensees shall indicate "broker owned" or "agent owned." "By Owner" newspaper ads shall use the term "broker owned" or "agent owned."

B) If an inoperative licensee runs an ad, for the purpose of purchasing real estate, he shall disclose in that ad that he is a licensee.

3) In addition to subsections (c)(1) and (2), all advertising shall comply with the provisions of Section 1450.90.

d) No cause of action shall arise against a licensee for the failure to disclose that an occupant of that property was afflicted with Human Immunodeficiency Virus (HIV) or that the property was the site of an act or occurrence which had no effect on the physical condition of the property or its environment or the structures located thereon (Section 31.1 of the Act).

Such acts shall include, but not be limited to murder or suicide. This provision is intended to apply to actions taken by the Office of Banks and Real Estate under the Act as well as to all civil actions in Illinois.

(Source: Amended at 15 Ill. Reg. 10416, effective July 1, 1991)

Section 1450.55 Agency Disclosure Pursuant to Section 18.2 of the Act

a) All disclosures shall be made in writing at or before the time of the first significant contact and shall be dated. However, if the first such contact is by telephone or in a similar manner, then oral disclosure should be made at that time and confirmed by written disclosure as required by this Section.

1) For the agent of a prospective buyer, "significant contact" shall mean the time at which the agent contacts the seller or seller's agent on behalf of one or more prospective buyers concerning the availability, price, condition of, or a showing of, a particular property or properties.

2) For the agent of a seller, "significant contact" shall mean the following:

A) the beginning of the showing of real property to the prospective buyer other than at an open house;

B) the beginning of the preparation of an offer to purchase real property for the prospective buyer; or

C) the beginning of an agent's prequalifications of a prospective buyer to determine the prospective buyer's financial ability to purchase real estate or the agent's request for specific financial information from a prospective buyer to determine ability to purchase or finance real estate in a particular price range.

3) Written disclosure may be provided in person, by mail, telefax, or other similar means sufficient to satisfy the written notice requirement of this Section (i.e. electronic mail, telegram).

b) The prospective buyer or seller shall be provided with a copy of the disclosure, and the employing broker shall retain a copy of the disclosure in the employing broker's files.

c) Disclosure to a seller can be made through the seller's agent.

d) The listing office is not required to make disclosure to a prospective buyer unless the listing office has significant contact with the prospective buyer.

e) The office that holds the listing is not required to ensure that a cooperating office has complied with the disclosure requirements of the Act.

f) A written disclosure of agency must be made to a prospective buyer even though the licensee or licensee's employing broker has previously entered into a written agreement with the prospective buyer to represent the prospective buyer if the licensee is acting as the agent of the seller in regard to a particular property or transaction in which the prospective buyer is involved.

g) The written disclosure of agency to the seller or prospective buyer can be a general disclosure and does not need to be site or party specific unless:

1) As to a prospective buyer, the licensee is a seller's agent as to some properties and an agent of the buyer in regards to the purchase of other properties.

2) As to a seller, the licensee is a subagent or cooperating agent of the seller, as to some prospective buyers and an agent of the buyer as to other prospective buyers.

h) Section 18.2 of the Act does not apply to lease or rental transactions unless the lease or rental agreement includes an

option to purchase the real property.

i) Disclosure of a licensee's interest as a principal in a transaction shall satisfy the agency disclosure requirements of the Act.

j) A licensee selling real property at auction may make the disclosure required by Section 18.2 of the Act by including that disclosure in advertising or in information sheets distributed to bidders at the time of the auction.

k) No disclosure of an agency relationship need be made by a licensee when the licensee is merely making a referral of a prospective buyer or seller to another real estate brokerage entity even though consideration or compensation is or may be paid to the referring licensee, unless the licensee has significant contact with the prospective buyer or seller.

(Source: Added at 15 Ill. Reg. 10416, effective July 1, 1991)

Section 1450.60 Employment Contracts

a) Every broker who employs salespersons or brokers or is associated with other licensees as independent contractors shall have a written agreement with each such person. The agreement shall be dated, signed by the parties and shall cover the salient aspects of their relationship, including, but not necessarily limited to, supervision, duties, compensation and termination.

b) Licensed activity. A broker may continue to make payments directly to a terminated licensee if such payments are pursuant to terms of an employment agreement and such payments are for licensed activity

performed while employed by that broker.

c) If it is the duty of an employed associated broker to supervise a branch office, the agreement shall so state and contain the address of the branch office supervised by such employed associated broker. A copy of the agreement shall be kept and available for inspection in the branch office supervised by each employed associated broker.

(Source: Amended at 15 Ill. Reg. 10416, effective July 1, 1991)

Section 1450.70 Listing Agreements

a) All written listing agreements shall contain the following:

1) the list price;
2) the agreed basis or amount of commission and the time of payment,
3) the duration of the contract, clearly set forth;
4) name of broker and seller;
5) identification of property involved (address or legal description); and
6) signatures of the parties.

b) Pursuant to Section 19 of the Act, no licensee shall obtain any written listing agreement containing a clause automatically extending the listing period.

Every written listing shall provide that no amendment or alterations in the terms, with respect to the payment of commission: shall be valid or binding unless made in writing and signed by the parties.

No licensee shall use Sale Contract forms that change previously agreed commission payment terms unless seller and listing agent agree to such changes in a written memorandum separate from the Sale Contract. Any such Sale Contract forms may state that a commission is to be paid to a named licensee pursuant to a separate agreement.

d) If the terms of the listing agreement are such that seller may not receive the earnest money deposit, in the event of purchaser's default, a statement to this effect shall appear in the listing agreement, in letters larger than those generally used in the listing agreement.

e) Each listing agreement shall clearly state that it is illegal for either the owner or the broker to refuse to display or sell to any person because of their race, color, religion, national origin, sex, handicap, or familial status.

f) Each listing agreement for a residential property of four units or less, which provides for a protection period subsequent to its termination date, shall also provide that no commission or fee will be due and owing pursuant to the terms of the listing agreement if, during the protection period, a valid, written listing

agreement is entered into with another licensed real estate broker.

g) A broker may discuss a possible future listing agreement with a seller whose property is listed with another broker only under the following conditions:

1) when the seller initiates the contact; or
2) when the listing broker upon request fails to provide within 10 calendar days the type and expiration date of the listing agreement between the seller and the listing broker. The request and response shall be in writing and mailed return receipt requested. If the above information is not received within 14 calendar days, the broker may then contact the seller only if this information cannot be obtained from another source of shared broker information.

(Source: Amended at 15 Ill. Reg. 10416, effective July 1, 1991)

Section 1450.80 Written Agreements

a) No licensee shall solicit, accept or execute any contract or other document relating to a real estate transaction which shall contain any blanks to be filled in after signing or initialing such contract or other document.

b) No licensee shall make any addition to, deletion from or alteration of any signed contract or other document relating to a real estate transaction without the written, telefax or telegraphic consent or direction from all signatories. No licensee shall process any contract or other document that has been altered after being signed, unless each addition, deletion or alteration is signed or initialed by all signatories at the time of such addition, deletion or alteration.

c) A true copy of the original or corrected contract or other document relating to a real estate transaction shall be hand delivered or mailed within 24 hours of the time of signing or initialing such original or correction to the person signing or initialing any such contract or other document.

d) All forms used by licensees intended to become binding real estate contracts shall clearly state this in the heading in large bold type. No licensee shall use a form designated Offer to Purchase when it is intended that such form shall be a binding real estate contract.

(Source: Amended at 15 Ill. Reg. 10416, effective July 1, 1991)

Section 1450.90 Advertising

a) Except for inoperative licensees selling their own property, the broker's business name (which in the case of a franchise shall include the franchise affiliation as well as the individual firm) shall be displayed in all real estate advertisements, including but not limited to newspapers as defined by Section 4(14) of the Act.

b) No blind advertisements may be used by any licensee regarding the sale or lease of real estate, including his own, or regarding real estate activities or the hiring of all licensees under the Act.

c) No advertising is to be fraudulent, deceptive, inherently misleading, or proven to be misleading in practice. It is considered misleading or untruthful if, when taken as a whole, there is a distinct and reasonable possibility that it will be misunderstood or will deceive the ordinary purchaser, seller, renter, or owner. Advertising shall contain all information necessary to communicate accurately. The form of communication shall be designed to communicate the information contained therein to the public in a direct and readily comprehensible manner.

d) A sponsored licensee cannot advertise under his own name. All advertising shall be under the direct supervision of the employing broker and in the name of the employer.

e) No licensee shall list his name under the heading or title "Real Estate" in the telephone directory or otherwise advertise in his own name to the general public through any media of advertising as being in the real estate business without listing the business name of the broker with whom he is affiliated. Printed information relating to the licensee and his name cannot be larger in size than that pertaining to the broker's business name.

(Source: Amended at 15 Ill. Reg. 10416, effective July 1, 1991)

Section 1450.95 Unlicensed Assistants

a) Licensees under the Act may employ, or otherwise utilize the services of, unlicensed assistants to assist them with administrative, clerical, or personal activities for which a license under the Act is not required.

b) An unlicensed assistant, on behalf of and under the direction of a licensee, may engage in the following administrative, clerical, or personal activities without being in violation of the licensing requirements of the Act. The following list is intended to be illustrative and declarative of existing law and is not intended to increase or decrease the scope of activities for which a license is required under the Act. An unlicensed assistant of a licensee may:

1) answer the telephone, take messages, and forward calls to a licensee;

2) submit listings and changes to a multiple listing service;

3) follow up on a transaction after a contract has been signed;

4) assemble documents for a closing;

5) secure public information from a courthouse, sewer district, water district, or other repository of public information;

6) have keys made for a company listing;

7) draft advertising copy and promotional materials for approval by a licensee;

8) place advertising;

9) record and deposit earnest money, security deposits, and rents;

10) complete ordinary forms with business and factual information at the direction of and with approval by a licensee;

11) monitor licenses and personnel files;

12) compute commission checks and perform bookkeeping activities;

13) place signs on property;

14) order items of routine repair as directed by a licensee;

15) prepare and distribute flyers and promotional information under the direction of and with approval by a licensee;

16) act as a counter to deliver documents, pick up keys, etc.;

17) place routine telephone calls on late rent payments;

18) schedule appointments for the licensee (this does not include making phone calls, telemarketing, or performing other activities to solicit business on behalf of the licensee);

19) respond to questions by quoting directly from published information;

20) gather feedback on showings; and

21) perform other administrative, clerical, and personal activities for which a license under the Act is not required.

c) An unlicensed assistant of a licensee may not perform the following activities for which a license under the Act is required. The following list is intended to be illustrative and declarative of existing law and is not intended to increase or decrease the scope of activities for which a license is required under the Act. An unlicensed assistant of a licensee may not:

1) host open houses, kiosks, or home show booths or fairs;

2) show property;

3) interpret information on listings, titles, financing, contracts, closings, or other information relating to a transaction;

4) explain or interpret a contract, listing, lease agreement, or other real estate document with anyone outside the licensee's firm;

5) negotiate or agree to any commission, commission split, management fee, or referral fee on behalf of a licensee; or

6) perform any other activity for which a license under the Act is required.

d) Any licensee who employs an unlicensed assistant shall be responsible for the actions of the unlicensed assistant taken while under the supervision of or at the direction of the licensee.

e) Any licensee who is responsible for the actions of an unlicensed assistant by statute, regulation, contract, or office policy and who permits, aids, assists, or allows an unlicensed assistant to perform any activity for which a license under the Act is required shall be in violation of the Act.

(Source: Added at 20 Ill. Reg. 6492, effective April 30, 1996)

Section 1450.100 Discrimination

a) Pursuant to Section 18(b)(22) of the Act, no licensee shall enter into a listing agreement which prohibits the sale or rental of real estate to any person because of race, color, creed, religion, national origin, sex, handicap, or familial status.

b) No licensee shall act or undertake to act as a real estate broker or real estate salesperson with respect to any property the disposition of which is prohibited to any person because of race, color, creed, religion, national origin, sex, handicap, or familial status.

c) A judgment or conviction in any court of competent jurisdiction that any licensee or applicant for licensure has violated any constitutional or statutory provision prohibiting discrimination in housing shall be deemed a demonstration of "unworthiness or incompetency to act as a real estate broker or salesperson in such manner as to endanger the interest of the public" and is subject to discipline pursuant to Section 18(b)(12) of the Act.

(Source: Amended at 15 Ill. Reg. 10416, effective July 1, 1991)

Section 1450.110 Unworthiness or Incompetence to Act as a Broker or Salesperson

Unworthiness or incompetence on the part of a licensee as set forth in Section 18(e)(11) of the Act may consist of both acts and omissions to act.

Omissions to act and a failure to safeguard the interests of the public in the buying or selling, the negotiation of sales or exchange of real estate, the leasing or renting of real estate wherein the premises are known by the licensee to be in serious violation of ordinances made for the protection of the public in regard to fire, health, sanitation and zoning shall be deemed "unworthiness or incompetence."

(Source: Amended at 12 Ill. Reg. 8036, effective April 26, 1988)

Section 1450.120 Hearings

All disciplinary hearings brought before the Board under Section 18 of the Act shall be conducted in accordance with the Rules of Practice in Administrative Hearings, 68 Ill. Adm. Code 110.

(Source: Amended at 9 Ill. Reg. 341, effective January 3, 1985)

Section 1450.140 Assumed Name

If a real estate broker operates under any name other than that appearing on his license, he shall submit a certified copy of his registration under "An Act in relation to the use of an assumed name in the conduct or transaction of business in this State." [805 ILCS 405] at the time of application or within 30 days of such registration.

(Source: Amended at 15 Ill. Reg. 10416, effective July 1, 1991)

Section 1450.150 Reciprocal Licensure

a) A license shall be issued without examination to a real estate broker licensed under the laws of his home state or to a real estate salesperson licensed under the laws of his home state under the following conditions:

1) That the broker or salesperson is the holder of an active license in his home state;

2) That the standards of that state for licensing as a real estate broker or salesperson are substantially equivalent to the minimum standards in Illinois;

3) That the broker maintains a definite place of business in his home state and has been actively engaged in the real estate business as a broker during the immediately preceding 2 years;

4) That the broker's or salesperson's home state grants reciprocal privilege to brokers and salespersons licensed in Illinois; and

5) If he is a salesperson holding an Illinois reciprocal license, that he is employed by or under contract to a broker who also holds an Illinois license and resides in the same state.

b) The broker or salesperson shall file an application, on forms furnished by the Office of Banks and Real Estate, along with the required fee specified in Section 15 of the Act and a statement bearing the seal of the licensing authority in the state in which he is licensed, showing that he has an active license as a broker or salesperson in that state.

c) Upon request by the Office of Banks and Real Estate, the broker or salesperson shall attest in writing, on forms supplied by the Office of Banks and Real Estate, to the fact that his license in his home state is active and in good standing and that he understands that his reciprocal license is valid only as long as he remains a resident of that state and will be invalid on the date his home state license is expired, is suspended, is inactive or otherwise not in good standing.

d) A reciprocal license becomes invalid when the licensee changes his residence to Illinois or any other state. Such individual shall meet the licensure requirements of the Act and this Part in effect at the time of his application for relicensure in Illinois and shall obtain a license in accordance with Section 12 or Section 14 of the Act prior to practicing in this State.

e) All requirements for licensure by reciprocity shall be met within 1 year of the date of original application or the application shall be denied and the fee forfeited. Thereafter, to be considered for licensure, such applicant shall file a new application and fee.

(Source: Amended at 15 Ill. Reg. 10416, effective July 1, 1991)

Section 1450.170 Rental Finding Services

a) Definition–Application.

1) A rental finding service is any business which finds, attempts to find, or offers to find, for any person who pays or is obligated to pay a fee or other valuable consideration, a unit of rental real estate or a lessee to occupy a unit of rental real estate, not owned or leased by such business.

2) Any person, partnership, or corporation which operates a rental finding service shall be considered a broker or salesperson as defined in the Real Estate License Act, shall obtain a license pursuant to the Act, and shall comply with the provisions of this Section.

3) The provisions of this Section shall not apply to:

A) Newspapers as defined in Section 4(14) of the Act.

B) Listing contracts between owners or lessors of real estate and licensees.

b) Contract. A rental finding service shall, prior to accepting a fee or other valuable consideration for such services, enter into a written contract with the person for whom such services are to be performed and deliver to such individual a copy of such contract. Such contract shall include in the case of a rental finding service which finds, offers, or attempts to find a unit of rental real estate for an individual, at a minimum, the following provisions:

1) The term of the contract;

2) The total amount to be paid for the services to be performed and a clear designation of the amount paid in advance of the performance of such services;

3) A statement regarding the refund or nonrefund of the fee paid in advance, which shall include:

A) the precise conditions, if any, upon which a refund is based;

B) the fact that such conditions shall occur within 90 days from the date of the contract;

C) the fact that the refund shall be paid no later than 10 days after demand, provided the check has been honored.

4) The statements required by subsection (3) above shall be uniform in type of a size larger than that used for the balance of the contract;

5) The type of rental unit desired, the geographical area requested, and the rent the prospective tenant is willing to pay;

6) A detailed statement of rental finding services to be performed by the licensee, which services shall include, at a minimum, the delivery to such prospective tenant of all rental information as listed in subsection (c), below;

7) A statement that such contract shall be null and void if information concerning possible rental units or locations furnished by the licensee is not current or accurate with respect to the type of rental unit desired and described in subsection (b)(5) above. A listing for a rental unit which has not been available for rent for over two days shall be prima facie proof of not being current;

8) A statement that information furnished by the licensee concerning possible rental units may be up to 2 days old;

9) A statement requiring the licensee to refund all fees paid in connection with the contract if such contract is null and void for any reason. The licensee shall not impose any condition for such refund and the contract shall state when the refund will be paid.

c) Disclosure. Pursuant to subsection (b)(6) above, the following written information for each rental unit shall be provided to the person with whom such contract is entered into:

1) The name, address, and the telephone number of the owner of each rental unit, or his authorized agent;

2) A description of the rental unit;

3) The amount of rent requested;

4) The amount of security deposit required;

5) A statement describing utilities which are located in the rental unit and included in the rent;

6) The occupancy date and the term of lease;

7) A statement setting forth the source of the rental information (i.e., owner, agent);

8) All other information which may reasonably be expected to be of concern to the prospective tenant.

d) Permission of Owner. A rental finding service shall not list or advertise any rental unit without the express written authority of the owner or agent of each unit.

e) Violation. Without limiting the provisions of the Act or this Part, a licensee shall be deemed to have demonstrated unworthiness or incompetence as a broker under Sections 18 and 20 of the Act when such registrant shall have violated any provision of this Section, including, but not limited to, failing to refund, pursuant to proper demand, any rental finding fee to any person lawfully entitled to such refund.

(Source: Amended at 15 Ill. Reg. 10416, effective July 1, 1991)

Section 1450.175 Continuing Education

a) Continuing Education Hour Requirements

1) Pursuant to Article 3 of the Act, beginning with the March 31, 1993, renewal of licensure for salespersons and the January 31, 1994, renewal of licensure for brokers, and every renewal thereafter, each licensee who is required to comply with continuing education (CE) shall complete during each prerenewal period a minimum of 12 hours of CE that is relevant to the practice of real estate as set forth in subsection (b)(3) below and is approved by the Real Estate Education Advisory Council ("Advisory Council").

2) For salespersons, a prerenewal period is the 24 months preceding March 31 of the year of the renewal. For brokers, a prerenewal period is the 24 months preceding January 31 of the year of the renewal.

3) Pursuant to Section 37.1 of the Act, CE requirements apply only to those licensees who obtained initial licensure in Illinois on or after January 1, 1977. Individuals licensed in Illinois prior to January 1, 1977, either as salespersons or brokers, are exempt from the CE requirements. Continuous licensure is not required to be eligible for this exemption. However, if a license has been nonrenewed for a period of 5 years or more, the date of initial licensure, for purposes of this Section, shall be the date of licensure after that nonrenewed period.

4) A renewal applicant is not required to comply with the CE requirements for the first renewal following the original issuance of either the salesperson or broker license.

5) Salespersons and brokers licensed in Illinois but residing and practicing in other states shall comply with the CE requirements set forth in this Section, unless they are exempt pursuant to Section 37.1 of the Act or subsections (a)(3) and (4) above.

6) The Office of Banks and Real Estate shall conduct random audits to verify compliance with this Section.

b) Approved Continuing Education

1) CE credit may be earned for verified attendance at or participation in a course which is offered by an approved CE sponsor who meets the requirements set forth in subsection (c) below.

2) CE credit may also be earned for completion of a self-study course that is offered by an approved sponsor who meets the requirements set forth in subsection (c) below.

3) Pursuant to Section 37.4 of the Act, the CE requirement shall be satisfied by successful completion of the following:

A) Mandatory category. A minimum of 6 hours of CE in any one or more of the following mandatory courses:

i) License law and escrow;

ii) Anti-trust;

iii) Fair housing; and

iv) Agency.

B) Elective category. A maximum of 6 hours of CE in the following elective courses:

i) Appraisal;

ii) Property management;

iii) Residential brokerage;

iv) Farm property management;

v) Rights and duties of sellers, buyers and brokers;

vi) Commercial brokerage and leasing;

vii) Financing; and

viii) Other CE courses approved by the Advisory Council (e.g., real estate tax laws).

4) Pursuant to Section 37.3(b) of the Act, one hour of approved CE shall include at least 50 minutes of classroom instruction and shall be exclusive of any time devoted to taking the examination as set forth in subsection (b)(6) below.

5) Each CE course shall include one or more subjects from the mandatory category or elective

category set forth in subsection (b)(3)(A) or (b)(3)(B), where the individual is in actual attendance, or participates in, or completes self-study. All CE courses shall be a minimum of three hours and shall be offered in three-hour increments. Each three-hour increment shall be from topics in the mandatory or elective category. In no case shall topics from the mandatory and elective category be intermingled within the same three-hour period. The sponsor shall clearly indicate on the certificate of completion the number of hours earned from each CE course and identify whether the completed course was from the mandatory or elective category.

6) Each CE course shall include the successful completion of an examination which measures the attendee's understanding of the course material. A score of at least 70% is required on the examination for successful completion of any CE course.

A) The examination shall be given on-site immediately following any CE course. When a sequence of courses is offered, the examination may be given either at the end of each individual course or it may be given at the end of the sequence of courses so long as the examination covers all aspects of the course material.

B) All examinations, including self-study examinations and retake examinations, shall be proctored by a representative of the approved sponsor and shall include at least 25 questions for each three-hour increment of CE earned. No course material, notes, or other aides shall be referred to during the examination by the student with the exception of amortization tables, tax tables and calculators.

C) No credit for CE shall be given to any licensee unless the examination is successfully completed. The sponsor shall allow the attendee one retake within 30 days after a failed examination in order to receive credit for CE. No more than one retake shall be allowed. A licensee failing a retake shall not receive credit for that CE course unless the entire course is retaken and the examination is successfully completed.

7) Self-study CE shall comply with all of the requirements of this Section, except that:

A) Verified attendance is only required for taking the examination.

B) Classroom instruction is not required for self-study CE, as the intent is for the licensees to review and learn the material on their own.

C) Acceptable self-study materials include, but are not limited to, reading material and audio/video cassettes.

D) The examination site for self-study CE shall be determined by the sponsor, and it shall be proctored by a representative of the approved sponsor. An approved instructor is not required to proctor the examination.

8) All CE courses shall:

A) Contribute to the advancement, integrity, extension and enhancement of professional skills and knowledge in the practice of real estate;

B) Provide experiences (e.g., role playing, lectures, films) which contain subject matter and course materials relevant to that set forth in Section 37.4 of the Act; and

C) Be developed and presented by persons with education and/or experience in the subject matter of the CE course.

9) Nothing shall prohibit an approved sponsor and its instructors from utilizing audio-visual aides or satellite communications with two-way voice interaction in assisting in the presentation of CE courses.

10) Pursuant to Section 37.4, a maximum of 6 hours of CE credit per prerenewal period may be earned by an approved instructor for teaching an approved CE course or pre-license course. One hour of teaching is equal to one hour of CE.

11) As provided for in Section 37 of the Act, if licensees have earned CE hours offered in another state or territory for which they will be claiming credit toward full compliance in Illinois, each applicant shall submit an application along with a $25 processing fee within 90 days after completion of the CE course and prior to expiration of the license. The Advisory Council shall review and recommend approval or disapproval of the CE course provided the sponsor and CE course are substantially equivalent to those approved in Illinois and provided that the course included the successful completion of a closed book, proctored examination. In determining whether the sponsor and CE course are substantially equivalent, the Advisory Council shall use the criteria in Article III of the Act and this Section.

12) CE credit shall not be given for CE courses taken in Illinois from sponsors not pre-approved by the Office of Banks and Real Estate.

c) Continuing Education Sponsors and Courses

1) Sponsor, as used in this Section, shall mean a person, firm, association, corporation, real estate school approved under Article I of the Act, or any other group which has been approved and authorized by the Office of Banks and Real Estate upon the recommendation of the Advisory Council to coordinate and present CE courses.

2) Those entities seeking approval as CE sponsors shall maintain an office for maintenance of all records, office equipment and office space necessary for customer service.

Real Estate or its designee during regular business hours;

A) The CE sponsor's office may be subject to inspection by authorized representatives of the Office of Banks and Real Estate during regular working hours when the Office of Banks and Real Estate has reason to believe that there is not full compliance with the Act or this Part and that this inspection is necessary to ensure full compliance.

B) The Office of Banks and Real Estate shall, upon an on-site inspection of an out-of-state sponsor, be reimbursed by the sponsor for all expenses incurred by the inspector in the course of the inspection.

3) Entities seeking approval as CE sponsors shall file a sponsor application, on forms provided by the Office of Banks and Real Estate, along with the required fee set forth in Section 37.5 of the Act. The application shall include the following:

A) A list of all CE courses that the sponsor is planning to offer during the 12 month period following approval;

B) The description, location, date and time of each CE course to be offered;

C) A list of all instructors the sponsor plans to utilize in the offering of CE courses. Such list shall include the instructor's name, address, and approval number;

D) A copy of a certificate of attendance planned to be used which meets the requirements set forth in Section 37.5 of the Act;

E) As provided in Section 37.5(m) of the Act, an approved sponsor shall not be precluded from offering CE courses or from utilizing instructors not listed in the initial application or subsequent annual renewals if written notice of the CE course and the instructor to be utilized is submitted 30 days prior to the CE course date pursuant to subsection (c)(3)(F)(v) below.

F) On the application the sponsor shall certify to the following:

i) That the content areas of all CE courses offered by the sponsor for CE credit will conform to those listed in Section 37.4(a) and (b) of the Act and that CE sponsors shall not offer for approved credit any of the courses set forth in Section 37.9 of the Act;

ii) That all CE courses offered by the sponsor for CE credit will comply with the criteria in this Section;

iii) That the sponsor shall be responsible for verifying attendance at each CE course and provide a certificate of completion signed by the sponsor which meets the requirements of Section 37.5 of the Act. The sponsor shall maintain these records for not less than 5 years and shall make these records available for inspection by the licensee or the Office of Banks and

iv) That upon request by the Office of Banks and Real Estate, the sponsor will submit such evidence as is necessary to establish compliance with this Section and Section 37.5 of the Act. Such evidence shall be required when the Office of Banks and Real Estate has reason to believe that there is not full compliance with the Act and this Part and that this information is necessary to ensure compliance;

v) That each sponsor shall submit to the Office of Banks and Real Estate a written notice of a CE course 30 days prior to the CE course date if such program was not listed in the application or any subsequent renewal application. The notice shall include the description, location date and time of the CE course to be offered;

vi) That the sponsors shall only offer CE in an environment which is conducive to learning (i.e., adequate lighting, seating) and does not jeopardize the health, safety, and welfare of the attendee(s). This does not apply to self-study CE courses; and

vii) That financial resources are available to equip and maintain its office in a manner necessary to enable the sponsor to comply with Article III of the Act, this Section and this Part, documented by a current balance sheet, an income statement or any such similar evidence as requested by the Office of Banks and Real Estate.

4) Real estate schools approved to offer the courses required by Article I of the Act shall be deemed to be approved to offer CE programs upon completion of an application for approval and the submission of the $2,000 fee required by Section 37.5 of the Act. Any college or university exempt from paying a fee for school approval under Article I of the Act is also exempt from paying the fee to become an approved continuing education sponsor under Article III of the Act.

5) Within 30 days after the action by the Advisory Council, the Office of Banks and Real Estate shall issue approval to the sponsor or notify such sponsor, in writing, why approval cannot be issued.

6) Approved CE sponsors shall comply with the following:

A) No approved sponsor shall allow the premises or classrooms utilized during CE courses to be used by anyone to directly or indirectly recruit new affiliates for any company. Sponsors and instructors shall report to the Office of Banks and Real Estate any efforts to recruit licensees.

B) No approved sponsor shall advertise that it is endorsed, recommended, or accredited by the Office of Banks and Real Estate. Such sponsor, however, may indicate that the sponsor and the CE course have been approved by the Office of Banks and Real Estate.

C) Approved sponsors shall utilize in the teaching of approved CE courses only instructors who have been approved by the Office of Banks and Real Estate.

D) Approved sponsors shall specify in any advertising promoting CE courses the number of CE hours that may be credited toward Illinois CE requirements for license renewal. Further, approved sponsors shall specify the number of mandatory and elective CE course hours that may be earned as set forth in subsections (b)(3)(A) and (b)(3)(B) above.

E) All CE courses given by approved sponsors shall be open to all licensees and not be limited to members of a single organization or group.

7) The sponsor shall be responsible for assuring verified attendance at each CE course or self-study examination. No renewal applicant shall receive CE credit for time not actually spent attending the CE course or when a passing score of 70% on the examination was not achieved in accordance with Section 37.5 of the Act.

8) To maintain approved sponsor status, each sponsor shall submit annually during the 30 days preceding April 1 a sponsor renewal application along with the required fee set forth in Section 37.5 of the Act. The sponsor shall be required to submit to the Office of Banks and Real Estate with the renewal application the following:

A) A list of those CE courses planned to be offered in the 12-month period immediately following the renewal period. This list shall include a description, location, date and time the course is planned to be offered.

B) A list of those instructors the sponsor plans to utilize. This list shall include the name, address, and instructor approval number for each.

d) Continuing Education Instructors

1) An applicant seeking approval from the Office of Banks and Real Estate to become an approved CE instructor shall submit a completed application, on forms provided by the Office of Banks and Real Estate, along with the fee as provided for in Section 37.5 of the Act.

2) An individual applying to become an approved CE instructor shall meet the following criteria, as provided for in Section 37.5(i) of the Act:

A) Has held a real estate brokers license for at least the last three years and has been engaged in active practice as a real estate broker; or

E) Is currently admitted to practice law and for three years has been engaged in real estate related work as part of his/her active practice of law or has taught pre-licensure real estate courses; or

C) Is a properly credentialed instructor of real estate courses who is or has been engaged in the practice of teaching for at least three years; or as evidenced by a professional designation, such as but not limited to a designated real estate instructor (DREI); or approved by a college or university's governing body to teach in a real estate degree program; or

D) Is properly licensed or certified to engage in the business of appraisal, finance and/or related real estate occupations (not including real estate salespersons) and for at least three years has been engaged in such practice; or

E) Is qualified by experience or education, or both, to teach CE pursuant to the provisions of this Section. In determining whether a person is qualified to teach CE under this Section, the Director of Real Estate shall consider the following:

i) The individual's teaching experience;

ii) The individual's real estate experience;

iii) Any real estate, business or legal education of the individual; and

iv) The results of a personal interview with the individual. The personal interview may be conducted via telephone if it would be overly burdensome and unreasonable for the applicant to personally appear for the interview (e.g., applicant living out-of-state).

F) Any applicant who the Director has determined does not meet the requirements of subsection (d)(2)(E) shall be evaluated by the Advisory Council. The Advisory Council shall evaluate the application and make a recommendation to the Commissioner for approval or disapproval of the applicant as a CE instructor. The Office of Banks and Real Estate shall issue approval to the applicant or notify the applicant in writing why approval cannot be issued.

3) Instructors approved to teach salesperson and broker pre-license courses, pursuant to Section 1450.280 of this Part, are deemed approved as CE instructors as long as they maintain their approval under Section 1450.280 of this Part, submit an application to the Office of Banks and Real Estate for approval and pay the fee as provided for in Section 37.5 of the Act.

4) Within 30 days after receipt of an application, the Office of Banks and Real Estate shall issue approval to the applicant or notify such applicant in writing why approval cannot be issued.

5) To maintain approved status, CE instructors shall submit annually during the 30 days preceding April 1 an instructor renewal application, on forms provided by the Office of Banks and Real Estate, along with the fee as provided for in Section 37.5 of the Act.

e) Withdrawal of Approval

1) Upon written recommendation of the Advisory Council, the Office of Banks and Real Estate shall, withdraw, suspend or place on probation the approval of an approved CE sponsor or an approved CE instructor when, at any time, the quality of the CE fails to meet the established criteria as set forth in this Section and Article III of the Act or if sponsorship or instructor approval was based upon false or deceptive information or if any other related license of the sponsor or instructor is suspended, revoked or otherwise disciplined.

2) If the Office of Banks and Real Estate or Advisory Council has reason to believe there has been fraud, dishonesty, or lack of integrity in the furnishing of any documentation for the evaluation of a sponsor or instructor, it shall refer such matter to the appropriate personnel for investigation and any disciplinary action which might be appropriate under the Act in accordance with 68 Ill. Adm. Code 1110.

f) Certification of Compliance with CE Requirements 1) Each renewal applicant shall certify, on the renewal application, full compliance with the CE requirements set forth in subsections (a) and (b) above.

2) The Office of Banks and Real Estate may require additional evidence demonstrating compliance with the CE requirements (e.g., certificate of attendance). Such evidence shall be required in the context of the Office of Banks and Real Estate's random audit. It is the responsibility of each renewal applicant to retain or otherwise produce evidence of such compliance.

3) In the context of an audit, the Office of Banks and Real Estate shall accept verification (e.g., original transcript, certificate) submitted directly from the sponsor on behalf of the renewal applicant as proof of CE completed.

4) When there appears to be a lack of compliance with CE requirements, an applicant will be notified and may request an interview with the Disciplinary Board. At that time the Board may recommend that steps be taken to begin formal disciplinary proceedings as required by Section 10-65 of the Illinois Administrative Procedure Act [5 ILCS 100/10-65].

3) Waiver of CE Requirements

1) Any renewal applicant seeking renewal of a license without having fully complied with these CE requirements shall file with the Office of Banks and Real Estate a renewal application along with a $25 waiver processing fee and the renewal fee as provided by Section 15 of the Act.

2) Pursuant to Section 37.8(c) of the Act, to be granted an interview before the Advisory Council with respect to a request for waiver, the interview must be requested at the time the request for such waiver is filed with the Office of Banks and Real Estate. The renewal applicant shall be given at least 20 days written notice of the date, time and place of such interview by certified mail, return receipt requested.

3) CE requirements shall automatically be waived for those person listed as exempt pursuant to Section 37.1 of the Act and subsections (a)(3) and (a)(4) above.

(Source: Added at 16 Ill. Reg. 3204, effective February 14, 1992)

Section 1450.180 Renewals

a) Every salesperson's license issued under the Act shall expire on March 31 of each odd numbered year. The holder of a salespersons' license may renew such license during the month preceding the expiration date thereof by paying the required fee as provided by Section 15 of the Act, unless otherwise provided for in subsections (c) and (d) below.

b) Every broker's license issued under the Act shall expire on January 31 of each even numbered year. The holder of a brokers' license may renew such license during the month preceding the expiration date thereof by paying the required fee as provided by Section 15 of the Act, unless otherwise provided for in subsections (c) and (d) below, and shall submit a properly completed consent to audit and examine special accounts form.

c) Every license issued to a partnership, corporation or branch office under the Act shall expire on October 31 of each even numbered year. The holder of such license may renew that license during the month preceding the expiration date thereof by paying the required fee as provided by Section 15 of the Act and by submitting the following:

1) A properly completed consent to audit and examine special accounts form; and

2) A properly completed corporation/partnership information form, except for branch office.

d) It is the responsibility of each licensee to notify the Office of Banks and Real Estate of any change of address. Failure to receive a renewal form from the Office of Banks and Real Estate shall not constitute an excuse for failure to pay the renewal fee or to renew one's license.

e) Practicing or offering to practice on an expired or inoperative license shall constitute unlicensed or unauthorized practice and shall be grounds for discipline pursuant to Section 18 of the Act.

1) Any licensee whose license has been expired for less than 3 years may renew such license at any time by complying with the requirements of this Section and by paying the fees required by Section 15 of the Act.

2) A licensee whose license has been expired for more than 3 years but less than 5 years may renew such license only after providing the Office of Banks and Real Estate with evidence that the licensee has satisfactorily completed at least 15 hours of refresher courses at a program approved in accordance with Section 1450.210 and by otherwise complying with the requirements of this Section. The refresher course shall be completed within one year prior to renewal.

f) Any licensee referenced in subsections (a) and (b) above, whose license under this Act has expired is eligible to renew such license without paying any lapsed renewal fees or reinstatement fee provided that such license expired while the licensee was:

1) on active duty with the United States Army, United States Navy, United States Marine Corps, United States Air Force, United States Coast Guard, the State Militia called into the service or training of the United States, or

2) engaged in training or education under the supervision of the United States prior to induction into military service, or

3) serving as the Director of Real Estate in the State of Illinois, or as an employee of the Office of Banks and Real Estate (Section 13.1 of the Act).

4) Licensees renewing their license in accordance with this subsection may renew such license within a period of two years following the termination of such service and are not required to take a refresher course or a retest.

g) In accordance with Section 13.2 of the Act, any individual whose license under this Act has expired for more than 5 years shall not be eligible for renewal of such license.

h) All renewals shall include the name and license number of the sponsoring broker.

i) In accordance with Section 13 of the Act, within 60 days after the conclusion of the broker and salesperson renewal period, the Office of Banks and Real Estate shall prepare and mail to each licensed real estate broker a listing of licensees who, according to the records of the Office of Banks and Real Estate, are sponsored by that broker.

1) This list shall be mailed to the last known address of the broker.

2) The broker shall respond to the Office of Banks and Real Estate within 30 days after the receipt of this listing by either:

A) Submitting to the Office of Banks and Real Estate a statement verifying the accuracy of such list, or

B) Notifying the Office of Banks and Real Estate in writing of any discrepancies in the list.

3) Failure by a broker to respond to the Office of Banks and Real Estate as set forth in subsection (b)(2)(B) above shall serve as automatic verification by the broker that the information contained on the list is correct.

(Source: Amended at 15 Ill. Reg. 10416, effective July 1, 1991)

Section 1450.185 Granting Variances

a) The Commissioner of Banks and Real Estate may grant variances from these rules in individual cases where he finds that:

1) the provision from which the variance is granted is not statutorily mandated;

2) no party will be injured by the granting of the variance; and

3) the rule from which the variance is granted would, in the particular case, be unreasonable or unnecessarily burdensome;

b) The Commissioner shall notify the Board of his intention to grant a variance, and the reasons therefor, at a meeting of the Board, prior to his granting said variance.

(Source: Amended at 15 Ill. Reg. 10416, effective July 1, 1991)

Section 1450.190 Procedure to Contest An Automatic Termination

Procedure to Contest an Automatic Termination. A licensee who desires to contest an automatic termination for payment out of the Real Estate Recovery Fund pursuant to Section 25(e) of the Act, must submit a motion, in writing, specifying the particular grounds relied upon. This motion must be filed within twenty (20) days of receipt of the notice of termination. Oral argument shall be granted in those instances in which the Commissioner of Banks and Real Estate deems it necessary to clarify relevant issues. The Commissioner shall notify the licensee of his ruling on the motion within 45 days of its receipt. If a motion is filed, denial of the motion constitutes final administrative action for purposes of judicial review.

(Source: Added at 9 Ill. Reg. 341, effective January 3, 1985)

Section 1450.195 Penalties for Criminal Acts

The criminal acts referred to in the Real Estate License Act of 1983, Section 22, as misdemeanors bear the following penalties:

Individuals

	Class C (1st Offense)	Class A (2nd Offense)
Fine not to exceed:	$500	$1000
Imprisonment not to exceed:	30 days	1 year

Corporations

	Business Offense (1st Offense)	(2nd Offense)
Fine not to Exceed:	$2000	$5000

(Source: Added at 9 Ill. Reg. 341, effective January 3, 1985)

Section 1450.200 Real Estate Recovery Fund

a) Necessity of Notice

When any person commences, in the civil courts, an action for a judgement which may result in collection from the Real Estate Recovery Fund, that person shall notify the Office of Banks and Real Estate in writing at the time of commencement of the action.

b) Time of Notice

"Time of the commencement of the action" shall be construed to mean that notice must be dispatched to the Office of Banks and Real Estate not later than 7 days after the action is commenced in accordance with Section 2-201 of the Civil Practice Law [735 ILCS 5/2-201].

c) Place and Manner of Notice

Notice required by Section 25 of the Real Estate License Act of 1983 [735 ILCS 5/2-201] or by this Section shall be sent by certified mail, return receipt requested, or shall be delivered by hand, to the Director of Real Estate at the principal office of the Office of Banks and Real Estate in Springfield, Illinois.

d) Contents of Notice

Every notice required by Section 25 of the Real Estate License Act of 1983 or by this Section shall include:

1) a copy of the complaint which may lead to collection from the fund, showing the "Filed" stamp of the Clerk of the Court in which the complaint was filed;

2) copies of evidence of title to real property on which the claim is based, or if claimant does not possess title, evidence of the interest in real property on which the claim is based (evidence includes such documents as title policy, deed, or lease); and

3) an itemized statement of losses of actual cash money which the claimant alleges occurred as a result of conduct identified in Section 23 of the Real Estate License Act of 1983 by a broker, associate broker, salesperson, or unlicensed employee of a broker. Where no itemized statement is possible, the claimant must state under oath that his losses are estimated and that his calculation of estimated losses is as accurate as circumstances permit him to make.

e) Necessity of Natural Person as a Defendant

No notice of claim will be recognized or accepted where the underlying complaint does not name at least one natural person, either a broker, associate broker, salesperson, or unlicensed employee of a broker, as a defendant.

(Source: Added at 9 Ill. Reg. 341, effective January 3, 1985)

SUBPART B: SCHOOL RULES

Section 1450.210 Approval of Schools (Repealed)

(Source: Repealed at 15 Ill. Reg. 10416, effective July 1, 1991)

Section 1450.215 Home Study/Correspondence Programs

Home study/correspondence programs shall be affiliated with an approved school and meet the curriculum requirements set forth in Section 1450.280(c) of this Part.

a) The program shall:

1) Be approved by the Office of Banks and Real Estate in accordance with Section 1450.210;

2) Maintain a brief description of each lesson;

3) Maintain a list of approved instructors who prepare each specific lesson;

4) Maintain a list of titles, authors, publishers, and copyright dates of all instructional materials;

5) Require minimum passing scores for all examinations of no less than 75%;

6) Consist of at least 5 lessons and examinations plus one additional final examination of at least 100 questions.

b) The program shall develop a written statement of teaching methods to be employed and materials and equipment needed for each course of instruction.

c) The program shall establish written policies and procedures for grading examinations and lessons, which shall include provisions for instructor comments, suggestions and written correction of errors. There shall also be written procedures for the prompt return of materials.

d) The program shall establish performance objectives for each specific course of study.

e) The program shall maintain an average passing rate of at least 40% for all students who take the licensure examination for the first time over a 6 month period, either January through June or July through December.

f) An approved instructor shall be available during normal business hours to answer student questions.

g) Students shall be allowed to attend the school's regularly scheduled real estate courses.

(Source: Amended at 15 Ill. Reg. 10416, effective July 1, 1991)

Section 1450.220 Definition of Class Hour and Credit Hour (Repealed)

(Source: Repealed at 15 Ill. Reg. 10416, effective July 1, 1991)

Section 1450.230 Educational Requirements of Broker Applicant Who is a Licensed Illinois Real Estate Salesperson (Renumbered)

(Source: Section 1450.230 renumbered to Section 1450.11, new Section adopted at 15 Ill. Reg. 10416, effective July 1, 1991)

Section 1450.240 Class Attendance Requirements

a) Attendance at all classes is mandatory; however, credit for absences not to exceed 10% of the class hours may be made up by attendance at make-up classes as provided in subsection (b) below.

Absences in excess of 10% of class hours shall result in failure of the course.

b) Each school shall provide time and facilities for conducting make-up classes for students who were absent from the regularly scheduled class period.

(Source: Amended at 15 Ill. Reg. 10416, effective July 1, 1991)

Section 1450.250 Requirements for Minor in Real Estate (Renumbered)

(Source: Section 1450.250 renumbered to Section 1450.12, new Section adopted at 15 Ill. Reg. 10416, effective July 1, 1991)

Section 1450.260 Qualification of Applicants Under 21 Years of Age (Repealed)

(Source: Repealed at 15 Ill. Reg. 10416, effective July 1, 1991)

Section 1450.270 Educational Requirements for Reinstatement of License (Repealed)

(Source: Repealed at 15 Ill. Reg. 10416, effective July 1, 1991)

Section 1450.275 Recruitment at Test Center

Recruitment at test facilities where the Illinois Real Estate Licensing Examination is being conducted is not permitted before, during, or after the examination.

(Source: Added at 15 Ill. Reg. 10416, effective July 1, 1991)

Section 1450.280 Approval of Schools

a) In accordance with Section 31 of the Act, a school seeking approval shall submit an application on forms provided by the Office of Banks and Real Estate along with the appropriate fee required in Section 15 of the Act. The Office of Banks and Real Estate shall, upon the recommendation of the Real Estate Administration and Disciplinary Board approve a school of real estate if it meets the following minimum requirements:

1) Approved schools shall include the following:

A) Colleges and Universities chartered by their state education authority;

B) Private Real Estate Schools whether operated by corporations, community organizations or any other entity to meet the education requirements of applicants for real estate broker or salesperson license under the Act. (Referred to in Section 15(E) of the Act as Private, Business, or Vocational Real Estate Schools);

or

C) Public Real Estate Schools approved by their state education authority, and supported by public taxes.

2) The program shall:

A) Be approved by the school's governing and/or supervising body, except in the case of private real estate schools;

B) Have a faculty all of whom meet the qualifications of subsection (b) below;

C) Have a curriculum which conforms to the standards of subsection (c) below;

D) Administer a minimum 100 question final examination as outlined in subsection (c)(6) below.

3) Facilities

A) A school must provide an office in Illinois or a bordering state for the maintenance of all records, office equipment and office space necessary for customer service.

B) A school seeking approval of any classroom site shall furnish to the Office of Banks and Real Estate an affidavit setting forth the name of the owner of the premises to be utilized and a copy of the lease.

C) The premises, equipment and facilities of the school shall comply with all applicable community fire codes, building codes, and health and safety standards.

D) The school is subject to inspection prior to approval or thereafter by authorized representatives of the Office of Banks and Real Estate during regular business hours.

E) No school shall be maintained in a private residence.

F) Whenever an approved school operates a branch or extension location, then an application shall be filed for each branch or extension location. Each application shall be accompanied by the fee as required by Section 15 of the Act.

G) No approved school shall allow the school premises or classrooms to be used during class time by anyone to directly or indirectly recruit new affiliates for any company. Instructors and school administrators shall promptly report to the Office of Banks and Real Estate any efforts to recruit students.

4) Administration

A) Instructors within an adult education, community education or vocational education program at any approved real estate school shall meet the criteria for approval as set forth in subsection (b).

B) No approved school shall advertise that it is endorsed, recommended, or accredited by the Office of Banks and Real Estate. Such school, however, may indicate that the school and course of study has been approved by the Office of Banks and Real Estate.

C) Before each approved real estate course is to begin, an approved school shall submit notice to the Office of Banks and Real Estate where the class is to be taught, title of the course, who is to instruct the class, date and time of the class and estimated class enrollment.

D) The school shall provide the student with information which specifies the course of study to be offered; the tuition to be charged; the school's policy regarding refund of unearned tuition when a student is dismissed or withdraws voluntarily or through hardship; any additional fee to be charged for supplies, materials or books which become the property of the student upon payment; and such other matters as are material to the relationship between the school and the student (for example: cost of retaking a course, current status of licensure, any disciplinary action taken by the Office of Banks and Real Estate, attendance requirements).

E) Each school shall maintain for each student a record which shall include the course of instruction undertaken, dates of attendance, and areas of study completed satisfactorily. Each student's record shall be maintained by the school for a period of 5 years and shall be available for inspection by the student or by the Office of Banks and Real Estate or its designee during regular business hours.

F) Total tuition for any course of instruction offered by the school shall be the same for all students at any given time.

G) An approved real estate school shall upon request give evidence of the financial resources available to equip and maintain the school documented by a current balance sheet, an income statement or any such similar evidence as required by the Office of Banks and Real Estate.

H) The Office of Banks and Real Estate shall, upon an on-site inspection of an out-of-state school, be reimbursed by the school for all expenses incurred by the inspector in the course of inspection.

b) Qualifications of Instructors in Approved Schools. The approved school shall employ only instructors who have been approved by the Office of Banks and Real Estate and meet the following:

1) Except as provided in subsections (7) and (8) below, pass an examination approved by the Office of Banks and Real Estate with a minimum score of 70; and

2) Holds a real estate broker's license for at least the last 3 years and has been engaged in active practice as an Illinois real estate broker; or

3) Is currently admitted to practice law by the Supreme Court of Illinois and for at least 3 years has been engaged in the active practice of law in Illinois; or

4) Is a properly credentialed instructor of real estate courses who is or has been engaged in the practice of teaching for at least 3 years; or as evidenced by a professional designation such as but not limited to, a designated real estate instructor (DREI); or approved by a college or university's governing body to teach in a real estate degree program; or

5) Is properly licensed or certificated to engage in the business of appraisal, finance and/or related real estate occupations and who is a member of a nationally recognized association in that field and for at least 3 years has been engaged in such practice; or

6) In the judgment of the Director of Real Estate, is qualified by experience or education, or both, to supervise a course of study pursuant to the provisions of this Section. In determining whether a person is

qualified to supervise a course of study under this Section, the Director shall consider:

A) The individual's teaching experience;

B) The individual's real estate experience;

C) Any real estate, business or legal education of the individual;

D) The results of a personal interview with the individual.

7) Those instructors teaching in a college or university real estate degree program are subject to approval by the administrator of that program and are not required to meet the examination requirement.

8) Instructors approved on the effective date of this amendment are exempt from taking the examination as long as they maintain an active instructor's certificate and have no break in such active status greater than 5 years.

9) A school seeking the approval of the Office of Banks and Real Estate for real estate instructors shall submit an application on forms provided by the Office of Banks and Real Estate and the appropriate fee.

10) No approved instructor shall be seated for either the salesperson or broker licensure examination except for the purpose of securing a salesperson or brokers license.

c) Curricula.

1) The school shall offer classroom instruction in the following subjects:

A) Real Estate Transactions as outlined in subsection (3)(A) below;

B) Advanced Real Estate Principles and Contracts and Conveyances as outlined in subsections (3)(B) and (C) below; and

C) In addition to those listed in subsections (A) and (B) above, at least 3 optional courses as outlined in subsection (3) below shall be offered.

2) The application of the school requesting approval shall include an outline of the content of the courses to be offered. Each outline shall make reference to the textbook used and other material related to the course or subject matter, and shall conform to the approved curricula outlines prepared by the Office of Banks and Real Estate.

3) Approved courses shall meet the minimum criteria set forth below:

A) Real Estate Transactions shall include a minimum of 30 class hours. The course shall include instruction in real estate law, types of interest and ownership in real estate, home ownership, legal descriptions, titles, liens, taxes, encumbrances, listing, advertising, appraisal, finance, closings, and professional code of ethics.

B) Advanced Real Estate Principles shall consist of a minimum of 15 class hours and shall be mandatory for all broker candidates. The course shall include instruction in Illinois real estate law and licensure, listings, title search, forms for closing, contract forms, and the broker-salesperson relationship.

C) Contracts and Conveyances shall consist of a minimum of 15 class hours and shall be mandatory for all broker candidates. The course shall include instruction in deeds, fixtures, contracts, real estate closings, foreclosure and redemption, land use controls, landlord/tenant relationship, cooperatives and condominiums.

D) Appraisal shall consist of a minimum of 15 class hours. The course shall include instruction in the appraisal process, real property and value, economic trends, depreciation, land value.

E) Property Management shall consist of a minimum of 15 class hours. The course shall include instruction in fundamentals of tenant - management relationship, property modernization, property maintenance, leases, insurance, commercial property, industrial property, advertising.

F) Financing shall consist of a minimum of 15 class hours. The course shall include instruction in types of financing, sources of financing, mortgages, mortgage documents, closing a mortgage, interest, liens, foreclosure, insurance, mortgage risk, principles of property value for mortgage credit, mortgage analysis, construction loans.

G) Sales and Brokerage shall consist of a minimum of 15 class hours. The course shall include instruction in qualifications and functions of a real estate broker, land utilization; appraisal principles and methods; office organization; selection, training and supervision of salespersons and office personnel; compensation of salesperson listings; prospects; real estate markets; financial control; and government regulations.

H) Farm Property Management shall include a minimum of 15 class hours. The course shall include instruction in inventorying assets, determining method of operation, tenants, budgeting, crop and livestock production, marketing, tax planning and depreciation, government programs and regulations, insurance and ethics.

I) Real Property Insurance shall include a minimum of 15 class hours. The course shall include instruction in risk, functions of insurance, insurance contracts, types and purposes of insurance.

J) Refresher Course for License Reinstatement shall include a minimum of 15 class hours. The course shall include instruction in current Illinois real estate law and rules, appraisals, contracts, open housing, transfer of title, leases, landlords/tenant, property management and real estate brokerage. Courses which may be substituted for this are Basic Transactions and Advanced Principles.

4) The Office of Banks and Real Estate shall make available to the public upon request copies of curricula of any of the courses specified above.

5) If additional elective courses are developed, they shall be approved by the Office of Banks and Real Estate prior to implementation. Such courses shall be approved upon determination that the course is at least 15 clock hours in length and constitutes real estate related material.

6) Examinations. Each course shall end in a mandatory final examination for which the minimum pass rate shall be no less then 70%.

7) Changes in ownership, management and curriculum occurring subsequent to the approval of a program shall be approved by the Office of Banks and Real Estate prior to implementation in order for approval to continue uninterrupted.

d) The Office of Banks and Real Estate shall notify officials of the school in writing within 15 days of its approval or disapproval.

In the event the school is disapproved, the reasons thereof will be detailed and the officials advised that the disapproval may be appealed by notifying the Office of Banks and Real Estate, in writing, within 10 days of the receipt of the disapproval.

(Source: Amended at 15 Ill. Reg. 10416, effective July 1, 1991)

Section 1450.290 Withdrawal of Approval

a) Upon written recommendation of the Real Estate Administration and Disciplinary Board, the Office of Banks and Real Estate shall withdraw, suspend or place on probation the approval of the real estate school when the quality of the program fails to continue to meet the established criteria as set forth in this Section or if approval of the school or program was based upon false or deceptive information.

b) If the Board has reason to believe there has been any fraud, dishonesty, or lack of integrity in the furnishing of any documentation for the evaluation of a school or program, it shall refer such matter to the appropriate personnel for investigation and any disciplinary action which might be appropriate under the Act.

c) An approved real estate school which does not maintain an average passing rate of at least 40% for all students who take the licensure examination for the first time over a 6 month period, either January through June or July through December, shall at the recommendation of the Real Estate Administration and Disciplinary Board, receive a written warning of noncompliance from the Office of Banks and Real Estate. Approval may be suspended, withdrawn or other disciplinary action taken in accordance with 68 Ill. Adm. Code 1110 if the school fails to maintain an average passing rate of at least 40% of all students who take the licensure examination for the first time over the next 6 month period.

d) A probation period shall be further defined as a time during which an approved school cannot receive approval for any course additions or changes.

e) A real estate program whose approval is being reconsidered shall be given at least 30 days written notice prior to any reconsideration by the Board. The officials in charge may either submit written comments or request a hearing before the Board.

f) In the event the real estate license of the administrator of an approved school is suspended or revoked, the school approval shall automatically be rescinded.

(Source: Added at 15 Ill. Reg. 10416, effective July 1, 1991)

Section 1450.APPENDIX A Penalties for Criminal Acts (Repealed)

(Source: Repealed at 9 Ill. Reg. 341, effective January 3, 1985)